Clinical Assessment of Child and Adolescent Personality and Behavior

Handbook of Psychological Assessment, Second Edition
Gerald Goldstein and Michel Hersen (Editors)
ISBN: 0-205-14340-7

The MMPI-2/MMPI: An Interpretive Manual
Roger L. Greene
ISBN: 0-205-12525-5

Clinical Assessment of Children's Intelligence
Randy W. Kamphaus
ISBN: 0-205-13934-5

Tactical Psychotherapy of the Personality Disorders: An MCMI-III–Based Approach
Paul D. Retzlaff (Editor)
ISBN: 0-205-15932-X

Clinical Use of Story Telling: Emphasizing the T.A.T. with Children and Adolescents
Hedwig Teglasi
ISBN: 0-205-13938-8

Clinical Assessment of Child and Adolescent Personality and Behavior

Randy W. Kamphaus

THE UNIVERSITY OF GEORGIA

Paul J. Frick

THE UNIVERSITY OF ALABAMA

Allyn and Bacon

Boston   London   Toronto   Sydney   Tokyo   Singapore

Library of Congress Cataloging-in-Publication Data
Kamphaus, Randy W.
    Clinical assessment of child and adolescent personality and
  behavior   /   Randy W. Kamphaus, Paul J. Frick.
        p.   cm.
    Includes bibliographical references and index.
    ISBN 0-205-15043-8
    1. Behavioral assessment of children.   2.   Personality assessment
of children.   3. Behavioral assessment of teenagers.   4.   Personality
assessment of teenagers.   I. Frick, Paul J.   II. Title.
    [DNLM: 1. Personality Assessment—in infancy & childhood.
2. Personality Assessment—in adolescence.   3. Child Behavior
Disorders—diagnosis.   4. Adolescent Behavior.   5. Personality
Tests—in infancy & childhood.   6. Personality Tests—in
adolescence.   WM 141 K15c 1996]
RJ503.5.K36   1996
155.4′1828—dc20
DNLM/DLC
for Library of Congress   95-21934
                                                                CIP

Printed in the United States of America
10   9   8   7   6   5   4   3   2   1   00   99   98   97   96

To the memory of my parents,
Richard and Nancy Kamphaus (RWK)

To my inspiration,
Vicki, Josh, and Jordan (PJF)

CONTENTS

PART II
ASSESSMENT METHODS

Chapter 6
Self-Report Inventories 88

Chapter 7
Parent Rating Scales 121

Chapter 8
Teacher Rating Scales 153

Chapter 9
Behavioral Observations 181

Chapter 10
Peer-Referenced Assessment 199

Chapter 11
Projective Techniques 209

Chapter 12
Structured Diagnostic Interviews 233

PREFACE

Psychologists offer an increasing variety of services to the public. Among these services, psychological assessment of personality and behavior continues to be a central activity. One main reason is that other mental health professionals often do not possess a high level of competence in this area. When one views psychologists who serve children and adolescents, psychological assessment seems to take on an even greater role. It follows then that comprehensive and enlightened graduate-level instruction in assessment should be a high priority for educators of psychologists who are destined to work with youth.

This book is an outgrowth of our efforts to improve our own instruction of child and adolescent assessment skills. We found that existing textbooks were not serving us well. Most of them were encyclopedic, edited volumes that were (1) uneven in the quality across chapters and/or (2) not geared either in format or level of presentation for beginning graduate instruction. The few single- or co-authored volumes available tended to lack the breadth of coverage we deemed necessary. Some focused largely on theoretical issues related to psychological testing, with minimal discussion of practical applications and use of specific tests. Others focused solely on summaries of individual tests, without reviewing the theoretical or empirical context within which to use the tests appropriately. Hence, this volume reflects our desire to provide a more helpful tool for instruction—one that provides a scientific context within which to understand psychological testing with children and adolescents and which translates this scientific context into practical guidelines for using individual tests in clinical practice.

Among our specific objectives for this volume were the following:

- To focus on measures specifically designed to assess the emotional, behavioral, and social functioning of children and adolescents. Measures of child functioning are vastly different from their adult counterparts, and any discussion of the assessment of child and adolescent personality and behavior should focus on the unique considerations of this age group.

- To provide current research findings that enable students to draw heavily on science as the basis for their clinical practice

- To help in the translation of research into practice by providing specific and practical guidelines for clinical practice

- To include a broad coverage of assessment methods that emanate from a variety of theoretical, practical, and empirical traditions

- To systematically compare tests and assessment methods using research findings, reviews, and our own synthesis of positions

- To provide a readable volume that would enhance the interest and retention of students through the use of numerous case examples, research notes, and other "boxes" containing practical advice

In writing a readable text that goes beyond a cursory survey of available instruments, we were faced with the difficult task of determining what specific instruments to include in the book. As we struggled with this decision, we eventually chose several selection criteria. Our main criterion for inclusion was a test's ability to serve as an exemplar of some specific type of assessment instrument or theoretical approach to assessment. In many cases we looked for "prototypes" that we thought would highlight some key points to the reader that could then be used in evaluating other assessment instruments not covered specifically in the text. Other criteria included a test's popularity or our estimate of a new test's potential impact on the field. Granted, this decision making was highly subjective, but we strove to be analytic and to limit to the extent possible our personal feelings and biases. Fortunately, several external anonymous reviewers of earlier drafts of the text helped us to be more objective.

A final point that should be clearly outlined is our basic orientation to psychological assessment. We feel that the goal of psychological assessment is the measurement of psychological constructs and, for clinical practice, measurement of psychological constructs that have important clinical implications, such as documenting the need for treatment or the type of intervention that is most appropriate. For an individual child the constructs that need to be assessed will vary from case to case and depend on the referral question. But what is important from this conceptualization is that our view of psychological assessment is not test-driven but construct-driven. Without exception, assessment techniques will measure some constructs well and other psychological dimensions less well. Another important implication from this view of testing is that it is critical that assessors become familiar with and maintain familiarity with research on the constructs they are trying to assess. In short, the most critical component in choosing a method of assessment and in interpreting assessment data is understanding what one is trying to measure.

In this volume, we have focused on the measurement of psychological constructs that focus on a child's emotional, behavioral, and social functioning. There is still a great debate over definitional issues in this arena of psychological functioning in terms of what should be called "personality," "temperament," "behavior," or "emotions," with distinctions

usually focusing on the level of analysis (e.g., overt behavior vs. unconscious motivational processes) or assumed etiology (e.g., biologically determined vs. learned) or proven stability (e.g., transient problems vs. a stable pattern of functioning) (see Martin, 1988). Unfortunately, people often use the same terms with very different connotations. In writing this text, we tried to avoid this debate by maintaining a broad focus on "psychological constructs," which often vary on the most appropriate level of analysis, or on assumed etiology, or on stability. This definitional variability adds a level of complexity to the assessment process because assessors must always consider what they are attempting to measure in a particular case and what research suggests about the best way of conceptualizing this construct before they can select the best way of measuring it. It would be much easier if one could develop expertise with a single favorite instrument or a single assessment modality that could be used in all evaluations to measure all constructs. Since this is not the case, psychologists must develop broad-based assessment expertise. Hence, our overriding objective in writing this volume is to provide the breadth of coverage that we feel is needed by the psychologist-in-training.

We have organized the text into three sections consistent with our approach to teaching. Part I provides students with the psychological knowledge base necessary for modern assessment practice including historical perspectives, measurement science, child psychopathology, ethical, legal, and cultural issues, and the basics of beginning the assessment process. Part II gives students a broad review of the specific assessment methods used by psychologists, accompanied by specific advice regarding the usage and, strengths and weaknesses of each method. In Part III we help students perform some of the most sophisticated of assessment practices; integrating and communicating assessment results and, infusing assessment practice with knowledge of child development and psychopathology. We think that upon completion of this volume, and a similar one covering aspects of cognitive assessment, that the student psychologist has the background necessary for practicum experiences in the assessment of children and adolescents.

ACKNOWLEDGMENTS

We wish to express our gratitude to the anonymous external reviewers and our students who made many helpful comments on drafts of the manuscript. The insightful observations made by Carolyn Imperato-McCammon, Mary Lowman, John Lody, Kerry Schwanz, Heather Cody, and Patty Adkins are particularly appreciated.

Historical Trends

- Who were the major innovators in the field of personality assessment?
- What is meant by the terms *personality* and *behavior?*
- What is meant by the terms *objective* and *projective* personality assessment?
- Who coined the terms *internalizing* and *externalizing behavior problems?*

Personality assessment is a process that most individuals engage in throughout their lives (Martin, 1988a). Mothers label their children as happy, cranky, or what not shortly after birth, and often in utero (e.g., active). The musings of Binet about the personality of his two daughters were captured for posterity. He described Madeleine as silent, cool, concentrated, while Alice was a laugher, gay, thoughtless, giddy, and turbulent (cited in Wolf, 1966). Adolescents seem obsessed with personality evaluation as they carefully consider feedback from their peers in order to perform their own self-assessments.

PERSONALITY VERSUS BEHAVIOR

Early personality assessment emphasized the assessment of enduring traits that were thought to underlie behavior. In fact, some may consider a person's personality to be reflective of a constellation of numerous traits. Kleinmnutz (1967) describes personality as a unique organization of factors that characterizes an individual and determines his or her pattern of interaction with the environment. This definition is also consistent with the notion of a trait.

Traits

A *trait* is often conceptualized as an relatively stable disposition to engage in particular acts or ways of thinking (Kaplan & Saccuzzo, 1993). Children, for example, may be described by their parents as introverted or extroverted. The introverted child may tend to cope with stressful situations by withdrawing from social contact, whereas the extrovert approaches social contact. For parents and psychologists alike these traits are often thought to have value for predicting human behavior. In fact, parents may take special precautions to ensure that the introverted child adapts well to the social aspects of attending a new school by asking one of their child's friends who also attends the school to accompany the child on the first day. Similarly, a stable tendency to be introverted should manifest itself in numerous social situations such as interactions in the neighborhood, at church, and in ballet class.

The Big Five Personality Factors

In 1961, Tupes and Christal discovered five factors of personality that appeared in the reanalysis of numerous data sets from scales of bipolar personality descriptors. These central personality traits have recently become the focus of an extensive research effort. One of the well-known scales used to identify the big five is the NEO Personality Inventory (NEO-PI) (Costa & McCrae, 1985).

The big five factors are typically identified by bipolar comparisons as follows (Goldberg, 1992).

Factor I—Surgency (or Introversion-Extroversion)

unenergetic vs. energetic
silent vs. talkative
timid vs. bold

Factor II-Agreeableness (or Pleasantness)

cold vs. warm
unkind vs. kind
uncooperative vs. cooperative

Factor III—Conscientiousness (or Dependability)

disorganized vs. organized
irresponsible vs. responsible
negligent vs. conscientious

Factor IV—Emotional Stability (versus Neuroticism)

tense vs. relaxed
nervous vs. at ease

Factor V—Culture, Intellect, Openness, or Sophistication

unintelligent vs. intelligent
unanalytical vs. analytical
unreflective vs. reflective

These factors are typically assessed using forced-choice item formats where adjectives are used as personality descriptors. This item format is in direct contrast to the more commonplace true/false item format.

Commercially available instruments such as the NEO-PI have provided new opportunities to study and refine these constructs. Given the amount of research and development in this area, the big five personality factors could have a substantial impact on the field of child and adolescent personality assessment. To date, however, big five research has been limited primarily to adult populations.

Temperament

A related concept is *temperament*, which also emphasizes the measurement of specific traits that are hypothesized as underlying behavior across settings. Goldsmith and Reisser-Danner (1990) observe, "most researchers consider temperament to be the behavioral manifestation of biologically influenced processes determining both the infant's characteristic response to the environment and his or her style of initiating behavior (p. 250). Therefore, temperament is distinguished by some researchers from personality in that temperaments are thought to be highly biologically based and present at birth (Martin, 1988a). Predictably, much of the research on temperament is conducted with infants and young children. In this conceptualization, personality may be viewed as being superimposed on the person's temperament base. The distinction between temperament and personality, however, is often debated.

Behavioral Assessment

The assessment of behavior focuses on the measurement of observable behaviors, although recently the definition has been broadened to include cognitions as a type of behavior. Martin (1988a) provides a useful definition of behavior by observing:

When applied psychologists speak of behavior, they are usually referring to that range of human responses that are observable with the naked eye during a relatively brief period of time in a particular environment. This conception of behavior rules out biochemical and neurological events, for example, because they are not observable by the unaided eye. Behavior is differentiated from traits or dispositions because the latter may only be seen if behavior is aggregated over relatively long periods of time and in a number of environmental contexts. Classical examples of observed behaviors of interest to child psychologists include tantrum behavior among young children, aggressive interactions with peers, attempts at conversation initiation, and so forth. (p. 13)

There are several distinguishing features of behavioral assessment methods. First, behavioral assessment methods have a different theoretical foundation than so-called traditional or trait-based psychological assessment. Behavioral assessment methods draw heavily on the theory and research tradition of operant conditioning as exemplified by the work of B. F. Skinner. This research tradition also emanates primarily from laboratory research as opposed to clinical practice, thus it is often considered to be more empirically based.

Second, and related to the first point, behavioral assessment methods are more clearly distinguished from medical models of assessment than are trait-based methods (Kaplan & Saccuzzo, 1993). The medical model assumes that symptoms are caused by underlying conditions, and it is the medical condition that must be measured, diagnosed, and treated in order to remove the symptoms. In direct contrast, behavioral assessment emphasizes the measurement and treatment of the symptoms or behavior itself.

Third, behavioral assessment places a greater premium on the assessment of discrete behaviors. For example, behavioral assessment may emphasize the measurement of finger tapping while completing seatwork in school, as opposed to aggregating several behaviors to form a test or scale with several items that measure motor activity in the classroom. This situation is changing, however, with the work of Achenbach and others to be discussed later who began combining behaviors into dimensions of behavior that may or may not differ as clearly from trait-based assessment methods.

As we suggested in the preface, we think that it is premature to reify any of these approaches as the ultimate method for assessing child problems or assets. This cautious approach seems warranted as the distinctions between the methods have become blurred with the work of Achenbach and others, and as the science of assessment emerges. We think that each approach may be more or less helpful for answering particular assessment questions. Some of the questions leveled at psychologists are clearly trait-based, whereas others require the measurement of distinct behaviors. For example, a parent who asks, "Will my child ever become more outgoing like his sister?" is asking for trait assessment, but the parent who queries, "How can I get him to stop wetting the bed?" may require behavioral assessment expertise.

Because of this potential diversity of referral questions, our use of the terms *personality* and *behavior* throughout this text will likely be faulty. Such confusion is probably unavoidable, but it is certainly not intended to confuse the reader.

Early History

Formal personality measures emerged as a logical outgrowth of other efforts to measure individual differences, most notably the experimental methods of Wundt, Galton, and others (Chandler, 1990). Of the early assessment luminaries, Sir Francis Galton is one of the most notable. Although well known for his intelligence measurement contributions, he also studied the measurement of "character." In order to highlight the utility of personality measurement, Galton (1884) cited a personality test invented by Benjamin Franklin as a crude form of a personality measure. The scale was described in the tale of the Handsome and Deformed Leg where Franklin recounts how his friend tested people so as to avoid those who, "being discontented themselves, sour the pleasures of society, offend many people, and make themselves everywhere disagreeable" (p. 9). This friend sought to diagnose such pessimistic individuals by showing them an attractive leg and a malformed one. If the stranger showed more interest in the ugly leg, the friend became suspicious and subsequently avoided this person. Franklin astutely identified this as a grotesque but effective personality assessment device. Galton cited this story as an example of the utility of personality measurement. He concluded: "The other chief point that I wish to impress is, that a practice of deliberately and methodically testing the character of others and of ourselves is not wholly fanciful, but deserves consideration and experiment" (p. 10).

Intelligence tests, acknowledged as the first fruits of the psychometric movement, reached prominence early in the twentieth century with the original Binet scale and numerous variants (Kamphaus, 1993). In fact, Alfred Binet developed some intelligence test items that resembled stimuli used 30 years later in apperceptive techniques (DuBois, 1970). Test-development activity also received a boost from the World War I effort when ability testing became widespread (Kamphaus, 1993); it is no coincidence that the first formal and widely used measures of personality were developed around this time.

Robert S. Woodworth

The Woodworth Personal Data Sheet was published in 1918 as a result of the surge of interest in testing potential soldiers. Woodworth developed a list of 116 questions about daydreaming, worry, and other problems. Some sample items from the Woodworth Personal Data Sheet (Woodworth, 1918) are:

Do people find fault with you much?

Are you happy most of the time?

Do you suffer from headaches and dizziness?

Do you sometimes wish that you had never been born?

Is your speech free from stutter or stammer?

Have you failed to get a square deal in life?

The examinee responded to each question with yes or no (French & Hale, 1990).

According to French and Hale (1990), the Woodworth Personal Data Sheet served as the foundation for the development of the Thurstone Personality Scale and the Allport Ascendance-Submission Test among others. DuBois (1970) described the Personal Data Sheet as "the lineal ancestor of all subsequent personality inventories, schedules and questionnaires" (p. 94).

The Personal Data Sheet was an important practical innovation since prior to this time all recruits had to be interviewed by trained interviewers. The Personal Data Sheet allowed for the screening of large numbers of recruits without huge cadres of interviewers (Kleinmuntz, 1967).

The Societal Need

It was not basic research on personality or employee selection that led to the eventual popularity of personality testing. The need for diagnosis created by world wars I and II provided considerable evidence of the need for personality tests. The successful World War I applications of psychological testing proved that psychology could make practical contributions to society by identifying, accurately and time-efficiently, those in need of mental health services.

After World War II the mental health needs of citizens, veterans in particular, were the focus of greater attention. In the postwar years the U.S. Veteran's Administration began to hire psychologists in large numbers to diagnose and treat veterans suffering from significant emotional disturbance. Psychologists brought their psychometric expertise to bear again by contributing new methods to the diagnostic process. This increased need for postwar mental health services created the fertile ground in which personality testing flourished. As Kleinmnutz (1967) noted, "The most popular personality tests of the past 30 years grew out of the need to diagnose or detect individuals whose behavior patterns were psychopathological" (p. 10).

The use of personality tests after the war expanded beyond diagnosis into many areas including counseling, personnel selection, and personality research

(Kleinmuntz, 1967). At this time the number of personality assessment methods increased dramatically in response to these various societal needs.

PROJECTIVE TECHNIQUES

The major assumption underlying projective testing is that the use of stimuli that are prone to a variety of interpretations will encourage clients to reveal information that they otherwise would not share in response to direct questioning (Chandler, 1990). Projective testing depended heavily on the explicit or implicit personality theory that was favored by the test developer—or interpreter, for that matter. Without a theory, how does one determine the underlying nature or cause of the projected thoughts, emotions, or behaviors?

Of course, the most popular theory of the day was psychodynamic personality theory as popularized by Sigmund Freud and others. Psychodynamic personality theory provided very fertile ground for the growth of projective assessment measures. Projective methods remain popular, but it could be argued that their heyday was in the early half of this century, as is demonstrated in the following discussion of specific projective assessment methods.

Association Techniques

The use of association techniques for assessment purposes can be traced to Aristotle (DuBois, 1970). Sir Francis Galton, of intelligence-testing fame, began studying association techniques as early as 1879. Galton's contribution to the study of association was his introduction of scientific rigor to the enterprise. He used experimental methods to study association methods including quantitative measurement of the results (DuBois, 1970).

Subsequently Kraepelin, Wundt, Cattell, Kent, and Rosanoff studied the associations of subjects to word lists, recording such variables as response time and type of association. The latter names, Kent and Rosanoff, may be least familiar to readers because the other names are linked with the illustrious history of intellectual assessment. Kent and Rosanoff made their contribution solely to the study of associations by developing a list of 100 stimulus words and systematically recording the associations of 1,000 normal subjects (Dubois, 1970). In a sense, then, this was an initial attempt at developing norms to which researchers and clinicians could compare the responses of clinical subjects.

The famous psychoanalyst Carl Jung made extensive use of association techniques for the study of personality. In an address at Clark University in 1909, he described his research efforts in considerable detail and provided some insight into the types of interpretations commonly made of these measures. Jung described his association word list as a formulary. His list consisted of 54 words including *head, to dance, ink, new, foolish,* and *white.* According to Jung (1910), normality could be distinguished from psychopathology with this formulary using variables such as reaction time and the response content. In this speech he provided a transcript of the responses of a normal individual and of a hysteric. A sampling of their associations to the formulary follows:

STIMULUS	NORMAL	HYSTERICAL
to sin	much	this is totally unfamiliar to me, I do not recognize it
to pay	bills	money
bread	good	to eat
window	room	big
rich	nice	good, convenient
friendly	children	a man

Reaction time to the stimulus words was also interpreted by Jung. He gives a glimpse of one such interpretation in the following quote:

The test person waives any reaction; for the moment he totally fails to obey the original instructions, and shows himself incapable of adapting himself to the experimenter. If this phenomenon occurs frequently in an experiment it signifies a higher degree of disturbance in adjustment. (p. 27)

These early word association methods set the stage for the development of other association (projective) techniques such as the Thematic Apperception Technique and Rorschach's test, both of which used pictures in lieu of word lists to elicit associations.

Thematic Apperception Test

The Thematic Apperception Test of Henry A. Murray is a classic example of a projective device. Charles E. Thompson summarizes the central tenet of the projective approach in the following quote taken from his 1949 adaptation of Murray's TAT.[1]

If the pictures are presented as a test of imagination, the subject's interest, together with his need for approval, can be so involved in the task that he forgets his sensitive self and the necessity of defending it against the probing of the examiner, and, before he knows it, he has said things about an invented character that apply to himself, things which he would have been reluctant to confess in response to a direct question. (p. 5)

The TAT is unique among projective measures in that it has traditionally been interpreted qualitatively even though quantitative scoring methods have been available (Kleinmuntz, 1967). Murray's original approach to TAT scoring was entirely qualitative and psychoanalytically based. He proposed the following categories for analyzing the characteristics of the stories given by the subject (Murray, 1943; Kleinmuntz, 1967).

1. The Hero. This is the person with whom the subject seems to identify. The hero may share characteristics such as age, gender, occupation, or other features with the subject that aid identification. The hero's traits should be evaluated to determine the self-perceptions of the subject including superiority, in-telligence, leadership, belongingness, solitariness, and quarrelsomeness.

2. Needs of the Hero. Murray was primarily interested in identifying the needs of the hero including needs for order, achievement, and nurturance.

3. Environmental Forces. These factors that affect the hero are also referred to as *press*. An example would involve scoring aggression if the hero's property or possessions were destroyed in a story.

4. Outcomes. The success of the hero and the hero's competencies are assessed by evaluating the outcomes of stories.

5. Themas. This is a complex aspect of scoring that assesses the interplay of needs and presses. Themas reveal the primary concerns of the hero.

7. Interests, Sentiments, and Relationships. For this aspect of scoring the examiner records the hero's preferences for topics.

Murray's qualitative scoring system for the TAT is a prototypical example of the application of systems that dominated the early interpretation of many projective devices. Numerous quantitative scoring systems followed Murray's original work.

Rorschach's Test

Hermann Rorschach (1884–1922) was a major figure in Swiss psychiatric research who began his work as a physician in 1910. He married a Russian colleague who became his comrade and collaborator (Morgenthaler, 1951). He served as a physician in a hospital in Herisau until his death from complications of appendicitis in 1922. His death was described as a critical blow to Swiss psychiatry. In a 1951 eulogy to Dr. Rorschach, published in the English translation of his original work, Dr. W. Morgenthaler attempted to describe Rorschach for future generations.

Flexibility of character, rapid adaptability, fine acumen, and a sense for the practical were combined in Hermann Rorschach with a talent for introspection and synthesis. It was this combination which made him outstanding. In addition to this rare nature, which tempered personal emotional experience with practical knowledge, he pos-

---

[1]Thompson's modification is identical to the original TAT with the exception that African-American figures are used as characters on the stimulus cards. Thompson found that African-Americans did not respond optimally to the original TAT pictures. In fact, one of his patients asked if he could imagine that the people in the pictures were "colored," and if he could make up some stories about "colored people."

sessed sound traits of character most valuable in a psychiatrist. Most important of these were an unerring tendency to search for the truth, a strict critical faculty which he did not hesitate to apply to himself, and a warmth of feeling and kindness. (p. 9)

Rorschach's approach to personality assessment was novel in many respects. The test stimuli used were inkblots placed on paper that was then folded in half. More importantly, Rorschach was not interested in the content of the subject's response to the inkblots. Rather, he was interested in the form of the response (or its *function*). Some functions of interest include the number of responses, perception of color or movement, and perception of the whole versus the parts. These and other characteristics of Rorschach responses continue as part of modern scoring systems.

Rorschach first offered his method as an experiment. His original sample is described in Table 1.1. He expressed a desire for larger sample sizes but noted that the number of experiments was limited because the figures were damaged by passing through hundreds of hands.

Rorschach's legacy, his original inkblots and many of the associated scoring criteria, remains influential as the test continues to enjoy considerable popularity. Several scoring systems have been offered for the Rorschach, with the Exner Comprehensive System

TABLE 1.1   Rorschach's original research sample

Sample	N
Normal, educated	55
Normal, uneducated	62
Psychopathic personality	20
Alcoholic cases	8
Morons, Imbeciles	12
Schizophrenics	188
Manic-depressives	14
Epileptics	20
Paretics	8
Senile dements	10
Arteriosclerotic dements	5
Korsakoff and similar states	3

SOURCE: Adapted from Rorschach (1942).

(Exner & Weiner, 1982) contributing most to the continuing usage of the instrument.

Sentence Completion Techniques

Sentence completion techniques are venerable personality assessment methods of the association tradition that can trace their roots to Payne (1928). The sentence completion method, however, obtained a substantial boost in popularity because of its use by the U.S. Office of Strategic Services (OSS), the forerunner of the Central Intelligence Agency (CIA). Henry Murray was the coordinator of a sophisticated assessment effort. About 60 assessment stations, staffed by American psychologists, were situated in the United States and abroad to screen recruits for sensitive and dangerous assignments (Dubois, 1970). Some of the methods used in this ambitious program are described in the following quote from Dubois (1970).

In one of the stations near Washington, recruits in fatigue uniforms assumed a false identity and developed a cover story, which the staff members during the three-day stay endeavored to break. The procedures described in a comprehensive report (OSS, Assessment Staff, 1948) were varied: casual conversations, searching interviews, the sentence completion test, questionnaires about health and working conditions and personal history, conventional aptitude tests such as map memory and mechanical comprehension, and a number of situational tests. (p. 111)

After World War II the sentence completion technique continued to enjoy some favor among psychologists. The well-known Rotter Incomplete Sentences Blank was published in 1950 (Rotter & Rafferty, 1950).

Sentence completion methods have a lengthy history of use with children and adolescents. They enjoy worldwide use in Finland, Germany, Denmark, India, Japan, and Taiwan, to name a few places (Haak, 1990).

Projective Techniques for Children

The use of projective techniques with children dates back to the early part of this century when Florence

Goodenough began to study children's human figure drawings (DuBois, 1970). Goodenough noted, as did others, that children's drawings were affected by their emotionality. The typical paradigm for drawing techniques has been to have the child draw a picture of a person. Traditionally the content of the drawings has been interpreted as a measure of child adjustment and personality. Some aspects of content that were extensively studied for adults included (Swensen, 1968):

Size of the person depicted

Placement on the page (bottom, top, corner, etc.)

Stance (vertical, horizontal, balanced, etc.)

Line quality (heavy, light, etc.)

Shading

Erasures

Omissions (missing body parts)

Distortion (poor proportion of body parts)

Various interpretations have been associated with these and other content variables over the years. Heavy lines, for example, have been associated with assertive and aggressive individuals and light lines are more commonly drawn by passive individuals (Swensen, 1968). Swensen (1968) found such interpretations to be highly unreliable. The most reliable and valid interpretive approach involved making general judgments about the mental health status of the individual based on the overall quality of the drawing rather than specific content interpretations.

The TAT, among other projective methods, has also been adapted by many for use with children and adolescents. One of the most well-known TAT adaptations is the Children's Apperception Test (CAT) (Bellak & Bellak, 1949b), designed for ages 3 to 10. The CAT consists of 10 pictures with animals as stimuli in contrast to the TAT's depictions primarily of people. The Rorschach has also been widely used with children, and several compendiums of child responses have been published to aid interpretation (e.g., Ames et al., 1974).

The proper interpretation of children's projective responses remains a topic of debate. Indeed, the degree to which children obey the projective hypothesis is in question. Chandler (1990) elucidates the nature of the projective hypothesis:

Projection, in common usage, means to cast forward. In this sense, projection implies a direct extension of psychological characteristics onto the outer world. But projection also has a specific meaning within psychoanalytic theory. Freud (1936) used the term to refer to the process that occurs when the ego, faced with unacceptable wishes or ideas, thrusts them out onto the external world as a means of defense. In projection the individual attributes his or her own thoughts and actions to someone else. Thus, if one's own faults or feelings are unacceptable to the ego, they may be seen as belonging to someone else; in the process, the material may become distorted or remain partially repressed. From such a perspective, projective material would not be seen as direct representation of aspects of the personality—certainly not with the sort of one-to-one correspondence that the first meaning of projection implies. (p. 57)

Which meaning of *projection* should the psychologist use for interpretation? The process of projection remains a mystery for adults as well as children. This uncertainty makes interpretation of children's responses to projective devices an enterprise requiring a high level of inference. For some psychologists this level of inference is too high to allow them to feel comfortable using projective devices. Recently, however, psychologists have applied psychometric methods in order to strengthen projective techniques.

Roberts Apperception Test for Children (RATC)

The RATC (MacArthur & Roberts, 1982) is one example of this rapprochement between objective and projective methods. The RATC is a storytelling technique in the tradition of the TAT and CAT designed for ages 6 through 15. The RATC consists of 27 cards, 11 of which have parallel forms for males and females.

The RATC is unique among association measures in its emphasis on psychometric principles and methods. The manual provides a description of a normative sample and evidence of reliability and validity. Moreover, like other objective methods, raw scores are converted to standard scores (T-scores with M of 50 and SD of 10) to provide norm-referenced comparisons for clinical and adaptive scales and supplementary measures. The RATC has a comprehensive scoring system that results in adequate evidence of reliability. On the other hand, validity evidence is meager (Worchel & Dupree, 1990). Despite the unimpressive validity evidence, the RATC is emblematic of a 1970s and 1980s trend to objectify projective methods.

Exner's Comprehensive System

In the 1960s, John Exner began a research program designed to take the best of the Rorschach scoring systems and incorporate their features into a comprehensive system (Exner & Weiner, 1982). As a result of his work, normative data are available for children and adolescents, as is evidence of reliability. The good reliability evidence is a major technical advance for the Rorschach. As with the RATC, however, questions of validity remain. Chandler (1990) evaluates the Comprehensive System favorably by concluding that, "clearly, Exner's work represents a major contribution to the development of the Rorschach" (p. 66).

The application of psychometric standards to projective measures is a clear departure from a long history of qualitative analysis and interpretation. The efforts of Exner, Roberts, and others have set a clear standard for projective measures in that they are increasingly held to the same standard as that for so-called objective measures.

OBJECTIVE TECHNIQUES

While it is understood that the distinction between projective and objective testing is sometimes an oversimplification, the distinction is useful. In many ways, objective techniques have come to serve as antidotes to the projective methods that emerged dominant in the second half of the twentieth century.

Objective methods can be differentiated from projective tests in several ways. First, objective methods are often considered to be atheoretical and/or empirical. As opposed to requiring the examiner to use theory to interpret results, the results often derive their meaning from empirical procedures such as matching a person's results to those of a clinical sample such as the test results for a sample of children with autism.

Second, objective methods are not likely to be based on psychodynamic theory. Hence, the results of objective measures are often considered to be less useful for providing insight into the dynamics of an individual's interactions with the world.

Third, objective methods take greater advantage of psychometric science for the development of tests. Issues of item selection, reliability, and validity are often emphasized in the test manuals.

The objective assessment movement gained considerable stature after World War II. The fact that some of the measures developed then remain extremely popular today testifies to the allure of this empirical approach. Later chapters in this book, however, will identify some of the limitations or rigid empirical approaches to test development.

Minnesota Multiphasic Personality Inventory (MMPI)

Until the advent of the MMPI, projective techniques reigned supreme. In a 1961 survey of U.S. psychologists' test use, the MMPI was the only nonprojective measure mentioned among the top 10 most used tests. Of the top 10 tests, 5 were intelligence tests and 4 were projective measures (Sundberg, 1961).

A confluence of circumstances including the expansion of clinical psychology practice during and after World War II and the emergence of an extensive research base led to almost immediate acceptance of this self-report inventory (Kleinmuntz, 1967). The MMPI (Hathaway & McKinley, 1942; see Box 1.1 for a quote from Paul Meehl, a student of Hathaway) differed from its predecessors (such as the Personal Data Sheet) in at least one fundamental way. It was one of the first tests to use an empirical approach to objective personality test development. Most tests of the day used a priori or rational-theoretical approaches (Martin, 1988a). Rational approaches, as the name implies, depend heavily on the test authors' theory of personality for many aspects of test construction, including item development and scoring methods. Empirical approaches,

Meehl on Science and Technics

Paul Meehl, of MMPI fame, is considered one of the founders of modern personality assessment and diagnostic practice. His 1973 collection of selected papers published by the University of Minnesota Press provides a unique glimpse of the genius of an astute clinician. In the following quote, Dr. Meehl discusses the tension between science and practice in psychology and takes a stance against theoretical dogmatism:

Doubtless every applied science (or would-be science) presents aspects of this problem to those working at the interface between science and technics, as is apparent when one listens to practicing attorneys talking about law professors, practitioners of medicine complaining about medical school teaching, real engineers in industry poking ambivalent fun at academic physicists, and the like. So I do not suggest that the existential predicament of the clinical psychologist is unique in this respect, which it certainly is not. But I strongly suspect that there are few if any fields of applied semiscientific knowledge in which the practititioner with scientific interests and training is presented *daily* with this problem in one guise or another, or in which its poignancy, urgency, and cognitive tensions are so acute. I am aware that there are *some* clinical psychologists who do not experience this conflict, but I have met, read, or listened to very few such during the thirty years since I first began working with patients as a clinical psychology trainee. Further, these rare exceptions have seemed to me in every case to be either lacking in perceptiveness and imagination or, more often, deficient in scientific training and critical habits of mind. When I encounter a hard-nosed behaviorist clinician who knows (for sure) that Freud's theory of dreams is 100 percent hogwash and is not worth five hours of his serious attention; or, toward the other end of the continuum, when I converse with a devoted Rorschacher who knows (for sure) that the magic inkblots are highly valid no matter what the published research data indicate—I find both of these attitudes hard to understand or sympathize with. (p. viii)

used an item selection method called empirical criterion keying (Anastasi, 1988). Essentially, this method involves selecting items that meet an empirical criterion. In the case of the MMPI, items were selected if they were able to routinely differentiate clinical groups from samples of normal subjects and distinguish clinical groups from one another. For example, items for the Psychoasthenia scale (a scale designed to assess anxiety-related problems such as obsessions and fears) were selected based on a clinical group of 20 cases, the results for which were compared to normals and other clinical groups in order to identify items that best differentiated the target clinical group from the others.

The original version of the MMPI consisted of 550 statements printed on separate cards. The cards were separated by the patient into three categories: true, false, and cannot say.

The first MMPI clinical scales were linked to the major diagnostic nosology of the day (Kleinmuntz, 1967), which is another factor that contributed to its popularity (see Box 1.2). The 10 clinical scales of the original version included:

1. Hypochondriasis
2. Depression
3. Hysteria
4. Psychopathic Deviate
5. Masculinity-Femininity
6. Paranoia
7. Psychasthenia
8. Schizophrenia
9. Hypomania
10. Social Introversion

Four validity scales were also part of the original version:

1. Question Scale
2. Lie Scale
3. F Scale
4. Correction Scale

on the other hand, make greater use of empirical data to make such decisions (see Chater 2 for a more detailed discussion of this distinction). The MMPI

The MMPI has undergone many changes since its inception, with the most recent edition entitled

BOX 1.2

Sample Items from 1960s MMPI Spoofs

Personality testing eventually became popular enough to warrant derision by members of Congress, well-known humorists such as Art Buchwald, and others. Some of these alternate MMPI items were published in a 1965 issue of *American Psychologist* (p. 990).

When I was younger I used to tease vegetables.

I think beavers work too hard.

I use shoe polish to excess.

When I was a child I was an imaginary playmate.

the MMPI-2. In fact, some of the scale names (e.g., Psychasthenia) had fallen into disuse at about the time of original publication (Kleinmuntz, 1967). A chronology of MMPI developments is listed next (thorough discussion of the MMPI is presented in Chapter 6).

MMPI VERSION	PUBLICATION DATE
MMPI	1942
MMPI-2	1989
MMPI-A (Adolescent)	1992

The "Children's MMPI"

The MMPI eventually influenced child assessment practice. The Personality Inventory for Children (PIC), a variant of the MMPI, was developed for children in the 1950s. The PIC was developed based on a pool of 600 item, thus it is similar in length to the MMPI. A central difference between the MMPI and the PIC is the informant. The PIC is not a self-report measure; rather, a parent rates the child's behavior. Lachar (1990b) gives the following rationale for this decision.

Selection of the parents as the source of PIC test responses helps overcome two of the major obstacles posed by requesting the referred child or adolescent to respond to nu-

merous self-report descriptions in order to obtain a multiple-scale objective evaluation. The majority of children seen by mental health professionals in a variety of settings appear for such an evaluation because of their noncompliant behaviors and/or documented problems in academic achievement, most notably in the development of reading skills. Therefore, it seems unlikely that a technique requiring such children to read and respond to a large set of self-descriptions will find broad acceptance in routine clinical practice. (p. 299)

The scales of the PIC were derived using factor-analytic methods; hence, the PIC, like the MMPI, was developed with a heavy emphasis on empirical methods (see Chapter 6). In the 1960s, empirical methods of test development were applied to the development of other types of child assessment devices.

Rating Scales

Although the use of rating scales for the assessment of child psychopathology is increasingly widespread, the technique traces its roots to the assessment of adult psychopathology in hospital settings. Conceptualized as one type of observational method, rating scales were developed in the 1950s for use by nurses and other caretakers who worked closely with patients for extended periods of time.

One of the first such measures was the Wittenborn Psychiatric Rating Scales (1955). According to Lorr (1965), the scales were designed for recording currently observable behavior and symptoms in mental patients. The Wittenborn could be completed by a social worker, psychologist, psychiatrist, nurse, attendant, or other individual familiar with the patient's day-to-day behavior. The original scale consisted of 52 symptoms that were combined to yield nine scores for acute anxiety, conversion hysteria, manic state, depressed state, schizophrenic excitement, paranoid condition, paranoid schizophrenic, hebephrenic schizophrenic, and phobic compulsive. An item assessing withdrawal included the following options:

No evidence of social withdrawal

Does not appear to seek out the company of other people

Definitely avoids people

The Wittenborn was used for diagnostic purposes as well as for the design and evaluation of treatment (Kleinmuntz, 1967). Reviewers of the day found many attributes to recommend the Wittenborn, including a thorough research base (Eysenck, 1965) and easy administration and scoring (Lorr, 1965). There was considerable concern, however, about overlapping scales. The hebephrenic schizophrenic and schizophrenic excitement scales correlated .88 and the paranoid condition and paranoid schizophrenic scales correlated at .79. Based on these data, Eysenck (1965) and Lorr (1965) recommended that these scales be combined to reflect this overlap.

Other rating scales of adult psychopathology for use in inpatient settings of the day included the Hospital Adjustment Scale (McReynolds, 1952) and the Inpatient Multidimensional Psychiatric Scale (Lorr, 1962), a rating of symptomotology completed after a diagnostic interview. Such measures probably fell into decline for many reasons, one of the most prominent being the deinstitutionalization movement of the 1970s. These instruments did, however, clearly demonstrate the utility of ratings of behavior as useful assessment tools, thus setting the stage for the development of parent and teacher rating scales of child behavior.

Internalizing and Externalizing Dimensions

Research into the diagnosis of child psychopathology led to increased attention to the use of rating scales for child diagnosis. In a 1978 article in *Psychological Bulletin,* Thomas Achenbach and Graig Edelbrock introduced many clinicians to the terms *internalizing* and *externalizing* when referring to psychological disorders of childhood. These dimensions or types of child psychopathology are based on an empirical analysis (typically using factor analysis) of parent and teacher behavior problem rating scales. Children experiencing adjustment difficulties of the internalizing variety have also been described as over-controlled with problems of inhibition, anxiety, and perhaps shyness (Edelbrock, 1979). On the other hand, children with externalizing problems have been described as undercontrolled with difficulties such

as aggression, conduct problems, and acting-out behavior (Edelbrock, 1979).

These two dimensions of child psychopathology trace their roots to the work of Peterson (1961), who labeled the syndromes as conduct problem (externalizing) and personality problem (internalizing). The veracity of the broad internalizing and externalizing categorizations of child psychopathology is supported by many factor-analytic investigations of parent and teacher rating scales alike (Edelbrock, 1979).

This dichotomous characterization of child maladjustment is also supported by evidence of concurrent validity, for example, results from a study of 163 consecutive referrals to a child psychiatry outpatient department (Cohen et al., 1985). Children were classified as externalizers and internalizers based on the Achenbach Child Behavior Checklist Parent and Teacher Forms (see Chapters 6 and 7). The resulting analyses uncovered distinct differences between the two groups, particularly on the Teacher Form. Internalizers were more intelligent, better readers, less egocentric, and used more adaptive means of coping with stressful situations. Internalizers were generally rated as being less disruptive than externalizers (Cohen et al., 1985).

Such robust factor-analytic support for these two types of child difficulty and supportive validity data have contributed to the use of these broad categories for the development of many teacher and parent rating scales, most notably the Achenbach Child Behavior Checklist (Achenbach, 1991b) and recently the Behavior Assessment System for Children (BASC) (see Chapters 6 and 7). Furthermore, the terms *internalizer* and *externalizer* are now part of psychologists' everyday parlance when discussing child behavior problems.

THE DEVELOPMENT OF DIAGNOSTIC SYSTEMS

DSM-IV

Diagnostic systems have had a profound impact on child assessment by defining symptoms and other diagnostic indices that have subsequently been incorporated into various assessment methods. The most obvious link exists between the various editions of the *Diagnostic and Statistical Manual of Mental Disorders* (currently DSM-IV) and structured interview methods designed to assess symptomotology associated with various DSM diagnostic categories. Given this interdependence, a thorough knowledge of the nature of the DSM and its variants is prerequisite to the study of child assessment.

As mental disorders became recognized as bona fide conditions worthy of medical treatment, the need for diagnostic systems became more pressing. Consistent diagnosis was necessary for communication among clinicians and for the conduct of epidemiological research and other scientific investigations. The American Medico-Psychological Association (now the American Psychiatric Association) began efforts to standardize diagnostic procedures in 1917 (Widiger et al., 1991). The first diagnostic manual, a classification of mental disease, was produced by the American Psychiatric Association in conjunction with the U.S. Census Bureau (Widiger et al., 1991).

The first edition of the DSM *(Diagnostic and Statistical Manual)* appeared in 1952. Part of the impetus for the creation and frequent updating of the DSM has been provided by the *International Statistical Classification of Diseases, Injuries, and Causes of Death* (ICD). The ICD, currently ICD-10, is published by the World Health Organization. The DSM has been revised both to coordinate with the ICD and to add criteria for conditions that are of concern to U.S. clinicians and delete conditions that are not apparent in the United States (Widiger et al., 1991).

The DSM has also been revised recently due to a desire to make the diagnostic categories more empirically based. Prior to the development of the DSM-III, the system was based primarily on the expert judgment of a relatively small number of clinicians. The DSM-II, for example, was finalized after review by 120 psychiatrists in February of 1967 (Widiger et al., 1991).

The DSM-IV (APA, 1994) is based on a more comprehensive research base than any of its predecessors. According to Widiger et al. (1991), three research methods have formed the empirical cornerstone for the development of DSM-IV.

1. Literature Reviews: Comprehensive reviews of the research were completed in order to advise the various committees charged with proposing diagnostic criteria for conditions. These reviews were seen as a way to mitigate against biases on the part of some committees (Widiger et al., 1991).

2. Data Reanalyses: Existing data sets have been made available to the DSM-IV committees supported by funding from the John D. and Catherine T. MacArthur Foundation. According to Widiger et al. (1991), these data set reanalyses allow the committees to evaluate the validity of current diagnostic algorithms and pilot-test new proposals for making diagnoses.

3. Field Trials: These studies are particularly useful for testing the reliability and validity of diagnostic categories (Widiger et al., 1991).

The DSM-IV, because of its greater reliance on empirical methods, is likely to have an even more substantial impact on the personality assessment process (see Chapter 3). The chronology of the DSM follows.

CHRONOLOGY OF DIAGNOSTIC SYSTEMS DEVELOPED UNDER THE AUSPICES OF THE AMERICAN PSYCHIATRIC ASSOCIATION

1917	Classification of Mental Disease
1933	Standard Classified Nomenclature of Disease
1952	*Diagnostic and Statistical Manual of Mental Disorders I* (DSM-I)
1968	*Diagnostic and Statistical Manual of Mental Disorders II* (DSM-II)
1983	*Diagnostic and Statistical Manual of Mental Disorders III* (DSM-III)
1987	*Diagnostic and Statistical Manual of Mental Disorders III—Revised* (DSM-III-R)
1993	*Diagnostic and Statistical Manual of Mental Disorders IV* (DSM-IV)

PL94-142, IDEA, and Special Education

The 1974 Education of Handicapped Children's Act, better known as Public Law 94-142, and its reauthorization, the Individuals with Disabilities Education Act (IDEA), mandated special education and related services for children diagnosed as seriously emotionally disturbed. Under IDEA, severe emotional disturbance was defined as follows:

> The term means a condition exhibiting one or more of the following characteristics over a long period of time and to a marked degree which adversely affects school performance: (a) an inability to learn which cannot be explained by intellectual, sensory, or health factors; (b) an inability to build or maintain satisfactory relationships with peers and teachers; (c) inappropriate types of behavior or feelings under normal circumstances; (d) a general pervasive mood of unhappiness or depression; or (e) a tendency to develop physical symptoms or fears associated with personal or school problems. (Federal Register, 42, 474, 1977)

These laws effectively forced U.S. public schools to identify and serve children with emotional disorders, who had previously been educated in a variety of settings including residential treatment programs. Consequently, these laws expanded school-based diagnostic practices to include evaluation for the presence of emotional disorders just as had been more commonly done for developmental and learning disorders. These federal mandates also enhanced the popularity of rating scales (particularly teacher ratings) as assessment methods of choice in many school systems.

The IDEA nosology of severe emotional disturbance has long been the target of criticisms that it is inadequate, restrictive, or otherwise flawed (Forness & Knitzer, 1992). Bower (1982), the recognized developer of the conceptual basis of the IDEA diagnostic categories, has raised similar questions about the system. He noted that:

> Section ii [which excludes the socially maladjusted from the IDEA act] is, one would guess, a codicil to reassure traditional psychopathologists and budget personnel that schizophrenia and autism are indeed serious emotional disturbances on the one hand, and that just plain bad

> boys and girls, predelinquents, and sociopaths will not skyrocket the costs on the other hand. It is clear what these modifications and additions were intended to do. It is perhaps not clear what such public policy and fiscal modifications do to the conceptual integrity of the definition and the nature and design of its goals. (p. 56)

Despite such controversy, the IDEA classification system remains a nosology to be reckoned with when considering eligibility for special education and related services. Furthermore, the relationship of IDEA and DSM-IV has yet to be clarified, resulting in tension between the diagnostic needs of school authorities versus other regulatory bodies.

FUTURE TRENDS

The pace of change in personality assessment appears to be hastening (see Box 1.2). There is renewed interest in the development of new techniques, including child assessment methods. Tuma and Elbert (1990) identify several test development and research trends:

- While projective techniques have fallen from favor, new projective techniques with stronger psychometric properties are likely to appear. In addition, projective techniques may find new uses. One example is the use of the Rorschach as an interview method.

- Behavioral assessment will likely be strengthened by theoretical and psychometric improvements and adoption of cognitive-behavioral methods.

- The use of structured and semistructured interview methods will continue to gain popularity.

- Considerable evidence will be placed on conceptualizing a child's behavior in the context of the larger social system in which he or she functions. This emphasis will result in the development of systematic methods for gauging the effects of family, community, and cultural factors on the child's functioning.

Tuma and Elbert (1990) characterize this latter assessment trend more eloquently in the following quote:

It is apparent that personality assessment is undergoing rapid development in all areas: projective, objective, and behavioral assessment; clinical interviewing and informal assessment; and environmental assessment. The developments outlined above encompass observable behavior, structured and unstructured use of tests and interviews, and assessment of broad- and narrow-band aspects of personality, all within the context of a person's situation/environment. Thus, in spite of various criticisms and some apparent decrease in the use of personality assessment instruments, all indications point to vigorous activity in the area that promises to continue. (p. 23)

CONCLUSIONS

While the technology of personality assessment has been viewed as lagging behind other areas of assessment such as intelligence and achievement testing (Martin, 1988a), there are signs that the technology is undergoing rapid change. New scientific rigor is being applied to the development of projective devices, interview methods, and diagnostic systems. The history of personality and behavior assessment is fraught with false starts and failed methods despite evidence of some practical contributions. The history of this field, however, is also marked by progress that appears to be hastening.

CHAPTER SUMMARY

1. Formal personality measures emerged as a logical outgrowth of other efforts to measure individual differences, most notably the experimental methods of Wundt, Galton, and others.

2. The Woodworth Personal Data Sheet was published in 1918 as a result of the surge of interest in testing potential soldiers.

3. The needs for diagnosis created by World War I and World War II provided considerable impetus for the development of personality tests.

4. The use of association techniques for assessment purposes can be traced to Aristotle.

5. The major assumption underlying projective testing is that the use of stimuli that are prone to a variety of interpretations will encourage clients to reveal information that they otherwise would not share in response to direct questioning.

6. The TAT is unique among projective measures in that it has traditionally been interpreted qualitatively even though quantitative scoring methods have been available.

7. Hermann Rorschach (1884–1922) was a major figure in Swiss psychiatric research who began his work as a physician in 1910.

8. The Rorschach test stimuli were originally inkblots placed on paper that was then folded in half.

9. Several scoring systems have been offered for the Rorschach, with the Exner Comprehensive System (Exner & Weiner, 1982) contributing most to the continuing usage of the scale.

10. The use of projective techniques with children dates back to the early part of this century, when Florence Goodenough began to study children's human figure drawings.

11. The proper interpretation of children's projective responses remains a topic of debate.

12. Sentence completion techniques are venerable personality assessment methods of the association tradition that can trace their roots to Payne (1928).

13. The MMPI was one of the first tests to use an empirical approach to objective personality test development.

14. The MMPI used an item selection method called empirical criterion keying.

15. The MMPI has undergone many changes since its inception, with the most recent edition entitled the MMPI-2.

16. The Personality Inventory for Children (PIC) is a variant of the MMPI that was developed for children.

17. The use of rating scales for the assessment of child psychopathology traces its roots to the

assessment of adult psychopathology in hospital settings.

18. One of the first rating scale measures was the Wittenborn Psychiatric Rating Scales (1955).

19. In a 1978 article in *Psychological Bulletin,* Achenbach and Edelbrock introduced many clinicians to the terms *internalizing* and *externalizing* when referring to psychological disorders of childhood.

20. Children experiencing adjustment difficulties of the internalizing variety have also been described as overcontrolled with problems of inhibition, anxiety, and perhaps shyness (Edelbrock, 1979). On the other hand, children with externalizing problems have been described as undercontrolled with difficulties such as aggression, conduct problems, and acting-out behavior (Edelbrock, 1979).

21. During the past couple of decades there has been an attempt to increase the psychometric sophistication of projective tests in an effort to increase their utility.

22. The Roberts Apperception Technique for Children (RATC) is a storytelling technique in the tradition of the TAT and CAT designed for ages 6 through 15.

23. In the 1960s John Exner began a research program designed to take the best of the extant Rorschach scoring systems and incorporate these features into his comprehensive system.

24. The first edition of the DSM *(Diagnostic and Statistical Manual)* appeared in 1952.

25. The DSM-IV is based on a more comprehensive research base than any of its predecessors.

26. The 1974 Education of all Handicapped Children's Act, better known as Public Law 94-142, and its reauthorization, the Individuals with Disabilities Education Act (IDEA), have mandated special education and related services for children diagnosed as seriously emotionally disturbed.

27. In 1961 Tupes and Christal discovered five factors of personality that appeared in the reanalysis of numerous data sets from scales of bipolar personality descriptors. The big five factors are typically identified by bipolar comparisons as: Factor I—Introversion-Extroversion, Factor II—Agreeableness, Factor III—Conscientiousness, Factor IV—Emotional Stability, and Factor V—Intellect.

28. Personality is typically considered to be a molar construct including components of cognition and temperament. It is often also considered to be composed of traits, a more enduring set of characteristics of the individual.

29. Behavior is typically considered to be a more molecular unit of analysis than is personality. Personality is usually defined by traits, which in turn are defined by constellations of behaviors often considered to be markers of such traits.

30. In the future, considerable evidence will be placed on conceptualizing a child's behavior in the context of the larger social system in which he or she functions. This emphasis will result in the development of systematic methods for gauging the effects of family, community, and cultural factors on the child's functioning.

CHAPTER 2

Measurement Issues

CHAPTER QUESTIONS

- What type of score is a T-score?
- How does skewness affect scaling decisions?
- How has factor analysis been used to develop personality tests and diagnostic schedules?

Users of personality tests should have a thorough understanding of measurement principles. The discussion that follows, however, hardly qualifies as thorough since measurement instruction is not the purpose of this book. This chapter merely points out some of the most useful measurement concepts that students have already learned in previous coursework. We assume that the user of this text has had, at a minimum, undergraduate courses in statistics and tests and measurements and at least one graduate-level measurement course. If a user of this text is not acquainted with some of the principles discussed here, then a statistics and/or measurement textbook should be consulted. There are a number of excellent measurement textbooks available, including Kaplan and Saccuzzo (1993) and Anastasi (1988).

This chapter begins by defining the nature of the personality test. Then a review of basic principles of statistics and measurement is presented, including topics ranging from measures of central tendency to factor analysis. The last part of the chapter introduces measurement issues that are more specific to the use and interpretation of personality tests.

DEFINING PERSONALITY TESTS

There is a Milky Way of tests designed to assess similar-sounding constructs, including personality scales, behavior rating scales, and diagnostic schedules. The available personality measures differ to such an extent that they can be subtyped in order to clarify their psychometric properties. A definition for a psychological test, taken from an early well-known personality assessment text, may be a good starting point. Kleinmuntz (1967) defines a psychological (including personality) test by observing, "A psychological test is a standardized instrument or systematic procedure designed to obtain an objective measure of a sample of behavior" (pp. 27–28). This rather broad definition provides a useful starting point for conceptualizing the great variety of measures available.

The central characteristic of this definition is the notion of standardization of behavioral sampling. *Standardization* can have two meanings: standardization in the sense of collecting a sample for the purpose of norm referencing and standardization as administration of the measure according to a consistent set of rules. Most of the measures discussed in this volume are norm-referenced in that they use norm groups for gauging a child's performance in comparison to some standard. The principle of administration structure or consistency applies to all of the measures in this text. Standardized procedure emanates from experimental psychology, where laboratory control is central to obtaining reliable and valid results (Kamphaus, 1993). Similarly, in the case of personality assessment, standardized administration procedure is necessary to produce reliable and valid measurements of behavior.

All psychological tests take a sample of behavior from which the findings are subsequently generalized (Anastasi, 1988). This ability to generalize findings is the central strength of psychological tests and is probably the reason for their widespread use. Without these tests, psychological measurement would be impractical because of the time and expense required. Of course a sample can always be in error, a fact that should always be considered when interpreting results (Dahlstrom, 1993).

Types of Tests

How does one identify a personality test? How do personality tests differ from interest inventories, behavior rating scales, or aptitude measures? Such questions are not easily answered, but an attempt will be made.

Personality tests have traditionally attempted to assess personality traits such as introversion, agreeableness, and anxiety. Traits are usually considered to be relatively stable characteristics of the individual (Martin, 1988a).

Behavior rating scales, a most popular child assessment method, fall into yet another category of

test called diagnostic schedules (Kamphaus et al., 1995). Kamphaus et al. (1995) define a diagnostic schedule as a specialized psychometric method that provides a structured procedure for collecting and categorizing behavioral data that correspond to diagnostic categories or systems. A diagnostic schedule, then, is not designed to assess a trait, but rather to diagnose a syndrome. How does one identify a diagnostic schedule? One clue is the source of the item pool. The Children's Depression Inventory (CDI; Kovacs, 1992) is a popular measure of childhood depression that used the DSM as its item source. It was designed to assess the symptoms of depression in order to assist with making the diagnosis of depression. It was not designed to assess a stable personality trait or temperament, but rather to allow the examiner to make the diagnosis of depression with confidence. In fact, a cut score that indicates the presence of depression is advised (Kovacs, 1992). Such a measure is consistent with the previous definition of a diagnostic schedule.

The difference between diagnostic schedules and personality tests is important for conceptualizing the two purposes of using such measures: assessment and diagnosis. Shepard (1989) articulates the essential differences in the approaches thusly:

It should be obvious that assessment of emotional disturbance relies almost entirely on clinical judgment. Measurement techniques consist mainly of strategies for collecting direct evidence of behavior patterns. Personality tests and measures of self-concept might be relevant, but they are not primary diagnostic indicators. Once a reliable picture of behavior and changes in behavior across situations and time has been established, the process of diagnosis rests on normative comparisons and the ruling out of competing explanations. Formal checklists and observation schedules do not make the clinician more insightful about what behaviors to observe, but they are helpful if they provide a basis for judging how extreme a pattern is in relation to the normal range of individual differences. (p. 565)

Diagnostic schedules have evolved from behavioral assessment methods, as has the DSM, which now emphasizes the tally of behaviors (symptoms) in order to make a diagnostic decision. Personality tests' on the other hand, are rooted in the psychometric tradition where tests are designed to assess traits across a continuum. While personality tests may not lead directly to a diagnostic decision, they can play other important roles by identifying traits that have implications for the course or prognosis of a disorder, or even for treatment.

While diagnostic schedules are practical for making diagnostic decisions, such measures have limitations for studying the nature of individual differences or for contributing to other important aspects of the assessment process because they often lack a clear theoretical basis or evidence of a priori defined trait(s) that can be supported with construct validity evidence. The emergence of diagnostic schedules as the instruments of choice for much of assessment practice is evidence of the profound impact of behavioral-based diagnostic systems on psychometric test development, particularly over the last decade.

Appropriate conclusions that could be drawn based on diagnostic schedules include statements like the following:

- Tonya suffers from major depression, single episode, severe.
- Tony exhibits nearly enough symptoms to be diagnosed as having conduct disorder.
- Traci has attention problems that are worse than those of 99% of the children her age.

Alternatively, conclusions that could be offered based on psychometric tests could include:

- Allison shows evidence of poor adaptability to new situations and changes in routine, which puts her at risk for school adjustment problems.
- Patrick's high score on the sensation seeking scale warrants consideration as part of his vocational counseling and educational planning.
- Maria's somatization tendencies reveal the need for counseling in order to reduce her frequency of emergency clinic visits.

A central difference between these interpretive statements is that those made based on diagnostic

schedules are dependent on diagnostic nosologies. A variation of this premise is the third statement exemplifying diagnostic-based conclusions, which may result from a norm-referenced behavior rating scale that has a scale devoted to inattention. The interpretive statements made based on psychometric tests, however, can be offered independent of diagnosis. These conclusions are based on the measurement of traits that may or may not represent diagnostic symptoms or signs and, yet, these conclusions contribute substantially to the assessment process.

In this volume the term *personality test* will be used in its generic form to apply to personality trait measures, diagnostic schedules, and related measures, always assuming that the reader is aware of the distinctions between subtypes of measures.

SCORES, NORMS, AND DISTRIBUTIONS

Types of Scores

In this section some of the basic properties of score types are reviewed, with particular emphasis on the T-score standard score metric and its variants. The properties of these scores will be highlighted in order to encourage psychometrically appropriate score interpretation.

Raw Scores

The first score that the clinician encounters after summing item scores is usually called a *raw score*. Raw scores on most tests of personality are simply the sum of the item scores. The term *raw* is probably fitting for these scores in that they give little information about a child's performance as compared to his or her peers. Raw scores are not particularly helpful for norm-referenced interpretation.

Raw scores are often used for interpretation of non–norm-referenced measures such as diagnostic interviews. The Diagnostic Interview Schedule for Children (DISC; Shaffer et al., 1991) (see Chapter 12) is one such measure. On this measure and other interview schedules, one merely tallies the number of items (symptoms) endorsed and makes a diagnosis if this number meets or exceeds a cut score. This tally in effect is nothing more than a raw score. This measure does not yield particular insight into a child's behavior; it merely identifies the number of symptoms present, not how deviant this amount of symptomotology is from the norm. Behavior observation schedules often yield only raw scores. The Student Observation Scale (SOS) of the Behavior Assessment System for Children (BASC; Reynolds & Kamphaus, 1992) (see Chapter 9) is one such scale. As with the DISC, the only result yielded is a frequency count of various classroom behaviors. While the raw scores yielded by non–norm-referenced measures have some utility for diagnosis, these scores are not useful in answering questions of deviancy, as discussed next.

Norm-Referenced Scores

Personality test interpretation often focuses on *norm-referenced interpretation,* the comparison of children's scores to some standard or norm. For the purposes of personality test interpretation, scores are usually compared to those of children the same age. Achievement tests, by contrast, may compare children's scores to those of others in the same grade, and college admission counselors may compare an incoming student's GPA to that of freshmen who entered the year before.

Norm referencing is of importance in personality assessment because it allows the clinician to gauge deviance, which is often the central referral question. Parents who refer a child for a psychological evaluation often have norm referencing in mind. They ask questions such as "Is her activity level normal for her age?" or "Everyone says he is just a boy but fire setting isn't normal, is it?" Norm referencing allows the clinician to answer such questions objectively, which those who do not have access to personality tests with good normative samples cannot do. The remaining scores discussed in this section are norm-referenced scores that allow the clinician to make comparisons.

Standard Scores

The *standard score* is a type of derived score that has traditionally been the most popular for personality test interpretation. Standard scores convert raw scores to a distribution with a set mean and standard deviation and with equal units along the scale (Anastasi, 1988). The typical standard score scale used for personality tests is the T-score, which has a mean of 50 and standard deviation of 10. Another popular standard score that is coming into more frequent use for personality test interpretation has the mean set at 100 and the standard deviation at 15, similar to the IQ metric (Kamphaus, 1993) (see Table 2.1). Because they have equal units along the scale, standard scores are useful for statistical analyses and for making comparisons across tests. The equal units (or intervals) that are characteristic of standard scores are shown in Figure 2.1 for various standard scores and percentile ranks. In the T-score metric the distance between 20 and 30 is the same as that between 45 and 55.

Standard scores are particularly useful for personality test interpretation because they allow for comparisons among various subscales, scales, and composites yielded by the same personality test, allowing the clinician to compare traits. In other words, standard scores allow the clinician to answer questions such as "Is she more anxious than depressed?", thus facilitating profile analysis. Most modern personality tests use T-scores, including the MMPI-2, BASC, Achenbach, and Revised Children's Manifest Anxiety Scale (RCMAS, Reynolds & Richmond, 1985). The relationship between two popular standard score scales is shown in Table 2.1. This table may also be useful for converting a score from one scale to another.

Wechsler popularized the *scaled score* metric for intelligence test subtest scores. Scaled scores have enjoyed some use in personality testing (Kamphaus, 1993). They have a mean of 10 and a standard deviation of 3 (see Table 2.1).

In a normal distribution (a frequently untenable assumption in personality assessment, as is shown in a later section) a normalized standard score divides up the same proportions of the normal curve. As can be seen in Table 2.1, a standard score of 85, T-score of 40, and scaled score of 7 all represent the same

TABLE 2.1 Standard score, T-score, scaled score, and percentile rank conversion table

Standard Score M = 100 SD = 15	T-score M = 50 SD = 10	Scaled Score M = 10 SD = 3	Percentile Rank	Standard Score M = 100 SD = 15	T-score M = 50 SD = 10	Scaled Score M = 10 SD = 3	Percentile Rank
				118	62		88
				117	61		87
				116	61		86
160	90		99.99	115	60	13	84
159	89		99.99	114	59		83
158	89		99.99	113	59		81
157	88		99.99	112	58		79
156	87		99.99	111	57		77
155	87		99.99	110	57	12	75
154	86		99.99	109	56		73
153	85		99.98	108	55		71
152	85		99.97	108	55		69
151	84		99.96	107	55		67
150	83		99.95	106	54		65
149	83		99.94	105	53	11	65
148	82		99.93	104	53		62
147	81		99.91	103	52		57
146	81	19	99.89	102	51		55
145	80		99.87	101	51		52
144	79		99.84	100	50	10	50
143	79		99.80	99	49		48
142	78		99.75	98	49		45
141	77		99.70	97	48		43
140	77	18	99.64	96	47		40
139	76		99.57	95	47	9	38
138	75		99	94	46		35
137	75		99	93	45		33
136	74		99	93	45		31
135	73	17	99	92	45		29
134	73		99	91	44		27
133	72		99	90	43	8	25
132	71		98	89	43		23
131	71		98	88	42		21
130	70	16	98	87	41		19
129	69		97	86	41		17
128	69		97	85	40	7	16
127	68		97	84	39		14
126	67		96	83	39		13
125	67	15	95	82	38		12
124	66		95	81	37		11
123	65		94	80	37	6	9
122	65		92	79	36		8
121	64		92	78	35		8
120	63	14	91	78	35		7
119	63		89	77	35		6

(Cont.)

TABLE 2.1 *(Continued)*

Standard Score M = 100 SD = 15	T-score M = 50 SD = 10	Scaled Score M = 10 SD = 3	Percentile Rank
76	34		5
75	33	5	5
74	33		4
73	32		3
72	31		3
71	31		3
70	30	4	2
69	29		2
68	29		2
67	28		1
66	27		1
65	27	3	1
64	26		1
63	25		1
63	25		1
62	25		1
61	24		.49
60	23	2	.36

Standard Score M = 100 SD = 15	T-score M = 50 SD = 10	Scaled Score M = 10 SD = 3	Percentile Rank
59	23		.30
58	22		.25
57	21		.20
56	21		.16
55	20	1	.13
54	19		.11
53	19		.09
52	18		.07
51	17		.06
50	17		.05
49	16		.04
48	15		.03
48	15		.02
47	15		.02
46	14		.01
45	13		.01
44	13		.01
43	12		.01
42	11		.01
41	11		.01
40	10		.01

amount of deviation from the average. These scores are also all at the 16th percentile rank (see Figure 2.1).

However, because many scales on personality measures are heavily skewed (the most frequent scenario is that most individuals are not experiencing psychopathology and a few are, resulting in positive skewness), some test developers opt for the use of linear T-scores. Linear T's maintain the skewed shape of the raw score distribution, which means that the same T-score on different scales may divide up different portions of the norming sample. Specifically, 50% of the norming sample may score below a linear T-score of 50 on the Activity scale, whereas 55% of the norming sample may score below a linear T-score of 50 on the Aggression scale. Essentially, then, the use of linear T-scores makes the relationship of percentile ranks to T-scores unique for each scale.

Percentile Ranks

A percentile rank gives an individual's relative position within the norm group (Kamphaus, 1993). Percentile ranks are very useful for communicating with parents, administrators, educators, and others who do not have an extensive background in scaling methods (Kamphaus, 1993). It is relatively easy for parents to understand that a child's percentile rank of 50 is higher than approximately 50% of the norm group and lower than approximately 50% of the norm group. This type of interpretation works well so long as the parent understands the difference between percentile rank and percent of items passed.

Figure 2.1 shows that percentile ranks have one major disadvantage in comparison to standard scores: Percentile ranks have unequal units along their scale.

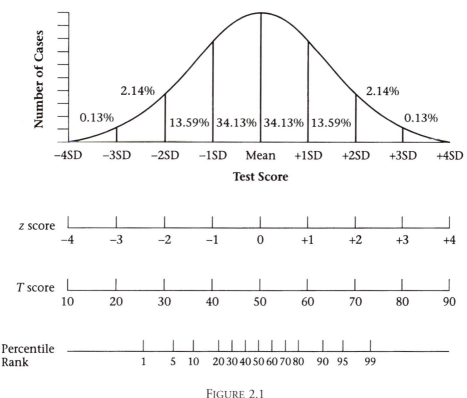

FIGURE 2.1

The relationship of T-scores, Z-scores, standard deviations, and percentile
ranks to the theoretical normal curve

The distribution in Figure 2.1 (and in Table 2.1) shows that the difference between the 1st and 5th percentile ranks is larger than the difference between the 40th and 50th percentile ranks. In other words, percentile ranks in the middle of the distribution tend to over emphasize differences between standard scores, whereas percentile ranks at the tails of the distribution tend to under emphasize differences in performance (Kamphaus, 1993).

Here is an example of how confusing this property of having unequal units can be. A clinician would typically describe a T-score of 55 as average. When placed on the percentile rank distribution, however, a T-score of 55 corresponds to a percentile rank of 69 in a normal distribution of scores (see Table 2.1). The percentile rank of 69 sounds as though it is higher than average. Examples such as this show clearly the caveats needed when dealing with an ordinal (unequal scale units) scale of measurement such as the percentile rank scale. It is important to remember that the ordinal properties of the scale are due to the fact that the percentile rank merely places a score in the distribution. In most distributions the majority of the scores are in the middle of the distribution, causing small differences between standard scores to produce large differences in percentile ranks.

Uniform T-scores

A uniform T-score (UT) is a specialized type of T-score that was used for development of the MMPI-2 norms (Tellegen & Ben-Porath, 1992). This derived score is a T-score like all other normalized standard scores with the exception that it maintains some (but not all) of the skewness of the original raw score distributions. The UT is like a normalized T-score in that the relationship between percentile ranks and T-scores is constant across scales, and it resembles a linear T-score metric in that some of the skewness in the raw score distribution is retained. The problem of a lack of percentile rank comparability across scales is described by Tellegen and Ben-Porath (1992) as follows:

> For example, the raw score distribution of Scale 8, Schizophrenia (Sc), is more positively (i.e., right-) skewed than that of Scale 9, Hypomania (Ma). This means that a linear T-score of, say, 80 represents different relative standings on these two scales in the normative sample. For women in the MMPI-2 normative sample, the percentile values of a linear T-score of 80 are 98.6 for Scale 8 and 99.8 for Scale 9; for men, the corresponding values are similar, 98.6 and 99.7. (p. 145)

In order for the UT scale score to have the properties of percentile rank comparability across scales and reflection of raw score distribution skewness, the UT-score is based on the average skewness value across clinical scales (Tellegen & Ben-Porath, 1992). This approach meets the objectives outlined by the developers, but it relies on the assumption that the skewness of the MMPI-2 clinical scales is similar. There is, however, evidence that some MMPI-2 clinical scales (e.g., Hypochondriasis and Schizophrenia) are far more skewed than others (see Tellegen & Ben-Porath, 1992). It appears that the UT is a compromise metric that meets test development objectives while at the same time not addressing completely the issue of different skewness across scales. More clinical experience with the UT metric will likely determine whether or not this method is adopted by other test developers.

Norm Development

Sampling

The technology of personality assessment has generally lagged behind that of intelligence or achievement

testing (Martin, 1988a). Intelligence tests, for example, have routinely collected stratified national samples of children to use as a normative base. Stratification is used to collect these samples in order to match, to the extent possible, the characteristics of the population at large. Common stratification variables include age, gender, race, geographic region, community size, and parental socio-economic status (SES, e.g., parent education and/or occupation) (Kamphaus, 1993). These variables are used presumably because they are related to score differences. Of these widely used stratification variables, SES is known to produce the most substantial score differences on intelligence measures (Kamphaus, 1993). The precedent then is set for personality assessment norming.

This precedent, however, has not been followed in several important respects. Until recently, many relatively popular personality scales have not done a good job of stratifying their samples. Some norming samples do not control for geographic region and others fail to control for SES. The result is a normative standard of unknown utility. While poor norming is less likely to be tolerated in intelligence and academic achievement assessment, it is less frequently criticized or even noted in discussions of personality assessment. (We will, however, note the characteristics of norming programs in subsequent sections of this text.) The savvy user of personality tests will want to know the characteristics of a test's norming sample in order to make test use decisions and gauge the amount of confidence to place in their obtained scores.

Intelligence, achievement, and adaptive behavior tests typically feature interpretation based on a normative standard, the national norm sample. In contrast, a national normative standard has often not been offered for personality tests. A substantial number of personality tests offer only local norms, a subset of the national normative sample. Local norms answer different questions than do national norms. Hence, their use has to be considered prior to test selection and interpretation.

Local Norms

Local norms may sometimes be more useful than national norms (Petersen, Kolen, & Hoover, 1989).

In order for local norms to be meaningful, however, the range of their usefulness must be defined clearly.

Typical norm-referenced questions of interest to psychologists are diagnostic ones. Common questions might include:

- Does Leah have attention deficit hyperactivity disorder?
- Is José clinically depressed?
- Is Stephanie more anxious than other children her age?

One of the goals of diagnostic practice is consistency, which is fostered by the publication of diagnostic criteria (DSM-IV). Consistent methods of diagnosis allow clinicians to communicate clearly with one another. If, for example, Dr. Ob Session in Seattle says that a patient is suffering from conduct disorder, then Dr. Sid Ego in Atlanta will know what to expect from this adolescent when he enters her office for follow-up treatment.

National norms similarly promote consistency. If a clinician concludes that a child has clinically significant attention problems based on a deviant score on an inattention scale, then others may reasonably conclude that this child has attention difficulties that are unusual for her age. Popular tests, however, may offer different local norms that may hamper consistent communication.

Gender-Based Norms

Personality measures are unusual in that gender-referenced (local) norms are often preferred by test developers. This practice is unusual in comparison to other domains of assessment where, although significant gender differences exist, national combined gender norms are typically the only ones provided. Specifically, intelligence, academic achievement, and adaptive behavior scales produce mean score differences between gender groups, but rarely are local norms by gender offered. Why then are gender local norms commonly offered for personality tests? Tradition could be the most parsimonious explanation.

When comparing a child to his or her gender group, the effects of gender differences in behavior are removed. Another way of expressing this is to say that when gender norms are utilized, the same proportion of boys as girls are identified as having problems. Since, for example, boys tend to have more symptoms of hyperactivity than girls (DSM-III-R, APA, 1987), the use of gender local norms would erase this difference in epidemiology. Gender norm referencing would identify the same percentage of girls and boys as hyperactive. Depression is another example of how gender norms may affect diagnostic rates. Much evidence suggests that girls express more depressive symptomotology than boys in adolescence (Weiss & Weisz, 1988). The use of gender norms for a depression scale would result in the same number of adolescent boys as girls exceeding a particular cut score, whereas general national norms would retain the known greater prevalence among adolescent females.

Are gender local norms a problem? Not so long as clinicians are clear about the questions they are asking. A gender norm question would be "Is Traci hyperactive when compared to other girls her age?" whereas a national norm question would be "Is Traci hyperactive in comparison to other children her age?"

Age-Based Norms

Since there are substantial differences across age groups, intelligence and academic achievement tests routinely offer norms separately by age groups, typically using age ranges of 1 year or less. By contrast, age ranges as large as 5 to 7 years are frequently used for personality tests. This tradition of articulating norms for larger age groups may be attributable to at least a couple of factors: a tendency to have poorer psychometric properties (Martin, 1988a) and a lack of age group differences in personality characteristics (Reynolds & Kamphaus, 1992).

Clinical Norms

A more unique norm group is a sample of children who have been previously diagnosed as having a mental health problem. This clinical norm-referenced comparison can answer questions such as:

- How aggressive is Sheila in comparison to other children who are receiving psychological services?
- Are Tonya's psychotic behaviors unusual in comparison to other children who are referred for psychological evaluation?

There is not a clear precedent for the development of national or local clinical norms. The relevant stratification variables have not been identified, making it difficult to judge the quality of the clinical norms. Should clinical norms, for example, attempt to mimic the epidemiology of childhood disorders including 10% depression cases, 12% ADHD cases, et cetera? Should norms be offered separately by diagnostic category to offer a more exact comparison, or both? Until such standards emerge, clinicians should seek clinical norms that are at least well described.

A clear description of the sample will allow the clinician to determine if the clinical norm group has the potential to answer questions of interest. For example, the clinician who works in an inpatient setting may have more interest in a clinical sample of inpatients, whereas others may prefer that clinical norms be based on a referral population. If the clinical norm group for a test is not well described, the clinician cannot meaningfully interpret the norm-referenced comparisons.

NORMALITY AND SKEWNESS

The Normal Curve

The *normal curve* refers to the graphic depiction of a distribution of test scores that is symmetrical (normal), resembling a bell. In a normal distribution there are a few people with very low scores (these people are represented by the tail of the curve on the left in Figure 2.1), a few with very high scores (the tail on the right), and many individuals with scores near the average (the highest point in the curve).

When a distribution is normal or bell-shaped, as is the case in Figure 2.1, the standard deviation always divides up the same proportion. Specifically, a

± 1 standard deviation always includes approximately 68% of the cases in a normal distribution, and a ± 2 standard deviation always includes approximately 95% of the cases. The normal curve is also sometimes referred to as the normal probability or Gaussian curve.

Skewed Distributions

Normal distributions, however, cannot be assumed for personality tests. While intelligence and academic tests often produce near-normal distributions, personality tests often produce skewed distributions. Examples of skewed distributions are shown in Figure 2.2 and Figure 2.3. The distribution depicted in Figure 2.2 is negatively skewed; a positive skew is shown in Figure 2.3. A mnemonic for remembering the distinction between positive and negative skewness is to note that the valence of the skewness applies to the tail, where positive is on the right and negative is on the left.

It is understandable that diagnostic schedules such as behavior problem rating scales produce skewed distributions. After all, only a small proportion of the population is experiencing a particular disorder at some point in time, and the majority of individuals are free of such symptomotology (positive skew). The distribution depicted in Figure 2.2, on the other hand, is negatively skewed.

The often skewed distributions obtained for personality measures, particularly diagnostic schedules, produce more controversy regarding scaling methods. If, for example, a distribution is heavily skewed, should normalized standard scores (which force nor-

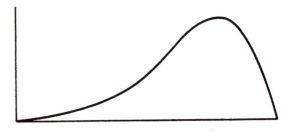

FIGURE 2.2

A hypothetical example of a negatively skewed distribution of scores

FIGURE 2.3

A hypothetical example of a positively skewed
distribution of scores

mality on the shape of the standard score distribution regardless of the shape of the raw score distribution) or linear transformations (which maintain the shape of the raw score distribution) be used? Petersen et al. (1989) maintain that "usually there is no good theoretical reason for normalizing scores" (p. 226), and we concur with this opinion.

What differences does the scaling method make (i.e., normalized versus linear transformations)? The primary difference is in the relationship between the standard scores (T-scores) and percentile ranks yielded by a test. The positively skewed distribution shown in Figure 2.3 is a good example of how this relationship can be affected. If this distribution was normalized (i.e., forced normal by converting raw scores to normal deviates and then the normal deviates to T-scores), then a T-score of 70 will *always* be at the 98th percentile. If linear transformations were used for this scale distribution shown in Figure 2.3, then the corresponding percentile rank could be 94 or something other than 98. Clearly the type of standard score used for scaling a test affects diagnostic, and perhaps treatment, decisions. If normalized standard scores were used for a positively skewed scale, then potentially fewer adolescents would be identified as having significant problems. On the other hand, normalized standard scores make the clinician's job easier by fostering interpretation across scales. Herein lies the debate: Is the interpretive convenience of normalized standard scores worth the trade-off in lack of precision?

Clinicians will find that many personality tests

use normalized standard scores (usually expressed in a T-score metric) even when clear evidence of significant skewness exists. We suggest that readers note the scaling method used by tests discussed in this volume as they consider the strengths and weaknesses of each measure.

COMPARING THE RESULTS OF DIFFERENT RATERS

Teachers, parents, children, and clinicians are all participants in the child assessment process. This multiaxial approach (McConaughy & Achenbach, 1989) is not requisite in adult assessment practice, where, not unlike medical assessment practice, the patient/client is the primary source of assessment information. Because of the perceived limited self-assessment capabilities of children, numerous additional raters and methods are used. As McConaughy and Achenbach (1989) observed: "Because children cannot provide a full account of their own functioning, it is necessary to obtain data from multiple sources" (p. 92). The veracity of adults, however, has also come under serious scrutiny (Nicholls, Licht, & Pearl, 1982). The presumption of children's inability to report on their own feelings and behavior requires careful empirical analysis. Some studies have evaluated the utility (validity) of various raters of child psychopathology, as summarized in the following sections. These findings are more than psychometric trivia; they are crucial for making the comparisons among informants that are required daily in child assessment practice.

Teachers

Teachers have sometimes been considered to be among the more accurate raters of child behavior (Martin, 1988a). They have the advantages of being able to observe children in a structured setting, and they have a comparison (norm) group against which they can compare the behavior of the child they are rating for the clinician. On the other hand, teachers may not use these advantages to their benefit. A recent study (Daniels, 1993) has shown that teachers do not differentiate ratings of child behavior as well as parents do.

Daniel (1993) performed a clever study of parent and teacher ratings by comparing the subtest specificity values yielded by raters using the BASC (see subsequent section for a review of the concept of subtest specificity). The rationale behind this study is that the better rater of child behavior would yield higher subtest specificity values (estimates of reliable specific variance). Higher specificities would suggest that the rater is more sensitive to behavioral differences across domains. Lower values would indicate that the rater tends to rate children more globally consistent with a kind of halo effect. The optimal rater would have higher specificities.

Daniel's (1993) specificities were clearly higher for parents than teachers. Parent specificities averaged .28 and 29; teacher values averaged .21. These results are striking given that the initial reliabilities of the parent ratings were lower than for teachers. Daniel (1993) concluded:

> *The implication of this finding is that parents are better able than teachers to describe children's behavior differentially. The ratings they give on one scale are less predictable from their ratings on other scales than is the case with teachers. Two explanations readily come to mind. One is that parents have a much longer time period than teachers in which to observe their child's behavior. A second is that a teacher, who comes into contact with a large number of children, may tend to form unidimensional or fairly simplified impressions of individual children, whereas a parent can more easily keep in mind the subtle variations in their own child's behavior. (p. 3)*

If these results are replicated with other samples and rating scales, new respect for parent ratings will be gained. Such findings suggest that at this time, parent and teacher ratings add unique information to the diagnostic process.

Parents

Parent–Teacher Agreement

There is some evidence that parents and teachers generally agree when reporting about externalizing behaviors when a structured interview assessment is used, although parents give higher estimates of behavior problems (Loeber et al., 1991). In the Loeber et al. (1991) investigation, parent, teacher, and child structured interview results were compared for a clinic population of 177 boys who were referred primarily for externalizing behavior problems. All reporters in this study were interviewed using the Diagnostic Interview Schedule for Children (DISC); Costello et al., 1987). Several findings from this investigation are of interest, particularly the finding that teachers reported fewer oppositional behavior, conduct problems, and hyperactive/inattentive behaviors than did parents.

Reynolds and Kamphaus (1992) evaluated parent–teacher agreement in a large national sample of 1,423 teacher-parent pairs. They drew the following conclusions:

1. Correlations between parent and teacher ratings are low to moderate.

2. These parent–teacher correlations increase after preschool. Median correlations between ratings at the preschool, child, and adolescent levels were .24, .37, and .35 respectively.

3. Parent and teacher ratings of externalizing problems (e.g., hyperactivity and conduct problems) and adaptive skills (e.g., social skills) correlate more highly (about .50) than ratings of internalizing problems (e.g., anxiety and depression).

4. Parent and teacher ratings correlated more with scales measuring the same construct (e.g., parent-rated attention problems versus teacher-rated attention problems) than with scales measuring differing constructs.

5. In spite of modest correlations, in some cases the level of agreement at the scale level for this large sample of nonreferred children showed considerable agreement in the T-scores obtained. All means hovered at about 50.

Mother–Father Agreement

A study by Christensen, Margolin, and Sullaway (1992) evaluated item rating agreement between parents in a sample of 137 families. The CBCL was used to rate children age 3 to 13 years. Several methods of assessing parental agreement revealed that both item characteristics and family distress affected item rating agreement.

The study's authors asked students to rate the characteristics of CBCL items across four dimensions: objectivity, observability, molarity, and social undesirability. Analyses revealed that the items most likely to produce parental agreement were characterized by greater objectivity, observability, and social undesirability and by less molarity. Since CBCL externalizing items were rated more favorably on these dimensions, there was greater item agreement on this scale than for the internalizing dimension.

Another factor identified by Christensen et al. (1992) as related to parental rating disagreement was family distress. For this study, family distress was defined as marital distress and/or the severity of child problems. Furthermore, families experiencing dual-system distress (i.e., blended families) versus single-system distress produced greater interparental disagreement.

The Christensen et al. (1992) investigation, however, ironically found that parents agreed on the total number of behavior problems identified (M = 11.1); they apparently just disagreed on the specifics. This finding is borne out by data presented in Reynolds and Kamphaus (1992), who compared the ratings of mothers and fathers for a large national sample using the Parent Rating Scale (PRS) of the BASC. These researchers tested mean T-score differences for mothers and fathers for children ranging in age from 4 through 18. Interestingly, there was little disagreement at the scale level with the exception of the Social Skills scale. What does this seemingly contradictory finding mean? It appears that while there may be considerable disagreement between mothers and fathers at the item level on rating scales, there is substantial agreement regarding the absolute number of problems that their child possesses.

Maternal Depression

The most frequently used rater of child behavior is the child's mother (Richters, 1992). There seem to be three commonly held perceptions about mothers' ratings of current and past behavior: (1) Mothers are inherently accurate raters of their children's behavior, (2) Mothers' ratings are a source of informant variance, and (3) Mothers tend to overrate child behavior problems if they are depressed. The third "conventional wisdom" sometimes results in a backward interpretive logic whereby a clinician considering highly significant maternal ratings of child behavior will begin to hypothesize about the mental status of the mother and question the veracity of her ratings.

Richters (1992) calls into question the causal link between maternal depression and ratings of child behavior suggested by results of many studies (e.g., Friedlander, Weiss, & Traylor, 1986; Schaughency & Lahey, 1985). Richters (1992) conducted a thorough review of this literature and found that few of the studies that hypothesized a link between maternal depression and distortion of children's behavior failed to control for a crucial variable—the level of behavior problems exhibited by the child. Richters (1992) found that 16 of the 17 studies he reviewed did not meet the minimal and necessary conditions to demonstrate evidence of distortion. He also noted that, "in contrast, all 5 studies that presented evidence counter to the distortion hypothesis examined mother–informant agreement using an appropriate metric. And in every case, the authors found that depressed mothers agreed with criterion informants about their children's functioning as well or better than did nondepressed mothers" (p. 496). This critical review calls into question a finding that is nearly axiomatic and calls on psychologists to no longer assume ratings distortion by depressed mothers without considerable clinical evidence and/or new research that unequivocally establishes such a link.

Children

Child–Adult Agreement

Loeber, Green, and Lahey (1990) found that boys significantly underreported conduct problems. They concluded: "On the whole, these prospective data appear to confirm that adults are better informants than children on disruptive child behavior problems" (p. 93). Children may be better able to accurately describe internalizing problems such as anxiety and depression. Furthermore, although children may be more adept at rating certain behaviors, it appears that it is important to routinely collect child perceptions in most assessment situations. Rater agreement issues are discussed further in subsequent chapters.

RELIABILITY

The *reliability* of a test refers to the degree to which its scores are free from errors of measurement (APA, 1985). The type of reliability that is of particular interest to personality test users is stability, or the degree to which a child's personality test scores are likely to be similar from one measurement to the next. The various theories of personality all suggest that it is a fairly stable trait over the course of development. If an individual has a personality trait, it is likely to remain this way barring any unusual circumstances.

The Reliability Coefficient

The reliability of a personality test is expressed by the computation of a reliability coefficient, which is a special type of correlation coefficient. One essential difference between a reliability coefficient and a correlation coefficient is that reliability coefficients are typically not negative, while negative correlation coefficients are eminently possible. Reliability coefficients range, then, from 0 to +1. Reliability coefficients represent the amount of reliable variance associated with a test. In other words, a reliability coefficient is not squared, as is the case with correlation coefficients, to calculate the amount of reliable variance (Anastasi, 1988). For example, the reliable variance of a test with a reliability coefficient of .90 is 90%, an unusually easy computation!

The error variance associated with a test is also easy to calculate. It is done by subtracting the reliability coefficient from 1 (perfect reliability). Taking the previous example, the error variance for a test with a reliability coefficient of .90 is 10% (1 − .90).

Test-Retest Method

The most popular method for computing the stability of personality test scores is the test-retest method. In this method the same test, for example the MMPI-A, is administered to the same group of individuals under the same or similar conditions over a brief period of time (typically 2 to 4 weeks). The correlation between the first and second administrations of the test is then computed, yielding a test-retest reliability coefficient that is typically very close to 1.0, usually somewhere between .90 and .98.

Internal Consistency Coefficients

Another type of reliability coefficient typically reported in personality test manuals is an internal consistency coefficient. This estimate is very different from test-retest or stability coefficients in that it does not assess directly the stability of the measure of personality over time. Internal consistency coefficients assess what the name implies—the average correlation among the items in a personality test, or, in other words, the homogeneity of the test item pool. Internal consistency coefficients are valuable primarily because they are inexpensively produced, since they only require one administration of the test, and serve as good estimates of test-retest or stability coefficients. Typical formulae used for the computation of internal consistency coefficients include split-half coefficients, Kuder Richardson 20, and Coefficient Alpha (Anastasi, 1988).

On occasion there are differences between internal consistency and test-retest coefficients that can affect personality test interpretation. A test may, for example, have a relatively poor internal consistency coefficient and yet have a strong test-retest coefficient (Kamphaus, 1993). Because internal consistency coefficients are imperfect estimates of stability coefficients, both types of coefficients should be recorded in the manual for a personality test (see also the test standards of the American Psychological Association, 1985).

In some cases a high test-retest coefficient may be undesirable. If a test professes to assess a personality state that is hypothesized to be unstable over time, a strong test-retest coefficient may call into question the theory underlying the test.

Variables That Affect Reliability

Clinicians who use personality tests should be especially cognizant of factors that can affect reliability. Foremost among these is test length (Nitko, 1983). The longer the test, the more likely the clinician is to obtain an accurate assessment of a child's personality. For this reason, short forms of personality tests are generally frowned upon. Other factors that the clinician should keep in mind when estimating the reliability of a test for a particular child include the following:

1. Reliability is affected by homogeneous samples. Differentiating among the very disturbed may be difficult since these individuals represent a very small range of scores (Nitko, 1983).

2. Reliability can change for different ability levels. A test that is very reliable for emotionally disturbed students is not necessarily as reliable for nonhandicapped students without research evidence to support its use (Nitko, 1983).

3. Reliability can suffer when there is a long interval between assessments (Nitko, 1983).

4. Reliability can be affected by child characteristics such as age, reading level, and fatigue. Reliability of personality measurement, for example, may drop if the child does not understand the test items.

Reliable Specific Variance

Another reliability coefficient that has recently become more popular is the estimate of reliable specific variance, more commonly referred to as *subtest specificity* (Kaufman, 1979). Subtest specificity is the amount of reliable specific variance that can be attributed to a single subtest or scale. Kaufman popularized the use of subtest specificity in clinical assessment as a way of gauging the amount of confidence a clinician should have in conclusions that are based on a single subtest. In effect, knowledge of subtest specificity makes clinicians more cautious about drawing conclusions based on a single scale.

A reliability coefficient represents the amount of reliable variance associated with a scale. An example would be an anxiety scale taken from a larger battery of 13 tests, all of which are part of a major personality test battery. The anxiety scale has a test-retest reliability coefficient of .82. On the surface this test looks reliable. If this scale produces the child's highest score, the examiner may wish to say that the child has a problem with anxiety. The examiner can then make this statement with confidence because the test is relatively reliable, right? Not necessarily. As Kaufman (1979) points out, the conclusion being drawn by the clinician is about some skill, trait, or ability (in this case anxiety) that is specific or *measured only by this one scale*. The reliability coefficient, on the other hand, reflects not just reliable specific variance but also reliable shared variances. Subtest specificity is typically computed in the following way (Kamphaus, 1993):

1. Compute the multiple correlation (R) between the scale in question and all other scales in the battery and square it (R^2). This computation yields the amount of reliable shared variance between the scale in question, in this case anxiety, and the other scales in the battery.

2. Subtract the squared multiple correlation coefficient from the reliability coefficient, or r_{tt}. If $R^2 = .30$, $.82 - .30 = .52$. This formula yields the reliable specific variance.

3. Compare the amount of reliable specific variance (.52) to the amount of error variance ($1 - .82 = .18$). If the reliable specific variance exceeds the error variance by .20 or more, then the scale is considered to have adequate specificity for interpretive purposes. If the reliable specific variance exceeds the error variance by .19 or less, then the test lacks specificity, and it should be cautiously interpreted. If the reliable specific variance does not exceed the error variance, then interpretation of the scale is ill advised.

Fortunately, subtest specificity values are sometimes computed for tests, and summary tables of values are provided. Clinicians new to practice should remember that the observed reliability coefficients for a scale are not adequate for gauging the reliable specific variance of a scale.

Standard Error of Measurement

The standard error of measurement (SEM) gives an indication of the amount of error associated with test scores. In more technical terms, the SEM is the standard deviation of the error distribution of scores. The reliability coefficient of a personality test is one way of expressing the amount of error associated with a personality test score in order to allow the user to gauge the level of confidence that should be placed in the obtained scores. An examiner may report a personality test score for a child as being 63 with a test reliability coefficient of .95. This practice, however, is unorthodox and clumsy. The typical practice is to report a personality test score along with the test's standard error of measurement, as is frequently done for opinion polls conducted by the popular media (e.g., the error rate of this poll is . . .). The standard error of measurement simply is another way of reflecting the amount of error associated with a test score.

In theory, if a child were administered a personality test 100 times under identical conditions, he or she would not get the same composite score on all 100 administrations. The child would not obtain the same composite score because the reliability of a personality test is imperfect. Rather, the child would obtain a distribution of scores that approximates a normal curve. Hence, in theory, *error is also normally distributed.* This error distribution would have a mean. The mean of this theoretical distribution of scores is the child's true score. *A true score is a theoretical construct that can only be estimated.* This error distribution, like other normal distributions, not only has a mean; it also can be divided into standard deviations. In an error distribution, however, instead of being called a standard deviation it is called the SEM. As one would predict, then, in this error distribution of scores ±1 SEM divides up the same portion of the normal curve (68%) as does a standard deviation and ±2 SEMs divides up the same proportion of the error distribution (95%) as ±2 standard deviations does for a normal distribution of obtained scores.

Confidence Bands

A *confidence band* is a probability statement about the likelihood that a particular range of scores includes a child's true score. As is done with opinion polls, clinicians use the SEM to show the amount of error, or unreliability, associated with obtained scores on personality tests. Obtained scores are banded with error. Banding is frequently accomplished by subtracting 1 SEM from and adding 1 SEM to the obtained score. If, for example, the child obtained a T-score of 73 on the Reynolds Child Depression Scale (RCDS; Reynolds, 1989), one could apply the theory of standard error of measurement to band this score with error. For the total RCDS sample the standard error of measurement rounds to 4 T-score points (Reynolds, 1989). Given that ±1 SEM includes approximately 68% of the error distribution of scores, the clinician could then say that there is a 68% likelihood that the child's true score lies somewhere in the range of 69 to 77. Or an examiner who wanted to use a more conservative ±2 SEMs could say that there is a 95% probability that the child's true score lies somewhere between 65 and 81. Confidence bands can be obtained for a variety of levels if one knows the SEM of the scale. Some manuals include confidence bands at the 68%, 85%, 90%, 95%, and 99% levels.

Regression Effects

Regression effects are the well-known phenomenon of discrepant scores tending to regress toward the mean upon retesting. Using the obtained score to make a probability statement about the child's true score is probably a very reasonable practice for scores in the middle of the distribution, that is, for children with scores near the average. However, at the tails of the distribution for the severely impaired or the exceedingly stable, use of the obtained score with its associated confidence band is more questionable because of regression effects. In theory and in everyday practice, scores at the tails of the distribution are less reliable and, as such, they are more likely to regress (move) toward the mean upon retesting. Because of such effects, some test manuals (e.g., WISC-III) include asymmetrical confidence bands. This practice, however, has not been applied frequently in personality assessment. If asymmetrical bands are used, a child's estimated true T-score rather than the obtained T-score is banded with error.

If, for example, a child has an obtained T-score of 73 on a test with a reliability coefficient of .90 (such as is the case for the RCDS), there is little regression to the mean when a theoretical true score is computed (the formula for an estimated true score in this case would be estimated by the formula $T = 50 + r_{xx} (X - 50)$, where r_{xx} is the reliability of the RCDS and X is the obtained T-score. The resulting estimated true score in this example (where $r_{xx} = .90$ and X = 73) is 70 (70.7). Using ± 1 SEM in this case yields a confidence band of 66 to 74, which reflects the greater likelihood that regression effects would be obtained on retesting.

Most test manuals ignore regression effects and simply use *a symmetrical confidence bands,* where the obtained T-score is assigned a confidence band. This practice has become customary but clinicians should insist otherwise.

VALIDITY

Validity is the foundation upon which the use of modern tests of personality is based. *Validity* is defined as the degree to which tests measure what they purport to measure. There are a number of different ways of evaluating the validity of a test (APA, 1985). Some of the more common types of validity evidence will be discussed in this section. Validity is the most important psychometric characteristic of a personality test. A test can be extremely well normed and extremely reliable and yet have no validity for the assessment of personality. One could, for example, develop a very good test of fine motor skill, but if one were to try to call this a test of personality, there would likely be a number of opponents to this point of view.

Content Validity

One of the reasons that many people would disagree with using a test of vocabulary knowledge as a measure of personality is that it does not appear to possess valid content. *Content validity* refers to the appropriate sampling of a particular content domain.

Content validity has been most closely associated with the development of tests of academic achievement (Anastasi, 1988). Typically procedures for the establishment of content validity are judgmental (Petersen, Kolen, & Hoover, 1989). In the process of developing an academic achievement test a group of consulting editors (experts) will be used to define the appropriate content for reading, mathematics, spelling, and other areas included in the battery. This board of editors will define the content and determine the match between the content used in the test and the curricula typically used in schools.

Personality test developers have often relied on empirical test development methods where items are assigned to scales based on statistical properties only (such as factor loadings, to be discussed later), and many manuals do not provide a clear indication of the source of items. In some cases the item source is clear, such as with the Children's Depression Inventory (CDI), whose items were based on accepted diagnostic nosologies such as the DSM. Even in such cases, however, personality test developers usually do not go to the lengths of achievement test developers to document adequate sampling of the content (or psychopathology) domain. Few personality tests, for example, use panels of experts to develop item content. One exception is the Student Observation Scale (SOS) of the BASC (Reynolds & Kamphaus, 1992) (see Chapter 9).

Criterion-Related Validity

Criterion-related validity assesses the degree to which personality tests relate to other tests in a theoretically appropriate manner. There are two kinds of criterion-related validity—concurrent and predictive.

Concurrent Validity

This type of validity stipulates that a personality test should show substantial correlations with other measures to which it is theoretically related. One of the important criteria for the evaluation of personality measures since their inception was that they show a substantial correlation with other indications of psychopathology such as well-validated tests or clinicians' ratings or diagnoses. The typical concurrent validity investigation involves administering a new personality test and an existing well-validated measure of psychopathology to a group of children. If a correlation of .20 is obtained, then the concurrent validity of the personality test would be in question. A .75 correlation, on the other hand, would be supportive of the validity of the new personality test.

Predictive Validity

The other important type of criterion related validity is *predictive validity,* the ability of a personality test to predict (as shown by its correlation) some later criterion. This type of research investigation is conducted very similarly to a concurrent validity study, with one important exception. This difference is that in a predictive validity study the new personality test is first administered to a group of children, and then sometime in the future—perhaps 2 months, 3 months, or even 2 years—a criterion measure (such as clinicians' ratings of adjustment) is administered to the same group of children.

Construct Validity

Virtually every aspect of a personality test either contributes to or detracts from its ability to measure the construct of personality or, in other words, its *construct validity.* Construct validity is the degree to which a test measures some hypothetical construct such as personality. As such, the construct validity of a personality test cannot be established based upon a single research investigation or the study of only one type of validity (e.g., factor analysis). Construct validity is based upon the long-term accumulation of research evidence about a particular instrument, using a variety of procedures for the assessment of validity. In fact, a statement that a test is valid or invalid is inappropriate. Tests are validated or invalidated for specific uses or circumstances (APA, 1985).

Correlations with Other Tests

One can use correlations with other tests to evaluate the validity of a personality test. In a sense this method is a special type of concurrent validity study. The difference here is that the correlation is not between a personality measure and some criterion variable, such as clinicians' ratings of adjustment, but between a personality test and a measure of the same construct, another personality measure. For example, if a new test of anxiety is published, it should show a substantial relationship with previous measures, but not an extremely high relationship (Anastasi, 1988). If a new personality test correlates .99 with a previous personality test, then it is not needed, as it is simply another form of an existing test and does not contribute any to increasing our understanding of the construct of personality (Anastasi, 1988). If a new anxiety scale correlates only .15 with existing well-validated anxiety scales, it is likely also to not be a good measure of personality. New personality tests should show a moderate to strong relationship with existing tests of personality, yet contribute something new to our understanding of the personality construct of interest.

Convergent/Discriminant Validity

Convergent validity is established when a personality test construct correlates with constructs with which it is hypothesized to have a strong relationship. Discriminant validity is supported when a personality measure has a poor correlation with a construct with which it is hypothesized to be unrelated.

If one were assessing the convergent and discriminant validity of the BASC-PRS Depression scale in relationship to the Achenbach CBCL, the following predictions would be in order.

1. The BASC-PRS Anxiety scale should correlate significantly with the CBCL Anxious/Depressed scale since this is another internalizing problem scale (convergent validity).

2. The BASC-PRS Anxiety scale should *not* correlate highly with the CBCL Delinquent Behavior scale since this is an externalizing problem scale (discriminant validity).

The BASC manual reveals that results are consistent with these predictions. The BASC-PRS Anxiety scale correlates with a measure of a similar construct on the CBCL at .52, which is evidence of convergent validity. Yet, the BASC-PRS Anxiety scale did not correlate well at .00 with the measure of a dissimilar construct, the CBCL Delinquent Behavior scale (Reynolds & Kamphaus, 1992).

Factor Analysis

Factor analysis is a popular technique for validating modern tests of personality that traces its roots to the work of the eminent statistician Karl Peterson (1901). Factor analysis has become increasingly popular as a technique for test validation because of the onset of high-speed computers that greatly facilitate what was formerly a very laborious statistical procedure. A wealth of factor-analytic studies dates to the 1960s.

Factor analysis is difficult to explain in only a few paragraphs. Those readers who are interested in learning factor analysis need a separate course on this particular technique and a great deal of independent reading and experience. A very thorough discussion of factor-analytic techniques can be found in Gorsuch (1988). An introductory-level discussion can be found in Anastasi (1988) and Keith (1990).

Factor analysis is a data reduction technique that attempts to explain variance the most efficient way (Anastasi, 1988, Keith, 1990). Most scales or items included in a personality test correlate with one another. It is theorized that this correlation is the result of one or more common factors. The purpose of factor analysis is to reduce the correlations between all scales (or items) in a personality test to a smaller set of common factors. This smaller set of factors will presumably be more interpretable than all of the scales in a personality test battery considered as individual entities.

Factor analysis begins with the computation of an intercorrelation matrix showing the correlations among all of the items or scales in a personality test battery (most studies of personality tests use item intercorrelations as input). These intercorrelations then serve as the input to a factor-analytic program that is part of a popular statistical analysis package.

The output from a factor analysis that is frequently reported first in test validation research is a factor matrix showing the factor loading of each subtest on each factor. A *factor loading* is in most cases the correlation between a subtest and a factor.[2] Factor loadings range from –1 to +1 just as do correlation coefficients. Selected factor loadings for the MMPI-A factor analysis of the standardization sample (Butcher et al., 1992) are shown in Table 2.2. A high positive correlation between a scale and a factor means the same thing as a high positive correlation between two subtests in that they tend to covary to a great extent. One can see from Table 2.2 that the Hysteria scale is highly correlated with Factor 1, for example, and that Mania is not highly correlated with Factor 1, but it is rather highly correlated with Factor 2.

Once the factor matrix, as shown in Table 2.2, is obtained, the researcher must label the obtained factors. This labeling is not based upon statistical procedures but upon the theoretical knowledge and skill of the individual researcher (Anastasi, 1988; Keith, 1990). For the MMPI-A there is general agreement as to the names of the factors. The first factor is typically referred to as general maladjustment, and the second as overcontrol. The third and fourth factors are named after the scales with the highest loadings on each, social introversion and masculinity-femininity (Butcher et al., 1992).

Test developers often eliminate scales or items based upon factor analyses. They also commonly design their composite scores based on factor-analytic results. This process was not followed in the development of the MMPI-A, as this test was developed long before the ready availability of factor-analytic procedures. Although the MMPI-A appears to be a four-factor test, it produces 10 clinical scale T-scores, and no composite scores corresponding to the four obtained factors are offered. More recently developed tests such as the CBCL made heavy use of factor-analytic methods in the development of scale and composite scores (see Chapter 6).

Generally, then, consumers of factor-analytic

---

[2]When orthogonal (independent or uncorrelated) rotation techniques are used (and these techniques are very frequently used in test validation research), the factor loading represents the correlation between the subtest and a factor. This is not the case when oblique or correlated methods of factor analysis are used (Anastasi, 1988).

TABLE 2.2   Selected MMPI factor loadings

	Factors			
	1	2	3	4
	General Maladjustment	*Overcontrol*	*Social Introversion*	*Masculinity Femininity*
Hs	.77	.09	.31	.05
D	.69	−.23	.51	−.08
Hy	.88	−.15	−.22	−.15
Pd	.71	.28	.21	.19
Mf	.08	.01	.07	−.84
Pa	.70	.19	.23	.25
Pt	.52	.39	.67	.06
Sc	.61	.38	.53	.36
Ma	.31	.78	−.04	.33
Si	.19	.10	.91	.02

NOTE: These are varimax rotated factor loadings.

SOURCE: Adapted from Butcher et al., 1992.

research seek comparability between the factors and composite scores offered for interpretation. If there is, for example, a one-to-one relationship between the number of factors found and the number of composite scores produced, then the validity of the composite scores is likely enhanced.

Confirmatory Factor Analysis

The procedures discussed thus far are generally referred to as *exploratory factor-analytic procedures.* A newer factor-analytic technique that is receiving increasing attention is called *confirmatory factor analysis* (Joreskog & Sorbom, 1986). These two factor-analytic procedures differ in some very important ways. In exploratory factor analysis the number of factors to be yielded is typically dictated by the characteristics of the intercorrelation matrix. That is, the number of factors selected is based upon the amount of variance that each factor explains in the correlation matrix. If a factor, for example, explains 70% of the variance in the correlation matrix, then it is typically included as a viable factor in further aspects of the factor analysis. If, on the other hand, the factor only accounts for 2% of the variance in a factor matrix, then it may not be included as a viable factor.

In direct contrast, in confirmatory factor analysis the number of factors is not dictated by data, but rather by the theory underlying the test under investigation. In confirmatory factor analysis the number of factors is selected *a priori,* as well as the scales that load on each factor (Keith, 1990). In addition, the general fit between the factor structure dictated a priori and the obtained data are assessed. If there is a great deal of correspondence between the hypothesized structure and the obtained factor structure, then the validity of the personality test is supported (hence the term *confirmatory*) and the theory is confirmed. If, for example, a researcher hypothesized the existence of four factors in a particular personality test, the confirmatory factor analysis will, in fact, yield four factors. Statistics assessing the fit of these four factors to the data may, however, indicate a lack of congruence (correlation) between the hypothesized four factors and the obtained four factors.

Thorough confirmatory factor-analytic studies use a variety of statistics to assess the fit of the hypothesized factor structure to the data. These include a chi square statistic, goodness-of-fit index (GFI), adjusted goodness-of-fit index (AGFI), and root mean square residual (RMR). Several statistics are desirable for checking the fit of a confirmatory factor analysis because all of these statistics have strengths and weaknesses. The chi square statistic, for example, is highly influenced by sample size (Glutting & Kaplan, 1990). Some general guidelines for assessing the fit of a confirmatory factor analysis solution include the following (Kline, 1989):

1. Nonsignificant chi square statistic
2. GFI > .90
3. AGFI > .80
4. RMC < .10

Consequently, confirmatory factor-analytic procedures may yield the number of factors hypothesized by the test developer, which, in exploratory factor analysis, would lend support to the theory and structure of the test. In confirmatory factor analysis, however, consumers of the research have to evaluate the statistics that assess the fit between the hypothesized and the obtained factor structure. These statistics will indicate whether or not the evidence is strong or weak for the validity of the scores yielded by the test under study.

Another issue in confirmatory factor analysis is that some researchers use it in an exploratory factor-analytic manner (Keith, 1990). Some authors specify a model a priori and then modify that model numerous times until adequate fit statistics are obtained which is essentially an exploratory approach. Ideally researchers should conduct studies comparing competing theoretical models (see Kline, 1989, for an example) in order to evaluate the theoretical structure of a test. An excellent nonmathematical introduction to confirmatory factor-analytic procedures can be found in Kline (1989).

Cluster Analysis

Cluster analysis is similar in many ways to factor analysis. Specifically, similarly to factor analysis, cluster analysis attempts to reduce the complexity of a data set. In factor analysis it is typical to try to reduce a large number of variables (e.g., items) to a smaller set. In cluster analysis, researchers are most often interested in grouping individuals (as opposed

to variables) into groups of people who share common characteristics. Ward's (1963) method is a popular cluster-analytic technique.

Several steps are common to cluster-analytic techniques, including the following:

1. Collect a sample of individuals who have been administered one test or a battery of tests.

2. For each variable (e.g., depression scores) compute the distance between each pair of children.

3. These distances between each individual on each variable are then used to produce a proximity matrix. This matrix serves as the input for the cluster analysis in the same way that correlation or covariance matrices are used as input in factor analysis.

4. Apply a cluster-analytic method that sorts individuals based on the distances between individuals that were plotted in the proximity matrix. In simple terms, clustering methods in this step match individuals with the smallest distance between individuals on a particular variable.

5. This sorting process continues until groups of individuals are formed that are homogeneous (i.e., have profiles of scores of similar level and shape). These groups are analogous to the factors formed in factor analysis.

6. Just as in factor analysis the researcher next has to decide on the number of groups that is the most clinically meaningful.

Cluster-analytic techniques are useful in psychopathology research for identifying subtypes of disorders or for designing diagnostic systems (Borgen & Barnett, 1987). Cluster-analytic techniques have frequently been applied to identify subgroups based on their performance on a particular personality measure (e.g., LaCombe et al., 1991).

Threats to Validity

Readability

An obvious but easily overlooked threat to validity is lack of ability of the parent, teacher, or child to understand the personality test items. While concern is often expressed about the ability of children to read test items, parents also have difficulty due to limited educational attainment or cultural or linguistic differences. Harrington and Follett (1984) found that most tests available at the time they conducted their study failed to address the issue in their test manuals. They provide several suggestions to the practitioner for screening informants in order to guard against readability serving as a threat to validity.

For parents, Harrington and Follett (1984) recommend having them read the test instructions for the informant and paraphrase. Children can be asked to read some items from the beginning, middle, and end of the instrument aloud so the examiner can gauge the child's reading skill.

Response Sets

A *response set* is a tendency to answer questions in a biased fashion, thus masking the true feelings of the informant. These response sets are often mentioned, and in some personality tests addressed in construction and interpretation.

The *social desirability response set* is the tendency of the informant to respond to items in a socially acceptable way (Anastasi, 1988). Some personality tests include items and scales to assess the potential effects of such a response set. "I like everyone that I meet" might be an item on such scales. The *acquiescence response set* is the tendency to answer true or yes to a majority of the items (Kaplan & Saccuzzo, 1993). A third response set is called *deviation,* and it comes into play when an informant tends to give unusual or uncommon responses to items (Anastasi, 1988).

Guarding Against Validity Threats

Personality tests often include other validity scales or indexes in order to allow the examiner to detect validity threats. Some tests include fake bad scales, which assess the tendency to exaggerate problems. Computer scoring of personality tests has allowed for the inclusion of consistency indexes. One such index allows the examiner to determine if the infor-

mant is answering questions in a predictable pattern. A consistency index might be formed by identifying pairs of test items that correlate highly. If an informant responds inconsistently to such highly correlated items, then his or her veracity may be suspect.

Examiners often also conduct informal validity checks. One quick check is to determine whether or not the informant responded to enough items to make the test valid. Another elementary validity check involves scanning the form for patterned responding. A form that routinely alternates between true and false responses may reflect a patterning of responses.

One way to limit the influence of response sets is to ensure that informants are clear about the clinician's expectations. Some clients may also need to take the personality test under more controlled circumstances. If an examiner has reason to believe, for example, that a child is oppositional, then the self-report personality measure may best be completed in the presence of the examiner.

CONCLUSIONS

Knowledge of psychometric principles is crucial for the proper interpretation of personality tests. As psychometrics become more complex, clinicians have to become increasingly sophisticated regarding psychometric theory. Since personality assessment technology has generally lagged behind other forms of child assessment, knowledge of psychometric theory must more often be considered by the clinician when interpreting scores.

Some personality tests, for example, do not include basic psychometric properties such as standard errors of measurement in the manual (the MMPI-A manual only includes SEM's for the scale raw scores and not for T-scores). Such oversights discourage the user from considering the error associated with scores, which is a basic consideration for scale interpretation. Omissions like this are rare in academic and intelligence assessment. The application of the SEM is merely one example of the psychometric pitfalls to be overcome by the user of personality tests.

CHAPTER SUMMARY

1. A T-score is a standard score that has a mean of 50 and standard deviation of 10.

2. A percentile rank gives an individual's relative position within the norm group.

3. In order to select a representative sample of the national population for any country, test developers typically use what are called *stratification variables.*

4. *Local norms* are those based on some more circumscribed subset of a larger population.

5. Children are likely better at rating internalizing than externalizing behaviors.

6. Parents tend to produce more differentiated ratings than do teachers.

7. The *reliability* of a test refers to the degree to which its scores are free from errors of measurement.

8. *Subtest specificity* is the amount of reliable specific variance that can be attributed to a single subtest.

9. The *standard error of measurement* (SEM) is the standard deviation of the error distribution of scores.

10. A *confidence band* is a probability statement about the likelihood that a particular range of scores includes a child's true score.

11. *Regression effects* are the tendency of discrepant scores to regress toward the mean upon retesting.

12. *Validity* is the degree to which tests measure what they purport to measure.

13. *Content validity* refers to the appropriate sampling of a particular content domain.

14. *Concurrent validity* stipulates that a personality test should show substantial correlations with other measures with which it should theoretically correlate.

15. *Predictive validity* refers to the ability of a personality test to predict (as shown by its correlation) some later criterion.

16. *Convergent validity* is established when a personality test construct correlates with constructs with which it is hypothesized to have a strong relationship. *Discriminant validity* is supported when a personality measure has a poor correlation with a construct with which it is not supposed to have a relationship.

17. *Factor analysis* is a data reduction technique that attempts to explain the variance in a personality test parsimoniously.

18. A *factor loading* is in most cases the correlation between a subtest and a factor.

19. A newer factor-analytic technique that is receiving increasing attention is *confirmatory factor analysis.*

20. In confirmatory factor analysis, however, consumers of the research have to evaluate the statistics that assess the fit between the hypothesized and the obtained factor structure.

21. *Cluster-analysis* researchers are most often interested in grouping individuals (as opposed to variables) into groups of individuals who share common characteristics.

22. Personality tests often include other validity scales or indexes in order to allow the examiner to detect validity threats.

Classification and
Developmental Psychopathology

CHAPTER QUESTIONS

- Why is understanding basic research on children's and adolescents' emotional and behavioral functioning important to clinical assessment?

- How are classification and assessment related?

- What are some of the models that have been used for the classification of the emotional and behavioral functioning of children and adolescents?

- What are some of the advantages and dangers of classification?

- What are some of the most important implications from basic research in the field of developmental psychopathology for the clinical assessment of children and adolescents?

SCIENCE AND ASSESSMENT

A basic assumption that underlies the writing of this text is that to be competent in the clinical assess-

ment of children and adolescents, much more knowledge is required than simple cognizance of the techniques of test administration. This is actually the easy part. Many other crucial areas of expertise are necessary if one is to appropriately select which tests to administer and interpret them after administration. One such area of expertise was the focus of the previous chapter: an understanding of the science of measuring psychological constructs. However, a more basic level of knowledge is needed even to appropriately use measurement theory. That is, one must have an understanding of the nature of the phenomenon one is attempting to measure before one can determine the best method for measuring it. Specifically, the phenomenon of interest in this text is the emotional and behavioral functioning of youth. The first hint at the importance of this basic understanding of psychological constructs came in the previous chapter on psychometrics. It should have become clear that good psychometric properties are not absolutes. They depend on the nature and characteristics of the *specific* psychological construct one is trying to assess. For example, childhood depression is frequently characterized by multiple episodes of depression interspersed with periods of normal mood (Kovacs et al., 1984). Therefore, high stability estimates over lengthy time periods should not be expected. In fact, if such stability occurs, then one is measuring something that is not episodic depression.

In addition to appropriately utilizing psychometric theory, understanding the nature of the phenomenon to be assessed is crucial to almost every aspect of a clinical assessment, from designing the assessment battery and selecting the tests, to interpreting the information and communicating the information to the child and parent. For these reasons, science and clinical practice are inextricably linked. There are many areas of basic research that enhance an assessor's ability to conduct psychological evaluations, but we have selected two that we feel are most critical to the clinical assessment of children and adolescents. First, understanding the theories that guide different models of classification are necessary because the framework that one uses to define and classify psychological functioning determines how one designs and interprets an assessment battery. Second, the clinical assessment of children must be conducted within the context of a broad knowledge of developmental psychopathology.

Developmental psychopathology refers to an integration of two scientific disciplines: child development and child psychopathology. The integration rests on the basic assumption that the most appropriate way to view the emotional and behavioral functioning of children, both normal and problematic, is within a comprehensive framework that includes the influence of developmental processes (Rutter & Garmezy, 1983). A noted developmental psychopathologist, Judy Garber, summarized her view of this field as being "concerned with both the normal processes of change and adaptation and the abnormal reactions to stress or adversity, as well as the relationship between the two" (Garber, 1984, p. 30). Developmental psychopathology, then, is a framework for understanding children's emotions and behaviors that has many implications for the assessment process.

It is beyond the scope of this book to provide an intensive and exhaustive discussion of theories of classification or of the many important findings in the field of developmental psychopathology. Instead, this chapter will illustrate how critical these two areas of knowledge are to the assessment process and will provide at least a basic framework for applying knowledge in these areas to the assessment of children and adolescents. The discussion that follows highlights some of the issues in both areas that we feel have the most relevance to the assessment process.

CLASSIFICATION

Classification refers to the process of placing psychological phenomenon into distinct categories according to some specified set of rules. There are two levels of classification. One level of classification is a method of determining when psychological functioning is abnormal, deviant, or in need of treatment. On a second level, classification is a method of distinguishing between different dimensions or types of psychological functioning. When classification is viewed this way, it becomes clear that clinical assessment is at least partly a process of classification. It involves (1) determining whether some areas of psychological functioning are pathological and in need of treatment and (2) determining the types of pathology that are present. Stated another way by Achenbach (1982), "assessment and classification are two facets of what should be a single process: assessment aims to identify the distinguishing features of individual cases; taxonomy (classification) is the grouping of cases according to their distinguishing features" (p. 1). Therefore, understanding the issues involved in classification is essential to clinical assessment.

The first issue involves the inherent imperfection in any classification system of psychological functioning. Psychological phenomena don't fall neatly into categories of normal and abnormal or into clear nonoverlapping types of dysfunction. This seems to be especially true with children, where there is often no clear demarcation of when a dimension of behavior should be considered pathological and there is often a high degree of overlap between the various forms of psychopathology. Therefore, any system of classification is bound to be imperfect. Due to this imperfection, many experts have argued against the need for any *formal* classification system. Instead, they argue that psychological functioning should be assessed and described idiosyncratically for each individual person. That is, each person is a unique individual whose psychological functioning should simply be described in ways that maintain this uniqueness without being compared with other individuals or fitted into artificial categories. This argument has quite some intuitive appeal given the complexity of human nature. However, there are several compelling arguments for why we need *good* classification systems, in spite of the fact that even the best system will be imperfect.

The Need for Classification Systems

Communication

The main purpose of classification systems is to provide a means of communication among professionals (Blashfield, 1984; Quay, 1986). A classification system defines the rules by which psychological constructs are defined. Without such systems, psychological constructs are defined by idiosyncratic rules developed by each professional, and one cannot understand the terminology used by a professional unless one understands the rules he or she employed in defining the terms. For example, the term *depression* is a psychological construct that has had many meanings in the psychological literature on children. It can refer to Major Depressive Episodes, as defined by the *Diagnostic and Statistical Manual of Mental Disorders, Fourth Edition* (DSM-IV; APA, 1994). In contrast, it can refer to elevations on a rating scale of depression (Curry & Craighead, 1993) or to a set of responses on a projective technique (Exner & Weiner, 1982). There is even the concept of masked depression that has been used to describe the belief that many childhood problems (e.g., hyperactivity, enuresis, learning disabilities) are the result of an underlying depressive state (Cytryn & McKnew, 1974). Not surprisingly, each of these definitions identifies a unique group of children.

With all of these uses of the term *depression,* simply saying that a child exhibits depression does not communicate much to another professional without a further explanation of how this classification was made. In contrast, if one states that the child meets criteria for Major Depression according to DSM-IV criteria, then you have made a classification using a system with clearly defined rules. Another professional will have a clear idea of how you are defining depression, even if he or she does not agree with the DSM-IV system. However, this communication requires precision in the use of terms. In this example, using the term *Major Depression* would be misleading and actually hurt communication if the term was used without ensuring that the DSM-IV criteria were met (e.g., based on responses from a projective technique).

Applying Research to Practice

In the introduction to this chapter we argued that clinical assessment should be based on the nature and characteristics of the phenomenon being assessed. Classification systems are critical for this purpose. Unless clinical assessment identifies features of a case that can be related to other cases *with similar features,* then the field's accumulated knowledge cannot be applied to the individual case (Achenbach, 1982). For example, there have been many definitions of the hyperactive child syndrome or Attention-Deficit Hyperactivity Disorder (APA, 1994) that have been used over the past several decades, and research findings often differ depending on which definition is used (see Frick and Lahey [1991]). Therefore, what research findings may be applicable to a given case will depend on how attention deficit disorder is defined. A scientific approach to clinical assessment requires classification.

Documentation of Need for Services

Classification systems allow for the documentation of the need for services. This encompasses documenting the need for special education services for a child, determining the need for mental health services within a given catchment area, attempting to determine appropriate staffing patterns within an institution, or documenting the need for services to third-party payers (e.g., insurance companies). These uses of classification systems have been the most controversial because the imperfections inherent in existing systems can lead to very deleterious outcomes for many people. Unfortunately, the task of documenting need is inextricably linked to classification because it requires some method of *classifying* those in need of services and those not in need of services. The solution cannot be to eliminate classification systems, but instead it should be (1) to develop better systems of classification that more directly predict the need for services and (2) to educate other professionals on the limitations of classifications systems, so that they can be used more appropriately for documenting the need for services.

Dangers of Classification

Due to the reasons already stated, we feel that classification systems are needed. However, users of classification systems must be aware of the dangers and limitations of such systems. Since clinical assessment is a process of classification, the clinical assessor especially must be cognizant of these dangers. Many of these dangers can be limited if classification systems are used appropriately. Therefore, in the discussion that follows we have tried to not only outline the dangers of classification but also to present practices that limit potentially harmful effects.

Because psychological phenomena, and the persons they represent, do not fall neatly into categories, one loses information by attempting to fit people into arbitrary categories. People within the same category (e.g., Major Depression) share certain characteristics (e.g., dysphoria, disturbances in sleep, impaired concentration), but there also will be many differences among persons within a category (e.g., the number of depressive episodes, whether the depression started after the death of relative). The shared characteristics should provide some important information about the persons in the category (e.g., prognosis, response to treatment) or the classification is useless. However, given the loss of information in-

herent in any classification grouping, classification should not be considered the only criterion necessary for an adequate case conceptualization. Instead, any classification, whether it is a diagnosis or an elevation on a behavior rating scale, should be one part of a larger description of the case. This approach allows one to take advantage of the positive aspects of formal classification yet acknowledges the limits of such systems and integrates classification into an idiographic formulation. Throughout this book, we provide case studies that illustrate this approach. In each case, diagnoses or other methods of classification are integrated into a more complete clinical description of the child being assessed.

A second danger of classification systems is that they foster the illusion of a clear break between normal and pathological psychological functioning. For example, if you are classifying based on elevations of a rating scale (over a T-score of 70), it gives the illusion of dramatic difference between children with T-scores of 69 (not classified) and children with T-scores of 70 (classified). Stating that this is an illusion does not imply that all psychological traits are on a continuum with normality, because some clearly are not. For example, in Jerome Kagan's work with behaviorally inhibited children there seem to be a number of qualitative differences between children with the behaviorally inhibited temperament and those without this temperamental style (Kagan & Snidman, 1991). However, if one was using a measure of behavioral inhibition with some cut-off for classifying inhibition (e.g., a T-score of 65), there may be some children close to this threshold (e.g., T-scores of 60–64) who were not classified due to imperfections in the measurement technique (Ghiselli, Campbell, & Zedeck, 1981). Therefore, whether the illusion of a clear break is due to a normally distributed trait or due to measurement error, it is still an illusion. Thus, users of classification systems must understand the often arbitrary line between categories and make interpretations accordingly.

A third danger of classification is the danger of stigmatization associated with psychological labels, often the end result of classification. How strong the effect of labeling is on psychological functioning is not clear from research; it does not seem that the act of labeling creates significant pathology through a self-fulfilling prophesy. However, it is also clear that labels can affect how others interact with a person (e.g., Snyder, Tanke, & Berscheid, 1977). Given this potential danger, classificatory terms (labels) should be used cautiously and only when there is a clear purpose for doing so (e.g., when it influences treatment considerations). Also, when such terms are used, great efforts should be made to clearly delineate the meaning and limitations of the term to limit the potential for misinterpretations. And, finally, terms should be worded to emphasize the classification of a psychological construct and not classification of the person. For example, it is better to use the phrase "a child with conduct disorder" rather than stating "a conduct-disordered child."

Evaluating Classification Systems

Thus far, we have argued that classification systems are necessary despite some potential dangers and misuses. However, this is only the case for good classification systems. If a classification system tells little about a person, then nothing is gained in terms of communication and all of the dangers we have discussed (e.g., loss of information, stigmatization) are maintained. Therefore, it is essential to critically evaluate any system of classification and, even within a system, to evaluate the individual categories.

Once again illustrating the arbitrary distinction between classification and assessment, how one evaluates classification systems is quite similar to how one evaluates assessment instruments and procedures in general, as discussed in the previous chapter. Specifically, the primary quality considerations of a system are its reliability and the validity of interpretations made from the classification (Quay, 1986). In terms of reliability, a user of a system must be able to make classifications consistently, such as over short periods of time (test-retest reliability) or between two independent users who are making the classification (interrater reliability). In order for classification systems to be reliable, the rules for making classifications must be simple and explicit. However, reliability is important primarily because it places limits on a classification system's validity. Therefore, the validity of a system is of paramount importance. Classifi-

cation must allow for some valid interpretations to be made based on the classification. That is, the classification must mean something. For example, a classification should tell something about the etiology, course, associated features, or treatment of the phenomenon being classified.

Models of Classification

So far our discussion of classification systems has been on issues that transcend any single type of classification system. The uses of a system, the dangers inherent in classification, and the methods of evaluating systems are all pertinent, irrespective of the model on which a system is based. However, there are several different theoretical models on which a classification system can be based. A *model* is a specific framework for viewing classification, such as whether abnormal behavior is viewed as statistical deviance ("Is this level of functioning rare in the general population?") or in terms of its functional impairment ("Does it affect a person's adaptive functioning?"). The theoretical model of a system will determine the rules by which classifications are made. As will become evident, the different types of assessment techniques discussed throughout this book were designed to provide information for different models of classification. The following sections will review two general models of classification that have heavily influenced the classification of children and adolescents and have had a major influence on the types of assessment procedures that have been developed.

Medical Models

The first major model of classification, the medical model, was largely derived from clinical experience with disturbed children and adolescents (Achenbach, 1982; Quay, 1986). In this type of classification a diagnostic entity is assumed to exist and the system defines what characteristics are indicative of this diagnosis. The approach is called a medical model approach because it assumes there is a disease entity, which is the psychiatric disorder, and then defines the symptoms that are indicative of the presence of the disorder.

There are two primary characteristics of medical model approaches to classification. First, because of the emphasis on a core deficit in medical models of classification, systems will differ dramatically depending on what theory or theories are used to define the deficits of psychological disorders. That is, medical model systems are heavily influenced by the theory of abnormal behavior espoused by the system, such as psychodynamic theories or organic theories. Second, because of the emphasis on a pathological core, medical model systems typically make sharp distinctions between disordered and nondisordered individuals. There is typically an underlying assumption that there are qualitative differences between individuals with and without a disorder.

Multivariate Approaches

The second major approach to classification that has been extremely influential in the clinical assessment of children has been labeled the multivariate statistical (Quay, 1986) or the psychometric approach (Achenbach, 1982). In this approach, multivariate statistical techniques are used to isolate interrelated patterns of behavior. Therefore, unlike the clinically derived syndromes that are defined by theory and clinical observations, behavioral syndromes are defined by the statistical relationship between behaviors or their patterns of covariation. In this approach, behaviors form a syndrome if they are highly correlated with each other, and there is no necessary assumption of a pathological core to underlie the symptoms, as is the case in medical models of classification. One of the primary statistical methods used to determine the patterns of covariation among behaviors has been factor analysis, which was discussed in the previous chapter.

In addition to being based on statistical covariation, the psychometric approach is also different from medical models of classification by emphasizing quantitative distinctions rather than qualitative distinctions. Once behavioral syndromes are isolated through statistical analyses, then a child's level of functioning along the various dimensions of behavior is determined. Behavioral syndromes are conceptualized along a continuum from normal to deviant. Interpretations are typically made by comparing an individual case to a representative normative sample and choosing some level of functioning as being so rare in the average population that it should be considered deviant. Classifications are thus based on how a child falls on a certain dimension of functioning (e.g., anxiety/withdrawal) relative to some comparison group (e.g., compared to other children of the same sex and age group).

In Box 3.1, we provide a summary of two multivariate approaches to classification of childhood emotional and behavioral functioning. The Quay classification system was based on a qualitative review of 61 factor-analytic studies spanning 40 years (Quay, 1986). Quay summarized the patterns of behavioral covariation across these studies into the eight dimensions of behavior that seem to emerge most consistently in factor analyses. In contrast, the ACQ system is based on factor analyses in a single large sample (n = 8,194) of children (ages 6–16) referred to American and Dutch mental health clinics (Achenbach et al., 1989). These two methods (a review of factor analyses from a large number of studies and a single study using factor analyses with a large number of behaviors in a large sample of children) exemplify the multivariate approach to determining behavioral syndromes.

Classification in the Future: An Integration of Medical and Multivariate Approaches

These two basic approaches to classification are important for clinical assessment because the design of assessment instruments often is consistent with one of these basic approaches. More importantly, interpretation of assessment instruments is basically a process of classification and therefore it is often guided by these models or some variation of them. The clinical assessor should be aware of the issues involved in classification generally, and the advantages and disadvantages of these two models of classification specifically, to aid in interpretation. Research has indicated that both the medical and the multivariate models have flaws that make the exclusive

BOX 3.1

Two Examples of Multivariate Classification Sytstems

QUAY'S SYNDROMES	ACQ SYNDROMES
Undersocialized Aggressive Conduct Disorder	Aggressive
Socialized Aggressive Conduct Disorder	Delinquent, Mean
Attention Deficit Disorder	Attention Problems
Anxiety-Withdrawal-Dysphoria	Anxious/Depressed
Schizoid Unresponsive	Schizoid
Social Ineptness	Socially Inept
Psychotic Disorder	Somatic Complaints
Motor Overactivity	Withdrawn

NOTE: Quay's syndromes were based on a qualitative review of 61 factor-analytic studies of children's emotional and behavioral functioning (Quay, 1986). The ACQ syndromes are core factors that replicated across gender and age in a large sample (n = 8,194) of 6- to 16-year-olds referred for mental health services (Achenbach et al., 1989).

use of either approach problematic (see Quay, 1986). For example, the reliance of medical model approaches on theory has led to many "disorders" being created with little support from research. Also, the medical model approach, with its emphasis on qualitative distinctions, masks a continuum with normality that seems most appropriate for understanding *some* dimensions of functioning. In contrast, the multivariate approach with its reliance on statistical analyses in the absence of clear theory has resulted in syndromes that are hard to generalize across samples. Whereas some psychological phenomena in children and adolescents are best conceptualized on a continuum with normality, there are others that may fit with more qualitative distinctions (e.g., Kagan & Snidman, 1991; Lahey et al., 1990) and are not captured well by the multivariate approach.

As a result, classification of the future should look toward an integration of the approaches. For example, clinical diagnoses can be improved by conducting multivariate analyses to see if the covariation of symptoms for the diagnosis is supported (e.g., Frick et al., 1993). However, there are many other ways in which the correspondence between statistically derived syn-

dromes and clinically derived diagnoses can be explicitly tested (e.g., Edelbrock & Costello, 1988), thereby improving the validity of both approaches and leading to classification systems that accommodate the diverse nature of psychological constructs. In the following section, we provide an overview of one of the most commonly used classification systems, the *Diagnostic and Statistical Manual of Mental Disorders,* which is published by the American Psychiatric Association. Although initially this system of classification was based largely on a medical model system of classification, more recent revisions have attempted to capture the best characteristics of the two major classification approaches.

Diagnostic and Statistic Manual of Mental Disorders—Fourth Edition (DSM-IV; APA, 1994)

The DSM approach to defining psychiatric disorders has undergone dramatic changes in its many revisions since its first publication in 1952. The biggest changes came with the publication of its third revision in 1980. In the first two editions the definitions of disorders were clearly based on a medical model approach to classification. The definitions assumed an underlying pathological core, and the conceptualization of the core was largely based on Freudian psychodynamic theory. In the third edition there was an explicit switch from a medical model view of disorders and the reliance on psychodynamic theory. In the third edition and continuing into later editions a functional approach to viewing disorders was used in which mental disorders were viewed as "a clinically significant behavioral or psychological syndrome or pattern that occurs in an individual and that is typically associated with either a painful symptom (distress) or impairment in one or more important areas of functioning (disability).

Another major change with the third edition that has been maintained in subsequent revisions is an increase in the level of specificity with which disorders are defined. In the first two editions of the manual, disorders were often poorly defined, which led to problems obtaining high levels of reliability in the diagnostic classifications (Spitzer & Cantwell, 1980). In contrast, later revisions include more detailed diagnostic definitions with explicit symptom lists, which has led to an increase in the reliability of the system (e.g., Spitzer, Davies, & Barkley, 1990). To illustrate this change, the DSM-III (APA, 1968) definition of Hyperkinetic Reaction of Childhood is contrasted with the analogous DSM-III-R definition of Attention-Deficit Hyperactivity Disorder in Box 3.2.

Box 3.2

A Comparison of DSM-II and DSM-III-R Diagnostic Criteria

DSM-II: Hyperkinetic Reaction of Childhood (Adolescence)

This disorder is characterized by overactivity, restlessness, distractibility, and short attention span, especially in young children; the behavior usually diminishes in adolescence. If this behavior is caused by brain damage, it should be diagnosed under the appropriate nonpsychotic *organic brain syndrome.*

DSM-III-R: Attention-Deficit Hyperactivity Disorder

Note: Consider a criterion met only if the behavior is considerably more frequent than that of most people of the same mental age.

A. A disturbance of at least 6 months during which at least eight of the following are present:

1. Often fidgets with hands or feet or squirms in seat
2. Has difficulty remaining seated when required to do so
3. Is easily distracted by extraneous stimuli
4. Has difficulty awaiting turn in games or group situations
5. Often blurts out answers to questions before they have been completed
6. Has difficulty following through on instructions from others (not due to oppositional behavior or failure of comprehension), e.g., fails to finish chores
7. Has difficulty sustaining attention in tasks or play activities
8. Often shifts from one uncompleted activity to another
9. Has difficulty playing quietly
10. Often talks excessively
11. Often interrupts or intrudes on others, e.g., butts into other children's games
12. Often does not seem to listen to what is being said to him or her
13. Often loses things necessary for tasks or activities at school or at home (e.g., toys, pencils, books, assignments)
14. Often engages in physically dangerous activities without considering possible consequences (not for the purpose of thrill seeking), e.g., runs into street without looking

B. Onset before the age of 7.
C. Does not meet criteria for a Pervasive Developmental Disorder.

SOURCE: *Diagnosis and Statistical Manual of Mental Disorders, Second Edition,* American Psychiatric Association, 1967 and *Diagnosis and Statistical Manual of Mental Disorders, Third Edition, Revised,* American Psychiatric Association, 1987. Reproduced with permission of the publisher.

As a result of these changes, the most recent revision of the manual (DSM-IV; APA, 1994) has characteristics of both the medical and multivariate models of classification. For example, its functional approach to defining disorders, which does not assume a pathological core, is consistent with the multivariate approach to classification. Also, many of the disorders are based, at least in part, on patterns of symptom covariation, which is the hallmark of multivariate models (e.g., Frick et al., 1994). In contrast, DSM-IV definitions classify disorders into discrete categories, which is more consistent with a medical model approach, although many of the cut-offs were empirically determined rather than being based purely on theoretical considerations (Lahey et al., in press).

One of the major changes in DSM-IV from all of its predecessors is the emphasis on users having access to the basic research underlying the various diagnostic categories. For example, in the manual itself, each disorder is initially introduced by summarizing current research on its basic characteristics; associated features; age, gender, and cultural trends; prevalence; course; and familial pattern (APA, 1994). In addition, there are five volumes that accompany the DSM-IV, (e.g., Widiger et al., 1994) called DSM-IV Source Books, which provide more extended discussions of the scientific bases of disorders in the DSM-IV. This focus on understanding the scientific underpinnings of the disorders is clearly a welcomed advance in the classification system.

DSM-IV maintained the multiaxial system of classification that was started in DSM-III. As was discussed previously in this chapter, a major disadvantage of any classification system is the inability to capture all relevant dimensions of a person's functioning within a single given category or diagnosis. In an attempt to take a broader view of classification, DSM-IV specifies several dimensions of functioning (axes) that are relevant to understanding a person's functioning. Specifically, Axis I (Clinical Disorders) and Axis II (Personality Disorders/Mental Retardation) are fairly typical of other classification systems and comprise the major categories of mental disorders. Box 3.3 provides a summary of the Axis I and Axis II diagnoses that are most relevant

---

BOX 3.3

A Summary of DSM-IV Axes I and II Diagnoses Relevant to Children and Adolescents

Intellectual	Mental Retardation
Learning	Mathematics Disorder
	Disorder of Written Expression
	Reading Disorder
	Language and Speech
	Expressive Language Disorder
	Mixed Receptive-Expressive Language Disorder
	Phonological Disorder
	Stuttering
	Selective Mutism
Motor Skills	Developmental Coordination Disorder
Pervasive Developmental	Autistic Disorder
	Rhett's Disorder
	Childhood Disintegrative Disorder
	Asperger's Disorder
Behavioral	Attention-Deficit Hyperactivity Disorder
	Oppositional Defiant Disorder
	Conduct Disorder
Emotional (Anxiety)	Separation Anxiety Disorder
	Generalized Anxiety Disorder*
	Panic Disorder*
	Agoraphobia*
	Social Phobia*
	Obsessive Compulsive Disorder*
	Post-Traumatic Stress Disorder*
	Adjustment Disorder with Anxious Mood*
Emotional (Mood)	Major Depression*
	Dysthymia*
	Bipolar Disorders (I & II)*
	Cyclothymia*
	Adjustment Disorder with Depressed Mood*
Identity	Gender Identity Disorder of Childhood
	Reactive Attachment Disorder of Infancy or Early Childhood
Physical (Eating)	Anorexia Nervosa*
	Bulimia Nervosa*
	Pica
	Rumination Disorder

(Cont.)

Box 3.3	(Continued)
Physical (Motor)	Tourette's Disorder
	Chronic Motor or Vocal Tic Disorder
	Transient Tic Disorder
	Stereotypic Movement Disorder
Physical (Elimination)	Encopresis
	Enuresis
Physical (Somatic)	Somatization Disorder*
	Conversion Disorder*
	Pain Disorder*
	Hypochrondriasis*
	Body Dysmorphic Disorder*
	Adjustment Disorder with Physical Complaints*
Psychosis	Schizophrenia*
Substance-Related Disorders	Alcohol (Amphetamine, Cannabis, etc.) Dependence*

*Denotes disorders that have the same criteria for children and adults.

NOTE: The selection of which disorders are most relevant to children and adolescents and the way the disorders are grouped were done by the authors of the text and not by DSM-IV.

for children and adolescents. However, DSM-IV includes three other dimensions on which a child can be classified. Axis III allows for the user of the system to indicate any physical disorder that is potentially relevant for the understanding or managing of a case. Axis IV allows for a reporting of psychosocial and environmental stressors that may affect the diagnosis, treatment, and prognosis of mental disorders in Axes I and II. Axis V provides a scale to indicate the highest level of adaptive functioning (psychological, social, and occupational/educational) that is currently being exhibited or the highest level of adaptive functioning that has been exhibited within the past year. Clearly this multiaxial approach of DSM-IV is not sufficient to take the place of an adequate case formulation. However, it highlights the need to place diagnoses in the context of many other important aspects of a person's psychological functioning.

DEVELOPMENTAL PSYCHOPATHOLOGY

As mentioned previously, the overriding principle of developmental psychopathology is that children's emotional and behavioral functioning must be understood within a developmental context (Rutter & Garmezy, 1983). Therefore, it follows that *the assessment* of children's emotional and behavioral functioning must also be conducted within a developmental framework. Such themes as understanding behavior in a developmental context and conducting assessment within a developmental framework are broad principles that have several important implications for the assessment process.

Developmental Norms

First, a developmental approach recognizes that a child's emotional and behavioral functioning must be understood within the context of developmental norms. To be specific, there are numerous behaviors of children that are common at one age but relatively uncommon at others. For example, bedwetting is quite common prior to age 5, and even at age 5 is present in from 15%–20% of children (Doleys, 1977; Walker, Milling, & Bonner, 1988). Similarly, childhood fears tend to be quite common and the types of fears that are most common show a logical progression with the development of the child (Campbell, 1986). For example, separation anxiety is not uncommon in infants toward the end of the first year of life (Bowlby, 1969), whereas fears of the dark and imaginary creatures are quite common in preschool and school-age children but decrease in prevalence with age (Bauer, 1976).

These are just a few of the many developmentally related changes in the prevalence of specific child behaviors. Knowledge of these developmental changes in the behavior of children is crucial to clinical assessment because the same behavior may be developmentally appropriate at one age but indicative of pathology at another. Therefore, assessment of children and adolescents must allow for developmentally based interpretations. The critical nature of these interpretations means that selection of assessment techniques must be based at least in part on the availability of age-specific norms. Further, given the rapid developmental changes experienced by children and adolescents, comparisons must be made within fairly limited age groups. Whereas for adults using a comparison group that spans the ages from 25 to 35 may be justifiable, a comparison group of children that spans the ages 5 to 15 would be meaningless, given the many changes in development that are subsumed within this period. Because the normative information provided by an assessment instrument and the appropriate use of norm-referenced information by the assessor are critical components to the clinical assessment of children, these issues are discussed in great detail throughout this book.

Developmental Processes

Unfortunately, many assessors believe that simply comparing assessment information to age norms is all that is needed to take a developmental approach to child and adolescent assessment. This is a much too limited view of development. In order to interpret assessment information, an assessor must also understand developmental processes. Each stage of development is a function of the dynamic interplay of several interrelated maturational processes (e.g., socio-emotional, cognitive, linguistic, biological). At any given stage, some behaviors may be more likely due to the unique demands (i.e., developmental tasks) that result from this interaction of developmental processes. These unique demands lead to the age-related changes discussed previously. However, simply comparing a child's behavior to developmental norms and determining whether or not a level of behavior is *deviant* for a child's age does not allow one to determine whether (1) it should be conceptualized as an exaggeration of normal developmental processes or (2) it should be conceptualized as a qualitative deviation from normal development that is more indicative of a pathological process.

These two different interpretations of deviations from developmental norms can be illustrated in the assessment of conduct problems in children and adolescence. Research has documented an increase in acting-out behavior for both boys and girls that co-incides with the onset of adolescence (e.g., Offord et al., 1989). The first implication of this finding is that the assessment of adolescent conduct problems should be based on a comparison to adolescent norms so that *age-specific* deviations can be determined. However, to interpret these age-specific deviations, it is also helpful to realize that an increase in acting-out behavior in adolescence is consistent with the identity formation process outlined in Erik Erikson's psychosocial theory of personality development (Erikson, 1968). Specifically, Erikson characterizes adolescence as a time when youths are struggling with the development of an individual identity, one that is separate from their parents. Rebellion and questioning of authority are manifestations of adolescents' rejection of parental and societal values, as they struggle to develop their unique identity. Understanding this process allows for an additional interpretation when one documents deviations from age norms. If a youth exhibits developmentally deviant levels of conduct problems for the first time in adolescence, the conduct problems may be best conceptualized as an exaggeration of a normal developmental process (e.g., identity development). In contrast, a preadolescent child who exhibits deviant levels of conduct problems is showing a behavior that seems more qualitatively different from what is expected from normal developmental processes. It may, therefore, be an indication of more severe pathology. This is consistent with research indicating that conduct problems that have onset in adolescence are more likely to be transient, whereas conduct problems with a prepubertal onset tend to be more severe and chronic (Loeber, 1991).

Stability and Continuity

Issues regarding the stability of childhood behavioral and emotional functioning are important to a developmental perspective to psychopathology. These complex issues have important implications for the assessment process. The basic issue of stability is not unique to the assessment of children and adolescents but has been a longstanding controversy in psychological assessment throughout the life span. For example, many have questioned the whole concept of personality because it implies a consistency of behavior over place and time that is often not apparent in human behavior (Mischel, 1968). This issue is even more relevant to children because childhood behavior seems even less stable over time and situations than that of adults, making the concept of personality in children even more controversial. Our view of the debate, which is similar to the view of many other theorists (e.g., Martin, 1988a), is that the concept of personality can be useful if conceptualized appropriately, but dangerous if viewed wrongly.

For example, many measures of children's behavior (e.g., anxiety—Agras, Chapin, & Oliveau, 1972) or other aspects of personality (e.g., locus of control—Connell, 1985; Rorschach responses—Exner & Wiener, 1982) show much less stability in children than do analogous constructs in adults. This is not surprising given the rapid developmental changes that are occurring in childhood. However, this has important implications for the interpretation of personality measures in children. Specifically, interpretations of dispositional characteristics must be made cautiously in children so that there is no implication of stability over time, unless data are available to support such an interpretation. Given that the data are lacking in most cases, the term *personality* may be misleading for many domains of child behavior.

Although we feel that this caution is warranted, there are also several ways in which this general statement must be qualified. First, there is clearly *some* continuity in children's behavior, and the degree of stability (or instability) seems dependent on which domain of behavior is being assessed. For example, research generally indicates that externalizing behaviors (e.g., hyperactivity, aggression, antisocial behavior) tend to be more stable over time than internalizing behaviors (e.g., fears, depression) (e.g., Agras, Chapin, & Oliveau, 1972; Gittelman et al., 1985; Kovacs et al., 1984; Robins, 1966). Therefore, interpretations of the stability of behavior must be dependent on the dimension of behavior that is of interest.

In addition, aggregates of behaviors (behavioral domains) tend to be more stable than discrete behaviors. For example, Silverman and Nelles (1989) reported on the 1-year stability of mothers' reports

of fears in their children between the ages of 8 and 11. Over the 1-year study period, there was only a 10% overlap between Time 1 and Time 2 in the 10 specific objects or situations that mothers reported eliciting the most fear in their child. However, the correlation between the absolute number of fears was quite high. Therefore, although the specific types of fears were not stable over the study period, the level of fears was stable. Some have argued that aggregation allows one to pick up generalized response tendencies (Martin, 1988a) that are not captured by discrete behaviors. However, this increase in stability through aggregation of behaviors can also be conceptualized from basic measurement theory. It has consistently been shown that increasing the number of items on a measure of a trait also increases its reliability (Ghiselli, Campbell, & Zedack, 1981). Hence, the increased stability may be a function of a more reliable method of measurement.

The stability or lack of stability in the assessment of children's emotional and behavioral functioning, then, depends on the type of functioning that is assessed and whether it is assessed as discrete behaviors or as an aggregated dimension of behavior. There is one further issue that is relevant to a discussion of stability in child behavior. That is, stability of behaviors may be related to the level of analysis. For example, Garber (1984) states that in some instances the poor stability in children's psychological functioning may truly reflect the fact that the maladjustment is a transient phenomenon, possibly a developmental response to an environmental stressor. However, she goes on to propose that "some apparent discontinuity may also reflect changes in the behavioral manifestation of a continuous pattern of behavioral organization" (p. 34). That is, the child may maintain some maladaptive means of organizing and integrating information or experiences, but how it is expressed in terms of behavioral dysfunction may change over the course of development. Therefore, the apparent instability in some forms of childhood psychopathology may be a function of viewing the behaviors themselves rather than the pattern of behavioral organization. Although this view makes intuitive sense and is consistent with many developmental theories, it also must be considered tentative due to the lack of any well-defined method of assessing behavioral organization, the level of analysis that would be predicted to demonstrate a higher degree of stability.

Situational Stability

A second issue in the personality debate is the cross-situational specificity of the behavior and emotional functioning of children. Providing some of the best data on this issue, Achenbach, McConaughy, and Howell (1987) conducted a meta-analysis of 119 studies that reported on the correlations between the reports of different informants on children's and adolescents' (ages 1½ to 19 years) emotional and behavioral functioning. The correlations between different types of informants (e.g., parent–teacher) were fairly low, averaging about .28. This low correlation is not a good indicator of cross-situational specificity by itself, because reduced correlations could also be due to the individual biases of different informants rather than to actual differences in a child's behavior across settings. However, the mean correlations between informants who typically observe the child in similar situations (between two parents or two teachers) were generally much higher, averaging about .60. The relatively (.28 vs. .60) low correlations across types of informants serves as a more relevant indicator of the high variability in children's behavior across settings.

Achenbach, McConaughy, and Howell (1987) make several interesting statements on the relevance

analysis included studies that correlated ratings of parents, teachers, mental health workers, observers, peers, and the subjects themselves. The overall findings suggested that correlations between different types of informants (e.g., parents and teachers) are fairly low, averaging about .28. This indicates a high degree of variability in the report of a child's emotional and behavioral functioning across different types of informants. The correlations were higher when the correlations between similar informants were calculated (e.g., between two parents or between two teachers), averaging about .60. This suggests that the low correlations between different informants may be due to differences in children's behavior in different settings, rather than to idiosyncratic methods of rating behavior.

The authors of this meta-analysis discuss several important implications of their findings to the clinical assessment of children.

1. "The high correlations between pairs of informants who see children in similar settings suggest that data from a single parent, teacher, observer, etc. would provide a reasonable sample of what would be provided by other informants of the same type who see the child under generally similar conditions" (p. 227).

2. "In contrast, the low correlations between different types of informants suggest that each type of informant provides substantially unique information that is not provided by other informants. The high degree of situational specificity poses a specific challenge to clinical assessments intended to categorize disorders according to fixed rules" (p. 227), such as the *Diagnostic and Statistical Manual of Mental Disorders—Fourth Edition, Revised* (APA, 1994). Such systems specify symptoms that must be judged present or absent, and the low correlations across settings suggest that in most cases the presence or absence will depend on the setting.

3. As a result of the high degree of specificity, clinical assessments of children must be multiaxial by including data obtained from different informants in specific contexts. "In such assessments, disagreements between informants' reports are as instructive as agreements because they can highlight variations in judgments of a child's functioning across situations" (p. 228). In Chapter 16, we discuss the issues involved in deciding how to interpret these variations in reports of a child's or adolescent's emotional and behavioral functioning.

BOX 3.4

Research Note: Meta-Analysis of Cross-Informant Correlations for Child/Adolescent Behavioral and Emotional Problems

---

As noted in the text, Achenbach, McConaughy, and Howell (1987) conducted a meta-analysis of 119 studies that reported correlations between different informants on children's and adolescents' emotional and behavioral functioning. The meta-

---

SOURCE: T. M. Achenbach, S. H. McConaughy, & C. T. Howell (1987). Child/adolescent behavioral and emotional problems: Implications of cross-informant correlations for situational specificity. *Psychological Bulletin, 101,* 213–232.

of these findings to the assessment process. These are summarized in Box 3.4. In addition, there are several issues on cross-situational specificity that are analogous to those discussed on the stability of childhood behavior. First, like stability, the low correlations across situations may depend on the type of behavior assessed. Specifically, the 1987 study authors reported that externalizing problems tend to show higher correlations across informants than internalizing problems. Second, the situational specificity of behavior may be a function of whether or not aggregated domains of behavior are studied or whether discrete behaviors are studied. For example, Biederman, Keenan, and Faroane (1990) compared parent and teacher reports on the symptoms of attention deficit disorder (ADD). Individual symptoms showed an average correlation across home and school settings of about .20. In contrast, on a diagnostic level, there was much higher agreement. There was a 90% probability of a teacher reporting enough symptoms to reach a diagnosis of ADD if the child was diagnosed by parents' report. Similar to the findings on stability, this suggests that although individual behaviors (symptoms) may show a high level of specificity across situations, the broader construct (diagnosis) of aggregated behaviors seems to show greater consistency across situations.

Comorbidities

Comorbidity is a medical term that refers to the presence of two or more diseases that are occurring simultaneously in an individual. This term has also been applied in the psychological literature to denote the presence of two or more disorders or two or more problematic areas of adjustment co-occurring within the same individual. There can be several reasons for comorbidity. For example, comorbidity can involve the co-occurrence of two independent disorders, two disorders having a common underlying etiology, or two disorders having a causal relation between them (Kendall & Clarkin, 1992). Unfortunately, research in most areas of psychology has not allowed for a clear delineation of the various causes of comorbidity among psychological problems.

Despite this imperfect understanding of the causes

of comorbidity, this concept is important for the clinical assessment of children for it is clear that comorbidity is the rule, rather than the exception, in children with psychological difficulties (Bird, Gould, & Staghezza, 1993). Specifically, children's problems are rarely circumscribed to a single problem area; instead, children tend to have problems in multiple areas of adjustment. For example, in children with severe conduct problems, 50%–90% have a co-occurring ADD, 62% have a co-occurring anxiety disorder, 25% have a learning disability, and 50% have substantial problems in peer relationships (see Frick & O'Brien, 1994; Strauss et al., 1988). Similar rates of comorbidity are found in many other types of child psychopathology (see Frick et al., 1993).

Research attempting to understand comorbidity in childhood psychopathology has had a major impact on our understanding of the causes of several childhood disorders (e.g., Hinshaw, 1987). However, comorbidity also has a more immediate impact on the clinical assessment of children and adolescents. In a special issue of the *Journal of Consulting and Clinical Psychology* (Kendall & Clarkin, 1992), several articles highlighted the unique treatment needs of children with various types of comorbid psychopathological conditions. The high degree of comorbidity and its importance to the design of effective treatment programs makes the assessment of comorbid conditions crucial in the clinical assessment of children and adolescents.

Because of the importance of comorbidity, most clinical assessments of children and adolescents should be comprehensive. Specifically, assessments must cover multiple areas of functioning so that not only are the primary referral problems assessed adequately, but potential comorbid problems in adjustment are also assessed. As discussed in the next chapter in planning evaluations, exactly how comprehensive an assessment should be and with what rigor certain areas should be assessed will depend on the specific referral reason. However, the clinical assessment must be designed with a thorough understanding of the high degree of comorbidity present in child psychopathology generally and the most common patterns of comorbidity that are specific to the referral question.

Practical Implications for Assessment

Although we have tried to summarize some of the major findings in the field of developmental psychopathology that have particular relevance to clinical assessment, sometimes it is difficult to translate research into guidelines for practice. The following is a summary of some of the major implications of the findings discussed in this section applied to the clinical assessment of children and adolescents. These implications for the clinical assessment of children are expanded on and applied to specific situations throughout this book.

1. A competent assessor needs to be knowledgeable in several areas of basic psychological research to competently assess children and adolescents. In addition to competence in measurement theory, knowledge of developmental processes and basic characteristics of childhood psychopathology is also essential.

2. Children's behaviors and emotions must be understood within a developmental context. Therefore, an important characteristic of assessment instruments for children is their ability to provide developmentally sensitive normative comparisons. On a more general level, appropriate interpretations of test scores, even if they are based on age-specific norms, should be guided by a knowledge of developmental processes and their effect on a child's behavioral and emotional functioning.

3. Children's behavior is heavily dependent on the contexts in which the child is participating. Therefore, assessments of children must be based on multiple sources of information that assess a child's functioning in multiple contexts. In addition, an assessment of the relevant aspects of the many important contexts in which a child functions (e.g., at school, at home, with peers) is crucial to understanding the variations in a child's behavior across settings.

4. Most assessments of children must be comprehensive. This is necessary not only because of the need to adequately assess the many important situational contexts that influence a child's adjustment. Children often exhibit problems in multiple areas of functioning that span emotional, behavioral, learning, and social domains. Effective treatments must be based on the unique strengths and weaknesses of the child across these multiple psychological arenas.

CONCLUSIONS

The main theme of this chapter, and in fact of this entire text, is that appropriate assessment practices are based on a knowledge of the basic characteristics of the phenomenon one is trying to assess. As a result, the competent assessor is knowledgeable not only in test administration but is well versed in psychometric theory, child development, and childhood psychopathology.

Clinical assessment can be conceptualized as a process of classification. Therefore, understanding the issues involved in classifying psychological functioning is important. Formal classification systems are needed to promote communication between professionals, to utilize research for understanding individual cases, and to document the need for services. However, classification systems can also be quite dangerous if they are poor systems or if they are not used appropriately.

Two models to classification have had a great influence on our understanding of and assessment of children's emotional and behavioral functioning: clinically derived medical models and multivariate models. Understanding the basic assumptions of these approaches to classification and understanding the advantages and disadvantages of each are important for interpreting assessment information.

Being knowledgeable of basic research within the field of developmental psychology is also crucial to conducting and interpreting psychological assessments of children and adolescents. This research illustrates the importance of conducting and interpreting assessments within a developmental context, the importance of understanding the stability and situational-specificity of children's psychological functioning, and the importance of comorbidity in childhood psychopathology. These research findings have many practical applications to the assessment process; and these applications are discussed throughout this text.

CHAPTER SUMMARY

1. To be competent in the clinical assessment of children and adolescents, one must be knowledgeable of the current research base on emotional and behavioral disorders.

2. *Classification* refers to a set of rules that delineates some levels or types of psychological functioning as pathological and places these significant areas of pathology into distinct categories or along certain dimensions.

3. Appropriately developed and competently used classification systems can aid in communication among professionals, aid in applying research to clinical practice, and document the need for services.

4. Poor classification systems or inappropriately used classification systems can foster an illusion of few differences within a given category, can foster an illusion of a clear break between normality and pathology, and can lead to stigmatization.

5. Medical model approaches to classification assume an underlying disease entity and tend to classify people into distinct categories.

6. Multivariate approaches base classification on patterns of behavioral covariation and tend to classify behavior along continuous dimensions from normality to pathology.

7. The *Diagnostic and Statistical of Mental Disorders, Fourth Edition* (APA, 1994) is one of the most commonly used classification systems with characteristics of both medical model and multivariate approaches.

8. Developmental psychopathology provides a framework from which to understand children's and adolescents' adjustment.

9. Based on this framework, assessments must be conducted with a knowledge of age-specific patterns of behavior, with a knowledge of developmental processes, and with consideration of issues regarding the stability of behavior over time and across situations.

10. Because research has shown that children with problems in one area of adjustment typically have problems in multiple areas, most assessments of children need to cover multiple domains of functioning.

11. Because research has shown that children's behaviors are heavily dependent on the contexts in which they occur, clinical assessments must assess a child across multiple contexts and assess the characteristics of the most important contexts in which a child functions.

CHAPTER 4

Ethical, Legal, and Diversity Issues

CHAPTER QUESTIONS

- Are there professional standards that give guidance regarding how to best assess individuals from diverse cultures?

- Is it permissible for a clinic secretary to administer and interpret some tests?

- What are some useful sources that give clinicians guidance for adhering to high standards of practice?

This chapter addresses some of the most important issues in psychological assessment. It now seems appropriate to conclude that many problems in assessment are due not to inherent flaws in the tests but to the inappropriate use of tests, and their results, by clinicians (Anastasi, 1992). Even a psychometrically valid test can become a tool for disserving a client. Many of us can cite cases of misuse. Recently, for example, one of our clients was not allowed services for his learning disability because he was gifted and therefore did not meet the criterion of "normal" intelligence. In the behavioral assessment realm some children are diagnosed as ADHD based on rating scale results without regard to non–test-based criteria for diagnosis such as age of onset (more discussion of this topic is provided in a later chapter). If the standards or ethical principles in this chapter are not heeded, then all of the information in other chapters is of no value because these principles represent the centerpiece of competent practice, not the periphery.

The modern clinician is faced with standards and ethical guidelines that encourage a higher level of practice than was the case a decade or two ago. Moreover, clinicians are also held to higher standards of multicultural practice that require them to develop specific competencies for more appropriately interacting with and assessing a culturally and linguistically diverse clientele. This chapter provides some preliminary guidance for practice based on some of the most widely cited ethical principles, test standards, and recent treatises that give suggestions for assessing diverse clientele. (A self-examination for enhancing retention of these issues is given in Box 4.1.)

BOX 4.1

Ethics and Standards Self-Examination Checklist

It is entirely too easy to forget relevant ethical and practice standards under the pressure of everyday practice. This checklist may serve as a quick reference for the clinician to cue adherence to optimal practice methods.

Principle/Guideline Questions

1. Do I have adequate training to use the tests/methods that I plan to use?

2. How might the individual's background—cultural, linguistic, social, economic, or otherwise—affect the planning of my evaluation or the interpretation of my results?

3. Are the tests that I am using validated for the specific purposes that I have in mind?

4. Are there particularly unreliable scales that I should refrain from interpreting?

5. Have I received informed consent and assent prior to initiating the evaluation?

6. Will I provide feedback to the client or to others concerned such as the child's parents, teachers, or pediatrician?

7. Did I personally perform the services for which I am billing the insurer?

8. Do I have written permission to share confidential information with concerned parties?

9. Whom do I need to assist with this examination—a translator, parent, social worker, community member, etc.?

10. Have I consulted a professional colleague regarding questionable issues as needed?

Much of the instruction in this chapter is provided via anecdote. We hope that this storytelling technique will convince the clinician-in-training of the frequency (virtually daily) with which the psychologist has to access knowledge of ethics, standards, and cultural issues.

THE APA ETHICAL PRINCIPLES OF PSYCHOLOGISTS

Virtually every professional organization adopts some responsibility for the ethical practice of its members. An initial step is the development and dissemination of ethical principles for the members of the organization. Many organizations also adjudicate ethical complaints against members.

Psychology has a long history of involvement in test development and assessment practice, resulting in the development of the term *psychometrics.* Hence, the ethical standards published by the American Psychological Association (which uses the same acronym as the American Psychiatric Association) are among the most well-known sets of ethical principles providing high standards of assessment practice (see Box 4.2). This section presents some of the relevant principles (as numbered by the APA) and provides sample applications of their use.

2.01 Evaluation, Diagnosis, or Intervention in Professional Context

Psychologists are admonished to only provide assessment services in the context of a professional relationship. If a neighbor, for example, came to you, a psychologist, described his daughter's behavior problems, and asked for your diagnosis, you would be hard pressed to give advice without violating this principle. The most appropriate course of action in this case is to refer the neighbor to a qualified professional, who will conduct an evaluation within the context of a professional (as opposed to your personal) relationship.

This is an important principle for several reasons, but, most importantly, it encourages clinicians to not be haphazard with their assessment practice by offering premature or uninformed opinions. Even the most capable clinician needs to study the client's situation carefully to ensure an accurate conceptualization of the child's problems. This thorough analysis is especially important for young clients because of the

BOX 4.2

Excerpts from the APA Ethical Principles of Psychologists Regarding Assessment Practice

---

2.02 Competence and Appropriate Use of Assessments and Interventions

(a) Psychologists who develop, administer, score, interpret, or use psychological assessment techniques, interviews, tests, or instruments do so in a manner and for purposes that are appropriate in light of the research on or evidence of the usefulness and proper application of the techniques.

(b) Psychologists refrain from misuse of assessment techniques, interventions, results, and interpretations and take reasonable steps to prevent others from misusing the information these techniques provide. This includes refraining from releasing raw test results or raw data to persons, other than to patients or clients as appropriate, who are not qualified to use such information. (See also Standards 1.02, Relationship of Ethics and Law, and 1.04, Boundaries of Competence.)

2.03 Test Construction

Psychologists who develop and conduct research with tests and other assessment techniques use scientific procedures and current professional knowledge for test design, standardization, validation, reduction or elimination of bias, and recommendation for use.

2.04 Use of Assessment in General and With Special Populations

(a) Psychologists who perform interventions or administer, score, interpret, or use assessment techniques are familiar with the reliability, validation, and related standardization or outcome studies of, and proper applications and uses of, the techniques they use.

(b) Psychologists recognize limits to the certainty with which diagnoses, judgments, or predictions can be made about individuals.

(c) Psychologists attempt to identify situations in which particular interventions or assessment techniques or norms may not be applicable or may require adjustment in administration or interpretation because of factors such as individuals' gender, age, race, ethnicity, national origin, religion, sexual orientation, disability, language, or socioeconomic status.

2.05 Interpreting Assessment Results

When interpreting assessment results, including automated interpretations, psychologists take into account the various test factors and characteristics of the person being assessed that might affect psychologists' judgment or reduce the accuracy of their interpretations. They indicate any significant reservations they have about the accuracy or limitations of their interpretations.

2.06 Unqualified Persons

Psychologists do not promote the use of psychological assessment techniques by unqualified persons. (see also Standard 1.22, Delegation to and Supervision of Subordinates.)

2.07 Obsolete Tests and Outdated Test Results

(a) Psychologists do not base their assessment or intervention decisions or recommendations on data or test results that are outdated for the current purpose.

(b) Similarly, psychologists do not base such decisions or recommendations on tests and measures that are obsolete and not useful for the current purpose.

2.08 Test Scoring and Interpretation Services

(a) Psychologists who offer assessment or scoring procedures to other professionals accurately describe the purpose, norms, validity, reliability, and applications of the procedures and any special qualifications applicable to their use.

(b) Psychologists select scoring and interpretation services (including automated services) on the basis of evidence of the validity of the program and procedures as well as on other appropriate considerations.

(c) Psychologists retain appropriate responsibility for the appropriate application, interpretation, and use of assessment instruments, whether they score and interpret such tests themselves or use automated or other services.

2.09 Explaining Assessment Results

Unless the nature of the relationship is clearly explained to the person being assessed in advance and precludes provision of an explanation of results (such as in some organizational consulting, preemployment or security screenings, and forensic evaluations), psychologists ensure that an explanation of the results is provided using language that is reasonably understandable to the person assessed or to

(Cont.)

BOX 4.2 *(Continued)*

another legally authorized person on behalf of the client. Regardless of whether the scoring and interpretation are done by the psychologist, by assistants, or by automated or other outside services, psychologists take reasonable steps to ensure that appropriate explanations of results are given.

2.10 Maintaining Test Security

Psychologists make reasonable efforts to maintain the integrity and security of tests and other assessment techniques consistent with law, contractual obligations, and in a manner that permits compliance with the requirements of this Ethics Code. (See also Standard 1.02, Relationship of Ethics and Law.)

Reprinted with permission of the American Psychological Association.

variability of their behavior across settings. Adherence to this principle precludes the psychologist from offering less than well-informed opinions that are endemic to an informal or personal relationship.

Most of the users of this text are clinicians-in-training, who may not yet appreciate the value that will be placed on their opinions by their church members, families, professional colleagues, and others. This principle is especially important for the new clinician to recall when the requests for advice multiply concurrently with increasing professional stature.

2.02 Competence and Appropriate Use of Assessments and Interventions

Psychologists are advised to interpret tests in a manner consistent with research findings regarding the validity of the instrument. This principle further asks psychologists to take steps to prevent others from misuse of test results.

It is, of course, very difficult to interpret tests in a way consistent with research evidence if the clinician is not properly trained in the use of the instrument and is not receiving adequate continuing education. In order to use the Rorschach, for example, with any acumen, considerable training is required. For that matter, even some of the seemingly straightforward self-report anxiety scales seem easier to use than is actually the case. For example, a clinician may be inclined to interpret an anxiety scale as a measure of anxiety for an individual. Even this deceptively obvious interpretation can be contravened by research. The reader will discover in Chapter 6 that it is becoming increasingly apparent that some scales of this nature are measuring more than one construct such as general distress or even depression.

Continuing education is important for valid test use. We were routinely reminded of the need for continuing education to stay abreast of validation research as we prepared this book and found that much that we learned during our training is now obsolete or, worse yet, constitutes substandard practice.

An example of this latter situation is overly rigid use of cut-off scores to make a diagnostic decision. A clinician may use a T-score of 70 or greater on an attention problems scale in order to diagnose ADHD, whereas a T-score of 69 would not trigger the diagnosis. Such simplistic methods of interpretation are not easily supported by research and diagnostic standards.

2.03 Test Construction

Test developers are responsible for producing tests that meet current psychometric standards. Presumably the *Standards for Educational and Psychological Tests* (APA, 1985), which will be discussed next, would serve as a useful guide in this regard.

Test developers are asked to address issues such as bias, adequate norming, validation, and appropriate recommendations for use. This standard, however, is not easy to apply. For example, is it ethical to publish a behavior rating scale that is recommended for use for diagnostic purposes although the developers did not control for SES when collecting the norming sample? Precedents for applying this standard are not yet plentiful. We recommend that individual psychologists make their best decision, based on the context of the assessment purpose, as to whether or not they think that use of a scale may be unethical due to the existence of psychometric inadequacies.

One clue to the existence of psychometric inadequacies is a brief test manual or lack of a manual. The days of minimalist test manuals that do not describe the norming of the scale or give any criterion-related validity evidence are now behind us. Increasingly psychologists have had to defend their conclusions in legal and other settings that require specific citations of psychometric properties. Poor documentation cannot be tolerated by the clinician, as is demonstrated by the next standard.

2.04 Use of Assessment in General and with Special Populations

This is a relatively high standard for the practicing psychologist to meet; it states that *psychologists must be familiar with the reliability, validation, and related standardization or outcome studies of, and proper applications and uses of, the techniques they use.*

Aspiring to this standard requires continuing education for the psychologist, as the interpretation of each scale can be altered by newly published research. At the very least, we suggest that psychologists occasionally review some of the basic research, such as reliability indices, on the instruments they use and become familiar with criterion-related validity studies on the primary measures they use. Some psychologists may be surprised to find that some of the most famous self-report inventories they use have paltry reliability estimates for some of their scales (see Chapter 6).

This standard also asks the psychologist to try to gauge the influence of background variables, such as culture, race, gender, et cetera on test results to ensure that test results are not compromised. The standard states further that administration and interpretation methods should be altered when certain situations arise. Methods for gauging the effects of culture are provided in the last section of this chapter.

2.05 Interpreting Assessment Results

There are two important implications of this standard. First, *the psychologist must use caution when characteristics of the person may be affecting test results or the psychologists' interpretation of them.* Secondly, *psychologists must state when they think their results have been compromised.*

This latter principle has led to the oft-read statement in reports that "the current test results appear to be an accurate assessment of _____'s functioning" (see Chapter 17). A judgment like this, however, is qualitative, requiring considerable experience on the part of the examiner. Clinicians-in-training are advised to seek the advice of their supervisors when making statements of this nature in their written and oral reports of assessment results. Perhaps new clinicians can counter their lack of experience by using the "norms" that their supervisors have garnered through years of experience.

2.06 Unqualified Persons

Although it seems axiomatic *to not endorse the use of psychological tests by unqualified persons,* this standard is difficult to apply. Is a person with a bachelors' degree in psychology capable of conducting a background interview, administering but not interpreting an MMPI, or coding the scores for a Rorschach? Optimally, the reader will have a better sense for how to apply this standard after reading this book. Again, however, questions about this standard are often best answered by consulting with others, particularly psychologists who have dealt with such circumstances in the past.

Obvious violations of this standard probably occur with disconcerting frequency. It seems to us that most practicing psychologists receive requests to use tests by individuals who have little or no training in psychology.

2.07 Obsolete Tests and Outdated Test Results

The two aspects of this standard include, (1) *prohibitions against using outdated tests* and (2) *admonishment against using outdated test results.* As an example, we think that the first prohibition precludes use of the original MMPI since a more current form, with new norms, is available.

The second part of this standard is more nebulous. When would a decision based on the Rorschach be antiquated—after 2 weeks, 6 weeks, 3 months, 9 months? It is clear that the clinician needs to think about the age of test results and either have a rationale for using results collected during a previous evaluation or decide that they are irrelevant and collect new data.

Recently one of us was asked by a lawyer representing a former client to determine whether or not a child possessed mental health problems that were significant enough to warrant additional public assistance. The child was originally evaluated 1½ years ago. In this case it did not seem sensible to complete the eligibility form based on 18-month-old data, and a new evaluation was requested prior to completing the necessary eligibility form. This example represents one of a myriad number of possible cases where this ethical principle comes into play.

2.08 Test Scoring and Interpretation Services

As technology becomes more intertwined with the psychological assessment process, the relationship between computer-assisted assessment and examiner responsibilities for test interpretation becomes more important to articulate. *Psychologists are advised to retain appropriate responsibility for the interpretation of tests.* This standard becomes extremely important when clinicians are faced with computer-generated interpretations that are at odds with their own impressions.

Additionally, *the validity of software programs should be evaluated by the psychologist.* We suggest that the user of interpretation programs become familiar with the algorithms underlying various interpretations and determine whether or not the author(s) has adequately documented the validity of each algorithm. It is also likely that the validity evidence for some of the software algorithms used will change as a result of new research, making it necessary for the psycholo-

gist to stay abreast of current findings for each software program used.

Ultimately, however, it is clear that the psychologist is responsible for test interpretation regardless of the technology utilized. A Simpsonian plea (i.e., Bart Simpson) that it is "not my fault" would likely not prevail.

2.09 Explaining Assessment Results

When writing this text, we decided that failure to give children and adolescents feedback is one of our pet peeves. The standard states that *psychologists ensure that an explanation of the results is provided using language that is reasonably understandable to the person assessed or to another legally authorized person on behalf of the client.* We have often encountered colleagues who do not provide feedback to children and, more distressingly, to adolescents. In addition, some psychologists rarely provide results directly to parents or other significant caregivers. As a first step, we suggest that students-in-training ask all of their clients, including young children, if they would like to meet with the clinician some time after the testing to discuss the results. This procedure will optimally build a habit that will last for an entire career.

2.10 Maintaining Test Security

Psychologists should make reasonable efforts to ensure that item content is secured from unqualified users. Violations of this standard are more obviously detrimental for intelligence and achievement assessment but problems can arise in the use of personality tests and behavior rating scales. An adolescent, for example, could coach others to mark commonly used lie scale items such as "I always tell the truth" as false in order to fake a personality test and avoid being identified as less than truthful.

We were reminded of this standard when writing this chapter. A fourth-grade female was referred to one of our clinics with a history of academic underachievement. She appeared to be a bit too familiar with the test materials considering that she had not been tested previously. As it turns out, her mother possessed a master's degree in counseling and she had obtained some assessment training. She was now working in another field. We are suspicious that this child was coached on the WISC-III.

Recently one of us was asked for an interview for a newspaper story. The reporter asked if sample items could be printed alongside the story. This ethical principle had to be shared with the reporter in order to protect test content.

What if a parent or nonpsychologist colleague wishes to have a copy of the protocols used, which may violate efforts to maintain test security? In the case where a parent asks to see the child's entire record, Koocher (1993) offers the following response:

> *Although my formal report is a part of your child's record and you are welcome to a copy of it, the notes I take and test forms I complete during the course of my evaluation are working notes. These are not a finished product, and even the actual test responses could not be effectively interpreted without specialized training. Although I would be glad to share specific test response data with another qualified professional of your choosing, it would be unethical for me to provide these materials to untrained people.* (p. 60).

TEST STANDARDS

The *Standards for Educational and Psychological Tests* (APA, 1985) complement the APA ethical principles by discussing desirable technical properties, including three primary types of validity evidence that should be provided for tests. These types are content-related, criterion-related, and construct-related evidence of validity. One of the important points presented by the test standards is that it is incorrect to use the phrase "the validity of the test" because it cannot be concluded that a particular test is valid for all children under all assessment situations (APA, 1985). The validity of a test should be gauged properly in relation to every assessment situation where it may be put to use. Clinicians who assess children's personalities must therefore learn how to use more than one personality test well in order to validly assess children from a number of different backgrounds.

Some of the important aspects of personality test validation are given in the following excerpts from the standards (APA, 1985).

1. Evidence of validity should be presented for the major types of interpretations for which a test is recommended.

If, for example, a personality test is used as part of the evidence in making the diagnosis of depression, then specific validation of the test for this purpose should be included in a test manual or technical manual. If this type of validity evidence is not presented, the manual should discuss why it is not presented and caution the user about using the test for this purpose. This type of validity evidence favors existing tests that have accumulated considerable validity studies. Another implication of this standard is that new tests must have considerable validity evidence reported in their manuals. Gone are the days when a test can be published with only evidence of reliability and factorial validity. New personality tests will have to possess thorough manuals if the tests are going to be immediately usable. Otherwise, the tests should lie dormant until some evidence is gathered.

2. When the interpretation of subtest profiles is encouraged by a test manual, the validity evidence for this type of interpretation should be presented. If this type of evidence is not presented, the user should be warned that validity evidence for this type of interpretation is not available.

The issue of profile analysis is currently of concern to researchers and clinicians alike. New tests often advise interpretive methods based on views of the validity of profile analysis dating to the World War II years (Kamphaus, 1993). The practice of interpreting high-point pairs (i.e., the two scales with the highest elevations on a personality inventory) is essentially profile analysis. Examiners are wise to use such interpretive systems cautiously without appropriate validity evidence.

3. Test manuals should give detailed descriptions of the nature of the samples used in reliability and

validity studies that allow the test user to gauge accurately the strength or weakness of the evidence presented.

Such detailed information might include the number of participants, age/grade range of the sample, gender and ethnic group composition, language background, whether or not subjects were considered handicapped, and dates of data collection. Sampling information like this is crucial for determining the generalizability of the research findings to the client currently being evaluated.

4. Internal consistency coefficients should not be presented in the manual as substitutes for stability or test-retest coefficients.

This guideline is self-explanatory. It is relatively rare for stability coefficients to differ substantially from internal consistency coefficients, but it does happen, as will be shown in later chapters. All new tests must include evidence of test-retest reliability.

The APA test standards (1985), which are currently under revision, represent considerable professional opinion regarding the construction and use of tests of personality and behavior. They cannot be represented fairly in brief form. Because of the popularity of these standards and their potential use in legislation and litigation, it behooves the clinician to have a copy on the bookshelf for easy reference. Most importantly, adherence to the standards will signal test developers to aspire to a higher level of psychometric sophistication for their products.

SELECTED LEGAL ISSUES

Bryn is a 16 year-old female who is experiencing significant family strife. One day at school she enters the student health center at her high school and asks to see the school psychologist. She tells the psychologist that her problems are frightening her. She is unable to sleep, she cries frequently, she is failing school, and she is considering suicide. She expresses,

however, that her parents are opposed to her seeking assessment and treatment. Should the school psychologist schedule an appointment for further assessment?

This scenario involves several legal and ethical issues that require consideration by the psychologist. Some of these issues will be elucidated further.

Consent for Assessment

Consent for evaluation and treatment is an important issue for minor children. At what age can a child/adolescent request services without having parental consent? The statutory age for consent in all states is 18 years, which is of little guidance in Bryn's case. Bryn could be seen for assessment and treatment under some circumstances in spite of her age.

A minor child should be assessed and treated without parental consent in some cases of emergency (Jonsen, Siegler, & Winslade, 1992), especially medical emergency. Suicidal intent, however, could be considered an emergency if, for example, Bryn told the psychologist that she had plans to drive her car off of a bridge immediately after school that day.

Provisions may vary depending on the jurisdiction (such as state) of practice. Some states may allow a minor child to seek treatment without parental permission in cases of contraception, abortion, or mental illness (Jonsen, Siegler, & Winslade, 1992). The psychologist needs to become familiar with any exceptions that may be allowed in the practice location that may allow Bryn to be assessed further.

An emancipated minor may seek assessment without parental consent. An emancipated minor is a young person who lives independently of parents, physically, financially, or otherwise—for example, in marriage, living out of town at college, or in the armed forces. Bryn would not likely meet this condition.

There is a trend to recognize the rights of the mature minor (Jonsen, Siegler, & Winslade, 1992). A mature minor is one who may still be dependent on parents but who is able to make reasoned judgments regarding his or her own well-being. Jonsen et al., 1992 suggest that an adolescent may be considered a mature minor if he or she:

1. Has reached the age of discretion (age 15) and understands the procedures well enough to give informed consent.

2. Undergoes procedures that are for his or her benefit (e.g., not research purposes).

3. Is administered treatments that are conservative and consistent with accepted practice standards for the profession.

4. Can provide a good reason as to why parental consent is unobtainable.

The psychologist must also recognize that there may be some legal risk in providing services to a mature minor. Traditionally, however, parents have not been awarded judgments in such cases (Jonsen, Siegler, & Winslade, 1992).

In Bryn's situation, even if she is considered a mature minor, the psychologist should likely try to communicate with her parents and reconcile differences. This communication, however, raises another issue—confidentiality.

Confidentiality

Bryn's confidentiality should be maintained unless she specifically waives this right (Jonsen Siegler, & Winslade, 1992). In many states, licensed psychologists have legal protection for their clients' confidentiality, which is usually referred to as *privileged communication.* Privileged communication statutes not only allow for confidentiality but also mandate it.

While the well known Tarasoff case, which highlighted the professionals' duty to warn, continues to set a precedent for breaking confidentiality, this should only be done under the extreme circumstances of danger to self or others. In these exceptional cases the psychologist should seek wise counsel from colleagues and/or legal counsel before violating confidentiality.

Threats to confidentiality are legion during the assessment process. Some of the possible breaches include:

- Parent questions such as "Did she tell you about . . . .?"

- Billing insurers
- Office workers who conduct computer scoring and type reports
- Paraprofessionals who administer and score some tests
- Publisher mail in scoring services
- Other clients or the public who see the child in your office

Billing

Increasing concern has recently surfaced about billing practices of psychologists for assessment services. Specifically, some insurers are unwilling to reimburse for services that are not specifically provided by the psychologist. Some insurers may allow paraprofessionals or other assistants to conduct testing, but only with stipulations.

At the time of this writing one large insurer was only allowing paraprofessionals to conduct testing under the supervision of a licensed psychologist if these individuals were salaried employees of the psychologist (Calhoon, 1994). These individuals could not be graduate students, for example, who worked for a psychologist on a consulting basis. Of course, the licensed psychologist is often required to be present during the assessment and conduct part of the assessment, and is solely responsible for preparing written reports.

The changing nature of insurance reimbursement makes this an especially murky area. A psychologist dealing with these issues is wise to consult with a state organization or other group that keeps abreast of developments within the psychologist's jurisdiction of practice.

DIVERSITY ISSUES

Test Bias

The perception that bias is inherent in psychological tests has spurred many challenges and accusations

(Kamphaus, 1993). Psychologists-in-training must be aware of these issues because of questions they are likely to receive from the various publics that they serve.

Mean Score Differences

Psychometric studies of test bias do not usually consider the issue of mean score differences as a meaningful test of bias (Reynolds & Kaiser, 1990). The psychometrician is assessing the validity of a personality test across groups as opposed to evaluating mean score differences. In this approach to bias there would have to be evidence that the *construct validity* for a personality test differs across groups. Numerous studies have addressed these technical issues. For the purpose of this chapter, the definition of test bias offered by Reynolds and Kaiser (1990) is most appropriate.

> Test bias refers in a global sense to *systematic* error in the estimation of some true value for a group of individuals. The key word here is systematic; all measures contain error, but this error is assumed to be random unless shown to be otherwise. Bias investigation is a statistical inquiry that does not concern itself with culture loading, labeling effects, or test use/test fairness. (p. 624)

An important point of this definition is that test bias is different from test misuse. The concept of test misuse will be revisited later; the ensuing discussion concerns only technical evaluation of bias.

Content Validity Bias

Content validity was one of the first areas of investigation of test bias. This search for bias is highly understandable given that the most frequent accusation of bias is usually directed at item content that seems inappropriate or perhaps even offensive to a group of individuals. Again, a very helpful definition of content validity bias can be taken from Reynolds and Kaiser (1990).

> An item or subscale of a test is considered to be biased in content when it is demonstrated to be relatively more difficult for members of one group than for members of another in a situation where the general ability level of the groups being compared is held constant and no reasonable theoretical rationale exists to explain group differences on the item (or subscale) in question. (p. 625)

Numerous procedures have been proposed for assessing bias in individual items, but the logic behind item bias detection techniques is fairly simple (Kamphaus, 1993). The central aspect of most statistical methods that assess for bias across cultural or gender groups is at the first step in the procedure, which is to match the groups on overall score level. If, for example, one was looking for gender bias in a pool of personality test items, one would first match boys and girls on their overall personality test score be it standard or raw score. So if one wanted to evaluate biased items in the MMPI-A, for example, one would first statistically group the cases, with perhaps all of the boys and girls with T-scores above 90 on a particular scale as one group, those between 80 and 89 as another group, those between 70 and 79 as another group and so on (it should be understood that this is not the exact procedure used by most item bias techniques but an oversimplification of such procedures). Then some statistical test of significance is applied to see if, within these various score groups, there are still significant differences in responses for the items for one gender group or another.

This discussion relates to another popular item bias technique, judgmental bias reviews. The procedure used by many publishers is to have groups of individuals review the items carefully. This procedure ensures that members of a number of cultural groups review the items to determine not only potential bias but also items that may be insulting or inappropriate for various cultural groups. There is, however, much disagreement between judgmental reviews of items and statistical analyses of bias. It appears that statistical analyses of bias are more reliable (Reynolds and Kaiser, 1990). In an investigation of judgmental bias reviews for intelligence test items, Sandoval and Mille (1979) compared the ratings of 45 WISC-R items by 38 African-American, 22 Mexican-American, and 40 undergraduate students. This study found that minority and nonminority judges did not differ in their ability to identify culturally biased items. The conclusions of Sandoval and Mille (1979) were that: (1) Judges are not able to detect items that are more difficult for a minority child than for an Anglo child, and (2) the ethnic background of the judges makes no difference in accuracy of item selection for minority children. It should also be noted that in the Sandoval and Mille investigation the most biased WISC-R items were used to try to make it easier for the judges to select biased items.

Construct Validity Bias

A workable definition of construct validity bias by Reynolds and Kaiser (1990) suggests that:

> Bias exists in regard to construct validity when a test is shown to measure different hypothetical traits (psychological constructs) for one group or another, or to measure the same trait but with differing degrees of accuracy. (p. 632)

The most popular method used for the study of construct validity bias is factor analysis. Numerous researchers have used similar procedures. The central characteristic of these procedures is to conduct factor analyses separately for various cultural and gender groups and determine if a similar factor structure is yielded for each group. The most popular procedure for assessing agreement between factor structures across groups is a coefficient of congruences, which is interpreted similarly to a correlation coefficient.

Lachar and Gruber (1994) provide an example of this method for the Personality Inventory for Youth (in press; see chapter 6). They conducted factor analyses separately by gender and ethnicity and then compared the factors yielded separately for the groups. Their findings were similar to those for ability tests (Kamphaus, 1993) in that correlations between the obtained factors were uniformly high, in the low .90s at their worst.

Predictive Validity Bias

The final type of bias that has received a great deal of attention is predictive validity bias. A working defini-

tion of predictive validity bias by Reynolds and Kaiser (1990) is:

> A test is considered biased with respect to predictive validity if the inference drawn from the test score is not made with the smallest feasible random error or if there is constant error in an inference for prediction as a function of membership in a particular group. (p. 638)

The issue of predictive or criterion-related validity is that these coefficients (see Chapter 5) should not differ significantly across cultural or gender groups. One of the typical procedures in this research literature is to compare the predictive validity coefficients across groups. A study might compare the ability of a depression measure to predict future adjustment for various groups, for example.

If different predictive validity coefficients were obtained for two or more groups, the results would be called *slope bias*. In order to understand the concept of slope bias, it is helpful to recall how correlation coefficients are learned in introductory statistics courses. Such procedures are typically taught by having the students collect data on two variables and plot the scores of a group of individuals on these two variables. This plot results in a scatter plot. Then students compute a correlation coefficient and draw a line of best fit through the scatter plot. This line of best fit is a visual representation of the slope. A correlation coefficient (predictive validity coefficient) of .90 would produce a very different slope than a correlation coefficient of .30. Consequently, the predictive validity is referred to as slope bias.

Summary Comments on Bias

While psychometric evidence of test bias can be found, little compelling evidence of bias is found for various groups residing in the United States (Figueroa, 1990). As a result, the focus has now changed to implicate test misuse as the major contributing factor to improper assessment of some groups of children. This misuse, however, includes more than individuals. Governmental, school district, or other entities may impose strict cut scores that affect assessment and conceptualization of the case.

MULTICULTURAL EXPERTISE

The renewed focus on test use comes at a time when psychologists are seeking to improve test use for various cultural and subcultural groups. Cultural plurality has posed a challenge to assessment and diagnostic practice since the early days of the mental testers. The testing movement was forced early on to change tests and testing practice in the United States because of the tremendous influx of new immigrants. Between 1901 and 1910, over nine million immigrants entered the United States—more immigrants than the combined populations of New York, Maryland, and New Hampshire in 1900 (French & Hale, 1990). One component of the initial appearance of the Wechsler scales as an alternative to the Stanford-Binet monopoly of the time was the fact that Wechsler included a Performance scale that could be used with some success with non-English speakers (Kamphaus, 1993).

Nothing has changed since the days of mass migration to the United States. Psychologists working in other cultures are also challenged to develop new competencies because of increased recognition of minorities.

In many ways, psychologists have used the same strategies for dealing with clients from diverse cultures. A popular approach involves adapting existing assessment instruments. The Thompson adaptation of the TAT for adults of African-American heritage during the 1930s (see Chapter 1) is one of the early examples of such attempts.

More recently a movement is afoot to train clinicians to address the needs of a wider range of clients. Presumably, psychologists with multicultural expertise should be able to adequately assess the needs of a child from a culture that may differ from their own, even if test instruments that are not specifically designed for the child's culture are the only ones available.

This latter approach of improving multicultural assessment expertise is perhaps more fruitful than modifying instruments, especially in light of the lack of frank evidence of test bias for many tests. In addition, few technological gains have been made in devising specific tests for specific populations. As Figueroa (1990) observes:

Currently, bilingual testing is an art form. The tester must infer and estimate the impact of language, culture, and schooling in the English versions of intelligence tests, and then do the same with even more marginal tests in another language (p. 687).

Additionally, recent concerns about testing problems have focused on the test user as a critical variable (Anastasi, 1992). The test user is being studied as it becomes clear that even results from a flawless test can produce flawed action by the test user. In many cases, clinicians choose the wrong test(s) and make inappropriate interpretations of the data (Shepard, 1989). The following section provides some advice to the psychologist who is faced with a referral for personality or behavior problems for a child who differs substantially from the examiner on cultural variables ranging from language to values.

Emic versus Etic Perspectives

The term *emic perspective* refers to behavior that is thought to be specific to a culture, whereas an *etic perspective* presupposes that much of behavior and laws of psychology are applicable cross-culturally. Anastasi (1992) proposes that both perspectives are valid by theorizing that learned behavior may be culture-specific (emic) but that the "laws of learning" apply cross-culturally. She hypothesizes further that hierarchical models of personality may be most useful for the study of behavior, as is the case for studies of intelligence where supporting evidence can be found for a "g" factor and for specific traits (e.g., spatial ability) at lower levels of the hierarchy. There is, for example, evidence that temperament traits can be identified cross-culturally (Martin, 1988).

Inappropriate, ill-informed, or insensitive interpretations may also be made of "clinical" data. An examiner may conclude that a 13-year-old girl of Asian heritage is socially introverted, shy, and perhaps in need of assertiveness training because of her behavior during an interview with a male clinician. She may have been demure and made no eye contact. The examiner may draw such a conclusion despite the fact that she appeared friendly and outgoing when she was observed on the school playground and seemed to interact openly with her family members. This client may not in fact be pathologically shy; rather, she may be adhering to a prohibition against making eye contact with a male because of cultural values that suggest that this is sexually seductive behavior (or an indication of a lack of respect) that is deemed inappropriate for her (Hasegawa, 1989). In this case the clinician was simply ignoring relevant data, and the clinician's lack of familiarity with the child's culture resulted in an erroneous interpretation.

An additional example may help clarify the need for multicultural knowledge. Perhaps a psychologist is working in a neighborhood where most of the inhabitants are children of African and Indian/Pakistani descent and Italian-American children are in the minority. Yet the Italian immigrant children are making up a large percentage of the referrals for mental health services, much more than would be expected based on their proportions in the neighborhood. A psychologist who is not schooled in multicultural research may conclude that there is something awry with the Italian-American family, physical constitution, or whatever. If, however, the psychologist is familiar with multicultural issues, he or she may more appropriately conclude that community/preventive interventions may be most appropriate since research shows that minority status itself is a stressor for any cultural group (Mintz & Schwartz, 1964).

The clinician, however, must remember the importance of individualizing interpretation. Within a cultural group, variability can be substantial (Zuckerman, 1990). It may be assumed by some that Vietnamese and Chinese children have similar values due to earlier Chinese domination and inculcation with Confucian ethics. There have also been other influences on this culture that may affect a child's behavior, including European Roman Catholicism brought by the French conquest of 1958, the influence of American culture from the Vietnam War, and Buddhist influences from neighboring Cambodia (Huang, 1990). Classifying children by race, culture, or language background is an appealing approach for researchers and clinicians alike that is fraught with errors primarily due to the tendency to overgeneralize about a particular group of people (Zuckerman, 1990).

Inclan and Herron (1985) cite the "culture of poverty" as another subculture that may affect a variety of groups. This "culture" is formed by a clash between those who have achieved material wealth and prosperity and those who struggle to achieve economic parity with little hope of doing so. Children reared in a culture of poverty possess characteristics such as an orientation to present time; inability to delay gratification; impulsivity; sense of predetermined fate; resentment of authority; alienation and distrust of others; and lack of emphasis on rigor, discipline, and perseverance (Inclan & Herron, 1989). They note that some impoverished parents of adolescents may be assessed by a therapist as being too rigid and controlling of their youngsters at a time when parents should be allowing their children more freedom. It is possible, however, that poor parents may be all too familiar with the culture of poverty and may be seeking control not for its own sake but rather to ensure that their child or adolescent does not fall prey to the negative consequences of behavior associated with that culture (Inclan & Herron, 1989).

These citations demonstrate the need for clinicians to develop an enlarged knowledge base in order to deal effectively with their referral population. Just as clinicians have to have knowledge of behavioral principles, psychometrics, child development, child psychopathology, and physiological psychology to conduct an evaluation competently, it is increasingly clear that they must know the history, culture, and language of their community extremely well in order to not use assessment procedures inappropriately and make naive interpretations.

Guidelines for Assessing Children from Diverse Backgrounds

Resources for assessing children from diverse groups are now more readily available (e.g., Geisinger, 1992). Two developments that can assist practitioners are (1) the availability of guidelines from blue ribbon panels and committees and (2) the increasing availability of formal measures of acculturation.

Numerous sets of guidelines provide specific advice for the psychologist who is unsure of what procedures to use in questionable situations. The recently released *Guidelines for Providers of Psychological Services to Ethnic, Linguistic, and Culturally Diverse Populations* give specific and helpful advice to the clinician seeking to carry out a competent evaluation of a child for whom cultural/social/linguistic issues loom large (see Box 4.3).

BOX 4.3

Guidelines for Providers of Psychological Services to Ethnic, Linguistic, and Culturally Diverse Populations

---

Preamble: The Guidelines represent general principles that are intended to be aspirational in nature and are designed to provide suggestions to psychologists in working with ethnic, linguistic, and culturally diverse populations.

1. Psychologists educate their clients to the processes of psychological intervention, such as goals and expectations; the scope and, where appropriate, legal limits of confidentiality; and the psychologists' orientations.

   a. Whenever possible, psychologists provide information in writing along with oral explanations.

   b. Whenever possible, the written information is provided in the language understandable to the client.

2. Psychologists are cognizant of relevant research and practice issues as related to the population being served.

   a. Psychologists acknowledge that ethnicity and culture impact on behavior and take those factors into account when working with various ethnic/racial groups.

   b. Psychologists seek out educational and training experiences to enhance their understanding and thereby address the needs of these populations more appropriately and effectively. These experiences include cultural, social, psychological, political, economic, and historical material specific to the particular ethnic group being served.

   c. Psychologists recognize the limits of their competencies and expertise. Psychologists who do not possess knowledge and training about an ethnic group seek consultation with, and/or make referrals to, appropriate experts as necessary.

   d. Psychologists consider the validity of a given instrument or procedure and interpret resulting data, keeping in mind the cultural and linguistic characteristics of the person being assessed. Psychologists are aware of the test's reference population and possible limitations of such instruments with other populations.

3. Psychologists recognize ethnicity and culture as significant parameters in understanding psychological processes.

   a. Psychologists, regardless of ethnic/racial background, are aware of how their own cultural background/experiences, attitudes, values, and biases influence psychological processes. They make efforts to correct any prejudices and biases.

   Illustrative Statement: Psychologists might routinely ask themselves, "Is it appropriate for me to view this client or organization any differently than I would if they were from my own ethnic or cultural group?"

   b. Psychologists' practice incorporates an understanding of the client's ethnic and cultural background. This includes the client's familiarity and comfort with the majority culture as well as ways in which the client's culture may add to or improve various aspects of the majority culture and/or society at large.

   Illustrative Statement: The kinds of mainstream social activities in which families participate may offer information about the level and quality of acculturation to American society. It is important to distinguish acculturation from length of stay in the United States and not to assume that these issues are relevant only for new immigrants and refugees.

   c. Psychologists help clients increase their awareness of their own cultural values and norms, and they facilitate discovery of ways clients can apply this awareness to their own lives and to society at large.

   Illustrative Statement: Psychologists may be able to help parents distinguish between generational conflict and culture gaps when problems arise between them and their children. In the process, psychologists could help both parents and children to appreciate their own distinguishing cultural values.

(Cont.)

BOX 4.3 *(Continued)*

d. Psychologists seek to help a client determine whether a "problem" stems from racism or bias in others so that the client does not inappropriately personalize problems.

   Illustrative Statement: The concept of "healthy paranoia," whereby ethnic minorities may develop defensive behaviors in response to discrimination, illustrates this principle.

e. Psychologists consider not only differential diagnostic issues but also the cultural beliefs and values of the client and his/her community in providing intervention.

   Illustrative Statement: There is a disorder among the traditional Navajo called "Moth Madness." Symptoms include seizure-like behaviors. This disorder is believed by the Navajo to be the supernatural result of incestuous thoughts or behaviors. Both differential diagnosis and intervention should take into consideration the traditional values of Moth Madness.

4. Psychologists respect the roles of family members and community structures, hierarchies, values, and beliefs within the client's culture.

   a. Psychologists identify resources in the family and the larger community.

   b. Clarification of the role of the psychologist and the expectations of the client precede intervention. Psychologists seek to ensure that both the psychologist and client have a clear understanding of what services and roles are reasonable.

      Illustrative Statement: It is not uncommon for an entire American Indian family to come into the clinic to provide support to the person in distress. Many of the healing practices found in American Indian communities are centered in the family and the whole community.

5. Psychologists respect clients' religious and/or spiritual beliefs and values, including attributions and taboos, since they affect world view, psychosocial functioning, and expressions of distress.

   a. Part of working in minority communities is to become familiar with indigenous beliefs and practices and to respect them.

      Illustrative Statement: Traditional healers (e.g., shamans, curanderos, espiritistas) have an important place in minority communities.

   b. Effective psychological intervention may be aided by consultation with and/or inclusion of religious/spiritual leaders/practitioners relevant to the client's cultural and belief systems.

6. Psychologists interact in the language requested by the client and, if this is not feasible, make an appropriate referral.

   a. Problems may arise when the linguistic skills of the psychologist do not match the language of the client. In such a case, psychologists refer the client to a mental health professional who is competent to interact in the language of the client. If this is not possible, psychologists offer the client a translator with cultural knowledge and an appropriate professional background. When no translator is available, then a trained paraprofessional from the client's culture is used as a translator/culture broker.

   b. If translation is necessary, psychologists do not retain the services of translators/paraprofessionals who may have a dual role with the client, to avoid jeopardizing the validity of evaluation or the effectiveness of intervention.

   c. Psychologists interpret and relate test data in terms understandable and relevant to the needs of those assessed.

7. Psychologists consider the impact of adverse social, environmental, and political factors in assessing problems and designing interventions.

   a. Types of intervention strategies to be used match the client's level of need (e.g., Maslow's hierarchy of needs).

      Illustrative Statement: Low income may be associated with such stressors as malnutrition, substandard housing, and poor medical care; and rural residency may mean inaccessibility of services. Clients may resist treatment at government agencies because of previous experience (e.g., refugees' status may be associated with violent treatments by government officials and agencies).

   b. Psychologists work within the cultural setting to improve the welfare of all persons concerned, if there is a conflict between cultural values and human rights.

8. Psychologists attend to, as well as work to eliminate, biases, prejudices, and discriminatory practices.

   a. Psychologists acknowledge relevant discriminatory practices at the social and community level that may be affecting the psychological welfare of the population being served.

(Cont.)

BOX 4.3 *(Continued)*

    Illustrative Statement: Depression may be associated with frustrated attempts to climb the corporate ladder in an organization that is dominated by a top echelon of White men.

b. Psychologists are cognizant of sociopolitical contexts in conducting evaluations and providing interventions; they develop sensitivity to issues of oppression, sexism, elitism, and racism.

    Illustrative Statement: An upsurge in the public expression of rancor or even violence between two ethnic or cultural groups may increase anxiety baselines in any member of those groups. This baseline of anxiety would interact with prevailing symptomatology. At the organizational level, the community conflict may interfere with open communication among staff.

9. Psychologists working with culturally diverse populations should document culturally and sociopolitically relevant factors in the records. These may include, but are not limited to

    a. number of generations in the country

    b. number of years in the country

    c. fluency in English

    d. extent of family support (or disintegration of family)

    e. community resources

    f. level of education

    g. change in social status as a result of coming to this country (for immigrant or refugee)

    h. intimate relationship with people of different backgrounds

    i. level of stress related to acculturation.

Reprinted with permission of the American Psychological Association.

A good example of the guidance to be gained from such publications deals with the frequently occurring situation of a language difference between examiner and child or other family members. Guideline 6a suggests to the examiner faced with such a case that a cascade of three options applies: (1) Refer the child to a clinician who can communicate in the client's preferred language; (2) if this is not possible,

use a translator who also possesses professional training; and, lastly, (3) one is advised to use a paraprofessional from the community to translate. Moreover, the next guideline, 6b, highlights the potential threat to validity of using a translator who has a dual relationship with the client (e.g., a grandparent).

Assessing Acculturation

The previously discussed guidelines for assessing diversity issues hint at the need to more carefully assess an individual's level of adoption of the so-called "dominant culture," which, of course, could change from neighborhood to neighborhood. The guidelines point out the need to collect information such as the number of generations of residence within the dominant culture, number of years of residence, dominant language fluency, community resources, and so forth. This data collection is an informal means of assessing level of acculturation.

There are now, however, more formal (some are quantifiable) methods for assessing acculturation. In fact, it has been argued that the ready availability of such measures warrants their routine use in assessment practice (Geisinger, 1992).

Marín (1992) defines the constructs relevant to assessing ethnic identity and acculturation. He cites three components of ethnic identity: (1) "birth and gestational history," (2) "culture-specific behaviors and practices" (e.g., language), and (3) "culture-specific attitudes that include adherence to a culture's values and norms as well as in-group and out-group attitudes." (p. 236) The process of acculturation is defined as the ". . . changes in individuals that are produced by contact with one or more cultural groups" (p. 237). Several instruments are now available for assessing the ethnic identification of individuals and the degree to which acculturation has taken place.

Dana (1993) provides a detailed compendium of measures of acculturation and identification with a particular culture. Some of these scales are listed below.

African-American Measures

    Developmental Inventory of Black Consciousness (DIB-C; Milliones, 1980)

Racial Identity Attitude Scale (RIAS; Helms, 1986

African Self-Consciousness Scale (ASC; Baldwin & Bell, 1985)

Asian-American Measures

Ethnic Identity Questionnaire (EIQ; Masuda, Matsumoto, & Meredith, 1970)

Hispanic American Measures

Acculturation Rating Scale for Mexican Americans (ARSMA; Cuellar, Harris, & Jasso, 1980)

Children's Acculturation Scale (Franco, 1983)

Cuban Behavioral Identity Questionnaire (CBIQ; Garcia & Lega, 1979)

Hispanic Acculturation Scale (Marín et al., 1987)

Children's Hispanic Background Scale (Martinez, Norman, & Delaney, 1984)

Cultural Life Style Inventory (Mendoza, 1989)

Multidimensional Scale of Cultural Differences (Olmedo, Martinez, & Martinez, 1978)

Multicultural Experience Inventory (Ramirez, 1984)

Behavioral Acculturation Scale (Szapocznik, Scopetta, & Aranalde, 1978)

Bicultural Involvement Questionnaire (Szapocznik & Kurtines, 1980)

CONCLUSIONS

The child psychologist of today has to become steeped in the various ethical, legal, professional, and diversity issues that face the profession. For some trainers of psychologists these are relatively new issues that are therefore not routinely included in the graduate curriculum. Insurance billing issues are excellent examples of such content. It is necessary for the practitioner to seek this knowledge through experiences other than graduate school. Continuing education activities and consultation services sponsored by professional organizations are excellent resources for such information.

CHAPTER SUMMARY

1. The ethical standards published by the American Psychological Association (which uses the same acronym as the American Psychiatric Association) are among the most well-known sets of ethical principles providing high standards of assessment practices.

2. Some of the APA ethics principles of relevance to assessment deal with:

   Evaluation, diagnosis, or intervention in professional context

   Competence and appropriate use of assessments and interventions

   Test construction

   Use of assessment in general and with special populations

   Interpreting assessment results

   Unqualified persons

   Obsolete tests and outdated test results

   Test scoring and interpretation services

   Explaining assessment results

   Maintaining test security

3. The *Standards for Educational and Psychological Tests* (APA, 1985) complement the APA ethical principles by discussing the technical properties that should be desired by test users, including three primary types of validity evidence that should be provided for tests.

4. Some legal issues of relevance to assessment practice include confidentiality, consent for assessment, and billing practices.

5. While psychometric evidence of content-, construct-, or criterion-related validity test bias can be found, little compelling evidence of bias is found for various groups residing in the United States. As a result, the focus has now changed to implicate test misuse as the major contributing factor in improper assessment of some groups of children.

6. The renewed focus on test use comes at a time

when psychologists are seeking to improve test use for various cultural and subcultural groups.

7. The emic perspective refers to behavior that is thought to be specific to a culture, whereas an etic perceptive presupposes that much of behavior theory and laws of psychology are applicable cross-culturally.

8. The recently released *Guidelines for Providers of Psychological Services to Ethnic, Linguistic, and Culturally Diverse Populations* give specific and helpful advice to the clinician seeking to carry out a competent evaluation of a child for whom cultural/social/linguistic issues loom large.

9. Examiners faced with a linguistic difference between themselves and an examinee have at least three options: (1) Refer the child to a clinician who can communicate in the client's preferred language; (2) if this is not possible, use a translator who also possesses professional training; and, lastly, (3) use a paraprofessional from the community to translate.

10. There are now more formal (some are quantifiable) methods for assessing acculturation.

Planning the Evaluation and Rapport Building

NONSPECIFICS IN CLINICAL ASSESSMENT

A recurrent theme in this text is that an assessor needs to have a knowledge of several areas of basic research to appropriately select and interpret psychological tests for children and adolescents. In this chapter we tackle another area of competence crucial to clinical assessment that goes beyond knowing how to administer specific tests. This competence is much harder to discuss in objective terms because it relates to topics that are difficult to research and, as a result, there is not a body of knowledge to guide practice. Instead, much in this chapter is guided by clinical experience, not just our own experience, but the experience of other practicing psychologists that have written in the area.

This chapter deals with setting an appropriate context in which testing takes place. This context is not simply the physical context of testing, but also the activities of the assessor that allow the clinical assessment to achieve its goals. Many of the issues we discuss involve clinical skills that are difficult to teach but which often require refinement based on practical experience in testing children and adolescents. However, an analogy can be made with the literature on psychotherapy. Many useful guides for practicing clinicians have been published that deal with the nonspecifics of psychotherapy. This term *nonspecifics* has been used to refer to several contextual factors within which the techniques of psychotherapy take place, such as the relationship between therapist and client or the process by which a therapist engages a client in a therapeutic setting (e.g., Shoham-Salomon, 1991; Strupp, 1973). In this chapter we attempt to deal with the nonspecifics in the clinical assessment of children and adolescents.

One critical component to setting an appropriate context for evaluations is careful planning. In the following section we discuss a basic framework for designing clinical assessments for children and adolescents. Within this basic framework, however, evaluations must be tailored to the needs of the individual case. The critical developmental issues, the most relevant areas of adjustment to assess, and the most important elements of a child or adolescent's environment will all vary from case to case. As a result, it is inappropriate to develop specific guidelines for designing evaluations. Instead, in this section we attempt to provide a framework for designing assessments that can be tailored to most assessment situations.

CLARIFYING THE REFERRAL QUESTION

A crucial part of planning any evaluation is having enough information prior to beginning testing to make at least some initial decisions on the structure and content of the assessment process. This is not to say that the assessment process should be so structured from the outset that changes after testing is underway are not possible. However, obtaining crucial information before the first testing session enhances the likelihood that one will provide a focused and appropriate assessment. Almost every testing

agency, whether clinic, school, hospital, or private practitioner, has some established intake through which preliminary information on the child or adolescent being tested is obtained. There is no single best way to structure the intake procedure. However, there are some pieces of information that should be obtained routinely in any intake process, in addition to any business information (e.g., name, address, phone number, insurance coverage) that is required by the agency.

Purpose of Testing

The most important piece of intake information for planning an evaluation is the intended purpose of the evaluation. A major flaw in many clinical assessments is a lack of focus. From the outset an evaluation should have clearly specified goals and objectives. As discussed previously, it is erroneous to think in terms of an assessment technique or battery being valid or invalid. Results of the evaluation can be valid for *specific interpretations*. Therefore, what interpretations one anticipates making at the end of the evaluation should guide what tests are selected for the assessment battery. For example, if an assessment is primarily to determine school placement, then the focus of the evaluation will not be to determine whether or not a psychiatric diagnosis is warranted, but to determine whether or not the child meets eligibility requirements of the school system. The assessor may feel that more information is needed to make appropriate recommendations for what interventions are needed to meet a child's psychological and educational needs than is required by these criteria. However, enough information to determine eligibility should be part of the assessment, if this is the primary referral question. In our experience, it is not uncommon for an otherwise sound and competently conducted evaluation to be useless for the specific purposes for which a child was referred.

There are many other examples of how the intended use of the assessment information will determine which measures should be used. This may be as broad as defining what areas need to be covered for a certain purpose (e.g., some residential treatment centers require a personality assessment prior to acceptance) to as specific as requiring certain tests (e.g., some school systems require the Rorschach for special education placement). The assessor should not give a test that, in his or her professional judgment, is inappropriate for a particular use or is inappropriate for a particular client. However, if at the time of referral the intended use of the assessment is clarified and there is some question as to how appropriate certain requirements are for a given case, the assessor can attempt to address these issues before beginning the evaluation.

Often the person or agency referring a child or adolescent for testing is not sure how the test results will be used. Instead, the child is referred because the agency is unsure of the nature of a child's problem (or even whether there is a problem) and the referrer is unsure of what can be done to help the child. There are many variations on this theme, but, in essence, the goal of the assessment then is to diagnose the source of a child's difficulty and to make treatment recommendations based on this diagnosis. In the previous chapter we discussed many important issues in making diagnostic decisions. However, Martin (1988) provides a succinct and practical analysis of the specific goals involved in diagnosis. These are to (1) predict future behavior, (2) differentiate between abnormal and normal behavior, (3) make differential diagnoses, and (4) delineate individual differences in competencies and disabilities. Martin (1988) provides some interesting recommendations for planning the evaluation to maximize the reliability of the diagnostic process. These are summarized in Box 5.1.

Box 5.1

Planning the Evaluation to Enhance Reliability

In our chapter on psychometric theory we discussed reliability as a key concept in understanding psychological measurement. Reliability is often considered as a property of individual tests. However, Martin (1988) discusses sev-

eral issues in planning an assessment battery that can maximize the reliability of the information that is obtained. Key to Martin's approach is his conceptualization of four primary sources of error variance that can affect the reliability of measurement of children's social and emotional functioning: (1) temporal variance—changes in behavior over time, (2) source or rater variance—differences in information due to characteristics of the informant, (3) setting variance—differences due to different demand characteristics across settings, and (4) instrument variance—unreliability inherent in individual instruments.

Martin uses a basic concept in measurement theory to describe how these sources of error variance can be controlled in an assessment. Specifically, the primary method of controlling error variance and increasing reliability is through *aggregation*. As the length of a test increases, the reliability of the scores increase. As a result, to control for temporal variance, repeated measurements on several occasions should be obtained. Similarly, to reduce source and setting variance, information should be obtained from multiple sources and across multiple settings. The implication of these psychometric considerations, the need for a comprehensive evaluation, is similar to the conclusion reached in Chapter 3 on developmental psychopathology. In that chapter there were several other rationales for a comprehensive evaluation based on research on the nature of children's emotional and behavior disturbances.

The final source of error variance in Martin's scheme is *instrument variance*. Like the other sources of variance, aggregating information across instruments is a crucial method of increasing reliability. However, this is only the case if the additional tests provide reliable information. If one adds unreliable tests to a battery, then aggregation actually *decreases* the reliability of the battery. Clinicians who have a favorite test that they use in batteries will often justify their use of the test, even if it has been proven unreliable, by the statement "I only use it as one part of a more comprehensive battery." This is clearly better than using the test in isolation. However, adding a piece of unreliable information will only reduce the reliability of the aggregated information. In a separate publication, Martin (1982) gives the example of three umpires calling a baseball game. If one of the umpires is blind, her calls will only serve to reduce the reliability of the calls made by the entire umpiring team. The moral to the story: Aggregation only increases the reliability of the information obtained if the individual tests are selected to enhance reliability.

SOURCE: R. P. Martin. (1988). *Assessment of Personality and Behavior Problems: Infancy through Adolescence.* New York: Guilford Press.

Description of Referral Problems

In addition to understanding the purpose of the testing referral, it is also important to obtain an initial description of the difficulties that a child is experiencing that led to the referral. One of the reasons that clinical assessments are so fascinating is that, if done right, the assessment should be a type of scientific inquiry. Based on the intake information, the assessor should have some initial hypotheses for understanding a given case that will be tested during the evaluation. These hypotheses will guide the initial planning of the evaluation and initial test selection. As in any good scientific endeavor, it must be clear what information would support and what information would contradict the various hypotheses. In contrast to many other scientific enterprises, however, the hypotheses can and should change during the investigation. As data accumulate on a case and it becomes clear that initial impressions of a case were wrong, the assessor must revise the assessment accordingly. To employ this scientific approach to clinical assessment, enough preliminary information on a child's functioning must be obtained prior to starting the evaluation, so that initial hypotheses can be formed. A case example that utilizes this approach is provided in Box 5.2.

DESIGNING THE EVALUATION

We ended Chapter 3 by providing several guidelines for clinical assessments of children that followed from research in developmental psychopathology. In this section we take these research-based guidelines and use them to develop practical considerations in designing clinical assessments of children. Once again, these recommendations are designed to provide a generic framework, which can be tailored to the needs of the individual case.

BOX 5.2

A Scientific Approach to Clinical Assessment: A Case Example

Joshua is a 10-year-old boy who was referred to the outpatient psychiatry department of a large inner-city pediatric hospital for testing. The intake worker determined that Joshua was being referred by his parents because he was in danger of failing the fifth grade. According to the intake information, Joshua was having great difficulty paying attention in class and completing assignments. He was also described as being excessively fidgety and restless. The intake information indicated that these school problems were new this school year. He had been an A\B student in the four previous school grades, which made his current poor performance especially puzzling.

Based on this information, several initial hypotheses were formulated. It could be that similar problems had been going on in past grades but they had just increased in severity in the fifth grade; in which case, dispositional causes were possible such as an attention deficit disorder and/or a learning disability. Alternatively, if this recent onset was supported in the evaluation (through history taking, obtaining school records, interviewing past teachers), it may be that the child had experienced or was experiencing some type of newly occurring stressor (e.g., parental divorce, sexual abuse) that was resulting in the deterioration in behavior. The evaluation was designed to test these initial hypotheses.

Interestingly, during the assessment of potential stressors Joshua's mother reported that he had been involved in an automobile accident during the summer prior to entering the fifth grade. He had sustained a closed head injury and had lost consciousness for several minutes. He was released from the hospital with no noticeable effects of the injury. After obtaining this information, another hypothesis became possible. The child might have sustained neurological damage from the accident that was affecting his behavior. As a result, he was referred for a neurological exam, which uncovered neurological damage that seemed to be the most likely cause of his behavioral difficulties. Although the initial hypotheses were not correct, this illustrates how a scientific approach to hypothesis testing can be useful in structuring the assessment process.

Developmental Considerations

The basic tenet of developmental psychopathology is the need to place a child's emotional and behavioral functioning in a developmental context. As a result, it is essential that a clinical assessor consider developmental issues in designing an assessment battery. The first important area in which developmental issues will influence the design of the evaluation is in the selection of specific tests or specific testing modalities. For example, some tests provide good norm-referenced scores (e.g., T-scores based on a large representative sample of children within a specific age group) for some age groups, whereas at other ages the normative base is much weaker or nonexistent. Because this issue is so crucial for selecting assessment instruments appropriate for a given child, a significant focus of our discussion of specific tests in later chapters is on the adequacy of the norm-referenced scores provided by the test. In addition to specific tests, some testing modalities may be more or less appropriate depending on the developmental level of a child. For example, in our chapter on structured interviews we discuss research suggesting that child self-report on such interviews tends to be unreliable prior to age 9.

The second way that developmental issues will influence the design of the evaluations is by suggesting certain initial hypotheses that will be tested in the evaluation regarding the most likely explanation for a child's referral problems. As we discussed in Chapter 3, certain behaviors tend to be more prevalent at some ages than at others due to the unique developmental tasks that arise at various ages. As a result, if the referring concern is for behavior (e.g., oppositional behavior) that is consistent with a developmental task appropriate for that age (e.g., development of autonomy around 24 months of age), one hypothesis to be tested is whether or not the problem may simply be an exaggeration of a developmentally normal behavior pattern.

Determining the Relevant Psychological Domains

A fairly ubiquitous finding in research on childhood psychopathology is the high degree of overlap or comorbidity in problem behaviors. That is, children with problems in one area of emotional or behavioral functioning are at high risk for having problems in other areas of emotional and behavioral functioning, as well as problems in social and cognitive arenas. As a result, most evaluations of children and adolescents must be fairly comprehensive to ensure that other problematic areas that could be relevant to treatment planning are assessed. In planning an evaluation, one should consider the most likely comorbidities associated with the referral problem and design the evaluation to provide an adequate assessment of these areas. From the referral information one may also gather some clues as to how intensive the assessment of these potentially important domains should be.

As an example of these two factors, consider a referral of a 7-year-old boy who is having significant problems of being unorganized, being very impulsive, and having difficulty staying in his seat. Your initial hypothesis may be that the child has attention-deficit hyperactivity disorder (ADHD), and you will design an evaluation to test this hypothesis (see Chapter 16). You know from research on ADHD that approximately 30% of children with the disorder have a co-occurring learning disability (Hinshaw, 1992). Therefore, you consider how you will assess for this likely comorbidity. However, in the initial intake, the child's mother states that her son has no real problems academically, other than losing his assignments frequently, and, in fact, he has only made two B's on his report cards since entering school. Based on this piece of information, you may decide not to conduct an intensive evaluation of a potential learning disability unless during the course of the evaluation you discover additional evidence of learning problems.

Screening of Important Contexts

Research has indicated that children's behavior is heavily influenced by factors in a child's psychosocial environment. Therefore, an important consideration in planning an evaluation is determining what aspects of a child's environment should be assessed (e.g., teaching styles of specific teachers, affective style of family) and how these should be assessed (e.g., naturalistic observations, behavior rating scales). However, which contexts are most relevant will vary from child to child. The intake information should provide enough information so that an evaluation can be planned in which (1) informants from each of a child's relevant contexts provide information on a child's functioning and (2) the contexts that seem to have the most impact on a child's functioning can be assessed in greater detail.

One of the most influential contexts for the majority of children is the family. A whole chapter in this text (Chapter 13) is devoted to the assessment of a child's family environment. However, what constitutes a family for a child is becoming increasingly diverse, and the intake can yield some preliminary information on the family structure (e.g., marital status of parents, degree of contact with nonresident parents, other adult caretakers in the home) that provides the assessor with some clues as to the best method of structuring an evaluation of the family context.

Practical Considerations in Designing an Evaluation

In an important clinical endeavor like psychological testing that can have important outcomes for a child one does not like to consider such mundane factors as time and expense in designing the evaluation. Clearly, these factors should not outweigh what is in the best interest of the child or adolescent being tested. However, sometimes these factors are unavoidable and often expediency is in the best interest of the child. For example, an adolescent who has an impending court date for a juvenile offense may need to have an evaluation completed before this date to help in determining the most appropriate placement and the most appropriate services. One would take care to not be so influenced by expediency that treatment decisions are misguided by poor assessment results. But one must consider what can meaningfully be obtained within the time frame available and possibly make as part of the outcome of the evaluation a recommendation for what additional testing might be beneficial as time allows.

How much to weigh cost and time constraints will vary from case to case. However, we feel that one should ask two questions in designing any evaluation:

1. What is the essential information needed to answer the referral question(s)?
2. What is the most economical means of obtaining this essential information without compromising the usefulness of information?

TO TEST OR NOT TO TEST

After a child is referred for testing, an important question that should be asked is whether or not an evaluation is in the child's best interest. We feel that simply because an evaluation is requested by someone is not sufficient reason to conduct the evaluation. A professional must make the decision as to whether or not an evaluation would benefit the child or adolescent. Often this question is ignored for financial reasons. If you don't do the evaluation, you don't get paid. However, we feel that a clinical assessor has the ethical obligation to determine whether or not a child would benefit from the evaluation and then convey this determination to the referring agency.

There can be several reasons why an evaluation would not be in a child's best interest. For example, a child's parent may seek multiple evaluations because the parent does not agree with the findings of previous evaluations. We feel that second opinions are not inappropriate in many cases. However, if this is not considered carefully, a child may be subjected to numerous intrusive evaluations that are not necessary and the evaluator may inadvertently reinforce a parent's denial of a child's special needs. Alternatively, the person referring a child or adolescent may have unrealistic expectations for what an evaluation can accomplish, or the reason for the evaluation may be insufficient to justify performing the evaluation. An example that illustrates both of these issues is a child who is referred by a parent to determine his future sexual orientation.

Even if one determines that a child or adolescent

may benefit from an evaluation, one must also question whether or not the assessor is the appropriate person to conduct the evaluation. The appropriateness of an assessor may simply be a matter of one's competence, either because of unique characteristics of the child (e.g., age, culture) or because of the specific nature of the referral question. Assessors must hold closely to the principle included in the APA Standards (see Chapter 4) that "Psychologists provide services, teach, and conduct research only within the boundaries of their competence, based on their education, training, supervised experience, or appropriate professional experience" (American Psychological Association, 1992, Standard 1.04).

In addition to competence, a clinical assessor must also question whether or not personal reasons might prevent him or her from conducting an objective evaluation. For example, an examiner may have a personal relationship with a child or family that might interfere with the ability to objectively administer and interpret tests. Alternatively, the assessor may have personal issues related to the referral problem that might prevent him or her from being able to competently perform the evaluation. For example, a psychologist who himself is dealing with memories of a past sexual abuse may not be able to conduct an evaluation of another sexual abuse victim because he is unable to transcend his own issues related to the abuse. There are no clear-cut guidelines for determining when personal issues would interfere with an evaluation. Our point is to suggest that assessors should routinely question whether or not they are appropriate to conduct an evaluation, and they should consult with colleagues if there is any question regarding their ability to appropriately conduct the evaluation.

RAPPORT BUILDING

There is no aspect of the assessment process that is as difficult to define and to teach as the concept of rapport. However, rapport is a critical component to testing children and adolescents (Fuchs & Fuchs, 1986), although it is rarely discussed in child assess-

ment texts (e.g., Achenbach & McConaughy, 1987; Ollendick & Hersen, 1993) or in administration manuals for tests designed for children (see Fuchs, 1987). The *Longman Dictionary of Psychology and Psychiatry* (1984) defines *rapport* as "a warm, relaxed relationship that promotes mutual acceptance, e.g., between therapist and patient, or between teacher and student. Rapport implies that the confidence inspired by the former produces trust and willing cooperation in the latter" (p. 619). To paraphrase and apply this definition to the testing situation, rapport refers to the interactions between the assessor and the person being assessed (client) that promote confidence and cooperation in the assessment process. Rapport building is not something that is done at the outset of testing and then forgotten. Instead, it is a process that evolves throughout the entire assessment endeavor (Barker, 1990; Sattler, 1988).

The importance of rapport is not specific to psychological assessment; it is a critical concept in most clinical endeavors. There are several recommendations that can be drawn from other clinical situations that apply equally well to child testing. For example, Phares (1984) described the basic elements of establishing rapport in psychotherapeutic relationships as "having an attitude of acceptance, understanding, and respect for the integrity of the client" (p. 195). Phares goes on to point out that this attitude is not synonymous with establishing a state of mutual liking but is more related to a clinician's ability to convey to the client a sincere desire to understand the client's problems and to help him or her to cope with them. This general attitude of the assessor is the basic component of establishing rapport with the client. As a result, our specific recommendations are designed to foster this attitude in testing situations.

While the importance of rapport is not confined to the psychological assessment of children and adolescents, there are several unique aspects to the assessment of youth that make rapport building a complicated process in this context. First, the clinical assessment of children typically involves many people (e.g., child, parent, teacher) who have varying levels of understanding of the assessment process and who possess varying levels of motivation for the assessment.

Therefore, the assessor must be skilled in enlisting and fostering the cooperation of many different participants. The issue of motivation is especially salient in the evaluation of youth because children and adolescents often are not self-referred. Children are often referred for evaluations because their behavior is causing problems for significant others in their environment (Frick et al., 1993). Therefore, enlisting their cooperation and trust is a critical, but often difficult, process. Later in this chapter we provide examples of how testing can be presented to children and adolescents in ways that foster the establishment of a working relationship.

A second factor that complicates the development of rapport in testing situations is the presence of severe time limitations. In many, if not most, testing situations the assessor has limited time in which to develop rapport with all participants. Often testing is confined to one or several discrete testing periods and testing starts early in the first session. This is quite different from many other clinical contexts, such as the psychotherapeutic context (see Strupp, 1973), in which there is likely to be more flexibility in the time allowed for developing rapport prior to the initiation of some clinical intervention.

Based on this discussion, it is evident that establishing rapport in the typical assessment situation for children and adolescents involves enlisting the cooperation of *multiple participants* to divulge personal and sometimes distressing information, despite a potential *lack of motivation* and despite the fact that the testing must be completed within a *limited time frame.* It should be obvious from this description that rapport building is not always an easy task in clinical assessments of youth. Therefore, we feel it is important to outline what we consider some of the more important considerations in the development of rapport in child and adolescent evaluations.

Informed Consent

We view informed consent in two ways in this book. The first way, which is the more traditional way, is to view it as a legal right of the recipients of any psychological service. The assessor has the legal and ethical responsibility of ensuring that informed consent is provided for the assessment. The ethical and legal issues involved in informed consent, as well as guidelines for obtaining such consent, were discussed in the previous chapter. However, we also view informed consent in a second way: as a basic element of rapport building. As discussed previously, a fundamental element in developing rapport is conveying a respect for the integrity of the individual participating in the evaluation. There is no more basic way of conveying respect than by focusing on the informed consent process.

In Chapter 4, we discussed the legal requirements of obtaining informed consent from a child's legal guardian. However, the assessor can communicate a sincere respect for the child's parents (or other legal guardian) by spending a great deal of time reviewing all testing procedures in very clear and specific terms, by discussing the limits to confidentiality in sensitive terms, by clearly reviewing the intended uses of the test results, and by allowing and encouraging the parents to ask questions about these issues. In essence, the assessor should convey to the parent that the consent procedures are not just a legal formality, but are intended as the first step in establishing a collaborative effort between the parent and assessor. Also, there is no greater damage to the development of rapport than a parent's *perception* that some procedures were used without his or her full knowledge and consent.

The need to transcend legal requirements is even more important with the child. With the view that minors may not be competent to make decisions regarding their need for certain medical or psychological procedures, like psychological testing, the right to informed consent generally rests with a child's parent or legal guardian. Unfortunately, many assessors take this to mean that a child does not have the right to have procedures explained to him or her in understandable language. Although in some situations we agree that a child may not have the right to refuse to participate in an evaluation, we feel that *in all situations,* irrespective of a child's age, the assessor should explain to the child all of the procedures that he or she will undergo as part of the testing. Clearly, the degree of depth and sophistication of this explanation should be made with recognition of the possible fears about the evaluation that a child or adolescent might experience and with recognition of his or her varying levels of motivation. Boxes 5.3, 5.4, and 5.5 provide examples of how testing procedures can be explained to children and adolescents of various ages in ways that enhance the establishment of rapport.

BOX 5.3

Explaining Procedures to a 5-Year-Old Boy

We have argued that all children should have testing procedures explained to them in terms that are understandable given their developmental level. This is a crucial aspect of developing rapport with a child. However, many beginning clinical assessors have difficulty describing testing in terms comprehensible to young children and fail to recognize some of the fears and motivations that children bring to the evaluation. To help in this regard, the following is an example of an explanation of procedures that is given to a 5-year-old boy referred to a private psychologist for testing.

> Hello, Johnny. My name is Dr. Test. I'm not the type of doctor you come to when you're sick, like with a stomachache or headache, but I'm the type of doctor who likes to get to know kids better, like how they feel about some things and how they act sometimes. So what I'm going to do today is find out a lot more about you. I'm going to ask you to draw some pictures for me and tell me about them. I also have some pictures and I want you to make up stories about them. And then, I have a bunch of questions about how you feel about certain things that I'm going to help you answer. We will have to work pretty hard together but I think it will be fun, too. We're going to take a lot of breaks and please let me know if you need to stop and go to the bathroom. Now, your mom and dad have already been telling me a lot about you and I'm also going to be talking to your teacher at school. After I do this, I'm going to take what you tell me, and what your folks and teacher tell me and try to get a good picture of what you're like, how you feel about things, all the things you're doing well in, and anything you

might need help in. And then I will talk to your parents and to you about what I find and let you know if there is anything that I can suggest that might help you.

This explanation is designed to be an example of the types of terms and phrasing that can be used in explaining psychological procedures to very young children. As you can see from the content of the explanation, we feel that in this age group, one of the most important sources of anxiety is the fear of the unknown. Therefore, we try to let the child know that the procedures will be pretty innocuous (e.g., answering questions, drawing). Obviously the actual content of the description will depend on the procedures that are planned. But we feel strongly that *all* procedures to be used should be explained to the child, albeit in a language that is understandable. Also, to illustrate the level of explanation, the discourse was presented in narrative form. In actual practice it is helpful to involve the child in the discussion by asking simple questions (e.g., Do you like to draw?) and encouraging him or her to ask you questions if there is anything he or she does not understand. This all helps the child to feel more respected and valued in the assessment process. Finally, we often find it helpful in this age group to present this information with the child's parent(s) present. When children see that their parents are comfortable with the procedures, they often develop a greater sense of comfort themselves.

BOX 5.4

Explaining Procedures to a 10-Year-Old Girl

Older, pre-adolescent children often have a better understanding of the basic nature of the testing situation than do younger children. However, the procedures should still be explained in very clear and simple terms to ensure that there are no misconceptions. In this age group we find that the explanation must be sensitive to the potential

(Cont.)

Box 5.4   *(Continued)*

threat to a child's self-concept that the testing may present. One of the major emotional tasks during the pre-adolescent period is the development of a sense of mastery and a sense of competence. Testing can be a threat to a child in these areas for several reasons. First, just the term "testing" conveys the possibility of failure. Second, the child may have implicitly or explicitly been told that the reason for the testing is to see "what's wrong with you." The explanation of testing in this age group should be sensitive to these issues. Here, we provide a sample explanation to a 10-year-old girl referred for a comprehensive evaluation.

Jessica, I want to explain exactly what we are going to be doing together today and give you a chance to ask me any questions you may have. Your parents were concerned about some of the problems you have been having at school and they wanted to know if there was anything more they could be doing to help you. In order for me to answer this question, I have to find out a lot more about you—what you like to do, how you feel about different things, what things you're good at, what things you might not be so good at. To do this, we are going to do a lot of different things together. First I am going to ask you to do some reading and math problems with me. Then I will ask you to fill out some questionnaires that will tell me how you feel about different things, how you get along with kids in your class, and how you see your family. Finally, I am going to show you some pictures and ask you to tell me some stories about them. Before we start each of these activities, I will tell you what we're going to do and how to do each thing and I will give you a chance to ask me any questions you have about the task. I have already talked to your mother about how things go at home and I am going to ask your teacher to fill out a questionnaire about how she sees you at school. After I get all the information, I should understand you a little better and I will then talk about what I found with you and your parents. Jessica, it is very important that you understand that I'm not looking for things that are wrong with you. My guess is that you are like most kids. You have things that you're good at and some things that you're not so good at, and there are things you like and other things you don't like. I am just trying to get a good picture of all these different parts of you.

Box 5.5

Explaining Procedures to an Adolescent

There are several crucial issues that one must keep in mind when explaining testing to an adolescent. First, adolescents spend a great deal of energy trying to convince people that they are no longer children. Therefore, one must be very careful not to come across as condescending to them. Second, because of the importance of peers in adolescence, adolescents are very concerned with fitting in. Coming in for psychological testing may be viewed as a threat to this by making them feel different from other adolescents. Therefore, the explanation should attempt to normalize the testing as much as possible. Third, privacy is a major issue for adolescents. In testing, adolescents may be asked many personal questions. They must be warned of these questions and informed as to how the information from the testing will be conveyed to other people. This is very threatening to most adolescents, and the explanation should be sensitive to this issue. Fourth, the majority of adolescents referred for testing do not see the need for such testing and don't want to be there. A major flaw we often see in presenting testing to adolescents is that the assessor tries to cajole the adolescent into being happy to be there and into appreciating the potential benefits of testing. Clearly, the potential benefits of testing should be discussed with the adolescent in an attempt to enhance motivation. However, this often has a minimal affect on motivation, and often one must simply acknowledge to the adolescent that you understand that he or she is not wild about being there but, if you work together, you will get through it quickly and painlessly. The following is a sample explanation of psychological testing provided to a 16-year-old male.

Jeff, I want to explain what we will be doing today and, please, feel free to ask me any questions about what I say. You probably know that your parents are concerned about your behavior. They have seen some changes in you recently and they want to know if they should be doing anything to help you. I understand that you are not wild about being here, but if we work together, maybe we can see if there is anything that I can recommend to help you or at least put your parents' minds at ease. But if we're going to get anything out of this we have to work together. I work with a lot of people your age who don't want to be here at first, but end up getting a lot out of the experience. I will
(Cont.)

Box 5.5 *(Continued)*

start out just asking you about some of the things that have been going on with you lately to get your view on things. I have already talked to your parents about their views of what's going on. Then I will have you fill out some questionnaires about your feelings, your behaviors, and your attitudes. Some of these questions are pretty personal, but they are important for me to get a better understanding of you. Finally, we are going to do an inkblot test that helps me understand how you view things. After all of this testing I will summarize the results in a report and go over it with you and your parents. At that time we can discuss anything that I think might help you.

Discussing testing with the child or adolescent is critical to respecting the integrity of the child as a person and it helps enlist the child as a collaborative participant in the process. It reduces the feeling of the child that the testing is being done to him or her rather than for or with him or her. Also, many children arrive for testing with substantial misconceptions about what the testing will entail (e.g., thinking that the psychologist is going to operate on their brain or that they are coming to be punished for being bad). Simply spending the time to clearly review why the child is being tested, what the child should expect during testing, and what will happen with the test results helps to eliminate misconceptions and reduce unnecessary anxiety.

Building Rapport with the Child

Establishing rapport with a child is not a simple process, for several reasons. First, as mentioned previously, the child is often not the one seeking an evaluation but is usually referred by some significant adult who feels that the child or adolescent needs the testing. Therefore, the motivation for the evaluation on the part of the child is often low. Another reason for low motivation is that the child often realizes, or has been explicitly told, that the evaluation is prompted by problems either at home or school. As a result,

the child is legitimately concerned about the outcome of the evaluation (i.e., getting into more trouble). Third, the testing situation is often unique in most children's experiences. Children have had few similar experiences, and therefore they often have little idea of what to expect in the testing situation. Fourth, the many developmental stages that characterize childhood and adolescence means that assessors must be familiar enough with development to be able to tailor their rapport-building strategies to the unique needs of children at various stages.

We have already mentioned that rapport building is a process that evolves throughout testing. It starts at the very first contact between the assessor and the child. When an assessor greets a child, the assessor should (1) use a warm, friendly, and interested tone of voice; (2) be sure to greet the child by name (don't simply greet the child's parents); and (3) introduce him- or herself using his or her title (e.g., Dr., Ms., Mrs.). This last recommendation is a subject of considerable debate by practicing psychologists (Barker, 1990). However, we feel that using a title is important in the time-limited, task-oriented assessment situation because it sets the stage that you are a professional (albeit a caring, friendly, and respectful one) who will be working with the child, and not a friend who will play with the child.

After informed consent, many authors recommend a period of time for discussing innocuous and pleasant topics, such as the children's hobbies, pets, friends, or other interests (Barker, 1990). For younger children, some authors even recommend a period of play to allow the children to become more accustomed to the examiner. In our experiences, such rapport-building strategies should be used cautiously and sparingly. For many children the assessor may be perceived as simply delaying the inevitable by using these strategies. This could have the paradoxical effect of increasing their anticipatory anxiety. In our experience, one of the best rapport-building strategies is to begin the assessment tasks quickly, so that the children begin to realize that the procedures will not be as bad as they imagined.

Periods of play before the evaluation are especially problematic if structured testing is to follow. Young children often have difficulty switching from unstructured to structured tasks (Perry, 1990). Therefore, it is usually best when testing preadolescent children to start with the more structured parts of the evaluation (e.g., rating scales, structured interviews) rather than starting with less structured tasks (e.g., projective tests). This is not only because of the greater difficulty in switching from unstructured to structured tasks, but also because the structured tasks have clearer demand characteristics. That is, it is usually quite clear to children what is expected of them on these tasks and this, in turn, helps the children become more comfortable in a situation that is different from anything they have experienced in the past. Box 5.6 provides a summary of some additional rapport-building strategies for use with children that were proposed by Barker (1990) in his book on interviewing children.

Box 5.6

Rapport-Building Strategies

Phillip Barker (1990), in his book on conducting clinical interviews with children and adolescents, discussed several helpful strategies for establishing rapport. These can be summarized as follows:

1. A critical basis for rapport building is an assessor's communication style. The assessor who is able to adopt a warm, friendly, respectful, and interested communication style is more likely to develop a good working alliance with a child.

2. The assessor's physical appearance also can enhance rapport. Overly formal dress can make a child feel ill at ease.

3. Assessors should attempt to match or pace the behavior of the person being tested. The assessor should attempt to conform his or her posture, movements, speed of speech, voice tone and volume, etc. to the style of the person being tested. This should be done sensitively and unobtrusively.

4. Assessors should tailor their vocabularies to the vocabularies of the person being tested. Few things impede the establishment of rapport as much as repeatedly us-

ing words and expressions that are unfamiliar to those with whom you are speaking.

5. Respect the views of those you are testing. This does not necessarily mean agreeing with or approving of the views expressed.

6. Occasionally the assessor should adopt a one-down position. To reduce the intimidation that children sometimes feel with experts, the assessor can sometimes ask a child, from a position of ignorance, about something with which a child has expertise, such as video games, television shows, or soccer.

7. Taking time during the testing to talk of experiences and interests that the assessor and child have in common can also increase the trust between assessor and child.

Barker (1990) also emphasizes that the development of rapport is continuous throughout the testing process. "Rapport can always be developed further; the reverse is also possible. Although it is certainly true that once it is well established, rapport can withstand a lot of stress, it nevertheless can be damaged or even destroyed at any time if continuing attention is not paid to maintaining it" (p. 35).

SOURCE: P. Barker (1990). *Clinical Interviews with Children and Adolescents.* New York: Norton.

Building Rapport with the Parent

There are also some unique considerations in building a working relationship with a child's parents. Of course, the importance of rapport with parents will depend on the degree of their involvement in the testing. However, in most situations their involvement will be substantial. Although many evaluations are conducted at the request of a parent, there are also many situations in which a child is referred by others (e.g., school, court), and in these situations, building rapport with the child's parent is critical. In these circumstances the assessor must allow the parents to express their views on the need for the evaluation very early on in the testing process. The assessor need not necessarily agree with these views, but the assessor should convey to the parent a sincere interest in understanding their views in order to build a working relationship with a reluctant parent.

Even for parents who have instigated the referral for testing the assessor should be aware of the potential threat to a parent's self-esteem that many testing situations present. For many parents, acknowledging that their child might have any type of disability is quite traumatic and can evoke a sense of failure. Also, parents often are struggling with feelings of blame for their child's problems and may be reluctant to have testing confirm their potential role in their child's difficulties. An assessor should be sensitive to these dynamics and allow the parents to express their concerns at some point during the testing. Additionally, the parents should be supported in their role of getting help for their child. For example, an assessor might tell the parents how lucky their child is to have parents who care enough to obtain help for him or her, and not just let things get worse. This helps to reframe the testing situation to one that could increase the parents' self-esteem, rather than one that is a threat to their self-concept.

Several reasons were given for starting with structured tasks in testing children in an effort to enhance rapport. In our experience, the opposite is true in rapport building with parents. Even prior to obtaining specific background information from a parent, it is important to let the parent discuss his or her concerns about the child in an unstructured format. The unstructured clinical interview is discussed in more detail in a later chapter. However, placing such an interview at the start of the evaluation conveys to the parent (1) a genuine concern with his or her perceptions of the child's functioning and (2) that the evaluation will be personalized to the individual child. If parents are immediately asked to fill out rating scales or administered a structured interview as part of a standard evaluation, they often develop the impression that the assessor is more interested in administering tests than in actually understanding the child's psychological adjustment. As one would expect, such an impression is very damaging to the development of rapport.

Building Rapport with Teachers

It is becoming increasingly clear that evaluations of children must involve information from teachers (Loeber, Green, & Lahey, 1990). The degree of teachers' involvement varies considerably depending on the focus of the evaluation. However, many assessors who are not used to working in school settings find themselves ill-equipped to collaborate with teachers to conduct psychological evaluations (Conoley & Conoley, 1991).

In the introduction to the concept of rapport we defined the basic ingredient to rapport building as exhibiting an attitude of respect toward the client or informant. Although many psychologists work hard at respecting and developing rapport with parents and children, often this respect is lost when dealing with other professionals, such as teachers. A key way to demonstrate this attitude is by respecting the importance of teachers' time. Matching phone calls to planning times, eliminating all but the most essential work for the teacher, and always personally thanking the teacher for his or her efforts in the evaluation are very simple, yet important, rapport-building strategies.

If a teacher is to be sent a portion of the assessment to complete (e.g., rating scales, sociometric exercise), it is important for the assessor to call the teacher and personally request the teacher's participation in the evaluation, acknowledging and thanking the teacher for his or her efforts, rather than simply sending the material to the teacher via the child, parent, or mail. Such a call is a professional courtesy that greatly enhances the collaborative effort. It sets the tone for the teacher being involved in the evaluation as a valued professional who has much to offer to the assessment of the child.

CONCLUSIONS

In this chapter some nonspecifics of the clinical assessment of children were discussed. That is, a successful evaluation is not simply a matter of appropriately administering and interpreting psychological tests. It is also dependent on an assessor's ability to provide an appropriate context in which the testing takes place.

The first major issue discussed was the importance of good planning. A good evaluation is focused and goal-oriented. The purpose of the evaluation and the intended uses of the assessment results will have a major impact on how the assessment is structured. Enough information should be available prior to actual testing so that the assessor has some initial hypotheses that will be tested in the evaluation.

The second part of the chapter focused on rapport-building strategies with all participants in the evaluation. Developing a collaborative, respectful, and trusting working relationship is crucial to a successful evaluation. Being able to develop rapport is a skill that often takes years of practical experience to develop fully. However, in this chapter we have tried to highlight some of the important issues in rapport building, and we have tried to make some practical recommendations based on these issues.

CHAPTER SUMMARY

1. The first step in planning an evaluation is to clarify the reason for referral both in terms of the purpose of testing and the types of behavior that led to the referral.

2. Two important decisions that a clinical assessor should make prior to starting any evaluation is whether or not a formal evaluation is warranted and whether he or she is the most appropriate person to conduct the evaluation.

3. In addition to competently administering tests, clinical assessors must create the appropriate environment within which the evaluation can take place.

4. Building rapport with a child refers to efforts at developing a collaborative and supportive relationship with the child for the purpose of conducting the evaluation.

5. Building rapport with other important people who will be involved in the evaluation (e.g., parents, teachers) is also critical to the assessment process.

6. A thorough and sensitive informed consent procedure can play a major role in showing respect to the child client and his or her parents and thereby can greatly aid in the establishment of rapport.

7. An explanation of the testing procedures with a child must be sensitive to various motivational and developmental issues.

CHAPTER 6

Self-Report Inventories

CHAPTER QUESTIONS

- How does the MMPI-A differ from its adult counterpart?
- What are some of the key differences between omnibus measures and single domain measures?
- Which of the self-report measures possess good evidence of content validity?
- What are validity scales and how can they be used to interpret self-report measures?

OMNIBUS PERSONALITY INVENTORIES

The use of self-report inventories with children is a relatively new phenomenon. Heretofore it was commonly believed that children did not yet possess the reading comprehension necessary to accurately report on their own feelings, perceptions, and behaviors. Similarly, the degree to which children could accurately report on their own behavior without resorting to response sets has also been in question.

For these reasons, parent and teacher reports have routinely been preferred over the use of self-report inventories in child personality assessment. One of the first popular child assessment instruments, for example, the Personality Inventory for Children (PIC; (Wirt et al., 1984), resembled a "junior" MMPI. It included a large item set similar to the MMPI, and the name conveys similarities to omnibus personality inventories. Yet the PIC was and is a *parent* rating scale.

In this chapter the use of child self-report inventories is discussed. The reader will note that many of the omnibus scales described here are new, and those familiar with the adult self-report literature will discover that it is eminently feasible and useful to use self-report inventories with older elementary grade children and adolescents.

Unfortunately, the complexity of an omnibus self-report inventory cannot be conveyed in one chapter. Most of the inventories discussed herein have entire volumes devoted to their interpretation. The following discussion serves primarily as a reader's guide for studying the larger literature that is available for an instrument. The eventual user of any of the omnibus inventories discussed will have to spend considerable time with the test manuals and additional readings and seek supervised interpretation practice. This necessary additional study is also required for the single-construct measures that are discussed, some of which have extensive literatures associated with them. We begin with an overview of some of the major omnibus scales that are currently available.

Behavior Assessment System for Children— Self-Report of Personality

The Behavior Assessment System for Children—Self-Report of Personality (BASC-SRP; Reynolds & Kamphaus, 1992) is a relatively new entrant onto the omnibus self-report scene. The SRP is one of many components of the BASC that attempts to gauge the child's perceptions and feelings about school, parents, peers, and his or her own behavior problems. The SRP has two forms for ages 8 through 11 (SRP-C) and 12 through 18 (SRP-A). The estimated minimum reading level of the SRP is the third grade.

Scale Content

The SRP includes 14 scales, 10 clinical and 4 adaptive. The scales were developed using a combination of rationale/theoretical and empirical approaches to test development. Specifically, scales were first defined, items were developed based on these definitions, and covariance structure analysis was used to enhance the homogeneity of scale content (Reynolds & Kamphaus, 1992). The scales included in the SRP range from the typical, such as anxiety and depression; to the practical, such as attitude toward parents; to the novel, such as social stress and sensation seeking; and to the school-focused, such as attitude toward school and teachers (see scale definitions in Table 6.1).

TABLE 6.1   SRP Scale Definitions

Scale	Definition
Anxiety	Feelings of nervousness, worry, and fear; the tendency to be overwhelmed by prolems
Attitude to School	Feelings of alienation, hostility, and dissatisfaction regarding school
Attitude to Teachers	Feelings of resentment and dislike of teachers; beliefs that teachers are unfair, uncaring, or overly demanding
Atypicality	The tendency toward gross mood swings, bizarre thoughts, subjective experiences, or obsessive-compulsive thoughts and behaviors often considered
Depression	Feelings of unhappiness, sadness, and dejection; a belief that nothing goes right
Interpersonal Relations	The perception of having good social relationships and friendships with peers
Locus of Control	The belief that rewards and punishments are controlled by external events or other people
Relations with Parents	A positive regard for parents and a feeling of being esteemed by them
Self-Esteem	Feelings of self-esteem, self-respect, and self-acceptance

Four composites were constructed for the SRP using factor analysis: Clinical Maladjustment, School Maladjustment, Personal Adjustment, and Emotional Symptoms Index (ESI). The Clinical Maladjustment composite includes traditional scales for self-report measures such as atypicality, locus of control, somatization, social stress, and anxiety. The School Maladjustment composite is relatively unique in the annals of self-report assessment because of its emphasis on schooling as an important domain of child functioning, just as occupational adjustment would be for adults. The School Maladjustment composite seems intuitive to interpret. It seems reasonable to say that if a child dislikes teachers and school (attitude toward school and teacher scales) and prefers less sedate activities such as sky diving (sensation-seeking scale), school difficulties could present themselves. The Personal Adjustment composite assesses self-perceived personal strengths such as self-esteem and relationships with parents. The ESI represents the scores for the six scales with the highest loadings on an unrotated first factor. Borrowing the logic of intelligence assessment, this factor could be called general psychopathology (Kamphaus, 1993).

Administration and Scoring

The SRP is available in three administration formats: a carbonless hand-scored form, a computer-scorable form, and computer-based on-line administration (with the BASC+Plus software program). SRP administration has been simplified for children by using item stems that are less than one sentence in most cases and a true/false response format. The SRP has a reasonable administration time given that there are 186 items on the SRP-A and 147 items on the SRP-C. Although the SRP has a reasonable reading level and is fairly brief, clinicians will find many children and adolescents who will not be able to use it. Children with handicapping conditions such as mental retardation or reading disabilities will undoubtably have difficulty with the items. An audiotape is available, but the use of this still requires adequate reading comprehension on the part of the child.

Validity Scales

The SRP includes three validity scales in the hand-scored version and five in the computer-scored version. These scales provide a variety of checks on the validity of a child's results. It is still quite possible, however, to have the SRP (or any other self-report measure for that matter) invalidated by a response set or lack of cooperation. A commonsense validity check should be conducted if a child yields a "hypernormal" profile; that is, nearly all T-scores on the clinical scales are below 50 (see Box 6.1).

BOX 6.1

An Example of Fake Good Response Set

Self-report inventories, despite the efforts of test developers, always remain susceptible to response sets. The following case is an authentic example. In this case the BASC-SRP was utilized.

Maury was admitted to the inpatient psychiatric unit of a general hospital with the diagnoses of impulse control disorder and major depression. She is repeating the seventh grade this school year because she failed to attend school regularly last year. When skipping school, she spent time roaming the local shopping mall or engaging in other relatively unstructured activities. She was suspended from school for lying, cheating, and arguing with teachers. She failed all of her classes in both semesters of the past school year.

Maury's responses to the diagnostic interview suggested that she was trying to portray herself in a favorable light and not convey the severity of her problems. When asked about hobbies, for example, she said that she liked to read. When questioned further, however, she could not name a book that she had read.

Maury's father reported that he has been arrested many times. Similarly, Maury and her sisters have been arrested for shoplifting. Maury's father expressed concern about her education. He said that Maury was recently placed in an alternative education program designed for youth offenders.

Maury's SRP results show evidence of a social desirability or fake good response set. All of her clinical scale scores were lower than the normative T-score mean of 50

(Cont.)

BOX 6.1 *(Continued)*

and all of her adaptive scale scores were above the normative mean of 50. In other words, the SRP results suggest that Maury is optimally adjusted, which is in stark contrast to the background information obtained.

Maury's response set, however, was identified by the Lie scale of the SRP, where she obtained a score of 9, which is on the border of the caution and extreme caution ranges. Her full complement of SRP scores are:

SCALE	T-SCORE
Clinical Scales	
Attitude to School	41
Attitude to Teachers	39
Sensation Seeking	41
Atypicality	38
Locus of Control	38
Somatization	39
Social Stress	38
Anxiety	34
Depression	43
Sense of Inadequacy	41
Adaptive Scales	
Relations with Parents	53
Interpersonal Relations	57
Self-Esteem	54
Self-Reliance	52

lected at 36 sites in the United States and 3 sites in Canada.

Reliability

The reliability of the SRP scales is good as indicated by a variety of methods. Median internal consistency coefficients are generally in the .80s (see Table 6.2) for the general and clinical samples. Test-retest coefficients taken at a 1-month interval are generally in the .70s. The SRP manual also includes a 7-month stability study. The results of this study varied widely, with a coefficient of .05 for the Interpersonal Relations scale and a .74 for the Atypicality scale.

Validity

The BASC manual provides an extensive report of SRP exploratory and confirmatory factor analyses. Three factors were yielded in the analyses, as shown

TABLE 6.2   BASC SRP Median Internal Consistency Coefficients

Scale	Coefficient
Anxiety	0.87
Attitude to School	0.82
Attitude to Teachers	0.79
Atypicality	0.81
Depression	0.88
Interpersonal Relations	0.82
Locus of Control	0.85
Relations with Parents	0.77
Self-Esteem	0.86
Self-Reliance	0.61
Sensation Seeking	0.71
Sense of Inadequacy	0.78
Social Stress	0.84
Somatization	0.64
Median	0.81
Composites	
School Maladjustment	0.88
Clinical Maladjustment	0.95
Personal Adjustment	0.90
Emotional Symptoms Index	0.95

Norming

The SRP was normed with the remainder of the BASC components on a national sample of 5,188 children and 4,423 adolescents. Weighting methods were used to ensure a match between the sample and 1990 U.S. Census figures using gender, geographic region, community size, age, and race/ethnicity as stratification variables. The SRP includes norms for the general national sample and separate gender norms. T-scores are available for four age groups: 6–7, 8–11, 12–14, and 15–18. These age groups were selected based on evidence for significant differences between average raw scores for some scales at these age breaks (Reynolds & Kamphaus, 1992).

The SRP offers clinical norms for a sample of 270 children and 140 adolescents. Clinical cases were colin Table 6.3. The school maladjustment factor is relatively unique. This survey of attitudes toward school could be of value for consulting with school personnel. The clinical maladjustment factor is more traditional in that measures of psychoticism (Atypicality) and stress (Anxiety) are featured. The personal adjustment factor is also unique in that many personality scales typically do not include measures of adaptation or potential strengths. An interesting and needed study would involve determining if elevations on this scale portend a more favorable prognosis. The Depression and Sense of Inadequacy scales were apparently too complex to place on a composite. Depression was related to the clinical maladjustment factor and it showed an inverse relationship to the personal adjustment factor. Sense of Inadequacy also loaded on the clinical maladjustment factor while possessing a secondary loading on the school maladjustment factor.

The criterion-related validity of the SRP was evaluated by correlating it with the MMPI, Achenbach Youth Self-Report, Behavior Rating Profile, and Children's Personality Questionnaire. These investigations will be difficult to evaluate throughout this chapter since self-report inventories have such differing item content and scale names.

The Depression scale of the BASC is one scale that has similarly named scales on other measures. The SRP Depression scale correlated .43 with the Depression scale of the MMPI and .59 with the Depressed scale of the Youth Self-Report for females and .43 for males. Similarly, the Anxiety scale of the SRP correlated .76 with the Psychasthenia scale of the MMPI. These results suggest the SRP Depression and Anxiety scales are at least within range in terms of their relationship to other well-known measures of similar constructs.

Further supportive evidence for the Depression scale of the SRP is provided in the profiles for clinical samples. In the case of the sample of 33 depressed children and adolescents, the Depression scale produced the highest mean T-score of the clinical scales (Reynolds & Kamphaus, 1992).

Since the SRP is relatively new on the assessment scene, one can expect many more validity studies to be forthcoming. A self-report inventory with this large

TABLE 6.3   BASC SRP Factors and Scale Members

School Maladjustment
  Attitude to School
  Attitude to Teachers
  Sensation Seeking (adolescent only)

Clinical Maladjustment
  Atypicality
  Locus of Control
  Somatization
  Social Stress
  Anxiety

Personal Adjustment
  Relations with Parents
  Interpersonal Relations
  Self-Esteem
  Self-Reliance

Other Scales
  Depression
  Sense of Inadequacy

number of scales will require many studies to determine the validity of the many scales with a range of clinical populations.

Interpretation

Although the composites of the SRP have some factor-analytic evidence to support their validity, they suffer from a lack of other validity evidence. The composite's relationship to external criteria such as prognosis, course, recidivism, and so on, for example, is unknown. The composites are also difficult to interpret since they were not formed theoretically but rather empirically. Consequently, until clinical experience and research studies are available, initial efforts at SRP interpretation should focus on the scale level since these item pools have some rationale, theoretical, and research basis.

Some guidelines for scale interpretation are provided in the following section. Given their speculative nature, however, these guidelines should be considered tentative in every case and should be supported by clinical data (e.g., history) external to the SRP.

Item-level factor-analytic results provide one empirical clue to the meaning of SRP scales. Some of the items with the most substantial factor loadings on each scale are identified in Table 6.4. These symptoms can be linked to background information in order to interpret SRP results with greater confidence. This interpretation method can be bidirectional. If, for example, background information suggests considerable family dysfunction, including parent–child strife, the Locus of Control scale could be predicted to be elevated (see Table 6.4) since the items that load highest on this scale have to do with feeling controlled by parents. Similarly, a low Self-Esteem score would lead a clinician to investigate the child's self-evaluation of attractiveness to others, if concerns about physical attractiveness have not already been elicited (see Table 6.4).

Other psychometric properties can influence in-

TABLE 6.4   SRP Key Symptoms as Indicated by Items with the Highest Factor Loadings per Scale

Scale	Key Symptoms
Anxiety	Nervousness, worry, guilt, dread, fear, sensitivity to criticism
Attitude to School	Expressions of school hatred, expressions of boredom at school, unwillingness to discuss school issues
Attitude to Teachers	Says that teachers are unfair, says that teachers are unfair or unconcerned, complains about teacher demands
Atypicality	Has urges to hurt self, hears name when alone, cannot control thoughts, hears voices
Depression	Complains that nothing goes right, no one listens to respondent, nothing about respondent is right, no one understands respondent, nothing goes respondent's way, and he or she always has bad luck
Interpersonal Relations	Is liked by others, is not liked by classmates (scored negatively), is ridiculed by others (scored negatively)
Locus of Control	Complains of being blamed for things that he or she can't help or didn't do, parents expect too much from respondent, and parents are always telling respondent what to do
Relations with Parents	Says that parents listen to what respondent says, parents trust respondent, and parents tell respondent that they are proud of him or her
Self-Esteem	Says that he or she is nice looking, respondent likes the way he or she looks, wishes to be different (scored negatively), and wishes to be someone else (scored negatively)
Self-Reliance	Says that he or she is dependable and is good at making decisions
Sensation Seeking	Likes to ride in a car going fast, has been sent to the principal's office at least five times, likes to take chances, and likes to play rough sports
Sense of Inadequacy	Complains of being disappointed by his or her grades, of wanting to do better but being unable to, of failing, and of not being able to think when taking tests
Social Stress	Complains of feeling out of place around other people, of people acting as if they don't hear him or her, of being lonely, of feeling left out of activities, and of friends having more fun than he or she does
Somatization	Complains of stomach upsets, nausea, and headaches

terpretation. The reliability estimates shown in Table 6.2 can help a clinician gauge the level of confidence in an obtained score. If, as an example, an adolescent's scores are elevated primarily on scales that are less reliable, the results may be of less import. High scores on the reliable scales may be of greater concern.

Among the scales that inspire confidence because of their reliability are Anxiety, Depression, Locus of Control, and Social Stress. Scales with lower reliabilities include Self-Reliance and Somatization. The application of a psychometrically influenced approach to interpretation of the SRP is presented in the following case study.

Sample Case

This case is the result of a referral from a child protective agency to a psychologist in private practice. The evaluation was sought as input for the residential placement of the client.

Mary Ann is a 16-year-old high school sophomore who was living in temporary foster care at the time of the evaluation. This is her second foster care placement since being taken from the home 5 months earlier. She had problems following rules in the first foster home. Her father has not been cooperative with court proceedings and did not attend the evaluation session.

Mary Ann arrived for the evaluation with evidence of depressed affect. She cried several times during the evaluation. She complained about living with her father and his girlfriend and her past tendency toward rebelliousness, her lack of contact with her birth mother, her history of recent stomach pain and the diagnosis of a sexually transmitted disease, her long history of school failure, low self-esteem, and poor relationships with some peers.

Mary Ann's SRP results are consistent with background information:

Attitude to School	49
Attitude to Teachers	43
Sensation Seeking	55
Atypicality	72

Mary Ann said that she sometimes heard voices or other noises. This finding could not be corroborated; hence, further evaluation is warranted to rule out beginning psychotic thought processes.

Locus of Control	76

She feels dominated by the will of her father, consistent with her complaints during the interview.

Somatization	86

She has bona fide medical concerns about her STD and dental problems. She expressed great worry about the STD.

Social Stress	73

Mary Ann often feels uncomfortable around others because of embarrassment about her living arrangements and fear of being teased about her weight, school difficulties, or other problems.

Anxiety	68

She often frets about her difficulties, especially since being taken from her father's household.

Depression	80

This finding is consistent with observations during the evaluation and background information suggesting recent weight gain, energy, and anhedonia.

Sense of Inadequacy	74

Mary Ann expressed little confidence about her ability to do well in school. Her Differential Ability Scale GCA obtained in this evaluation of 61 is within the mental retardation range. This result is consistent with considerable school failure and frequent moves by the family resulting in her avoiding being tested for special class placement in the past. She said, "The more I study, the less goes in."

Relations with Parents	32

The adaptive scale score is reasonably low given a long history of parent–child enmity.

Interpersonal Relations	50
Self-Esteem	30

Mary Ann views herself as considerably less attractive than others, primarily due to obesity.

Self-Reliance	52

Mary Ann feels unable to accomplish tasks and to take responsibility for her behavior.

Strengths and Weaknesses

The SRP is an important addition to the assessment armamentarium of psychologists (Sandoval & Echandia, 1994). Previously few omnibus self-report inventories other than the MMPI have been available to clinicians. The SRP has numerous strengths that make it a serious competitor for use with children and adolescents. Notable strengths include:

1. A broader age range than is typically available for omnibus inventories designed for children

2. A realistic number of items which makes administration in one session the norm

3. Good reliability estimates

4. Ease of administration and scoring (Kline, 1995)

5. Availability of a range of derived scores and norms for general, clinical, and gender-referenced samples

6. Good manual (Kline, 1995).

7. Scales that are relevant to the milieus of children, such as attitude toward teachers and schooling and parent–child relations

8. A clear link between teacher and parent rating scales (BASC-PRS and TRS)

9. Good national norming

Although all of the data are not in yet, there is some early evidence of SRP weaknesses, such as:

1. Lack of range for norms (Several scales are incapable of yielding scores well within the clinical range.)

2. Lack of external validity evidence, particularly for the composites (Kline, 1995)

3. A lack of clinical history, which requires training for large numbers of clinicians

4. Lack of case studies in the manual (Kline, 1995)

5. Lack of validity evidence for the validity scales

6. An excessive number of Self-Esteem scale items that deal with self-perceptions of personal appearance (Hoza, 1994)

Minnesota Multiphasic Personality Inventory— Adolescent

The Minnesota Multiphasic Personality Inventory— Adolescent (MMPI-A; Butcher et al., 1992) has strong roots in the original work of Hathaway and McKinley (1940) and the authors of the revision tried to maintain continuity with the original work (Butcher et al., 1992). This objective was achieved, as all of the clinical and validity scales were retained.

Scale Content

Knowledge of the history, rationale, psychometric properties, and item content of the MMPI-A scales is important for proper interpretation. Consequently, each of the featured clinical scales is discussed in turn.

SCALE 1, Hs: HYPOCHONDRIASIS. Items for this scale were originally developed to identify respondents with a history of symptomatology characteristic of hypochondriasis (Butcher et al., 1992). Items of this scale assess topics such as nausea, vomiting, upset stomach, sleep problems, chest pain, numbness, muscle twitching, head pressure, bodily tenderness, dizziness, weakness, and lack of general feeling of wellness.

SCALE 2, D: DEPRESSION. Hathaway and McKinley (1942) described this measure as an index of general dissatisfaction with one's life, including feelings of discouragement, hopelessness, and low morale. Item content includes appetite changes, health worries, anhedonia, work problems, tension, constipation, increased swearing, concentration problems, anergy, sleep problems, withdrawal, teasing animals, low self-confidence, low self-esteem, worry at bedtime, crying easily, decreased reading comprehension, weight change, and impaired memory, among other things. The item content of this scale is diverse, reaching far beyond diagnostic criteria for depression such as those included in the DSM. This item content diversity is also a likely contributor to mediocre internal consistency reliability coefficients, to be discussed subsequently.

SCALE 3, HY: HYSTERIA. According to Butcher et al. (1992), this scale consists of 60 items that were originally selected to identify individuals who respond to stress with hysterical reactions that include sensory or motor disorders without an organic basis. Some of the item content includes poor appetite, fatigue, cold extremities, decreased work productivity, nausea and vomiting, urges to curse, poor concentration, disturbed sleep, hot flashes, health concerns, chest pain, unhappiness, difficulty persuading others, muscle twitching, irritability, worry about contracting diseases, dysfunctional relationships with family members, tolerance for others' trickery, concern about others' opinion, and dislike of school. Like D, this item pool is very diverse, resulting in mediocre internal consistency coefficients. It is also clear that the first three scales of the MMPI-A share considerable item overlap, particularly scales 2 and 3.

SCALE 4, PD: PSYCHOPATHIC DEVIATE. This scale was originally constructed based on the responses of individuals with histories of lying, stealing, sexual promiscuity, and alcohol abuse (Butcher et al., 1992). Furthermore, high scores on this scale are associated with family, legal, and school difficulties (Butcher et al., 1992). Item content includes loss of interest in daily activities, desire to leave home, feeling misunderstood, feeling used, poor concentration, having unusual experiences, history of trouble because of sexual behavior, history of stealing, unhappiness, disapproval by family members, winning arguments, inability to tolerate ridicule, regretting actions, admissions of misbehavior, history of school disciplinary action, feeling like someone is out to get him/her, feeling responsible for own behavior, and weight changes. For the most part this is the first scale with item content that is distinctive from the first three.

SCALE 5, MF: MASCULINITY-FEMININITY. This scale was originally developed on a sample of adult males, described by Hathaway (1956) as male sexual inverts (Butcher et al., 1992). Presumably males with high scores are more feminine, and women with clinically significant scores were thought to have more masculine interests. Item content includes topics such as lack of interest in mechanics magazines, reluctance to incriminate oneself, a desire to be of the opposite gender, interest in love stories and poetry, sensitive feelings, lack of interest in forest ranger work, being a soldier or hunting, expressing the need to argue to make a point, attending few parties, dislike for wagering, interest in gardening and cooking, having racing thoughts, a belief in eternal life, maintaining a diary, fear of snakes, worry, and talks about sex (scored if true for male and false for female). This scale is, to say the least, unique, and, by most current understanding, out of step with the times.

SCALE 6, PA: PARANOIA. This scale is designed to assess paranoid symptomatology. The scale includes item content such as feelings of persecution, having evil thoughts, feeling misunderstood, emotional lability, feeling possessed by evil spirits, unhappiness, sensation seeking, distrust of others, crying easily, feeling as though one is being followed or poisoned by someone, ideas of reference, feeling controlled by someone, and history of legal trouble.

SCALE 7, PT: PSYCHASTHENIA. The item content of Scale 7 includes health worries, loss of interest in activities, having shameful thoughts, emotional lability, poor concentration, fatigue, unhappiness, low self-esteem, feelings of regret, guilt, impaired reading comprehension, impaired memory, weakness, worry, restlessness, excitability, fear of speaking in front of school class, loneliness, being easily embarrassed, impatience, avoiding greeting others, counting unimportant things, ruminating sometimes about unimportant things, and overreaction to failure. This scale has many items in common with scales 2, 3, and 8.

SCALE 8, SC: SCHIZOPHRENIA. This scale was designed to identify patients with diagnoses of various forms of schizophrenia (Butcher et al., 1992). Scale 8 items sample content such as lack of interest in daily activities, having unwanted thoughts, desire to leave home, poor concentration, bizarre experiences, stealing, anergy, feelings of persecution, avoidance of others, daydreaming, muscle twitching, urges to do something socially unacceptable, changes in speech pattern, decreased reading comprehension, impaired memory, black-out spells, fear of losing control, impaired balance, restlessness, difficulty initiating activity, excitability, numbness, decreased taste sensitivity, sexual preoccupations, impaired relationships with parents and other family members, loneliness, worry about money, lack of intimacy, impatience, and feelings of unreality. This scale shares many items with scales 2, 3, and 7. It is a long scale with 77 items making item overlap with other scales a central characteristic. Its high correlations with other scales is discussed in a later section. Some of the items that differentiate this scale from others have to do with impaired social relationships and poor reality contact.

SCALE 9, MA: HYPOMANIA. This scale includes items assessing tension, desire to leave home, crying spells, urges to do something socially unacceptable, indecision, sensation seeking, racing thoughts, feelings of persecution, lack of fear of heights, black-out spells, occasional ability to make decisions very easily, self-righteousness, restlessness, satisfaction with personal appearance, sweatiness, excitability, excessive thirst, and admiration for cleverness even if it is criminal.

SCALE 10, SI: SOCIAL INTROVERSION. Si score elevations are produced by content such as failure to face crises or problems, poor concentration, poor sociability, unhappiness, fear of ridicule, lack of interest in parties, easily losing arguments, low sensation seeking, change in speech pattern, distrust of others, indecision, shyness, difficulty with small talk, brooding, concerns about personal appearance, embarrassment in front of groups, failure to initiate conversation, difficulty making friends, loneliness, envy of others' successes, and low self-esteem.

CONTENT SCALES. Content scales are a relatively unique feature of the MMPI that were developed differently from the original clinical scales. While empirical approaches, including empirical criterion keying, were used for the development of the original scales, content scales depend more on a rational/theoretical approach to test development (Williams et al., 1992) (see Chapter 2).

The first step in the content scale development process was to select 22 content categories based on

a review of the adult experimental version (the predecessor to the MMPI-2. In the second step a total of three raters (the qualifications of whom were not stated) assigned items from the adult experimental form to the 22 categories (Williams, et al., 1992). A group consensus was reached on the assignments and some items were discarded. A total of 21 content scales remained after this step. In the next step, correlations and reliability indices were used to enhance the reliability and homogeneity of each scale. The fourth stage involved another "rational review" of the items in response to the aforementioned statistical data. Some scales were renamed and some dropped at this stage. In the fifth and final step, items that correlated higher with a scale of which they were not a member were removed. The result was 15 "MMPI-2" content scales (Williams et al., 1992).

These same procedures were applied to the development of the MMPI-A content scale, where the MMPI-2 content scales served as the foundation. Items were added and removed, and some new scales were developed (Williams et al., 1992). This step resulted in the retention of the majority of the MMPI-2 content scales for adolescents and the addition of three scales—Alienation, Low Aspirations, and School Problems. Descriptions for the scales can be found in Williams et al. (1992).

The content scales offered with the MMPI-A by the publisher include:

A-anx, Anxiety

A-obs, Obsessiveness

A-dep, Depression

A-hea, Health Concerns

A-aln, Alienation

A-biz, Bizarre Mentation

A-ang, Anger

A-cyn, Cynicism

A-con, Conduct Problems

A-lse, Low Self-Esteem

A-las, Low Aspirations

A-sod, Social Discomfort

A-fam, Family Problems

A-sch, School Problems

A-trt, Negative Treatment Indicators (no external validity data collected to date.)

A, Anxiety

R, Repression

MAC-R, MacAndrew Alcoholism Scale—Revised (cut score of 28 with internal consistency indices ranging from .44 to .55 and test-retest coefficients of .47.)

ACK, Alcohol/Drug Problem Acknowledgment

PRO, Alcohol/Drug Problem Proneness

IMM, Immaturity

Administration and Scoring

The MMPI-A is unusually long compared to other self-report inventories designed for children and adolescents which calls for special administration guidelines. Some adolescents may have to take the test in more than one session (Butcher et al., 1992). Furthermore, since many adolescents require supervision during the administration of these scales, considerably more examiner time may be required.

Checks on the adolescent's reading comprehension level are also required. Readability analyses of individual items show adequate readability in most cases as reported in the manual. Unfortunately, however, many candidates for MMPI-A administration will lack even rudimentary English language reading comprehension skills. When in doubt, an examiner may ask the child to read some items aloud to get some sense for the child's ability to comprehend the item content. The validity checks provide another useful alert to possible readability problems.

Validity Scales

The MMPI series's long tradition of the use of validity indexes is reflected in the adolescent version. Brief descriptions of the scales follow (Butcher et al., 1992):

CANNOT SAY (?). This scale is comprised of the total number of items that the respondent either failed to answer or endorsed as both true and false.

LIE (L). This scale is intended to detect naive attempts by adolescents to put themselves in a favorable light.

F, F1, AND F2 (INFREQUENCY). The F scale is the antithesis of the L scale in that it assesses the tendency of individuals to place themselves in an unfavorable light, or fake bad. Items were selected for this scale if they were endorsed in their deviant direction by less than 20% of the normative sample.

K (DEFENSIVENESS). This scale was designed originally to identify adults in psychiatric settings who displayed significant degrees of psychopathology but produced profiles that were within normal limits. Butcher et al. (1992), however, suggest that an MMPI-A profile should not be invalidated solely on the basis of an elevated K score.

VRIN (VARIABLE RESPONSE INCONSISTENCY). The VRIN scale consists of pairs of items that have either similar or opposing item content. The score yielded by the VRIN scale reflects the number of item pairs answered inconsistently. A high score may reveal a careless response style on the part of the client.

TRIN (TRUE RESPONSE INCONSISTENCY). This scale is analogous to the VRIN scale in that it is made up of pairs of items. It differs in that the TRIN scale consists solely of items with opposite content. An elevated score may reveal an acquiescence response set, or the tendency for the test subject to indiscriminately answer True to the items. Conversely, a low TRIN score may reveal nonacquiescence.

Norming

The MMPI-A was normed in eight states in the continental United States. One state, however (Washington), contributed only 14 cases to the norming.

The distribution of sample by variables such as gender, age, grade, and parental education and occupation are given in the manual. These variables were not, however, used as stratification variables in order to match U.S. Census or other criteria as is common for clinical test instruments. The Hispanic population, for example, is clearly undersampled, constituting only 2.2% of the female sample and 2.0% of the male sample, which is smaller than the sample of Native American children. Similarly, the SES distribution may be skewed toward higher levels of SES than the national population, as the authors noted that, "This rough classification of occupations suggests that mothers and fathers are described by many children as having professional and managerial occupations, while relatively low percentages are recorded for homemaker and unskilled" (Butcher et al., 1992, p. 13). The age distribution of the sample is also highly variable. At age 18, only 42 cases male cases and 45 female cases were collected.

The clinical sample is somewhat smaller, consisting of 420 boys and 293 girls. All of the clinical cases were taken from the Minneapolis area (Butcher et al., 1992). Further detail regarding the clinical sample can be found in Williams et al. (1992). The majority of cases, 71% of the boys and 56% of the girls, were undergoing treatment on acohol/drug units (Williams et al., 1992) suggesting that the clinical sample could be renamed to more accurately reflect the preponderance of substance abuse cases.

Reliability

There are distinct scale differences in the internal consistency estimates for the MMPI-A (see Table 6.5). Some of the clinical scales have typical and respectable estimates: Hs, Pt, and Si are among these. In direct contrast, some of the scales have internal consistency estimates that raise questions about the inclusion of the scale. The desirability of including a scale that possesses more error than reliable variance is not clear. The Mf coefficients of .43 (boys) and .40 (girls) are the worst of those reported. Other MMPI-A scales are unusually unreliable. The Pa and Ma scales are also less reliable than most of the scales described in this chapter. The D scale is less reliable than many of the Depression scales presented in this chapter.

Internal consistency estimates for the validity scales range from unacceptably low to impressively high with most being moderate (.70s and .80s). The lowest coefficients were obtained for the L scale, where coefficients ranged from .53 (girls clinical sample) to

TABLE 6.5 MMPI-A Median Internal Consistency Reliability Estimates

	Normative Sample		Normative and Clinical Sample
	BOYS (N=805)	GIRLS (N=815)	BOYS AND GIRLS
Scale 1, Hs	0.78	0.79	A-anx .80
Scale 2, D	0.65	0.66	A-obs .74
Scale 3, Hy	0.63	0.55	A-dep .83
Scale 4, Pd	0.63	0.68	A-hea .82
Scale 5, Mf	0.43	0.40	A-aln .74
Scale 6, Pa	0.57	0.59	A-biz .75
Scale 7, Pt	0.84	0.86	A-ang .72
Scale 8, Sc	0.88	0.89	A-cyn .80
Scale 9, Ma	0.61	0.61	A-con .73
Scale 10, Si	0.79	0.80	A-lse .74
			A-las .61
			A-sod .78
			A-fam .82
			A-sch .70
			A-trt .76
			A .89
			R .53
			MAC-R .48
			ACK .66
			PRO .69
			IMM .82

NOTE: Medians are based on the coefficients presented in Table 22 of Butcher et al. (1992).

.64 (boys normative sample). In contrast, the F scale produced coefficients ranging from .81 (girls clinical sample) to .90 (boys normative sample).

The internal consistency estimates for the "content" scales of the MMPI-A are generally better than those for the original clinical scales (see Table 6.5). The A-dep scale coefficients are considerably better than those of the original D scale, ranging from a low of .80 for the normative sample of boys to a high of .89 for the clinical sample of girls.

The lowest internal consistencies of the content scales are produced by the A-las scale, which has coefficients ranging from .55 to .66. These coefficients, however, are better than those of the MF scale.

Some of the supplementary scales are also plagued by poor reliability estimates. The revised MacAndrew scale yields a median coefficient of .48, which is again lower than most of the scales cited in this chapter. This lack of reliability also makes the MAC-R scale difficult to validate since reliability is a necessary condition for validity (although some supportive validity evidence will be cited later). This coefficient is also disappointing given the frequent referral concern of substance abuse or dependence.

Although the manual cautions that a cut-off raw score of 28 on the MAC-R may result in false positives, the existence of such poor reliability estimates makes one question the reliability of any cut score or, for that matter, the inclusion of the scale. Reliability coefficients in the .40s are typically not seen as adequate for clinical decision making.

If one orders all of the MMPI-A clinical and content scales by their reliability estimates, some implications for interpretation become clear. Scales can be grouped by reliability coefficients with guidance for interpretation as shown:

GOOD RELIABILITY
(median Coefficient ≥ .80) Scale 7, Pt

Scale 8, Sc
A-anx
A-dep
A-cyn
A-hea
A-fam
A
IMM

ADEQUATE RELIABILITY
(median Coefficient = .70 to .79)

Scale 1, Hs
Scale 10, Si
A-obs
A-aln
A-biz

A-ang
A-con
A-lse
A-sod
A-sch
A-trt

POOR RELIABILITY
(median Coefficient = .60 to .69)

Scale 2, D
Scale 3, Hy
Scale 4, Pd
Scale 9, Ma
A-las
ACK
PRO

INADEQUATE RELIABILITY
(median Coefficient ≤ .59)

Mf
Pa
R
MAC-R

This reliability-based interpretive hierarchy is of course overly simplistic because the validity of these scales is not equivalent for all purposes. The hierarchy, however, is useful in that there is a relationship between reliability and validity. The four scales with median coefficients below .60 are less likely to be the beneficiaries of substantial validity evidence, as will be noted in the next section.

As is typical for such scales, test-retest coefficients differ from internal consistency estimates. Test-retest coefficients are somewhat more difficult to interpret, however, since it is unclear whether or not some scales measure traits that theoretically should be stable over at least short periods of time. Regardless, test-retest data can be of value when gauging changes from one evaluation to another.

One scenario might involve an adolescent who was hospitalized with paranoid ideation that was reflected by a high T-score (.78) on the PA scale. It is conceivable that this individual would obtain a lower score of 61 on retest prior to discharge 2 weeks after the initial assessment. One interpretation of these results is that treatment has been effective. Another interpretation is that PA scale results are relatively unstable (r = .65) and the T-score of 78 was spuriously high or the 61 was erroneously low. These test-retest data do provide an alternative hypothesis for this score difference that, in this case, may have implications for discharge planning. In such a scenario, where MMPI-A results may not be well corroborated by other clinical findings, more careful outpatient follow-up may be warranted to ensure that PA ideation has abated significantly enough so as to not adversely affect functioning in school or other settings.

Over all, the reliability estimates for the MMPI-A are more variable than might be expected. Such variability requires a more discerning user who evaluates the reliability of results on a scale-by-scale basis, which would not be necessary with more uniform reliability coefficients. It is also noteworthy that the new content scales appear to be more reliable on average than the original clinical scales. The user may more confidently assume that the content scales possess adequate reliability.

Validity

An important fact to keep in mind when interpreting the factor structure of the MMPI-A is the extent of item overlap (Archer, Belevich, & Elkins, 1994). The scales were designed with many overlapping items that serve to strengthen the correlation between the scales. Item 31, for example, is included on six scales (2, 3, 4, 7, 8, 0). An analogous situation would be to have some WISC-III items included on several subtests or composites. It is difficult to imagine, but what if several Block Design items were allowed, because of their correlations with the Verbal scale, to be included in calculations of the Verbal IQ composite? Such a move would probably be greeted by

skepticism, causing clinicians to wonder about the distinction between the Verbal and Performance scales.

Analogously, scales 7 (Pt) and 8 (Sc) correlate highly with one another at .85 for females and .83 for males (Butcher et al., 1992). Not remarkably, these scales both "load" highly on the first factor. A reading of table E-1 of the manual reveals that these scales have 17 items in common, which parsimoniously explains the similar factor loadings of these scales. This validity evidence is potentially important in that it warns against routinely interpreting these scales as measures of distinct constructs, traits, or symptom clusters.

An early factor analysis of the MMPI-A revealed four factors: general anxiety, overcontrol or repression, and the Si (third factor) and Mf (fourth factor) scales (Butcher et al., 1992). This factor solution reported in the manual is highly similar for both males and females.

The general anxiety factor accounts for the vast majority of the variance in the correlation matrix. Factor 1 is marked by loadings for the Hs, D, Hy, Pd, Pa, Pt, and Sc scales. This factor looks like a measure of general distress.

The second, overcontrol factor is identified by loadings for L and K for males and Ma for females. The Si factor is clear-cut for both genders, whereas the Mf factor is clearcut for males only.

A recent factor analysis of the same normative sample produced somewhat different findings, with 14 factors being yielded from an exploratory factor analysis at the item level and 8 factors when conducted at the scale level (Archer, Belevich, & Elkins, 1994).

Since the MMPI basic structure was defined before the ready availability of factor-analytic methods, it would be unrealistic to expect strong factor-analytic support for the structure of the MMPI-A. Unfortunately, the factor-analytic evidence for the MMPI-A produces more questions than answers.

Why not offer a composite score corresponding to the robust first factor? Does the existence of a large first factor suggest that for the most part the MMPI-A measures essentially one latent trait (general distress or something similar)? Despite the large number of MMPI studies, these and other intriguing questions need to be researched more vigorously since factorial validity remains a centerpiece of psychological test validation.

Criterion-Related Validity

There is a wealth of external validity evidence for the MMPI-A content scales (see Williams et al., 1992). This evidence requires cross-validation, and much of it is difficult to interpret.

For example, the A-dep (Depression content scale) was correlated with several criteria/variables for the normative and clinical samples. Correlations with these criteria ranged from a low (considering the absolute magnitude of the correlation) of −.18 with marks in school and outstanding personal achievement to a high of .24 for increase in disagreements with parent(s). The correlations between a high A-dep score and suicidal ideation/gestures and history of depression were .23 and .22 (Williams et al., 1992). By comparison, the A-anx (Anxiety) scale correlated .23 with a history of depression, and the A-lse (Low Self-Esteem) also correlated .26 with depression history. The majority of the external validity coefficients seem to be in the range of .20 to .30. The authors suggest several reasons for these results and numerous methodological caveats, including the appropriateness of the criterion measures, sample sizes, composition of the clinical samples, and other factors (Williams et al., 1992). Much cross-validation research appears necessary to address these various caveats but the mere presence of such studies is laudable.

The A-cyn (Cynicism) and the A-trt (Negative Treatment Indicators) scales, for example, produced little external validity data to support their use (Williams et al., 1992, and Butcher, et al., 1992). The A-sch (School Problems) fared better than most by producing 44 significant correlates with meaningful external criteria. The MAC-R scale is one of the MMPI scales that has been the beneficiary of considerable criterion-related validation conducted specifically with adolescents (Archer, 1992)(see Box 6.2). Studies have used external criteria to devise cut scores for this scale. For example, raw scores of 28 for males

Box 6.2

Research Report

The differential validity of the MAC scale of the MMPI was thoroughly evaluated in a 1992 study by Gantner, Graham, and Archer. These authors begin by providing a comprehensive review of research on the use of the MAC scale with adolescents. They note inconsistencies in previous research. Specifically, some studies found the MAC to correctly differentiate adolescent substance abusers from other adolescent psychiatric populations with a correct classification rate as high as 74%. On the other hand, other investigators have found that high scores on the MAC scale are more likely associated with delinquent behavior and adolescent conduct problems than with substance abuse per se. The authors address the differential validity issue in their study with relatively large samples.

Their investigation included three groups. Group one (mean age = 15 years) included 164 consecutive admissions to a residential substance abuse treatment program. Individuals who were admitted to this treatment program did not have significant comorbid psychiatric problems. The second group (mean age = 15 years) included 124 psychiatric inpatients who were admitted for short-term treatment. The most frequently occurring diagnoses for this sample were conduct disorder, dysthymia, and major depression. Substance abuse cases were referred to other settings. The third sample comprised 155 high school students (mean age = 16 years). The latter sample was part of the MMPI restandardization program.

The authors performed several discriminant function analyses in order to determine the classification rate for the MAC. The resulting classification rates differed by gender. The classification rate for the first group of males was a modest 62.5%. In other words, 62.5% of the cases were correctly classified by the MAC scale into their original three groups. In the cross-validation sample of males the classification rate fell to only 53.2%. The first female sample yielded a classification rate of 52.4% and the cross-validation sample 57.1%.

While these classification rates are significantly better than chance, they are less than impressive. In fact, given that the MAC correctly identifies only 50% to 60% of adolescents, the scale should be interpreted cautiously and not in isolation. It appears that the MAC does not differentiate well between substance abuse and other adolescent psychiatric samples. This finding lends credence to the

(Cont.)

position that the MAC measures other types of psychopathology such as delinquency and conduct problems. In the authors own words,

> Results from the current study indicate that the MAC may be sensitive to characteristics found among adolescent substance abusers but also among adolescents receiving inpatient psychiatric treatment. These characteristics may be related to an overall level of psychopathology which, presumably, would be higher in an inpatient group regardless of their specific diagnoses. (p. 136)

and 27 for females have been found to be useful cut scores for identifying risk of substance abuse in psychiatric inpatient populations (Archer, 1992). High scores on the MAC have also been related to abuse of a variety of substances, not just alcohol. Such extensive external validation is needed for all of the self-report inventory.

Interpretation

The MMPI-A manual supplies several aids to interpretation. Considerable psychometric information is provided, including reliability and factor-analytic validity information. The potential import of reliability information for interpretation was outlined earlier. Similarly, factor-analytic data can help clinicians understand MMPI-A results.

If an adolescent obtains high score elevations on all of the clinical scales save Si and Mf, for example, then the client is producing a high factor 1 score. This client, consistent with the factor-analytic research, is showing a high level of general anxiety or distress. This result may not be of particular import for differential diagnosis, but it is a sensible and predictable finding that, accompanied by nonsignificant validity scale findings, is lawful and likely not spurious.

The previous description of scale item content can be most useful for understanding scale elevations. The MMPI-A manual (Butcher et al., 1992) also provides a list of items and their scale membership (table E-1), which can be useful for scale interpretation. The clinician can review table E-1 to develop a better understanding as to the behaviors, feelings, and perceptions that an adolescent would have to acknowledge in order to obtain a high score.

Some questions to ask oneself when interpreting the MMPI-A could include:

- How does an adolescent get a high score on this scale? What are the behaviors, perceptions, and feelings assessed by this scale (i.e., the item content)?
- How reliable are the scales that I wish to interpret as being of some clinical value in this case?
- Is there a content scale analogue that is more reliable (e.g. D versus A-dep) than the clinical scale?
- Is this scale elevation consistent with factor analytic research?
- How is this scale reflective of non-test based clinical symptomatology?
- Does external validity evidence exist (e.g. differential validity studies) to support my interpretation of this scale?
- Has the validity study been independently replicated?

Various interpretive methods are utilized in the following sample case.

Sample Case

Jean is a 17-year-old high school senior. She was referred for psychological evaluation after being admitted to the hospital with the diagnosis of Major Depression, Recurrent, Severe.

Jean currently resides with a roommate who is reportedly also having some adjustment difficulties. She is taking vocational courses in preparation for a career as a secretary. She reports no history of academic difficulties in school.

Jean reports a history of depressive symptomatology dating to her childhood years. She has always had feel-

(Cont.)

Sample Case *(Continued)*

ings of inadequacy and unhappiness that seem more pronounced than those of her peers.

Jean was cooperative and attentive throughout the test session. She was dressed casually in a sweatshirt and slacks. She was neatly groomed, and her response style to the cognitive test items showed good achievement motivation.

Jean demonstrated tendencies toward perfectionism and anxiety during some of the WAIS-R subtests. During the arithmetic subtest she began to tremble and remarked, "This is making me nervous." She had considerable difficulty concentrating, which resulted in the examiner having to repeat many of the test items for her. On another subtest, when faced with some of the more difficult items, she remarked, "Now I'm nervous." Her perfectionism was evidenced by her unwillingness to give up on difficult items and considerable concern with the neatness of her constructions on the Picture Arrangement and Block Design subtests.

Jean displayed depressed affect during the test session, although she did smile on occasion. She was very eager to obtain good test results, and she expressed some fear that her responses to some of the test items were inadequate.

Jean's intellectual test findings were all within the Average range. Her Full Scale Score on the WAIS-R was 104. These findings are consistent with her educational history.

Her responses to the Schedule of Affective Disorders and Schizophrenia revealed that she meets the diagnostic criteria for Dysthymia. She admitted to problems since childhood with crying spells, feeling sorry for herself, feelings of inadequacy, feeling resentful and angry, a lack of enjoyment from praise or rewards, and feeling that she is not as good as other people. Furthermore, the SADS revealed evidence of Generalized Anxiety Disorder. Jean acknowledged problems with muscle tension in her neck, fidgeting and restlessness, experiencing a dry mouth, nausea, frequent urination, difficulty falling asleep, occasionally feeling "keyed up", difficulty concentrating, and impatience. Jean elaborated by saying that she is impatient frequently about issues such as getting to school on time.

Jean scored in the moderate to severe range of depression on the Beck Depression Inventory. She obtained a total score of 28, and she rated her feelings of hopelessness and suicidal ideation in a manner consistent with risk for suicidal behavior. She noted severe unhappiness, no hope about improving, feeling like she is a failure, hatred of herself, a desire to kill herself, feeling unattractive, a lack of energy, and loss of appetite. From a norm referenced standpoint, her Beck score reveals a need for intensive intervention to alleviate the severity of her symptomatology.

An analysis of her responses to individual items suggests some issues that need to be addressed in psychotherapeutic interventions. Specifically, Jean's self-deprecation and related negative cognitions may provide a useful focus for psychotherapeutic interventions.

The findings of this evaluation support the need for intensive treatment at this time. Jean continues to demonstrate considerable risk of suicidal behavior. Moreover, she appears to possess comorbid difficulties, including generalized anxiety disorder that have been impairing her functioning for as long as she can remember. No psychotic symptomatology has been elicited thus far. A possible focus of psychotherapeutic interventions may be on the self-deprecating nature of her cognitions.

Jean's MMPI-A results suggest that she holds high standards for herself that cannot be achieved. She never meets her own expectations for success and becomes self-critical. This behavior pattern produces feelings of inferiority, low self-esteem, and poor self-confidence.

She also displays evidence of anxiety accompanied by ruminations. She also gives indications of fatigue.

Jean's MMPI-A results also suggest that she may be shy and difficult to get to know. Moreover, her shyness may be so severe that she cannot take the interpersonal risks necessary to form rewarding intimate relationships.

PSYCHOMETRIC	SUMMARY
L	52
F	79
K	50
HS	63
D	86
HY	73
TD	73
MF	50
PA	59
PT	79
SC	65
MA	49
SI	76
A	66
R	70
MAC-R	53

Strengths and Weaknesses

The MMPI-A's long history is simultaneously its greatest asset and liability. On the one hand the volumes of MMPI research guides practice. The downside is that loyalty to the original MMPI structure is untenable; it assumes that all of the original clinical scales have been the beneficiary of strong validation support and our understanding of adolescent psychopathology and personality have not progressed since the inception of the scales.

Strengths of the MMPI-A include:

1. Its familiarity to a large group of devoted users (This familiarity allows users to develop their own "internal" norms and conduct "informal" validation studies. By this we mean that clinicians who have used the MMPI-A with hundreds of cases that are referred for similar purposes have developed a knowledge base that allows them to develop a full appreciation of the strengths and weaknesses of the MMPI-A for a specific population. While this sort of data collection is no substitute for scientific research, it is a very useful adjunct to clinicians.)

2. The existence of a number of valuable validity scales

3. Interpretive flexibility because of the numerous scales available; as well as excellent reliability estimates of some of the newer content scales, leading to the hope that favorable validity evidence will follow (Black, 1994)

4. A thorough evaluation of the adolescent's self-appraisal due to the variety of items presented

5. The availability of numerous books and chapters devoted to MMPI interpretation, many of which offer highly sensible interpretive guidance

Potential weaknesses of the MMPI-A include:

1. Retention of scales that have not been well supported by validity evidence.

2. Retention of scales that lack internal consistency. According to Black (1994), "the low magnitude of the internal consistency reliabilities of many of the clinical scales are of considerable concern with respect to decisions about individual diagnosis" (p. 12).

3. Failure to incorporate factor-analytic evidence into the test development process (e.g., consideration of composite scores or clarifying how scales measure differing traits or problems despite the fact that they load on the same factor).

4. Duplicating items on different scales which produces high intercorrelations, thus bringing into question the distinctiveness of measurement of individual constructs (Kline, 1995)

5. Lack of a complete description of the normative sample and little evidence that the sample matches well a particular population (e.g., U.S. Census bureau statistics).

6. In spite of the extraordinary amount of MMPI research available, much remains to be done. The majority of the available research is based on adult samples, and little research on scale validity (particularly criterion-related validity) has been conducted specifically with adolescent populations (Archer, 1992).

Personality Inventory for Youth

The Personality Inventory for Youth (PIY; Lachar & Gruber, 1995) is a new entrant onto the child personality self-report measure scene that has its roots in the well-known Personality Inventory for Children which is designed as a parent rating scale (see Chapter 7). The PIY is designed to assess emotional and behavioral adjustment, school adjustment, family characteristics and interactions, and academic ability in children age 9 through 19 years (Lachar & Gruber, 1994). The PIY offers a substantial array of scales designed to assess these issues.

Scale Content

The PIY features four broad band factor scales; Externalizing/Internalizing, Cognitive Impairment, Social Withdrawal, and Social-Skills Deficit. The scales and subscales that contribute to these factors include:

Cognitive Impairment
    Poor Achievement and Memory
    Inadequate Abilities
    Learning Problems

Impulsivity and Distractibility
    Brashness
    Distractibility and Overactivity
    Impulsivity

Delinquency
    Antisocial Behavior
    Dyscontrol
    Noncompliance

Family Dysfunction
    Parent–Child Conflict
    Parent Maladjustment
    Marital Discord

Reality Distortion
    Feelings of Alienation
    Hallucinations and Delusions

Somatic Concerns
    Psychosomatic Syndrome
    Muscular Tension and Anxiety
    Preoccupation with Disease

Psychological Discomfort
    Fear and Worry
    Depression
    Sleep Disturbance

Social Withdrawal
    Social Introversion
    Isolation

Social Skill Deficit
    Limited Peer Status
    Conflict with Peers

The PIC item pool served as the basis for developing items for the PIY (Lachar & Gruber,1994). In fact, only a few new items were added. The vast majority of PIY items are adapted from the PIC. The manual does not give a compelling rationale for this method of item development by demonstrating the content validity of the original PIC item pool.

Validity Scales

Four validity scales are also featured. A Validity scale measure is intended to assess for the presence of inattentive, oppositional, or provocative responses (Lachar & Gruber, 1994). The Inconsistency scale indicates if a protocol was answered haphazardly. Dissimulation measures the tendency of the informant to fake bad or malinger. Finally, the Defensiveness scale provides an index that may reflect a fake good or a social desirability response set (Lachar & Gruber, 1994). See Table 6.6 for summary information on PIY scales and reliabilities.

The CLASS

A unique feature of the PIY is the availability of an 80-item short form that may have utility for classroom screening for adjustment difficulties. The CLASS also offers some indication of validity.

Administration and Scoring

The PIY manual (Lachar & Gruber, 1994) provides several helpful guidelines for administration. The manual suggests, for example, that the examiner explain the directions to the examinee even though the directions are included on the Administration Booklet in order to ensure compliance and enhance rapport. The administration requires two components, the booklet, and WPS Autoscore™ Answer Forms.

Hand-scoring of the PIY does not require the use of acetate templates as was common for older tests. Rather, a single "template" is included in the answer form. The examiner adds rows and columns in order to obtain raw scores. These scores are then converted to gender-based T-scores. The PIY does not offer combined norms by gender as an interpretive option.

Norming

The PIY norming sample consists of 2,327 regular education students tested in five states. The sample was stratified to meet U.S. Census Bureau statistics

TABLE 6.6 PIY Scales and Test-Retest Reliabilities for the Clinical Samples

Scales and Subscales	Test-Retest Coefficient
Cognitive Impairment	.80
Poor Achievement and Memory	.70
Inadequate Abilities	.67
Learning Problems	.76
Impulsivity and Distractibility	.84
Brashness	.70
Distractibility and Overactivity	.71
Impulsivity	.58
Delinquency	.91
Antisocial Behavior	.88
Dyscontrol	.88
Noncompliance	.80
Family Dysfunction	.83
Parent–Child Conflict	.73
Parent Maladjustment	.76
Marital Discord	.73
Reality Distortion	.84
Feelings of Alienation	.74
Hallucinations and Delusions	.78
Somatic Concerns	.76
Psychosomatic Syndrome	.63
Muscular Tension and Anxiety	.72
Preoccupation with Disease	.59
Psychological Discomfort	.77
Fear and Worry	.75
Depression	.69
Sleep Disturbance	.71
Social Withdrawal	.82
Social Introversion	.77
Isolation	.77
Social Skill Deficit	.79
Limited Peer Status	.76
Conflict with Peers	.72

SOURCE: Adapted from table 46 in Lachar and Gruber (1994).

for ethnicity, parental educational level (SES), and community size. In addition, the marital status of the parent(s) was also considered. There was a slight undersampling of African-American children. An additional norming sample of 1,178 cases was collected to produce clinical norms. These cases were collected from 50 facilities that served a variety of inpatients and outpatients.

Reliability

Internal consistency coefficients are available for the PIY for both the norming and clinical samples. The reliabilities for the scales for the clinical sample are generally good, producing a median of .85. The median reliability for the subscales is much lower at .73. In fact, for the clinical sample, several (a total of eight) of the internal consistency coefficients fall below .70. The internal consistency coefficient for the learning problems scale, for example, was the lowest at .44.

The test-retest coefficients for the clinical sample are also good at the scale level, with a median of .82. The median coefficient at the subscale level was again lower at .73. At the subscale level a total of seven subscales yielded test-retest coefficients of .70 or less. The lowest coefficient was .58 for the Impulsivity subscale and the highest was .88 for the Antisocial Behavior and Dyscontrol scales (Lachar & Gruber, 1994).

The manual also reports useful estimates for the standard error of measurement for each scale and subscale in T-score units. The typical SEM at the scale level is about 4 or 5 T-score points for the test-retest estimates. These data may be valuable for the practitioner who needs to gauge the level of confidence in the obtained scores.

Validity

The manual suggests that factor analytic techniques were the primary methods used for deriving scales and subscales as opposed to using rational methods (see Chapter 2). The item content of some of the subscales appear to reflect the use of this methodology. Why, for example, is the item "Money is my biggest interest" placed on the Distractibility/

Overactivity subscale? Finally, why is the item "Several times I have said I wanted to kill myself" included on the Sleep Disturbance subscale as opposed to the Depression subscale? If, for example, the DSM-IV system were used as one method for classifying items by content, a suicidal ideation item would be much more likely to be placed on the Depression subscale. The extent to which rational methods of item selection were used for item placement is not clear in the manual (Lachar & Gruber, 1994). The major argument presented for content validity is that the items were derived from the PIC-R item pool.

Several criterion-related validity studies are included in the manual. A study of 152 adolescents who also took the original MMPI produced very modest relationships between the PIY and the MMPI clinical scales. Among the highest correlations were Reality Distortion and MMPI Schizophrenia (.66), and Psychological Discomfort and Psychasthenia (.65). The majority of correlations were in the .20 to .50 range, and many of the correlations were not statistically significant.

Another study correlated the PIY with the State-Trait Anxiety Inventory and the Reynolds Adolescent Depression Scale for 79 cases. These data allow for the evaluation of the criterion-related validity of the PIY Psychological Discomfort scale and its component subscales. The correlations ranged from modest to strong. The State-Trait correlated .51 and the Reynolds .70 with the Psychological Discomfort scale, suggesting that this scale may measure more depressive than anxiety symptomatology. It is difficult to summarize the wealth of data included in these studies in the limited space available here. The clinician who is seriously interested in the PIY would be served well by reading the criterion-related validity studies included in the manual very carefully prior to interpreting the scales and subscales.

Several samples were also used to assess the factor invariance of the PIY by gender and ethnicity (Lachar & Gruber, 1994). The results were generally supportive of the hypothesis of factor invariance across groups, although cross-validation with independent samples should be sought before drawing definitive conclusions.

Interpretation

A five-step interpretive system for the PIY is offered by the authors (Lachar & Gruber, 1994). The first step involves assessing the validity of the obtained results using the four validity scales and a review of the completed form.

The second interpretive step suggests identifying primary profile elevations. A primary scale elevation is defined as a clinical scale with a T-score ≥ 60 and subscale member of this same scale with T ≥ 65 (for the majority of scales although this cut score varies). These primary scale elevations may identify the diagnostic issues most likely to require additional attention and/or study.

The third interpretive step pertains to secondary scale elevations. These significant profile elevations are defined as scales that exceed the clinical cut score that are not accompanied by corresponding subscale scores that exceed the clinical cut score. In addition, subscales that exceed the cut score (without a corresponding high scale score) are also interpreted in this step. These secondary scale elevations may reveal mild problems and/or frequently occurring personality characteristics (Lachar & Gruber, 1994).

Step four includes tallying and interpreting items labeled as critical. This extensive list is intended to identify items that suggest clinical issues that should be examined in greater detail (Lachar & Gruber, 1994).

The last interpretive step is probably the most crucial—the integration of PIY results with other findings. The relationship of the PIY and PIC-R is highlighted in this regard. The complexity of this interpretive step, however, cannot be overstated. Our methods for integrating information are described in detail in Chapter 16.

Strengths and Weaknesses

The PIY is so new that it has not had the benefit of clinical experience, which would provide the best indication of its utility. The data presented in the manual do provide some initial suggestions for cautious and promising uses. Some tentative strengths of the PIY are:

1. The PIY is supported by a relatively thorough manual that gives considerable statistical data, guidelines for interpretation, and case studies. The PIY manual is more comprehensive than, for example, the one accompanying the MMPI-A.

2. The PIY appears to assess a broad spectrum of child and adolescent behavior, and it has a larger age range than does the MMPI.

3. The PIY may be of a more practical length than the MMPI.

4. The availability of a screening form provides an interesting option for the user.

5. Computer-scoring options are available for the PIY, which should enhance practicality.

Some potential weaknesses of the PIY may include:

1. Evidence of content validity is not compelling. Some of the item placements on scales do not seem consistent with rational/theoretical approaches to test development, which are gaining favor in personality assessment as exemplified by the new content scales of the MMPI, many of which produce better internal consistency coefficients than the traditional MMPI clinical scales.

2. The use of norm-referenced scores at age 9 seems questionable given the much smaller norming sample at this age (N = 70 for the regular education sample)(Lachar & Gruber, 1994).

3. The internal consistency and test-retest reliability of several of the subscales are substandard, and the reliability of the subscales is also consistently lower than that obtained at the scale level. The subscales should likely be used with caution, or not used by the inexperienced PIY user, until further reliability studies are conducted.

4. While the PIY manual reports considerable valuable statistical information, some of the most crucial information is not clearly integrated with the interpretive process. Specifically, the standard error of measurement values are not used for defining clinical cut scores. The advised use of rigid cut scores tends to undervalue the unreliability that is associated with the scales and subscales.

Given that the SEM for most of the scales is either 4 or 5, it would be advisable to not suggest cut scores of T ≥ 65. In order to ensure that clinicians account for error variance, it may be more appropriate to suggest a cut score for most of the scales of T ≥ 60 to 70. Incorporation of more appreciation of the SEM into an interpretive scheme seems especially important given the continuing concerns about test misuse (see Chapter 4). Of course, the MMPI and other measures share a deemphasis of the SEM in interpretive practice. The BASC at least features the SEM (in the form of confidence bands) in the hand scoring and computer scoring options.

Youth Self-Report

The Youth Self-Report (YSR; Achenbach & Edelbrock, 1991) is one component of the larger set of assessment instruments offered by Achenbach that includes a parent rating scale, a teacher rating scale, and a classroom observation measure among other instruments (these are discussed in subsequent chapters). The YSR is designed for ages 11 through 18, to obtain adolescents' reports about their own competencies and problems in a format similar to that of the CBCL (Achenbach, 1991). This latter point is an important one in that the YSR content is highly similar to that contained in the parent form of the system, the *Child Behavior Checklist* (CBCL, Achenbach, 1991a).

Scale Content

Composite scores reflecting the familiar externalizing and internalizing dimensions and a total composite are offered. The following clinical scales contribute to these composites.

Withdrawn—prefers to be alone, shy, sulks, sad, depressed, etc.

Somatic Complaints—nausea, headaches, fatigue, etc.

Anxious/Depressed—fears, depressed, suicidal ideation, nervous, etc.

Social Problems—immature, withdrawn, disliked by peers, etc.

Thought Problems—hoarding objects, ruminations, hallucinatory experiences

Attention Problems—immature, impulsivity, nervous, daydreaming, etc.

Delinquent Behavior—lying, substance abuse, truancy, stealing, etc.

Aggressive Behavior—bragging, arguing, fighting, destruction of property, etc,

Scales labeled Social Competence are also included that assess participation in a variety of activities (e.g., sports) and social interactions (e.g., friendships). A social competence composite is also offered.

The clinical scales are empirically derived (via factor analysis), and the competence scales are rationally derived. One clinical scale was identified only for males—Self-Destructive/Identity Problems. The existence of such a scale (or syndrome) for males only has not been independently corroborated.

As is evident from the preceding, this empirical procedure for scale development does result in some scales that share items, and some items may have been placed differently had rational methods also been used. Depressed affect, for example, is included on more than one scale.

Administration and Scoring

The YSR is designed to be self-administered and requires a minimum of 15 minutes. The YSR uses a three choice response format—Not True, Somewhat or Sometimes True, and Very True or Often True. Some items also require written responses, for example, "Please describe any other concerns you have."

Achenbach (1991a) also recommends that the informant be reassured of the confidentiality of results. This, however, can be difficult to guarantee, especially for younger respondents (see Chapter 4). The YSR may be read to adolescents with limited reading skill.

Templates are used for hand-scoring and computer-scoring is also available. An integrative computer program can be used to compare results for several raters (e.g. a parent, two teachers, and the YSR). The correlations between the scales derived from the 89 common clinical items for the various raters can also be computed. The level of comparability facilitates the study of interrater agreement in clinical or research settings.

Norming

The design of the YSR norming sample attempted to mimic the national population of school children for ages 11 through 18 by controlling for factors such as SES, geographic region, and ethnicity. The sample included 637 males and 678 females. The sample systematically excluded children with any handicapping conditions.

The derived T-scores for the YSR are normalized, which results in changing the shape of the raw score distribution (i.e., reducing skewness). Furthermore, the T-score distributions are truncated, which limits the range of low scores on the clinical scales and high scores on the competence scales. For example, T-scores for the clinical scales were not allowed to be articulated below a value of 50. The transformation to reduce skewness and truncated score range both serve to make the T-score distribution for the YSR different from original sample results. This lack of reflection of the sample characteristics in the T-scores makes them of dubious value for research purposes in particular. These T-score characteristics also render some clinical questions unanswerable, such as "How well developed are his competencies?"

Reliability

Internal consistency estimates are reasonable for the clinical scales falling into the .70 to .90 range for the most part. The Withdrawn scale is an exception at about .60. Internal consistency estimates are also lower for the competence scales.

Short-term (approximately 1-week interval) test-retest coefficients are substandard in some cases. At ages 15 to 18 the Thought Problems and Somatic Complaints scales produce coefficients below, and in some cases well below, .70. At ages 11 to 14 the Thought Problems, Delinquent Behavior, and Social Problems scales all yield coefficients below .70.

Validity

The YSR manual does not report evidence of content- or criterion-related validity. No correlational studies with the MMPI or other important measures are presented.

Some differential validity data are presented, but these are of little importance. Specifically, the ability of the YSR to differentiate nonhandicapped from clinical samples is presented. The more important question, the ability of the YSR to differentiate *among* clinical samples, is not answered. The amount of validity evidence in the manuals is curious given the similarity of content of the current and previous edition and the number of studies conducted with the previous edition.

A study by Thurber and Hollingsworth (1992) compared YSR results with the results of several other measures (e.g., California Personality Inventory and Beck Depression Inventory) in a factor-analytic investigation. The sample for this study included 102 adolescent inpatients. Support for the existence of the internalizing and externalizing dimensions was found as these factors converged with measures of similar constructs to form recognizable factors. Of interest was an additional finding that the Externalizing scale may be affected by a tendency to respond in a socially desirable way and deny problems. The Internalizing scale also showed some sensitivity to response sets in that it was affected somewhat by minimizing symptoms (Thurber & Hollingsworth, 1992).

Interpretation

While the accompanying manual provides some case studies, it does not provide adequate interpretive guidance. This omission is remedied to some extent by the existence of other articles on the YSR and other components of the system (see later chapters).

The interpretive emphasis that embues the YSR is empirical. In this regard the YSR offers statistical methods for comparing the degree of correspondence with its parent and teacher companion instruments. The software program yields correlation coefficients as estimates of agreement, the implication being that agreement is good, and that agreement regarding specific behavior problems suggests the presence of psychopathology.

More detailed information regarding interpreting data from multiple sources is found in figure 5.3 of the Integrative Guide (Achenbach, 1991). This figure suggests useful courses of action for the clinician based on patterns of agreement and disagreement between raters. Again, agreement is prized, and it is suggested that T-scores across comparable scales for different raters can be averaged to obtain a composite T-score. This emphasis on agreement stands in contrast to the philosophy that different raters make unique contributions to the understanding of a child's referral difficulties (see Chapter 16).

Strengths and Weaknesses

The YSR has some advantages in comparison to the PIY and BASC-SRP. Among the strengths of the YSR are (see Table 6.7):

1. Brief administration time

2. A large research base

3. A large base of experienced users

4. Considerable item overlap with its parent and teacher report counterparts

However, the YSR lacks many features of newer scales such as the BASC-SRP and PIY. Its weaknesses include (Kline, 1995):

1. Lack of differentiation of the constructs of anxiety and depression

2. Little assessment of school-related problems

3. A manual with limited psychometric data

4. The absence of validity scales, which seems to be of considerable importance for adolescents

5. Some very poor test-retest reliability estimates for some of the scales

SINGLE CONSTRUCT PERSONALITY INVENTORIES

Children's Depression Inventory

The Children's Depression Inventory (CDI; Kovacs, 1991) is a 27-item depression self-report scale for ages 6 through 17. A derivative of the Beck Depression Inventory (Semrud-Clikeman, 1990), the CDI, enjoys a long history of clinical use, particularly in research investigations.

Scale Content

The 27 items of the CDI assess a wide range of depressive symptomatology, much of which is included in popular diagnostic systems such as the DSM. Items assess sadness, cognitive symptoms, social problems, somatic complaints, and acting out behaviors. Subscales are not offered.

Administration and Scoring

Contributing to the popularity of the CDI is its ease of administration and scoring. The scale can be completed in minutes by a competent reader. Each item is composed of three stems from which the child must choose one. The three stems typically represent differing levels of severity of depressive symptomatology. Items are assigned scores of 2, 1, or 0, where a higher raw score reflects more severe symptomatology.

Raw scores are used for interpretive purposes in that a raw score cut-off of 11 is advised as adequate for screening purposes; 18 is considered evidence of significant depressive symptomatology. No other derived scores, such as T-scores, are offered.

Norming

The CDI possesses essentially local norms based on a sample of 1,463 Florida school children (Finch, Saylor, & Edwards, 1985). The norm sample gives little evidence of national representation; hence, the degree to which CDI norms can be recommended as a national or some other standard is not known.

Reliability

Reliability of the overall CDI score is good with internal consistency coefficients typically in the .80s. Test-retest coefficients are only slightly lower.

Validity

Internal evidence of validity has been assessed via numerous factor-analytic investigations. Kovacs (1991) suggests using a five-factor solution for conceptualizing subscales. The presence of more than one factor, however, does not necessarily support the validity of the CDI. The factor studies do suggest dominance by a large first factor (Cooper, 1990).

Criterion-related studies are generally supportive of the CDI as a measure of internalizing symptomatology. The CDI correlates significantly with other measures of anxiety and depression.

Strengths and Weaknesses

The CDI promises to be a widely used measure for some time given its current popularity. Knowledge of the CDI's strengths and weaknesses, however, are crucial for proper use. Among the CDI's strengths are:

1. A long research history that has contributed to considerable trust by the psychological research community
2. Ease of administration and scoring
3. Low cost
4. Evidence of concurrent validity with measures of internalizing symptoms

The CDI, however, has some noteworthy weaknesses that caution against overinterpretation.

1. The wisdom of offering such rigid cut scores for screening or diagnostic purposes in the manual is questionable as these suggestions are often applied rigidly by the end user (Kamphaus, 1993).
2. The CDI may not be appropriately labeled. Some have argued that the CDI is more a measure of

general distress rather than a measure primarily of the depression syndrome (Cooper, 1990).

3. The norm-referenced scores from the CDI should be interpreted cautiously given their lack of representativeness. In fact, a crucial flaw such as this suggests that the CDI may be more useful for research purposes than for clinical assessment and diagnostic decisions. The CDI, in fact, does have an impressive history of research utility where norm-referenced scores are often of little interest.

Reynolds Adolescent Depression Scale

The Reynolds Adolescent Depression Scale (RADS; Reynolds, 1986) is designed to assess symptomatology associated with depression, and not to provide a diagnosis of a specific and definitive depressive disorder (Reynolds, 1986). Furthermore, the RADS is designed for use in individual assessment, screening, and research.

Scale Content

The RADS is designed to provide a thorough sampling of depressive symptoms that are included in the DSM and other nosologies for children age 13 to 18.

Administration and Scoring

The RADS uses 30 items to which the client responds to one of four choices of frequency: almost never, hardly ever, sometimes, and most of the time. The items are placed on a single page where a template is used to easily sum item scores to obtain raw scores. Raw scores are then converted to percentile ranks based on the total sample and by gender and grade. T-scores are not offered, which is unfortunate given that the unequal units of the percentile rank distribution may be misinterpreted (Kamphaus, 1993).

Norming

The RADS was normed on a local sample, as was the CDI. A total of 2,460 adolescents were tested at one high school and two junior high schools in the Midwest. The sample is described as socioeconomically diverse, with representation reported by age, gender, and ethnicity. The match of the sample to meaningful national criteria such as census data is not given. Other details are missing, such as the proportion of the sample that is of Hispanic origin. Without further details the degree to which the norming sample represents a useful standard is unknown.

Reliability

Reliability indices for the RADS total score are high, with many studies yielding internal consistency coefficients in the low .90s. The internal consistency estimate reported for the total sample in the manual is .92 (Reynolds, 1986). A test-retest coefficient of .80 is reported for a 6-week interval.

Validity

Considerable validity data are reported in the RADS manual. Reynolds (1986) presents evidence of content validity showing that the RADS systematically assesses many of the symptoms commonly associated with the syndrome. These data reassure the user that items were not developed capriciously but with careful attention to the research on depression.

Many studies show reasonable correlations between the RADS and measures of depression and similar internalizing constructs. Several studies with the Beck Depression Inventory (BDI) produced consistently significant correlations ranging from .68 to .76.

Several studies have shown similarly high correlations between the RADS and anxiety measures. These studies produced correlations ranging from .73 to .80, suggesting considerable overlap between RADS scores and other measures of distress. The RADS could be similar to the CDI in that it may serve as a general measure of distress.

Strengths and Weaknesses

The RADS has gained popularity because of many strengths, including:

1. A thorough assessment of depressive symptomatology rooted in content validity
2. Good evidence of criterion-related validity
3. Ease of administration and scoring
4. Good caveats regarding interpretation in the manual

Weaknesses may include:

1. Unknown representativeness of the norming sample
2. Featuring the percentile rank as the derived score of choice, which results in undue interpretive emphasis being placed on a derived score based on an ordinal scale of measurement with its attendant problems

Reynolds Child Depression Scale

The Reynolds Child Depression Scale (RCDS; Reynolds, 1989) is a downward extension of the RADS designed for ages 8 through 12. It is designed with the same rationale and intended uses as the RADS.

Scale Content

The scale includes 29 items that use a likert-type four-choice format. The four response options measure frequency of symptomatology with the following options: almost never, sometimes, a lot of the time, and all the time. A 30th item uses a rebus response format with five faces depicting a range of happy to sad faces. As with the RADS, some items are reverse-scored in order to discourage response sets.

The items were selected with diagnostic criteria clearly in mind, ensuring that the RCDS assesses a good range of depressive symptoms.

Administration and Scoring

An attempt was made to make all items readable by second-graders to enhance its utility with this younger age range. The RCDS is also self-contained on one sheet for convenience, and a scoring template is provided. A machine-scannable form is also available for group or other large-scale administration of the RCDS. Although a cut score is provided, the author cautions against its use for diagnostic purposes (Reynolds, 1989). Of course, cut scores are always questionable, even for screening purposes. Again, only percentile rank scores, with their attendant problems, are offered in lieu of standard scores.

Norming

The RCDS was normed with a sample of 1,620 children in the Midwest and other portions of the country (Reynolds, 1989). Reynolds (1989) presents data showing similar raw scores for samples tested in Sacramento, California and Beloit, Wisconsin and concludes that geographic representation is adequate for the sample. This point could be debated, particularly given the SES differences across regions (Kamphaus, 1993). Unfortunately, SES was not specifically controlled in the norming study, with the exception that some students had teachers estimate their SES. This procedure is also easily questioned given its unusual nature.

Gender, ethnicity, and grade data are reported for the sample. Like the RADS, however, the representation of the sample in comparison to criteria such as census data is not given.

Reliability

The internal consistency of the RCDS is strong, with coefficients at most grade levels of .90. A coefficient of .87 was obtained even at grade 3. Test-retest at 2- and 4-week intervals is strong, with coefficients ranging from .81 to .92.

Validity

Reynolds (1989) makes a good case for content validity. In addition, five studies of the relationship of the RCDS to the CDI produced significant correlations, mostly in the .70s. Correlations with the

RCMAS are also significant, ranging from .60 to .67 in three studies.

A five-factor solution is reported for the RCDS, with the first factor clearly dominant. The presence of a strong first factor argues for an emphasis on total score interpretation.

Strengths and Weaknesses

The RCDS is strikingly similar to the RADS in terms of its strengths and weaknesses. In fact, there is no need to repeat the same lists here.

Revised Children's Manifest Anxiety Scale

The Revised Children's Manifest Anxiety Scale (RCMAS; Reynolds & Richmond, 1985) is a revision of the CMAS designed to improve upon its predecessor by enhancing content validity, improving readability, and extending the age range. The RCMAS measures the expression of anxiety symptomatology whether or not the construct is conceptualized as being a state or a trait.

Scale Content

The RCMAS includes 37 items distributed among four subscales: physiological anxiety (10 items), worry/oversensitivity (11), social concerns/concentration (7 items), and lie (L, 9 items). The content of the subscales appears diverse. Items from the physiological anxiety subscale, for example, range from "difficulty making decisions" (the physiological nature of this item is not apparent) to "awakening scared from sleep" to "having sweaty hands."

The L scale is a rather unique feature of a single-construct measure. The RCMAS L scale measures children's tendency to portray themselves in a favorable light (i.e., fake good). To obtain a high score on this scale, children would have to deny ever getting angry and liking everyone they know. This scale is likely to be transparent to adolescents.

Administration and Scoring

Children have simply to respond yes or no to RCMAS items that are read from a one-page response form that is accompanied by a template for scoring. Group administration is feasible for older children. A high score is indicative of anxiety.

The Total Anxiety score is a T-score conversion of a raw score. Standard scores with a mean of 10 and standard deviation of 3 are also provided for the subscales. A standard score of 13 on the L scale should lead the clinician to suspect the child's report (Reynolds & Richmond, 1985). Norm-referenced scores are provided by gender, age, and ethnicity, giving the user a variety of interpretive options. Non–gender-based norms are not offered.

Norming

The RCMAS was normed using 4,972 children age 6 through 19 years. The sample was collected from 13 states, which appears to be a broader national sampling than was used for the CDI and RADS. Age, gender, and ethnic information is given in the manual (Reynolds & Richmond, 1985). The representation of Hispanic students is again lacking, and no formal measure of SES is included. Consequently, while the sample size is large and the geographic representation better than for other single-trait measures, the representativeness of the sample is still open to question.

Reliability

Internal consistency reliability of the composite score is good with overall coefficients in the low .80s. Subscale reliabilities are somewhat lower particularly for the physiological anxiety and social concerns/concentration scales. The physiological anxiety scale produced a coefficient of .67 for the total score. The social concerns/concentration estimate was highly similar at .64. The worry/oversensitivity coefficient was somewhat higher at .76. Clearly, the worry/oversensitivity subscale is the most trustworthy.

The L scale yielded an overall coefficient of .77. This finding suggests some utility for this subscale as a measure of veracity.

Validity

Considerable validity evidence is provided in the manual. Factor studies of the standardization data do not suggest that the RCMAS is dominated by a single factor. A review of the factor loadings suggest that some of the scale placements were based on minimal loadings. The item about having difficulty making decisions, for example, had a .26 loading on both the first and second factors for the norming sample. Yet the item is placed on the physiological anxiety factor, not worry/oversensitivity. Theoretical or logical considerations may have helped with the item-placement process.

The RCMAS demonstrates lawful relationships with other measures of anxiety. A correlation of .65 is reported between the RCMAS Total Anxiety score and the State Trait Anxiety Inventory for Children Trait Anxiety score.

Interestingly, the RCMAS is one of the few measures of this variety to systematically study item bias. Considerable item bias was found, but it appeared to be random across groups. Specifically, about as many items were found to be biased against whites and black children as were found to favor boys or girls.

Strengths and Weaknesses

Strengths of the RCMAS include:

1. A broad sampling of anxiety symptomatology
2. Ease of administration and scoring
3. A larger and more geographically diverse norming sample than is typical for single-construct measures
4. A reliable Total Anxiety score
5. The presence of an L scale

Weaknesses of the RCMAS include:

1. A lack of information about relevant ethnic and SES representation of the norming sample
2. Subscales with questionable external evidence of validity

CONCLUSIONS

Reviews of the current state of self-report personality assessment are consistent with Martin's 1988 impressions. Namely, this method of personality assessment continues to lag behind intelligence and achievement testing. Poor norming is common and some subscale reliabilities are too low to support diagnostic decisions. In some cases they are too low to support hypothesis generation. Few of the instruments discussed herein empirically checked for item bias, and few have used modern statistical methods such as structural equation modeling and latent trait methodology as is commonly done for intelligence and achievement tests. Moreover, even the revered MMPI-A fails to satisfy some basic psychometric standards (see Table 6.7.)

While all of the instruments discussed in this chapter are improvements over the technology available just a decade ago, their shortcomings present problems for clinicians. At the most basic level, psychologists make conclusions about behavior based on multiple data sources in order to enhance the reliability of their impressions. In many cases, clinicians cannot safely assume that self-report personality tests add reliable findings to this decision-making process.

CHAPTER SUMMARY

1. Until recently, parent and teacher reports have routinely been preferred over the use of self-report inventories in child personality assessment.
2. The SRP is one of many components of the BASC that attempts to gauge children's perceptions and feelings about school, parents, peers, and their own behavior problems.
3. Three composites were constructed for the SRP using factor analysis: Clinical Maladjustment, School Maladjustment, and the Emotional Symptoms Index (ESI).
4. The SRP includes three validity scales in the hand-score version and five in the computer-scored version.

TABLE 6.7 Overview of Self-Report Inventories

Scale	Authors	Publisher	Content	Ages	NO	Reliability	Validity	MI
BASC-SRP	Reynolds & Kamphaus (1992)	American Guidance Service	Clinical Maladjustment, School Maladjustment, Personal Adjustment, Emotional Symptoms Index composites, 10 clinical scales, 4 adaptive scales, 5 validity indexes (152–186 items)	8–18	E	Internal consistency, test-retest, & interrater (.70s–.90s)	Support for factor structure, modest to high correlations with existing scales, lawful profiles for clinical samples	E
MMPI-A	Butcher et al., 1992	National Computer Systems	10 original clinical scales, 6 validity scales, 15 content scales, 6 supplementary scales, 28 Harris-Lingoes scales and 3 Si subscales, no composites (478 items)	14–18	G	Internal consistency and test-retest, better coefficients for content scales than original scales	Four-factor structure that is not reflected in obtained scores; item overlap detracts from content validity	P
PIY	Lachar & Gruber, 1994	Western Psychological Services	9 clinical scales (additional subscales), 4 validity scales (270 items, 80 items on screening form)	9–18	G	Internal consistency and test-retest (.70s–.80s), lower estimates for subscales	Differential validity (nonhandicapped vs. clinical groups, modest to high correlations with other measures, case history correlates	F

(Cont.)

TABLE 6.7 (Continued)

Scale	Authors	Publisher	Content	Ages	NO	Reliability	Validity	MI
YSR	Achenbach, 1991	Author, University of Vermont	Internalizing, Externalizing, Competence (112 items)	11–18	G	Internal consistency, test-retest (.70s–.90s), and interrater	Support for factor structure, differential validity (nonhandi-capped vs. clinical groups), interrater comparisons	E

NO = Evaluation of the scales' normative base evaluated as either E = Excellent, G = Good, F = Fair, and P = Poor.
MI = evaluation of the scales' enhancement of a multi-informant assessment.

5. The SRP was normed with the remainder of the BASC components on a national sample of 5,188 children and 4,423 adolescents.

6. The reliability of the SRP scales is good as indicated by a variety of methods.

7. Until clinical experience and research studies are available, initial efforts at SRP interpretation should focus on the scale level since these item pools have some rationale, theoretical, and research basis.

8. The MMPI-A has strong roots in the original work of Hathaway and McKinley (1940), which is the source of its greatest strengths and most disconcerting weaknesses.

9. The MMPI-A has 10 clinical scales, 8 validity scales, and a growing number of content scales.

10. The MMPI-A is unusually lengthy in comparison to other self-report inventories designed for children and adolescents; this length entails special administration guidelines.

11. There are distinct differences in the internal consistency estimates for the MMPI-A, with many adequate scales and some that are below minimum standards.

12. Factor analysis of the MMPI-A reveals four factors; the first two are labeled general anxiety, overcontrol or repression, and the third and fourth factors are composed solely of the Si and Mf scales, respectively.

13. Strengths of the MMPI-A include:

    a. Its familiarity to its large group of devoted users

    b. The existence of a substantial research base that allows users to have a good understanding of the value of particular scores

    c. Interpretive flexibility because of the numerous scales available

    d. A thorough evaluation of the adolescent's self-appraisal due to the variety of items presented

    e. The availability of numerous books and chap-

ters devoted to MMPI interpretation, many of which offer highly sensible interpretive guidance

14. Weaknesses of the MMPI-A include:

    a. Retention of scales that have not been well supported by validity evidence

    b. Retention of scales that lack internal consistency

    c. Failure to incorporate factor-analytic evidence into the test-development process (e.g., consideration of composite scores or clarifying how tests measure differing traits or problems despite the fact that they load on the same factor)

    d. Duplicating items on different scales, which produces high intercorrelations thus compromising the distinctiveness of measurement of individual scales

    e. Lack of a complete description of the normative sample and little evidence that the sample matches well a particular population (e.g., U.S. Census Bureau statistics)

15. The CDI is a 27-item depression self-report scale for ages 6 through 17 (Kovacs, 1991). The CDI enjoys a long history of clinical use, particularly in research investigations.

16. The CDI possesses essentially local norms based on a sample of 1,463 Florida school children.

17. Reliability of the overall CDI score is good, with internal consistency coefficients typically in the .80s.

18. The RADS is designed to assess symptomatology associated with depression, and not to provide a diagnosis of a specific and definitive depressive disorder (Reynolds, 1986).

19. Reynolds (1986) presents evidence of content validity showing that the RADS systematically assesses many of the symptoms commonly associated with the syndrome. These data reassure the user that items were not developed capriciously but with careful attention to the research on depression.

20. The RCDS is a downward extension of the RADS designed for ages 8 through 12.

21. Five studies of the relationship of the RCDS to the CDI produced significant correlations, mostly in the .70s.

22. The RCMAS measures the expression of anxiety symptomatology whether or not the construct is conceptualized as being a state or a trait.

The RCMAS includes 37 items distributed among four subscales: physiological anxiety (10 items), worry/oversensitivity (11), social concerns/concentration (7 items), and lie (L, 9 items).

23. The RCMAS demonstrates lawful relationships with other measures of anxiety.

24. While all of the self-report instruments discussed

Parent Rating Scales

CHAPTER QUESTIONS

- How reliable are parent ratings of child behavior problems?
- What domains of behavior are assessed by parent rating scales?
- What is the typical factor structure of parent rating scales?
- Which rating scales have the best psychometric properties?
- How are parent rating scales used in the typical psychological evaluation?

EVALUATING CHILDREN VIA PARENT RATINGS

It has long been recognized that children are often less than accurate reporters of their own behavior. Furthermore, children may not have sufficient reading or oral expression skills for self-report purposes

(Lachar, 1990b). Problems with underreporting and response sets have always been well recognized by clinicians and, to some extent, have been documented by research (see Chapter 2). These concerns about child self-reports have undoubtedly contributed to the popularity of parent rating scales.

Parent ratings of child behavior possess additional advantages including brevity and cost efficiency. The time-efficient nature of parent ratings makes it easy to collect additional information about child behavior. Furthermore, the parental perspective, regardless of its validity, is often valuable when conceptualizing a case. Given the importance of parental influence on child behavior, parental perceptions of behavior should routinely be collected.

These scales also provide a broad coverage of problems. For example, while the unstructured interview may allow the clinician to carefully evaluate a specific area of functioning, other important behavior problems may be missed (Witt, Heffer, & Pfeiffer, 1990).

Parent or caretaker ratings also foster objectivity and clarity in the assessment process. Because of the behavioral specificity of the typical item content of these measures, parents are "forced" to operationally define their previously vague reports of hyperactivity, depression, nervousness, and the like (Witt, Heffer, & Pfeiffer, 1990).

Finally, ratings by parents ensure increased assessment of children's behavior across settings. In this way, parent ratings allow the clinician to conduct a more ecologically valid (Witt, Heffer, & Pfeiffer, 1990) evaluation of children's functioning.

All rating scales can be accused of bias and susceptibility to response sets (Witt, Heffer, & Pfeiffer, 1990). Even biased reporting, however, can be of value. If parent ratings provide very different results when compared to the ratings of others, the clinician can develop some important insights into child or family functioning. If, for example, a child's father rates his son as having significantly more behavior problems than the mother rates him, the clinician can explore the dynamics behind the ratings. A straightforward explanation may be that the father is doing the majority of the child care. This could be important information to acquire if the presumption had been that the child's mother was providing most of the care.

Parent rating scales, however, are not interchangeable and, with the seemingly exponential growth of such measures, psychologists have to make many decisions about the utility of various measures. This chapter attempts to aid the clinician in decision making by providing an overview of the variety of scales available, with particular attention devoted to defining the strengths and weaknesses of each measure. Writing such a chapter requires selectivity. Hence, if a scale is not mentioned in this chapter, it should not be construed as a judgment of the quality of the scale. Scales may have been omitted for a variety of reasons including recent availability, lack of widespread use, or simply the authors' lack of knowledge of them. Optimally, however, the principles applied to evaluating parent rating scales in this chapter can be used by psychologists to evaluate newly available scales.

Several subgroups of parent rating scales are discussed in this chapter, including multidomain/multisyndrome/omnibus measures, single-domain/syndrome measures, and scales designed to measure specialized traits (e.g., temperament). Although these scales are discussed in isolation, it should be recalled that many are parts of larger multimethod/multitrait/multisource assessment methods that are discussed in various chapters of this book. The integration of components is discussed in the context of interpretation in Chapter 16 and in subsequent chapters that address specific syndromes.

OMNIBUS PARENT RATING SCALES

BASC Parent Rating Scales

The BASC Parent Rating Scale (BASC-PRS; Reynolds & Kamphaus, 1992) is part of the larger BASC system. The PRS was published concurrently with the SRP (discussed in Chapter 6) and other components (Reynolds & Kamphaus, 1992). Although the PRS is relatively new, early reviews have been positive (e.g., Sandoval & Echandia, 1994).

The PRS has three forms composed of similar items and scales that span the preschool (4–5 years), child (6–11 years), and adolescent (12–18 years) age ranges. The PRS takes a broad sampling of a child's behavior in home and community settings.

Scale Content

The PRS was developed using both rational/theoretical and empirical means in combination to construct the individual scales (see scale descriptions). The resulting scales have relatively homogenous content. The uniqueness of the scales was also enhanced by not including items on more than one scale.

PRS scale definitions are provided next (as taken from Reynolds & Kamphaus, 1992).

Adaptability. The ability to adapt readily to changes in the environment.

Anxiety. The tendency to be nervous, fearful, or worried about real or imagined problems.

Aggression. The tendency to act in a hostile manner (either verbal or physical) that is threatening to others.

Attention Problems. The tendency to be easily distracted and unable to concentrate more than momentarily.

Atypicality. The tendency to behave in ways that are immature, considered "odd," or commonly associated with psychosis (such as experiencing visual or auditory hallucinations).

Conduct Problems. The tendency to engage in antisocial and rule-breaking behavior, including destroying property.

Depression. Feelings of unhappiness, sadness, and stress that may result in an inability to carry out everyday activities (neurovegetative symptoms) or may bring on thoughts of suicide.

Hyperactivity. The tendency to be overly active, rush through work or activities, and act without thinking.

Leadership. The skills necessary for interacting successfully with peers and adults in home, school, and community settings.

Social Skills. The skills necessary for interacting successfully with peers and adults in home, school, and community settings.

Somatization. The tendency to be overly sensitive to and complain about relatively minor physical problems and discomforts.

Withdrawal. The tendency to evade others to avoid social contact.

Two types of scales are included at each age level; clinical and adaptive. Clinical scales of the PRS are designed to measure behavior problems much like the PIC-R and CBCL in that behavioral excesses (e.g., hitting others) are the focus of assessment. The adaptive scales, by contrast, measure behavioral deficits (e.g., compliments others) or skills that are associated with good adaptation to home and community. The content of the scales is defined further in Table 7.1, where behaviors that are highly correlated with particular scales are listed for interpretive purposes.

Administration and Scoring

The PRS uses a four-choice response format (never, sometimes, often, almost always) with no space allowed for parent elaboration. Each age level of the scale takes about 20 minutes for parents to complete.

A variety of derived scores and interpretive devices are offered. Linear T-scores are available for all scales and composites. Other scores available include percentile ranks, confidence bands, and statistical methods for identifying high and low points in a profile. T-scores can also be obtained for three norm groups.

Scoring of the PRS is self-contained by virtue of using a carbonless record form. While the procedure is straightforward, the potential for scoring errors is still present (Adams & Drabman, 1994). The BASC Enhanced ASSIST is an easy to use software scoring program that considerably reduces the potential for clerical errors.

Norming

The PRS provides three norm-referenced comparisons depending on the questions of interest to the clinician. Some examples of questions and their implications for norm group selection include the following.

QUESTION	NORM GROUP
Is Adrian hyperactive in comparison to U.S. children of the same age?	General national sample
Is Adrian hyperactive in comparison to a large sample of U.S. children who are currently diagnosed and receiving treatment?	Clinical national sample
Is Adrian hyperactive in comparison to U.S. children of the same gender and age?	Male national sample

TABLE 7.1   PRS Key Symptoms as indicated by Items with the Highest Factor Loadings per Scale

Scales and Key Symptoms	
Adaptability	Adjusts to changes in routines and plans, adjusts well to new teachers, shares toys or other possessions with others
Aggression	Argues with, bullies, teases, hits, threatens, and blames others
Anxiety	Exhibits nervousness, worry, guilt, dread, fear, and sensitivity to criticism
Attention Problems	Does not complete work, has difficulty concentrating and attending, forgets things, and does not listen to directions
Atypicality	Has urges to hurt self, hears name when alone, cannot control thoughts, and hears voices
Conduct Problems	Drinks alcohol, uses illegal drugs, or chews tobacco; steals and lies, has been suspended from school, or is in trouble with police
Depression	Complains that no one listens to or understands him or her; cries, is sad, pouts, whines, and complains of loneliness
Hyperactivity	Acts impulsively, interrupts others, and has tantrums; is restless, leaves seat, and climbs on things
Leadership	Is creative, energetic, and good at facilitating the work of others; joins clubs and participates in extracurricular activities
Social Skills	Compliments and congratulates others, and makes suggestions tactfully; has good manners and smiles at others
Somatization	Complains about health, dizziness, heart palpitations, pain, shortness of breath, and being cold; has headaches and stomach problems
Withdrawal	Avoids others and competition; is extremely shy and refuses to join group activities

NOTE: Adapted from table 10.4 of the BASC manual (Kamphaus & Reynolds, 1992).

Is Adrian hyperactive in comparison to U.S. girls of the same age?	Female national sample

These various norm referenced comparisons are more than are typically offered for such scales. The general national norming sample is advised as the starting point for most purposes (Reynolds & Kamphaus, 1992).

The general norm sample for the PRS included 309 preschoolers; 2,084 children, and 1,090 adolescents. Cases were collected at 87 test sites in 26 states. A close match between the norm sample and U.S. Census statistics for variables such as race, ethnicity, and SES was achieved by weighting the sample.

Reliability

The median reliability coefficients provided in the manual suggest good evidence of reliability for the individual scales and composites. All scales and composites have median reliability estimates of .80 and above, with the exception of the Adaptability, Conduct Problems, Hyperactivity, and Somatization scales. The Atypicality scale has the lowest median coefficient at .67.

Validity

Considerable factor-analytic validity evidence is provided in the manual showing the existence of three factors; externalizing, internalizing, and adaptive. The strongest measures of the externalizing factor are the Aggression, Conduct Problems, Hyperactivity, and Attention Problem scales. The Internalizing factor is marked by loadings on the Atypicality, Depression, Anxiety, Somatization, and Withdrawal scales. Adaptive skills scales that load highly on this factor include Adaptability, Leadership, and Social Skills.

Some of the secondary loadings for the scales may have implications for interpretation. Specifically, the factor-analytic data suggest that the following profiles are reasonable:

- Poor Adaptive Skills with Attention Problems and Withdrawal
- Externalizing Problems coexisting with Depression, Atypicality, and poor Adaptability
- Internalizing Problems accompanied by Poor Adaptability

Criterion-related validity studies have produced lawful relationships between the PRS and other parent rating scales. Scales with similar names on other measures generally show significant correlations with the PRS. Some examples of the results of these studies are shown in Table 7.2.

Interpretation

An interpretive system for the BASC is given in the manual (Reynolds & Kamphaus, 1992). This interpretive approach includes detailed descriptions of the individual scales. In addition to descriptions of the scales, the manual includes factor analytic findings for items. Details of the items that contribute to the scales are given in Table 7.1.

The same logical interpretive steps that were outlined for the BASC-SRP (discussed previously) also apply to the BASC-PRS. Briefly, Reynolds and Kamphaus (1992) recommend the following steps.

1. Assess validity using validity indexes and informal means.
2. Interpret scores on scales and composites.
3. Interpret items as warranted.
4. Set objectives for treatment/intervention.

5. Clarify scale scores using item responses.

Sample Case

Lonnie was referred for a psychological evaluation by his mother. He is a 12-year-old sixth-grader. Lonnie's mother is primarily concerned about school difficulties. She suspects that Lonnie has an unidentified disability. She also is unsure that Lonnie is in the appropriate class at school. This is the third psychological evaluation sought by Lonnie's mother.

Lonnie has had trouble completing schoolwork since the first grade. Lonnie was retained in the second grade because of poor work completion and academic progress. A psychological evaluation in the second grade revealed a visual-motor weakness, but no diagnosis was made. He was placed in special education in the third grade in a learning problem class. He was placed in a regular class again in the fourth grade. A psychological evaluation conducted at the end of the fourth grade resulted in the conclusion that he was a slow learner. This year Lonnie is in a remedial class that, according to his mother, has many disruptive children. He is again having difficulty concentrating, and he rarely completes his assignments. Academic progress is still unacceptable to his mother and teachers.

Lonnie's 7-year-old sister is doing very well in school. Both of his parents completed high school, although his father has a history of school behavior problems. His mother has a history of depression for which she has received antidepressants intermittently.

Lonnie's developmental milestones were slightly delayed. He still has problems drawing and using scissors. Last year he was diagnosed with juvenile diabetes.

Lonnie was exceedingly cooperative during the evaluation. He addressed the examiner politely and would occasionally answer questions by saying "yes sir." He had considerable difficulty comprehending instructions on the WISC-III. He was reluctant to admit to not knowing an answer, and he worked extremely slowly. The test session had to be conducted over 2 days because of his slow response style.

He did respond impulsively to items on occasion. He also wiggled in his seat and frequently looked around the room and asked questions of the examiner.

His Full Scale intelligence test score in this evaluation was 85. His achievement test scores were similarly below average.

(Cont.)

TABLE 7.2   Summary of PRS Criterion-Related Validity Studies

PRS Scale	Criterion Correlations
Aggression	CBCL Preschool (N = 30); Aggressive Behavior = .74 CBCL Child (N = 57); Aggressive Behavior = .82 CBCL Adolescent (N = 56); Aggressive Behavior = .58
Hyperactivity	CBCL Preschool (N = 30); Attention Problems = .63 CBCL Child (N = 57); Attention Problems = .71 CBCL Adolescent (N = 56); Attention Problems = .71 PIC-R Preschool (N = 39); Hyperactivity = .12 Conners Child (N = 46); Hyperactive-Immature = .48, Restless- Disorganized = .59
Anxiety	CBCL Preschool (N = 30); Anxious/Depressed = .52 CBCL Adolescent (N = 56); Anxious/Depressed = .76 PIC-R Preschool (N = 39); Anxiety = .53 Conners Child (N = 46); Anxious/Shy = .45
Depression	CBCL Preschool (N = 30); Anxious/Depressed = .66 CBCL Child (N = 57); Anxious/Depressed = .66 CBCL Adolescent (N = 56); Anxious/Depressed = .74 PIC-R Preschool (N = 39); Depression = .56
Conduct Problems	CBCL Child (N = 57); Delinquent Behavior = .76 CBCL Adolescent (N = 56); Delinquent Behavior = .78 Conners Child (N = 46); Antisocial = .71
Somatization	CBCL Preschool (N = 30); Somatic Complaints = .55 CBCL Child (N = 57); Somatic Complaints = .44 CBCL Adolescent (N = 56); Somatic Complaints = .68 PIC-R Preschool (N = 39); Somatic Concern = .12 Conners Child (N = 56); Psychosomatic = .40
Atypicality	CBCL Preschool (N = 30); Thought Problems = .36 CBCL Child (N = 57); Thought Problems = .62 CBCL Adolescent (N = 56); Thought Problems = .42 PIC-R Preschool (N = 39); Psychosis = .46
Attention Problems	CBCL Preschool (N = 30); Attention Problems = .67 CBCL Child (N = 57); Attention Problems = .78 CBCL Adolescent (N = 56); Attention Problems = .76 PIC-R Preschool (N = 39); Hyperactivity = .35 Conners Child (N = 46); Restless/Disorganized = .29; Hyperactive/ Immature = .37
Withdrawal	CBCL Preschool (N = 30); Withdrawn = .61 CBCL Child (N = 57); Withdrawn = .36 CBCL Adolescent (N = 56); Withdrawn = .70 PIC-R Preschool (N = 39); Withdrawal = .57 Conners Child (N = 46); Anxious/Shy = .78

His BASC-PRS (completed by his mother) results are highly consistent with background information.

Hyperactivity   63

The lack of hyperactivity symptomatology is consistent with his history, which gives no suggestion of overactivity or externalizing problems.

Aggression   50
Conduct Problems   58
Anxiety   53
Depression   47
Somatization   67

This score was elevated for his teacher ratings consistent with his history of juvenile diabetes and its attendant difficulties.

Withdrawal   57
Atypicality   68
Attention Problems   76

This scale was the highest elevation for his mother and for two teachers.

Social Skills   57
Leadership   39

His teachers noted delays on all adaptive scales similar to his mother's Leadership T-score.

Lonnie's results were strikingly similar for both teachers and parents. The diagnosis of attention-deficit hyperactivity disorder, primary inattentive type was made based on these and other findings. Note was made of below-average intelligence and visual-motor problems when making recommendations for teachers and referrals to other service providers.

Strengths and Weaknesses

The BASC-PRS has been cited as possessing assets including:

1. Good psychometric properties (Adams & Drabman, 1994; Jones & Witt, 1994)
2. A variety of scales that may be useful for differen-

tial diagnosis (e.g., Attention Problems vs. Hyperactivity, and Anxiety vs. Depression) (Adams & Drabman, 1994)

3. The availability of validity indexes (Adams & Drabman, 1994).

4. Several norm referenced adaptive scales such as social skills (Adams & Drabman, 1994). Jones & Witt (1994) observed, by delineating positive as well as negative behaviors, that the BASC may be more useful than other similar scales in identifying target alternative behaviors for intervention.

Among the weaknesses of the PRS are:

1. A lack of interpretive information in the manual
2. A response format that does not allow parents to provide additional detail about their responses
3. The unavailability of a form for ages 2 and 3
4. The cumbersomeness of the hand-score answer sheets for the new user (Adams & Drabman, 1994)
5. Cross-scale comparisons not as readily made as on the Achenbach because of an emphasis on maintaining content validity (Adams & Drabman, 1994)
6. Greater utility of the computer scoring program to the clinician than to the researcher because fields for research information (e.g., an ID number) are not included (Hoza, 1994)

The BASC-PRS still lacks substantial independent research. More independent validation studies are needed to clarify its strengths and weaknesses.

Child Behavior Checklist

The Child Behavior Checklist (CBCL; Achenbach, 1991) has long been considered one of the premier measures of child psychopathology (Merrell, 1994). This scale is the product of an extensive multiple-decade research effort, and it has a distinguished history of research usage.

The CBCL is part of an extensive system of scales including teacher rating, self-report (YSR), and classroom observation measures. The newest version of the CBCL (Achenbach, 1991b) has an extended age range of 4 through 18 years.

The development of the CBCL reflects the author's belief that parent reports are an important part of any multi-informant system of child evaluation. In Achenbach's (1991b) own words:

> Parents (and parent surrogates) are typically among the most important sources of data about children's competencies and problems. They are usually the most knowledgeable about their child's behavior across time and situations. Furthermore, parent involvement is required in the evaluation of most children, and parents' views of their children's behavior are often crucial in determining what will be done about the behavior. Parents' reports should therefore be obtained in the assessment of children's competencies and problems whenever possible. (p. 3)

Scale Content

The CBCL scales are primarily empirically derived, with substantial use of factor-analytic methods. As Achenbach (1991b) describes, "Our syndrome scales were derived from principal components analyses of the correlations among items" (p. 69).

The CBCL scales were also derived separately by gender and age group, and only for referred samples. For example, the item scores of a referred sample of 6- to 11-year-old girls were first submitted to a principal components analysis (Achenbach, 1991b). Then varimax methods of factor rotation were applied to the data for each sample. Additional analyses were conducted to refine the scales (which are also referred to as core syndromes).

Throughout the test development process the CBCL developers also emphasized the derivation of scales that were common across raters (e.g., parents and teachers). The CBCL parent and teacher scales have closely articulated items and scales that should make it easier for clinicians to make cross-scale comparisons.

The CBCL includes competence scales that are designed to discriminate significantly between children referred for mental health services and nonreferred children (Achenbach, 1991b). Competence scales assess Activities, Social, and School competencies. The selection criteria for the competence scales and their items, above and beyond the criterion of discrimination between groups, is not clear.

The Sex Problems scale is an optional and relatively unique scale that is only available for ages 4 through 11. This brief six-item scale includes items assessing sexual preoccupations and gender identity issues, among others.

Sample item content from the individual syndrome scales follows:

Aggressive Behavior. Cruelty, "meanness", fighting, bullying, bragging, attacking others, temper tantrums, and arguing.

Delinquent Behavior. Lying, cheating, lack of guilt, stealing, swearing, runaway behavior, and associating with children who are in "trouble".

Anxious/Depressed. Sadness, unhappiness, perfectionism, feeling unloved, feeling self-conscious, crying, worry, and suicidal ideation.

Somatic Complaints. Fatigue, physical problems that are lacking a medical basis, aches, stomach problems, and dizziness.

Social Problems. Unpopular, being teased by others, acting immature, and difficulty working with others.

Attention Problems. Inattention, confusion, poor schoolwork, nervousness, difficulty concentrating, overactivity, and impulsivity.

Thought Problems. Staring, obsessions, hearing and seeing things that are not present.

Withdrawn. Avoids interaction with others, secretive, shy, sad, and seeks to be alone.

The CBCL was a forerunner in the provision of composite scores, reflecting the now customary internalizing and externalizing dimensions (Achenbach & Edelbrock, 1979). In addition, a total T-score is offered, which is a composite of the internalizing and externalizing T-scores.

Administration and Scoring

The CBCL is easily administered via a four-page record form. The CBCL is somewhat unique in that adaptive behavior is assessed with fill-in-the-blank responses and some of the problem behavior items require the parent to elaborate. This format is advantageous in that it allows the parent to respond in an open ended format. Clinicians can gain access to qualitative information of value using this format. Open-endedness, however, also has a disadvantage: It extends administration time and requires more decision making on the part of the parent.

Hand-scoring via templates can be cumbersome, making the computer scoring program an attractive alternative (Merrell, 1994) . The CBCL offers normalized T-scores as the featured interpretive scores. Percentile ranks are also provided. T-scores are available for all scales and three composites: Externalizing, Internalizing, and Total. T-scores are not offered for adaptive items.

The advantages and disadvantages of using normalized versus linear T's are debatable (see Kline, 1995). On the one hand, the advantage of comparable percentile ranks across scales was recognized by the MMPI-A author team (see Chapter 5). Normalized scores, however, clearly change the shape of the many skewed raw score distributions (see Chapter 2).

Norming

The norming of the CBCL is based on a large national sample of children age 4 through 18 years. This sample was collected in 48 states in the spring of 1989 (Achenbach, 1991b). The sample included 2,368 cases that were selected in order to represent the national population. Relevant stratification variables such as age, gender, ethnicity, region, community size, and SES were controlled to closely match U.S. Census statistics. The respondents were mothers in 82% of the cases and fathers in 15% of the cases (3% of the cases used "others").

Children were excluded from the sample if they "had received mental health or special education classes during the previous 12 months (Achenbach,

1991b). Separate clinical norms are not offered for the CBCL.

Reliability

The CBCL has good evidence of reliability with median internal consistency coefficients for the scales and composites of .76 and .92 respectively. The data from a 1-week interval test-retest study for a sample of 80 children yielded coefficients ranging from .70 for the Activity scale (a competence scale) to .95 for the Somatic Complaints scale (Achenbach, 1991).

A 2-year interval test-retest study of 70 children, which is a strict test of reliability, yielded coefficients ranging from .39 for Sex Problems to .87 for Aggressive Behavior. Although these coefficients are considerably lower, they may in some cases reflect the instability for syndromes rather than a test development problem. The meaning of the results of such a long interval test-retest study for a behavior rating scale may not be clarified without further studies involving a variety of measures.

The optional Sex Problems scale appears to have more reliability problems than many others in the test-retest studies. This scale attained a coefficient of .83 in the 1-week interval study but dramatically lower coefficients of .20 to .41 in the 1- to 2-year interval studies. Apparently caution is the watchword when interpreting this scale.

Validity

The CBCL does a thorough job of assessing the differential validity of individual items. Appendix D of the manual reports data for all items indicating their ability to differentiate clinical from nonclinical samples (Achenbach, 1991b). Some of the items are clearly better than others (see Table 7.3) leading to the conclusion that characteristics in addition to sample discrimination were used in the item-selection process.

An additional validation method involved evaluating the ability of the individual scales and composites to differentiate clinical and nonclinical samples. Four studies comparing the performance of referred boys and girls for two age groups show good differ-

TABLE 7.3   Selected Items Differential Validity Data (means) for the CBCL for Ages 4–11

Item	Referred Boys	Referred Girls	Nonreferred Boys	Nonreferred Girls
Items with strong differential validity				
Argues a lot	1.36	1.31	.91	.84
Can't concentrate	1,26	1.09	.55	.40
Items with weak differential validity				
Asthma	.12	.08	.14	.12
Shy	.51	.65	.50	.56

Data were selected from appendix D of Achenbach (1991b).

ential validity for the composites. In each study the referred samples obtained mean T-scores (in the range of 60 to 62) that were 10 to 12 points higher than the means for the nonreferred samples (Achenbach, 1991b).

Factorial validity evidence for the CBCL raises some questions in that less robust forms of factor analysis were used. The choice of exploratory factor analysis for the construction of this latest edition is questionable given the long history of this scale. More modern confirmatory methods would have at least been good supplements to exploratory methods.

The question of the choice of factor-analytic methods for test development is raised by the structure of the scales. It is unusual by today's standards to combine constructs such as anxiety and depression, and hyperactivity and inattention, into single scales (see discussion of the CTRS in Chapter 8). Although choice of factor analytic method may play a role in the lack of separation of these constructs, other variables, such as an inadequate item pool, could also be culprits. This question is raised because it contributes to a lack of potential for differential diagnosis by this widely used scale.

Interpretation

Interpretation of the CBCL is bolstered by many articles by Achenbach and colleagues devoted to its clinical use (e.g., McConaughy & Achenbach, 1989). The CBCL user is fortunate to have many interpretive resources available.

One source, McConaughy and Achenbach (1989), provides an assessment methodology for the identification of severe emotional disturbance in the schools. Their multiaxial empirically based assessment model proposes five axes for such assessment situations: (1) parent reports (Achenbach, CBCL), (2) teacher reports (Achenbach Teacher Report Form), (3) cognitive assessment, (4) physical assessment, and (5) direct assessment of the child (Achenbach Direct Observation Form and Youth Self-Report).

McConaughy and Achenbach (1989) then propose three assessment phases that take the practitioner through the steps of assessment and intervention. The authors describe the phases by proposing that:

> Phase I utilizes rating procedures for initial data gathering based on teacher ratings, direct observations in the classroom, and parent ratings. Phase II includes a trial classroom intervention and evaluation of outcomes to determine whether further assessment or more intensive interventions are needed. Phase III begins with a psychoeducational evaluation of the child and determination of SED eligibility for special education interventions, followed by development of an Individual Education Plan (IEP) and evaluation of the IEP interventions. (pp. 95–96)

McConaughy and Achenbach (1989) assist the psychologist working in schools further by linking each CBCL scale to the accepted criteria for severe emotional disturbance. High scores on the Anxious/Depressed scale may, for example, indicate the presence of a general pervasive mood of unhappiness, which, in turn, may qualify a child as SED and document eligibility for special education and related services.

Some of these interpretive methods are used in the following sample case.

Sample Case

Doug is an 11-year-old, fifth-grade male who was referred because of parental and teacher concerns about his school performance. He is suspected of having significant attention problems.

Doug also has significant trouble in peer and other relationships. He often fights and argues with peers, resulting in his often playing by himself.

Doug has a history of significant medical difficulties. He is the product of an at-risk pregnancy. Although he achieved most developmental milestones within normal time frames, he has a history of motor delays. In second grade he was diagnosed with muscular dystrophy. He also suffers from inflammatory bowel disease, resulting in on-going treatment for ulcers. He does not tolerate many foods well and consequently his appetite is poor.

In first grade Doug was also diagnosed as learning-disabled, with problems in reading. He is in a resource special education program. He is described by his teacher as "socially inept." He is often disrespectful of teachers and peers. His grades deteriorated significantly toward the end of the last academic year. His teachers consider him to be a capable underachiever with behavior problems such as inattention, excessive talking, fighting, arguing, and poor work completion.

Doug's CBCL results for his mother and father reflect the multitude of his difficulties as follows:

CBCL Scale	Mother/Father
Internalizing T	83/60
Withdrawn	70/61
Somatic Complaints	91/64

Anxious/Depressed	79/55
Externalizing T	78/66
Social Problems	80/70
Thought Problems	79/67
Attention Problems	78/69
Delinquent Behavior	73/63
Aggressive Behavior	85/65
Total T	82/67

This set of results is not unusual given that Doug's mother is the primary caregiver who is involved in monitoring his medical status. His mother's report, however, was also more severe than the majority of the three teacher ratings. His mother's responses to the Parenting Stress Index were also highly significant revealing stress beyond the 99th percentile on the majority of the PSI scales.

All raters and observations were needed in order to clarify the CBCL results. Comparisons of all raters, self-report measures, and historical and observational data corroborated some of the CBCL results. Aggressive behavior, attention problems, somatic complaints, and depression symptoms were identified by the majority of indices. Enough information was gleaned to make the diagnoses of attention-deficit hyperactivity disorder and oppositional defiant disorder. Recommendations for intervention also included treatment for significant sadness, although the criteria for a depressive disorder were not met at the time of the evaluation.

Indications of thought problems were not corroborated by other findings. The clinicians thought that the thought problems scale was elevated for some raters due to interpretation of the items by raters as indicators of hyperactivity or inattention.

CBCL Social Problems scores were corroborated by low scores on social skills measures. The social-skills measures were used to develop behavioral objectives for Doug's intervention.

This CBCL profile highlights the need, more pressing in a case like this, to complement the CBCL with other measures. In this case, teacher ratings, observations, self-reports, measures of parent stress, history taking, and observations were all needed to clarify diagnostic impressions and identify treatment objectives.

Strengths and Weaknesses

The CBCL has many strengths that continue to make it a popular choice for clinicians. Noteworthy strengths include:

1. A large research base that continues to provide evidence of differential validity for many of the scales

2. Several journal articles that provide interpretive guidance above and beyond that provided by the manual

3. Familiarity to a large number of clinicians

Weaknesses of the CBCL include:

1. A lack of empirical profile typing that has been validated against external criteria that may assist in interpretation (Kline, 1995)

2. Item overlap of scales that may hinder the interpretation of individual scales

3. Lack of adaptive scales and some clinical scales (e.g., anxiety versus depression) that may hinder differential diagnosis. The CBCL assesses a limited range of social competencies (Orotar, Stein, & Perrin, 1995) that are particularly important for the assessment of ADHD (Stein, Szumowski, Blondis, & Roizen, 1995).

The CBCL continues to be a preferred choice of many child clinicians due to its history of successful use and popularity with researchers. The continuing development of the CBCL database bodes well for its future.

Merrell (1994) notes that the CBCL item pool contains more items than some scales that assess relatively rare behaviors that are of substantial severity (e.g., handling one's genitals in public). He then suggests that because of such items, "The Child Behavior Checklist system is perhaps the best rating scale currently available for assessing severe symptoms of childhood psychopathology; however, as a rating scale for garden-variety behavioral problems in home and school settings, it may not always be the best choice" (p. 75).

The CBCL would benefit from research aimed at assessing the adequacy of its item pool and the distinctiveness of its scales. Such research efforts are necessary to define further the degree of confidence that a clinician can place on specific scales for making differential diagnostic decisions.

Connors Parent Rating Scales

The Conners (1989) is a widely used behavior rating scale that was frequently used as a research instrument until it was commercially published in 1989. The Conners was originally used extensively in clinical trials of drugs (Conners, 1989). It is designed to be used to characterize the behaviors of a child and compare them to levels of appropriate normative groups (Conners, 1989). The parent forms are designed for ages 3 through 17. Two parent forms are available; a 93-item version (Conners-93) and a 48-item version (Conners-48). The short form, however, is somewhat unique in that its content is not drawn exclusively from the long form.

Conners (1989) notes several strengths of parent behavior rating scales. He observes:

> The most important strength of parent ratings is that the parent may spend more time in a day with the child than the teacher does, and has the advantage of having seen the child over a number of years in a very large number of situations. The parent also has a greater knowledge of the situational context of the child's behaviors, and whether there are certain environments where there are relatively greater levels of problems encountered. (p. 7)

Scale Content

The Conners-93 includes Conduct Disorder, Anxious-Shy, Restless-Disorganized, Learning Problem, Psychosomatic, Obsessive-Compulsive, Antisocial, and Hyperactive-Immature scales. The Conners-48 provides Conduct Problem, Learning Problem, Psychosomatic, Impulsive-Hyperactive, and Anxiety scales.

A distinguishing feature of both Conners is the Hyperactivity Index. This scale is based on ten items most sensitive to drug effects (Conners, 1989). This empirically derived scale differs from many scales in that items were not selected based on their ability to differentiate diagnostic groups, but rather, items were selected if they could show the most responsivity to the psychostimulant medication often taken by children diagnosed with ADHD. The Hyperactivity Index may also be used in isolation without administering either Conners form in its entirety. Conners (1989) does emphasize that the Hyperactivity Index differs from the other Conners scales that carry the Hyperactive or similar label.

In an unusual approach, the Hyperactivity Index is only norm-referenced on the Conners-48 form and, in fact, the manual advises using the 48-item form if a norm-referenced Hyperactivity Index is desired (Conners, 1989).

Administration and Scoring

The Conners-93 uses a four choice response format where 1 = not at all, 2 = just a little, 3 = pretty much, and 4 = very much. The Conners'-48, in contrast, uses a slightly different scoring system where 0=not at all, 1 = just a little, 2 = pretty much, and 3=very much. Suggested administration time of the Conners-93 and Conners-48 is 30 and 20 minutes, respectively. According to Conners (1989), both mothers and fathers can use the same form and norms.

A QuikScore™ form is used for computing scores, which eliminates the need for templates. An IBM-compatible computer program is available that allows for computerized administration and scoring. A scoring system is integrated with the response form by using carbon paper. Raw scores are easily computed by adding item values vertically.

The profile form that is included with the response form is used to convert raw scores to T-scores. Separate sides of the form are used for obtaining male and female norm-referenced scores. In addition, separate norms for various age groups on each profile form require the examiner to carefully enter the appropriate column in order to obtain T-scores. On the Conners-48, for example, there are five age group columns on the profile form.

The Conners-93 has norms for ages 6 through 14; the Conners-48 provides norms for a larger age range of 3 through 17 years.

Norming

Conners (1989) provides no information on the standardization of the scales in the manual above and beyond the sample sizes. Reference is made to a study

by Goyette, Conners, and Ulrich (1978) that describes a sample of 570 children that was used to produce norms for the Conners-48. The development of the Conners-93 is described in an article by Conners (1970). In a section on factorial validity of the parent forms the Conners manual (1989) alludes to a sample of 683 children age 6 through 14 who participated in the original norming. The age of the citations suggests that the norms for the Conners are suspect.

The Conners-48 was normed based on the responses of parents residing in the greater Pittsburgh area (Goyette, Conners, & Ulrich, 1978). The sample is made up of ratings primarily of Caucasian children (98%). Gender and SES data were also collected. The match of any of these variables, which would demonstrate representativeness, is not reported by Goyette, Conners, and Ulrich (1978).

The sample sizes upon which some of the norm-referenced scores are based are small. Specifically, the Conners-48 offers norms separately by age and gender making the samples, for some age groups, inadequate. At ages 15–17, for example, only 38 males and 34 females were available for norms development.

Reliability

Conners (1989) reported that no studies of the short-term test-retest reliability of the Conners-93 and -48 were available. Similarly, internal consistency data, such as coefficient alpha, are not available for either parent scale except for those reported in an older study by Sandberg, Wieselberg, and Shaffer (1980). Generally speaking, more reliability data are available for the Conners Teacher Rating Scales (see Chapter 8).

Validity

Similarly, more validity data are available for the teacher forms of the Conners. According to Conners (1989), some studies of discriminant validity have shown either the Conners-93 or -48 to differentiate boys with attention deficit disorder, specific learning disabilities, and matched normal controls (Kuehne, Kehle, & McMahon, 1987), as well as attention-deficit–disordered boys and developmental reading–disordered boys (Dalby, 1985).

Factor loadings and a few of the details of a factor-analytic study of the Conners-93 are reported in the manual (Conners, 1989). Factor-analytic data reported for the Conners-48 do not support the organization of the scales. The fifth factor, for example, labeled anxiety, includes only two items.

Interpretation

Conners (1989) suggests that interpretation can occur at various levels including integrating information from other scales, individual scale interpretation, and interpretation of individual items. A T-score elevation of 65 or higher is generally suggested to be of potential clinical value (Conners, 1989).

Sample Case

Doug, whose evaluation with the CBCL was reported earlier in this chapter, was also evaluated with the Conners-48. The results are very similar to those obtained from the CBCL, with his mother giving the most severe ratings by far:

Scale	Mother/Father
Conduct Problem	82/66
Learning Problem	91/67
Psychosomatic	91/53
Impulsive-Hyperactive	68/51
Anxiety	62/52
Hyperactivity Index	85/60

It is noteworthy that the Conners produces lower Impulsive-Hyperactive scores than were obtained on the CBCL Attention Problems scale. The Hyperactivity Index, however, does suggest considering the ADHD diagnosis based on maternal ratings.

These scores, like those of the CBCL, raise questions that require further data collection. Why are mother's ratings so much more severe than father's? (The answer to this is already known, as mother's stress was documented earlier.) With so many scale elevations how can a differential diagnosis be made? Given all of the scale elevations, where should intervention be targeted initially? None of these questions is answered by the Conners in isolation.

Finally, administration of the Conners' and CBCL seems somewhat redundant in this case. If a child's problems are localized to inattention, impulsivity, and hyperactivity, the Conners-48 may suffice. If, however, other problems are suspected or need to be screened (e.g., depression) then the breadth of the CBCL is more desirable.

Strengths and Weaknesses

Some of the strengths of the Conners are:

1. The availability of complementary teacher and parent forms
2. Response forms that are easily completed by parents and easily scored by clinicians

Some characteristics that may be considered weaknesses are:

1. Response forms that provide little space for demographic information
2. Uniform negative wording of items, which does not discourage a negative response set
3. Meager reliability and validity evidence for the scales
4. Few details of norming, scaling, or other psychometric topics included in the manual. (The Conners (1989) manual exemplifies an inadequate test manual.)

There is serious question as to whether or not the Conners-93 and -48 can be used as norm referenced measures. They may be useful for pre- and post-testing purposes in drug studies, but their diagnostic usage is compromised by little evidence to support the adequacy of the norm-referenced scores. Consequently, until further evidence of psychometric integrity is offered, the T-scores yielded should be considered suspect unless they are corroborated by other sources. Merrell (1994) reinforces this opinion by observing that "the size of the CPRS-48 norm population is relatively small, and the geographic and racial composition of the norm sample is so limited that the generalizability of the norm-based scores should be questioned" (p. 81). Aman (1994) expresses additional reservations about the use of the Conners with children who have diagnoses of mental retardation.

Devereux Scales of Mental Disorders

The Devereux Scales of Mental Disorders (DSMD; Naglieri, LeBuffe, & Pfeiffer, 1994) is essentially a new instrument, although it is based on an older form. This new version is designed for ages 5–18 (two forms with 111 items for ages 5–12 and 110 items for ages 13–18).

The DSMD is somewhat novel in that either parents or teachers can serve as raters. This unusual approach makes the assumption that the item content is appropriate for both audiences. Only time will tell if this is the case. Teachers or parents will likely inform the DSMD user if they think that some of the item content is inappropriate for them. The research on parental use of the scale will be discussed here, and the separate school form that is used exclusively by teachers will be presented in Chapter 8.

The DSMD is designed to indicate whether a child or adolescent is experiencing or is at risk for an emotional or behavioral disorder. In addition, the DSMD is based on DSM-IV categories and is purportedly useful for intervention planning and evaluation.

Scale Content

The items were reportedly selected using both rational and empirical means, with special attention given to sampling DSM-IV criteria. Three composite scores are available, based on two scales associated with each. A fourth total composite score is also available that summarizes all of the scales. The DSMD only samples problem behaviors, to the exclusion of adaptive scales or behaviors.

Sample item content for the scales and the contributors to each composite are shown as follows:

INTERNALIZING COMPOSITE

Anxiety Scale (Anx)—appetite problems, sleep problems, fears, somatic complaints, compulsions, easily duped by others, fatigue, and self-deprecation

Depression Scale (Dep)—social anxiety, depressed affect, withdrawal, suicidal ideation, and school refusal

CRITICAL PATHOLOGY COMPOSITE

Autism Scale (Aut)—excitable, confused, easily startled, lack of fear of injury, and restricted or stereotypic interests

Acute Problems Scale (AP)—self-injurious behavior, pica, runaway behavior, bowel problems, substance abuse, fire setting, hallucinations, and animal torture

EXTERNALIZING COMPOSITE

Conduct Scale (Con) (ages 13–18 only)—ill tempered, fighting, deceit, concentration problems, blames others, vengeful, and failure to finish activities

Delinquency Scale (Del) (ages 13–18 only)—truancy, cheating, theft, and substance abuse

Attention Scale (Att) (ages 5–12 only)—concentration problems, restlessness, daydreaming, distractibility, and inattention

The degree to which DSM-IV criteria and rational means were used to assign items to scales is not clear. For example, at ages 5 to 12 years, items related to runaway behavior and substance abuse are included on the Acute Problems scale and not on the Conduct scale. This item placement is potentially confusing to users who are aware that runaway behavior is listed in DSM-IV under the criteria for the diagnosis of conduct disorder. This lack of adherence to DSM-IV criteria is not explained fully. Item placement that is obviously inconsistent with the DSM-IV suggests that the examiner may have to carefully review item content before drawing conclusions about scale elevations.

Administration and Scoring

According to the manual, the DSMD can be completed by any adult (parent, teacher, or other) who has known the child for at least 4 weeks. The form can be completed in approximately 15 minutes.

Only hand scoring is currently available. While the forms are not particularly difficult to use, they require enough effort to suggest that many users may prefer computer-scoring.

Norming

Separate sex norms are available and based on a recent national sample of 3,153 cases. The sample was selected to represent 1990 U.S. Census Bureau and other governmental agencies' statistics.

The match of the sample to these statistics is typically good, although it appears that low SES groups are slightly underrepresented. The norms at some age groups are also based on rather small samples. The norms for girls and boys at age 5, for example, are based on 66 and 78 cases respectively. The size of the norming sample at age 18 is unacceptable. The sample of 18-year-old boys is only 38, and for girls only 48.

The derived T-scores are based on a linear transformation that maintains the shape of the original raw score distributions. Each composite is based on the sum of scores for its two constituent scales, and the total composite is based on the sum for the six scales.

Reliability

The internal consistency coefficients for the composites are generally good, usually exceeding .90. The internal consistency estimates for the scales are similarly high, with most coefficients being in the .80s and .90s. The lone exception is the Delinquency scale as rated by parents, where the coefficients were .74 for males and .70 for girls.

Some of the test-retest and interrater data suggest that attention should be paid to the qualifications of

the rater. The test-retest coefficients for a sample of teachers, for example, were significantly higher than the coefficients for a sample of residential staff. The staff test-retest coefficients dipped to .41 on the Anxiety scale and .49 for the internalizing composite. The result, however, should be considered tentative because of the minimal sample size of 18 cases. In an interrater study comparing the ratings of teachers and teachers aides the coefficients again faltered. The median coefficient for the scales in this study was .50. This coefficient seems a little low given that the teachers and aides seemed to be working for some time in the same classrooms with the same children. Until the results of future studies produce better reliability coefficients, these early studies suggest that the ratings may not be comparable for teachers, parents, and, particularly, others, even though the item content is identical.

Validity

To the credit of the DSMD, several aspects of validity are addressed in the manual. Facets of content, criterion, and construct validity are discussed in some detail.

Efforts were made to enhance content validity of the item pool at large by ensuring good correspondence between the items and DSM criteria. It is not clear, however, whether efforts were made to apply similar methods to establish the content validity of the scales, as alluded to earlier.

Exploratory factor analyses were also conducted with item level data in order to define the number of scales. This procedure suggests that items were initially assigned to scales based exclusively on empirical means.

The differential validity (Anastasi, 1988) of the scales was assessed by comparing the results of various clinical samples including children diagnosed with conduct disorder, attention-deficit hyperactivity disorder, anxiety disorders, depressive disorders, autistic disorder, and psychotic disorder (Naglieri, LeBuffe, & Pfeiffer, 1994). Further validity studies were conducted comparing nondiagnosed children with those carrying some sort of diagnosis such as seriously emotionally disturbed. As would be expected, large T-score differences were found between such groups. These studies provide a good starting point for future studies that assess differential validity with discriminant function and other more sophisticated analyses.

Evidence of criterion-related validity, using other tests as a standard, are notably lacking in the manual. Hence, the degree to which the DSMD measures constructs similar to those of other instruments is not yet known.

Interpretation

Several interpretive procedures are described in the DSMD manual, accompanied by a couple of case studies. Some of the advised interpretive algorithms include (Naglieri, LeBuffe, & Pfeiffer, 1994):

1. Individual scale elevations of T-scores of greater than or equal to 60 as indicative of significant problems in a domain
2. A means for making intraindividual (ipsative) comparisons)
3. Guidance for identifying individual items that signify significant problems
4. Comparisons of T-scores across raters
5. Advice for considering pretest-posttest comparisons
6. A procedure described by the authors as treatment outcome–based interpretation

Strengths and Weaknesses

The DSMD possesses strengths of:

1. A modern normative base that engenders confidence in the obtained scores
2. Reasonable and practical test length
3. A brief but helpful manual that includes information about expected changes in scores over time that may be useful for treatment evaluation
4. High level of reliability for the three composites

Among the weaknesses of the DSMD are:

1. A limited number of scales (six) which hinders problem coverage and creates more opportunity to miss important information (For example, assessment of ADHD is limited because of the lack of an attention problems scale at the adolescent level and the unavailability of a hyperactivity scale at either level.)
2. A lack of evidence of content validity for the construction of the scales
3. No computer-scoring option
4. No formal validity scales

Personality Inventory for Children-Revised

The Personality Inventory for Children (PIC-R; Wirt et al., 1990) was one of the earliest and remains among the most well known of parent rating scales. In fact, the development of the PIC followed closely on the heels of the MMPI, with much of the early development work taking place in the 1950s. The PIC is a 420-item rating scale designed for use with parents of children between the ages of 3 and 16 years.

Scale Content

The PIC scales, for the most part, have a long clinical history. The PIC includes scales that were developed via empirical means with considerable use of external validation techniques and scales developed through rational/theoretical means.

Scales developed through rational means include Lie, Development, Somatic Concern, Depression, Family Relations, Withdrawal, Anxiety, and Social Skills. Lachar (1990) gives a glimpse of the method used to develop these scales in the 1960s and 1970s by Klinedinst:

Items were nominated for the PIC item pool by four or more experienced judges who were provided detailed instructions and material describing the content areas for which they were to select items. Items included in an initial scale met two criteria: 1) At least three-fourths of the judges had to nominate the item for placement on the scale, and 2) a majority of the judges had to key the item in the same direction. (p. 40)

In the following list, each scale is identified in parentheses as being developed primarily by either empirical or rational means.

Lie Scale (L). The (rational) L scale was intended to "identify a defensive response set manifested by a tendency to ascribe the most virtuous of behaviors and to deny minor, commonly occurring behavior problems in the child described" (Lachar, 1990a).

Frequency Scale (F). This (empirical) scale was designed to identify two response sets, either exaggeration of problems or random responding.

Defensiveness Scale (DEF). As its name states, this (empirical) scale is designed to measure the tendency of a parent to be defensive about a child's behavior during an evaluation (Lachar, 1993).

Adjustment Scale (ADJ). The (empirical) Adjustment scale serves as a screener. Elevated scores may reflect poor mental health adjustment and a need for psychological evaluation.

Achievement Scale (ACH). The (empirical) Achievement scale is intended to reveal problems with academic underachievement. Significant scores would cause a psychologist to consider assessing for the presence of a learning disability or other problem that could be adversely affecting academic attainment.

Intellectual Screening Scale (IS). The (empirical) IS scale serves as an intelligence screener. Follow-up testing with an individually administered intelligence measure would be warranted when low scores are obtained that cannot be explained by other variables.

Development Scale (DVL). The (rational) DVL scale was constructed by asking clinicians to identify items that were indicators of delayed intellectual and/or physical development. Again, significant scores suggest further testing in the intellectual, adaptive behavior, and perhaps other domains.

Somatic Concern Scale (SOM). The (rational) SOM scale is composed of items that judges identified as measuring variables related to a child's health status, including frequency and seriousness of somatic complaints and illnesses, adjustment to illness, appetite and eating habits, sleep patterns, energy and strength, headaches and stomachaches, as well as the physical basis for symptoms (Lachar, 1990a).

Depression Scale (D). The (rational) D scale was also designed by expert judges who defined the content. Items were selected that fit the judges' definition of depression as proposed by the Group for the Advancement of Psychiatry (Lachar, 1990a). An interesting study would be to have expert judges check this scale against current DSM diagnostic criteria to see if the items have stood the test of at least a quarter century of change.

Family Relations Scale (FAM). This (rational) content scale was designed to assess family effectiveness and cohesion. Furthermore, FAM was constructed to assist in determining the role that family and parental characteristics play in the development of child psychopathology, as well as to measure the need for in-depth assessment of family and parental characteristics (Lachar, 1990a).

Delinquency Scale (DLQ). This (empirical) scale shows its age similarly to the D scale. The term *delinquent* has become colloquial and is not supported by the DSM nomenclature. Again, the degree to which the items would be identified by experts as overlapping with current diagnostic criteria such as those for conduct disorder would be of interest. Items assess opposition to limits imposed by others, smoking, alcohol use, runaway behavior, irritability, unhappiness, impulsivity, school problems, swearing, and nervousness.

Withdrawal Scale (WDL). The (rational) WDL scale includes items designed to measure withdrawal from social contact. According to the authors, the dimensions used to guide item selection included degree of enjoyment of social interactions, desire to remain isolated, number of friends, discomfort in social situations, preference for isolated activities, distrust of others, avoidance of people, and emotional detachment (Lachar, 1990a). Items assess lethargy, social isolation, excessive television viewing, fear of meeting new people, shyness, tendency to play alone, lack of self-disclosure, interest in working puzzles and reading the dictionary.

Anxiety Scale (ANX). The (rational) Anxiety scale is composed of items nominated by judges as measuring the various manifestations of anxiety: limited frustration tolerance, exaggeration of problems and concerns, worries that reflect parental concerns, behavioral and physiological correlates of anxiety, irrational fears and worries, and nightmares (Lachar, 1990a). Items assess unhappiness, moodiness, fears, worry, seriousness, crying spells, and seeking reassurance. The ANX scale shares an excessive number of items with the D scale making the scales virtually indistinguishable. In fact, 17 of the 30 items (57%) are common, which leads one to question why both scales are offered. The amount of correlation due to overlap between the two scales is given as .46 (Lachar, 1990a, table 52). The correlation between the two scales is substantial at .81 for a clinical sample (Lachar, 1990a, table 53). In this way the PIC-R reveals its MMPI lineage in that both instruments can be criticized for item overlap across scales.

Psychosis Scale (PSY). The (empirical) PSY scale was designed by selecting items that differentiated children with behavior typically defined as psychotic from normal, behaviorally disturbed nonpsychotic children and retarded children (Lachar, 1990). Items assess lack of friendships, delayed toilet training, screaming, disrobing outdoors, limited verbalization, delayed ability to ride a tricycle, crying spells, and lack of belief in God.

Hyperactivity Scale (HPR). The (empirical) HPR scale, like the D scale, was constructed based on dated criteria—the DSM III (1983). Consequently, hyperactivity items were selected if they differentiated hyperkinetic children from children with other types of clinical problems, while ADHD subtypes such as the new ADHD Primary Inattentive Type were apparently not con-

sidered. Items assess cheating, stubbornness, temper outbursts, distrust of others, sloppiness, peer problems, bragging, and worry about hurting someone.

Social Skills Scale (SSK). The (rational) SSK is a measure of adaptive skills in the social realm including the ability to lead and to follow, level of active participation in organized activities, self-confidence and poise in social situations, and social comprehension and tact in interpersonal relations. SSK items assess lack of friends, peer rejection, lack of leadership, preference for interacting with adults, stubbornness, little participation in clubs, and being a sore loser.

Critical Items. These items were selected based on both rational and empirical methods. Items were initially selected if it was thought that they contained information that required further investigation (Lachar, 1990a). Then these selections were checked for the rarity of their endorsement in the normative and clinical samples.

Administration and Scoring

The PIC-R includes three forms containing 131, 280, and 420 items respectively. The PIC-R has often been perceived as impractical because of its length. While this concern has been muted by the availability of the 131-item short form, this form offers only four factor scales as compared to the full complement of scales that can be obtained with the CBCL, BASC-PRS, or other measures.

Items are read by the parent from a booklet and the responses are placed on a separate response sheet. This format introduces more opportunity for error, as alignment of the items with answer spaces becomes the responsibility of the parent. The PIC-R differs from other parent rating scales in using a dichotomous (true/false) response format for each item.

The WPS Test Report is also offered for the PIC-R in both personal computer and mail-in formats. The computerized version can reduce clerical errors and it offers more assistance for interpretation, such as actuarially based interpretations.

For the hand-scoring version (which records the

parent's responses for profiling with carbon paper inserts) raw scores are computed with the assistance of self-contained templates. The use of carbon paper eliminates the need for separate templates or overlays.

A separate Profile Form is required in order to compute T-scores. The use of this form is rather cumbersome; it requires the clinician to select the correct form (or side of the form) based on the child's age (3–5 or 6–16), gender, and the length of the version used (131- and 280-item versions are on one side of the form with the 420-item version on the reverse). The 420-item version, however, can be obtained only on the computer-scored version. At any rate, the potential confusion to the new PIC-R user is obvious.

The primary reason for the onerous Profile Form selection process is that it eliminates the need for selecting norm tables. The raw score to T-score conversion is offered on the form itself. PIC-R, then, offers linear T-scores based on gender and two age groups. According to Lachar (1990a) analyses were conducted in order to determine whether or not separate norms were required for specific age groups. The developers used a criterion of a 1/4 to 1/2 SD difference between age group and total group means as an indication that age differences were large enough to warrant separate norms by age group. The Intellectual Screening scale was the only one found to produce age group differences of this magnitude.

It is not clear, however, if this same criterion was applied to gender differences. A perusal of the gender norms for ages 6 to 16 does not argue strenuously for gender norms. Entering tables B-1 and B-2 with a raw score of 20 produces only four gender differences of 1/2 SD or more in T-score units (5 points) and only two on the clinical scales. The girls had a Delinquency T-score of 80 versus 73 for boys and the boys had an Anxiety score of 92 versus 87 for girls. The average T-score by gender for the 18 scales represented in these norm tables is 83.7 for boys and 84.3 for girls. This crude analysis of gender differences merely generates a question about the necessity of gender-differentiated norms for all scales. Norms are not offered for the total standardization sample or for a clinical sample.

The PIC-R manual (Lachar, 1990) provides one of the more thorough treatises on interparent agreement. Lachar (1990a) concludes that:

> In general, interparent agreement is lower than that found for mothers over repeated testings. Because the normative data and most of the validity and reliability studies are based on maternal report, fathers should serve as the sole informant only when a mother or mother surrogate is unavailable. (p. 118)

Norming

The PIC norming sample does not meet modern norming standards. Among other questionable practices the sample was only collected in the Minneapolis area, SES data were collected only for a subset of the sample, race or ethnicity data are not reported, and the match of the sample characteristics to U.S. Census or some other standard is not given.

The norm sample could be dated. Although it is not absolutely clear from reading the manual, it appears that much of the normative data were collected in the 1960s. The effect of renorming on parent rating scale norms is not as clear as it is for intelligence or adaptive behavior scales where there is abundant evidence that the date of the norming sample affects the derived scores (Kamphaus, 1993). A study comparing the PIC-R norms to a modern sample is needed to lay this issue to rest.

PIC-R T-scores are linear conversions rather than normalized standard scores, with the skewness of the individual scales clearly reflected. These norms then differ from the CBCL normalized T-scores which serve to mute the skewness of the CBCL scales.

Reliability

Internal consistency coefficients for the scales are for the most part acceptable, ranging from .57 for Intellectual Screening to .86 for Depression (Lachar, 1990). Scales with the lowest internal consistency coefficients include Intellectual Screening, Achievement, and Hyperactivity.

The results of test-retest studies are also generally supportive (see Table 7.4). These studies show good short-term stability for the scales, with the exception of the Defensiveness scale, which also produced a mediocre internal consistency coefficient. The utility of the Defensiveness scale is questionable based on these findings.

Validity

A factor analysis of the PIC-R scales reported in the manual (Lachar, 1990a) produced five factors; Acting Out/Conduct Disorder/Externalization, Cognitive Development, Psychopathology/Internalization, Activity Level, and Somatic Concern. These factors were used for the selection of scales to use in subsequent validity studies (Lachar, 1990a). Factor scales, however, were not constructed for use in these analyses.

The PIC-R has been the recipient of considerable creative validation work including external validation of core profile types. LaCombe et al. (1991), for ex-

TABLE 7.4   PIC-R Scales and Reliability Estimates

Validity Scales	Median Reliability
Lie (L)	.82
Frequency (F)	.72
Defensiveness (DEF)	.50
Adjustment (ADJ)	.91
Clinical Scales	
Academic Achievement (ACH)	.90
Intellectual Screening (IS)	.82
Developmental (DVL)	.86
Somatic Concern (SOM)	.68
Depression (D)	.93
Family Relations (DAM)	.94
Delinquency (DLQ)	.81
Withdrawal (WDL)	.92
Anxiety (ANX)	.85
Psychosis (PSY)	.89
Hyperactivity (HPR)	.81
Social Skills (SSK)	.93

NOTE: These scales are for the 280- and 420-item versions of the PIC-R. Reliability estimates are medians based on three studies from Lachar (1990a).

ample, made an effort to identify case history correlates of PIC-R core profiles in previous cluster analysis studies (see Chapter 2). Previous studies have identified 12 core profiles, and each profile has been associated with concurrent variables such as intelligence, achievement, and special education placement. As an example, members of profile type 12 (Intellectual Screening T < 70, and Achievement and Development > 60) were found to have learning problems without obvious cognitive impairment (LaCombe et al., 1991).

In the Lacombe et al. (1991) investigation, profile types 1 through 12 were linked to historical information available for each case fitting the profile. Children who displayed profile 12 were found to have lower rates of problems as infants and preschoolers than base rates; also, about one half (43%) of these cases were recommended for regular classrooms but with remedial instruction (e.g., resource rooms; base rate = 21%) (LaCombe et al., 1991). Studies of this nature not only provide validation evidence for various empirically identified profiles but also yield considerable interpretive guidance for the clinician.

Interpretation

Lachar (1990a) suggests interpreting the PIC-R using three methods; (1) analysis of individual scale elevations, (2) interpretation of scale profile patterns, and (3) comparison of profiles to those obtained for various clinical and nonclinical samples.

Much of the 1990(a) manual by Lachar is devoted to the presentation of mean profiles of various samples (e.g., general child, mentally retarded, and cerebral dysfunction samples). Some of these samples, however, may not be current and hence their meaningfulness as criterion samples is suspect. The general sample (Seat, 1969), for example, was collected at a time when referral reasons may have differed. If a clinical sample were collected at many clinics today, there would likely be many more ADHD referrals than years ago given increased parental knowledge about the syndrome due to media coverage. The mentally retarded sample could also benefit from cross-validation since it is not current and it was made up of only 85 boys and 53 girls (Lachar, 1990a).

A PIC-R sample case is offered next.

Sample Case

Crew is a 4-year-old boy who was referred by the preschool intervention team because of concerns about inattention, overactivity, poor peer interactions, and delayed language development.

Crew was born at home without the benefit of any medical attention. The delivery was reportedly unexpected. He fell to the floor at some point during parturition, sustaining some head injury.

Most of Crew's developmental milestones were delayed, especially language. He did not speak his first words until age 2 years. His medical history is significant, with frequent upper respiratory infections and ear infections.

As a toddler, Crew began demonstrating significant behavior problems including frequent temper tantrums, overactivity, inability to sleep, and oppositional behavior. At age 2 he had frequent episodes of head banging. In preschool he rarely speaks, and he has significant behavior problems. His mother reports numerous difficulties with child care, saying that no one wants to baby-sit for him after a single experience.

The following observations were made during testing.

Throughout the evaluation, Crew demonstrated short attention span and a high level of motor activity. He shifted frequently from one toy to another, did not sit still, was easily distracted by other objects in the room, squirmed when attempts were made to keep him from running down the halls, and ran without looking where he was going when not held firmly. When he was unable to take toys with him, Crew displayed tantrum behavior (e.g., kicking and crying).

Crew's cognitive assessment results revealed strengths in motor skill areas with scores in the average range. On the other hand, his verbal skill measures were found to be far below the second percentile rank. Although he passed an audiological screening, he showed significant deficits in both expressive and receptive language skills.

Behavior ratings revealed significant problems in many areas. Crew's PIC-R T-scores are:

Factor I—Undisciplined	86
Factor II—Social Incompetence	58
Factor III—Internalization	54

Factor IV—Cognitive Development	73
Lie	49
Frequency	80
Defensiveness	50
Adjustment	97
Achievement	58
Intellectual Screening	76
Development	59
Somatic Concern	55
Depression	59
Family Relations	53
Delinquency	85
Withdrawal	54
Anxiety	60
Psychosis	117
Hyperactivity	65
Social Skills	66

The PIC-R findings confirm other sources of information about Crew. His developmental delays, particularly in language, are revealed on the Development and Psychosis scales. His behavior problems are reflected on the Delinquency and Psychosis scales. Crew's overactivity is revealed to some extent by the Hyperactivity scale score in the borderline range.

After considering the results from several additional measures, the psychologists assigned to this case made the diagnosis of expressive language disorder, receptive language disorder, and attention-deficits hyperactivity disorder, combined type.

Recommendations for Crew included continued speech/language therapy, medical evaluation, increased use of visual cues in school, preferential seating, provision of more opportunities for movement, minimizing distraction, contingent use of positive reinforcement, and more use of manipulatives during instruction, among others.

Strengths and Weaknesses

PIC-R strengths include:

1. A thorough manual by Lachar (1990a) that summarizes important validity studies

2. A large pool of research studies that provides insights into the value of individual scales and profiles

3. The inclusion of valuable interpretive guidance in the manual

Weaknesses of the PIC-R are:

1. Longer test length than many of its competitors
2. Dated normative sample, item selection criteria, and terminology
3. Excessive item overlap between scales (e.g., D and ANX)

The PIC-R is an innovator that could be considered the grandparent of many modern rating scales. As the first of its genre, it is probably more difficult to keep the scale updated.

Despite its original strengths, the PIC-R is plagued by more weaknesses in comparison to other scales. Unlike the CBCL, BASC, and others the PIC-R has not developed complementary teacher rating scales. In addition, the lack of modern norms is a glaring inadequacy. The most significant limitation of the PIC-R is a practical rather than high-minded one—test length. The availability of a short form that offers a limited number of scores is probably of little solace to clinicians. The CBCL, BASC, and others have successfully developed reliable and useful rating scales that are of roughly the same length as the shortest form of the PIC-R.

OTHER PARENT RATING SCALES

Attention Deficit Disorders Evaluation Scales

Scale Content

The ADDES (McCarney, 1989a) was designed specifically to assess for the presence of the core symptoms of ADHD; inattention, impulsivity, and hyperactivity. The ADDES includes a parent form that is labeled the Home Version for use with children 4½ to 20 years of age. The subscales were developed using rational-theoretical means.

Administration and Scoring

The ADDES Home Version rating form has some unusual characteristics. First, it is telegraphic. The form has the name of the disorder that it is trying to assess placed prominently on the front of the record form. Similarly, the three symptom clusters are listed on the front with the standard score and percentile rank score scales. Items are also grouped by symptom cluster.

The 46-item rating scale uses a 5-point scale where the parent has to place the number (value) associated with a rating in a box adjoining the item. For example, to indicate that a behavior occurs one to several times per hour, the parent has to place a 4 in the box next to the item. This system is unusual in that 5-point response scales are less common and, more importantly, the parent is required to remember this coding system, which may require considerable reference to the key given on the top of the page.

In lieu of using T-scores, a standard score scale with a mean of 10 is utilized. While most psychologists are used to this metric popularized by the Wechsler scales, it is a somewhat unconventional choice for a behavior rating scale.

Norming

Norms were computed based on a sample of 1,754 ratings of children. The sample was stratified by gender, race, community size, geographic area, grade level, and parental occupation.

The match of the standardization sample characteristics to U.S. Census data is good in comparison to many of the other measures discussed in this chapter. The racial/ethnic group representation of the sample, however, appears flawed. Citing census data as indicating that 86% of the population in 1980 is white is likely based on statistics for the entire population rather than on children who are of the target age for use of the ADDES. At younger age groups the U.S. population, even in 1980, is more diverse. The Kaufman Assessment Battery for Children (K-ABC), for example, which based its norming on the same census, selected 73.1% of their sample as white, reflecting the fact that for young children the proportion of cultural and/or racial minorities in the U.S. population is considerably larger than 14% (see Kaufman & Kaufman, 1983). It looks as though the ADDES underrepresented the diversity of the U.S. population.

Reliability

Internal consistency estimates for the ADDES are good, ranging from .93 to .95 for the subscales. Test-retest coefficients are similarly high, ranging from .90 for the Impulsive scale to .92 for Hyperactivity.

Validity

A factor analysis of the ADDES does not provide strong support for its rationally derived scale organization. The most questionable aspect of the ADDES is the Impulsive scale. This construct has proven difficult to measure with other tests because it overlaps so substantially with hyperactivity scales that the two are indistinguishable (Reynolds & Kamphaus, 1992). Similarly, the ADDES Hyperactivity scale correlates highly at .79 with the Impulsive scale.

A review of the factor-analytic results in the ADDES manual produces further questions. The Impulsive factor identified is very complex. Of the 15 items on the scale, 13 of them have significant secondary loadings on the Hyperactivity factor. Based on the loadings presented the evidence that the Impulsive scale measures a distinct construct is not compelling. Unfortunately, at the time of this writing an independent factor analysis of the ADDES could not be found.

In a related development the DSM-IV combines the hyperactivity and impulsivity symptoms rather than separating them. While it is conceptually appealing to separate the symptoms as part of assessment with the ADDES, there is more evidence in support of the contrary position (see Box 7.1 for an alternative method of ADHD assessment).

Strengths and Weaknesses

On the positive side the ADDES is
1. Brief and easy to administer and score

Weaknesses of the ADDES include:

1. A telegraphic record form that could encourage response sets

2. Questionable validity, particularly for the impulsivity construct

3. A focus on ADHD that requires that the scale be supplemented with other measures in order to rule out conduct disorder, a frequently comorbid problem

The ADDES may be too good to be true. It is brief, easy, and apparently highly interpretable. Some of these characteristics, however, are cause for concern given that the DSM-IV suggests that behavioral impulsivity is an elusive construct to measure. Similarly, the notion that ADHD occurs in isolation is disavowed by the ADDES, although its structure suggests the opposite. The ADDES is less practical when one considers that other parent rating scales would have to be used in addition to the ADDES, and several of these scales measure the inattention and hyperactivity symptoms as well as or better than the ADDES.

A recent comprehensive review of the ADDES by Silverthorn (1994) concluded that:

> However, the ADDES suffers from the inclusion of non-ADHD behaviors and the artificial use of a three scale structure when two would be more appropriate. In addition, it is unclear whether or not the ADDES is able to differentiate children with ADHD from other clinic-referred children. Based on correlations with other child behavior measures (e.g., Conners parent and teacher scales), which showed high correlations with other behavioral domains, it is not likely that the ADDES will be helpful in making differential diagnoses within behaviorally disordered children. (p. 12)

Temperament Assessment Battery for Children

The Temperament Assessment Battery for Children (TABC; Martin, 1988) was developed as a measure of broad behavioral tendencies of children age 3 through 7 years of age. This questionnaire is a modi-

Box 7.1

A Global Impairment Index

Recently, overall estimates of level of impairment are increasingly used in studies of child psychopathology. One such scale, the Child Global Assessment Scale (CGAS; Shaffer et al., 1983), is an adaptation of an adult scale designed to assess overall level of impairment at home, in school, or with friends (Wiessman, Warner, & Fendrich, 1990). The scale extends from a low of 1 (extremely impaired) to a high of 100 (no impairment). A parent, teacher, or interviewer is asked to rate the child on this scale where deciles are accompanied by a descriptor (e.g., 51–60, "some noticeable problems"). Previous studies have demonstrated some evidence of reliability and validity. A cut score is commonly used in studies of child psychopathology (e.g., CGAS ≤ 70 identifies a clinical case).

The CGAS was used as one of the criteria for validating the DSM-IV criteria for the diagnosis of ADHD (Lahey et al., in press). Lahey et al. used a CGAS score of 60 or less as an indication of significant impairment associated with symptoms of ADHD. A noteworthy finding of this study was the differential results for the parent and teacher CGAS scores. The parent CGAS scores were significantly related to symptoms of hyperactivity/impulsivity but not to inattention. Teacher CGAS scores were not significantly related to hyperactivity/impulsivity problems. These same teacher scores were, however, related to ratings of academic problems. The Lahey et al. investigation then used the relationship between teacher and parent CGAS scores and inattention symptoms to shape the DSM-IV criteria for inattention problems associated with ADHD.

What is the future of impairment indexes such as the CGAS? Several measurement issues are yet to be resolved, such as the time frame of the rating. Some recommend that the impairment rating be based on average lifetime functioning, while others have suggested that average level of functioning in the 1 year prior to evaluation is a better time frame for everyday clinical assessment practice (Weissman, Warner, & Fendrich, 1990).

Furthermore, the accuracy of CGAS ratings (as is the case for all ratings) depends heavily on the rater's knowledge of the child's functioning in a variety of spheres (Weissman, Warner, & Fendrich, 1990). Can parents, for example, validly rate school and peer functioning as is required by the CGAS?

Are there better substitutes for impairment indexes? A study by Bird et al. (1990) found a strong association between CGAS scores and the Total T-score of the CBCL. The most impaired group had a mean Total T of 70, the next most impaired group had a mean of 67, the next group produced a mean of 59, and the no-diagnosis group mean was 53 (Bird et al., 1990). Future studies may reveal that there are other psychometrically sound options for the CGAS, but it is even more likely that measures of impairment will see increasing use in clinical assessment practice.

fication of the Thomas, Chess, and Korn Teacher Temperament Questionnaire (Thomas & Chess, 1977) and is based on the Thomas and Chess model of the structure of early childhood temperament. It consists of three forms: a parent (48 items), teacher (48 items) and brief clinician form, the latter being designed to code the behavior of children seen in a traditional psychometric evaluation. Each item of the parent and teacher forms is rated on a 7-point scale based on the frequency of occurrence of the behavior described in the item.

The construct of temperament, as utilized in this measure, was defined as a set of traits that are a subset of the broader construct of personality, but are distinguished from personality in that they (1) appear earlier in development, with most being apparent during the first year of life; (2) are grounded in the biology of the individual; (3) are conceptualized to be distinct from motivation; and (4) are the building blocks from which other personality traits are constructed through experience and maturation. There is no assumption that the traits that are measured in the preschool years by the TABC are a direct expression of genetic or biological effects, since by the 3rd through 7th year of life the expression of temperamental characteristics can be significantly altered through the interplay between experience and biological disposition.

Scale Content

The TABC was designed to assess six characteristics: Activity Level (primarily gross motor vigor and control of motor activity), Adaptability (the speed and ease of adjustment to an altered or novel social environment), Approach/Withdrawal (very similar to the concept of inhibition, it is a measure of the initial behavioral tendency in response to novelty), Emotional Intensity (variation in the vigor with which negative emotions are expressed), Distractibility (the ease by which a socialization agent can distract the child from an inappropriate behavior [parent form], or the tendency to have attention diverted by non task-relevant stimuli [teacher form]), and Task Persistence (a measure of attention span and the ability to continue working on a difficult learning task).

Examples of items used to assess each characteristic on the teacher form are as follows:

Activity Level: Child seems to have difficulty sitting still, may wiggle a lot or get out of seat. Child runs rather than walks.

Adaptability: Child will quickly adjust to a game if someone wants to play in a different way. If initially hesitant about entering into new games and activities, child quickly gets over this.

Approach/Withdrawal: Child will get up and perform before the class (sing, recite, etc.) with no hesitation, even the first time. When given a new school assignment, child responds with immediate interest.

Emotional Intensity: Child overreacts (becomes very upset) in a stressful situation. Child's responses are loud.

Distractibility: Child is among the first to notice if a messenger, parent, or another teacher comes into the room; child is distracted by other children's movement or talk when teacher is reading a story.

Task Persistence: If an activity is interrupted, the child tries to go back to the activity. Child practices new skills over and over.

Reliability

The internal consistency reliabilities for the six teachers scales of the TABC are: Activity .86; Adaptability, .83; Approach/Withdrawal, .83; Emotional Intensity, .76; Distractibility, .57; Task Persistence, .74 (Martin, 1988). Internal consistencies for parent scales tend to be marginally lower. Temporal stability has been documented in several studies. In one example the stability of the teacher form was assessed in four different samples (Martin et al., 1986). For the two samples with a test-retest interval of 6 months the stability coefficients ranged from .70 (Adaptability and Distractibility) to .87 (Approach/Withdrawal). For the two samples in which the test-retest interval was 12 months and involved different teachers at test and retest, the coefficients ranged from .40 (Approach/Withdrawal-sample 1) to .57 (Activity Level and Approach/Withdrawal-sample 2) with one exception. The stability coefficients for Adaptability were not significantly different from zero.

Validity

The validity of the TABC has been examined in a number of different studies, with strongest data available on the teacher form. For the teacher form, TABC scores have been found to be correlated with scholastic achievement contemporaneously and over 1, 5, 7, and 9 years (Dresden, 1994; Martin, 1989; Martin, Nagle, & Paget, 1984), with individually and group-measured cognitive ability (Martin & Holbrook, 1985), teacher attitudes toward children (Martin, Nagle, & Paget, 1984) and observed behavior in the classroom (Martin, Nagle, & Paget, 1984). It has also been shown to differentiate between children with learning disabilities and children without disabilities (Cardell & Parmer, 1988), and among ADHD, emotionally/behaviorally disordered, and normal children (Love & McIntosh, 1994).

Some of the most interesting work with the parent measure is Brody and Stoneman's studies of parenting of siblings. They found that parents who view their children as less well-adjusted are more likely to rate their children as having temperaments that are less persistent and highly active, or more emotionally intense (Brody, Stoneman, & Burke, 1988). Also, in families in which the younger sibling displays more antagonistic behavior (pushing, hitting, yelling, etc.) during sibling interaction, the older sibling is more likely to have rated as having a highly active temperament (Brody, Stoneman, & Burke, 1987). Parental ratings of temperament have also been found to relate to behavior in school. For example, Newman and Matsopoulos (1994) found that parent ratings of negative emotionality, poor adaptability, high activity level, and lowered task persistence predicted teacher ratings of first-grade reading ability.

The TABC is in the process of being reformulated and renormed. Called the TABC-R, the new measure will be more strongly based on current temperament research, on factor-analytic results from several countries of temperament measurement instruments, and of extensive factor analytic study of the TABC. Many of the scales will be very similar to those previously assessed; the TABC-R will additionally assess five characteristics in a somewhat shorter format.

(The authors wish to express their appreciation to Dr. Roy P. Martin, who contributed the section on the TAB-C.)

CONCLUSIONS

Parent rating scales are now common methods for assessing child problems. This shift is substantial given that not long ago there was not a specific technology for assessing child difficulties, characteristics, and assets. Formerly much of child assessment was conducted with adapted adult assessment methods (e.g. projective techniques).

Most importantly, the quality of parent rating scales has improved considerably. Scales such as the CBCL, DSMD, and BASC have national normative samples, which was an anomaly not that long ago (see Table 7.5).

The conclusion made by Martin (1988) unfortunately is still true—the psychometric properties of parent rating scales are still often lacking when compared to other domains of psychological assessment. Many scales lack national norms and supportive validity evidence for their scales. There is much work to be done to bring many parent rating scales to a

level of sophistication similar to that of intelligence and achievement testing. Even the best parent rating scales have to do a better job of scale construction and validation and make further attempts to eliminate threats to validity (see Box 7.2).

Box 7.2

Assessing Change

Assessment of change is important in clinical practice, particularly in light of increasing calls for accountability for the delivery of health care. Demonstration of utility for intervention planning and assessment is a tricky endeavor since psychometric evidence of validity is not clearly applicable. A measure designed for evaluating change, for example, may not need norms. Consequently, the quality of the norming sample is not relevant. Furthermore, it may not be necessary to total scores if one is interested only in change in individual behaviors. The Eyberg Child Behavior Inventory (ECBI; Eyberg & Ross, 1978) is an instrument that has a history of use for evaluating treatment results. Its usefulness for assessing particular constructs, however, is not well supported.

The ECBI is a 36-item parent rating scale designed to assess behavior problems in children for children age 2 through 17 years (Eyberg & Ross, 1978). Each item is rated in two ways: (1) a likert-type scale that is used for marking frequency, and (2) a dichotomous scale that the parent uses to identify if the scale is in fact a problem.

Recently the ECBI has been used as a measure of conduct-problem behaviors (Burns & Patterson, 1990). The ECBI does possess some advantages, including the fact that it provides an indication of both frequency and severity for individual behavior problems, which is not common for parent rating scales. This characteristic may make the scale particularly useful for planning and evaluating treatment.

The ECBI also produces total scores for both the frequency (Intensity) and severity (Problem) measures. The ECBI has been normed recently in the Seattle metropolitan area (Burns & Patterson, 1990).

We have expressed our belief that both theoretical and empirical means should be used for scale construction, including the assignment of items to scales. We favor this approach for several reasons, including the fact that many

(Cont.)

TABLE 7.5 Overview of Parent Rating Scales

Scale	Authors	Publisher	Content	Ages	NO	Reliability	Validity	MI
BASC-PRS	Reynolds & Kamphaus (1992)	American Guidance Service	Clinical Maladjustment, School Maladjustment, Personal Adjustment, Emotional Symptoms Index composites, 10 clinical scales, 4 adaptive scales, 5 validity indexes (152–186 items)	4–18	E	Internal consistency, test-retest, and interrater (.70s–.90s)	Support for factor structure, modest to high correlations with existing scales, lawful profiles for clinical samples	E
CBCL	Achenbach (1991)	Author, University of Vermont	Internalizing, Externalizing, Total T, Competence, 8 clinical scales, (113 items)	4–18	G	Internal consistency, test-retest, (.70s–.90s), and interrater	Support for factor structure, differential validity (non-handicapped vs. clinical groups),	P
CPRS	Conners (1989)	Multi-Health Systems, Inc.	CPRS-93, 9 clinical scales; CPRS-48, 5 clinical scales	3–17	P	Poorly documented	Scales based on factor analysis and Hyperactivity Index of both scales have consistently been proven to be sensitive to treatment effects	F

Scale	Authors	Publisher	Content	Ages	NO	Reliability	Validity	MI
DSMD	Naglieri, LeBuffe, & Pfeiffer (1994)	The Psychological Corporation	Autism, Acute Problems, Conduct, Anxiety, and Depression Scales. Internalizing, Externalizing, Critical Pathology, and Total Composites, 6 clinical scales, Attention (ages 5–12 only), and Delinquency (ages 13–18 only)	5–18	E	Coefficients in the .80s and .90s for scales and composites with few exceptions; test-retest and interrater coefficients suggest lack of interchangeability of raters	Content validity for total item pool, initial differential validity evidence	G
PIC-R	Lachar & Gruber (1994)	Western Psychological Services	9 clinical scales (additional subscales), 4 validity scales (270 items, 80 items on screening form)	9–18	G	Internal consistency and test-retest (.70s–.80s), lower estimates for subscales	Differential validity (nonhandicapped vs. clinical groups), modest to high correlations with other measures, case history correlates	F

NO = Evaluation of the scales' normative base evaluated as either E = Excellent, G = Good, F = Fair, and P = Poor.
MI = evaluation of the scales' enhancement of a multi-informant assessment.

BOX 7.2   *(Continued)*

of the statistics used to construct parent (and other) rating scales are fraught with problems, and, at least as often, scale construction statistics are misapplied. This is an example of a scale that is rather difficult to interpret in any sophisticated way for at least two reasons: (1) Rational/ theoretical approaches were not used extensively in scale construction, and (2) empirical methods of test construction may have been misapplied.

In the case of the ECBI an item blueprint is never specified. Were the items selected in order to measure a single syndrome (which is the suggestion since only total scale scores are provided) such as conduct disorder or ADHD? If so, what was the source of the item pool— research on conduct problems, epidemiological data regarding conduct problems, or the DSM? Is the scale intended to measure a theoretical construct? If so, what is the definition of this construct, do content experts such as eminent child clinicians agree on this definition? Such information would help clinicians understand the meaning of the obtained ECBI scores. In the absence of such content information they are left to interpret the scores as measures of behavior problems in children. Is it necessary to administer a scale and compute a score in order to draw such conclusions?

Psychometrically the ECBI is said to be internally valid (Eyberg & Ross, 1978) and homogeneous (Burns & Patterson, 1990). Again the clinician is given the impression that the ECBI measures a single construct. But the psychometric data for the ECBI call such conclusions into question. Burns and Patterson (1990), for exampale, noted that while the average item–total correlations for the items was .49, the values ranged from –.01 to .76. Why retain an item with an item–total correlation of –.01? A defensible reason would be content validity, but, failing that, an item with such a low item correlation may actually detract from the homogeneity and reliability of the scale (Anastasi, 1988).

Burns and Patterson (1990) also conducted principal component analyses of the two scores yielded by the ECBI and found that in both cases the first factor accounted for most of the variance in the scale (29% in one case and 24% in the other). Additional principal components accounted for significant amounts of variance, as much as 7%, but factor rotation was not conducted in order to evaluate these factors further (see Chapter 2), and multiple methods for selecting the number of relevant factors were not used (Gorsuch, 1983). Hence, while the authors' conclusion is that the ECBI is a homogeneous measure of

a single construct, this conclusion is not clearly supported by the data reported. Also of relevance is the fact that Burns and Patterson (1990) point out the heterogeneity of the scale later in their article by concluding, "Our hypothesis is that ECBI scores in the clinical range for younger children (ages 2–7 years) would show a mixture of oppositional defiant and attention-deficit hyperactivity disorders" (p. 396). Is this then a guide for interpreting the total ECBI score for younger children? Is the best conclusion that can be drawn something like "I think that your child has a mixture of oppositional defiant and ADHD disorders"? Such a conclusion would hardly be satisfying to referral sources such as parents.

The available research suggests that the ECBI may be useful for identifying treatment objectives for children referred for disruptive behavior problems and for evaluating response to treatment. When the ECBI is used for other purposes, such as norm-referenced assessment of constructs, research to date does not reveal significant evidence of construct validity (using the term as outlined by Anastasi, 1988). The ECBI is an excellent example of a scale that has some value only in the hands of the well-informed clinician who applies the scale only in circumstances where it possesses empirical strengths.

The utility of parent ratings for various purposes is just becoming understood. Their apparent ease of use and low cost will probably further enhance their popularity for both clinical and research purposes. In contrast, interpretation of these instruments can be fraught with problems due to the characteristics of the scales and the limitations of the psychologist's knowledge base. Much research is necessary to improve interpretive practice.

CHAPTER SUMMARY

1. Concerns about child self-reports and practicality have made parent rating scales commonplace in modern child assessment practice.

2. The Achenbach CBCL has long been considered one of the premier rating scale measures of child psychopathology.

3. The CBCL was a forerunner in the provision of composite scores reflecting the now customary internalizing and externalizing dimensions.

4. It is unusual by today's standards for the CBCL to combine constructs such as anxiety and depression, and hyperactivity and inattention, into single scales.

5. The CBCL continues to be a preferred choice of many child clinicians due to its history of successful use and popularity with researchers.

6. The development of the Personality Inventory of Children (PIC) followed closely on the heels of the MMPI, with much of the early development work taking place in the 1950s.

7. The PIC is a 420-item rating scale designed for use with parents of children between the ages of 3 and 16 years.

8. The PIC includes scales that were developed via empirical means with considerable use of external validation techniques, as well as scales developed through rational/theoretical means.

9. The PIC-R norming sample lacks sophistication. Among other questionable practices the sample was only collected in the Minneapolis area, SES data were collected only for a subset of the sample, race or ethnicity data are not reported, and the match of the sample characteristics to U.S. Census or some other standard is not given.

10. A factor analysis of the PIC-R scales produced five factors; Acting Out/Conduct Disorder/ Externalization, Cognitive Development, Psychopathology/Internalization, Activity Level, and Somatic Concern.

11. Despite its original strengths, the PIC-R is plagued by more weaknesses in comparison to other scales.

12. The Conners Parent Rating Scales are designed for ages 3 through 17. Two parent forms are available; a 93-item version and a 48-item version. The short form, however, is somewhat unique in that its content is not drawn exclusively from the long form.

13. Conners (1989) provides no information on the standardization of the scales in the manual above

and beyond the sample sizes. A section on norming is not included in the chapter on psychometric properties.

14. According to Conners (1989), some studies of discriminant validity have shown either the Conners-93 or -48 to differentiate boys with attention-deficit disorder and specific learning disabilities from matched normal controls, as well as boys with attention-deficit disorders and developmental reading disorders.

15. There is serious question as to whether or not the Conners-93 and -48 can be used as norm referenced measures. They may be useful for pre- and post-testing purposes in drug studies, but their diagnostic usage is compromised by the lack of evidence for the adequacy of the norm-referenced scores.

16. The Behavior Assessment System for Children (BASC) Parent Rating Scales (PRS) has three forms of similar items that span the preschool (4–5), child (6–11), and adolescent (12–18) age ranges. The PRS takes a broad sampling of a child's behavior in home and community settings.

17. The PRS was developed using both rational/ theoretical and empirical means in combination to construct the individual scales.

18. The general norm sample for the PRS included 309 preschoolers; 2,084 children; and 1,090 adolescents. Cases were collected at 87 test sites in 26 states.

19. Considerable factor-analytic validity evidence is provided in the PRS manual showing the existence of three factors; externalizing, internalizing, and adaptive.

20. The Attention Deficit Disorders Evaluation Scale (ADDES) Home Version was designed specifically to assess for the presence of the core symptoms of ADHD; inattention, impulsivity, and hyperactivity.

21. The ADDES Home Version rating form has some unusual characteristics. It telegraphs its intent more than other scales, which may contribute to response sets. The form has the name of the disorder that it is trying to assess placed

prominently on the front of the record form. Similarly, the three symptom clusters are listed on the front with the standard score and percentile rank scales. Items are also grouped by symptom cluster.

22. A factor analysis of the ADDES does not provide strong support for its rationally derived scale organization.

23. The DSMD is a new scale that is designed for ages 5–18 (two forms with 111 items for ages 5–12 and 110 items for ages 13–18). It includes six clinical scales and can be completed by parents, teachers, and other adults.

24. The DSMD norms at some age groups are also based on rather small samples. The norms for girls and boys at age 5, for example, are based on 66 and 78 cases respectively. The size of the norming sample at age 18 is unacceptable.

25. The Temperament Assessment Battery for Children (TABC; Martin, 1988) was developed as a measure of broad behavioral tendencies of children age 3–7 years of age.

26. The TABC was designed to assess six characteristics: Activity Level, Adaptability, Approach/Withdrawal, Emotional Intensity, Distractibility, and Task Persistence.

CHAPTER 8

Teacher Rating Scales

CHAPTER QUESTIONS

- Why are teachers important sources of information about a child's emotional and behavioral adjustment?

- What factors can influence how one interprets teacher information in clinical assessments of children and adolescents?

- What are some important differences between the major global rating scales that are available for use with teachers?

- What are some rating scales that allow teachers to provide information specific to a single dimension of psychological adjustment or to provide information on the degree of impairment associated with a child's emotional and behavioral functioning?

Although teachers have traditionally been considered an important source of information on children's academic performance, they often have not been used in the assessment of children's behavioral and emotional functioning. However, knowing how a child behaves in the classroom is important for several reasons. First, school is a setting in which the child spends the majority of his or her time. Therefore, a child's adjustment to the school setting can have a dramatic impact on his or her overall psychological functioning. Second, the multiple demands of the school environment (e.g., to stay seated, to follow demands of adults, to interact with classmates) present many challenges to the child, challenges that may not be present in other settings and that the child may experience problems in meeting. Third, the demands of the school setting change as a child progresses through school (e.g., demands for organization, the importance of social acceptance). Therefore, understanding school-related problems that are unique to a given period can provide clues to specific problems in adaptation that a child or adolescent might experience.

Based on these considerations, there is increasing interest in assessing a child's behavioral and emotional functioning in the school setting. Given the many advantages of behavior rating scales, such as time-efficiency and objectivity, it is not surprising that the primary assessment instruments for children's school behavior have been teacher-completed behavior rating scales. Suggestions for appropriate use of rating scales in general are presented in previous chapters and will not be repeated in full here. However, there are several considerations for interpreting information from teachers that warrant special attention.

FACTORS THAT INFLUENCE TEACHER RATINGS

The usefulness of teacher information may vary depending on what type of behavior is being assessed. Teachers are often considered the best source of information on a child's attention problems and overactivity because they have the opportunity to observe the child in a situation with high demands for sustained attention and inactivity (Loeber, Green, & Lahey, 1990; Loeber et al., 1991). In contrast, teachers' ratings tend to be less useful in assessing many types of antisocial behavior that are unlikely to occur in the school environment (e.g., fire setting, cruelty to animals) or for internalized types of problems that may not be readily observable in the classroom setting (Loeber et al., 1991).

The usefulness of teacher information may also vary according to the age of the child. Children in early elementary school frequently have one teacher who observes a child across several class periods, if not the entire school day. In contrast, high school teachers frequently have students for one class period during the day. Therefore, the usefulness of information decreases as a child advances in school and contact with any single teacher decreases (Edelbrock et al., 1985).

A final issue in interpreting teacher rating scales is understanding the "frame of reference" or standard used by teachers. As discussed in previous chapters and elsewhere (e.g., Piacentini, 1993), a number of characteristics of a rater can influence his or her judgment of the intensity, quality, and/or frequency of a child's behavior. In the case of teacher ratings a characteristic of teachers that can influence their ratings is their experience with many children

of the same age. This allows the teacher to make some internal normative comparison of a child's behavior with the behavior of other children the teacher has taught. This internal norm is a double-edged sword. It often gives the teacher a unique perspective of knowing both the individual child and knowing what are age-appropriate behaviors. However, some teachers, such as teachers who work in special education classrooms, may have a skewed base of comparison that could influence their ratings. That is, their ratings of a child's behavior may be influenced by a comparison of the child to other disturbed children.

Despite these cautions and limitations, we feel strongly that teacher ratings are an essential element of a comprehensive clinical assessment of children's behavioral and emotional functioning. The rest of this chapter is a selected review of several widely used teacher rating scales. Carlson and Lahey (1983), in an earlier review of teacher ratings, reported that most of the teacher rating scales available at that time suffered from significant psychometric problems in development and inadequate norming. As a result, the available scales were severely limited in their usefulness for clinical evaluations. Fortunately, since this 1983 review there have been numerous advances in the teacher rating scales or the emergence of new scales, with many of the inadequacies of earlier scales eliminated or greatly reduced. The following review of teacher rating scales highlights the basic characteristics of some specific scales, summarizes important psychometric properties of the scales, and summarizes the unique strengths and weaknesses of the scales that are most relevant to their use in clinical assessments of children and adolescents. As was stated in previous chapters, this broad overview of the various scales is not designed to replace information provided in the technical manuals that accompany these instruments, which should be reviewed by any user of the scales.

OMNIBUS RATING SCALES

The primary focus of this chapter is on rating scales that assess a broad array of children's emotional and behavioral functioning (omnibus scales), rather than on scales that focus on a single aspect of a child's functioning. In some cases a focused assessment in a single area (e.g., social skills) is warranted, and an overview of several single-domain rating scales is provided later in the chapter. However, the decision to focus primarily on omnibus rating scales was made based on research in developmental psychopathology. As discussed previously in Chapter 3, research on children's and adolescents' emotional and behavioral problems consistently indicates that youth with problems in adjustment typically have problems in multiple domains, spanning emotional, behavioral, social and learning arenas. Therefore, assessment instruments that span multiple psychological domains are required in most clinical assessments. As a result, we feel that most clinical assessments benefit from the use of global rating scales that cover multiple domains of child functioning. A summary of basic information on the omnibus rating scales reviewed in this chapter is provided in Table 8.1.

Behavior Assessment System for Children— Teacher Rating Scales

The BASC Teacher Rating Scales (BASC-TRS; Reynolds & Kamphaus, 1992) was designed to gather information on a child's observable behavior from the child's teacher and to place this information in the context of other information obtained in the overall BASC system (e.g., self-report scale, parent rating scales, classroom observation system). There are three forms of the BASC-TRS for preschool (ages 4–5), elementary school (6–11), and middle/high school (12–18) children. The three forms contain behavioral descriptors that are rated by the teacher on a 4-point scale of frequency, ranging from "Never" to "Almost Always". The three forms have 109 items, 148 items, and 138 items for the preschool, elementary school, and middle/high school versions respectively.

Content

The items of the BASC-TRS were chosen to measure multiple aspects of a child's personality and be-

havior, including both positive (adaptive) and pathological (clinical) dimensions. The rationale underlying the selection of the initial item pool was to include items indicative of constructs that (1) were found to be most useful to the authors in their own clinical practice, and (2) were frequently included in other behavior rating scales. The BASC-TRS items are grouped into five composite scales across all age ranges, with 14 narrow-band scales in the elementary and middle/high school versions and 10 narrow-band scales in the preschool version. The descriptive labels given to the composite scales and narrow-band scales are provided in Table 8.2. The content coverage of the BASC-TRS scales has several unique features relative to other teacher rating scales. First, it provides comprehensive coverage of several areas of adaptive behavior. Second, there are separate scales for motor hyperactivity and attentional difficulties, which aids in the differentiation of subtypes of attention-deficit hyperactivity disorder. Third, there are separate scales for anxiety, depression, and withdrawal, which aid in the assessment of emotional difficulties. Fourth, the BASC-TRS includes items that screen for learning problems that often accompany emotional and behavioral problems in children.

Administration and Scoring

The BASC-TRS is a relatively lengthy rating scale and takes approximately 15 to 20 minutes to complete. The cover of the record provides instructions to the teacher for completing the form and space for recording background information about the child and teacher (e.g., age, gender, type of class, length of time in class). The BASC-TRS was designed for easy hand-scoring. The top answer sheet is attached to a scoring sheet on which the teacher's responses appear by scale. This facilitates the summing of all items on a scale to determine the raw scale scores. Norm tables in the BASC manual are provided so that any of four sets of norms can be used: general, female, male, and clinical. Both T-scores and percentile ranks are listed for each set of norms.

An interesting and unique feature of the BASC-TRS scoring system is a table on the scoring sheet that allows one to compare the composite scores.

TABLE 8.1 Overview of Broad Teacher Rating Scales

Scale	Authors	Publisher	Content	Ages	NO*	Reliability	Validity	AI**
BASC-TRS	Reynolds & Kamphaus (1992)	American Guidance Service	Externalizing, Internalizing, Learning, Attention, & Adaptive, (109–148 items)	4–18	E	Internal consistency (m = .80), test-retest (m = .89), and interrater (m = .71)	Support for factor structure and high correlations with existing scales	E
CBCL-91-TRS	Achenbach (1991)	Author, University of Vermont	Internalizing, Externalizing, Social, & Attention (113 items)	4–18	F	Internal consistency (m = .87), test-retest (m = .92), & interrater (m = .55).	Support for factor structure and extensive research base on correlations with important criteria	E
CBRSC	Neeper, Lahey, & Frick, (1990)	Psychological Corporation	Attention, Anxiety, Learning, Cognitive, Conduct, & Social (70 items)	6–14	F	Internal consistency (median = .91) & test-retest (median = .94)	Support for factor structure and correlates with DSM diagnoses	P
CTRS-39 (& CTRS-28)	Conners (1989)	Multi-Health Systems, Inc	Attention, Hyperactivity, Conduct, & Anxiety—39 items (Conduct, Hyperactivity, & Attention—28 items)	4–12 (& 3–17)	P	Internal consistency (median = .84) & test-retest (.72–.91) (no reliability data available for CTRS-28)	Scales based on factor analysis; Hyperactivity Index of both scales has consistently been proven to be sensitive to treatment effects	F

Scale	Authors	Publisher	Content	Ages	NO*	Reliability	Validity	MI**
DBRS-SF	Naglieri, LeBuffe, & Pfeiffer (1993	Psychological Corporation	Interpersonal Problems, Inappropriate Behaviors/ Feelings, Depression, & Physical Symptoms/Fears (40 items)	5–18	E	Internal consistency (median = .87), test-retest (median = .83), & interrater (median = .52).	Discriminates between emotional disturbed and undisturbed children	E
RBPC	Quay & Peterson (1983)	Author, University of Miami	Conduct Problems, Attention/ Hyperactivity, Anxiety/ Withdrawal, Psychotic Behavior (89 items)	5–18	P	Internal consistency (.68–.95), test-retest (.49–.83), & interrater (.63–.97)	Factor structure consistently replicated; most scales show good concurrent validity	G

NOTE: BASC-TRS = Behavioral Assessment System for Children—Teacher Report Scales; CBCL-91-TRS = Teacher Rating Scales of the Child Behavior Checklist—1991 Version; CBRSC = Comprehensive Behavior Rating Scale for Children; CTRS = Conners Teacher Rating Scales; DBRS-SF = Devereux Behavior Rating Scales—School Form; RBPC = Revised Behavior Problem Checklist.

*NO = Evaluation of the scales' normative base evaluated as either Poor (P), Fair (F), Good (G), or Excellent (E).

**MI = Evaluation of the scales' aid in a multi-informant evaluation.

TABLE 8.2   Composites and Scales of BASC-TRS

Composite	Scales
Externalizing Problems	Aggression
	Hyperactivity
	Conduct Problems
Internalizing Problems	Anxiety
	Depression
	Somatization
School Problems	Attention Problems
	Learning Problems
Other Problems	Atypicality
	Withdrawal
Adaptive Skills	Adaptability
	Leadership
	Social Skills
	Study Skills

For example, one can determine whether the difference in T-scores between a child's Internalizing and Externalizing composite is statistically significant, and one can determine the frequency with which a discrepancy of this magnitude occurs in the normative sample. These data provide a basis for examining a child's unique strengths and weaknesses. Finally, the BASC-TRS scoring sheet highlights critical items (e.g., "I want to kill myself") that are clinically important.

Norming

The standardization and development of norms were conducted at 116 sites across the United States and Canada. The norming group included 333 preschoolers, 1259 elementary school children (ages 6–11), and 809 middle/high school students (ages 13–18) with fairly equal sex distributions in all age groups. The sampling procedures for obtaining the normative sample were designed to ensure an adequate representation of ethnic minorities, and, in fact, the sample had a slightly larger representation of African-American and Hispanic children than

would be expected based on 1986–88 U.S. population figures. However, the scores based on this normative sample are statistically weighted to more closely approximate census data. The normative sample closely approximates population statistics on the distribution of parental education level and percentage of children receiving special education services. The T-scores derived from this normative sample are based on a linear transformation of raw scores, which preserves the shape of raw score distributions. This means, however, that the various scales will not possess the same distribution and, as a result, the same T-score on different scales will not reflect the same percentile rank.

Reliability

The manual for the BASC-TRS (Reynolds & Kamphaus, 1992) provides evidence on three types of reliability: internal consistency, test-retest reliability, and interrater reliability. With very few exceptions the scales of BASC-TRS proved to be quite reliable in the normative sample. Coefficient alpha was used to make estimates of the internal consistency of scales, and these estimates tended to average above .80 across all age groups. In fact, across the 485 internal consistency coefficients (covering all scales across age and gender) only one, the Conduct Problems scales for girls ages 6–7, had questionable internal consistency (coefficient alpha = .48). Similarly, test-retest reliability over 2 to 8 weeks in samples of preschool (n = 58), elementary school (n = 90), and middle/high school (n = 98) children was high, with median correlation coefficients of .89, .91, and .82 in the three age groups respectively. Finally, the consistency of ratings between two teachers was tested in samples of preschool (n = 57) and elementary school–age (n = 30) children with high reliability estimates emerging in both samples (median coefficients of .63 and .71 respectively). Correlation coefficients were lower between teachers on internalizing (.43) than on externalizing (.65) behaviors, consistent with past research (Achenbach, McConaughy, & Howell, 1987). The only scale that emerged with questionable consistency between teachers was the Somatization scale in preschoolers (r = .27).

Validity

The manual of the BASC-TRS provides factor analytic support for the construct validity of the scales and provides correlations between the BASC-TRS scales and several other teacher rating scales. In general, the BASC-TRS scales exhibit high correlations with analogous scales from other teacher rating scales. However, validity information for the preschool version is limited to one study of 92 preschool children (mean age 4 years, 8 months) correlating the scores on the BASC-TRS with analogous scales on the Conners Teacher Rating Scales (CTRS-39; Conners, 1989). The BASC-TRS manual provides mean T-scores of several clinical groups so that clinical profiles of children in these groups, relative to the normative sample, could be determined. However, there were no tests directly testing the BASC-TRS scales' utility in distinguishing *within* these clinic groups. In fact, it appears that many of the clinic groups share scale elevations. Therefore, the *specificity* of scale elevations on the BASC-TRS to single clinic groups is still in question.

Interpretation

The BASC-TRS contains a fake bad index (F), which helps to assess the possibility that a teacher rated a child in an overly negative pattern. Therefore, interpretation of this scale should be the first step in the interpretative process, providing a context for the interpretation of the remainder of the BASC-TRS protocol. However, while high scores on the F-scale often indicate a negative bias, in rare cases it can indicate the presence of extraordinary maladaptive behaviors.

Because of the lack of specific associations with elevations on the individual clinical scales and because higher reliability is obtained at global scale levels, it is recommended that interpretation start at a global level and move toward a more specific level. The most global level of interpretation is the Behavioral Symptoms Index, which is a combination of the clinical composite scales and provides an index of the overall level of problem behavior, much like the concept of "g" in the interpretation of intelligence tests. The next level of interpretation is the four composite scales of Adaptive Skills, School Problems, Internalizing Problems, and Externalizing Problems. The third level of interpretation is at the level of the 14 clinical scales, all of which generally have proven to have acceptable levels of reliability.

There are two reasons why one may want to interpret individual items. However, in both cases, interpretations must be made quite cautiously due to the low reliability of individual items. First, it is often informative to see which items led to a child's or adolescent's elevation on a given clinical scale. For example, it may be informative for a child with an elevation on the Adaptability scale to determine if this elevation was largely due to problems specifically within interpersonal domains or due to more general problems in adapting to changes in routine. This level of analysis is not as important as it is with some other rating scales with more heterogeneous item content within scales. Also, given the questionable reliability of individual items, one would not want to interpret individual items in the absence of elevations on the clinical scale level. Second, critical items should be reviewed, since these items tend to be clinically important indicators that deserve careful follow-up assessment.

Strengths and Weaknesses

The BASC-TRS is a psychometrically sophisticated rating scale for teachers that is attractive for clinical use for several reasons. It is part of a multimethod, multi-informant system that aids in a comprehensive clinical evaluation. The item content covers the major domains of classroom behavioral and emotional functioning, similar to many other teacher rating scales, but it also has some fairly unique content features. Specifically, the BASC-TRS covers several aspects of adaptive behavior (adaptability, leadership, social skills, and study skills), includes separate anxiety and depression scales, and has separate hyperactivity and attention scales. The BASC-TRS is also unique in having a preschool version for children ages 4–5, an age group often not included in the development of teacher rating scales. The BASC-TRS has a large nationwide normative sample on which norm-referenced scores are based, allowing for one to confidently make many norm-referenced interpretation of scores.

One weakness in the normative base of the BASC-TRS is a somewhat limited sample of cases in the adolescent age range, especially for ages 14–18. Therefore, the norm-referenced scores for adolescents should be used cautiously. Because the BASC-TRS was published more recently than many of the other scales reviewed in this chapter, there is less research on the validity of its scales. The manual reported encouraging initial findings on validity, especially the factor-analytic support for its scale structure and correlations with other teacher rating scales. However, the use of the BASC in clinical populations, especially the usefulness of the scales for discriminating within a clinic population, needs further testing before the instrument can confidently be considered useful for making differential diagnoses.

Child Behavior Checklist-91—Teacher's Report Form

The CBCL Teacher's Report Form (TRF; Achenbach, 1991) is designed to be completed by teachers of children between the ages of 5 and 18. It is part of a multi-informant system that has a long and prominent history of assessing children's emotional and behavioral functioning (Achenbach & Edelbrock, 1978). The parent report form, the child self-report form, and a direct observation system, which are the other components of the CBCL system, are all discussed in different chapters of this book. The CBCL is a widely used rating scale system, and the dimensions of functioning covered by these scales are often considered the standard by which the content of other rating scales is judged. The 1991 revision of the TRF includes many psychometric improvements from the original version of TRF. However, its item content remained virtually unchanged in the revision. The content of the TRF was designed to be analogous to the original parent-completed CBCL, which explicitly attempted to be atheoretical in the development of an item pool.

Content

The TRF answer sheets include several background questions (How long have you known this pupil? How well do you know him/her?"), a teacher's rating of a child's academic performance, and a four-item screening of a child's adaptive behavior with scoring on a 1–7 scale (How hard is he/she working? How appropriately is he/she behaving? How much is he/she learning? How happy is he/she?). The major portion of the TRF consists of 113 items describing problematic behaviors and emotions that the teacher rates as being Not True, Somewhat True or Sometimes True, or Very True or Often True of the child. The problem behavior items cover a broad array of both internalizing (e.g., anxiety, depression, somatic complaints) and externalizing (antisocial behavior, aggression, oppositionality) behaviors. The behaviors form eight clinical scales, which are summarized in Table 8.3.

Administration and Scoring

Most teachers can complete the TRF in about 10 minutes. The instructions to the teacher are printed on the front of the answer sheet. Scoring of the TRS can be done by hand using the CBCL Profile Sheets with separate profile sheets available for boys and girls. This hand-scoring system is rather tedious, since item scores must be individually transferred from the answer sheet to the profile sheet. A computer scoring system is available from the author that greatly

TABLE 8.3   Scales of the CBCL-91-TRS

Broad-Band Scales	Narrow-Band Scales
Internalizing	Withdrawn
	Somatic Complaints
	Anxious/Depressed
	Social Problems
	Thought Problems
	Attention Problems
Externalizing	Delinquent Behavior
	Aggressive Behavior

facilitates scoring by automatically calculating raw scale scores and converting them to norm-referenced scores appropriate for the child's age and gender.

Both the Profile Sheets and the computer scoring program provide raw scores and norm-referenced scores for several scales including a Total Problem score, which is an overall indicator of a child's classroom adjustment, and two broad-band scores consisting of Internalizing and Externalizing behaviors. These broad dimensions are further divided into eight narrow-band scales. One of the major changes in the recent revision of the TRF is that these narrow-band scales were designed to have analogous item content for both boys and girls and to have item content analogous to the other scales in the CBCL system (i.e., CBCL-1991 Parent Form, and CBCL-91 Youth Self-Report Form), which allows for easier cross-informant integration of information.

Norming

Another major improvement in the revision of the CBCL system is a greatly improved normative sample. The earlier versions of the CBCL were standardized on a sample that was unrepresentative of the general population geographically, ethnically, and socioeconomically (Achenbach & Edelbrock, 1985; Sandberg, Meyer-Bahlburg, & Yager, 1991). The normative sample for the 1991 TRF is a subset of the nationwide sample for the parent version of the CBCL. It includes 1,391 children and adolescents between the ages of 5 and 18 distributed across four groups: boys age 5–11 (n = 334), boys age 11–18 (n = 309), girls age 5–11 (n = 379), and girls age 12–18 (n = 369). Although the normative sample is geographically representative and includes representation of African-American and Hispanic children that approximates the U.S. population, there is an overrepresentation of middle to upper socioeconomic classes in the sample. Also, the normative sample excluded children who had received mental health services or special remedial school classes within the preceding 12 months. Therefore, the sample should be considered a normal comparison group, rather than one that is normative and representative of the general population.

The TRF allows for raw scores on all scales to be converted to T-scores and percentile ranks based on the standardization sample. The T-scores are normalized standard scores. That is, the raw score distributions are transformed to a normalized distribution. This procedure allows T-scores on all scales to have similar distributions and corresponding percentiles based on the assumptions of a normal distribution. However, it assumes that the dimensions assessed by the scale *should* be normally distributed in the general population, an assumption that is questionable since most children tend to cluster in the normal end of the distributions. One must be aware that norm-referenced scores based on either the hand-scoring or computer-scoring formats are based on gender and age-specific norms. Without additional information from the author, it is impossible to score the TRF in comparison to the entire normative sample, if this is desired.

Reliability

The TRF manual presents three types of reliability information. Internal consistency estimates were determined *for the behavior problems scales only* in a sample of 1,275 children referred for emotional and behavioral problems and 1,275 matched children from the normative sample. Coefficient alpha averaged .87 for the TRF scales across all age and gender groups. The only coefficients to drop below a .70 level were for the Thought Problem scale in girls age 5–11 (.63) and 12–18 (.65) and the Delinquency scale in girls age 5–11 (.69). Test-retest reliability over a 15-day interval is presented on a sample of 44 children (27 boys, 17 girls) age 8 and 9. The test-retest coefficients were high, averaging .92 in the full sample and .90 and .95 for boys and girls respectively. The only coefficient to show unacceptable reliability was the Thought Problems scale for girls, which showed a coefficient of .43. The manual also provides correlations between two different teachers for 207 children with emotional and behavioral problems. The correlations were modest across scales, with a mean coefficient for the full sample being .55 for the adaptive behavior scales and .54 for the behavior problem scales. Lower coefficients emerged in older children (age 12–18) and for ratings of internalizing problems.

Validity

The manual of the TRF provides only limited validity information, mainly providing data from a sample of 45 children between the ages of 5 and 16, in which significant correlations are reported between externalizing scales on the TRF and analogous scales on the Conners Revised Teacher Rating Scale (Goyette, Conners, & Ulrich, 1978). However, the manual points out that the earlier version of the TRF has been extensively used in research, having been used in over 100 published studies (Achenbach, 1991). In fact, in the development of many of the rating scales reviewed in this chapter, correlations with the TRF have been viewed as the standard for determining construct validity. Given the high degree of correlation between scales in the 1991 revised TRF and the original TRF scales (most being over .90), it is likely that much of this validity information is still applicable to the 1991 version. These studies generally support the validity of CBCL scales in (1) differentiating clinic-referred children from non-referred children, (2) correlating with classroom observations of children's behavior, and (3) correlating with independent clinical diagnoses (see Achenbach, 1991; Piacentini, 1993; Witt et al., 1990). One note of caution is in order, however. Most of these studies on the TRF scales have focused primarily on the externalizing scales and the Attention Problem scale, with much less information being available on the usefulness of the internalizing and Thought Problems scales.

Interpretation

Information on the reliability and validity of the competence scales of the TRF is lacking; therefore, interpretations of these scales should be done very cautiously, if at all. In the interpretation of the behavior problem scales, it is recommended that one start with global levels of interpretations and move toward more specific interpretations. The first level of interpretation is the Total Problems scale, which gives a global

indicator of a child's emotional and behavioral functioning. The next level of interpretation is on the level of the Internalizing and Externalizing composites. The third level of analysis is based on the eight clinical scales. As mentioned previously, these scales generally have been shown to be reliable across age groups.

Because the initial development of the TRS item pool was done in an attempt to be atheoretical, the item content of the TRS scales tends to be more heterogeneous than other rating scales that used a more explicit guiding theory for scale development. For example, the Attention Problems scale consists of items traditionally associated with inattention (difficulty concentrating) but also includes items associated with immaturity, overactivity, poor school achievement, and clumsiness. Therefore, it is imperative that the items that led to a clinical scale elevation be viewed to understand the meaning of the elevation. For example, a child may show an elevation on the Attention Problems scale because of problems with immaturity, clumsiness, or academic problems, or a child may have an elevation due to problems of inattention and/or hyperactivity. However, because of the unreliability of individual items, this item-level analysis should be conducted only when there is an elevation on the clinical scale.

Interpretation of the Thought Problems scale deserves several cautionary notes. This scale has an especially heterogeneous content, consisting of items describing obsessions (e.g. Can't get mind off certain thoughts), compulsions (e.g., Repeats acts over and over), fears (e.g., Fears certain animals, situations, or places), and psychotic behaviors (e.g., Hears sounds or voices that aren't there), many of which are fairly ambiguous (e.g., Strange behavior, Strange ideas). Also, the restricted range in the normative sample leads to significant elevations resulting from the endorsement of only a few items. These factors probably led to the poor reliability of the scale in many analyses, especially in samples of girls. As a result, interpretations of elevations on the Thought Problems scale should be made very cautiously.

One final note is in order for interpreting TRS scales. Since the norm-referenced scores of the TRS are based on a normal sample and not a normative sample, it is recommended that a more conservative cut-off score be used than would be the case for other rating scales. This is compounded by the fact that the normative sample tends to be somewhat skewed to upper socioeconomic levels, which may hinder interpretations in some low income samples (e.g., Sandberg, Meyer-Bahlburg, & Yager, 1991).

Strengths and Weaknesses

The TRF is one of the most widely used of the teacher-completed behavior rating scales. Therefore, there is a large literature showing correlations between CBCL scales and important clinical criteria, especially for the externalizing scales. Further, the newest revision of the TRF has overcome many of the most problematic features that limited the clinical utility of the original version. The scale content is now constant across age and gender groups, and, most importantly for fitting into a comprehensive assessment procedure, the scale content is consistent with the parent and youth self-report versions of the CBCL. The author of the CBCL provides manuals and computer programs that aid in integrating information across the various rating scales. Also, the geographical and ethnic representativeness of the revised normative base is a great improvement over the normative sample for the original TRF.

Despite the improvements in the normative base, there are still several problematic areas in the norm-referenced scores provided by the TRF. First, the normative sample is relatively small by contemporary standards, and it seems to be unrepresentative of the population in terms of an abundance of children from upper socioeconomic strata. Second, the normative sample excluded children who had received mental health or special education services and therefore should not be considered representative of the general population. Third, the TRF utilized normalized T-scores in which the raw score distributions were converted to a normalized distribution. In effect, this forces a normal distribution on scores that are likely to be positively skewed. Each of these three factors hinders the use of norm-referenced scores from the TRF in making clinical interpretations. Also, the two scoring systems of the TRF, hand-scoring and

computer-scoring, do not allow for the calculation of norm-referenced scores that are not specific to a child's gender and age. (In Chapter 2, we discussed some of the issues in using gender and age-specific norms in the interpretation of test results.)

Two other weaknesses of the TRF deserve note. Although the TRF purports to assess children's competencies and deficits, the content related to competencies is somewhat limited. It basically involves the teacher's subjective rating of a child's academic performance and four global items on a child's diligence, behavior, learning, and happiness. This is a somewhat limited assessment of a child's classroom competencies. Also, as mentioned previously, the attempt to be atheoretical in the scale development led to somewhat heterogeneous scale contents. This leads to many problems in the interpretation of scale elevations.

Comprehensive Behavior Rating Scale for Children

The Comprehensive Behavior Rating Scale for Children (CBRSC; Neeper, Lahey, & Frick, 1990) is a 70-item teacher rating scale designed to assess the classroom functioning of children age 6 to 14. Teachers rate 70 behaviors on a 5-point scale based on whether the child exhibits the behavior Not at all (1) to Very Much (5). Unlike many other rating scales reviewed in this chapter, the CBRSC is not part of a multi-informant assessment system and it targets a more limited age range of children. However, while both of these factors limit its usefulness in many situations, it did allow for a scale with a content that is uniquely suited for assessing the classroom adjustment of elementary school-age children.

Content

The development of the CBRSC was based on several considerations. Items were developed to assess the traditional areas of behavioral, emotional, and social functioning, thereby making it similar in content to other teacher rating scales. However, an attempt was made to make the following refinements in item content. First, there was an attempt to make items more comparable to the symptoms of the behavioral and emotional disorders of childhood and adolescence included in the DSM-III and DSM-III-R (American Psychiatric Association, 1980, 1987). Second, the authors wanted to refine the assessment of children's social competence by including items that more directly assessed teachers' judgments on peer interactions (e.g., Relates to children in a friendly, positive manner) and peer acceptance (e.g., Is a child one that many classmates 'like the most'), whereas other rating scales focus more on social withdrawal or on the general socialization of the child (e.g., Blames others for mistakes, Uncooperative with adults). Third, the authors of the CBRSC wanted to include behaviors more specifically related to cognitive and learning difficulties (e.g., Reverses letters, Has difficulty sounding out words, Confuses directions) in the item content.

The CBRSC items are arranged in nine scales. Three scales focus on learning problems and cognitive processing (Reading Problems, Cognitive Deficits, Sluggish Tempo), three scales are related to attention deficits and motor hyperactivity (Inattention-Disorganization, Motor Hyperactivity, Daydreaming), and one scale each assesses conduct problems (Oppositional-Conduct Disorders), anxiety (Anxiety), and peer relations (Social Competence).

Administration and Scoring

The CBRSC can be completed by teachers in about 10 to 15 minutes. The questionnaire contains instructions to the teacher and requests the teacher to provide basic background information on the student being rated. This is followed by the 70 items that form the nine clinical scales of the CBRSC.

A scoring key accompanying the CBRSC helps in the calculation of raw scores for the nine scales. The front of the questionnaire provides a profile sheet that aids in determining clinical elevations by a conversion of raw scores to T-scores based on the entire normative sample. The authors made the explicit assumption in designing the profile sheet that primary interpretations should be made based on a comparison of a child's score to the entire normative sample. However, in the manual that accompanies

the CBRSC, tables are provided that allow one to covert raw scores to T-scores and percentiles based on age- and gender-specific norms.

Norming

The normative database for the CBRSC consists of a nationwide sample of 2,153 children between the ages of 6 to 14, fairly equally divided by sex (54% male). While the normative sample is large and shows good geographic representation, there is no information presented on the socioeconomic status of the sample, and there is a an underrepresentation of African-American (9.2%) and Hispanic children (3.4%) relative to 1988 U.S. population statistics. The normative sample did include representation of children receiving special education services at a level that approximates the general population (12.1%). The CBRSC manual allows for the calculation of T-scores and percentile ranks based on the normative sample as a whole, or specific to age and gender groups. However, the profile sheet that is part of the CBRSC questionnaire allows for plotting of T-scores based on the entire normative sample only. All T-scores are nonnormalized T-scores that preserve the raw score distributions.

Reliability

The reliability of the CBRSC scales was assessed by determining the internal consistency of scales and by evaluating their test-retest reliability. The internal consistency estimates of the CBRSC scales were all quite high, with a median internal consistency coefficient in the full normative sample being .91. The lowest estimate for any scale across all age and gender groups was .76 for the Social Competence scale for girls age 13 to 14. Two-week test-retest correlations were calculated for a sample of 98 children between the ages of 6–14. It is important to note that the correlations were based on factors from an earlier version of the CBRSC (Neeper & Lahey, 1986). The factors closely approximate the final nine CBRSC scales, but they are not identical. The reliability estimates were all quite high, ranging from .84 to .97 with a median coefficient of .94.

Validity

The manual of the CBRSC reports on extensive factor-analytic testing that resulted in the nine scales of the CBRSC. These scales were then tested in a sample of 284 elementary school-age children referred to three outpatient mental health clinics for emotional, behavioral, or learning problems. The clinic sample was primarily composed of boys (91%). In general the CBRSC scales showed high correlations with other teacher rating scales. Importantly, the CBRSC makes an attempt to more specifically assess peer acceptance on its Social Competence scale. In the validation sample the Social Competence scale was significantly correlated with peer sociometric nominations of "liked most" (.26). Although this correlation is statistically significant, it is still somewhat low. This indicates that the relationship between teachers' report of social competence on the CBRSC and actual ratings of acceptance by peers does not show high convergence.

A second goal of the CBRSC was to assess behaviors related to learning, and the data are more supportive of its ability to accomplish this. Specifically, the Reading Problems scale was negatively correlated (-.52) with reading scores on a individually administered achievement test, and it was also positively correlated with reading achievement below a level predicted by intelligence. Also, the Cognitive Deficit scale was negatively correlated with verbal (−.37), performance (-.32), and full scale (−.38) intelligence as measured by the Wechsler Intelligence Scale for Children—Revised (WISC-R; Wechsler, 1974).

A third goal of the CBRSC was to more closely approximate DSM-III and DSM-III-R definitions of emotional and behavioral problems. Several scales were associated with DSM definitions of attention-deficit disorders. First, the Intention-Disorganization scale was positively correlated with teacher ratings of DSM-III symptoms of inattention (.79) and impulsivity (.72), and the Motor Hyperactivity scale was significantly correlated with DSM-III symptoms of overactivity (.79). Also, the Inattention-Disorganization, Motor Hyperactivity, and Daydreaming scales differentiated children clinically diagnosed with a DSM-III-R diagnosis of Attention-Deficit Hyperactivity Disorder (ADHD) from other clinic-referred

children. Interestingly, three scales differentiated children with DSM-III Attention Deficit Disorder with Hyperactivity (ADD/H) from children with Attention Deficit Disorder without Hyperactivity (ADD/WO). Children with ADD/WO scored lower on the Motor Hyperactivity scale and higher on the Sluggish Tempo and Daydreaming scales than children with ADD/H. The CBRSC scales of Oppositional-Conduct Disorders and Anxiety also differentiated children with analogous DSM-III-R diagnoses from other clinic-referred children.

Interpretation

Unlike many of the other rating scales reviewed in this chapter, the CBRSC does not include any global scales and, therefore, interpretation is primarily conducted at the level of the nine clinical scales. Development of the CBRSC was explicitly geared to forming scales with relatively homogeneous item content. This aids in the interpretation of scale elevations, since the items generally correspond closely to the construct purported to be measured by the scale. Also, research on the CBRSC scales supports the correspondence between scale elevations and DSM diagnoses and the ability of scales to aid in differential diagnoses in clinic-referred children.

Although all of the CBRSC scales generally have proven to have acceptable reliability, one must be cautious in the interpretation of the short (three-item) Daydreaming scale. Also, despite the significant correlations between the Reading Problems and Cognitive Deficit scales and individually administered intelligence and achievement tests, interpretation of these scales should not replace psychometric testing. A more appropriate use would be to use these scales as a screener to determine if a more intensive assessment of learning is warranted.

Strengths and Weaknesses

The CBRSC is a relatively short rating scale that offers several unique features. Its Reading Problems and Cognitive Deficit scales show good correlations with standardized achievement and intelligence measures, making these scales good screeners for children with learning problems who might warrant a more comprehensive learning evaluation. Also, the CBRSC seems to have met its goal of providing an item content that more closely corresponds to DSM-III and DSM-III-R diagnostic definitions. This correspondence may not be important in some assessment situations, but it may be desirable as part of a more comprehensive diagnostic evaluation in which other assessment procedures are closely tied to the DSM nomenclature.

One area in which the CBRSC seems especially strong is in the assessment of ADHD. Four of the nine scales seem relevant to the assessment of this domain. The Inattention-Disorganization and Motor Hyperactivity scales are related to the Hyperactive and Combined Types of ADHD as specified in the DSM-IV (American Psychiatric Association, 1994), and the Daydreaming and Sluggish Tempo scales are uniquely related to the Inattentive Type. Having scales that distinguish between the subtypes of ADHD is important based on research showing important differential correlates to the two subtypes (Frick & Lahey, 1991). A case study of a child with the Inattentive Type of ADHD using the CBRSC is provided in Box 8.1.

Unfortunately, the CBRSC does not have analogous rating scales for other informants (e.g., parents, child self-report) to aid in a multi-informant assessment, and the age range of the CBRSC norms (6–14) is somewhat limited. Also, the underrepresentation of ethnic minority students and the lack of information on the socioeconomic strata of the children in its general normative sample limits the usefulness of its norm-referenced scores in many diverse samples of children. Although the validity information reported in the manual, especially the association between CBRSC scales and DSM-III-R diagnoses, is promising, independent replication of these results in more diverse samples is needed. Also, the CBRSC is limited in its assessment of adaptive behaviors, assessing only adaptive social skills.

Conners Teacher Rating Scales

The Conners Teacher Rating Scales (CTRS; Conners, 1989) is another rating scale with an extensive his-

tory of use for both research and clinical purposes. It was originally developed as a research instrument to test the effects of treatment on hyperactive children (Conners, 1969). Although the the scale was first published in 1969, a manual for its use was not available until 1989, when it was published commercially by Multi-Health Systems, Inc. In the intervening two decades there were many different versions of the CTRS in use, each with different scales and associated normative data (see Piacentini, 1993). The presence of numerous versions of the CTRS has led to a great deal of confusion in terms of what information applies to the specific version of the scale being used. This discussion focuses on the two versions of the CTRS (CTRS-39, CTRS-28) published in 1989 by Multi-Health Systems, Inc.

Content

The CTRS-39 has 39 items describing behaviors that are scored on a 4-point frequency scale ranging from Not at all (0) to Very Much (3). The CTRS-39 was the original scale published in 1969, and the six scales that are included in this version are summarized in Table 8.4. The CTRS has been normed for use with children between the ages of 4 and 12. The CTRS-28 is a 28-item version of the CTRS that includes three scales that are also summarized in Box 8.5. For both versions of the CTRS there is a 10-item scale, labeled the Hyperactivity Index, composed of the 10 items most sensitive to drug effects in the treatment of childhood hyperactivity (Conners, 1989).

Administration and Scoring

Both versions of the CTRS are relatively brief, thus requiring less time for teachers to complete (5–10 minutes) than most of the other rating scales reviewed in this chapter. The 1989 versions of the CTRS consist of a response sheet, which includes the behavioral items to be rated, connected to a scoring key. A teacher's responses are automatically copied onto the attached scoring key, which aids in calculating raw scale scores.

Also attached to the response sheet and scoring key is a profile form, which allows a conversion of the raw scores to T-scores. There is a separate profile form for males and females. Unfortunately, there are

BOX 8.1

Use of the CBRSC for Assessment of ADD: A Case Example

Nicholas was a 9-year-old boy who was referred to an university-based outpatient mental health clinic for a comprehensive psychological evaluation by his parents. Nick's teacher had reported that he was having academic problems in the classroom, which she had attributed to problems in concentration and remaining on task. Both his parents and teacher reported that Nick seemed to be unmotivated to complete work and frequently daydreamed rather than doing his work. Nick was in the third grade at the time of his evaluation, and his parents reported that he had similar problems in the second grade, although they were much less severe that year.

On standard individually administered intelligence and achievement tests, Nick scored in the average to high average range in all areas, with no consistent cognitive or academic weaknesses emerging. As part of an emotional and behavioral assessment, Nick's teacher completed the CBRSC; the following is a graph of the resulting scale scores. Because the CBSRC uses nonnormalized T-scores, both T-scores and percentile ranks are reported. Nick was rated in the clinically significant range on the Daydreams, Sluggish Tempo, and Inattention-Disorganized scales. However, the Motor Hyperactivity scale was within normal limits. Therefore, Nick seemed to show the pattern of scores that is consistent with Attention-Deficit Hyperactivity Disorder—Inattentive Type.

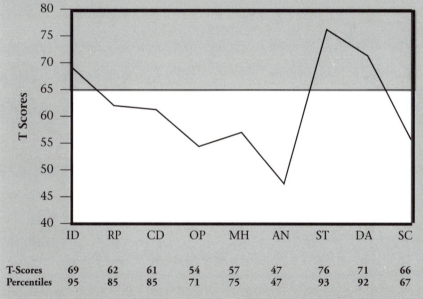

	ID	RP	CD	OP	MH	AN	ST	DA	SC
T-Scores	69	62	61	54	57	47	76	71	66
Percentiles	95	85	85	71	75	47	93	92	67

NOTE: ID = Inattention-Disorganization, RP = Reading Problems, CD = Cognitive Deficit, OP - Oppositional-Conduct Disorders, MH = Motor Hyperactivity, AN = Anxiety, ST = Sluggish Tempo, DA = Daydreams, and SC = Social Competence.

These results were supported by structured clinical interviews with Nick's parents and teacher and rating scales completed by his mother. As a result of this evaluation, Nick's parents began consultation with a psychologist, who developed behavioral programs with Nick's teacher to increase on-task behavior. The psychologist also helped Nick develop organizational strategies to aid in school performance. Finally, Nick's pediatrician instituted a trial of a low dose of stimulant medication to help reduce the problems associated with inattention and disorganization.

no tables provided, either on the profile form or in the accompanying manual, for conversion of raw scores to T-scores based on the entire normative sample.

Norming

One of the most confusing aspects of the CTRS is matching the correct scale version to the appropriate normative base. Unfortunately, the manual for the CTRS-39 and CTRS-28 does little to help clear up this confusion. Unlike the manuals of other rating scales, the CTRS manual contains only brief descriptions of the samples on which the norm-referenced scores are based, and one must search through journal articles to obtain basic information on the source of norm-referenced scores. The norms for the CTRS-39 were based on a large (n = 9,583) sample of Canadian school children between the ages of 4–12. The sample included English-speaking children from 53 schools in the Canadian province of Ottawa (Trites, Blouin, & Laprade, 1982). The norms for the CTRS-28 are based on 383 Canadian children age 3–17 years.

The profile form that accompanies the rating scales helps to convert the scale scores to T-scores based on these normative samples. These T-scores are nonnormalized T-scores that preserve the shape of the raw scores distribution. Unfortunately, the CTRS profile sheets do not allow for the conversion of the raw scores to percentiles, an important piece of information when using nonnormalized T-scores.

Reliability

The manual of the CTRS reports reliability data for only the CTRS-39. Internal consistency estimates of the CTRS-39 range from .61 to .94 with a median of .84 in the large Canadian standardization sample (Trites, Blouin, & Laprade, 1982). Only one scale, the Daydream-Attention Problem scale, had a questionable internal consistency estimate (.61). One-month test-retest reliability on the CTRS-39 is reported from several samples, with reliability coefficients generally ranging from .72–.91.

Validity

The major strength of the CTRS is its extensive use in the research literature. It is difficult to accurately interpret this literature because of the many different forms of the CTRS that have been employed, making it difficult to compare the results across studies. The most definitive finding across the various forms of the CTRS is the sensitivity of the Hyperactivity Index to treatment effects in samples of children with attention deficit disorders, especially in studies on the effects of the stimulant Ritalin (see Conners, 1989; Piacentini, 1993). Other studies showing the predictive, discriminant, and concurrent validity of the two versions of the CTRS have generally also focused on the assessment of attention deficit disorders (Piacentini, 1993). Therefore, the validity of the CTRS in assessing other domains of behavior is less clear.

Interpretation

The use for which the CTRS scales are uniquely suited is monitoring treatment affects in children with ADHD. The Hyperactivity Index on both scales provides a short (10 items), reliable assessment that has been well validated for this purpose. Because of its time-efficiency, the Hyperactivity Index can be administered frequently to assess the ongoing effectiveness of an intervention program for children with ADHD.

Because of the inadequacy of the normative samples, interpretations using the norm-referenced T-scores should be made cautiously, if at all. Also, like other rating scales that lack a clear theoretical basis for scale development, the scales tend to be very heterogeneous in item content. For example, the Inattentive-Passive scale of the CTRS-28 includes inattentive items (Daydreams) but also includes items related to immaturity (Childish), passivity (Easily led by other children), poor frustration tolerance, (Easily frustrated), and learning problems (Difficulty learning). It is difficult to know how to interpret high scores on this very heterogeneous cluster of behaviors without viewing the individual items that led to the scores.

Strengths and Weaknesses

The unique contribution of the CTRS is the short Hyperactivity Index which has proven to be an effective method of monitoring the effectiveness of medication trials for children with ADHD. This strength is not surprising given that it was for this purpose that the Conners scales were originally developed.

Unfortunately, the clinical utility of the CTRS is severely limited in several other respects. Although the author of the CTRS recommends use of the CTRS-28 (Conners, 1989), this seems questionable for most clinical uses for a number of reasons. The CTRS-28 norm-referenced scores are based on a very small sample (n = 339) that spans a large age range (3–17) and is limited to Canadian school children. Such a limited normative base does not seem to justify use of clinical cut-offs based on it. Also, no reliability estimates are reported for this scale, so it is impossible to determine the degree of confidence (i.e., standard error) that one can place on a child's scores on this form.

Although the CTRS-39 normative base is much larger (n = 9,583), it was limited to children age 4–12 and to Canadian school children. The manual does not provide any data to support the contention that these norms would adequately represent the U.S. general population or even be representative of Canadian children because it was limited to English-speaking Canadian children. Therefore, diagnostic decisions that require norm-referenced interpretations (e.g., scale elevations above a T-score of 70) cannot be made with much confidence from any of the CTRS scales.

Three other difficulties with the development of norm-referenced scores also deserve note. First, the test manual provides minimal information on the normative samples, which severely limits one's ability to interpret the norm-referenced scores. Second, neither the profile sheets attached to the CTRS response forms nor the accompanying manual allows for a determination of percentile ranks. Since the T-scores are not based on normalized scores, but on different distributions across clinical scales, interpretation of percentile ranks becomes quite important (see Chapter 2). Third, only T-scores separated by gender are provided either on the profile sheet or

accompanying manual. These gender-specific norms may be particularly misleading for one of the primary uses of the CTRS, assessment of the behaviors associated with ADHD. Behaviors associated with ADHD are consistently found to be more prevalent in males than females. Comparing a girl's scores only to those of other girls artificially eliminates what seem to be true gender differences. This practice will make elevations more likely in girls than would be the case if scores were compared to those of both boys and girls. As we stated in Chapter 2, there are many arguments on both sides of the issue of using norms specific to gender (or age-, race, etc.), but we feel that scales should at least allow the user to make the comparisons he or she feels are most appropriate in a given situation.

In addition to the problems in the norm-referenced scores produced by CTRS, the item content is also quite limited in comparison to many other teacher rating scales that are currently available. The CTRS content consists largely of externalizing behaviors, and even within this category, its primary item content focuses on behaviors associated with ADHD. In fact, none of the four scales of CTRS-28 is specific to internalizing problems (e.g., anxiety, depression/withdrawal), and only one of the CTRS-39 scales (Anxious-Passive) includes behaviors from this domain. Therefore, its breadth of coverage is more limited than many of the other broad rating scales that are currently available. Also, as mentioned in the previous section, the scale content of the CTRS tends to be very heterogeneous, which hurts the interpretation of scale scores.

Another limitation of the CTRS is that, despite the fact that both parent and teacher forms are available, multi-informant assessment is hurt by a lack of correspondence in item content between parent and teacher scales. As a result, it is impossible to determine whether discrepancies between parent and teacher reports on a child are simply a result of different questions being asked of the two raters.

Devereux Behavior Rating Scale—School Form

The Devereux Behavior Rating Profile—School Form (DCBS-SF; Naglieri, LeBuffe, & Pfeiffer, 1993) is a revision of the Devereux rating scales published in the 1960s by the Devereux Foundation (Spivack & Spotts, 1966; Spivack, Spotts, & Haimes, 1967). The revision was designed to (1) make the scale easier to complete and interpret (e.g., contain only one response format), (2) update the item content to more closely approximate current psychiatric and educational classification systems, (3) develop a new nationwide normative sample, and (4) provide further evidence of the scales reliability and validity. The DCBS-SF contains two 40-item forms, one for children age 5–12 and a second for adolescents age 13–18. The behaviors are rated on a 5-point frequency scale from Never to Very Frequently based on their occurrence in the past 4 weeks. DCBS-SF was designed to be completed by either a parent or teacher, and therefore, analogous forms are used, which aids in a multi-informant assessment.

Content

The DCBS-SF contains two distinct sets of items for the child and adolescent forms. However, both forms have four analogous scales. The first scale encompasses problems in socialization and interacting with peers (e.g., annoys others, teases or bullies others, appears uncomfortable and anxious with others) and is labeled the Interpersonal Problems scale. The Inappropriate Behaviors/Feelings scale involves problems of impulse control and aggression (e.g., expresses anger in a poorly controlled way, has temper tantrums, has difficulty playing or working quietly), whereas the Depression scale focuses on symptoms of dysphoria and social withdrawal (e.g., appears discouraged or depressed, remains alone or isolated, fails to show pride in accomplishments). The fourth scale assesses somatic complaints and fearful behaviors (e.g., refuses to go to school, shows strong fear of rejection, overreacts to minor pain) and is labeled the Physical Symptoms/Fears scale.

Administration and Scoring

The DCBS-SF is a relatively short (40 items) rating scale and takes only 5 to 10 minutes to complete. The record form containing the DCBS-SF is a two-sheet, perforated, self-carbon form. The front of the first sheet includes basic identifying information about the child and rater, instructions to the rater, and the 40 scale items. Printed on the back of the first sheet are abbreviated instructions for scoring responses, computing raw scores, and deriving standard scores. A teacher's ratings are automatically copied onto the third page of the record form, where they appear in one of four columns, corresponding to the appropriate scale. Raw scale scores are calculated by summing the items within a column.

Raw scores can then be converted to standard scores (m = 15 and SD = 3) and percentile ranks using conversion tables in the DCBS-SF manual. These tables only allow for conversion into norm-referenced scores that are specific to discrete age and gender groups. These tables also provide 90% and 95% confidence intervals around the standard scores, which aids in calculating the relative strengths and weaknesses of a child or adolescent across the DCBS-SF scales.

Norming

A sample of 3,153 children and adolescents between the ages of 5 and 18 was the normative base for the DCBS-SF. The sample was obtained from 51 sites nationwide and was designed to have an adequate sample at all ages, with the median number of children at each age level being 248 (range 68–295). The sample matches the U.S. population well in relation to ethnic composition and parental education. Based on scores from this sample, raw scores on the DCBS-SF can be transformed into standard scores (m = 10, SD = 3) for each scale based on a linear (nonnormalized) transformation of raw scores. Because of the importance of also interpreting percentile ranks for nonnormalized standard scores, the DCBS-SF provides tables that aid in the conversion of raw scores to percentile ranks for each scale.

Reliability

The internal consistencies of the DCBS-SF scales completed by teachers range from .83 to .94 (median .87). One week test-retest coefficients were calculated in a sample of 133 children and adolescents in regular education classrooms. Test-retest coefficients were generally higher for children (range .80–.84, median .84) than for adolescents (range .53–.82, median .61) with an overall median coefficient of .83. Interrater reliability estimates were calculated across several samples, with estimates ranging from .36 to .77 (median .52).

Validity

There is no factor-analytic support provided in the manual for the four DCBS-SF scales. The validity information provided for the DCBS-SF demonstrates the ability of the four scales to differentiate children receiving special education services or psychiatric services from normal control children in six samples. Scale scores were viewed both continuously and dichotomously using clinical cut-offs, with both methods showing significant associations with group membership.

Interpretation

The interpretation of the DCBS-SF is primarily conducted at the scale level. All four scales seem to have proven reliability across many samples and many age groups. However, due to the relatively recent publication of the DCBS-SF, information on the validity of the four scales is somewhat minimal, which greatly hurts interpretation of scale elevations. As a result, only very gross interpretations (e.g., child is in need of further evaluation and treatment) should be made until more information on the validity of the scales is obtained.

Strengths and Weaknesses

The DCBS-SF is a relatively brief rating scale that shows acceptable reliability and has an excellent normative base with which to make norm-referenced interpretations. Also, the scales have shown to discriminate emotionally disturbed children from undisturbed children. The main limitation in the DCBS-SF is in its item content. It is quite limited in the behavioral domains assessed, especially in its as-

sessment of externalizing behaviors. This is unfortunate given that it is in this domain that teachers are most useful in providing information. The most severe limitations are the lack of items corresponding to attention deficits or motor hyperactivity and the confounding of social competence and conduct problems on similar scales. Therefore, the DCBS-SF is not likely to add much to an assessment of externalizing behaviors.

Also, validity information has largely focused on the scales' utility in making gross distinctions between disturbed and normal children, but no information is provided for more specific associations within clinic-referred children. Therefore, the DCBS-SF is limited in its ability to aid in differential diagnosis within disturbed children. Finally, the failure to provide factor-analytic support to the scale structure leaves open to question the construct validity of the scales, although the high internal consistency estimates and high item-total correlations lend some support to these dimensions of behavior.

Revised Behavior Problem Checklist

The Revised Behavior Problem Checklist (RBPC; Quay & Peterson, 1983) is a revised version of one of the first standardized rating scales for child psychopathology (Peterson, 1961). The original Behavior Problem Checklist (BPC) contained four dimensions of behavior that were so consistently replicated that they have been used to form an entire system of classifying childhood behavioral disorders (Quay, 1986). The revision of the BPC was undertaken to increase the reliability of the scales by increasing the item pool, deleting unreliable items, and dropping items that were not specific to a given dimension of behavior (Lahey & Piacentini, 1985).

Content

The resulting RBPC is an 89-item scale that can be completed by a parent or teacher. Each behavior is rated on a 3-point scale from Not at all (0) to Severe problem (2). The six scales that form the RBPC include four dimensions that correspond closely to the original BPC scales (Conduct Disorder, Socialized Aggression, Attention Problems-Immaturity, and Anxiety-Withdrawal) and two new scales that are unique to the revised version (Psychotic Behavior and Motor Excess). One of the unique and important factors in the content coverage of the RBPC is the large number of items assessing conduct problems and antisocial behavior. This large item pool resulted in two scales covering two dimensions of conduct problems based on a distinction between socialized (antisocial behavior in the context of deviant peer group) and undersocialized (irritable and argumentative) antisocial behavior.

Administration and Scoring

The RBPC takes about 15–20 minutes to complete. The front of the questionnaire requests several pieces of background information and provides instructions for completion. There are no aids or keys for calculating the raw scale scores. Since no norm-referenced scores are available, calculation of the raw scale scores is the only scoring necessary.

Norming

The authors explicitly acknowledge the absence of representative national norms for the RBPC and recommend the formation of local norms by users of the test (Quay & Peterson, 1983). They provide data for the RBPC scales from a sample of 869 school children (K–12) from predominantly middle- and working-class families in four states as one source of local norms. The authors provide data from a second unselected sample of children that is a large-scale normative study conducted in New Zealand that also provides some normative information (Aman et al., 1983). However, there are several differences in the means and distribution of scores across these various samples. Therefore, the lack of any single representative sample makes interpreting norm-referenced scores difficult.

Reliability

As was its goal, the revision process led to an increase in the reliability of the RBPC scales. The manual reports 2-month test-retest reliability coefficients ranging from .49 (Socialized Aggression) to .83 (Attention Problems-Immaturity). The internal consistency estimates also tend to be adequate, ranging from .68 to .95. The correlations between two teachers reportedly ranged from .52 to .85 in several samples.

Validity

Although there has been less research on the RBPC than on the original BPC, correlations between scales on the RBPC and analogous scales on the BPC are reported in the manual to be quite high, ranging from .63 to .97. Therefore, it is likely that the wealth of research on BPC will be applicable to the RBPC scales as well. RBPC scales have been shown to correlate with other analogous scales completed by teachers and with several external criteria in expected directions (see Lahey & Piacentini, 1985) with two notable exceptions. The five-item Motor Excess scale has not proven to be highly correlated with behavioral observations of motor activity (Quay & Peterson, 1983) or with a diagnosis of ADHD (Lahey et al., 1987). This is likely due to the fact that the content of the Motor Excess scale mixes behavioral descriptors of motor overactivity (e.g., Restless; Unable to sit still) with behavioral indicators of anxiety (e.g., Nervous, jittery, jumpy; Easily startled). Also, the clinical correlates of the six-item Psychotic Behavior scale have not been well defined (Quay & Peterson, 1983).

Interpretation

Since the RBPC relies on the determination of local norms, clinical interpretation of the RBPC will be dependent on the norms collected. This has led to the RBPC being primarily used as a research tool, with more limited use in purely clinical settings. Research has generally shown that the RBPC scales are correlated in expected ways with important clinical correlates. Two notable exceptions are the Motor Excess and Psychotic Behavior scales. As already mentioned, because the Motor Excess scale combines indicators of motor restlessness and nervous tension, it tends to have weak correlations with other measures of these psychological constructs (e.g., diagnoses of ADHD). Also, the Psychotic Behavior scale tends to have items that are very infrequently endorsed in most settings (Lahey et al., 1987). Therefore, it has been hard to establish the validity of this scale.

Strengths and Weaknesses

The RBPC scales were based on a factor structure that has been widely replicated and researched. For some systems of classification (e.g., Quay, 1986), it has become the standard on which to base classification of childhood psychopathology. Its large item pool of conduct problems and its scale structure that distinguishes between socialized and undersocialized antisocial behavior make it especially suitable for situations in which this distinction is of primary interest to the assessor. Also, the primary goal of the revision process has been met. That is, the scales have generally proven to show acceptable levels of reliability. In addition, the use of the same forms and analogous scale structures between parents and teachers enhances the use of the RBPC in a multi-informant evaluation, although there is no youth self-report version available.

The RBPC, however, has some troubling limitations for clinical use. The major limitation is in the lack of a representative national normative sample. Although the authors recommend the development of local norms within the population of interest (Quay & Peterson, 1983), the development of such norms is unfeasible in many clinical settings. Therefore, it is difficult to make norm-referenced interpretations from the RBPC scales. Second, the item content of the RBPC is somewhat limited in the domains assessed, in comparison with other broad rating scales. It does not include the assessment of adaptive behaviors, social skills/peer acceptance, or behavioral indicators of learning problems. Third, the two scales that are new to the revised version of the RBPC, the

Motor Excess and Psychotic Behavior scales, need to be interpreted with caution. The validity of these two scales is more open to question than that of the other RBPC scales.

SINGLE-DOMAIN RATING SCALES

In this chapter we have primarily focused on teacher rating scales that cover multiple dimensions of a student's emotional and behavioral functioning. There are also numerous specialized rating scales that are completed by teachers but which focus specifically on a single dimension of behavior. Such rating scales often provide a more in-depth, yet focused, assessment of some specific area of functioning that may be of particular relevance for a given assessment. Because of their specificity, the single-domain rating scales may not be as uniformly relevant across many assessment situations. However, in some testing situations they can be used to supplement more comprehensive assessment techniques such as omnibus rating scales.

The four most common domains for which teacher rating scales have been developed are the areas of (1) learning problems/academic skills, (2) ADHD, (3) conduct problems in preschoolers and (4) social skills/peer interactions. Assessment of the first domain, learning problems/academic skills, is beyond the scope of this book, which specifically focuses on the assessment of children's emotional and behavioral functioning. However, in this section we provide a brief overview of several scales that assess behaviors in the latter three domains to serve as examples of single-domain teacher rating scales.

Attention Deficit Disorders Evaluation Scale—School Version

The ADDES (School Version; McCarney, 1989) is a 60-item rating scale with three subscales designed to assess the primary dimensions of ADHD: Inattention (27 items), Impulsivity (18 items), and Hyperactivity (15 items). It is unclear what guided the development of items to tap these dimensions other than the statement that "behavioral descriptors were gathered for the educational environment from diagnosticians and educators working with Attention-deficit Disordered students" (McCarney, 1989, p. 6). Extensive normative data are available for the ADDES based on the ratings of 4,876 students nationwide, a base that is fairly representative of the U.S. population in sex, ethnicity, and parental occupation.

Internal consistency, test-retest reliability, and interrater reliability of the ADDES scales all tend to be quite high. The primary problem with the ADDES is its construct validation. Although the ADDES items are divided into three scales, results of the factor analysis reported in the manual seem to be more consistent with a two-dimensional conceptualization, which divides behaviors into inattention-disorganization items and impulsivity-overactivity items. This two-dimensional method of viewing ADHD symptoms is more consistent with much past research (Frick & Lahey, 1991) and with the criteria for ADHD in the DSM-IV (American Psychiatric Association, 1994).

Important for the assessment of ADHD, the manual reports an association between ADDES scores and students identified as having attention-deficit disorder in a sample of 102 children (McCarney, 1989). Unfortunately, it is unclear what criteria were used to define ADHD and how these criteria were assessed. This lack of clarity makes it difficult to interpret scale scores in relation to diagnostic groups.

In summary, the ADDES provides a comprehensive list of items related to inattention, impulsivity, and hyperactivity. It has been shown to have high reliability, and there is a large, nationwide, normative base to aid in making interpretations. However, more needs to be done on validating this instrument, especially in determining its relation with a diagnosis of ADHD.

Social Skills Rating System

The teacher form of the Social Skills Rating System (SSRS; Gresham & Elliott, 1990) was designed to be part of a multi-rater (the SSRS includes parent and self-report forms) assessment of children's social behaviors that affect teacher–student relations, peer acceptance, and academic performance. The SSRS teacher version includes three scales measuring cooperation (e.g., helping others, sharing materials, complying with rules and directions), assertion (e.g., initiating interactions, making friends, responding to the actions of others), and self-control (e.g., responding to teasing in an appropriate manner, taking turns, and compromising). The SSRS also includes items assessing conduct problems, hyperactivity, emotional difficulties and academic competence. There are three forms of the SSRS designed for preschoolers (40 items), elementary school–age children (57 items), and secondary school–age children (51 items).

The standardization sample on which norm-referenced scores consisted of 1,335 children age 3–18. The sample was representative geographically but had higher rates of special education children and children of college-educated parents and lower representation of Hispanic children than U.S. population statistics. Internal consistency, test-retest reliability, and interrater reliability estimates of the SSRS scales are all adequate. Further, the manual reports factor-analytic support for the scale structure and correlations with other rating scale measures of social skills.

In summary, the SSRS is a reliable assessment tool for screening problems in children's social relationship. The national normative sample is adequate for making many norm-referenced interpretations of scale scores. The behavioral and emotional problem scales should be interpreted cautiously due to the limited item content and should not be considered an adequate replacement for other more comprehensive assessments of these areas. Also, the validity information on the SSRS teacher version is somewhat limited. Although the scales correlate highly with other teacher ratings, it is unclear how well these ratings correlate with measures of social skills from other sources, such as observations of actual peer interactions or indices of social acceptance provided directly from a child's peer group.

Sutter-Eyberg Student Behavior Inventory

The Sutter-Eyberg Student Behavior Inventory (SESBI; Sutter & Eyberg, 1984) was designed to be a companion rating scale to the parent-completed Eyberg Child Behavior Inventory (Eyberg & Robinson, 1983). The unique feature of these rating scales is that their development specifically focused on assessing conduct problems in preschool children. The authors state that the SESBI was "designed to discriminate normal children from children in need of treatment for conduct problem behaviors" (Funderbunk & Eyberg, 1989, p. 299). As a result, the item content is uniquely applicable to very young children. The SESBI consists of 36 items that are rated on a 1–7 frequency scale with the markers of Never (1) to Always (7). In addition to rating frequency, each behavior is rated as to whether or not the teacher considers it to be a problem. From these ratings, two scores are calculated. The first score is the Intensity Score, which is the sum of the 7-point frequency scale for all items. The second score, the Problem Score, is the number of behaviors rated by the teacher as being problematic.

In a sample of 55 preschoolers age 3–5, Funderbunk and Eyberg (1989) found very high internal consistency and 1 week test-retest correlations for both the Intensity Score (Cronbach's alpha = .98, test-retest r = .90) and the Problem Score (Cronbach's alpha = .96, test-retest r = .89). These authors also provided data indicating that the SESBI was able to discriminate between children referred for school conduct problems and normal nonreferred children, which was one of the primary goals in the inventory's development. Other research has shown that the SESBI is sensitive to treatment effects in clinic-referred preschoolers (McNeil et al., 1991).

In summary, the SESBI appears to be a reliable method of assessing conduct problems in preschoolers that can differentiate children in need of treatment from other children and which is sensitive to treatment effects. Therefore, the SESBI can play an important role in the clinical assessment of very young children. However, there are relatively few normative data on the SESBI, with the exception of the small (n = 55) preschool sample reported by Funderbunk and Eyberg (1989). In addition, while the authors report that the SESBI is applicable to children between the ages of 2 and 17; (Funderbunk & Eyberg, 1989), the content seems most suitable for the assessment of preschool children.

Swanson, Nolan, and Pelham Rating Scale

The Swanson, Nolan, and Pelham Rating Scale (SNAP; Atkins, Pelham, & Licht, 1985) was designed to obtain standard ratings that correspond *exactly* to DSM-III (American Psychiatric Association, 1980) definitions of Attention Deficit Disorder (ADD). This was later revised to include items corresponding to the DSM-III-R (American Psychiatric Association, 1987) definitions of Attention-Deficit Hyperactivity Disorder (ADHD; 14 items) and items corresponding to the related diagnoses of Oppositional Defiant Disorder (ODD; 9 items) and Conduct Disorder (CD; 13 items) (Pelham et al., 1992). The item content of the revised SNAP simply takes each symptom from the DSM-III-R criteria, maintaining as closely as possible o the DSM-III-R wording, and has the teacher rate each symptom on a 4-point scale from Not at all (0) to Very Much (3). Scales on the SNAP are based on the DSM-III-R criteria. A symptom is considered present if endorsed by the teacher as being present Very Much, and the number of symptoms present for each disorder is compared to DSM-III-R criteria (e.g., eight symptoms of ADHD are required for a diagnosis).

The scale was standardized in a nationwide sample of 931 boys between the ages of 5 and 14 attending regular school classrooms (Pelham et al., 1992). Internal consistency estimates for the three scales were .75 (CD), .95 (ODD), and .96 (ADHD). By design the SNAP corresponds to DSM-III-R definitions. This has both positive and negative implications. On the positive side, if the goal of an evaluation is to determine the presence of a DSM-III-R diagnosis, then it is essential to assess the criteria exactly, which is not accomplished by most other rating scales. The SNAP provides a standardized and time-efficient way to do so. On the negative side, as the criteria change, the scale becomes outdated. Therefore, even the revised item content does not correspond to the DSM-IV definitions. Further, since it was designed to approximate DSM-III-R definitions, it maintains the problems associated with these definitions. Specifically, there is convincing evidence from factor analyses that the ADHD criteria is not unidimensional, as listed in DSM-III-R. Instead, symptoms seem to form two dimensions of behavior: inattention/disorganization and impulsivity/hyperactivity (Pelham et al., 1992; Lahey et al., 1988). Finally, much of the work with the SNAP has been done in samples of boys and therefore its use in samples of girls is questionable.

Walker-McConnell Scale of Social Competence and School Adjustment

The Walker-McConnell scale (Walker & McConnell, 1988) is a 43-item rating scale that includes items in three primary domains of social competence. The Teacher-Preferred Social Behavior scale includes 16 items measuring peer-related social behavior highly valued by teachers (e.g., cooperates with peers, controls temper, shows sympathy to others). The Peer-Preferred Social Behavior scale consists of 17 items that measure peer-related social behavior that is highly valued by classmates (e.g., makes friends easily, compromises when the situation calls for it, plays games skillfully). The third scale is the 10-item School Adjustment Behavior scale, which measures adaptive social behaviors (e.g., displays study skills, has good work habits, listens carefully to directions).

Normative scores on the three scales of the Walker-McConnell are based on a nationwide sample of 1,812 school children grades K–6. The sample is fairly equally distributed between boys and girls across grade levels and provides a cross-section of urban, suburban, and rural school districts. The sample is somewhat unrepresentative in having a higher percentage of white children (80%) than would be expected in the general population. It is unclear whether this sample included children who were receiving special education services. Tables are provided to convert all subscales to nonnormalized scaled scores (m = 10, SD = 3) and percentile ranks based on the normative sample.

Internal consistency of all scales on the Walker-McConnell was quite high across all age ranges (.94–.98) in the normative sample, and test-retest correlations are reported as generally being above .80. The manual reports several studies showing factor-analytic support for the three scales. Perhaps the most important validity information comes from several studies reported in the manual on the association between the Walker-McConnell scales and sociometric exercises. In a study of 80 school children the Teacher-Preferred Social Behavior and School Adjustment Behavior scales differentiated children classified as amiable by their peers from children who were nominated as rejected and isolated by peers. In a larger study of 323 students in grades 2 and 4, discriminant function analysis revealed that the Walker-McConnell scales helped to discriminate groups of children classified as Popular, Rejected, Neglected, and Average on peer sociometrics, with the Peer-Preferred Social Behavior scale being especially effective in differentiating Rejected subjects from the other sociometric groups.

In summary, the Walker-McConnell scale provides a reliable method of assessing several domains of social competence, and it is one of the few such scales completed by teachers to show an association between teachers' judgments of social competence and peer ratings of social acceptance. For the latter reason, the Walker-McConnell seems to be an especially useful screening instrument for potential problems in peer relations. Two notes of caution are in order on the use of the Walker-McConnell, however. First, its normative sample did not sufficiently sample ethnic minorities, especially African-American and Hispanic students, and therefore the scales should be interpreted cautiously in ethnically diverse samples. Second, the School Adjustment Behavior scale is somewhat limited in its item content and therefore should not be used in place of a more complete behavioral and emotional assessment.

IMPAIRMENT RATING SCALES

Rating scales in general, and teacher rating scales in particular, have traditionally assessed the number, type, and frequency of problematic behaviors. There is a fairly recent trend to also obtain measures of the *degree of impairment* associated with a child's emotional or behavioral disturbance. That is, children with the same type of emotional and behavioral disturbance may differ on the degree to which the disturbance impacts day-to-day functioning. Assessing the degree of impairment is crucial to diagnostic and treatment decision making. In fact, DSM-IV diagnoses often by definition require documentation that the symptoms result in substantial impairment in a person's adaptive functioning (American Psychiatric Association, 1994). Because the trend in developing impairment-focused rating scales is so recent, there are few standardized assessment instruments available. Two notable exceptions are described here as examples of these instruments for use with teachers to assess the level of impairment in a child's classroom functioning associated with behavioral or emotional disturbance.

School Situations Questionnaire

The content of the School Situations Questionnaire (SSQ; Barkley & Edelbrock, 1987) is markedly different from the other teacher rating scales reviewed in this chapter. Rather than having items that describe different types of child behaviors, SSQ includes 12 situations (e.g., During Individual Desk Work, At Recess, On the Bus) in which a child may have problems. It was not designed to assess specific behaviors but to assess specific situations in which problem behaviors can occur. This has led to our inclusion of the SSQ in this section on impairment-oriented rating scales.

On the SSQ the teacher rates whether or not the child has any problem in a given situation and then rates the severity of the problem on a 1–9 scale. The SSQ was originally designed to assess the pervasiveness of problems associated with ADHD (Barkley, 1981). Although this is still one of the most important uses of the SSQ, other types of emotional and behavioral difficulties may vary in their impact across situations. Therefore, the SSQ may be beneficial for other types of clinical assessment as well.

Unfortunately, the psychometric development of the SSQ is still in its early stages, which limits its clinical usefulness to some extent. Normative data are available on a sample of 599 school children age 6–11 years from several schools in central Wisconsin (Barkley & Edelbrock, 1987). The sample is fairly equally distributed between younger and older children and between boys and girls. However, besides the geographical limitations, the sample had very limited representation of ethnic-minority children.

Test-retest reliability of the SSQ in a sample of 119 regular education children was estimated at .68 for number of problem situations and .78 for the mean severity score. It is difficult to decide the best type of validity information to obtain for the SSQ, since its uniqueness makes it difficult to find some criterion against which to judge it. Barkley and Edelbrock (1987) reported numerous significant correlations between the SSQ and rating scale measures of externalizing behavior problems and evidence that the SSQ differentiates children with ADHD from children without ADHD. However, empirical evidence for its ability to detect true situational variability in behaviors is not available. This aspect of its validity relies on face validity.

Academic Performance Rating Scale

The Academic Performance Rating Scale (APRS; DuPaul, Rapport, & Perriello, 1991) was designed to assess the effect of childhood behavior problems on a child's academic skills. For many childhood emotional and behavioral disorders an important consideration in diagnosis and treatment is the degree of impairment in school functioning associated with the psychological dysfunction. The APRS includes 19 items that assess a child's academic productivity (e.g., percentage of work completed), academic success (e.g., percentage of work completed accurately), and impulse control (e.g., neatness of work, amount of work begun carelessly).

Normative data for the APRS is available for 493 children in grades 1–6 from 45 public schools in Worcester, Massachusetts, that included 29% ethnic-minority students. The internal consistency of the APRS scales was quite high for the academic productivity and academic success scales (both .94) but somewhat lower for the impulse control scale (.72). Two-week test-retest reliability for a sample of 25 children ranged from .88 for the impulse control scale to .95 for the total scale. Significant correlations were reported between the academic success scale and standardized achievement measures (.61–.62), and the academic productivity scale was significantly correlated with behavioral observations of on-task behavior (.31) and objective measures of academic efficiency (.57). Also, the impulse control measure was negatively associated with ratings of ADHD symptoms (−.61). Therefore, the initial development of the APRS suggests that it is a reliable method of obtaining teacher ratings of how impaired a child's academic performance is as a result of an emotional or behavioral disturbance and can outline some specific targets of intervention.

CONCLUSIONS

Obtaining teacher information is a crucial part of any comprehensive evaluation of the emotional and behavioral functioning of children and adolescents. In fact, for some problems and in some age groups (e.g., ADHD in elementary school–age children), teachers may be the most important source of information in making diagnostic and treatment decisions. Rating scales provide a time-efficient and reliable method for obtaining assessment information from teachers. In this chapter we summarized the content and properties of several scales that are available for use in clinical evaluations.

We focused primarily on global scales that assess multiple domains of functioning because the nature of childhood problems is such that dysfunction in one domain is often associated with problems in other areas of functioning. Our review of rating scales was not intended to be exhaustive but was designed instead to focus on some of the most commonly used scales and to illustrate what we feel are some crucial areas to consider in evaluating scales for use in a clinical assessment. Also, our overview was not intended to replace a careful reading of the technical manuals of these scales but to highlight some of the important features of the scales that might influence their use in clinical assessments. It is quite heartening that

many of the older rating scales have undergone revisions and new rating scales have emerged, resulting in a pool of more high-quality assessment instruments in the area of teacher ratings than was available over a decade ago (see Carlson & Lahey, 1983).

Teacher rating scales can also be used for more in-depth evaluations of specific problem areas. Two of the more common areas in which teachers provide crucial information are the assessment of attention deficits and overactivity and the assessment of social competence. An emerging trend in the clinical assessment of children and adolescents is to obtain reliable information on the degree of impairment in school and peer functioning that is associated with behavioral or emotional difficulties. Although the development of impairment-oriented rating scales for children is still in the early stages, two examples of scales that focus on level of impairment, rather than on the degree and type of childhood behaviors, were discussed.

CHAPTER SUMMARY

1. Teachers are a critical source of information in most clinical assessments of children.

2. The utility of information provided by a teacher may vary depending on what domain of psychological functioning is being assessed and the age of the child being assessed.

3. The BASC-TRS is a relatively new rating system that covers a broad range of psychological dimensions. Its major strengths include:

   a. It is technically sophisticated in its development.

   b. It fits well into a multi-method and multi-informant assessment using other components of the BASC system.

   c. It covers a range of adaptive behaviors, in addition to assessing the major domains of behavioral and emotional functioning.

   d. Good normative information is available from a large nationwide standardization sample for most ages.

Its major weaknesses include:

   a. Limited norms for adolescents (ages 14–18)

   b. Because of its relatively recent publication, limited amount of research on its validity, especially for discriminating within clinical groups

4. The CBCL-TRF is another omnibus rating scale that is also part of a multi-method and multi-informant system. It has several other advantages as well:

   a. It assesses both adaptive behaviors and emotional and behavioral problems.

   b. Its standardization sample is large, well-distributed across the age ranges and is geographically and racially representative.

   c. The TRF items have a long and extensive research base, which aids in interpretation.

Its major weaknesses include:

   a. The normative sample is somewhat skewed toward upper socioeconomic strata and children receiving mental health or special education services are not represented.

   b. It is difficult to calculate norm-referenced scores that are not gender- and age-specific.

   c. The Thought Problems scale should be used cautiously because of its questionable reliability and validity.

   d. The item content of most of the scales tend to be quite heterogeneous, which hurts interpretation of scale elevations.

5. The CBRSC is also an omnibus rating scale specifically designed for use with teachers. Its major strengths include:

   a. It has scales that can help screen for learning problems.

   b. Its items are closely aligned with the DSM system, which enhances its compatibility with other assessment instruments that are based on this system (e.g., structured interviews).

   c. It provides scales that help to differentiate children with subtypes of ADHD.

Its major weaknesses include:

   a. No analogous forms for other informants

   b. Underrepresentation of ethnic minority students in the standardization sample and no information on socioeconomic status distribution in this sample

   c. Limited assessment of adaptive behaviors

6. CTRS is an omnibus rating scale that has been extensively used in research. Additional strengths include:

   a. The Hyperactivity Index is a 10-items index that has clearly shown to be sensitive to the effects of stimulant medication and provides an efficient way to obtain teacher information when evaluating a medication trial.

Major weaknesses include:

   a. The many forms of the CTRS make it difficult to match validity information to the appropriate form.

   b. The normative base for the CTRS is severely limited making use of normative cut-offs questionable.

   c. The item content of CTRS is limited for the assessment of emotional functioning.

   d. Scales tend to include heterogeneous items hurting interpretation of scale scores.

   e. Different items across parent and teacher versions hinder integration of information across informants.

7. The DCBS-SF is relatively brief (40-items) when compared to other omnibus rating scales. Additional advantages include:

   a. A large and representative normative sample allows one to have confidence in making norm-referenced interpretations.

The weaknesses of the DCBS-SF include:

   a. Poor coverage of behaviors associated with externalizing behaviors

8. The RBPC is an omnibus rating scale frequently used in research. Major strengths include:

a. Consistent factor-analytic support for its scale structure

b. Items worded to have analogous forms for parents and teachers

Major weaknesses include:

a. No representative normative sample with which to make norm-referenced interpretations

b. Somewhat questionable reliability and validity of the Motor Excess and Psychotic Behavior scales

9. In addition to the omnibus rating scales that cover many dimensions of functioning, there are several rating scales that assess specific domains. For example, several scales obtain teacher ratings of ADHD symptoms (e.g., ADDES-School Version, SNAP Checklist), teacher ratings of conduct problems in preschool children (e.g., SESBI), and teacher ratings of a child's or adolescent's social competence (e.g., SSRS; Walker-McConnell scale).

10. A new trend in teacher rating scales is the development of scales that focus on the degree of impairment associated with a child's problems in adjustment.

CHAPTER 9

Behavioral Observations

CHAPTER QUESTIONS

- Why have direct observations often been considered the standard by which other assessment techniques are judged?

- What are some of the characteristics of behavioral observations that limit their usefulness in many clinical situations?

- What are the basic components of observational systems?

- What are some examples of observational systems that might be used as part of a clinical assessment of children and adolescents?

Direct observation of a child's or adolescent's overt behavior has held a revered status in the clinical assessment of youth. Frequently the validity of other methods of assessment is judged by their correspondence with direct observations of behavior. In fact, behavioral observation is often viewed as synonymous with the practice of behavioral assessment (Shapiro & Skinner, 1990). There are two primary reasons

for this infatuation with direct observations. First, as the term *direct* implies, observations of behavior are not filtered through the perceptions of some informant. Instead, the behaviors of the child are observed directly. As we have discussed in the chapters on behavior rating scales, information provided by others in the child's environment or by the child himself/herself can be influenced by a host of variables and biases. This increases the complexity of interpreting these types of assessment by requiring assessors to account for these influences in their interpretations. Therefore, direct observations of behavior eliminate some of the complexity in the interpretive process. Second, direct observations of behaviors frequently allow for the assessment of environmental contingencies that are operating to produce, maintain, or exacerbate a child's behavior. For example, direct observations can assess how others respond to a child's behavior, or they can detect environmental stimuli that seem to elicit certain behaviors. By placing the behavior in a contextual framework, behavioral observations often lead to very effective environmental interventions.

While these characteristics of behavioral observations make their use an important component of many clinical assessments, we feel that the importance of direct observation is often overstated. Like any assessment technique, direct observations have several limitations. One of their major limitations is that direct observations are often expensive and time-consuming, if one is to obtain high-quality information. Because of their cost, many assessors simply eliminate this source of information from their assessment battery. Alternatively, assessors may attempt less-rigorous observations than are appropriate. For example, an assessor may observe a child interacting on a playground for a 20-minute period and record the child's behavior in a narrative form, without clearly specifying what behaviors will be observed or how they will be recorded. These informal observations are dangerous if the assessor is unaware of the severe limitations and potential biases in the data that are collected and instead interprets the data as if they were objective (see Harris & Lahey, 1982a).

Another result of the costliness of direct observations is that the development of many observational systems has ignored basic psychometric considerations (Hartmann, Roper, & Bradford, 1979). In the previous chapters on rating scales, we focused a great deal of attention on the psychometric properties of scales such as the different types of reliability that have been established, the information on the validity of the scales, and the normative base with which to compare scores. Because of cost factors, few systems have established the reliability or validity of observation results in multiple samples. An even more widespread problem for observational systems is the lack of a representative normative sample that would allow a comparison of a child's scores with those from the general population. As we have discussed in earlier chapters, having norm-referenced scores is crucial in clinical assessments of children and adolescents given the rapid developmental changes they are experiencing.

Even if one were to use an observational system in the most sophisticated manner, direct observations are still limited by (1) the reactivity of the observational setting, (2) difficulties in obtaining an adequate sample of behaviors, and (3) an inability to detect internal events such as cognitions and emotions. *Reactivity* refers to a well-documented phenomenon that a person will change his or her behavior when it is being observed (Kazdin, 1981; Mash & Terdal, 1988). As a result, the sample of behavior may not be as objective as one would hope. There is a significant amount of research on factors that influence the degree of reactivity that results from direct observations (Harris & Lahey, 1982b; Kazdin, 1982). For example, the age of the child can affect the degree of reactivity, with preschool children showing less reactivity to observation than older children (Keller, 1986). Also, steps can be taken to reduce reactivity during observation such as allowing the child time to get used to (habituate to) the observational setting and reducing the conspicuousness of the observational system (Keller, 1986). But even under optimum conditions, reactivity is still likely to affect the results of the assessment to some unmeasurable degree.

Another liability of direct observations is the difficulty of obtaining an adequate sample of behaviors. There are several facets to this issue. The first issue involves ensuring that the sample of behavior is obtained under the most ecologically valid conditions—that is, under conditions that will generalize to other times and situations. Although the issue of ecological validity is most important for observational systems that use contrived (analog) conditions (e.g., observing the child in a clinic playroom), it is also important in selecting the natural setting most appropriate for conducting the observation. The second issue is that even if one selects the best setting, one must ensure that a large enough time frame is used, so that the behaviors will be representative and generalizable to other times and settings. In the previous example of a child being observed in a playground setting for a 20-minute period, it cannot be determined how typical a child's behavior was during this observational period. He or she may have had an especially good or especially problematic day on the playground. A third issue, which encompasses both the selection of settings and adequacy of the observational period, is the difficulty in assessing many behaviors that are very infrequent (e.g., cruelty to animals, hallucinations, panic attacks) or by nature covert (e.g., stealing, lying). In most cases, one would not ethically want to contrive a situation that would prompt such behaviors and the behaviors are often too infrequent to be observed naturally occurring in the child's environment.

A final issue in the use of behavior observations is the fact that observations are limited to the assessment of overt behaviors. They do not provide a means for assessing the cognitive, affective, and motivational components of a child's functioning (Mash & Terdal, 1988). This does not negate the importance of having a good assessment of a child's overt behavior in making diagnostic and treatment decisions. However, it has become increasingly clear that overt behavior is only one piece of a complex puzzle. Research in several areas of child psychopathology has supported the importance of intrapsychic variables for both assessing (e.g., Farrington, 1993) and treating (e.g., Kendall & Braswell, 1985) children and adolescents.

In summary, direct observations are affected by some factors that often preclude their use in many clinical settings and limit the usefulness of the data obtained. We spent a great deal of time reviewing the factors that affect behavioral observations, not because of a bias against this form of assessment, but because we have found that too often assessors ignore these issues and overvalue the importance of observations. We feel that a clinical assessor should be aware of these issues in deciding whether or not direct observations should be included in an assessment battery and should consider these issues when interpreting observational data. However, these limitations should not be considered any greater than those associated with other assessment techniques, and the limitations must be weighed against some very important advantages of direct observation (e.g., elimination of reporter bias and ready translation into environmental manipulations). Direct observations can be an integral part of many assessment batteries, but, as is the case for all assessment techniques, they also have limitations in the information they provide in isolation.

In the following section, we discuss basic issues in the development and use of observational systems. As was mentioned earlier in this chapter, many clinical assessors use informal observational techniques

in their assessment battery without establishing a well-defined system. Unfortunately, the information obtained from such systems is difficult to interpret. Unlike rating scales, there are few standardized observational systems that are readily available for clinical use that have well-established psychometric properties. Therefore, the next section focuses on basic considerations in designing an observational system for one's own clinical use. Following this discussion, some examples of observational systems that are commercially available or that have been used in research are reviewed.

BASICS OF OBSERVATIONAL SYSTEMS

Defining Target Behaviors

The basic components of observational systems can be broken down into the what, where, how, and by whom of the system. The first part of developing a system of direct observation involves defining *what* behaviors one wishes to observe. Defining the behaviors of interest first involves deciding on the level of analysis one wishes to use (Barrios, 1993). Specifically, the level of analysis can be at the level of isolated behaviors, at the level of constellations of behaviors (syndromes), or at the level of interactions within a social unit. As an example of the social unit level of analysis, many observational systems allow for the recording of how a child behaves in response to parental behavior and how a parent responds to a child's behavior (Gelfand & Hartmann, 1984). Because these systems allow one to document events (stimuli) that elicit a behavior and responses to the behavior that may help to maintain or increase it, this level of analysis provides important information on potential targets of intervention. An example of a simple antecedent-behavior-consequence (A-B-C) type of observation is provided in Box 9.1. From this example it is clear that recording antecedents and consequences allows one to determine the sequence of events within which a behavior is embedded.

Box 9.1

A Hypothetical Example of Simple A-B-C Observational System of an 8-Year-Old Boy (B)

Time/Setting	Antecedent	Behavior	Consequence
8:30 / Math class— copying from board		B takes pencil from another child	Child ignores him
	Child ignores him	B tears paper on child's desk	Child tells teacher and teacher reprimands B
	Teacher reprimands B	B sulks	Teacher allows B to erase board
8:35 / Math class— doing seatwork		B leaves seat to sharpen pencil	Teacher asks B to raise hand to leave seat
		B raises hand	Teacher continues to work with other student
	Teacher ignores B	B gets out of seat & pulls on teacher's shirt to get attention	Teacher scolds B for leaving seat and places name on board
	Teacher puts B's name on board	B starts to cry	Child teases B
	Child teases B	B tries to hit other child	B sent to office
8:55 / Math class— completing seat work	B returns to class	B sullen and refuses to work	Teacher allows B to collect assignments

---

After the level of analysis is chosen, one must operationally define what behaviors, what constellation of behaviors, or what antecedents/consequences will be observed within this window. These definitions are made prior to beginning a direct observation and must be specified in objective and understandable terms in order to reduce the potential for bias and increase the reliability of the observation. Some ex-

amples of target behaviors used in observational systems are described in Table 9.1.

The target behaviors in Table 9.1 are simply lists of behaviors from several domains that can be assessed by observational systems. In order to be reliable, coding systems must have very explicit definitions of each behavior. This is necessary to reduce the possibility that the observer will use some sub-

TABLE 9.1   Examples of Target Behaviors from Several Behavioral Domains

ADHD (Milich) 1984)	Conduct Problems (Patterson, 1982)	Social Competence (Dodge, 1983)	Depression (Kazdin, 1988)	Autism (Freeman & Schroth, 1984)
Off task	Noncompliance	Solitary play	Talking	Preoccupation with objects
Fidgeting	Destructiveness	Cooperative play	Playing alone	Resisting being held
Vocalization	Aggressive play	Smiling	Negativism	Rubbing surfaces
Plays with objects	Insults/threats	Compliments	Frowning	Ignoring others
Out of seat	Aggression	Rule making	Complaining	Holding hands
	Arguing	Turn taking	Whining	
	Teasing			
	Yelling			
	Humiliating			

jective and idiosyncratic definition of the behavior and thereby making interpretations from the observations difficult. Without such definitions the primary advantage of direct observations, objectivity, is severely compromised. One would think that behaviors such as those in Table 9.1 are easy to define and that simple definitions would lead to different observers being able to code the same behavior in the same way. Decades of research have found that this is not true. To reliably code behaviors, one must develop very detailed definitions. Box 9.2 provides an example of a very detailed definition of behavior from a frequently used coding system.

Setting

Once the target behaviors are defined, the next decision is to determine *where* is the most appropriate place to observe these target behaviors. Naturalistic observations involve observing the child in his or her natural setting (e.g., in the classroom, at home). The kind of behaviors of interest (e.g., social interactions during free play) often determines what natural setting is best to conduct the observation (e.g., on the playground). In its purest form, naturalistic observations involve placing no constraints on a child's behavior other than those naturally occurring in the observational setting. However, sometimes it is necessary to place some restrictions on the observational setting to enhance the quality of the observations. For example, an observer who is in the home of a child to observe parent–child interactions may need to place some constraints on the child and parents to ensure that there are sufficient opportunities to observe interactions during the observational session. For example, one may wish to place the restrictions that parents and children must stay in the same room, that there is no talking on the telephone, and that there is no watching TV. Another example is an observational system designed to observe a child's anxious behavior. The observer may wish the teacher to "create" a situation that seems to lead to anxiety in the child, such as being called on in class or taking a test, in order to observe the child's response.

Naturalistic observations are often preferred because they generally provide more ecologically valid data. However, time and cost constraints may prevent one from conducting a naturalistic observation. For many clinical assessments, it is often impossible

BOX 9.2

Criteria for "Whine" from the Dyadic Parent–Child Coding System

---

Definition

A whine consists of words uttered by the child in a slurring, nasal, high-pitched, falsetto voice.

Examples

When can we go home?

Mommy, I hurt my finger?

I have to go to the bathroom.

This is too hard.

I don't want to play this anymore.

Guidelines

1. The voice quality of the word or phrase is the primary distinguishing element for coding whine.

2. Each whined sentence constitutes a separate whine. Whined phrases separated from one another by a pause of 2 seconds or longer are coded as separate whines.

Examples:

Child: I have a <u>headache.</u> I want to go <u>home.</u> (2 whine)

Child: I don't <u>like</u> the red blocks . . . 2 second pause . . . and I don't <u>like</u> the Legos. (2 whine)

Child: <u>Please</u> let me take it home . . . 2 second pause . . . <u>Please.</u> (2 whine)

3. The content of the word or phrase may be anything except smart talk.

Examples:

I don't like this anymore.	(whine)
I hate you.	(smart talk)
I feel sick.	(whine)
You make me sick.	(smart talk)
You hurt my feelings.	(whine)
You're a jerk.	(smart talk)

4. Whining is a verbal behavior and can occur simultaneously with a nonverbal deviant child behavior (destructive or physical negative-child).

Decision Rules

1. When uncertain as to whether the child's voice quality is actually a whine or normal voice quality, do not code whine.

2. When uncertain as to whether a child's verbalization is a whine, smart talk, or a cry, code whine.

3. When uncertain as to whether the deviant behavior is a whine or a yell, code yell.

SOURCE: Summarized from the manual for the Dyadic Parent-Child Interaction Coding System (Eyberg & Robinson, 1983) with the authors' permission.

for the assessor to make several home visits to observe a child or adolescent interacting with his or her parents. Also, for some behaviors, there may not be a way of obtaining unobtrusive observations in a child's natural environment. As a result, the level of reactivity would be so high that the data would be meaningless. In addition to these more practical considerations, sometimes there is a need to exert more control over the situation than is possible in a natural setting. For example, one may wish to observe a child's activity level in a free play situation by determining how many times a child passes from one part of a room to another. To code this reliably, one can divide the room into sections with tape and then code the number of times a child crosses over a tape divider (Milich, 1984). This type of control (e.g., dividing the playroom into grids) may not be feasible in a child's natural environment.

For these reasons, it is sometimes necessary or desirable to conduct analog observations in a laboratory or clinic. *Analog* refers to the creation of a contrived setting that approximates the natural environment. Dividing a clinic playroom into grids to observe a child's activity level is one example of an analog setting. However, the key to these observations is how well the analog situation approximates the natural environment. Staying with our example, it would be imperative that the playroom be similar to a play area that a child would be in outside of the clinic (e.g., with age-appropriate toys available). There are many other examples of analog settings for behavioral observations, but each involves the basic component of *simulating* a child's natural environment in a clinic setting.

Sometimes it is not feasible to have the clinic setting approximate the natural setting. In these cases, children may be asked to imagine themselves in a situation, and their behavior is observed in this role-play situation. An area in which *role-play* observations have been frequently used is the assessment of children's social competence (e.g., Bornstein, Bellack, & Hersen, 1977; Dodge, McClaskey, & Feldman, 1985). For example, Dodge, McClaskey, and Feldman (1985) had children pretend that they were in certain social situations and then pretend that the assessor was another child. An explicit coding system was developed to code the degree of social competence of a child's behavior in each of the imagined situations. An example of one of the role-play situations used in this study is included in Box 9.3.

Data Collection

The next stage in developing an observational system is to determine *how* one will code the target behaviors in the selected setting. There are several data collection methods that can be used, with the method of choice depending on the characteristics of the behaviors of interest. Although there are many variations of these basic data-collection methods, the tech-

niques can be summarized into three categories: Event Recording, Duration Recording, and Time Sampling.

Event Recording

Event recording is the simplest of the data-collection methods. It involves recording the number of times that a target behavior occurred during preset intervals or during an entire observational session. Due to its simplicity, event recording is the most frequently used method of direct observation. However, to use event recording, target behaviors must have discrete beginnings and endings, such as hitting another child, raising one's hand, and asking to play a game (Shapiro, 1987). In contrast, behaviors that are continuous and persist for long periods of time are more difficult to code using event recording because it is difficult to distinguish the occurrence of one incident from the next. Examples of such continuous behaviors are off-task behavior, talking out loud, and engaging in solitary play. Event recording is especially useful for recording behaviors that occur only briefly and for recording low-frequency behaviors that only occur once or twice in an observational period, such as swearing or hitting another child (Keller, 1986; Shapiro, 1987).

Duration Recording

For some assessments, it may be more important to know how long a behavior occurs rather than the frequency of the behavior. In duration recording the observer records the length of time from the beginning to the end of an instance of behavior. Duration and event recording can be combined to provide an even richer source of information (Shapiro, 1987). For example, in observing the temper tantrums of a young child, it may be helpful to record not only the frequency of tantrums within a given period, but to also record the duration of each tantrum episode.

Time Sampling

In both event and duration recording techniques, all instances of the behaviors are recorded during the

Box 9.3

A Role-Play Situation from the Dodge Study of Social Competence

---

Situation #2

Let's pretend that I'm playing blocks with some of my friends after lunch. We're building a really neat house. You come in the schoolroom and see us. Pretend that you really want to play blocks with us. What do you and say?

   a. Was the child role playing?

   b. How competent was the response? Score:

        8—Complimentary or evaluative remark with a request to play.
            (Example: Boy, that's neat. Can I play?)

        6—A simple request to play: I'd ask, "May I please play?'

        4—Rhetorical question or evaluative remark: What are you doing? or That's neat.

        2—Suggestion for different activity: Want to play a game?

        0—Aggressive responses such as I'd knock the blocks over; subject would say nothing or sit down at
            desk without speaking; subject didn't know what to do, or didn't answer.

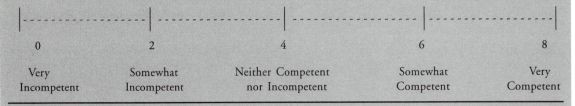

0	2	4	6	8
Very Incompetent	Somewhat Incompetent	Neither Competent nor Incompetent	Somewhat Competent	Very Competent

Reproduced with permission of author from the Scoring System for Child Role Plays: Role Playing Criteria used in K. A. Dodge, C. L. McClaskey, and E. Feldman, "Situational Approach to the Assessment of Social Competence in Children," *Journal of Consulting and Clinical Psychology, 53,* (1985).

observational period. However, some behaviors occur too frequently to obtain accurate counts, or there are no clear beginning or end points to the behaviors, which prevents effective event and duration recording. For these types of behaviors the observation period can be divided into predetermined intervals, and the behaviors are simply coded as being either present or absent during each interval. Therefore, rather than yielding an exact count of the number of times that a behavior occurred during the observational period, time sampling allows one to determine the proportion of intervals in which the behavior occurred.

Shapiro (1987) reviews three types of time-sampling techniques. In *whole-interval* recording one codes a behavior as present only if it occurs throughout a time interval. For example, an observational period in a child's classroom can be broken down into 20-second intervals and the number of intervals in which the child remained on task for the entire interval is recorded. In *partial-interval* recording, one records whether or not a behavior occurred at any time during the interval. Shapiro (1987) gives the example of a teacher dividing the day into 15-minute segments and noting whether or not certain behaviors occurred during each segment. A final type of time sampling is *momentary recording,* in which one records whether a behavior was present or absent only during the moment when a time interval ends. For example, when observing the degree of social withdrawal of a child, one may divide an observational period into 60-second intervals and record whether or not a child was engaged in interactions with other children at the end of each interval.

Selecting the Observers

After determining what behaviors will be observed, where the observations will take place, and how the observations will be conducted, one still must determine *who* is best suited to conduct the observation. Having someone who is in the child's natural setting (e.g., teacher or parent) conduct the observation is often useful in naturalistic observations because it helps to maintain unobtrusiveness. However, it is often difficult to teach people in the child's natural environment how to use a coding system and to ensure that it is being used appropriately.

In order to exert more control over the observational methodology, many observational systems require rigorously trained and monitored observers. Barrios (1993) provides a summary of the steps required in training and monitoring observers (see Table 9.2). As one can see from this summary, using specially trained observers is quite costly. Such stringent methodology is feasible only when a large number of children are being observed with the same observational system. Therefore, such stringent methodology may not be optimal in many clinical settings.

One type of observation that is frequently used in clinical assessments involves training a person to observe his or her own behavior. The same steps of selecting target behaviors, determining the setting for the observation, and determining how the target behaviors will be recorded are followed. However, in *self-monitoring* the child is trained to record his or her own behavior. Although self-monitoring has been used largely with adults, children have used self-monitoring systems to monitor such diverse behaviors as classroom attending, class attendance, talking out in class, room cleaning, aggression, and inappropriate verbalizations (Mash & Terdal, 1988).

Research suggests that children can self-monitor their behavior accurately if they are trained appropriately, have a clear and simple observational system, have an outside monitor of the accuracy of their recording, and are reinforced for the accuracy of their recording (Keller, 1986). The advantages of self-monitoring are that it is cost-effective and is less intrusive than many other forms of behavioral observation. However, research clearly suggests that children change their behavior as they become more aware of it through self-monitoring (Keller, 1986; Shapiro, 1987). Whereas this change in behavior may be a beneficial aspect of self-monitoring in a treatment program, this reactivity limits the usefulness of self-monitoring as a means of obtaining objective information on a child's behavior for assessment purposes.

EXAMPLES OF
OBSERVATIONAL SYSTEMS

In contrast to behavior rating scales, there are few observational systems that are widely used, have standardized procedures, and are readily available for clinical use. In this section, we review some notable exceptions. From the outset the goal of this overview is not to provide an exhaustive list of observational systems but to provide a carefully selected list of systems that vary in terms of target behaviors, settings of observation, method of data collection, and degree of training needed to reliably use the observational system. We feel that even if one does not choose to use one of the specific systems discussed here, these systems provide concrete examples of some of the issues discussed in this chapter and therefore can serve as a guide for the development and use of other observational systems.

Behavioral Assessment System for
Children—Student
Observation System

The BASC-Student Observation System (BASC-SOS; Reynolds & Kamphaus, 1992) is a commer-

TABLE 9.2   Steps in Training and Monitoring Observers

Step	Description
Orientation	Informing observers of the importance of objective assessment in the understanding and treating of childhood disorders. Informing observers of their duties and responsibilities, in particular their independent, unbiased, and faithful recording of the behaviors of interest.
Education	Instructing observers in the response definitions and recording scheme through the use of written materials, filmed illustrations, and live demonstrations.
Evaluation	Assessment of observers' knowledge of the response definitions, coding system, and recording scheme through the use of written and oral examinations. Representation of materials until observers are thoroughly acquainted with all aspects of tracking and recording of the behaviors of interest.
Application	Graduated implementation of the observation system across a range of situations, beginning with analog ones and ending with actual setting of interest. Transition from one situation to the next contingent upon observers achieving a criterion level of agreement and accuracy.
Recalibration	Assessment of the accuracy and agreement of observers' recordings in the setting of interest. Identification and correction of any breakdowns in the fidelity of observers' recordings.
Termination	Questioning observers as to the merits of the observation system. Informing observers of their contributions to the understanding and treating of the behaviors of interest. Reminding observers of the need to maintain confidentiality.

Reproduced with permission from Barrios (1993), "Direct observation." In T. H. Ollendick and M. Hersen (Eds.), *Handbook of Child and Adolescent Assessment* (pp. 140–164). Boston: Allyn & Bacon.

cially available, short (15-minute) observational system that is designed for use in a classroom setting. It is part of the comprehensive BASC system, which includes parent and teacher behavior rating scales and a child self-report form, all of which have been discussed in previous chapters. The BASC-SOS defines 65 specific target behaviors that are grouped into 13 categories—4 categories of positive/adaptive behaviors and 9 categories of problem behaviors. The 13 categories and examples of target behaviors in each category are provided in Table 9.3. The BASC-SOS is designed to use a momentary time-sampling approach in recording data. The 15-minute observational period is divided into 30 intervals. At the end of each 30-second interval the child's behavior is observed for 3 seconds. A checklist allows the observer to mark each category of behavior that oc-

curred during the 3-second observation interval. At the end of the observation period the observer is asked to provide narrative information on the interactions between the child and teacher.

The BASC-SOS is a simple and time efficient observational system that assesses, through direct observation, many behaviors that are crucial for the clinical assessment of children and adolescents. It is one of the few direct observational systems commercially available. However, the BASC-SOS lacks a number of crucial psychometric elements. First, there is no information on the reliability of the system. Establishing interobserver agreement is a crucial component in developing an observational system, to ensure that observations are largely objective and relatively free from bias. Second, there are no norms for the BASC-SOS and so norm-referenced interpreta-

TABLE 9.3 Behavioral Categories from the Student Observation System of BASC

Category/Definition	Example of Specific Behaviors
Response to Teacher/Lesson (appropriate academic behaviors involving teacher or class)	Follows directions Raises hand Contributes to class discussion Waits for help on assignment
Peer Interaction (appropriate interactions with other students)	Plays with other students Interacts in friendly manner Shakes hand with other student Converses with others in discussion
Work on School Subjects (appropriate academic behaviors that student engages in alone)	Does seatwork Works at blackboard Works at computer
Transition Movement (appropriate nondisruptive behaviors while moving from one activity to another)	Puts on/takes off coat Gets book Sharpens pencil Walks in line Returns material used in class
Inappropriate Movement (inappropriate motor behaviors that are unrelated to classroom work)	Fidgeting in seat Passing notes Running around classroom Sitting/standing on top of desk
Inattention (inattentive behaviors that are not disruptive)	Daydreaming Doodling Looking around room Fiddling with objects/fingers
Inappropriate Vocalization (disruptive vocal behaviors)	Laughing inappropriately Teasing Talking out Crying
Somatization (physical symptoms/complaints)	Sleeping Complaining of not feeling well
Repetitive Motor Movements (repetitive behaviors that appear to have no external reward)	Finger/pencil tapping Spinning an object Body rocking Humming/singing to oneself
Aggression (harmful behaviors directed at another person or property)	Kicking others Throwing objects at others Intentionally ripping another's work Stealing

(Cont.)

TABLE 9.3 *(Continued)*

Category/Definition	Example of Specific Behaviors
Self-Injurious Behavior (severe behaviors that attempt to injure one's self)	Pulling own hair Head banging Biting self Eating or chewing nonfood items
Inappropriate Sexual Behavior (behaviors that are explicitly sexual in nature)	Touching others inappropriately Masturbating Imitating sexual behavior
Bowel/Bladder Problems (urination or defecation)	Wets pants Has bowel movement outside toilet

From C. R. Reynolds and R. W. Kamphaus, *Behavior Assessment System for Children (BASC)* (Circle Pines, MN: American Guidance Services, 1992).

tion of scores is not possible. Third, there is limited information on the validity of BASC-SOS, such as whether or not the BASC-SOS code categories correlate with clinically important criteria (e.g., diagnoses, behavior rating scales, response to intervention). These psychometric considerations greatly limit the BASC-SOS's contribution to many clinical assessments. In addition, the BASC-SOS does not provide a standard method of assessing antecedents and consequences of a child's behavior that can provide a sequential analysis of a child's behavior and point the way to potential targets of intervention.

Behavioral Avoidance Tests

Behavioral Avoidance Tests (BATs) have been used to observe a person's behavioral response to an anxiety-producing stimuli since the early 1900s (Jersild & Holmes, 1935). Although there are many different versions of BATs (e.g., Morris & Kratochwill, 1983; Van Hasselt et al., 1979), they all involve exposing the child or adolescent to some feared stimuli (e.g. animal, dark, stranger, heights, blood), then requiring the child to approach the feared stimuli in graduated steps. BATs provide explicit and objective criteria for observing a child's behavioral reaction to

the feared stimulus, such as how closely the stimulus is approached, the number of steps in the gradual approach that are taken, or the time spent touching or handling the phobic stimulus. In quantifying these responses to anxiety-producing stimuli, BATs provide a measure of the severity of a child's anxiety and can help document changes brought about by interventions.

Barrios and Hartmann (1988) provide a good summary of the advantages and disadvantages of BATs. They describe the primary disadvantage of BATs as the absence of a single standardized BAT. Instead, there have been numerous different BATs developed that vary widely on the number of steps in the graduated approach, the types of instructions given to the child, and how the feared stimulus is presented. As a result, it is impossible to compare the findings across studies and therefore it is impossible to develop a significant body of knowledge on the reliability, validity, and normative base for any of the BATs. In addition, a hallmark of the BATs is the rigorous control over how the feared object is presented to the child and how the child approaches it. Barrios and Hartmann (1988) point out that this degree of control may prevent the behavior observed in the contrived setting from generalizing to the child's natural environment.

On the positive side, however, BATs are relatively simple and time-efficient in their administration. Many of the BATs have shown to have good inter-observer agreement with minimal observer training and to be sensitive to treatment effects (Barrios & Hartmann, 1988). Most importantly, they provide one of the only methods of assessing the behavioral components to childhood anxiety.

Child Behavior Checklist—Direct Observation Form

The CBCL Direct Observation Form (CBCL-DOF; Achenbach, 1986) is part of Achenbach's CBCL system and is designed to be interpreted in conjunction with the parent, teacher, and child self-report versions of the CBCL, all of which have been discussed in previous chapters. The CBCL-DOF is designed to provide a direct observation of a child in a classroom or group setting during a 10-minute period. The author recommends using the CBCL-DOF on three to six separate occasions to obtain a representative sample of the child's behavior and then averaging the ratings across occasions (Achenbach, 1986). There are three parts to the CBCL-DOF. First, the observer is asked to write a narrative description of a child's behavior throughout the 10-minute observational period, noting the occurrence, duration, and intensity of specific problems. Second, at the end of each minute the child's behavior is coded as being on- or off-task for 5 seconds. Third, at the end of the 10-minute period, the observer rates the child on 96 behaviors that may have been observed during the observational period using a 4-point scale (from 0 = behavior was not observed to 3 = definite occurrence of behavior with severe intensity or for greater than 3 minutes duration).

The 96 problem behaviors on the CBCL-DOF have a high degree of item overlap, with the behaviors rated on the parent and teacher rating scales of the CBCL system. Therefore, the CBCL-DOF is nicely suited for a multimodal assessment of a child's or adolescent's emotional and behavioral functioning. Like the other parts of the CBCL system, the CBCL-DOF can be used to calculate a Total Problem score, which is a sum of the ratings of all 96

problems, two broad-band scales (Internalizing and Externalizing), and six narrow-band scales (Withdrawn-Inattentive, Nervous-Obsessive, Depressed, Hyperactive, Attention-demanding, Aggressive) (McConaughy, Achenbach, & Gent, 1988).

There is evidence that the CBCL-DOF can be used reliably by observers with minimal training. Interobserver correlations have been calculated on the Total Problems scale in several samples. Correlations between observers range from .96 in a residential treatment center (Achenbach, 1983) to .92 in a sample of boys referred for special services in school (Reed & Edelbrock, 1983) to .75 in a sample of outpatient referrals to a child psychiatry clinic (McConaughy, Achenbach, & Gent,, 1988). Interobserver correlations for the On-task scores were .71, .71, and .88 in the three samples respectively. Reed and Edelbrock (1983) reported interobserver reliability in their sample of 25 boys for a selected set of individual items from the CBCL-DOF. In general, most items showed high inter-observer correlations (most above .80), with the exceptions of Nervous, highstrung, or tense (.20); Picks nose, skin, or other parts of body (.52); and Compulsions, repeats behavior over & over (.53).

Reed and Edelbrock (1983) reported that the Total Problems scale and On-task scores from the CBCL-DOF correlated in expected directions with teacher ratings of total problems and adaptive behaviors. In addition, the CBCL-DOF Total Problems scale and On-Task scores have been shown to differ in normal and disturbed children (McConaughy, Achenbach, & Gent al., 1988; Reed & Edelbrock, 1983). In terms of discriminating within disturbed children, the CBCL-DOF has also shown some degree of validity. McConaughy, Achenbach, and Gent (1988) reported that the Total Problems, On-task, and Externalizing scores differentiated children classified with internalizing or externalizing problems. However, the Internalizing scale of the CBCL-DOF did not demonstrate discriminant validity in this study. The narrow-band scales of Hyperactive, Attention-demanding, and Aggressive all were significantly higher in children with externalizing problems. In contrast, children with externalizing and internalizing problems did not differ on the Withdrawn-

Inattentive, Nervous-Obsessive, or Depressed scales. Therefore, the appropriate use of the internalizing scales of the CBCL-DOF has not been well established to date.

In summary, the CBCL-DOF is a time-efficient observational system that requires minimal observer training and fits into a multi-informant assessment system. The Total Problems and On-task scores have shown to be reliable between observers and to differentiate disturbed and undisturbed children. The use of the other scales is less clear-cut. There is some evidence that the Externalizing scale and the narrow-band externalizing scales differentiate children with externalizing problems from other disturbed children. However, it does not seem that the Internalizing scale or the narrow-band scales related to anxiety and depression possess the same degree of discriminant validity. Therefore, the clinical use of these scales does not seem justified at present. Like most other direct observational systems, the CBCL-DOF suffers from a lack of representative norms with which to compare scores. The author of the scale recommends that the observer use the CBCL-DOF to observe two control children of the same age and sex of a child identified for assessment, one observed prior to the identified child's observation and one observed subsequently. The scores of the control children can be compared with the identified child to provide a frame of reference. However, this provides very limited normative information. Therefore, the CBCL-DOF is not likely to provide good norm-referenced information on a child's emotional and behavioral functioning.

Dodge's Observation of Peer Interactions

Dodge (1983) developed a direct observation system that specifically assesses several components of peer interactions associated with acceptance in a peer group. Dodge developed his system in sample of 5-, 6-, 7-, and 8-year-old boys. Children were observed in 60-minute play groups of eight boys each by three observers who were stationed behind a one-way mirror. The boys wore numbered T-shirts to aid in quick identification by the observer. Each observer coded

the behaviors of one boy for a 6-minute period and then coded a second child according to a prearranged schedule.

There were 18 target behaviors of five types that were defined for the observation system (see Table 9.4). A complex event recording system was used for the observations. Each time a target behavior was observed, the observer coded the time, the context (structured vs. unstructured), the target behavior observed, and the peer target (number of child). Observers received extensive training over a 4-week period; a copy of the training manual is available from the author (Dodge, 1983). With this training, Dodge (1983) reported quite high interobserver agreement. Across the 18 target behaviors, 15 behaviors showed interobserver agreement of 65% or better. The three behaviors that showed poor interobserver agreement were watching peers, norm-setting statements, and supportive statements.

This observational system exemplifies the time-consuming process of developing a reliable method of obtaining direct observations. Although the rigor used by Dodge (1983) may be too costly for most clinical settings, this system was included in this review because it exemplifies observational systems that specifically assess peer interactions. Also, the target behaviors that are a part of the Dodge system were shown to be strongly associated with peer social status (Dodge, 1983). Therefore, these behaviors should serve as a basis for any observational system of peer interactions.

Family Interaction Coding System

One of the most common uses of behavioral observations is to observe parent–child interactions. For example, Patterson and colleagues at the Oregon Social Learning Center have developed a direct observational system designed to assess children's conduct problems in the home and to assess the interactional patterns in which the conduct problems are often embedded. The Family Interaction Coding System (FICS; Patterson, 1982) is composed of 29 code categories that include both child behaviors and parental reactions to the child behaviors. These cat-

TABLE 9.4 Target Behaviors in the Dodge Observational System of Peer Interactions

Behavior Category	Target Behaviors
Solitary Active	Solitary play Watching peers On-task behavior Off-task behavior
Interactive Play	Cooperative play Aggressive play Inappropriate play (e.g., standing on table)
Verbalizations	Social conversations with peers Norm-setting statements (e.g., rule making) Hostile verbalizations (e.g., insults, threats) Supportive statements (e.g., compliments, offers of help) Exclusions of peers from play Extraneous verbalization (e.g., laughs, cheers)
Physical Contact with Peers	Hits Object possession (e.g., grabbing an object from peer) Physically affectionate behavior (e.g., holding hands, hugging)
Interactions with Adult Group Leader	Social conversation with adult leader Reprimanded by adult group leader

From K. A. Dodge, "Behavioral Antecedents of Peer Social Status," *Child Development, 54* (1983).

egories are summarized in Table 9.5. The goal of the FICS was to observe children interacting with family members in natural home settings. However, as described by Patterson (1982), several restrictions had to be made in the home for the observational sessions. Specifically, to use the FICS, all family members must be present during the prearranged observation times with no guests present, and the family is limited to two rooms of the house. There can be no telephone calls out (only brief answers to incoming calls) and no TV. Finally, there is to be no talking to the observers during coding.

The FICS was designed to have data coded continuously and to provide a sequential account of the interactions between a child and other family members. The behavior of the child and the person(s) with whom the child interacts are coded in sequence. After initial coding, many of the child's behaviors are summarized in a rate-per-minute variable that combines both frequency and duration of the behavior. However, the most frequently used "score" from the FICS is the Total Aversive Behavior (TAB) score which is a sum of the number of aversive behaviors (see Box 9.8) which occurred during the observational session.

Patterson (1982) describes a moderate level of interobserver agreement for most code categories of the FICS, with the categories of Negativism and Self-Stimulation showing the most questionable levels of agreement. One-week test-retest reliability of the TAB was studied in a sample of 27 boys and was found to be quite high (.78). The TAB was also found to discriminate between families of children referred for behavior problems and nonreferred families and has proven to be sensitive to family-focused treatment for children's conduct problems (Patterson, 1982). Although most of the individual code categories of the FICS can be coded consistently by two observers, psychometric information is generally limited to the global index of aversive behavior, the TAB.

In summary, the FICS is an example of an observation system designed to assess a child's behavior in the home environment and to assess parent–child interactional patterns in which the behavior is embedded. The FICS is generally most useful for younger children (10 and under). Also, most of the psychometric information available for the FICS is for the aversive behaviors assessed by the TAB. This is not as severe a limitation as one might think, however, given that these aversive behaviors have proven to be quite important to understanding and treating children with conduct problems.

TABLE 9.5   Target Behaviors in the Family Interaction Coding System

Approval	High Rate*	Physical Negative*
Attention	Humiliate*	Physical Positive
Command	Ignore*	Receive
Command Negative*	Laugh	Self-stimulation
Compliance	Noncompliance*	Talk
Cry*	Negativism*	Tease*
Disapproval*	Normative	Touch
Dependency*	No Response	Whine*
Destructiveness*	Play	Yell*

Reproduced with author's permission from G. R. Patterson, *Coerceive Family Process* (Eugene, OR: Castalia, 1982).
* Denotes aversive behaviors that are included in the Total Aversive Behavior (TAB) score.

Structured Observation of Academic and Play Settings

Milich, Roberts, and colleagues (Milich, Loney & Landau, 1982; Milich, 1984; Roberts, Ray, & Roberts, 1984) have developed an observational system (Structured Observation of Academic and Play Settings [SOAPS]) to assess behaviors associated with ADHD in a clinic playroom analog setting. In this system a clinic playroom is designed with age appropriate toys, four tables, and a floor divided into 16 equal squares by black tape. The child is placed in two situations. Free Play involves the child being placed alone in the room and allowed to play freely with the toys. The Restricted Academic Playroom Situation involves the child being requested (1) to remain seated, (2) to complete a series of academic tasks, and (3) not to play with any of the toys.

Each observational situation lasts for 15 minutes. A combination of event recording and time sampling is used in this observation system. Event recording is used to determine the total number of grids crossed for the entire observational period. That is, the number of times that a child moves completely from one square of the divided room into another is counted. Event recording is also used to determine the number of times the child shifts his or her attention from one task to another during the entire observational period. A 5-second time sampling procedure is used to observe other target behaviors. These include the proportion of 5-second intervals that the child is out of his or her seat, that the child is fidgeting, that the child is noisy, and that the child is on task. In the Restricted Academic Situation, two additional categories are coded. The 5-second time sampling is used to determine the number of intervals that the child was observed touching forbidden toys. Also during the academic task the number of items completed is recorded.

This observational system seems promising in several respects for the clinical assessments of ADHD. First, it is a relatively easy observational system. As a result, high interobserver reliability has been obtained for most categories with minimal observer training (Milich, Loney, & Landau, 1982). Second, categories from this system have been correlated with clinicians' diagnoses of ADHD (Milich, Loney, & Landau, 1982), they have differentiated ADHD children from aggressive and other clinic-referred children (Milich, Loney, & Landau, 1982), and they have been relatively stable over a 2-year period (Milich, 1984). Third, a modified version of this task has been shown to be sensitive to treatment with stimulant medication (Barkley, 1988).

CONCLUSIONS

In this chapter, we have attempted to summarize both the advantages and disadvantages of direct observations of behavior as part of a comprehensive clinical assessment. Although we have argued that direct observations are often overvalued by many assessors, we also feel that they are a useful component to many assessment batteries. Probably the biggest detraction from the clinical utility of direct observations is the time and cost involved in conducting behavioral observations appropriately. We have attempted to outline some of the major considerations in developing and using observational systems so that clinical assessors can (1) evaluate existing observational systems appropriately, (2) develop their own observational systems as needed, and (3) recognize limitations in the data provided by observational systems that are not developed and used in a sound manner.

We concluded this chapter by providing an overview of several existing observational systems. This overview was not meant to be exhaustive; the observational systems included were specifically chosen to provide examples of the various domains of behavior that observational systems can assess, the different settings in which observations can be conducted, and the various methodologies that can be employed. Two of the systems are commercially available (BASC-SOS, CBCL-DOF) and cover a broad array of behaviors. The other systems reviewed focus on more narrowly defined dimensions of behavior such as anxiety, peer interactions, aggression, or ADHD. Whether or not a clinical assessor chooses to use these specific systems, we feel that concrete examples of observational systems help to illustrate the unique contribution that behavioral observations can make to an assessment battery.

CHAPTER SUMMARY

1. Direct observations of children's and adolescent's behavior are an important part of an assessment because they provide an objective view of behavior that is not filtered through an informant.

2. Direct observations are also helpful in assessing environmental contingencies that affect a child's behavior.

3. Direct observations also have a number of limitations:

   a. Conducting observations in a way that provides valuable information is often an expensive and time-consuming process.

   b. Because of the cost of obtaining observations, the development of observational systems often has ignored basic psychometric considerations such as testing the reliability of the system or developing an adequate normative base.

   c. Even well-developed observational systems are subject to reactivity. That is, persons change their behavior when they are aware of being observed, which reduces the validity of the observations.

   d. Other factors affecting the validity of observational systems include the difficulty in observing an adequate sample of behavior and the inability to observe internal events.

4. The basic components of observational systems include:

   a. *What*—defining target behaviors to be observed

   b. *Where*—selecting the most appropriate setting in which to observe the behavior

   c. *How*—determining how the target behaviors will be coded

   d. *Who*—determining who should observe the target behaviors

5. In defining target behaviors, one must consider the level at which behaviors will be defined and then clearly define the behaviors to be observed.

6. Observations conducted in a child's natural environment have greater ecological validity but allow less control over the observational setting than observations conducted in a laboratory or analog setting.

7. There are three basic ways in which behaviors can be recorded in an observational system:

   a. Event recording—the number of times a behavior occurred is recorded.

   b. Duration recording—the length of time from

the initiation to the desistance of a behavior is recorded.

   c. Time sampling—behaviors are recorded as to whether or not they have occurred during preset time intervals.

8. Observations can be conducted by outside observers, people in a child's environment (e.g., parents, teachers), or by the child or adolescent himself or herself.

9. The BASC-SOS is an observational system used to assess classroom behavior that can be integrated with other assessment components of the BASC system.

   a. It specifies 65 target behaviors and uses a momentary time-sampling procedure for observations.

   b. There is no normative information nor is there any information on the reliability or validity of this observational system.

10. BATs allows one to observe a child's response to an anxiety-provoking stimuli.

11. The CBCL-DOF is an observational system that can be used in conjunction with other components of the CBCL system.

   a. It allows for a direct observation of a child's classroom behavior during three to six 10-minute observational periods.

   b. There is evidence for the reliability and validity of the CBCL-DOF On-task and Externalizing scores.

   c. Evidence for the reliability and validity of the Internalizing scales is weaker, and there are no representative norms against which to compare scores.

12. Observational systems have also been developed to assess peer interactions, parent–child interactions, and behaviors associated with ADHD.

CHAPTER 10

Peer-Referenced Assessment

CHAPTER QUESTIONS

- What contributions can peer-referenced techniques make to clinical assessments of children and adolescents?

- What are some ethical concerns in the use of peer-referenced assessments?

- What are the different types of peer-referenced assessments?

- What do sociometric exercises measure and why might this be an important component of clinical assessments?

- Besides social status, what other areas of a child's behavioral, emotional, and social functioning can be assessed by peer nomination techniques?

Peer-referenced assessment strategies are assessment techniques in which a child or adolescent's social, emotional, or behavioral functioning is assessed by obtaining the *perceptions of the child's peers*. One of the most common types of peer-referenced assessment is the sociometric assessment, in which the child's acceptance in or rejection by his or her peer

group is determined. We discuss sociometric techniques in more depth later in this chapter. However, *sociometric assessment* should not be considered synonymous with *peer-referenced assessment*. There are many aspects of a child's adjustment, not just peer social status, that can be usefully assessed through the perceptions of a child's peers. A sampling of the most common psychological domains suitable for peer-referenced assessment and the different measurement strategies are the focus of this chapter.

The main reason for using peer-referenced assessment is that it provides important information that cannot be obtained from other sources. The importance of peer perceptions has both an intuitive and empirical basis. A child or adolescent's social milieu is considered a major influence on a child's psychological adjustment in most developmental theories. Therefore, one of the most devastating effects of a child's behavioral disturbance is the effect that it may have on his or her social environment (Coie & Kupersmidt, 1983). For these reasons, understanding how a child is viewed by peers is critical in developing a complete picture of a child's or adolescent's overall psychological functioning. Peer-referenced assessment, whether it focuses specifically on a child's social relationships or indirectly assess a child's social milieu by determining how peers perceive a child's emotional and behavioral functioning, allows for a better understanding of a child's social network.

The empirical literature supports this theoretical emphasis on peer relationships. Parker and Asher (1987) conducted a meta-analytic review of studies that have tested the utility of peer relationships (primarily acceptance and aggression) in predicting later outcomes (dropping out of school, criminality, and psychopathology). Two of the major findings of this review were that low peer acceptance was consistently related to dropping out of school and that peer-rated aggression was consistently related to delinquency. This literature, then, clearly supports the importance of peer perceptions in *predicting negative outcomes* for a child and hence it illustrates the need to assess and to intervene in a child's social milieu. Box 10.1 summarizes several other interesting findings from the Parker and Asher review that have implications for the use of peer-referenced techniques in clinical assessments.

of the studies reviewed, such as imprecise definitions of psychopathology.

However, in addition to illustrating the overall importance of peer relationships to clinical assessments of children, this review had several other interesting results that can guide the assessment process. For example, in terms of predictive accuracy, a consistent pattern of errors emerged in which peer-referenced procedures tended to make few false-negative errors in predicting which children would have poor outcomes, but there were many false-positive errors. That is, most children who have problems later in life had peer relationship problems. However, a large number of children with relationship problems do not show later difficulties. Knowledge of this type of predictive relationship can be quite helpful in interpreting peer-referenced assessments.

The authors of this review also caution users of the literature to be aware of the fact that, despite knowing that there is a predictive relationship between early peer relations and later adjustment, we do not know *why* this relationship exists. For example, it could be that because these children are excluded from normal patterns of peer interactions, they may also be excluded from normal socialization experiences and deprived of important sources of support. However, it is also possible that early forms of a pathological process that may emerge more fully in adulthood may have a negative influence on early peer relationships. In essence, peer relationships could be an accidental by-product of a pathological process and not really have a causal relationship with later adjustment.

A final relevant point made by the authors of this review is the fact that future research should attempt to obtain a more comprehensive picture of children's social relationships. For example, the authors found very limited data on shyness and social withdrawal in predicting later outcome, with most studies relying on indices of acceptance and aggression as the primary aspects of social relationships to be studied. Other aspects of peer relationships that could be studied systematically include impulsive/hyperactive behavior, bossy and demanding behaviors, and behaviors that define attributes that approximate how children choose their friends (e.g., Is this child fun to play with?). The development of peer-referenced assessment is still in its infancy and clinical assessors should be aware of or take part in new developments in the use of peer-referenced assessment techniques.

BOX 10.1

Research Note: Meta-Analysis of the Association between Peer Relationships and Later Psychological Adjustment

---

Parker and Asher (1987) completed a comprehensive meta-analytic review of the predictive association between peer relationships in early to middle childhood and later (adolescent and adult) psychological adjustment. As mentioned in the text, this review clearly supported the importance of a child's social milieu in general, and peer perceptions of a child specifically, in terms of predicting later adjustment. This review found that peer acceptance was consistently predictive of later school drop-out and that peer-rated aggression was consistently related to criminality. These authors found little consistency in the association between early peer relationships and later psychopathology. However, the authors argue that this last inconclusive finding is likely due to methodological inadequacies of most

SOURCE: J. G. Parker, and S. R. Asher (1987), "Peer Relations and Later Personal Adjustment: Are Low-Accepted Children at Risk?" *Psychological Bulletin, 102,* 357–389.

The assertion that peer perceptions cannot be obtained by other methods comes from the meta-analysis conducted by Achenbach, McConaughy, and Howell (1987). These authors calculated the average correlations across studies between peer reports of social, emotional, or behavior functioning with the reports of teachers and with the child's self-report. Across 23 studies reviewed, the average correlation across all psychological domains was .44 between peer and teacher ratings, with the correlation being somewhat higher for behavioral (.47) problems than for emotional (.35) problems. Similarly, across 20 studies in which the correlation between peer ratings and the child's self-report of adjustment was determined, the average correlation was .26, again with the correlation for behavioral difficulties (.44) being somewhat higher than for emotional difficulties (.31). These data suggest that there are substantial differences between how peers rate children and how teachers rate children and how children describe themselves. Therefore, to understand a child's peer network that is heavily influenced by peer perceptions, these perceptions must be assessed directly.

ETHICS OF PEER-REFERENCED STRATEGIES

Despite research on the unique and important contributions that peer-referenced techniques can make to clinical assessments, these techniques are probably one of the least used assessment techniques of any reviewed in this book. The failure to include peer-referenced techniques in many assessment batteries could be due in part to the paucity of standardized, well-normed, and readily available assessment procedures. This exclusion could also be due to the time-consuming nature of many of the peer-referenced techniques used in the research literature. However, as we discuss later in this chapter, there are several relatively time-efficient procedures that have been used extensively in research which could add to a clinical assessment battery. The low frequency of use then is likely the result of other considerations.

One such consideration could be the intrusiveness of peer ratings. Peer-referenced assessment typically involves the use of many peer raters, making it more intrusive than many other assessment techniques. For example, asking a teacher to complete a behavior rating scale adds only one person to the assessment process. In contrast, having a child's class participate in a sociometric exercise involves 15–30 additional people in the assessment process. In addition to the sheer number of people that must be involved, the people involved are typically children who may not appreciate the need for discretion and confidentiality. Therefore, special precautions to limit the intrusiveness of this intervention are essential.

There are several necessary precautions for the use of any peer-referenced strategy. First, it is important that both the parent and the child being assessed are clearly informed and give their consent to the peer-referenced assessment (Gresham & Little, 1993). Second, peer-referenced techniques should be designed to ensure that the child's classmates do not know that the assessment is focused on any one individual (see Box 10.2 for an example of instructions provided in a sociometric exercise). Finally, administration of peer-referenced techniques should be carefully monitored to ensure that answers are not shared, and those involved in the assessment should be instructed on the importance of the confidentiality of their responses after the assessment (McConnell & Odom, 1986).

One of the most controversial aspects of peer-referenced strategies is the use of negative ratings from peers (e.g., nominations of children who are not liked or who are aggressive). Teachers and parents are often concerned about the possibility that these negative ratings will lead to social rejection and other negative reactive effects (McConnell & Odom, 1986). Fortunately, 50 years of research using peer-referenced strategies has not found any evidence for these negative effects (McConnell & Odom, 1986). In fact, the potential for negative effects was specifically tested in one study whose authors did not find any adverse consequences resulting from the peer rating procedure (Hayvren & Hymel, 1984).

Despite the lack of evidence for reactive effects of negative ratings, it would be nice to be able to use

BOX 10.2

Instructions for Two Peer-Referenced Techniques

Assessor-Administered Exercise with Unlimited-Choice Format (Carlson, Lahey, & Neeper, 1984)

After discussing the importance of confidentiality, sheets are provided to each child with the class role and each of 32 nomination categories.

Now we're ready to begin. We have written down lots of things kids do, and we would like you to check which kids in your class do these things. Look across the list of names along the top of the page until you find your name. We'll ask you to tell us about what things you do later, but for now put a line through your name and draw a line down the column your name is in so you'll remember not to check these things for yourself. Go to the other pages and do this every time you see your name.

Now go back to the first page. See the number one? After the number one, it says, "Those who are tall? Now look across the names. Who is tall? Put an "X" under their name. Who isn't tall? Put an "O" under their name. Go through every name one at a time and put an "X" under it if they are tall, and an "O" under it if they aren't tall. Be sure to read every name on the top so you don't forget to check anyone. When you finish with number one, you may turn back to the first page and wait for the rest of the group to finish.

Following the completion of item one, all subsequent items were completed in a similar manner, with each item read aloud.

Items

1. Those who are tall
2. Those who say they can beat everybody up
3. Those who complain a lot
4. Those who bother people when they are trying to work
5. Those who stand back and just watch others who are playing
6. Those who get mad when they don't get their way
7. Those who start a fight over nothing
8. Those who act like a baby
9. Those who don't follow the rules when they play games
10. Those who tell other children what to do
11. Those who try to change the game when they join in
12. Those who help others
13. Those who speak softly and are difficult to understand
14. Those who do not pay attention when someone is talking to them
15. Those who daydream a lot
16. Those who keep talking even when someone is talking to them
19. Those who ask a lot of questions when they join a group
20. Those who always talk about themselves when they join the group
21. Those who don't want your help even if you offer it
22. Those who don't know how to join in the group
23. Those who show off in front of the class
24. Those who share their things
25. Those who give in to others too much
26. Those who are afraid to ask for help
27. Those who often change the subject
28. Those who are honest
29. Those who don't try again when they lose
30. Those who can't wait their turn
31. Those who never seem to be happy
32. Those who let others boss them around a lot

Teacher-Administered Exercise with Fixed-Choice Format (Strauss et al., 1988)

A. Pass out pages of paper to all of the children in the class.

B. Read the following statement to the children: Class, I want us to do an exercise now that will help me learn more about you as people and about your friendships. It will just take a couple of minutes and should be fun,

(Cont)

BOX 10.2   *(Continued)*

Instructions for Two Peer-Referenced Techniques

Teacher-Administered Exercise with Fixed-Choice Format (Strauss et al., 1988) *(Continued)*

but if anyone does not want to take part, you may feel free to sit quietly while the rest of us do the exercise. Because the questions that I will ask are about private feelings, I want to ask you not to discuss your answers with each other and not to let your neighbors see your paper.

C. Then ask the children to list the *three* children in the class that you . . .

1. Like the most
2. Like the least
3. Think fight the most
4. Think are the meanest
5. Think are the most shy

D. After the exercise is completed, collect the papers. To protect the feelings of the children, you may wish to briefly

look through the collected papers and state, "I haven't had a chance to look carefully at these, but it looks like everybody was named as most liked by at least one person. That's really nice." Reiterate the need for the children not to discuss their responses with each other.

E. Count the total number of children who participated in the exercise, and the number of times the child being evaluated was named in response to each of the five questions. Please write this information on the back of the page and mail it in the self-addressed stamped envelope provided.

F. Thank you again for your assistance. If the parent gives us permission to do so, a copy of the evaluation results will be sent to you. It is important to note that the fact that this child is being evaluated does not necessarily mean that he or she has psychological problems; many of the children that we evaluate turn out to be perfectly normal.

NOTE: Procedures are provided with permission of the authors.

---

only positive ratings, given the reluctance of many people to employ negative ratings in peer-referenced assessments. Unfortunately, research has clearly shown that negative ratings are not simply the opposite of positive ratings. Negative ratings add crucial additional information to the assessment. For example, rejected children are not simply nonaccepted children in terms of peer status, but they are actively disliked by their classmates (Coie, Dodge, & Copotelli, 1982). Therefore, one cannot simply assess peer acceptance and then consider those low on acceptance as being rejected by peers. As we discuss later in this chapter, this rejected status, which requires negative ratings to assess, is one of the most important indices of a child's social status. Therefore, negative ratings appear to be an important part of a peer-referenced assessment strategy. However, clinical assessors should be sensitive to concerns about

negative ratings and assure parents and teachers that appropriate safeguards are being used in the assessment procedures and explain to them the critical need for this information in the evaluation.

TYPES OF PEER-REFERENCED TECHNIQUES

Peer Nominations

Peer nominations are the oldest and most commonly used form of peer-referenced assessment (Asher & Hymel, 1981). The procedure involves asking children in a classroom to select one or more of their peers who display a certain characteristic (e.g., liked, fights, cooperates, shy, leader). Although this procedure is relatively simple and straightforward, there are several variations of peer nomination procedures. For example, there can be a predetermined number of children that can be selected in each category *(fixed-choice format)*. Alternatively, the number of peers nominated in each category can be left entirely to the child providing the nominations *(unlimited-choice format)*. An example of instructions for both a fixed-choice and an unlimited-choice format is provided in Box 10.2. Although some authors prefer the unlimited-choice format to avoid forcing a set number of children into categories, especially negative categories (McConnell & Odom, 1986), there is little empirical evidence for any clear advantage of one format over the other.

A second dimension on which peer nomination procedures can vary is the degree of explicitness that defines the nominating pool. For example, some procedures simply instruct the children to consider any child in their class (Strauss et al., 1988). In contrast, other nomination strategies provide children with a roster of names from which to choose (Coie & Kupersmidt, 1983) or may even provide pictures of classmates from which the rater selects nominees for the individual categories (Moore & Updegraff, 1964). The rule of thumb is that the younger the rater, the more explicit the definition of the nominating pool should be. Also, if the pool of potential subjects is not within a well-defined group (e.g., only part of a class is participating in the procedure), then more explicit definitions are required.

The typical level of interpretation of a peer nomination procedure is the number of times a child was nominated in a given category. This number is then compared to a normative base for that particular procedure to see if the child was nominated at a level that is atypical for children his or her age. However, there are some instances where more complex combinations or adjustments of peer nominations are desired. For some purposes it may be useful to compare the number of nominations obtained by a child in one area with the number of nominations that the same child received in another area. For example, in sociometric techniques, one often compares the number a times a child was nominated as Liked Least

with the number of times he or she was nominated as Liked Most by classmates. This allows one to determine the relative balance of the two nomination categories. However, to make such comparisons, the two scores should first be converted to standard scores (e.g., Z-scores; Coie et al., 1982) to equate for possible differences in the variance of the raw scores.

A second type of conversion is warranted if one wishes to compare nominations of one child with the nominations of another child from another nominating pool (e.g., different class). To make this comparison the number of nominations must be adjusted to equate scores for differing class sizes. For example, 5 nominations of Most Cooperative in a class of 12 should be interpreted differently than 5 nominations in a class of 30. As an example of this conversion, Strauss et al. (1988) divided the number of nominations obtained by a child by the number of children participating in the assessment. The quotient was multiplied by 23, so that the nominations were all expressed in terms of a common class size of 23.

Sociometrics

Sociometric techniques focus on a specific, important aspect of a child's peer relationships: a child's social status. It answers the question of whether or not a child is liked and accepted by his or her peer group. Sociometrics do not assess specific behaviors of the child. It answers the question of whether the child is liked and not what is the child like (Asher & Hymel, 1981). Sociometric exercises have appeared in the research literature since the 1930s (see Gresham & Little, 1993; Hughes, 1990), and the most commonly used procedure has changed very little in the past 60 years. An example of this basic technique is provided in Box 10.2 from Strauss et al. (1988).

There are two basic components of sociometric nominations. Children can be nominated by peers as a child who is *Liked Most* (sometimes defined as Most like to have as a best friend or Most like to play with) and/or they can be nominated by peers as a child who is *Liked Least* (or alternatively, Least like to have as a friend or Least like to play with). Although there is no definitive normative study that specifies exact cut-offs for when nominations are considered indicative of problems, in a fixed response format allowing 3 nominations in each category in a class size of approximately 20 students, Liked Most (LM) nominations of less than 2 and nominations of Liked Least (LL) of greater than 4 are generally considered indicative of problems in peer relations (Green et al., 1981; Dodge, Coie, & Brakke, 1982; Strauss et al., 1988).

A common way of interpreting sociometric nominations is by combining the LM and LL nominations into five distinct social status groups (Hughes, 1990). As mentioned previously, when combining LM and LL nominations, the nominations should first be converted to standard scores to equate for potential differences in the variance of the two cat-

egories. The five groups are based on two difference scores. The social preference score is the difference between LM and LL scores (LM − LL = Social Preference). High social preference scores indicate substantially more LM nominations than LL nominations. The social impact score is the sum of the LM and LL scores (LM + LL = Social Impact). High social impact scores simply determine the number of nominations a child receives, regardless of whether they are negative or positive. A combination of these scores leads to a child being considered in one of several social status groups: Popular, Rejected, Neglected, Controversial, and Average. The method of combining these scores to determine a child's social status and two computational formulas that have been used in research are provided in Box 10.3.

BOX 10.3

Determining Social Status from Sociometric Nominations

Category	Description	Computational Formula Using Standard Scores (Coie, Dodge, & Coppotelli, 1982)	Computational Formula Using Raw Scores (Strauss et al., 1988)
Popular	High social preference scores (LM − LL) but few LL nominations	1). ZLM − ZLL > 1 2). ZLM > 0 3). ZLL < 0	1). LM > 4.5 2). LL < 1.5
Rejected	Low social preference scores with few LM nominations	1). ZLM − ZLL < −1 2). ZLM < 0 3). ZLL > 0	1). LM < 1 2). LL > 4.5
Neglected	Low social impact scores (LM + LL) and no nominations in LM category	1). ZLM + ZLL < −1 2). LM = 0	1). LM < 1.5 2). LL < 1.5
Controversial	High social impact scores and above-average LM and LL scores	1). ZLM + ZLL > 1 2). ZLM > 0 3). ZLL > 0	
Average	Average social preference scores	1). ZLM − ZLL > −.5 2). ZLM − ZLL < .5	

NOTE: Both computational formulas are based on a fixed-choice format allowing for three nominations in both the Like Most (LM) and Like Least (LL) categories. ZLM refers to LM nominations converted to standard Z-scores and ZLL refers to LL nominations converted to standard Z-scores. The unstandardized formulas are based on scores adjusted to a class size of 23.

Although there have been several variations in the formulas for determining a child's social status, the validity of these groupings has been consistently shown in research (see Gresham & Little, 1993; Hughes, 1990; McConnell & Odom, 1986). Sometimes these ratings can be influenced by non-behavioral characteristics. For example, physically attractive girls tend to obtain higher social preference scores and therefore fall in the Popular category more often than other children (Vaughn & Langlois, 1983). Another characteristic that influences sociometric ratings is race. Research suggests that social preference scores tend to be higher when nominations are obtained from same-race peers (Singleton & Asher, 1979). This finding on race is especially important for interpreting sociometric ratings in mixed-race classrooms.

Social status has also been associated with emotional and behavioral characteristics of the child. One of the most consistent findings is that rejected children show higher levels of aggressive and acting-out behavior than nonrejected classmates (e.g., Dodge, 1983). However, neglected status is also associated with problems in adjustment, most notably with anxiety (Strauss et al., 1988). Several behavioral characteristics are associated with popular children, including being more likely to contribute to conversations during play, being more likely to engage in parallel play, receiving and initiating more positive social behavior, and using effective peer-entry strategies (Gresham & Little, 1993). Children in the controversial status group have been less well studied. However, one study suggests that children in this social status group tend to exhibit aggressive and disruptive behaviors, like the rejected children, but also tend to be viewed as socially skilled and as leaders, like the popular children (Coie et al., 1982).

From this research it is clear that a child's social status is intertwined with his or her behavioral and emotional functioning, both in terms of current and future functioning. This is especially true of rejected social status which has very severe consequences to a child's adjustment and is highly predictive of later problems in adjustment (Coie & Dodge, 1983). Therefore, sociometrics can contribute important information to many clinical assessments by providing a reliable (see reliability estimates in Gresham & Little, 1993; Hughes, 1990) method of assessing a crucial aspect of a child's social functioning.

Aggression

Another common aspect of a child's functioning that is assessed by peer nominations is aggression. The typical format is to have a class nominate the children in the class who Fight most. As with other nomination techniques, the format can either be in a fixed-choice or unlimited-choice format. Peer nominations of aggression have been shown to be correlated with a psychiatric diagnosis of conduct disorder and therefore can be considered an important indicator of the impairment associated with this syndrome (Walker et al., 1991). However, one of the most interesting and troubling characteristics of peer nominated aggression is its stability. In their 5 year study, Coie and Dodge (1982) found that peer nominations of Starts Fights showed the most stability across the 5 years of any of the peer-nomination categories that were obtained, exhibiting correlations of .83 between third and fourth grades and .84 across fifth and sixth grades. Huesmann et al. (1984) provide even more dramatic evidence for the stability of peer nominations of aggression. These authors found that peer nominations of aggression at age 8 significantly predicted aggression *30 years later.* Therefore, peer nominations of aggression assess an aspect of problematic interpersonal functioning that can be highly stable for a child and is thus an important target for intervention.

Hyperactivity

Assessment of inattention and motor hyperactivity, behaviors typically associated with ADHD, has relied primarily on information obtained from parents and teachers (Loeber et al., 1991). However, Schaughency and Rothlind (1991) provide some interesting data to suggest that peer nominations of inattentive and hyperactive behavior could aid in the assessment of ADHD. Specifically, these authors reported that peer nominations of Can't pay attention, Can't wait turn, and Can't sit still correlated with teacher and observer measures of inattention and hyperactivity. In a second study, these authors reported that peer nominations of Doesn't pay attention and Can't sit still significantly discriminated between youngsters diagnosed with ADHD from other clinic-referred children. Although these results are promising and suggest that peer nominations can aid in the assessment of ADHD behaviors, there is no evidence that these peer nominations should take the place of parent and teacher ratings as a primary information source for these behavioral domains. Also, it is unclear whether or not peer nominations add anything to the assessment of ADHD behaviors over the information provided by other assessment techniques.

Depression

Lefkowitz and Tesiny (1980) developed the Peer Nomination Inventory of Depression (PNID) to aid in the assessment of childhood depression. A list of 13 depression-related categories was developed by nine expert judges. These nomination categories are provided in Box 10.4. Lefkowitz and Tesiny (1980) found that the 2-month test-retest reliability of the individual depression items (mean r = .66) and the depression composite for all 13 items (r = .79) were acceptable. More importantly, the PNID Depression composite was significantly associated with teacher (r = .41) and child (r = .23) ratings of depression. As was the case with peer nominations of inattention and hyperactivity, peer assessment of depression is promising as a component to a comprehensive evaluation but has not been sufficiently tested to determine its contribution relative to more traditional measures of depression.

OTHER PEER-REFERENCED TECHNIQUES

Although we have focused most of our discussion on peer nomination techniques, there are other peer-referenced assessment strategies that have been used in research that may be applicable to some clinical settings. *Peer ratings* require children to rate on a

---

BOX 10.4

Depression Items on the Peer Nomination Inventory of Depression

---

Procedures

Children were provided a class roster. Each item was read aloud twice, and children were instructed to draw a line through all the names on their class roster "which best fit the question" (Lefkowitz & Tesiny, 1980, p. 45). Self-nominations were not permitted, but children could choose not to nominate anyone in a category.

Depression Items

  Who often plays alone?

  Who thinks they are bad?

  Who doesn't try again when they lose?

  Who often sleeps in class?

  Who often looks lonely?

  Who often says they don't feel well?

  Who says they can't do things?

  Who often cries?

  Who doesn't play?

  Who doesn't take part in things?

  Who doesn't have much fun?

  Who thinks others don't like them?

  Who often looks sad?

The 13 items are only the depression items on the PNID. The PNID includes 20 items, with additional items measuring happiness and popularity.

SOURCE: M. M. Lefkowitz, and E. P. Tesiny (1980). "Assessment of Childhood Depression, *Journal of Consulting and Clinical Psychology, 48,* 43–50.

Likert-type scale each member of their class or peer group (Gresham & Little, 1993; McConnell & Odom, 1986). Like any ratings scale, peer scales vary on the behavioral dimensions included on the scale, the number of points on the scale, and the behavioral descriptions used as anchors on the scale. For example, a rating scale for young children used a happy face to anchor the positive end of the continuum, a neutral face to anchor the middle, and a sad face to anchor the negative end of the continuum (Asher et al., 1979).

One of the most reliable forms of peer assessment, especially for very young children (McConnell & Odom, 1986), is the *paired comparison technique*. In this procedure, photographs are taken of all the children in the class and photographs of each possible classmate dyad are paired. The rater is then asked to choose between the two children in each dyad in reference to some criterion (e.g., Fights, Liked, Shy, Cooperative, etc.). The salient used cues in making the choices between peers make this procedure much more reliable for young children, especially of preschool age. However, it is so labor-intensive that it is not feasible for use in most clinical assessments. As McConnell and Odom (1986) point out, for a class of 20 children, each child will have to make 171 selections for each criterion.

CONCLUSIONS

Peer-referenced assessment strategies share the common characteristic of having a child or adolescent rated on important psychological dimensions by his or her peers. Due to several practical and ethical considerations, peer-referenced strategies are not commonplace in many clinical assessments. This is unfortunate because, if designed appropriately and with precautions taken to ensure safe administration, peer-referenced assessment can provide an invaluable picture of child's social milieu. This picture of a child's social relationship is essential for treatment planning given the importance of social relationships for a child's current and future psychological adjustment.

One of the most commonly used peer-referenced techniques is the sociometric exercise. This peer nomination technique allows one to determine whether or not a child is accepted, rejected, or ignored (neglected) by his or her peer group. These dimensions of social status cannot be adequately assessed by other methods of assessment, such as teacher ratings

or a child's self-report. In addition, this crucial aspect of a child's social context has been highly related to emotional and behavioral disturbances. Therefore, sociometric assessment is a type of peer-referenced assessment that could be an especially important component of many clinical evaluations.

CHAPTER SUMMARY

1. Peer-referenced assessments provide information on how a child or adolescent is viewed by his or her peers, and thereby provide important insights into a child's social milieu.

2. Peer-referenced assessments must be conducted in light of two important ethical issues, minimizing the intrusiveness of peer-referenced techniques and minimizing the potential reactive effects of negative ratings by peers.

3. Peer nominations are the most commonly used forms of peer-referenced assessments. They involve having a child's or adolescent's peers select one or more children who display certain characteristics.

4. Sociometric exercises are a type of peer nomination that determines whether a child is accepted, rejected, or neglected by his or her peers.

5. Aggression, hyperactivity, and depression have also been assessed through peer nomination procedures. Unfortunately, the relative utility of peer-reference assessments of these psychological dimensions, in comparison to other assessment modalities, has been untested.

6. In addition to peer nominations, perceptions of a child's peers can be obtained by peer ratings in which children rate each other along certain dimensions on a Likert-type scale.

7. A reliable method of peer-referenced assessment for very young children is a paired-comparison format. Children are given pictures of classmates in dyads, and the rater is asked to choose between the two children in reference to some criterion (e.g., Liked, Shy, Cooperative, Aggressive).

CHAPTER 11

Projective Techniques

CHAPTER QUESTIONS

- What are some of the key issues in the debate over whether and how projectives should be used in clinical assessments?

- What are some of the strengths and limitations of the clinical and psychometric approaches to interpretation of projectives?

- How would viewing projective techniques from either a traditional projection approach or as a behavioral sample influence what type of technique would be used and what interpretations would be made?

- What are the basic interpretive strategies for inkblot techniques, thematic techniques, sentence-completion techniques, and projective drawing techniques?

- What are some specific examples of administration, scoring, and interpretive systems for each type of projective technique?

THE CONTROVERSY SURROUNDING PROJECTIVE TECHNIQUES

No type of assessment has engendered as much controversy as projective techniques. For some, projectives are synonymous with personality testing and provide some of the richest sources of clinical information on children or adolescents (Rabin, 1986; Weiner, 1986). For others, projective techniques typically do not meet even the minimum of basic psychometric standards, and their use therefore detracts from the assessment process and tarnishes the image that psychological testing has with other professionals and with the general public (Anastasi, 1988; Gittelman-Klein, 1986). In Table 11.1, we have attempted to summarize some of the major arguments made on either side of this debate.

Our philosophy in writing this chapter was not to espouse either of the strong views on projective testing. Instead, our goal was to provide the reader

TABLE 11.1   The Projective Debate

Pro	Con
Less structured format allows clinician greater flexibility in administration and interpretation and places fewer demand characteristics that would prompt socially desirable responses from informant.	The reliability of many techniques is questionable. As a result, the interpretations are more related to characteristics of the clinician than to characteristics of the person being tested.
Allows for the assessment of drives, motivations, desires, and conflicts that can affect a person's perceptual experiences but are often unconscious.	Even some techniques that have good reliability have questionable validity, especially in making diagnoses and predicting overt behavior.
Provides a deeper understanding of a person than would be obtained by simply describing behavioral patterns.	Although we can at times predict things we cannot understand, it is rarely the case that understanding does not enhance prediction (Gittelman-Klein, 1986).
Adds to an overall assessment picture.	Adding an unreliable piece of information to an assessment battery simply decreases the overall reliability of the battery.
Helps to generate hypotheses regarding a person's functioning.	Leads one to pursue erroneous avenues in testing or to place undue confidence in a finding.
Nonthreatening and good for rapport building.	Detracts from the time an assessor could better spend collecting more detailed, objective information.
Many techniques have a long and rich clinical tradition.	Assessment techniques are based on an evolving knowledge base and must continually evolve to reflect this knowledge.

with an overview of this method of assessment that would allow for an informed view of the appropriate role of projective techniques in clinical assessments. Too often in the past the debate over projectives has focused on ideological arguments, or even on personal beliefs, without a critical and scholarly examination of the actual issues involved. Therefore, the first part of this chapter focuses on what we feel are the major issues in the use of projectives that determine *whether* they should be used and *how* they should be used in clinical assessments.

Irrespective of ones eventual stand on the projective controversy, projective techniques remain one of the most commonly used methods of clinical assessment by psychologists in general (Lubin, Larsens, & Matarazzo, 1984) and by child psychologists specifically (Tuma & Pratt, 1982). This fact is not cited

to defend their use. It is cited simply to indicate that projective techniques are a firmly entrenched part of the clinical assessment process that shows no signs of changing in the near future.

Clinical Technique or Psychometric Test

Much of the debate over the use of projective techniques comes from a confusion as to what are the most appropriate criteria with which to judge the usefulness of projectives. Traditional methods of evaluating psychological tests are grounded in measurement theory, which, as was discussed in Chapter 2, relies primarily on indices of the reliability and validity of the scores that result from the test

(Anastasi, 1988). When evaluated on these terms, most projectives techniques have not fared well. As Rabin (1986) states:

> An aspect of projective tests that is not to be overlooked is the frequent disappointment and disaffection with the adequacy, reliability, and validity of several projective methods. The psychologist, reared in the atmosphere of respect for science and for the psychometric purity of his instruments, often finds them wanting. (p. 8)

One way these criticisms have been addressed has been through the development of standardized administration, scoring, and interpretive procedures for certain projective techniques that are designed to provide scores that meet traditional psychometric standards. Two examples of such approaches that are frequently used for testing children and adolescents are the Rorschach Comprehensive System (Exner, 1974) and the Roberts Apperception Test for Children (McArthur & Roberts, 1982). Both of these approaches to projective testing are discussed in more detail later in this chapter. However, it is important to note that both systems share the goal of providing very clear and explicit guidelines on how the tests are to be given, scored, and interpreted. Such standardization is a prerequisite to further psychometric evaluation.

This method of addressing the criticisms of projective tests has not met with unanimous approval. Instead, it has been argued that projective tests should not be evaluated by traditional measurement theory and any attempt at standardization will limit the clinical utility of the technique. For example, Haak (1990) has argued that:

> The problem with all of these standardization efforts is the amount of destruction they wreak on the essential nature of projectives. All such approaches result in a huge loss of the rich and complex information that is obtained by using the technique in the first place. (p. 149)

This argument is based on the contention that projectives are part of the older clinical tradition that seeks to describe the individual person in depth, capturing all of his or her unique dispositions, motivations, conflicts, and desires. This is an idiographic approach that is not concerned with how the individual differs from the norm or how his or her scores compare to those of some other reference group (e.g., those with diagnoses of depression). Instead, the goal is simply to understand the person's unique qualities. In this conceptualization, "validity" takes on a very different meaning than the one that is typically used in measurement theory. One is not concerned with how a score compares to some objective criterion outside the person being tested.

For some psychologists this clinical approach might seem unscientific. However, all clinicians rely on intuition at some point in an evaluation to understand the nuances of an individual case. Our science of human behavior is not at a point where every clinical decision can be guided by well-established principles, and, given the complexity of psychological functioning, such pure empiricism may never be possible. Therefore, the clinical view of projectives considers these techniques as a structured way of obtaining these intuitions. By using this structure, one can use the judgments of other experienced clinicians as a guide to making interpretations.

The importance of understanding this debate is not to decide which view is right. What is more crucial is for one to recognize the two disparate ways of using projective techniques and the unique strengths and weakness of both. For example, using projectives as a psychometric technique allows one to compare a person's score with those from a normative group, or with those from some relevant clinic group, or with some other clinically important criterion (e.g., response to treatment). However, to use the scores in this way, one must maintain rigorous standardization in procedures and be willing to live within the confines of the data that are available. One of the frustrating parts of clinical assessments is realizing the limitations of what our assessments can provide.

On the other side of the issue, using projectives as a clinical tool allows one greater flexibility in administration and interpretation. However, with this flexibility the interpretations that result from the assessment are much more susceptible to influences that are idiosyncratic to the assessor. Interpretations of the same case material may vary widely across clinicians. As such, interpretations should be clearly viewed as *clinical impressions* and not be considered in the same way as empirically derived interpretations. In Box 11.1 we have provided a more detailed discussion of the importance of clearly defining ones approach to projective assessment and then recognizing the limitations inherent in either method.

Projection or Behavioral Sample

Even more basic than the debate over the method of interpretation is confusion over what psychological processes projective techniques are supposed to measure. The critical nature of this question is obvious from a psychometric viewpoint. Validity is the critical property of a test and it is often defined as evidence that the test is measuring what it is supposed to measure (Anastasi, 1988). Therefore, if it is unclear what a test is supposed to measure then it will be unclear as to what are the most appropriate methods of determining its validity.

Box 11.1

Two Approaches to Projective Testing: You Can't Have It Both Ways

---

The divergent approaches to the interpretation of projectives can be descriptively labeled as the psychometric approach and the clinical approach. The problem that arises in the use of projectives is that many clinical assessors aren't aware of the approach that they are using and therefore do not recognize the limitations of their approach. To put it bluntly, many assessors want the best of both worlds. They want the flexibility and the rich clinical information afforded by the clinical approach, but they do not want to recognize the potential biases in interpretation that are inherent in such usage. In contrast, many psychologists have found new promise in projective assessments with the advent of standardized administration and scoring procedures for some techniques. However, users of these systems are frustrated by the limited and often confusing databases on which to base interpretations and often slip back into making interpretations that are better considered clinical intuitions. In this box we provide two examples of the confusion resulting from these differing approaches to interpretation.

In the clinical tradition, interpretations are based on clinical judgment and experience. This is often considered bad practice, but we feel that such clinical intuition is unavoidable and even desirable in any assessment enterprise. The problem arises when users fail to recognize the potential unreliability of their clinical judgments. In fact, justification for their interpretations is often based on research on the Exner Comprehensive System for Rorschach interpretation, which has demonstrated acceptable levels of reliability for many scores (Exner & Weiner, 1982). Unfortunately, they use this argument to justify the reliability of *any* interpretation they make for the Exner system or to justify the reliability of their interpretations from *any* projective technique. This latter practice would be analogous to assuming that all self-report measures of anxiety have the same psychometric properties and therefore can be interpreted in the same way.

A second example comes from a common practice in using one of the newer standardized systems, like the Exner system for Rorschach interpretation. Psychologists have enjoyed the increase in reliability that such systems provide and which sets the stage for more empirically based interpretations. However, studies have not always been able to show empirical support for some of the interpretations that have been well established in the clinical tradition (Finch & Belter, 1993). This has led some to the conclusion that the richness of the Rorschach record is simply too complex for current methodology (Finch & Belter, 1993). This implies that the scores *cannot be tested adequately with current research methodology.* Because of this fact, these authors and others have recommended that one should use both the psychometric *and* clinical method of interpretation of Rorschach when using the Exner system. The problem arises when assessors make a clinical interpretation that does not have empirical support but place undue confidence in this interpretation because they are using a reliable and valid system. This goes back to a basic psychometric principle. Tests or interpretive systems are not themselves reliable and/or valid. The individual interpretations that one makes from them can be reliable and/or valid. Unfortunately, the Exner system, like most of the interpretive systems for the projective techniques, encourages interpretations based on clinical tradition, some of which have been supported in research and others of which have not garnered much research support. Users then are often unaware of the basis of their interpretations.

One dominant view of projective tests, which is the view that led to the name *projective,* is best described by Murray (1943): "There is the tendency for people to interpret an ambiguous human situation in conformity with their past experiences and present wants" (p .1). This forms the basis of the projective hypothesis. The projective hypothesis rests on the assumption that people, in the absence of clear environmental demands, will project basic aspects of themselves in their interpretations of environmental stimuli. Freudian theory, which dominated clinical psychology for decades, heavily emphasized unconscious conflict as the basic element of human personality. Projection is seen by many as being a window to these unconscious dynamics.

However, there is a second view of projectives. Rather than seeing them as windows to hidden or unconscious motives and drives, many assessors view projectives as a *behavioral sample.* For example, Knoff (1983) writes:

When a student completes an incomplete sentence blank with "I hate myself" or "My father beats me up all the time," and these hypotheses are confirmed through self-injurious behavior or a physically abusive father, is this a hidden aspect of *personality?* Or how is a student's response to a thematic approach which uses real photographs depicting significant interpersonal situations (i.e., peer group acceptance, attitudes toward schoolwork, reactions to new sibling) different from an interview question asking how she/he is getting along with peers on the playground? (p. 448)

It is evident from this quotation that one can view responses to projective tests as samples of behaviors from which one would like to generalize to behaviors in other situations, outside of the testing environment. In fact, this type of interpretation underlies Rorschach's original development of the inkblot test and has been the guiding principle for Exner's more recent system of interpretation. Rorschach, and later Exner (see Exner & Martin, 1983; Exner & Weiner, 1982), describe the inkblot test as a "perceptual test" meaning that a person's perception of the inkblot is used as a sample of behavior with which to generalize to the person's perception of other, more clinically relevant, stimuli.

These two competing views of what is measured by projectives have several important implications to the assessment process. As already mentioned, how one views the process will determine what evidence is used to establish the test's validity. For example, if one views the test as a behavioral sample, then one would want evidence that the behaviors obtained from the test are associated with behaviors outside the testing situation. Alternatively, if one views projectives as tapping unconscious conflicts, then the relationship to overt behavior is not expected to be one-to-one, since the same conflicts can be manifested in different behaviors (Koppitz, 1983). In this case, validity would be best established by showing that responses on a projective technique are associated with other indicators of unconscious conflicts.

Implicit in this discussion is the important point that how one views the psychological process that is being measured by projective tests will determine the types of interpretations that will be made from a child's or adolescent's responses. A person viewing the results in terms of projection will make interpretations about drives and motivations. It is these types of predictions that one wishes to make. In contrast, a person viewing the results in terms of a sample of behavior will make interpretations about behavioral tendencies that are likely to be manifested in situations outside of the testing situation. For example, if the Rorschach is used as a sample of perceptions, one would wish to make predictions about how these perceptual tendencies will be manifested in other situations.

The final impact of viewing projective techniques as either projection or a behavioral sample is its influence on the selection of the type of stimulus used. Specifically, if one is operating from the projective hypothesis, one would want as ambiguous a situation as possible. For example, the Thematic Apperception Test (Murray, 1943) contains a blank card that has no picture on it and the person is required to make up a story about this card. This is an example of a very ambiguous situation with few demand characteristics, or very little stimulus pull that would guide a person's response. This stimulus allows for the purest form of projection.

In contrast, if one wishes to obtain a behavioral

sample from the projective technique, high levels of stimulus pull may actually be beneficial. If one knows the demand characteristics that promoted the response, then one would have some clue as to what situations one might generalize (i.e., ones with similar demand characteristics). For example, cards from the Roberts Apperception Test for Children (McArthur & Roberts, 1982) were designed to pull for specific themes (e.g., peer conflict, school problems, marital discord in parents). This is not a desirable property from the pure projection viewpoint because it increases the demand characteristics of the stimulus and thereby limits the degree of projection required.

Summary

Our approach to the debate over the use of projective techniques is that assessors should use or not use projective testing based on a careful consideration of critical assessment issues. Assessors are often unclear about what approach to measurement they are using (i.e., clinical or psychometric) and often make inappropriate interpretations based on this confusion. Further, assessors are often unclear about what they are trying to measure with projectives, and, again, this leads to confusion in interpretations or to selection of a technique that is not well-suited for their purpose. The rest of this chapter will highlight characteristics of specific projective techniques. However, these general issues are paramount in understanding and using these techniques; therefore, several of the issues are revisited throughout this chapter.

INKBLOT TECHNIQUES

One of the most commonly used projective techniques is the ink-blot technique. The stimulus is simply an inkblot, and the child is asked to interpret this ambiguous stimulus in some way. The best known of the inkblot techniques, the Rorschach, consists of 10 cards with standardized inkblots. Although the Rorschach is often considered synonymous with inkblot techniques, a notable alternative

is the Holtzman Inkblot Technique (HIT). This technique was developed to overcome psychometric limitations in the Rorschach by constructing a completely new set of inkblots (Holtzman & Swartz, 1990). The HIT consists of two parallel forms, each of which contains 45 inkblots.

Volumes have been written on the different interpretive systems for inkblot techniques for children (e.g., Ames et al., 1974; Exner & Weiner, 1982). The primary variations among these systems are along the dimensions discussed in the introduction to this chapter: whether they view the inkblot test as a projective approach or as a behavioral sample and whether they take a clinical or psychometric approach to interpretation. Rather than giving a superficial overview of the different approaches to interpretation, we will focus on one of the most commonly used methods of interpretation for children: Exner's Comprehensive System (ECS) for Rorschach interpretation (Exner & Weiner, 1982). This system attempts to integrate five major approaches to Rorschach interpretation by combining the empirically defensible features of each system into a single Rorschach approach (Exner & Martin, 1983). Even limiting our focus to one system of interpretation does not allow us to do justice to the intricacies of Rorschach interpretation using the ECS; accordingly, the reader is referred to Exner and Weiner (1982) for a more in-depth discussion of this system of interpretation.

The Exner Comprehensive System for Rorschach Interpretation

Process Measured

The ECS treats the Rorschach as a *perceptual-cognitive task*. When viewed in this way:

> The Rorschach becomes a task to which people respond by exercising their perceptual-cognitive abilities and preferences. To articulate their answers, they must select parts of these variegated stimulus fields to which they wish to attend, use some mixture of the features

of the stimulus and their own needs to guide formulations, and identify objects that will give substance to
their impressions. In short, they decide how to scan
the stimulus, how to translate the stimulus input, and
what to report. (Exner & Weiner, 1982; p. 3)

Weiner (1986) outlines four basic factors that influence a child's response to the inkblot. First, the
nature of the stimulus itself may lead the child to
classify a blot in a certain way. Although the inkblots
were designed to minimize stimulus pull, there are
clearly some common or typical answers that are based
on the specific features of the blots. Second, responses
may be influenced by concerns about making a particular impression which could lead to some censor-
ing of responses in a socially desirable manner. Third,
responses are influenced by personality traits that
predispose a person to perceive the blots in idiosyncratic ways. Fourth, responses are partly a function
of situational psychological states that affect a person's
perception of examination. Each of these factors provides an important context for interpreting a child's
response to the Rorschach inkblots.

Administration and Scoring

In contrast to the complexity of Rorschach interpretation, administration of the task is relatively simple.
The subject is handed the individual cards with the
inkblot stimulus and merely asked, "What might this
be?" The only unacceptable response is, "It's an inkblot." If the child provides this answer, then he or
she is encouraged to see it as something it's not. All
10 cards are administered in this way, and the subject's
responses during this *free association* phase are recorded verbatim for later scoring. After the child responds to all 10 cards, the examiner enters the *inquiry phase*. The assessor readministers each card and
reads to the child his or her initial responses. The
child is instructed to show the examiner which part
of the blot led to the response and what made him
or her think it looked that way. The child is informed
that the assessor would like to see it "just the way
you did" (Exner & Weiner, 1982, p. 29). The child's
responses during this inquiry phase are also coded
verbatim to use in later scoring.

The heart of the ECS is the extensive and detailed scoring procedure of a child's test protocol (i.e.,
verbatim responses to Rorschach cards). This system
includes approximately 90 possible scores. There are
seven major categories of codes, which are described
in Table 11.2: Location, Determinants, Form Quality, Organizational Activity, Popularity, Contents, and
Special Scores. The ECS utilizes a Structural Summary, which shows all of the possible scores, plus
various summary scores that are ratios, percentages,
and other derivations of the individual scores that
provide important information for interpretation.

Norming

The best normative data on the Exner system were
obtained in a large (n = 1870) nationwide sample of
children between the ages of 5 and 16 (Exner &
Weiner, 1982). At each age in this 12-year age range,
there were at least 105 children. There is also fairly
equal gender representation at each age, and the inclusion of minority children is at a proportion that
approximates national census data. The only weakness evident in this normative data base is the
overrepresentation of children from higher socioeconomic strata.

From this normative sample, Exner and Weiner
(1982) documented several age-related trends in scores.
These trends are summarized in Table 11.3. Users of
the ECS with children should be aware of these developmental changes in the Rorschach responses and interpret scores within a normative perspective. The extensive normative database for children available with
the ECS aids in such interpretations. This normative
base is one of the major reasons for the popularity of
the ECS for use with children.

Reliability

Because of its explicit and standardized administration and scoring procedure, it is not surprising that
the ECS has proven to be more reliable than many
other inkblot interpretive systems, showing high
interrater and high test-retest reliability (Exner &
Weiner, 1982; Weiner, 1986). For example, in a
sample of 25 eight-year-old children, 1-week test-

TABLE 11.2   Summary of Scores Used in Exner's Comprehensive System to Rorschach Interpretation

Categories	Description	Examples of Scores
Location	Part of the blot used by respondent	W = Whole blot D = Common area Dd = Uncommon Area S = White space
Determinant	Features of the blot that contributed to the formation of the response	F = Form C = Color T = Texture/Shading M = Human Movement
Form Quality	Measures the perceptual accuracy of the response (i.e., does the area of the blot really conform to the child's perception)	+ = Superior—overelaborated o = Ordinary—common u = Unusual—rare but easy to see – = Minus—distorted, arbitrary, and unrealistic
Content	Places into categories the various persons, places, and things that form the child's response	H = Whole Human An = Anatomy Bl = Blood Fi = Fire Fd = Food Hh = Household Items
Popular	Codes the number of times the child gave a high-frequency (very common) response to a blot	P = Number of popular responses given in the entire protocol
Organizational Activity	Provides an estimate of the efficiency of a child's organization of the stimulus field	Z score = Higher scores indicate greater organizational effort
Special Scores	Denotes unusual verbal material in a child's responses	INCOM = Incongruous Combination—merges details or images in unrealistically way MOR = Morbid—response includes references to death or clear dysphoric feeling AG = Aggressive Movement—response includes action that is clearly aggressive

retest coefficients for individual and summary scores ranged from r = .49 to r = .95 with a mean coefficient of r = .84 (Exner & Weiner, 1982). In fact, the only coefficient to drop below r=.70 was the coefficient for Inanimate Movement (r = .49).

Validity and Interpretations

While Rorschach scores are reliable over short time intervals, the stability of the scores over longer periods is lower than the stability of adult scores. Spe-

TABLE 11.3   Age Trends in the Normative Data for the Exner Comprehensive System for Rorschach Interpretation

Score	Age Trend
Length of Record	Younger children tend to give fewer responses than older children. Protocols of less than 17 are not uncommon before age 15 and records of more than 25 are unusual prior to age 13.
Location	Younger children (less than 11) give more responses that include the whole blot rather than a specific area. Most children, and especially very young children, give at least one response that uses an infrequently identified area of the blot.
Developmental Quality	Younger children frequently give many vague responses in which diffuse impressions of the blot or blot area are given without clearly articulating specific outlines or structural features. Such vague responses account for one-third of the responses of children ages 5, 6, and 7.
Movement Determinants	Younger children give few human movement responses. It is not unusual for the responses of 5-, 6-, and 7-year olds to have few or none such determinants, whereas it is uncommon for this to occur after age 11.
Chromatic Color Determinants	It is not uncommon for children to give color responses that are *not* created based on the form features of the blot. The presence of such pure color responses is often interpreted as indicative of poor affective regulation. About 70% of 5-year-olds, 35% of 8-year-olds, 23% of 12-year-olds, and 8% of 16-year-olds give at least one pure color response.
Form Dimension	Answers that include the impression of depth, distance, or dimensionality increase with age such that by age 8, they appear at least once in over half of all subjects' records.
Reflection Responses	In contrast to responses of adults, images reported as a reflection or mirror image because of the symmetry of the blot are quite common in child protocols. Such responses appear in about half of the protocols of children under the age of 8. Although the incidence of such responses declines over time, they still are found in about 25% of the protocols of 15-year-olds.
Popular Responses	There is a steady increase in the number of popular responses with age, with adolescents giving approximately one-third more popular responses than children under age 8.
Special Scores	Many of the special scores that document unusual verbalizations and cognitive slippage are more common in young children than in adolescents and adults.

SOURCE: J. E. Exner, Jr. and I. B. Weiner, *The Rorschach: A Comprehensive System,* vol. 3 (New York: Wiley, 1992).

cifically, Exner, Thomas, and Mason (1985) tested 57 children at 2-year intervals from age 8 to age 16. In general, most scores showed only moderate consistency over each 2-year interval until the interval between the ages of 14 and 16. Some notable exceptions were the fairly stable coefficients for the use of good form, the use of popular responses, the number of active movement responses, and the use of shading features for making depth and dimension responses. The modest stability of Rorschach scores is not unique to this type of assessment but is characteristic of most assessment techniques in children (e.g., McConaughy, Stanger, & Achenbach, 1992). In fact, this is probably a positive attribute of the scores because it suggests that the scores capture the rapid developmental changes experienced by children and adolescents. However, there is a tendency to equate Rorschach responses with personality assessment and to equate personality with stable dispositions. These findings on the low stability of Rorschach scores clearly argue against making strong dispositional statements based on a child's Rorschach protocol.

One major use of the ECS has been to assess childhood depression. For this use the issue of determining the best method for validating Rorschach scores is compounded by confusion over the nature of depression in children (Kazdin, 1989). Exner (1983) initially developed a Depression Index (DEPI) based on six scores from a child's protocol. Unfortunately, the DEPI, based primarily on research in adults, showed very poor agreement with other measures of depression in children, which led Exner to revise the DEPI (Exner, 1990) in an effort to increase its correspondence with other measures of depression. Tests of the revised DEPI index have also failed to find consistent associations with other measures of depression (Ball et al., 1991). These findings could be a function of inadequate methods of assessing childhood depression in general, which results in the failure to have an appropriate standard with which to judge the Rorschach. Alternatively, Weiner (1986) has argued that the Rorschach "is a measure of personality processes, not diagnostic categories . . . it can only help to identify forms of psychopathology only to the extent that they identify personality characteristics associated with the types of disorder" (p. 155). However, these findings suggest that users of the DEPI from the ECS should not expect the scores to be highly related to other indices of depression.

An even more extreme caution is in order for the Suicide Constellation for Children, a set of scores based on an index used to assess for suicidal tendencies in adults (Exner, 1978). The suicide constellation was developed by selecting the eight best predictors of suicide from the ECS in a small sample (n = 39) of children who had attempted or committed suicide within fewer than 60 days after the Rorschach was taken (Exner & Weiner, 1978). Unfortunately, the predictive validity of these indices was not replicated in another sample, making the interpretation of this index questionable at present (cited in Allen & Hollifield, 1990).

Another common use of the Rorschach is in the detection of cognitive and perceptual irregularities that could be associated with schizophrenia (Weiner, 1986). Exner and Weiner (1982) outline four sets of Rorschach scores that can aid in this detection. First, disordered and illogical thought processes are the focus of several special scores in the Exner system. For example, the Incongruous Combination score identifies responses that condense blot details or images into a single incongruous percept in which the parts or attributes do not belong together: "a person with the head of a chicken" (Weiner, 1986, p. 217). Second, perceptual inaccuracies are suggested when the child has a protocol with many responses that do not correspond closely to the form structure of the blot (i.e., poor form quality) or protocols with few common or popular responses. Third, interpersonal inadequacies that are often associated with schizophrenia can be assessed in responses involving human movement. Movement responses with poor form quality are considered indicative of inaccurate or unrealistic interpretations of interpersonal situations (Exner & Weiner, 1982). Fourth, the irregular content of a protocol, such as one with very violent (e.g., two boys stabbing each other in the chest) or very bizarre content (e.g., flowers squirting poisonous gas) content can be considered suggestive of disturbed ideation that is often associated with schizophrenia.

Exner and Weiner (1982) reported data on 20 children (ages 9 to 16) reliably diagnosed with schizophrenia and 23 nonschizophrenic children. These data indicated that the use of these indices produced a high correct classification rate (90.7%). These positive findings must be interpreted with two cautions, however. First, while these indices appear to be correlated with a diagnosis of schizophrenia, it is unclear how much utility these indices possess over the actual behavioral symptoms of the disorder (Gittelman-Klein, 1986). In other words, there is no evidence to suggest that children who show elevations on these indices but who do not show overt behavioral manifestations of the disorder are at risk for developing Schizophrenia. Second, Gallucci (1989) studied a sample of 72 intellectually gifted children and found elevated rates on these indices compared to age norms, but no other signs of maladjustment in the children. Intellectually superior children may process the Rorschach stimuli in nonconventional ways, but these differences should not be considered indicative of a psychotic process.

Evaluation

These examples of the interpretations that are often made from Rorschach scores using the ECS are only a small sample of the common uses in clinical assessments of children and adolescents. However, these examples illustrate two issues that are important for interpreting all responses on the Rorschach using the ECS. In general, Rorschach responses do not typically correspond closely to behaviorally based diagnoses; therefore, use of the Rorschach for diagnostic purposes is not recommended. Second, many of the Rorschach scores and indices were developed and validated on adults. Unfortunately, the extension to children has not met with great success, as evident by studies on the Children's Depression Index and Suicide Constellation of Children. Therefore, users should be wary about using adult-oriented systems for interpreting the Rorschach responses of children.

THEMATIC (STORYTELLING) TECHNIQUES

The second type of projective technique for children are the storytelling or thematic approaches. In these techniques a child is shown a moderately ambiguous picture or photograph and asked to tell a story about it. For example, the instructions to the Roberts Apperception Test for Children (McArthur & Roberts, 1982) are:

I have a number of pictures I am going to show you one at a time. I want you to make up a story about each picture. Please tell me what is happening in the picture, what led up to this scene, and how the story ends. Tell me what the people are talking about and feeling. Use your imagination and remember that there are no right or wrong answers for the picture. (p. 7)

Thematic tests have been a popular type of projective technique with children because the storytelling format is usually nonthreatening and fun for children. However, it does require a significant level of verbal ability in the child.

There are many different thematic techniques that have been used with children and adolescents, which vary in the types of pictures that are used to promote children's stories. One of the most commonly used techniques for children and adolescents is the Thematic Apperception Technique (TAT; Murray, 1943). The TAT consists of 31 cards with black-and-white pictures of primarily adult figures involved in some relatively ambiguous action or interaction. Because the TAT was designed primarily for use with adults and contained adult pictures, the Children's Apperception Test (CAT; Bellak & Bellak, 1949) was developed especially for children. The original CAT contains 10 cards with pictures depicting animal figures, although a later CAT-H was developed with human figures. The pictures on both the CAT and the CAT-H were designed to ellicit typical childhood conflicts that are predicted from psychodynamic theory (e.g., sibling rivalry, oedipal urges, toileting concerns). Another thematic test heavily influenced by psychodynamic theory is the Blacky Picture Test (Blum, 1950). The Blacky Picture Test consists of 11 cartoons whose central figure is a dog named Blacky. Like the CAT, the pictures were designed to depict psychosexual conflicts common in children.

Two apperception tests, the School Apperception Method (Solomon & Starr, 1968) and the Michigan Picture Test—Revised (Hutt, 1980), were designed more specifically for use in educational settings. One of the more recent thematic tests designed specifically for use with children is the Roberts Apperception Test for Children (RATC; McArthur & Roberts, 1982). The RATC is quite explicit in the themes assessed by the stimulus pictures. Unlike many other thematic techniques, the themes the pictures were designed to assess are not specific to psychodynamic theory. Also, the RATC is one of the few thematic techniques that includes an explicit scoring system. The RATC is reviewed in greater detail later in this chapter.

Thematic approaches often have special sets of pictorial stimuli for specific groups of children. For example, many thematic techniques, such as the TAT and the RATC, contain some pictures that are gender-specific. Also, Thompson (1949) developed a TAT that contains pictures depicting African-American characters. The RATC also contains a supplementary set of pictures depicting African-American children (McArthur & Roberts, 1982). The Tell-Me-a-Story technique (TEMAS; Constantino, 1986) is a thematic test consisting of 23 colored pictures that was specifically designed for depicting minority (Hispanic and African-American) characters in primarily urban and familial settings.

General Interpretation of Thematic Techniques

One important issue in the use of thematic techniques is the lack of standardized administration or scoring procedures for most systems. For example, people administering the TAT often select certain cards to administer. Further, there are many different systems for obtaining scores, but most assessors do not use any systematic scoring system. Given the lack of consistency in administration and scoring, it is not surprising that evidence for the reliability and validity of thematic techniques is limited. Thematic techniques often are interpreted within an idiographic or clinical tradition in which *clinical impressions* of an individual child are obtained through an analysis of the child's stories.

Clinical interpretation of a child's story is typically based on two broad aspects of a child's response. The first step is a *process* interpretation. In this part of the interpretation, one notes such characteristics of the stories as how elaborate the stories were, whether the stories were coherent and tied to the stimulus card, and whether there were any specific cards for which the child had difficulty formulating

a story. This type of interpretation can be used to determine how invested the child or adolescent was in the assessment process, whether there were any potential disturbances or idiosyncrasies in thought processes, and whether there were any specific types of stimuli that elicit defensive reactions from the child.

The second part of the interpretive process is a *content* analysis. Children's stories are typically analyzed for (1) the characteristics of the hero or main character (e.g., motives, needs, emotions, modes of coping, self-image), (2) forces that affect the hero in his or her environment (e.g., rejection by peers, punitiveness from parents, frightening forces, support by parent, affection from sibling), (3) the coping or problem solving strategies used by the hero (e.g., aggression, compromise, nurturance), and (4) the outcomes of the story (e.g., positive or negative, outcomes brought about by hero are someone in his or environment, outcomes are realistic). The content analysis should determine whether there are any *consistent themes* in a child's story, especially themes that transcend the stimulus pull of a card. For example, an aggressive story provided for a card that shows two children fighting is less diagnostic than a story with an aggressive theme based on a picture of two people sitting next to each other in a park.

Roberts Apperception Technique for Children

We decided to provide a more in-depth focus on the Roberts Apperception Techniques for Children (RATC; McArthur & Roberts, 1982) because (1) the RATC was explicitly designed for use with children and (2) the RATC is one of the few thematic procedures with an explicit and standardized scoring system. This instrument illustrates some major components in the interpretive process of thematic techniques.

Content

The RATC is intended for use with children and adolescents ages 6 to 15. There is a standard set of 27 stimulus cards depicting common situations, conflicts, and stresses in children's lives (McArthur & Roberts, 1982). Eleven cards have parallel male and female versions, and there is a supplementary set of stimulus cards featuring African-American children. A description of the RATC cards and the themes the cards were designed to elicit are provided in Table 11.4.

Administration and Scoring

The administration procedures are quite simple (the instructions given to the child were provided earlier in this chapter). The RATC provides explicit instructions for scoring the stories provided by a child. Each story is scored on 16 coding categories. There are 8 Adaptive categories, 5 Clinical categories, and 3

TABLE 11.4 Depictions in the Stimulus Cards from the Roberts Apperception Test for Children

Card Number	Description	Common Themes
1 (B & G)	Both parents discussing something with child	Elicits themes of family confrontation and stories in which parents are giving advice or punishing a child
2 (B & G)	Mother hugging child	Elicits themes of maternal support and dependency needs in relation to a maternal figure
3 (B & G)	Child working on homework	Elicits themes related to child's attitude to school, teachers, tests, and homework
4	One child standing over another child in prone position	Elicits themes with aggression, accidents, and illnesses
5 (B & G)	Parents are shown in an embrace with child looking on	Elicits themes related to a child's attitude toward parental displays of affection
6 (B & G)	Two white children are shown interacting with a black child	Elicits themes related to peer interactions and racial attitudes
7 (B & G)	Child sitting up in bed awake	Elicits themes of anxiety and bad dreams
8	Both parents speaking to male and female child	Elicits themes related to family discussions, such as around discipline or planning a family activity
9	Child standing with clenched fists over a child sitting on the ground	Elicits themes related to peer aggression
10 (B & G)	Mother holding baby with child looking on	Elicits themes of sibling rivalry and attitudes toward the birth of a new sibling
11	Child cowering with hands in front of face	Elicits themes of fear and anxiety

(Cont.)

TABLE 11.4   *(Continued)*

Card Number	Description	Common Themes
12 (B & G)	Adult male glaring at a distressed adult female with child looking on	Elicits themes of parental conflict and parental depression
13 (B & G)	Child preparing to throw chair onto the ground	Elicits themes of anger and aggressive feelings
14 (B & G)	Child with paint on hands has put handprints on wall with mother looking on in distress	Elicits themes of maternal limit setting and child wrongdoing
15	Adult female in bathtub with male child looking through door	Elicits attitudes toward sexuality and nudity
16 (B & G)	Child and father in a discussion while father looks at a paper	Elicits themes of father–child relationships and paternal approval

NOTE: B & G = Separate cards for girls and boys.
SOURCE: D. S. McArthur and G. E. Roberts, *Roberts Apperception Test for Children* (Los Angeles: Western Psychological Service, 1982).

categories labeled Indicators. A description of these categories is provided in Table 11.5. As evident from this box, the RATC coding categories are quite similar to traditional content areas used to interpret other thematic techniques. Scores used in interpretations from the RATC are the total number of times a given code was present across all stories. This allows one to determine consistent themes (high scores within a category) across stories.

Norming

One objective of the authors of the RATC was to develop a standardized scoring system so that normative data could be generated and used by other users of the system (McArthur & Roberts, 1982). The importance of age-specific normative data in the interpretation of projective tests was already discussed in the previous section on the Rorschach. Unfortunately, the normative data provided in the RATC

manual are minimal. The normative sample on which norm-referenced scores are based consisted of 200 school children: 20 boys and 20 girls in the age ranges of 6–7 and 8–9 and 30 boys and 30 girls in the age ranges of 10–12 and 13–15. Not only is the size of the sample small, but its representativeness is also questionable. The sample was taken from three school districts in southern California. Although the manual states that an effort was made to select children from lower, middle, and upper socioeconomic family backgrounds (McArthur & Roberts, 1982), there is no evidence to show that this goal was met, nor is there any information given on the ethnic make-up of the sample. Therefore, the norm-referenced scores provided in the RATC manual are of questionable utility.

Reliability

A positive outcome of the explicit scoring system was an increase in reliability compared to other thematic

TABLE 11.5   Profile Scales and Indicators from The Roberts Apperception Test for Children

Scale	Purpose	Description of Scoring Criteria
Reliance on Others (A)	Designed to measure the adaptive capacity to use help to overcome problem	Main character (1) seeks assistance for handling problem or completing tasks, (2) asks permission, or (3) asks for approval or material objects
Support—Other (A)	Reflects tendency to support others	Main character (1) gives object or does something requested or (2) gives emotional support or encouragement
Support—Child (A)	Measures self-sufficiency, maturity, assertiveness, and positive affect	Main character (1) shows appropriate self-confidence, assertiveness, self-reliance, perseverance, or delay of gratification or (2) experiences positive emotions
Limit Setting (A)	Measures the extent that parents place reasonable and appropriate limits on child	Story describes some appropriate disciplinary action or constructive discussion following child wrongdoing
Problem Identification (A)	Measures child's ability to articulate problem situations	Character in story states a problem or obstacle or experiences contradictory feelings
Resolution—1 (A)	Measures child's tendency to seek easy or unrealistic solutions to problems	Story involves a situation in which a problem is solved without any clear mediating process or by some unrealistic or imaginary process
Resolution—2 (A)	Measures a child's tendency to use constructive resolutions to problems	Story involves constructive resolution of internal feelings, external problem, or conflicted interpersonal relationship. Solution is limited to present situation without an explanation of the process involved in working through the problem
Resolution—3 (A)	Measures a child's tendency to use constructive resolutions to problems	Same as Resolution—2, except the story explains how the character worked through problem
Anxiety (C)	Measures a child's tendency to interpret situations as dangerous and fearful	Story involves (1) character showing apprehension, self-doubt, or guilt or (2) themes of illness, death, or accidents
Aggression (C)	Measures a child's aggressive impulses	Story involves angry feelings, physical or verbal attack, or destruction of objects

(Cont.)

TABLE 11.5   *(Continued)*

Scale	Purpose	Description of Scoring Criteria
Depression (C)	Measures a child's tendency to depression	Stories involve dysphoric feelings, giving up, or vegetative symptoms of depression
Rejection (C)	Measures issues that a child might have concerning separation and rejection	Story involves physical separation, rejection, dislike of another person, needs unmet by others, or racial discrimination
Unresolved (C)	Measures a tendency toward having an external locus of control or an inability to control one's emotions	Story involves an emotional reaction without a resolution
Atypical Response (I)	Measures distortions in a child's thought processes or unusual ideation	Story involves a distortion of stimulus card, is an illogical story, involves homicidal or suicidal ideation/action, involves death, or involves child abuse
Maladaptive Outcome (I)	Measures poor problem-solving abilities or the presence of a pessimistic or hopeless cognitive style	Story involves characters that behave inappropriately to solve a problem or when the story ends with the main character dying
Refusal (I)	Measures a lack of investment in the task or extreme defensiveness to certain stimuli	Child refuses to respond or stops in the middle of a story and refuses to go on

NOTE: Descriptions of scoring criteria are not full criteria and should not be used in place of the explicit criteria provided in the RATC manual. Manual also provides concrete examples of each criteria.

(A) = Adaptive scale, (C) = Clinical scale, (I) = Indicator.

SOURCE: D.S. McArthur and G. E. Roberts, *Roberts Apperception Test for Children* (Los Angeles: Western Psychological Services, 1982).

approaches without standardized administration or scoring procedures. The manual reports that 17 doctoral-level raters averaged 89% agreement on three RATC protocols, and 8 master's-level clinicians reached 84% agreement. Evidence for the split-half reliability of the RATC was less impressive, however. Acceptable (above .70) reliability was found for only 6 of the 13 adaptive and clinical scales: Limit Setting, Unresolved, Resolution 2, Resolution 3, Problem Identification, and Support.

Validity and Interpretations

The increase in reliability afforded by the RATC scoring system has set the stage for the development of a database with which to judge the instrument's validity. However, the extent of this database is presently quite limited and the findings mixed. For example, the manual reported comparisons between 200 clinic-referred children and the 200 well-adjusted children in the standardization sample (McArthur & Roberts, 1982). In this broad test, all eight of the adaptive scales and all three indicators differed between the two groups. In contrast, the only clinical scale to show differences between groups was the Rejection scale. Thus, the clinical scales failed to differentiate maladjusted from well-adjusted children, which does not bode well for the likelihood of these scales accomplishing the more difficult tasks of differentiating types of problems within clinic-referred children.

Evaluation

Because of the lack of validity evidence, the RATC should not be used in diagnostic decision making, as is the case for other thematic approaches. Instead, the RATC should be used as a method of obtaining clinical impressions, with a consideration of all the strengths and weaknesses of this test. However, unlike many other thematic techniques, the explicit scoring system of the RATC has led to a reliable scoring procedure which sets the stage for further validation to guide interpretations. Another caution in interpreting the RATC stems from the poor normative base from which norm-referenced scores provided in the RATC are derived. These scores should be regarded as suspect until further information becomes available from a larger and more representative population of children and adolescents.

SENTENCE COMPLETION TECHNIQUE

Another type of projective technique that is frequently used in the clinical assessment of children is the sentence completion technique (SCT). The sentence-completion method involves providing the child, either orally or in writing, a number of incomplete sentence stems such as, My family is . . . or I am most ashamed of . . . . As evident from these examples, the stimulus employed in sentence completion techniques is much less subjective than the other projective methods reviewed in this chapter. That is, the sentence stems have a high degree of stimulus pull in prompting certain types of answers. As a result, many have debated whether sentence comple-

tion methods should even be considered projective, given their more objective nature (Hart, 1986).

Although clearly SCTs require a different level of inference than other projectives, they probably are closer to other projectives in design and interpretation than to self-report rating scales. However, a decision as to whether or not to use a SCT in a clinical assessment goes back to our initial discussion of projective techniques in general. If one wishes to interpret projectives as a behavioral sample, then the objective nature of the SCT and the lower level of inference required is a distinct advantage. In contrast, if one wishes to enhance projection, then the strong stimulus pull of the SCT is less desirable.

Features of SCTs

Content

Despite a common format, there are numerous SCTs available that vary on their content (e.g., fears, self-image, significant relationships, psychodynamic conflicts), length, complexity, and purpose. The Rotter Incomplete Sentence Blank (Rotter & Rafferty, 1950) is one of the oldest and most common of the SCTs. It was originally developed for use with adults and consists of 40 items designed to elicit information on psychosexual conflicts. It is available in three forms, and the authors provide a quantitative scoring procedure that can be used to determine the degree of conflict present in each response. Another commonly used SCT is the Hart Sentence Completion Test for Children (HSCT). The 40-item HSCT was designed specifically for use with children, and the content was designed to elicit children's perceptions of family, peers, school, and self (Hart, 1986). The HSCT is discussed in more depth later in this section. There are numerous other SCT procedures that are beyond the scope of this chapter to discuss in detail, such as the Rohde Sentence Completion Method (Rohde, 1957), and the Haak Sentence Completion Technique (cited in Haak, 1990).

Administration

Administration of SCTs are straightforward and typically includes instructions that inform children that they are to complete the sentences in whatever manner they choose, and that there are no right or wrong answers. There are two important dimensions on which the administration procedures of SCTs differ (Hart, 1986). First, some users of SCTs request that the child answer as quickly as possible by saying the first thing that comes to their mind, in an effort to elicit spontaneous and unguarded responses. In contrast, other users attempt to promote deliberation by telling the subjects that they can complete the sentences in any way they like and that the purpose of the test is to better understand their *real* feelings. The first use of the SCT is typically preferred if the goal of administration is projection. The second administration procedure is typically preferred if the goal is to obtain a behavioral sample.

The second major way in which SCTs differ in administration is in whether or not they include an inquiry process. In the inquiry phase children are asked to explain their responses in more depth. This questioning helps the assessor determine why a child may have completed the sentence in a particular way. This information is especially useful for responses that are unusual, ambiguous, or diagnostically important (Hart, 1986). Because of the important clinical information obtained by this inquiry, it is often an integral part of the administration of SCTs for many assessors' procedures (Haak, 1990).

Interpretation

Interpretation of SCTs typically relies on an analysis of the manifest content of a child's responses. As was the case with the thematic techniques, an assessor would analyze a child's response for consistent themes that might provide clues to the child's emotional adjustment or his or her perceptions of certain persons or situations. For example, positive responses to stems designed to assess perceptions of parents (My father is the best; What I like best about my father is he is nice) are thought to be an indication of a positive father–child relationship. This is an example of the low level of inference that is often applied to the interpretation of SCTs.

Some assessors also analyze the *process* of a child's responses, such as are they complex, are they perseverative, are they expressive and imaginative, and are they coherent and related to the sentence stem (Haak, 1990). This type of analysis can provide the assessor with insight as to how invested a child was in the task and some possible clues into a child's thought processes. Box 11.2 provides an overview of the most common approaches to interpreting responses on SCTs.

BOX 11.2

Research Note: Interpretive Approaches to Sentence Completion Techniques

---

The author of the Hart Sentence Completion Test for Children (Hart, 1986) provided an interesting summary of various interpretive approaches to sentence completion techniques (SCTs) in the clinical assessment of children and adolescents.

Strategy 1

The most common interpretive approach to SCT is to review each item's content and obtain clinical impressions about a child's personality dynamics. The assessor searches for patterns, clues, and thought processes and generates hypotheses consistent with the assessor's view of human behavior. This approach often leads to different interpretations of the same set of responses by different clinicians. What is viewed as important or diagnostic will depend on the assessor's theoretical orientation.

Strategy 2

The next approach places sentence stems into clusters with similar item content that are judged to elicit similar psychological information. The assessor determines if there are important patterns of responses within a cluster of items. However, like the first strategy, the interpretations are heavily dependent on the assessor's orientation. What items determine a meaningful cluster and what constitutes an important pattern of responses within a cluster are based on an assessor's theoretical orientation.

Strategy 3

The third approach is exemplified by the Rotter Incomplete Sentence Blank (Rotter & Rafferty, 1950) and is based
(Cont .)

on psychodynamic theory. Each response is analyzed according to the degree of intrapsychic conflict evident in the response. It is a quantitative scoring system in which the severity of the conflict is rated as negative, neutral, or positive.

Strategy 4

The fourth approach involves comparing responses on SCT to some predetermined criteria. This approach attempts to limit the unreliability inherent in the other strategies by minimizing the reliance on the assessor's theoretical orientation. An example of this approach is the Hart Sentence Completion Test for Children (Hart, 1972). In a standardization sample a large pool of responses were obtained for each sentence stem. The responses were placed into positive, negative, and neutral categories by expert judges. In each rating category, representative responses were identified for each sentence stem to aid assessors in making their determination of the valence of a child's response.

SOURCE: D. H. Hart, "The Sentence Completion Techniques," in H. M. Knoff (Ed.), *The Assessment of Child and Adolescent Personality*, New York: Guilford, 1986.

Evaluation

As evident from the discussion of SCTs to this point, most systems do not have explicit and standardized administration, scoring, and interpretive procedures. These decisions are often left to the judgment of the assessor who can be guided by the advice of the authors of the SCT or other experienced clinicians (e.g., Haak, 1990). As a result, most SCTs can be considered to fall in the clinical tradition of projectives, with most techniques failing to have well-established psychometric properties (Anastasi, 1988). Of particular concern is the lack of a normative base to guide the interpretation of SCTs in children and adolescents. Also, most SCTs were initially developed for adults and so the content is often inappropriate for children. A notable exception is the Hart Sentence Completion Test for Children (Hart, 1972).

Hart Sentence Completion Test for Children

The Hart Sentence Completion Test for Children (HSCT; Hart, 1972) is one of the few sentence completion tests specifically designed for children. As mentioned earlier, the HCST contains 40 sentence stems designed to assess a child's perceptions of family, peers, school, and self. The majority of items were designed to assess a child's self-perceptions by sampling his or her reactions to sentence stems involving achievement, security, aggression, materialism, affiliation, and isolation. There are also several self-concept items assessing a child's personal evaluation of his or her physical abilities, physical attributes, personal adequacies, and general self-worth.

The HSCT was designed for use with children and adolescents ages 6–18. The instructions request that the child complete the sentence with the first things he or she thinks of. There are two scoring approaches to the HSCT. The first system is a global subjective rating system in which the assessor rates the child on a 5-point positive-to-negative continuum on all items pertaining to a specific content area (e.g., perceptions of family, perceptions of peers, personal evaluation). A second, more systematic scoring procedure is also available. Each item is rated as either positive, negative, or neutral based on a comparison with representative responses from 250 children. Each response from the standardization sample for each sentence stem was rated as positive, negative, or neutral by five school psychologists (Hart, 1980). These ratings for individual items were combined within each content area to provide examples or anchors against which an assessor can judge a child's response.

Hart (1986) and Hart, Kehle, and Davies (1983) cite several studies showing high reliability estimates for the HSCT, especially for the item-by-item scoring system. Also, these authors cite studies showing that the HSCT scores can differentiate emotionally disturbed from well-adjusted students. Therefore, it appears the HSCT is a promising assessment approach. However, it should also be noted that these data do not support its use for making differential diagnoses within samples of disturbed children. Also, correlations between the HSCT and other measures of analogous constructs are lacking (e.g., HSCT scores on the Personal Evaluation scale with other measures of self-esteem).

DRAWING TECHNIQUES

A final popular approach to projective testing with children is through the interpretation of children's drawings. The popularity of drawing techniques in the assessment of children can be attributed to two factors. First, unlike other projective techniques that require substantial verbal ability often exceeding the capacity of some very young children, drawing techniques are primarily nonverbal. Second, most children are familiar and comfortable with drawing and thus it is an enjoyable assessment context for a child. Koppitz (1983) writes:

> Drawing is a natural mode of expression for boys and girls. It is a nonverbal language and form of communication; like any other language, it can be analyzed for structure, quality, and content. (p. 426)

From this description it is evident that the interpretation of children's drawings is based on the same assumptions that underlie the interpretation of other projective approaches—namely, that drawings contain nonverbal clues and symbolic messages about a child's self-concept, motivations, concerns, attitudes, and desires (Cummings, 1986).

Draw-a-Person Technique

One of the most common drawing techniques for children is the Draw-a-Person Technique (DAPT) made popular by a seminal publication by Koppitz (1968). In this technique a child is simply given a paper and lead pencil and asked to draw a picture of a whole person. It is left up to the child the type of person to be drawn (e.g., age, gender, race, context of figure). After finishing this first drawing, the child is given another sheet of paper and asked to draw another person of the opposite sex from the first drawing.

Koppitz (1968) provides one of the most explicit guides to interpreting children's figure drawings. She organizes her approach around three basic questions. The first question is *How did the child draw the figure?* Such content analysis is the focus not only of the Koppitz system but of most interpretive systems of children's drawing. In the Koppitz system the figure is viewed as reflecting a child's self-concept. Koppitz developed a series of 30 Emotional Indicators (EI) that were rare in children's drawings that were independent of age, and that differentiated undisturbed from maladjusted children. Examples of EI in the Koppitz system include poor integration of parts, slanting of figure by 15 degrees or more, omission of mouth, body, or limbs, and monster or grotesque figures. Figure size is another EI that is not only a part of the Koppitz system but is included in many interpretive systems and is considered to be a key indicator of a child's self-esteem. Small figures are interpreted as indicating low self-esteem (2 inches or less in height) and large expansive figures (9 inches or more in height) are interpreted as indicating high levels of self-esteem. Box 11.3 summarizes in more detail Koppitz's EI.

The second question around which the Koppitz interpretation is organized is *Whom does the child draw?* Most children tend to draw figures that are of the same gender as themselves (Cummings, 1986; Finch & Belter, 1993). Based on these findings, Koppitz considered a child's drawing an opposite-sex figure on his or her first drawing to be diagnostic, either of problems in gender identity or as a reflection of loneliness and isolation. There is also a tendency to view the figure as an indicator of the child's image of his or her own body (Cummings, 1986).

The final question in the Koppitz interpretive system is *What is the child trying to express via the drawing?* A child's self-figure may reflect his or her self-perceptions, or a drawing of someone else may reflect attitudes or conflicts toward this person. Koppitz notes that a child's drawing may (1) be a reflection of a child's wish, fantasy or ideal; (2) be an expression of real attitudes or conflicts; or (3) be a mixture of both. To help clarify this issue, many assessors note either a child's spontaneous verbalizations about a

BOX 11.3

**Research Note: Further Discussion of the Koppitz Emotional Indicators
for Human Figure Drawings**

As mentioned in the text, the writings of Elizabeth Koppitz (1968, 1983) have been quite influential in the interpretation of human figure drawings for children and adolescents. A key element to her projective interpretation of drawings is the presence or absence of 30 Emotional Indicators (EI). Koppitz's EI were chosen based on (1) their utility in differentiating disturbed from nondisturbed children, (2) their low prevalence (less than 6%) in the drawings of nondisturbed children, and (3) their occurring independent of age.

The EIs can be divided into three broad categories: Quality Signs, Special Features, and Omissions.

QUALITY SIGNS	SPECIAL FEATURES	OMISSIONS
Poor integration of parts	Tiny Head	No eyes
Shading of face	Crossed eyes	No nose
Shading of hands & neck	Presence of teeth	No mouth
Asymmetry of limbs	Short arms	No body
Slanting figures	Long arms	No arms
Tiny figure	Arms clinging to body	No legs
Big figure	Big hands	No feet
Transparencies of major	Hands cut off	No neck
body parts	Legs pressed together	
	Genitals	
	Monster/Grotesque figures	
	Multiple figures drawn	
	spontaneously	
	Clouds	

Koppitz explains that the EI are not scores but are clinical signs that may reveal underlying attitudes and characteristics of the child (Koppitz, 1983). There is evidence that the EIs occur at a greater frequency in the drawings of emotionally disturbed than nondisturbed children (see Finch & Belter, 1991). However, Koppitz describes the difficulty in interpreting EIs for the individual child:

> There is no relationship between an EI and overt behavior. For instance, long arms and big hands both reflect aggressiveness and anger, yet children who show these two EI on their drawings may act very differently. One boy may reveal his anger by refusing to do his homework or by truanting from school, another child may be physically aggressive to peers, while a third child may withdraw and soil himself when angry. The Human Figure Drawings indicate that all three pupils are angry; the youngsters' behaviors demonstrate how they express this anger. It is also important to recognize that different EI can reflect the same attitude. Thus, a girl may show acute anxiety by shading the body and face of her Human Figure Drawing and by omitting the arms. When she makes another drawing some time later, she may omit the figures' nose and hands and may draw a dark cloud above the figure. Similarly, a single EI may have different meanings depending on the situation. For example, a tiny figure may reflect underlying timidity or shyness, or it may indicate withdrawal or depression. The true meaning of a given EI can only be determined by other aspects of the personality battery, from observing the child in different work settings, and from studying his or her developmental and social background. (Koppitz, 1983; p. 423)

SOURCE: E. M. Koppitz. Projective Drawings with Children and Adolescents, *School Psychology Review, 12,* (1983), 421–427.

figure or ask the child to tell a story about the figure. The assessor may follow up with specific questions about the figure such as, Who is he/she in the figure? or Whom were you thinking about while you were drawing? or What is he/she thinking about? or How does he/she feel?

House-Tree-Person

A second projective drawing technique is the House-Tree-Person (HTP) technique (Cummings, 1986). In this technique the child is asked to draw a house, a tree, and a person. The order is always the same and the drawings are done on separate sheets of paper. After the drawing, children are asked a series of questions to give them an opportunity to describe and interpret the objects that were drawn (Cummings, 1986; Koppitz, 1983). According to one of the originators of the HTP technique, the three figures give insight into different facets of a child's functioning (Hammer, 1958). The house is thought to elicit feelings associated with the children's home situation and familial relationships. In contrast, the tree is thought to elicit deeper and unconscious feelings about themselves and their relationships with their environment. Unlike the self-portrait, the tree is thought to have less pull for conscious self-descriptions and therefore to involve a greater level of projection. And, finally, the drawing of a person is thought to reflect more of a conscious or semiconscious view of the child's self, the child's ideal self, or a significant other.

Kinetic Family Drawing

A third common projective drawing technique that is used in the assessment of children and adolescents is the Kinetic Family Drawing. In this technique a child is asked to "Draw a picture of everyone in your family, including you, *doing* something" (Burns & Kaufman, 1970, p. 5). These instructions emphasize the family engaging in some activity, hence the term *kinetic*. As was the case for the HTP technique, there is an inquiry phase in which a child is asked to describe and explain his or her drawing (Cummings, 1986). The first part of the inquiry typically involves

the child explaining who each figure is (e.g., name, relationship to the child, age). The child is then asked to describe all the figures, what they are doing in the picture, how they are feeling, and what they are thinking about. After these initial descriptive questions, the child is asked to tell a story about the drawing, saying what happened immediately before the actions depicted in the drawing took place and what happens next. Finally, the child is asked to describe anything that he or she would change about the picture if he or she could.

The popularity of the KFD lies in its ability to assess a child's perceptions of his or her family in a fun and nonthreatening way. Burns and Kaufman (1970) outline a three-part interpretative process that is heavily dependent, not just on the drawing, but on the inquiry phase that follows. The first part of the interpretive process is the analysis of the *actions* portrayed in the drawing. It not only refers to the movements between people but the energy (e.g., avoidance, conflict, nurturance) and emotion (e.g., love, anxiety, anger) captured in the picture. The next part of the interpretive process deals with the style of the family drawing. Style refers to the patterns of interactions among significant family members and often reflects a child's defense system (e.g., denial, isolation). The final stage of the interpretation is the *symbolic* interpretation which is analogous to the content interpretations of other projective drawing techniques.

Psychometric Cautions for Drawing Techniques

As with most other projective techniques, the best method of validating projective drawings has been hotly debated. In a review of the psychometric properties of drawing techniques, Cummings (1986) found that the lack of explicit scoring and interpretive guidelines for projective drawings has caused most systems to have poor reliability. Even for those systems in which high reliability estimates have been obtained, correlations between drawings and other measures of a child's adjustment have not been consistently shown. Most studies have found that clinicians are unable to distinguish clinically identified children from nonclinical controls using projective drawings. This inability to demonstrate the validity of projective drawings has led to the extreme position held by some authors that the use of drawings in clinical assessments of children is unethical (Martin, 1983). This strong stance has sparked a lively debate (Knoff, 1983).

It is clear that content analyses of drawings have rarely been shown to predict overt behavior, yet many users still try to make behavioral predictions (e.g., aggression, anxiety, history of sexual abuse) from drawing techniques. A quote from Cummings' (1986) review of projective drawing research seems to summarize a sensible way to view assessment with projective drawings and possibly a good way to view projective testing in general:

> The greatest value associated with projective drawings does not lie in the graphic symbols represented on the paper. Rather, the value of the technique may be in the practitioner's opportunity to observe the examinee's behavior while drawing. Drawings provide a non-threatening beginning point which should lead to an in-depth exploration of attitudes, feelings, and beliefs via the synthesis of direct interviews, third-party interviews, observations, and test data. (pp. 238–239)

CONCLUSIONS

In this chapter we have outlined some of the major issues in the debate of when and how to use projective testing in the clinical assessment of children and adolescents. As with most assessment techniques, the problem with projective testing lies not in the techniques themselves but in the inappropriate purposes for which they are often employed. This issue is exacerbated in the use of projective techniques because of widespread disagreement over the basic nature of these techniques. There is considerable dissension over what psychological processes they are designed to measure and there is lack of agreement over what method of interpretation (e.g., clinical or psychometric) is most appropriate for a given technique. The most important goal of this chapter was to provide the reader with a clear discussion of these issues so

that projectives can be used appropriately, with the assessor clearly recognizing the limitations of whichever interpretive approach is used.

We have also summarized some of the major methods of projective testing that are used with children. We have discussed inkblot techniques, thematic techniques, sentence completion techniques, and projective drawings. Space limitations prevent an exhaustive review of specific techniques and interpretive systems. However, we have attempted to provide selected examples of each type of projective method as a basis for developing greater expertise in the use and interpretation of these techniques through further didactic and clinical training.

CHAPTER SUMMARY

1. Projective techniques have been the focus of much controversy. However, they remain the most frequently used method of psychological assessment.

2. Much of the debate over projective techniques stems from confusion over what projective techniques were designed to measure and how best to evaluate their usefulness.

   a. The first area of confusion is whether projective techniques obtain samples of behavior or whether they assess unconscious personality dynamics.

   b. The second focus of debate is whether projectives are ways of obtaining highly individualized clinical impressions or whether they are psychometric tests that should be evaluated by traditional indices of reliability and validity.

3. The Exner Comprehensive System provides a structured method for administering, scoring, and interpreting responses to Rorschach inkblots.

   a. The inkblots are administered in two phases: a free association phase and an inquiry phase.

   b. Detailed scoring of responses provides 90 possible scores to be used in interpretation.

c. A large nationwide normative sample allows for norm-referenced interpretations, which is especially important in light of several age trends in children's Rorschach responses.

d. Scores from the Exner system have proven to be reliable.

e. The validity of scores for children has not been well established, although it has been difficult to determine the most appropriate way of testing the validity of Rorschach scores.

4. Thematic tests provide a child with a relatively ambiguous picture and require that the child "make up a story" about the picture.

5. Most interpretive systems of thematic tests use a two-part interpretation of a child's stories. The first step interprets the process of a child's stories (e.g., coherence of stories) and the second step interprets the content of the stories.

6. A popular thematic test for use with pre-adolescent children is the RATC.

a. The RATC contains pictures depicting common situations that children experience and provides a standard scoring system for children's responses.

b. The explicit scoring instructions allow for reliable scoring of children's responses.

c. The standardization sample on which norm-referenced scores are based is quite small and its representativeness is questionable.

d. Existing evidence for the validity of RATC scores is quite limited.

7. Sentence-completion techniques provide the child with a sentence stem and require the child to complete the sentence.

8. Most sentence-completion techniques do not have standardized scoring procedures for interpreting children's responses. It is left to clinical judgment how to interpret the content of the responses.

9. A notable exception is the Hart Sentence Completion Test for Children which provides two explicit methods of scoring children's responses.

10. Drawing techniques, such as the Draw-a-Person Technique, the House-Tree-Person, and the Kinetic Family Drawings are popular for assessing children because drawing is a familiar and enjoyable exercise for children.

11. Despite their popularity, there is no interpretive system of children's drawings that has shown high levels of reliability and validity.

CHAPTER 12

Structured Diagnostic Interviews

CHAPTER QUESTIONS

- What are the major differences between structured and unstructured interviews?
- What are the major similarities and differences among the most common structured diagnostic interviews used to assess children?
- What information can diagnostic interviews provide that cannot be obtained from other assessment techniques?
- What are some important guidelines for the appropriate use of diagnostic interviews in the assessment of children and adolescents?

HISTORY

Clinical interviews have a prominent place in the history of psychological assessment. The face-to-face verbal dialogue between assessor and client is the prototypical format for most clinical enterprises. Until recently the most common type of clinical interview was the unstructured interview. In the unstructured interview the interviewer determined what questions would be asked, how the questions would be framed, what follow-up questions would be asked, and what were acceptable responses from the client. This unstructured format was quite consistent with the clinical approach to assessment, which was discussed in the previous chapter on projectives. It allows the assessment to be tailored to the individual needs of the client and relies heavily on the individual clinician's orientation and expertise.

However, many clinicians were concerned about the unreliability inherent in unstructured interviews. The results and interpretation of the interview tended to be highly idiosyncratic to the clinician conducting the interview. This unreliability was especially problematic for research. Hence, many clinical assessors began to develop more structured diagnostic interview schedules that provided a clear and standardized format from which to conduct the clinical interview. Initially most of these instruments were designed for use with adults and were primarily used in research. Two of the better known of the early interview schedules were the Feighner Research Diagnostic Criteria (Feighner et al., 1972), which later became the NIMH Diagnostic Interview Schedule (DIS; Robins et al., 1981) and the Schedule for Affective Disorders and Schizophrenia (SADS; Endicott & Spitzer, 1978).

Over the past two decades, structured diagnostic interviews have moved from being strictly research instruments to being a part of many clinical assessments. In addition, several interview schedules have been developed for use with children and adolescents. This chapter focuses on these interview schedules and their potential role in the clinical assessment of children and adolescents.

OVERVIEW

Structured diagnostic interviews consist of a set of questions that the assessor asks the child or adolescent. There are explicit guidelines on how a child's responses are to be scored. Interview questions generally start with a stem question (e.g., Have you been involved in many physical fights?). If the stem is answered affirmatively, then follow-up questions are asked to determine other relevant parameters such as frequency (e.g., How many fights have you been in the past year?), severity (e.g., Have you ever used a weapon in a fight?), duration (e.g., When was the first time you got in trouble for fighting?), and impairment (e.g., Has fighting caused problems for you at school, home, or with kids your age?). An example of the question format from the NIMH Diagnostic Interview Schedule for Children—2nd Edition (DISC-2.3; Shaffer et al., 1991) is provided in Box 12.1.

Commonalities Across Interview Schedules

In Table 12.1 we summarize the basic characteristics of the most commonly used diagnostic interviews for children. It should be noted that the interviews are continuously updated to keep up with changing diagnostic criteria or modified for some specific ap-

---

BOX 12.1

Example of the DISC-2.3 Question Format

The following is an example of the stem/follow-up question format used by most diagnostic interview schedules. This question was taken from the questions assessing Social Phobia from the DISC-2.3 (Shaffer et al., 1991). Words in italics are not to be read to the child but are simply instructions to the interviewer.

13. In the past 6 months, have you been very nervous or anxious in any of these situations:

    A. . . . speaking to people you don't really know, like a clerk in a store?

    B. . . . speaking in class?

    C. . . . reading out loud in front of others?

    D. . . . writing in front of other people?

    E. . . . or eating in front of others?

    (IF NO FEARS NAMED, GO TO QUESTION 14)

IF MORE THAN 1 FEAR NAMED IN Q13, ASK F.
THEN ASK G TO N ABOUT FEAR NAMED IN F.
IF ONLY 1 FEAR NAMED, GO TO G

    F. Which of these are you most afraid of? *(WRITE IN)*

    G. Are you afraid of *{Name Fear}* because you are shy and get easily embarrassed?

    IF YES,   H. When you have to *{Name Fear}*, are you almost always nervous or anxious?

         I. Does *{Name Fear}* make you so nervous or anxious that you try not to do it or refuse to do it?

         J. When you have to *{Name Fear}*, do you become nervous or anxious right away?

         K. If you have to *{Name Fear}*, do you feel very nervous or anxious almost the whole time?

         L. Does being nervous or anxious about *{Name Fear}* keep you from

(Cont.)

Box 12.1 *(Continued)*

doing things you would like to do or should do?

M. Do you think you are much more nervous or anxious about this than you need to be?

N. Does being so nervous or anxious about *{Name Fear}* bother you a lot?

IF THREE OR MORE RESPONSES IN I TO N WERE YES, ASK:

O. How old were you when you started to be nervous or anxious about *{Name Fear}* ?

SPECIFIY AGE _____

This question sequence is reprinted with the permission of Dr. David Shaffer.

---

plication (e.g., outcome measure for treatment of childhood depression, screening device for an epidemiological study of child disorders). Therefore, many of the interviews have multiple versions and are continually being revised. The contents of these interviews were all based on the criteria specified in the *Diagnostic and Statistical Manual of Mental Disorders,* starting with the third edition (DSM-III; American Psychiatric Association, 1980) and continuing through its more recent revisions (DSM-IV; American Psychiatric Association, 1994).

Which DSM disorders are assessed is generally quite similar across the different interview schedules. All of the interviews can be used to assess for the disruptive behavior disorders, affective disorders, and anxiety disorders in children and adolescents. All interviews also allow for an assessment or at least a brief screening for schizophrenia. With the exception of the K-SADS, all of the interviews also assess for substance use and elimination disorders. With

the exception of the ISC, all of the interviews assess for symptoms indicative of eating disorders. The DISC is unique in including questions that assess for the presence of verbal and motor tics. Most interviews organize questions by diagnosis, with the exception of the Child Assessment Schedule (CAS; Hodges et al., 1982). The CAS has several sections in which questions are organized around specific topic areas (e.g., school, family, friends), rather than being organized around diagnostic criteria.

In order to promote multi-informant assessments, most interviews contain parallel forms to ask identical questions of both the child and a parent. There is even an experimental teacher version of the DISC 2.3 that was used in the DSM-IV field trials for the disruptive behavior disorders (Frick et al., 1994).

Most of the interviews were designed to assess children and adolescents between the ages of 8 and 17. Some interviews report applicability to younger children. However, there is some evidence that the reliability of children's self-report on diagnostic interviews is low before age 9 (Edelbrock et al., 1985; Hodges & Zeman, 1993). The length of time that it takes to administer a diagnostic interview is heavily dependent on the child being assessed. Because of the stem/follow-up question format, more symptomatic children will require more interview time because of the need to ask more follow-up questions. However, as evident from Box 12.2, the average time to administer the interviews does not vary much across the different schedules and is typically from 60 to 90 minutes.

Major Sources of Variation across Interview Schedules

From the previous discussion it is clear that the various interview schedules probably have more similarities than differences. However, one of the major differences across schedules is the *degree of structure* inherent in the interview format. All of the interviews provide some degree of structure and give guidelines for standardized administration and scoring. However, there is substantial variation in the amount of "leeway" given the assessor across the various interviews. For example, the K-SADS is one of

TABLE 12.1   Basic Features of Interview Schedules for Children

Name	Primary References	Time	Administration Age	Time Frame	Informants	Remarks
Child Assessment Schedule (CAS)	Hodges, Cool, & McKnew, 1989; Hodges	60–90 minutes	7–17	Present	Child and parent	Originally developed for ages 7 to 12. Shown to be reliable for both symptoms and diagnoses. Less structured than some other interviews and therefore requires trained clinicians to administer.
Diagnostic Interview for Children and Adolescents (DICA)	Reich et al., 1982	45–60 minutes	6–17	Lifetime	Child and parent	Highly structured format allows for trained lay interviewers and clinicians to administer. Shown to be reliable for assessing conduct disorder, attention deficit disorders, "any" depressive disorder, and "any" anxiety disorder.
Diagnostic Interview Schedule for Children (DISC-2.3)	Shaffer et al., 1993	60–90 minutes	6–17	Present	Child and parent (experimental teacher version available)	Highly structured format especially designed for administration by trained lay interviewers. Good reliability for major categories on both symptom and diagnostic level. Frequent use in epidemiological studies allows for a determination of base rates of disorders in community samples.
Interview Schedule for Children (ISC)	Kovacs, 1985; Last, 1987	60–90 minutes	8–17	Present	Child and parent (use single form)	Primarily developed for assessment of depression. One of the least structured formats and therefore requires experienced clinicians for administration. Limited data on psychometric properties.

(Cont.)

TABLE 12.1   *(Continued)*

Name	Primary References	Time	Administration Age	Time Frame	Informants	Remarks
Schedule for Affective Disorders and Schizophrenia for School-aged Children (K-SADS)	Ambrosini et al., 1989; Chambers et. al., 1985	60–90 minutes	6–17	Present and life-time (two versions)	Child and parent (use single form)	Primarily designed to study childhood depression. Semistructured format requires clinician administration. Allows for ratings of severity of symptoms on Likert-type scales. Some questionable reliability estimates, especially for anxiety disorders.

the least structured of the interviews. The manual for administration includes the following instructions:

> The K-SADS supplies a series of questions addressed to the child for each item to be rated. The aim is not to oblige the rater to ask all of the questions. They serve as a guide for questions which have been found most helpful and informative. The rater should ask as many questions as necessary to arrive at a well-documented rating. Needless to say, probing should be as neutral as possible and leading questions should be avoided. (Puig-Antich & Chambers, 1978, p. 2).

In contrast, the DISC-2.3 was designed to have a greater degree of structure in administration. The manual for its administration includes the following instructions:

> The DISC-2.3 symptom questions are designed to be read *exactly* as written. There is very limited scope for independent questioning. DO NOT deviate from the prescribed question sequence. DO NOT make up your own questions because you think you have a better way of getting at the same information, or because you think the question is poorly worded. (Fisher, Wicks, Shaffer, Piacentini, & Lapkin, 1992; p. 31).

The trade-off between leeway and structure is obvious. Less structure allows the assessor to tailor the interview according to the needs of the individual client. However, these interviews generally require a greater degree of experience to administer and often have lower levels of reliability (Gutterman, O'Brien, & Young, 1987; Hodges & Zeman, 1993).

Another major variation among the structured interviews for children is the time frame used to assess symptoms and diagnoses. All of the interviews assess whether problems are currently evident. This is called a *present episode* frame of reference. Most interviews consider present episodes to be within the last 6 months, although in some instances the time frame may be as short as within the last 2 weeks (ISC for emotional disorders) or as long as within the last year (DISC-2.3 for conduct disorder). The major source of variation is whether or not the interview is *limited* to present episodes. Most interviews only assess for problems that are being displayed within the given time window. For example, if a child exhibited a depressive episode prior to the 6-month time frame on the DISC-2.3, this disturbance would not be detected. In contrast, the DICA targets *lifetime* diagnoses by determining whether or not a child has ever shown symptoms of the disorder being assessed. A similar lifetime focus is used by one version of the K-SADS (K-SADS-E).

A third source of variation within the interview schedules is the answer format. For most interviews the interview responses are coded into a categorical format (yes, no, sometimes). This categorical format is consistent with the DSM orientation in which symptoms are considered either present or absent. In contrast, the ISC and the K-SADS have answer formats that can be placed on a Likert-type scale that allows one to rate the severity of a symptom. While this format makes it more difficult to translate responses into DSM diagnoses, it does not create an artificial dichotomy between the presence or absence of a symptom and allows symptom scores to reflect gradations in severity.

EVALUATION OF DIAGNOSTIC INTERVIEWS

Advantages

Structured interviews share with behavior rating scales the goal of obtaining a detailed description of a child's emotions and behaviors from multiple informants. The logical question is: What advantages do the time-consuming structured interviews offer in comparison to the more time-efficient behavior rating scales? The primary advantage of structured interviews is their usefulness in obtaining important parameters of a child's behavior that are not typically assessed by most behavior rating scales. Specifically, most interview schedules provide questions that elicit information on the duration of a child's behavioral difficulties and the age at which the problems began to emerge. This temporal information allows one to take a developmental perspective in understanding a case, a perspective that has proven to be crucial for assessing many forms of childhood psychopathology (e.g., Frick & Lahey, 1991; Lahey et al., 1992).

Interviews also allow one to determine the *temporal sequencing* among behaviors. For example, it is important in the assessment of childhood depression to determine whether periods of sadness occurred contiguously with other behaviors associated with

depression, such as sleep disturbances, eating disturbances, or thoughts of death (Kazdin, 1988). Another important parameter assessed by most structured interviews is the *level of impairment* associated with behaviors being reported. Most interviews have questions that elicit information on the degree to which a child's difficulties are affecting his or her functioning in major life arenas (e.g., at home, at school, and with peers).

In addition to assessing important parameters of behaviors, diagnostic interviews also enhance the *correspondence between assessment techniques and diagnostic criteria*. As mentioned previously, the most common structured interviews were specifically designed and revised to correspond to the changing DSM system. This means that the usefulness of the interview is in part dependent on the usefulness of the diagnostic definitions that are being assessed. There are some diagnostic categories that have been poorly validated and hence this dependency is not always beneficial to the assessment process. However, this tie between assessment and diagnosis can be advantageous for several reasons. First, it promotes revisions of the interviews to correspond with advances in our knowledge of the basic characteristics of child and adolescent psychological disorders. Second, it allows one to make a diagnosis based on strict adherence to diagnostic criteria. Either due to theoretical, empirical, or practical reasons (e.g., insurance reimbursement), many assessors attempt to make DSM diagnoses as a result of their assessments. Too often diagnoses are made based on information (e.g., rating scales, projective tests) that do not directly assess the diagnostic criteria. As a result, the meaning of the diagnosis is ambiguous.

Diagnostic interviews are also helpful in *training* clinical assessors. As assessors are developing their competence in interviewing, it is often helpful to have an explicit format from which to conduct the interview. It gives the assessor a good way to learn the basic characteristics of childhood emotional and behavioral disorders. After being trained in administration procedures and after conducting several interviews with actual clients, assessors often begin to internalize the diagnostic criteria for the most common disorders of childhood. This knowledge can then be applied in situations in which a structured interview is not possible.

Disadvantages

Two weaknesses in the use of diagnostic interviews have already been mentioned. These are the *time-consuming* nature of the interviews and the *dependence of the interviews on DSM criteria,* which is a strength for assessing well-validated syndromes but a weakness for assessing disorders with a weak empirical basis. Also, diagnostic interviews are subject to the same potential *reporter biases* that were discussed in previous chapters on self-report inventories and parent and teacher behavior rating scales.

A weakness that is more specific to structured interviews is the difficulty in making *norm-referenced interpretations* from interviews. Clinically significant levels of symptoms are often based on DSM criteria rather than based on a comparison with a representative normative sample. Therefore, the appropriateness of clinical elevations for a given age depends on the appropriateness of the diagnostic criteria for that age. Several community studies using an early version of DISC (e.g., Anderson et al., 1987; Costello, 1989) allow one to view the base-rates of disorders assessed by the DISC in community samples of school-age children. Although this provides some information on how a child who meets criteria would compare to others in the general population, this type of normative information is still much more limited than the type provided by other assessment techniques, most notably, behavior rating scales.

Another weakness of most diagnostic interviews is the failure to provide a format for obtaining information from a child's teacher. This source of information is crucial in the clinical assessment of elementary school-age children (Loeber et al., 1991). As a result, information from teachers must be obtained by some other method, thereby making it difficult to determine if discrepancies between a teacher's report and the report of others are due to real differences in a child's classroom behavior or whether they are due to differences in the assessment format.

RECOMMENDATIONS FOR USE OF STRUCTURED INTERVIEWS

Based on the strengths and weaknesses of structured interviews, several recommendations can be made on their appropriate use in the clinical assessment of children and adolescents. First, like any assessment technique, the diagnostic interview should never be used alone in a clinical evaluation. It should be one part of a comprehensive assessment battery. Information from diagnostic interviews should be supplemented by assessment techniques that provide better norm-referenced scores (e.g., behavior rating scales) and by assessment techniques that provide information on a child's classroom functioning (e.g., behavioral observations in the school).

In addition, the diagnoses derived from the diagnostic interviews should be viewed within the context of the overall assessment. A diagnosis can be viewed similarly to the way an elevation on a behavior rating scale is interpreted. Specifically, it is one piece of information that needs to be integrated with other sources of information to develop a good case formulation. Stated simply, diagnoses based solely on diagnostic interviews should not be considered final clinical diagnoses. Such final diagnoses should be based on an assessor's integration of multiple sources of information (see Chapter 16 for a detailed discussion of integrating multiple aspects of an assessment). A case example in which a diagnostic interview was used as part of a comprehensive assessment battery is provided in Box 12.2.

BOX 12.2

Case Example: The DISC 2.3 in the Evaluation of a 7-Year-Old Boy with Attention-Deficit Hyperactivity Disorder

---

Jordan is a 7-year, 3 month–old boy who was referred for a comprehensive psychological evaluation by his parents upon the recommendation of his teachers. His teachers had reported to Jordan's parents that he was having difficulty paying attention and was daydreaming, interrupt-

(Cont.)

Box 12.2   *(Continued)*

ing others, and making careless mistakes in his work. His parents requested a comprehensive evaluation to determine the severity and possible cause for these difficulties and to make recommendations for possible interventions to aid in his school adjustment.

Jordan's background, developmental, and medical history were unremarkable. During the testing Jordan had great difficulty concentrating and was easily distracted. He was also very fidgety and restless. Intellectually, Jordan had much better verbal comprehensive abilities, especially in the area of verbal reasoning, than nonverbal perceptual-organizational abilities. Consistent with his verbal abilities, Jordan scored in the above average range on measures of reading and math achievement.

Jordan's emotional and behavioral functioning was assessed through the use of structured interviews conducted with Jordan's parents and teachers and through rating scales completed by his parents, teacher, and Jordan himself. The structured interviews were the parent version of the DISC-2.3 and the experimental teacher version used in the DSM-IV field trials (Frick et al., 1994). The child version was not given to Jordan because he was below the age of 9 and the DISC has not proven to be reliable in this young age group. The following is a excerpt from the report of Jordan's evaluation that illustrates how information from the DISC-2.3 was integrated with other assessment information:

> The only problematic area that emerged from this assessment of Jordan's emotional and behavioral functioning were significant problems of inattention, disorganization, impulsivity, and overactivity that seem to be causing Jordan significant problems in the classroom. Jordan's teachers described him as being very restless and fidgety, being easily distractible, having very disorganized and messy work habits, having a hard time completing things, and making a lot of careless mistakes. Results from teacher rating scales suggested that these behaviors are more severe than would be typical for children Jordan's age. These behaviors are consistent with a diagnosis of Attention-Deficit Hyperactivity Disorder (ADHD). Also consistent with this diagnosis, his parents reported that many of these behaviors, especially the restless and fidgety behaviors have been present from very early in life, at least since age 4. These behaviors associated with ADHD seem to be causing significant problems for Jordan in school, affecting the amount and accuracy of schoolwork. A sociometric exercise also suggests that these behaviors may be starting to affect his peer relationships.

The child's age is also an important consideration in the use of structured interviews. Generally the reliability for most interviews schedules are low before the age of 9 for child self-report (Hodges & Zeman, 1993). It seems that the structured, face-to-face dialogue is not appropriate for assessing very young children. Although the parent versions of the interview are appropriate for young children, children's self-report should be obtained by other methods.

A final consideration in using structured interviews concerns when to administer diagnostic interviews in the assessment battery. There is no research on this issue, and these recommendations come from clinical experience. Diagnostic interviews should not be the first assessment administered to parents. The structured format does not facilitate the development of rapport between the interviewer and parent, and some parents become frustrated in trying to fit their descriptions of their child's behavior into the confines of the interview. Therefore, it is often helpful to precede diagnostic interviews with less structured questions that allow parents to express, in their own words, their concerns for their child. For children and adolescents we actually find that the structured format enhances rapport in many cases. Children often enter the assessment situation nervous because they are unsure about what is expected of them. The clear and explicit response format of diagnostic interviews makes the demands of the situation apparent for the child and thereby reduces his or her anxiety in many cases.

Up to this point we have tried to give an overview of structured interviews, looking at the various formats that are available, highlighting some of the advantages and disadvantages of using interview schedules in a clinical assessment, and providing guidelines for appropriate use. In the next section we provide a more in-depth look at one particular interview schedule, the DISC-2.3. We chose the DISC-2.3 as a prototypical example of a structured interview because it is one of the most widely used interview schedules for children and adolescents and it has been one of the most systematically developed. However, one must be aware that the DISC-2.3 is one of the most structured interview schedules, and therefore it has all of the advantages and disadvantages that accompany a high degree of structure.

FOCUS ON THE NIMH DIAGNOSTIC INTERVIEW SCHEDULE FOR CHILDREN

Development

The original version of the DISC (Costello, 1983) was designed to be a downward extension of the adult-oriented DIS (Robins et al., 1981), and its development was supported by a grant from the National Institute of Mental Health. Like the DIS, the original version of the DISC was designed for use in epidemiological studies and was explicitly tied to the version of the DSM being used at the time (DSM-III; American Psychiatric Association, 1980). In 1985, Dr. David Shaffer at the New York State Psychiatric Institute and his colleagues undertook a revision of the interview to (1) improve it reliability for use with children and for use by lay interviewers and (2) provide diagnostic compatibility with the DSM-III-R (American Psychiatric Association, 1987) and anticipated DSM-IV and ICD-10 criteria (Fisher et al., 1992).

Structure and Content

The DISC-2.3 (Shaffer et al., 1991) contains 231 core questions and 1,186 questions that are asked contingent on a child's responses to the core questions. There are two parallel versions of the DISC-2.3, the Child version (DISC-C) to be administered to children between the ages of 9 and 17 and the Parent version (DISC-P) to be administered to the parents of children ages 6–17. There is also an experimental Teacher version (DISC-T), which was developed for use in the DSM-IV field trials (Frick et al., 1994).

The DISC 2.3 is organized by "diagnostic modules." There are six modules that comprise sets of related disorders. A summary of the modules is provided in Box 12.3. For each diagnosis the DISC-2.3 is designed to obtain information about the presence of symptoms included in DSM criteria. If a certain threshold, usually below the DSM diagnostic threshold, is met, then questions regarding age of

---

Box 12.3

Organization and Content of the DISC-2.3

MODULE A: *Anxiety Disorders*
Simple Phobia
Social Phobia
Agoraphobia/Panic Disorder
Separation Anxiety Disorder
Avoidant Disorder
Overanxious Disorder
Obsessive Compulsive Disorder

MODULE B: *Miscellaneous Disorders*
Bulimia/Anorexia
Elimination Disorders
Tic Disorders

MODULE C: *Mood Disorders*
Major Depressive/Dysthymic Disorders
Mania/Hypomania

MODULE D: *Psychosis*
Schizophrenia

MODULE E: *Disruptive Behavior Disorders*
Attention-Deficit Hyperactivity Disorder
Oppositional Defiant Disorder
Conduct Disorder

MODULE F: *Alcohol and Substance Use Disorders*
Alcohol Abuse/Dependence
Marijuana Abuse/Dependence
Other Drug Abuse/Dependence

SOURCE: Shaffer et al., 1992.

---

first onset, impairment, and past treatment are asked. (See Box 12.1 for an example of the DISC-2.3 question format).

Administration

The DISC-2.3 was designed to be administered by interviewers without clinical experience after 3 to 4 days of training. Training includes (1) instruction on standard DISC-2.3 administration procedures, (2) viewing an actual administration of the DISC-2.3,

(3) supervised practice in administration with a confederate in a controlled situation, and (4) supervised practice with an actual case.

At the beginning of the interview the interviewer completes a Subject Profile Sheet which includes several pieces of demographic information (e.g., age and sex of child) that are necessary to properly administer the interview. After completing the Subject Profile Sheet, the interviewer establishes a time line with the interviewee. As discussed previously, the DISC assesses for symptoms that have been present within the past 6 months for most disorders and within the past year for symptoms of conduct disorder. The time line establishes very salient events (e.g., birthdays, vacations, start of the school year, holidays) that occurred 6 months and a year prior to the interview. This anchor helps the child or parent remember the time frame of the interview.

The verbal instructions given to the respondent are semistructured. That is, several points that must be covered are provided, but verbatim instructions are not required. The points include:

1. There are no right or wrong answers; the best answer is the one that tells the most about the child.

2. The informant should try to answer yes or no to each question.

3. The time frame is within the last 6 months, unless otherwise specified.

4. Some of the questions on the form will be left out.

5. Some questions may be asked more than once.

6. It is possible to take breaks, if needed.

Unlike the instructions, the administration of the actual DISC 2.3 questions is quite structured. The questions are designed to be read exactly as written and in the sequence prescribed. Interviewers are explicitly instructed not to make up their own questions or to ask for an example unless requested in the interview format. If a respondent does not understand the question, the interviewer should repeat the question, emphasizing the words that seemed to cause confusion. The interviewer is not allowed to interpret questions for the respondent (e.g. What do

you mean by often? or Is one or two times considered frequent?). The interviewer is instructed to simply ask the respondent to interpret the question as whichever way he or she thinks is best.

Reliability

The best source of information on the reliability of the newest version of the DISC-2.3 comes from a series of articles by Shaffer and colleagues; (Piacentini et al., 1993; Schwab-Stone et al., 1993; Shaffer et al., 1993). These authors tested the psychometric properties of the DISC-2.3 in a sample of 75 clinic-referred children ages 11–17. In 41 cases the child and/or parent were reinterviewed 1 to 3 weeks later by a second interviewer. There were sufficient cases to calculate the test-retest reliability for five DSM-III-R diagnoses (Attention-Deficit Hyperactivity Disorder, Oppositional Defiant Disorder, Conduct Disorder, Major Depression, and Separation Anxiety Disorder). The kappa statistics for the test-retest agreement are reported in Table 12.2. Also reported in this box are the intraclass correlations, which provide an estimate of the test-retest reliability of the symptom clusters that form the diagnostic criteria for DSM-III-R diagnoses. Finally, Table 12.2 also includes Chronbach's alpha as an index of the internal consistency of the symptom clusters.

On a diagnostic level all diagnoses showed relatively high test-retest agreement for the parent interview, the child interview, and the combined parent and child interview. A symptom was considered present if either parent or child endorsed it. The one exception was the low reliability of the Oppositional Defiant Disorder diagnosis by child report. The symptom cluster for this diagnosis also exhibited the lowest intraclass correlation according to child report. Most of the symptom clusters showed moderate to high internal consistency, with the exception of the Conduct Disorder symptoms. However, this low internal consistency of symptoms that form the Conduct Disorder criteria is not surprising for two reasons. First, only three symptoms are required for the diagnosis of CD and most of these symptoms tend to be of relatively low base rate. Second, these symptoms tend to be interchangeable rather than

TABLE 12.2   Test-Retest and Internal Consistency Estimates from the DISC-2.3

	Kappa	ICC	Alpha
Parent Only (n = 39)			
Attention-Deficit Hyperactivity	.55	.87	.87
Oppositional Defiant	.88	.82	.75
Conduct	.87	.86	.56
Major Depression	.72	.82	.88
Separation Anxiety		.77	.61
Child Only (n = 41)			
Attention-Deficit Hyperactivity		.72	.83
Oppositional Defiant	.16	.44	.67
Conduct	.55	.60	.59
Major Depression	.77	.68	.85
Separation Anxiety	.72	.66	.71
Combined Parent and Child (n = 37)			
Attention-Deficit Hyperactivity	.56	.84	
Oppositional Defiant	.59	.65	
Conduct	.50	.80	
Major Depression	.71	.66	
Separation Anxiety	.80	.72	

NOTE: Kappa is the agreement between diagnoses at Time 1 and diagnoses at Time 2 with a 1- to 3-week interval between interviews. ICC is the intraclass correlation between symptoms at Time 1 and Tiame 2. Alpha is Chronbach's alpha calculated for the symptoms at Time 1.

SOURCE: M. Schwab-Stone, P. Fisher, J. Piacentini, D. Shaffer, M. Davies, & M. Briggs (1993). "The Diagnostic Interview Schedule for Children—Revised Version (DISC-R): II. Test-Retest Reliability," *Journal of the American Academy of Child and Adolescent Psychiatry, 32,* 651–657.

intercorrelated, making internal consistency estimates a less than optimal method of determining the reliability of this symptom domain.

Validity

Piacentini et al. (1993) tested the associations between diagnoses based on the DISC-2.3 and diagnoses made by experienced clinicians. In general, there was moderate agreement between lay interviewers and clinician diagnoses based on the parent DISC-2.3 (average kappa = .50) and low agreement based on the child DISC-2.3 (average kappa = .34). Combining the two interviews gave agreement estimates between those of either informant alone (average kappa = .41). These authors reported that most of the cases with disagreements between clinicians and

lay interviewers were cases that were close to the diagnostic threshold. For example, several disagreements emerged in which children had seven symptoms of ADHD (rather than the required eight symptoms in DSM-III-R criteria) and were not given the diagnosis according to the DISC-2.3 but were given the diagnosis of ADHD by the clinician.

Other evidence for the validity of the DISC interview comes from earlier versions of the interview and must be applied to the revised version with some caution. For example, using the original DISC interview with parents, Edelbrock and Costello (1988) found strong associations between the diagnoses of Attention Deficit Disorder, Conduct Disorder, and Depression/Dysthymia from the DISC-P and the Hyperactive, Delinquent, and Depressed scales of the Child Behavior Checklist (Achenbach & Edelbrock,

1983) in a sample of 270 clinic-referred children between the ages of 6 and 16. High rates of agreement were also found between the original DISC-P and the CBCL in another study of 40 psychiatric referrals and 40 pediatric referrals (Costello, Edelbrock, & Costello, 1985). However, in this study the relationship between the CBCL and the child version of the DISC tended to be much lower. At this juncture it is impossible to determine whether the low correlations with the DISC-C were due to differences in informants (parent-completed CBCL and child-respondent DISC) rather than to differences in the assessment instruments themselves.

CONCLUSIONS

Structured diagnostic interviews have become an important part of many clinical assessments of children and adolescents. Like behavior rating scales, diagnostic interviews provide a reliable means of assessing a child's emotional and behavioral functioning. In this chapter we have attempted to highlight the advantages and disadvantages of using diagnostic interviews. Diagnostic interviews enhance clinical assessments by providing a format for determining how long a child's problems have been occurring, for determining the temporal sequencing of behaviors, and for estimating the degree of impairment associated with a child's emotional or behavioral problems. These important parameters of a child's emotional and behavioral functioning are often not assessed by other assessment modalities. In addition, diagnostic interviews are typically tied to the most recent revisions of the DSM, which closely links assessment with this system of classification.

On the negative side, diagnostic interviews are often time intensive, and they typically do not provide any norm-referenced information on a child's functioning above that which is accorded by DSM criteria. In addition, diagnostic interviews typically do not include a format for obtaining information from a child's teacher, and their reliability in obtaining self-report information for young children (below age 9) is somewhat questionable. As a result of

these weaknesses, diagnostic interviews are best used as part of a more comprehensive assessment battery. We have attempted to provide guidelines for their use in this capacity. We have also attempted to provide an overview of the most commonly used diagnostic interviews for assessing children and adolescents, highlighting the major commonalities and differences across interviews. We concluded the chapter with a more detailed discussion of the DISC-2.3, as an example of a typical diagnostic interview schedule designed for use with children and adolescents.

CHAPTER SUMMARY

1. Structured diagnostic interviews consist of a set of questions to be asked of a child or adolescent with explicit guidelines on how the youth's responses are to be scored.

2. Most of the commonly used structured interviews are designed to assess diagnostic criteria from one of the recent versions of the *Diagnostic and Statistical Manual of Mental Disorders.* Therefore, if a goal of the evaluation is to make a DSM diagnosis, structured interviews are an important assessment tool.

3. Interviews vary on the degree of structure inherent in the interview format and whether or not the interview assesses only current episodes of the disorders.

4. Structured interviews, like behavior rating scales, obtain detailed descriptions of a child's emotions and behaviors from multiple informants.

5. Unlike rating scales, however, structured interviews allow for the assessment of important parameters of a child's behavior, such as the duration of the behavioral difficulties, the temporal sequencing among problems, and the degree of impairment associated with the difficulties.

6. Most structured interviews are time-consuming and are not good for making norm-referenced interpretations.

7. Diagnoses derived from structured interviews

should be viewed within the context of other assessment instruments.

8. Child self-report from diagnostic interviews is typically not reliable before age 9.

9. The NIMH Diagnostic Interview Schedule for Children—Version 2.3 is a prototypical structured diagnostic interview for use with children and adolescents.

    a. The DISC is highly structured so that it can be administered by trained lay interviewers.

    b. There are child, parent, and experimental teacher versions of the DISC.

    c. The DISC contains 231 core questions and 1,186 follow-up questions that are asked contingent on a child's responses to the core questions.

    d. The DISC is organized in six modules: (1) Anxiety Disorders, (2) Miscellaneous Disorders (Eating Disorders, Elimination Disorders, Tic Disorders), (3) Mood Disorders, (4) Psychosis, (5) Disruptive Behavior Disorders, and (6) Alcohol and Substance Use Disorders.

Assessing Family Context

- Why is assessing a child's family context important in the clinical assessment of children's emotional and behavioral functioning?

- What dimensions of a child's family context are most important to the assessment process?

- How can one assess these important dimensions of family functioning?

INTRODUCTION

In the research on childhood psychopathology discussed in Chapter 3, one of the more important findings was that children's and adolescents' emotional and behavioral functioning was heavily influenced by the demands and stressors they experienced in their environment. As a result, to truly understand a child's or adolescent's psychological adjustment, one must not limit the assessment to obtaining characteristics of the youth but must also assess the impor-

tant contexts which shape a child or adolescent's behavior. There is no context more important to understanding a child or adolescent than the family context.

Causal Role of Familial Influences

Research on childhood psychopathology consistently suggests that factors within the family play a major causal role in the development of personality and psychopathology (Hetherington & Martin, 1986). At times the causal role of a child's family has been overemphasized, either by ignoring the potential effects that a child or adolescent can have on the family (Lytton, 1990), or by ignoring factors that can influence both the family and child (Frick & Jackson, 1993). These caveats indicate that a child's family context is only one piece of a very complex puzzle in understanding the psychological adjustment of a child or adolescent. However, research also suggests that it is a very important piece of the puzzle. Family factors play an integral role in the causal theories of many types of problems across many theoretical orientations. Box 13.1 provides examples of three different types of childhood problems from three different theoretical perspectives, all of which emphasize the family context as a causal agent in a child's adjustment problems. Therefore, if one goal of an assessment is to uncover the possible causes of a child's

teractions between parents and children, Patterson outlines the development of a coercive cycle that develops between parent and child and which escalates through aversive conditioning. The cycle starts when a parent makes a demand of a child and a child reacts aversively (e.g., whines, becomes defiant). Rather than pushing the child, the parent withdraws the demand, which reinforces the child's aversive response. During the next phase of the cycle the parent again makes a demand of the child but decides not to give in to the child's aversive behaviors. As the child becomes more aversive (e.g., temper tantrum), the parent becomes more aversive (e.g., yelling, spanking). As the parent becomes more aversive, the child eventually complies, which reinforces the parent's increase in aversive behavior.

This cycle repeats itself over and over again, leading to each party reinforcing increasing levels of aversiveness in the other. This training in coercive responses is then carried over by the child into other settings with other people (e.g., teachers, peers). It is evident that the cycle is transactional; that is, both the child and the parent contribute to the escalating cycle. However, for the purpose of the current discussion it is evident how important the child's family environment, especially parent–child interactions, is to the development of aggression within this theoretical framework.

BOX 13.1

Childhood Problems in a Family Context: Examples of Three Problems and Three Theoretical Orientations

---

Childhood Anxiety: An Operant Perspective

One way of conceptualizing the causes of childhood anxiety has been from an operant perspective. In this model a child receives reinforcement from his or her environment that functions to maintain and increase the anxious behavior. Often this reinforcement is provided in the family context. A good example is provided by Ross (1981) of a 8-year old girl, Valerie, with school phobia. Valerie refused to attend school, and an assessment of her home context revealed that the consequences of her refusal to go to school were indeed quite positive. Instead of going to school, Valerie was able to sleep an hour later than her three siblings who were attending school. Until her mother left for work, she was allowed to follow the mother around the house and then was taken to a neighbor's house for the day. At the neighbor's house Valerie was free to do whatever she pleased for the rest of the day, such as playing games and making occasional trips to a corner store where she bought candy, gum, and soft drinks. It was clearly a comfortable routine for both child and mother, who thereby avoided Valerie's temper tantrums.

Childhood Aggression: A Social Learning Perspective

Gerald Patterson (Patterson, 1982) and his colleagues at the Oregon Social Learning Center have developed a social learning model for the development of aggression. In this model, family interactions provide a training ground for a child to learn coercive methods of controlling interactions with others. Through analyses of micro-social in-

Eating Disorders: A Family Systems Perspective

Sargent, Liebman, and Silver (1985) describe family characteristics that provide a context in which the psychological features of anorexia nervosa fit and are adaptive. Families of a person with anorexia have been found to have parents who are overinvolved in their child's life. This overinvolvement prevents the child with anorexia from perceiving her own sensations, including hunger. It also prevents the child from developing a sense of self-competence and the ability to use problem-solving skills. As the anorexia worsens, the family becomes more protective and involved and further inhibits the affected child from acting more maturely and adaptively. Families of an anorexic child also tend to have difficulty resolving conflict. As a result of unresolved marital conflict, the parents have difficulty collaborating to handle the child's symptoms and actually counteract each other in their attempts. These are just a few of the family dynamics that family system theorists have proposed to explain the development and maintenance of anorexia nervosa in a child. However, it clearly illustrates the primary role of the family context for understanding the child with an eating disorder.

---

or adolescent's emotional or behavioral difficulties and thereby point the way to important treatment goals, then the assessment of family functioning is critical to the assessment process.

Family History and Differential Diagnoses

Two other facts emerge from research on childhood psychopathology that point to the importance of assessing a child's family context in clinical assessments. First, childhood emotional and behavioral problems tend to be rather amorphous, lacking clear boundaries, more so than is the case in adult psychopathology (see Frick et al., 1993). Stated another way, children with problems often have multiple types of problems and it is often difficult to know what is primary and what might be secondary. Second, there seems to be a parent–child link to many types of psychopathology, with parents and children showing similar patterns of adjustment. Taking these two facts together, assessment of the adjustment of parents, in whom the type of problem may be more clearly defined, may provide clues to the primary problem of the child.

An example from research on childhood affective disorders illustrates the use of family history data in making a differential diagnosis. Prior to adolescence, the diagnosis of a bipolar affective disorder is difficult to make. But research suggests that a significant proportion of children with a depressive disorder will develop a bipolar disorder later in life (Geller, Fox, & Fletcher, 1993). Geller, Fox, and Fletcher (1993) found that obtaining a family psychiatric history helped to predict which children with a depressive disorder were at most risk for developing a bipolar disorder. Specifically, the presence of a family history of a bipolar disorder significantly predicted which of the children with depression would later begin to cycle between manic and depressive states. This study also illustrates the important treatment implications for making differential diagnoses. Children who were depressed and had a family history of bipolar disorders were more likely to have manic behaviors develop following treatment with antidepressant medication than were the depressed children without a

family history of bipolar disorder. A case study in which family history information was used in making a differential diagnosis is provided in Box 13.2.

BOX 13.2

Family History and Differential Diagnosis: A Case Study of a 7-Year-Old Girl with Social Phobia

Claire was a 7 year, 2 month–old girl who was in the middle of the first grade when her teacher recommended that she be tested at an outpatient mental health clinic. Her teacher was concerned that she might have an attention-deficit disorder. Claire seemed bright and capable of learning and, in fact, performed quite well in one-on-one situations with the teacher or teacher's aide. However, in the general classroom setting, Claire rarely finished her work. She was often noted to be staring off into space and she had to be constantly redirected back to her work. Her teacher emphatically stated that Claire was not a behavior problem. In fact, Claire was quite quiet and reserved and even had difficulty asking for help when it was needed.

There were several differential diagnoses that were made in the psychological evaluation of Claire. A psychoeducational evaluation that included an intelligence test and an academic screener indicated that Claire was quite capable of learning at or above a level expected for her age. Therefore, her problems in school did not seem to be caused by the presence of an intellectual deficit or a learning disability. However, the differential diagnosis between an attention deficit disorder and an anxiety disorder was more difficult, since she exhibited many behaviors consistent with both types of problems. Several pieces of information helped make the decision that Claire's primary problem was one of anxiety, and particularly, social anxiety.

First, Claire's attentional difficulties tended to be much milder than would be expected for children with attention-deficit disorder, as indicated by structured interviews conducted with Claire's mother and teacher and rating scales completed by her mother and teacher. Second, Claire showed a number of other symptoms of anxiety in social situations. For example, she refused to go to Sunday school at church and to other social activities (e.g., parties) and

(Cont.)

she had one good friend in the neighborhood but would only spend time with her if they were alone. Third, Claire's mother had a history of agoraphobia that had led to several lengthy periods in which she could not leave the house because of her fears.

In this example a family history of anxiety was just one piece of the assessment that helped to make the differential diagnosis. However, it seemed to be an important piece. The diagnosis itself ended up being important because rather than treatment focusing on Claire's attentional problems, a treatment strategy that used systematic desensitization to social situations was implemented, with Claire's teacher reporting dramatic improvements in Claire's school performance by the end of the year.

Interpreting Information Provided by the Parent

Many of the assessment techniques discussed throughout this book rely on the report of family members in the assessment of child or adolescent adjustment. As a result, another important reason for assessing a child's family context is that factors within the family can affect the information provided by family members on the child's adjustment. To appropriately interpret the information obtained from parents and other family members, one must understand those factors that could influence a parent's accuracy in providing information on a child. For example, a non-custodial parent involved in a custody dispute may try to inflate the problems of a child in an effort to sway a more favorable court decision. In contrast, the custodial parent may have motivations to present the child in a more positive light. A second example would be parents who are trying to have their child placed in a residential treatment center and who may inflate problems in an effort to justify this placement. These are just two examples of a myriad of familial factors that can affect how one interprets the information provided by family members.

Another critical familial factor that can affect how one interprets the information provided by a parent

is the parent's psychological adjustment. There have been numerous studies that have called into question the accuracy of depressed mothers' reports about their children's behavior (see Richters, 1992). Numerous studies have indicated that depressed mothers report more problems in their children than are reported by nondepressed parents and teachers and more than are detected using direct behavioral observations of the children. These findings have led many authors to conclude that a parent's depression leads to a distorted view of the child's behavior. Richter's (1992) scholarly review of this literature is summarized in Box 13.3.

Like parental depression, there is also evidence that parental anxiety may influence a parent's report of childhood problems. Frick and colleagues (Frick, Silverthorn, & Evans, 1994) found that in a sample

John Richters (1992) conducted a critical review of the research on the effects of depression on a parent's rating of a child's behavior. Richters cited 17 studies that have been published calling into question the accuracy of depressed mothers' reports. In general, depressed mothers have tended to report more behavior problems in their children than the level reported by teachers, fathers, or children and greater than that observed in behavioral observations. All of these studies led researchers to the conclusion that depressed mothers' perceptions of their children's behavior was biased by their own level of depression. However, Richters's critical review of several methodological and interpretive problems that have plagued this body of research calls into question this depressive bias theory. The most pervasive of the problem was discussed here.

The first major problem in these studies was the fact that most of the comparisons between mothers and other informants used measures that were discordant on either the types of behaviors assessed or the situation in which the behaviors were assessed. The best example was the fre-

(Cont.)

BOX 13.3 *(Continued)*

quent comparison between mothers' and teachers' rating on a behavior rating scale that had a different item content for mothers and teachers. In this case, both the behaviors assessed and the situation in which the behaviors were being observed were discordant. As a result, it is unclear whether the differences between mothers and the other raters were due to maternal depression or to differences in the behaviors and/or situations being assessed. Only 27% of the comparisons between depressed mothers and other informants used ratings that were both behaviorally and situationally concordant.

The second pervasive problem in this literature is the fact that most of the studies (94%) did not demonstrate that the mothers' overreporting was systematically related to maternal depression. Twenty-four percent of the studies simply documented that depressed mothers reported more behavior problems in their children than did nondepressed mothers. Seventy-one percent indicated that maternal depression predicted variance in mothers' ratings of their children that was not accounted for by criterion ratings provided by other informants. Richters argues that the most direct evidence for the depression distortion hypothesis would be if mother-criterion disagreements were systematically related (correlated) with measures of maternal depression.

The third problem discussed by Richters is that most of the studies (94%) focused only on maternal depression. It is well established that depression is related to other factors within the individual (e.g., other forms of psychopathology) and the environment (e.g., marital satisfaction). Therefore, it is unclear whether or not mothers' disagreements with informants were due to the depression or to other aspects of the mothers' adjustment and/or concomitant stressors in the family environment.

As a result of these problems, Richters suggested that we must be cautious in accepting the depression distortion hypothesis until more refined research is conducted. In fact, Richters cites five studies that used better methodology and found that depressed mothers agreed with other informants as well or even better than nondepressed mothers. However, these are only a few studies, and they are not without flaws themselves. At this point, however, clinical assessors should at least be aware of the issues, many of which are unresolved, in this very important body of research.

SOURCE: J. E. Richters (1992). "Depressed Mothers as Informants about Their Children: A Critical Review of the Evidence for Distortion," *Psychological Bulletin, 112,* 485–499.

of 41 clinic-referred children between the ages of 9 and 13, mothers tended to report more symptoms of anxiety disorders than did the child. This overreporting was systematically related to anxiety in the mother. Specifically, the more anxious the mother, the greater the overreporting of anxiety in the child. These authors also reported that maternal anxiety was not associated with overreporting of other types of maladjustment but seemed to be more specifically related to anxiety. This pattern of results would be consistent with the possibility that anxious mothers project their anxiety symptoms onto their reports of anxiety in their children. These findings provide another example of the importance of understanding parental adjustment for interpreting the information parents provide on their child.

Making Recommendations for Intervention

The goal of most clinical assessments is to develop a psychological profile of the child so that appropriate recommendations for treatment can be made. We have already discussed the fact that treatment recommendations are typically based on the strengths and weaknesses of the individual child. The same is true for the child's family. Treatment should also be tailored to the strengths and weaknesses of a child's family.

As already mentioned, many childhood problems are caused or maintained by factors within the family (see Box 13.1). If an evaluation can uncover which familial factors seem to be operating for a given case, this information provides an important focus for intervention. Also, even if the primary causal agents are not familial (e.g., neurodevelopmental problems), an assessment of family functioning may document strengths within the family that can be used in treatment (e.g., having parents teach the child to cope with his or her difficulties).

FAMILY ASSESSMENT: GENERAL ISSUES

To this point we have discussed several reasons why assessing the family is an important part of clinical assessments of a child or adolescent. In this section we discuss more specifically *what* areas of family functioning should be assessed and *how* this can be accomplished. However, before discussing specific areas and techniques, two general points deserve mention.

First, many of the behavior rating scales that were reviewed in previous chapters have subscales that assess various aspects of a child's family context. For example, the parent-completed Personality Inventory for Children-—Revised (Lachar, 1982) and the child self-report Personality Inventory for Youth (Lachar & Gruber, 1992) both include a Family Relations scale. Included in this scale are items assessing marital stability, consistency in discipline, emotional tone of family, community connectedness, and parental adjustment. The MMPI-A contains a supplementary content scale, the Adolescent-Family Problems scale (A-FAM; Archer, 1992), which includes 35 items assessing an adolescent's perceptions of family conflict, level of love and acceptance in the home, family communication, and emotional support provided by the family. The BASC Self-Report Scale (Reynolds & Kamphaus, 1992) contains a Relations with Parent scale that assesses a child's perceptions of being important in the family, the quality of parent–child interactions, and the degree of parental trust and concern. All of these scales provide a time efficient screening of many important aspects of a child's family environment. The main drawback is that each scale combines many different aspects of a child's family environment making it impossible to uncover specific areas of strength and/or dysfunction that could be important in understanding a child and in making treatment recommendations.

This criticism leads to our next general comment for assessing a child's family context. What areas to assess and how rigorous the assessment should be within these areas will vary depending on the purpose of the evaluation. In the sections to follow we make the case that several aspects of the family should be routinely assessed: parenting style and parenting practices, marital conflict, and parental adjustment. The depth of the assessment in each area and which additional areas of family functioning should be assessed will vary depending on the individual case.

For example, the assessment of a child by a school psychologist to document emotional and behavioral factors that might be impairing academic performance may include only minimal assessment of the child's perception of the family environment and only as it may influence his or her behavior in the classroom. In contrast, an assessment designed to assess a child's adjustment to a recent parental divorce in order to make treatment recommendations on factors that could aid in the child's post-divorce adjustment may include a substantial family component. This assessment will likely include obtaining extensive information on the level of parental conflict and level of parental cooperation in child-related issues, since these factors are crucial to understanding a child's adjustment to divorce (Amato & Keith, 1991). Another type of assessment that requires very detailed and somewhat specialized assessment of family functioning is in the case of known or suspected child abuse. A recommended assessment strategy for cases of child abuse is summarized in Box 13.4. These examples illustrate the point that how intensive the assessment of family factors will be and which familial factors will be assessed may vary somewhat from case to case.

BOX 13.4

Research Note: A Child Abuse and Neglect Assessment Strategy

A primary part of assessing children who have been physically or emotional abused or who have been neglected is the assessment of their family context. While there are specialized instruments to assess families in which child abuse has occurred, like the CAPI discussed in this chapter, most evaluations require the use of general assessment strategies that have been covered throughout this book. The following is an outline of a child abuse and neglect assessment strategy that we have adapted from a chapter by David Wolfe (1988), one of the foremost authorities on child abuse. As you will see in this outline, most of the domains important to assess in these evaluations have been discussed in this and other chapters. Wolfe (1988) states

(Cont.)

Box 13.4   *(Continued)*

that the goals of this assessment strategy are to identify major strengths and problem areas of the family system in preparation for involvement of additional community resources, to provide directions for protective services, and to identify specific treatment needs.

Goal 1: Identify General Strengths and Problem Areas of Family System

A. Family Background

1. Parental history of rejection and abuse during own childhood.

2. Discipline experience during own childhood.

3. Family planning and effect of children on the marital relationship.

4. Parents' preparedness for and sense of competence in child rearing.

B. Marital Relationship

1. Length, stability, and quality of marital relationship.

2. Degree of conflict and physical violence in marital relationship.

3. Support from partner in child rearing.

C. Areas of Perceived Stress and Supports

1. Employment history and satisfaction of parents.

2. Economic stability of family.

3. Social support for parents, both within and outside the family (e.g., number and quality of contacts with extended family, neighbors, social workers, church members).

D. Parental Psychopathology

E. Parental Health Status

Goal 2: Assess Parental Responses to Child-Rearing Demands

A. Emotional Reactivity of Parent

1. Parents' perception of how abused child differs from siblings and other children.

2. Parents' feelings of anger and loss of control when interacting with child.

3. Typical methods of coping with arousal during stressful episodes.

B. Child-Rearing Methods

1. Appropriateness of parental expectations for child behavior given child's developmental level.

2. Typical methods used by parents for controlling/disciplining the child.

3. Willingness of parents to learn new methods of discipline.

4. Parents' perception of effectiveness of discipline strategies.

5. Child's response to discipline attempts.

Goal 3: Identify Needs of the Child

A. Child Emotional and Behavioral Problems

1. Behaviors that may place this child at risk for abuse.

2. Problems in adjustment resulting from abuse and living in family with multiple stressors.

B. Child Cognitive and Adaptive Abilities

1. Identify child's developmental level to determine most appropriate method and level of intervention.

2. Determine if abuse or chronic family stressors have led to cognitive delays or delays in the child's development of adaptive behaviors.

3. Child's comprehension and reaction to abuse and family difficulties.

SOURCE: D. A. Wolfe (1988), "Child Abuse and Neglect." In E. J. Mash and L. G. Terdal (Eds.), *Behavioral Assessment of Childhood Disorders* (2nd ed.), pp. 401–444. (New York: Guilford Press).

OMNIBUS RATING SCALES

In the subsequent sections we review several omnibus family assessment devices that assess multiple areas of family functioning. We focus on these rating scale measures of family functioning because they tend to be more widely applicable to clinical assessments of children and adolescents than other methods of family assessment. Some of the reasons why rating scale measures of family functioning are so widely applicable is that they are time efficient, they often provide a broad coverage of multiple areas of family functioning, and they often provide a format for obtaining the impressions of multiple family members. Also, most of these rating scales were standardized in large community samples that allowed for the testing of the reliability of scores.

Unfortunately, most of the standardization samples of these omnibus rating scales have glaring weaknesses in their representativeness of the general population, which greatly limits the ability of the assessor to use the norm-referenced scores from the scales. Another weakness of these family-focused rating scales is that, like all behavior rating scales, the information provided by these scales is filtered through an informant, whose biases and motivations can influence the ratings. Also, in some situations a more in-depth evaluation of a discrete aspect of family functioning may be desired (e.g., parent–child attachment, parent-adolescent problem-solving abilities). These strengths and weaknesses of rating scale measures of family functioning should be considered in designing clinical assessments of children and adolescents. They should also be considered when interpreting the information obtained from these rating scales.

Child Abuse Potential Inventory—Second Edition

The CAPI (Milner, 1986) is a 160-item rating scale completed by a child's parent. As the name implies, the CAPI was originally developed to assess dimensions of parental behavior that have proven to be risk factors for physical abuse of children. However, the CAPI assesses multiple areas of family functioning that are important in many clinical assessments. The items require a third grade reading level to complete and each item is presented in a forced-choice, agree-disagree format. It takes approximately 15 minutes to complete.

Content

The CAPI contains three validity scales: Lie, Random Response, and Inconsistency. The Lie scale was designed to detect tendencies to distort responses in a socially desirable manner. Both the Random Response and Inconsistency scales were designed to detect haphazard or random responses to items without regard to item content. There are six primary scales of the CAPI that are combined into a composite Abuse scale. The items were developed from an extensive review of the child abuse and neglect literature. The Distress scale assesses parental anger, frustration, impulse control, anxiety, and depression. The Rigidity scale assesses parents' flexibility and realism in their expectations of children's behavior. It includes such items as: A child should never disobey, A child should always be neat, A child should never talk back. The Unhappiness scale assesses a parent's degree of personal fulfillment as an individual, as a parent, as a marital/sex partner, and as a friend. Problems with Child and Self is a scale with items tapping parents' perceptions of their child's behavior and their perceptions of their own self-concept as a parent. The last two scales, Problems with Family and Problems with Others, assess the level of family conflict in the extended family and the level of conflict with persons outside the family or community agencies.

Norms

Normative information is available in the CAPI manual (Milner, 1986) from a sample of 836 parents, child care workers, and parent aides from Florida, California, North Carolina, Hawaii, Oklahoma, Illinois, New York, and West Germany. It is unclear how this normative sample was selected, and the representativeness of this sample in terms of parental education, socioeconomic status, and ethnicity is also unclear. This is crucial information since there is evidence that family functioning can vary as a function of these variables (Maccoby & Martin, 1983). As a result, lack of accessible information on the normative sample hinders the ability to make norm-referenced interpretations from the CAPI scales.

Reliability and Validity

The CAPI manual provides evidence that the composite Abuse scale and the Distress and Rigidity scales exhibit acceptable internal consistency and temporal stability. The reliability of the four other individual scales tend to be more inconsistent across samples. There is evidence that the composite Abuse scale can successfully discriminate between proven abusers and control subjects (Milner & Wimberley, 1980). Also, the Abuse scale has proven to be sensitive to the effects of intervention with high-risk parents (Wolfe et al., 1988). Therefore, it appears that the composite Abuse scale provides a reliable method of assessing dysfunctional elements of a child's family environment that are associated with child abuse. However, the appropriate use of the individual scales that make up the composite Abuse scale is not well established.

Family Environment Scale— Second Edition (FES)

The FES (Moos & Moos, 1986) 90-item true-false questionnaire is widely used to assess persons' perceptions of their family environment. It can be completed by the parent and/or child (over 11 years). There are three forms of the FES. We focus on the Real Form (Form R) of the FES, which measures the respondent's actual perceptions of the family environment. However, there are also two special forms of the FES. The Ideal Form (Form I) allows the respondent to answer items in terms of the type of family he or she would ideally like. The Expectations Form (Form E) allows the respondent to answer items in terms of what he or she expects family environments to be like.

Content

The FES is divided into 10 subscales from three domains: Relationships, Personal Growth, and System Maintenance. A description of the 10 subscales within each of these domains is provided in Box 13.5. The item content was based primarily on family systems theory. This is evident from the emphasis on family structure and organization and the focus on the transactional patterns between members of the family in the FES item content.

Norms

The FES manual reports information on a large normative sample that was administered the FES. It included 1,125 families from all areas of the country, single-parent and multi-generational families, families drawn from ethnic minority groups, and families of all age groups (Moos & Moos, 1986). It is unclear how representative the sample is on each of these variables. However, the authors note that 294 families from the normative sample were drawn randomly from specified census tracts in the San Francisco area, and the means and standard deviations of FES scales did not differ between this group and the rest of the normative sample.

Although the normative group includes families of all age groups, it is notable that the majority of the normative sample was based on the reports of adults, with much less data available on the reports of children and adolescents. This is important because the authors found small but systematic differences between the scales completed by parents and adolescents (Moos & Moos, 1986). Specifically, adolescents perceived less emphasis on cohesion, expressiveness, independence, and intellectual/religious orientation and more emphasis on conflict and achievement than did their parents.

Reliability and Validity

The 10 subscales of the FES generally have been shown to have acceptable levels of reliability in many samples. The manual reports internal consistency estimates in a large community sample (n = 1,067) ranging from alpha = .61 to alpha = .78 (Moos & Moos, 1986). Two month test-retest reliability in a smaller community sample (n = 47) ranged from r = .68 to r = .86. Moos and Moos (1986) provide a good summary of over 100 research articles using the FES, which attests to its correlation with other measures of family functioning, its ability to differentiate distressed from nondistressed families, and its sensitivity to treatment effects.

Probably the biggest threat to the validity of the FES is the failure to validate the scale structure through factor analyses. The scales were designed primarily based on content and face validity. Unfor-

BOX 13.5

Subscales of the Family Environment Scale

Dimension	Subscale	Description of Item Content
Relationship	Cohesion	Commitment, help, and support provided by family members
	Expressiveness	Extent to which family members are encouraged to express feelings
	Conflict	Amount of expressed anger, aggression, and conflict among family members
Personal Growth	Independence	Extent to which self-sufficiency, assertiveness, and independence are encouraged in family
	Achievement Orientation	Extent to which activities of family members are achievement-oriented and competitive
	Intellectual-Cultural Orientation	Degree of interest in political, social, and cultural activities
	Active-Recreational Orientation	Emphasis placed on participation in social and recreational activities
	Moral-Religious Emphasis	Importance placed on ethical and religious issues
System Maintenance	Organization	Importance of clear family structure and well-defined roles
	Control	Degree to which rules and procedures for family life are explicit

SOURCE: Moos and Moos, 1986.

tunately, factor analyses have generally isolated anywhere from two (e.g., Fowler, 1982) to seven (Robertson & Hyde, 1982) factors on the FES. No study has provided convincing evidence supporting the 10 scale structure that is the basis for most interpretations from the FES.

Parenting Stress Index— Second Edition (PSI)

The PSI (Abidin, 1986) is unique in its focus on factors that influence the family context of *preschool* children. As a result, the PSI is primarily useful for assessing the child-rearing environment of children between the ages of 1 and 4. Completion of the PSI requires at least a fifth-grade education. It contains 151 items and generally takes 20–30 minutes to complete.

Content

The items of the PSI are divided into two main categories: Child Domain (47 items) and Parent Domain (54 items). The Child Domain consists of items that assess qualities of a child that make it difficult for parents to fulfill their parental role. The Parent Domain assesses sources of stress and disability related to parental functioning. Box 13.6 provides a summary of the scales that constitute the Child and Parent domains. The PSI also allows for the computation of a composite score which provides a overall indicator of the amount of stress in the parent–child system.

Norms

The normative group for the PSI consisted of 534 parents of children referred to a small group of pediatric clinics in Virginia; the median age of the children was 9 months (SD = 23.2 months). The representativeness of the normative sample is one of the major weaknesses of the scale. The sample consisted of primarily White (92%), highly educated (1/3 with college degrees) parents from central Virginia. Thus, the use of norm-referenced scores for families that do not match these characteristics is questionable.

Reliability and Validity

The manual of the PSI provides convincing evidence for the internal consistency and temporal stability of the three composite scores: Total Stress, Parent Domain, and Child Domain. The reliability coefficients for the individual scales, however, are much more variable and typically exhibit relatively low reliability estimates. The manual provides one of the best summaries of the extensive use of the PSI in research on the family context of preschoolers. In general, the PSI scales have been correlated with other measures

of family functioning, have differentiated families who are experiencing major stressors from non-stressed families, and has proven sensitive to treatment effects. However, as would be predicted from the reliability data, much of the validity information on the PSI is based on the three composite scales, with much less information being available for the individual subscales of the PSI. Therefore, clinical interpretations are best limited to these three broad composite scales.

PARENTING STYLES
AND PRACTICES

In the introduction to the previous section we proposed that two advantages of the omnibus rating scales for assessing family functioning were their time efficiency and their ability to screen multiple aspects of the family environment. However, for many clinical assessments a more focused assessment of specific aspects of a child's or adolescent's family context may be desired. Starting in this section, we attempt to highlight several of the more important dimensions of the family context that may warrant a more focused assessment. We begin each section with a brief overview of the research documenting the importance of each aspect of the family environment for understanding a child's or adolescent's adjustment and for designing treatment strategies for the child or adolescent. This research overview also helps the clinical assessor understand the basic nature and characteristics of the different family constructs. This basic understanding of the various dimensions of family functioning is crucial given that most dimensions lack carefully developed and standardized assessment instruments. Some notable exceptions are discussed in the following sections.

The first area of focus is parenting behavior. There is broad consensus that parenting behaviors exert a significant influence on child development. There is less consensus regarding the specific aspects of parenting that are most crucial to child adjustment. The implications for clinical assessment are obvious. It is hard to determine how to assess something if

Box 13.6

Item Content of the Parenting Stress Index—Second Edition

Scale	Items	Characteristics of High Scorers
CHILD DOMAIN	47	Child displays qualities that make it difficult for the parent to fulfill parenting roles.
Adaptability	11	Child shows inability to change from one task to another without emotional upset, avoidance of strangers, is overreactive to changes in routine and difficult to calm.
Acceptability	7	Child is not as attractive, intelligent, or pleasant as the parent had hoped or expected.
Demandingness	9	Child is very demanding of parents' time and energy, with patterns such as frequent crying, frequent requests for help, and frequent minor problem behaviors.
Mood	5	Child is frequently unhappy, sad, and crying.
Distractibility/ Hyperactivity	9	Child displays overactivity, restlessness, distractibility, and short attention span, fails to finish things, and shifts from one activity to another.
Reinforces Parent	6	Interactions between child and parent fail to produce good feelings in the parent—associated with parental feelings of rejection and poor self-concept as parent.
PARENT DOMAIN	54	Indicates significant stress on the parent–child system that is related to dimensions of parental functioning.
Depression	9	Parent reports significant feelings of depression and guilt. High score may prevent parent from mobilizing sufficient levels of psychic and physical energy to fulfill parenting responsibilities.
Attachment	7	Parent does not feel emotional closeness to child and parent perceives an inability to accurately read and understand child's feelings and needs.
Restriction of Role	7	Parents feel that parental role restricts their freedom and impairs their attempts to maintain own identity.
Sense of Competence	13	Parents do not feel that they can adequately fulfill their parental roles either due to a lack of knowledge of child development or a limited range of child-management skills.
Social Isolation	6	Parents perceive themselves as socially isolated from their peers, relatives, and other social support systems.

(Cont.)

BOX 13.6 *(Continued)*

Scale	Items	Characteristics of High Scorers
Relationship with Spouse	7	Parents perceive that they do not receive emotional and physical support from their spouse in area of child management.
Parent Health	5	Parents report a deterioration in physical health that is impacting their ability to fulfill parental responsibilities.

SOURCE: Abidin, 1986.

one is unsure of what to assess. While acknowledging the unresolved status of this issue, we feel that a recent conceptual paper by Darling and Steinberg (1993) provides a good context for conceptualizing parenting and its effect on children and adolescents.

Darling and Steinberg (1993) divide parenting into two main components: parenting styles and parenting practices. These authors define parenting styles as "a constellation of attitudes toward the child that are communicated to the child and create an emotional climate in which the parents' behaviors are expressed" (p. 493).

These authors use Baumrind's (1971) typology to exemplify parenting style. Baumrind divides parenting styles into three types. The *authoritarian* style is characterized by a rule-adherence orientation that deemphasizes autonomy and emotional support. The *permissive* style is a child-centered style in which child autonomy is of primary importance and rules and demands are minimal. The *authoritative* style is characterized by emotional support and respect for appropriate autonomy in the child but in the context of clearly defined and consistently enforced rules. It is this last parenting style, Authoritative, that research has consistently linked to more healthy child adjustment. In contrast to parenting style, parenting practices are defined as the techniques used by the parent to socialize their child and enforce rules. For example, specific discipline practices (e.g., degree of corporal punishment), use of positive parenting (e.g., praise and rewards for appropriate behavior), consis-

tency in parenting, and appropriate supervision and monitoring of a child's behavior by a parent are all examples of parenting practices that have been linked to child adjustment (Frick, 1994).

The unique contribution of Darling and Steinberg's model of parenting is not only its explicit distinction between parenting style and parenting behaviors but also clear specification of how these factors interact to influence child development. Specifically, parenting style provides a context in which parenting behaviors influence a child's development. As a result, the same parenting behavior may have different effects on a child depending on the parenting style. For example, there is a generally accepted association between adolescents' school performance and their parents' involvement in their schooling. However, the effectiveness of parents' school involvement in facilitating academic achievement has been found to be greater among parents who have an authoritative parenting style than among parents who show an authoritarian parenting style (Steinberg et al., 1992).

The implications of this model of parenting are important for clinical assessments of children and adolescents. It suggests that to understand the effects of parenting on a child or adolescent's development, one must assess both parenting style and parenting practices. Unfortunately, there are few standardized methods of assessing either of these dimensions. The Family Environment Scale (FES; Moos & Moos, 1986), one of the omnibus rating scales discussed previously, contains several scales that are related to parenting style (e.g., Organization, Control, Independence, and Conflict). In addition, the Child Rearing Practices Report (CRPR; Block, 1965) was developed to specifically assess parenting style and it has been used fairly extensively in research. We will discuss the CRPR in more detail soon. There are also several behavior observation systems developed specifically to assess parent interactions with young children that provide information on both parenting style and practices. One example is the Dyadic Parent–Child Interaction Coding System (DPICS; Eyberg & Robinson, 1983), which will also be discussed in detail.

However, most assessors typically obtain information on parenting style and/or practices in an unstructured clinical interview (see Chapter 14) or through other unstandardized methods. In Box 13.7 we provide a summary of an assessment system in the preliminary stages of development that assesses parenting practices using four modalities: child and parent global report and child and parent telephone interview. Although this specific assessment strategy has not been adequately tested yet for widespread clinical use, the constructs assessed and the items that make up each construct illustrate how parenting is often assessed in clinical practice.

Child-Rearing Practices Report (CRPR)

The CRPR (Block, 1965) is a rating system that is commonly used in research to assess parenting style. Its 91 items, phrased in the first person, tap child-rearing attitudes, values, behaviors, and goals (Roberts, Block, & Block, 1984).

Content

Box 13.8 provides a summary of the domains of parenting assessed by the CRPR and examples of items in each domain. Although the CRPR content focuses primarily on parenting style, there are a number of items pertaining directly to type of parental discipline. The CRPR has an atypical administration format. It is administered using a forced-choice Q-sort format. The parent is asked to sort the CRPR items into seven piles of 13 items each, with each pile designating a point on a 7-point scale from most descriptive to least descriptive. That is, the items are ranked in terms of their relative descriptiveness rather than being rated on some anchored Likert-type scale.

BOX 13.7

The Alabama Parenting Questionnaire

To aid in the clinical assessment of parenting practices, the Alabama Parenting Questionnaire (APQ; Kuper, Frick, & Wootton, 1994) was developed. The multi-informant, multimodal APQ has four components. There are parent and child global forms in which the informant responds to questions about *typical* parentiang. The parenting practices are rated on a 1 (Never) to 5 (Always) Likert-type scale. The other two components are parent and child telephone interviews. They include analogous questions but ask the parent and child to estimate the *number of times in the past 3 days* that each behavior has occurred.

The development of the APQ is still in its infancy. Kuper et al. (1994) have tested the APQ in a large clinic sample and small normal control sample with promising results, at least for the parent report formats. However, there are insufficient psychometric data on the system to warrant standardized use in clinical assessments. However, the following summary of items illustrates the types of questions that are often used to obtain clinical impressions of parenting practices. The items were based on items used previously in research on parenting practices (see, for example, Loeber & Stouthamer-Loeber, 1986).

(Cont.)

BOX 13.7   *(Continued)*

Parental Involvement and Positive Parenting	Inconsistent Discipline	Supervision/Monitoring	Discipline Practices
You have a friendly talk with your child.	You threaten to punish your child and then do not actually punish him/her.	Your child fails to leave a note or to let you know where he/she is going.	You spank your child with your hand when he/she has done something wrong.
You let your child know when he/she is doing a good job with something.	Your child talks you out of being punished after he/she has done something wrong.	Your child stays out in the evening past the time he/she is supposed to be home.	You ignore your child when he/she is misbehaving.
You volunteer to help with special activities that your child is involved in (such as sports, scouts, church youth groups).	You feel that getting your child to obey you is more trouble than it's worth.	Your child is out with friends you do not know.	You slap your child when he/she has done something wrong.
You reward or give something extra to your child for obeying you or behaving well.	You let your child out of a punishment early (like lift restrictions earlier than you originally said).	Your child goes out without a set time to be home.	You take away privileges or money from your child as a punishment.
You play games or do other fun things with your child.	Your child is not punished when he/she has done something wrong.	Your child is out after dark without an adult with him/her.	You send your child to his/her room as a punishment.
You help your child with his/her homework.	The punishment you give your child depends on your mood.	You get so busy that you forget where your child is and what he/she is doing.	You hit your child with a belt, switch, or other object when he/she has done something wrong.
You compliment your child when he/she does something well.		You don't check that your child comes home at the time she/he was supposed to.	You yell or scream at your child when he/she has done something wrong.
You ask your child what his/her plans are for the coming day.		You don't tell your child where you are going.	You calmly explain to your child why his/her behavior was wrong when he/she misbehaves.
You drive your child to a special activity.		Your child comes home from school more than an hour past the time you expect him/her.	You use time-out (when he/she misbehaves).

BOX 13.7   *(Continued)*

Parental Involvement and Positive Parenting	Inconsistent Discipline	Supervision/Monitoring	Discipline Practices
You praise your child if he/she behaves well.		Your child is at home without adult supervision.	You give your child extra chores as a punishment.
You hug or kiss your child when he/she has done something well.			
You talk to your child about his/her friends.			
Your child helps plan family activities.			
You attend PTA meetings, parent/teacher conferences, or other meetings at your child's school.			

Norms

Despite its extensive use in research, there is very little normative information on the CRPR. Most studies using CRPR investigated the basic properties of the CRPR scores, such as their stability (Roberts, Block, & Block, 1984) or their correlations with observed parent behavior (Kochanska, Kuczynski, & Radke-Yarrow, 1989). Therefore, normative cut-off scores were not developed.

Reliability and Validity

The internal consistency of the CRPR factors have generally been found to be poor (McNally, Eisenberg, & Harris, 1991). In a community sample of 32 mothers of children ages 7–8, only the Negative Affect (alpha = .67), Independence (alpha = .53), and Openness to Experience (alpha = .50) had internal consistency estimates above .50 (McNally et al., 1991). However, the stability of CRPR scores seems to be more impressive. McNally et al. (1991) reported high

correlations for CRPR scores across a 4-year time period (coefficients ranging from r = .42 to r = .83) and across an 8-year time period (coefficients ranging from r = .31 to r = .73).

The correlations between CRPR scores and problems in child adjustment have been well established (Block, Block, & Morrison, 1981). One of the more interesting pieces of validity information on the CRPR comes from a sample of 68 mothers of young children (1 to 3 years) (Kochanska, Kuczynski, & Radke-Yarrow, 1989). In this study, CRPR factors were combined into those indicative of authoritative parenting styles (Rational Guidance, Independence, Expression of Affect) and authoritarian styles (Control, Supervision, Control by Anxiety Induction). The authoritative style was positively correlated with behavioral observations of the use of suggestions and positive incentives, and negatively related to the use of physical punishment, prohibitive interventions, and direct commands. The authoritarian style was positively correlated with the use of direct commands, physical enforcement, reprimands, and prohibitive

Box 13.8

Domains Assessed by the Child-Rearing Practices Report

Behavior Domain	Types of Items
Encouragement of Independence	Parents' respect for child opinions, encouragement of independence in child, and encouragement of child's input in decision making
Control	Strictness of parental control over child's behavior and emotions
Investment in Child	Parental enmeshment and overindulgence with child
Worry about Child	Parental anxiety over child's health and safety
Suppression of Aggression	Parental control over child's aggressive behavior
Enjoyment of Child	Parents' intrinsic enjoyment in child rearing
Emphasis on Early Training	Degree to which parents believe in early training in self-sufficiency
Suppression of Sex	Parental anxiety about avoidance of discussing sexual topics with child and acceptance of nudity
Control by Anxiety Induction	Parental control of child's behavior by threatening and warning of bad consequences
Control by Guilt Induction	Parental control of child's behavior by inducing shame and self-reproach
Negative Affect	Anger, conflict, and disappointment in parent–child relationship
Parental Independence	Parents' ability to separate and be independent from child
Emphasis on Achievement	Parents' emphasis on achievement, competition, and success
Expression of Affect	Parents' communication with both positive and negative emotion with children
Emphasis on Health	Parental concern over child's health and engagement in healthy lifestyle
Openness to Experience	Parents' encouragement of introspection and curiosity in child
Protectiveness	Parents' willingness to let child take risks
Supervision	Parental monitoring of their child's behavior
Inconsistency	Parental consistency in following through with punishments and promises made to child
Rational Guidance	Parents' use of praise, rewards, and reasoning as behavior change techniques
Nonphysical Punishment	Parents' use of noncorporal punishment, such as taking away privileges
Residual Items	Potpourri of items that do not fall into other dimensions

---

SOURCE: Block, 1965.

interventions, and negatively correlated with the use of suggestions. While this study provides support for the correlation between CRPR scores and behavioral observations of parenting behavior, it should be noted that it did not use the individual factors from the CRPR but used rationally derived groups of factors. Also, it is unclear how well this correspondence with behavioral observations would generalize to older children.

Dyadic Parent-Child Interaction Coding System (DPICS)

The DPICS (Eyberg & Robinson, 1983) is an observational system that was mentioned briefly in Chapter 9 in our discussion of direct observational systems. It is reviewed in more detail here because of its focus on parenting and parent-child interactions. The DPICS is a highly structured coding system designed to assess maternal behaviors and parent–child interactions in several standard settings. It has typically been used to code parents of preschool children (e.g., Eisenstadt et al., 1993; Robinson & Eyberg, 1981). Parents and children are observed in two 5-minute periods, typically in a clinic playroom setting. In the Child Directed Interaction (CDI) the parent is instructed to allow the child to choose any activity and to play along with the child. In the Parent Directed Interaction (PDI) the parent is instructed to select an activity and to keep the child playing according to parental rules.

Content

The 5-minute interactions are videotaped for later coding. The DPICS includes a detailed manual for coding several parent and child behaviors. A summary of the parent and child behaviors included in the DPICS is provided in Box 13.9. In addition to discrete behaviors, several additional categories are included in the DPICS to code *sequences of behaviors.* Parental responses (i.e., ignores or responds) to child's defiant behavior and child responses (i.e., complies, noncomplies, or no opportunity) to parental commands are coded. The coding system is a continuous frequency count of all behaviors observed during the 5-minute interaction periods.

BOX 13.9

Categories from the Dyadic Parent–Child Interaction Coding System

MATERNAL BEHAVIORS

1. Praise
   a. Labeled Praise
   b. Unlabeled Praise
2. Command
   a. Direct Commands
   b. Indirect Commands
3. Other Verbalizations
   a. Descriptive/Reflective Question
   b. Descriptive/Reflective Statement
   c. Irrelevant Verbalization
   d. Verbal Acknowledgment
4. Responses to Child Behavior
   a. Physical Positive
   b. Ignore
   c. Critical Statement
   d. Physical Negative

CHILD BEHAVIORS

1. Deviant
   a. Whine
   b. Cry
   c. Smart Talk
   d. Yell
   e. Destructive
   f. Physical Negative
2. Response to Commands
   a. Compliance
   b. Noncompliance
   c. No Opportunity

SOURCE: Eyberg and Robinson, 1983.

Norms

The normative information available on the DPICS is quite limited. Robinson and Eyberg (1983) provide data on 22 families with children between the ages of 2 and 7. The sample was primarily two-parent families (73%) and highly educated (mean of 15.2 years of education for parents). As a result, the generalizability of this information to other samples is questionable.

Reliability and Validity

Not surprisingly, given the very detailed behavioral descriptions provided by the DPICS manual, trained observers have been able to achieve quite high interrater reliability with the DPICS. In a sample of 42 families (20 clinic-referred and 22 normal control) the mean interrater reliability for parent behaviors was .91 and for child behaviors was .92 (Robinson & Eyberg, 1981). In addition, DPICS scores have been shown to differentiate families of clinic-referred children with conduct problems from families of normal control children (Robinson & Eyberg, 1983). Scores from the DPICS have also been shown to be sensitive to interventions for families of children with behavior problems (Eisenstadt et al., 1993; Eyberg & Robinson, 1982).

In summary, the DPICS appears to be a promising observational system for assessing parent–child interactions in preschool children. It has proven to provide reliable scores for trained observers, and its differential validity and sensitivity to treatment effects have been shown in several studies. However, the lack of normative data and the time required to train coders on its very detailed definitions of behaviors may limit its usefulness in many clinical situations.

MARITAL DISCORD AND DIVORCE

There is a long history of research showing a link between divorce and child behavior problems. The most comprehensive summary of this research comes from Amato and Keith (1991). These authors conducted a meta-analysis of 92 published studies of the impact of divorce on a child's psychological well-being. The combined samples from the 92 studies involved over 13,000 children. This meta-analysis revealed that divorce consistently had a negative impact on several types of child well-being (e.g., conduct problems, school achievement, social adjustment, self-concept). These studies suggested that the relationship between divorce and psychological difficulties in children was greatest within the 2 years immediately following a divorce.

The meta-analysis also provided intriguing data in support of the theory that it is the conflict that occurs between parents before and during the separation that has the most detrimental impact on a child's adjustment (see also Emery, 1982). Whereas children of divorced families tended to have poorer adjustment than children in low-conflict, intact families, children in *intact, high-conflict* homes tended to have the poorest adjustment of all three groups. Also consistent with this perspective, several studies found that less conflict and better divorce cooperation between parents predicted better post-divorce adjustment for children.

The implications of these findings are important to clinical assessments of children and adolescents. They suggest that it is not simply enough to determine the marital status of a child's parents for understanding the potential impact of the parents' marital relationship on the child. A more important focus of assessment is the overt conflict between parents that is witnessed by the child. Many of the omnibus family rating scales (i.e., CAPI, FES) and parenting scales (i.e., CRPR) contain items that assess the level of family conflict. Unfortunately, they tend to focus on general family conflict and not specifically on the conflict within the parents' marital relationship.

There are also two omnibus marital inventories that are frequently used in research and clinical practice. The Marital Adjustment Test (MAT; Locke & Wallace, 1959) and the Dyadic Adjustment Scale (DAS; Spanier, 1976) are two self-report instruments that have been shown to produce reliable scores and differentiate persons in distressed and nondistressed marriages. However, these inventories tend to focus on general marital satisfaction rather than on overt conflict per se. The O'Leary Porter Scale (OPS; Porter & O'Leary, 1980) is a brief rating scale that focuses on overt marital conflict and even more specifically on marital conflict that is witnessed by the child or adolescent. As a result, the OPS is uniquely suited for use in clinical assessments of children and adolescents.

O'Leary-Porter Scale (OPS)

The OPS (Porter & O'Leary, 1980) was developed specifically for studying the association between marital adjustment and child behavior problems. The OPS is 20-item self-report inventory within which are embedded 9 items that assess the degree of marital conflict witnessed by the child. A parent rates on a 5-point frequency scale (Never to Very Often) how often the child witnesses arguments between himself or herself and the spouse over money, discipline, wife's role in family, and personal habits of spouse. Two questions also ask for overall estimates of the amount of verbal and physical hostility between spouses that is witnessed by the child.

There is little normative data on the OPS. However, 2-week test-retest reliability in a sample of 14 families was found to be quite high (r = .92) (Porter & O'Leary, 1980). These authors also reported that the OPS was correlated with several types of maladjustment in children. Highlighting the importance of focusing specifically on overt conflict, these authors found that the OPS was more consistently associated with child adjustment difficulties than was a measure of general marital satisfaction (i.e., the MAT). Therefore, it appears that the OPS captures the critical component of marital discord in terms of its detrimental effect on child adjustment.

PARENTAL ADJUSTMENT

In the introduction to this chapter, we discussed several ways in which assessing parental psychiatric adjustment is critical to the clinical assessment of children. We discussed two areas of research, one on

parental depression and another on parental anxiety, that suggest that information obtained from a parent must be interpreted in light of the parent's level of emotional distress. We also discussed the importance of obtaining a family psychiatric history for making differential diagnoses and treatment recommendations. In this section we provide a brief overview of basic research showing the link between parent and child adjustment difficulties that can aid the clinical assessor in structuring assessments and making appropriate interpretations from the assessment information.

Parental Depression

One type of parental adjustment that has a well-documented link to child development is parental depression. Studies have found that between 40% (Orvaschel, Walsh-Allis, & Ye, 1988) and 74% (Hammen et al., 1987) of the children of depressed parents exhibit significant adjustment problems. Depression in parents places children at risk for a number of problems spanning academic, social, emotional, and behavioral domains (Downey & Coyne, 1990). Therefore, it seems that parental depression is a *nonspecific* risk factor for problems in children. That is, it is not specifically related to the development of a single type of child behavior problem.

There are two possible exceptions to this nonspecific relationship, both related to subtypes within affective disorders. First, Weissman et al. (1988) found some preliminary evidence that *early-onset* recurrent depression (depression that has its initial onset before adulthood) might have a more specific link with childhood depression. Second, family histories of bipolar disorders in parents predict a risk for subsequent bipolar disorder in adolescents with a childhood-onset of depressive symptoms (Geller et al., 1993). However, whether or not more specific links between parental affective disturbances and child adjustment are uncovered as research focuses more on depressive subtypes, the clear link between parental depression and child maladjustment makes the assessment of parental depression an important component of many clinical assessments of children and adolescents.

Parental Substance Abuse

A comprehensive review of the literature found that, like parental depression, parental alcoholism is associated with a number of child adjustment problems. West and Prinz (1987) reported studies finding an association between parental alcohol abuse and the following problems in their children: hyperactivity, conduct problems, delinquency, substance abuse, intellectual impairment, somatic problems, anxiety, depression, and social deficits. Like depression, some of the lack of specificity in its effect on child adjustment may be due to a failure to define subgroups within parents who abuse substances (Frick, 1993). Alternatively, West and Prinz (1987) reviewed several studies suggesting that the effects of having a substance-abusing parent on a child's adjustment may be mediated through the impact on the home environment and the impact on parent and child interactions.

Parental Antisocial Behavior

The intergenerational link to antisocial behavior is a consistent finding in research and one that has long intrigued social scientists and policy makers alike. Early studies tended to focus on the intergenerational link to criminality; this research found that the link was independent of socioeconomic status, neighborhood, and intelligence (Glueck & Glueck, 1968). More recent studies have focused on psychiatric definitions of antisocial disorders. As in studies of criminality, children diagnosed with antisocial disorders are significantly more likely to have parents with antisocial disorders than are children without conduct problems (Frick et al., 1992).

An important methodological point in the more recent family history studies was the fact that each used clinic control groups and found that histories of antisocial disorders in parents were specific to conduct problems in children. That is, children with conduct problems not only had higher rates of parental antisocial personality disorder (APD) than normal controls, but they also had higher rates of parental APD than clinic-referred children with other problems in adjustment (Frick et al., 1992). There-fore, unlike parental depression and substance abuse, parent antisocial behavior appears to have a specific relationship to child conduct problems.

Parental ADHD

There is preliminary evidence that parents and other biological relatives of children with ADHD show more attentional problems (Albert-Corush, Firestone, & Goodman, 1986) and a higher rate of ADHD (Faraone et al., 1991). However, these studies may have underestimated the link between parent and child ADHD by studying the parents' *current* adjustment. Given that 30–50% of ADHD children may not be so diagnosed as adults (Gittelman et al., 1985; Lambert, 1988), it may be that many of the parents of ADHD children exhibited ADHD as a child but are not currently showing symptoms.

To test this possibility, Frick et al.(1991) studied the childhood histories of parents of clinic-referred children. A child's biological parent reported on whether or not he or she had problems associated with ADHD before the age of 18 and then completed a similar family history questionnaire for all first degree relatives. Children with ADHD were more likely to have mothers, fathers, and other biological relatives who also exhibited ADHD as children than were other clinic-referred children. In fact, approximately 75% of the 103 children with ADHD had one biological relative with a significant history for ADHD (27% of mothers and 44% of fathers) and 46% had two biological relatives with a significant history for ADHD. This study suggests that an assessment of parents' childhood histories of behavior problems could aid in assessment of ADHD in children.

Parental Anxiety

Another type of problem that appears to have a familial link is anxiety. Last et al. (1987) reported that in their sample of children with an anxiety disorder (n = 58), 83% of the children had a mother with a lifetime history of anxiety disorders. Furthermore, 57% had a mother experiencing significant levels of anxiety concurrently with the child. Both of these proportions were significantly greater than what was found in parents of clinically referred children without anxiety disorders. Importantly, Frick et al. (1994) found similar results but also found that the link between mother and child anxiety could not solely be attributed to anxious mothers *reporting* more anxiety in their children. All of the children in the Frick et al. (1994) study who self-reported an anxiety disorder had a mother with a history of an anxiety disorder. It is clear from these findings that parental anxiety is an important area to be assessed in clinical assessments of anxious children.

Parental Schizophrenia

Another type of maladjustment with a clear familial link is schizophrenia. Children of one schizophrenic parent appear to have a 10% to 15% likelihood of developing schizophrenia; the children of two schizophrenic parents have about a 25–46% risk (Helzer, 1988). These rates of disorder in offspring of schizophrenic parents are striking given that the prevalence of schizophrenia in the general population is between 1 and 10 per 1000 individuals (Helzer, 1988). However, parents who either themselves have schizophrenia or who have another relative with schizophrenia are often quite concerned over the risk for their children, based on the evidence for a familial transmission. Therefore, it is often important for clinical assessors to also view these risk rates from the point of view that the vast majority of children with a schizophrenic relative, even if that relative is a parent, do not develop schizophrenia.

Assessment of Family History

From this very brief overview of the familial link to childhood disorders it is evident that obtaining a family history is a critical component of most clinical assessments of children and adolescents. However, like all aspects of the assessment process, what areas to be assessed and the depth at which they will be assessed depend on the individual case. In some cases a screening for psychiatric disorders in a child's relatives can be conducted as part of an unstructured

interview followed by a more in depth family history assessment only if this is judged to be warranted from the initial screening. In other cases a more detailed and structured assessment may be needed from the outset.

It is beyond the scope of this book to cover assessment of adult psychopathology in great detail. One decision that an clinical assessor can make, after determining the depth of the family assessment, is determining the breadth of assessment. One can assess a wide range of problems in parents or other relatives through omnibus rating scales or structured interviews. For example, the NEO-Personality Inventory (NEO-PI; Costa & McCrae, 1985) and the Minnesota Multiphasic Personality Inventory—Second Edition (MMPI-2; Hathaway & McKinley, 1989) are two widely used and readily available objective personality inventories that cover a number of areas of psychological functioning. There are also numerous structured diagnostic interviews that are available, like the NIMH Diagnostic Interview Schedule—Third Edition (DIS-IIIA: Robins & Helzer, 1985) and the Schedule for Affective Disorders and Schizophrenia (SADS; Endicott & Spitzer, 1978).

In considering what type of assessment may be needed, it is important to note that structured interviews tend to focus on more severe pathology, assessing for diagnosable disorders, than the objective personality inventories do. In addition, the structured interviews tend to be more amenable to the family history method of assessment, in which a family member reports on him- or herself and other relatives who cannot be assessed directly.

There may be some assessments when a more focused family history is deemed appropriate, such as when one wants to focus on some specific domain of parental adjustment. For example, the Beck Depression Inventory (BDI; Beck, Steer, & Garbin, 1988) and the State-Trait Anxiety Inventory (Spielberger, Gorsuch, & Lushene, 1970) are brief screening measures for depression and anxiety, respectively, that are often used to assess parental adjustment in clinic-referred children (see Richters, 1992, table 1). These are just a few of a host of domain-specific rating scales that can be used to assess a specific area of adjustment in a child's parent or other relatives.

CONCLUSIONS

In this chapter we discussed several reasons why assessment of the family environment is critical to most clinical assessments of children and adolescents. Family factors often play a critical causal role in child maladjustment, and familial factors can aid in making differential diagnoses and treatment recommendations, two important goals of many clinical assessments. Further, factors within the family are often important for interpreting information provided by members of the family on a child's or adolescent's adjustment. We reviewed several omnibus rating scales that assess many dimensions of a child's family context in a time-efficient manner. Many of these scales also facilitate obtaining analogous assessments from multiple family members, which allows one to compare different perceptions of the family environment.

Unfortunately, most of these rating scales lack a good normative base from which to interpret scores. This is a critical flaw given research that clearly documents differences in many aspects of family functioning depending on the age and gender of the child, the ethnicity of the family, and the socioeconomic status of the family. Further, many clinical assessments require a more focused assessment of specific areas of family functioning. To aid in designing these more focused assessments, we reviewed the research on several specific areas of family functioning that research has consistently linked to child adjustment: parenting style and parenting practices, marital discord, and parental psychological adjustment. Because of the consistent findings from research that each of these aspects of a child's or adolescent's family environment has an important impact on a child's adjustment, each area should be assessed as a standard part of clinical assessments of children and adolescents. However, the depth and breadth of coverage in each domain will be dependent on the goals of the assessment.

CHAPTER SUMMARY

1. There is no context more important to understanding a child's emotional and behavioral functioning than understanding the child's family context. This is because:

   a. Familial influences often play major causal roles in a child's or adolescent's psychological difficulties.

   b. A family psychiatric history can be instrumental in making differential diagnoses.

   c. Understanding a child's or adolescent's family context can help to interpret information provided by members of the family.

   d. Understanding a child's family context can help to determine the most important targets for intervention.

2. Many behavior rating scales reviewed in previous chapters such as the PIC-R, the PIY, the MMPI-A, and the BASC-SRS, have items that assess various aspects of a child's family context.

3. The Child Abuse Potential Inventory—Second Edition (CAPI) is a 160-item rating scale that assesses many important dimensions of family functioning.

   a. The CAPI contains three validity scales (Lie, Random Response, and Inconsistency) and six clinical scales (Distress, Rigidity, Unhappiness, Problems with Child and Self, Problems with Family, and Problems with Others).

   b. The best evidence for the reliability and validity of the CAPI scales is for the Abuse composite, which combines the six clinical scales.

   c. The representativeness of the CAPI normative sample is unclear.

4. Another omnibus measure of family functioning is the Family Environment Scale—Second Edition (FES). It is a 90-item true-false scale that can be completed by parents and by children over the age of 11.

   a. The FES is divided into subscales from three domains: Relationships, Personal Growth, and Systems Maintenance.

   b. Item content is based on family systems theory.

   c. There is good evidence for the reliability of the FES scales and for the ability of the FES scales to differentiate distressed from non-distressed families.

d. The normative sample was based primarily on parent report, making its use for interpreting child/adolescent report questionable, especially in light of documented differences in parent and youth report.

e. The scale structure of the FES has not been well validated.

5. The Parenting Stress Index—Second Edition (PSI) is an omnibus family assessment device that is unique in its focus on family functioning as it relates to preschool children (ages 1–4).

a. The two main item categories are the Child Domain, consisting of items assessing child qualities that make it difficult for parents to fulfill their parental role, and the Parent Domain, consisting of items assessing sources of stress and dysfunction related to parental functioning.

b. The best data on the reliability and validity of PSI scales are on the global scales (Total Stress, Child Domain, and Parent Domain).

c. The normative sample consists primarily of White, highly educated parents from central Virginia.

6. For many clinical evaluations of children and adolescents a more in-depth assessment of several important aspects of parental functioning may be required than that provided by the available omnibus rating scales.

7. Clinical assessors should be aware of the potential interactions between parenting style, which is the emotional climate provided by the parents, and parenting practices, which are techniques used by parents to socialize their children and enforce rules.

8. The level of marital discord and overt marital conflict in the home has proven to be important in understanding children's functioning.

9. Assessing parental adjustment can provide critical information in clinical assessments.

a. Research has shown that parental depression and anxiety can affect a parent's report on a child's emotions and behavior.

b. Since there seems to be a familial link to many psychological difficulties, obtaining a family history can aid in making differential diagnoses.

c. Parental depression, parental anxiety, parental substance use, parental antisocial behavior, parental ADHD, and parental schizophrenia have all been linked to increased risk for problems in children and adolescents.

d. Family histories can be obtained using unstructured clinical interviews, omnibus personality questionnaires, or structured interviews.

CHAPTER 14

History Taking

CHAPTER QUESTIONS

- What are the unique contributions of historical information to the child assessment process?
- What are the typical domains, variables, or behaviors, assessed by such measures?
- What structured and unstructured history taking methods are available?

THE ROLE OF HISTORY TAKING IN CHILD ASSESSMENT

Historical information is as crucial as other types of information for child assessment but it is often underutilized by nonphysician practitioners. This oversight is especially regrettable given the widespread availability of history-taking measures and their ease of use. It appears that history taking is simply not as well entrenched in child behavioral assessment as it is in medical assessment, where history taking (in-

terviewing) is central to making initial diagnostic decisions.

There are numerous reasons for taking histories as part of child assessment. Some of the important variables are simply not assessed by rating scales, self-report inventories, or other widely used measures. A few of the variables that are uniquely assessed by history taking include age of onset, course/prognosis, etiology, and previous treatment history.

Age of Onset

Most rating scales, self-report inventories, and even diagnostic interviews do not directly assess the age of onset of problems. Age of onset is particularly important in child assessment as it affects diagnosis directly. In the case of mental retardation, for example, age of onset must occur during the developmental period (DSM IV, APA, 1994). Furthermore, the age of onset is crucial for the diagnosis of ADHD, early infantile autism, learning disabilities and other so-called developmental disorders (DSM IV, APA, 1994).

Most psychologists have seen cases of suspected mental retardation with a reported age of onset in the early 20s. Similarly, children are often referred for ADHD with an age of onset after age 7. Sometimes, however, the age of onset is unclear or disputed, and the typically less structured format of history taking is ideal for clarifying the onset issue.

In one realistic scenario a mother may bring in a college freshman because he is suddenly having problems in school. On a rating scale or other more structured assessment format the clinician may be tempted to accept this age of onset. In the less structured history taking interview, one can pursue the issue of onset more thoroughly by asking the mother if her son was ever in special education or federally sponsored remedial programs or if he had received tutoring in an earlier grade. The clinician may also ask if there were any teacher complaints in the first grade.

It is not unusual for a clinician to find a much earlier age of onset than that initially stated by a child, teacher, parent, or other informant. If, in this sample case the college student did experience some difficulties in first grade that were associated with inattention and hyperactivity and he also struggled to pass both the ninth and twelfth grades, then the clinician may investigate more carefully the diagnosis of ADHD with its associated early age of onset. (See also the case study of James.)

The use of history taking to clarify age of onset is crucial for the diagnosis and conceptualization of several developmental disorders including:

Mental Retardation

Attention-Deficit Hyperactivity Disorder

Learning Disability

Pervasive Developmental Disorder

Autism

Case Study

James is a 15-year-old male who was referred by his father for suspected ADHD. The referral for evaluation was also supported by his high school teachers.

According to James's father, his school difficulties be-

came pronounced about 3 years ago. He rarely does homework and is described by his teachers as exhibiting hyperactivity, impulsivity, and inattention. He is also described as the class clown by his teachers. A recent classroom observation found that James was grossly inattentive in comparison to the other children. He, for example, was the only one who briefly rolled around on the floor in the rear of the room during part of a teacher's lecture. Previously, norm-referenced behavior ratings by four of his teachers identified him as highly hyperactive and inattentive.

Being mindful of the late onset of James' symptoms, the examiner asked James's father for more detail about the onset of his problems. His father could not identify significant symptomatology prior to age 12. It was also discovered that James's parents went through a contentious divorce concurrently with the onset of symptoms. It was further disclosed that James recently has threatened to attempt suicide on several occasions. An interview with James subsequently revealed significant evidence of depression with suicidal ideation.

In this case, history taking, by clarifying the age of onset, made a significant contribution to the conceptualization of James's difficulties and intervention design. Failure to use history taking to rule out ADHD in this case could have been disastrous as poor history taking could have resulted in a failure to treat his depression.

Course/Prognosis

The *course* of a child's difficulties refers to the assessment of the developmental trajectory of symptomatology. The remission of symptoms has substantial implications for differential diagnosis. Developmental disorders, for example, are not marked by significant remissions.

If a parent describes a child as having had severe hyperactivity in first grade that was not apparent in second grade but then emerged again in the fourth grade, then the diagnosis of a developmental disorder such as ADHD is called into question. Similarly, if a child displays symptoms of autism that seem to spontaneously remit and reappear then the diagnosis of autism becomes questionable.

Evaluation of course also provides evidence of the effectiveness of previous intervention strategies. A child's, or family's, failure to respond to previous interventions suggests that different and/or more intensive interventions are in order. The trajectory of behavioral excesses or deficits is uniquely accessed via history taking. Subtleties of this nature are difficult to assess even with many of the structured diagnostic interviews.

Etiology

Etiology refers to the likely presumed cause of a child's difficulties. The assessment of etiology is crucial in that it has important implications for treatment. The discovery that a child's learning difficulties in mathematics began in the ninth grade effectively rules out a developmental disorder such as a learning disability. A developmental disorder is also unlikely, given the epidemiology of learning disabilities which reveals that mathematics problems are rare. If the clinician then discovers that the child was for the first time placed in the advanced section of a mathematics class, then curriculum placement becomes a potential etiological agent. A simple change in classes may be an effective intervention for this suspected mathematics learning disability. Such a parsimonious intervention may not have been tried, however, without important historical information that led the clinician to a potential etiology.

Knowledge of etiology is of potential importance for at least four reasons (AAMR, 1992).

1. The etiology may be associated with other problems (e.g., Down Syndrome) that may impair other aspects of functioning—physical, social, etc..

2. The etiology may be amenable to treatment/intervention.

3. Knowledge of etiology may lead to the design of prevention programs for certain etiologies.

4. Etiologies may be useful for forming homogeneous groups for research or administrative purposes.

Unfortunately, for most childhood problems the range of potential single and multiple etiologies is often extensive. The potential etiologies associated with depression, for instance, are multitudinous, as is shown in Box 14.1. Moreover, multiple etiologies may be interacting to produce symptoms of a problem such as depression. It would not be unusual, for example, for a depressed child to be affected by parental depression, poverty, and the death of a friend—all of which may require simultaneous and/or coordinated intervention.

BOX 14.1

Selected Etiologies of Depression

MEDICAL DISORDERS ASSOCIATED WITH DEPRESSION

Autoimmune disorders—systemic lupus, rheumatoid disease, sarcoidosis

Cancers—head, pancreas, gastrointestinal, lung, renal

Central nervous system diseases—Parkinson's disease, degenerative dementias, normal-pressure hydrocephalus, subarachnoid hemorrhages, Huntington's disease, reversible dementias, focal lesions (nondominant), stroke, head trauma

Disabling/deforming disorders—all types

Endocrinopathies/metabolic disorders—hypothyroidism, Addison's disease, Cushing's disease, pituitary tumors, diabetes, hyperparathyroidism, prophyria

Intoxications—lead, mercury, thallium

Occult infections—genitourinary tract, liver

Viral infections—influenza, viral pneumonia, mononucleosis, hepatitis

DRUGS ASSOCIATED WITH MAJOR DEPRESSION OR DYSTHYMIA

Anticancer—vincristine, vinglastine
Antihypertensives—reserpine, methyldopa, propanolol, guanethidine, hydralazine, clonidine
Antiinfectives—cycloserine
Anti-Parkinson agents—levodopa, amantadine, carbidopa
Corticosteroids
Hormones—estrogens, progesterone
Psychotropics

(Cont.)

Commonly used history taking forms may not fully address the various etiologies associated with a problem or set of problems. Clinicians will often have to use their knowledge of child development, psychopathology, and other areas to go beyond the standard questions included on a history form (i.e., branching) to rule out important high-frequency etiologies.

This process of branching from a history form is difficult for even the most savvy clinician. For the majority of examiners the most realistic option will be to assess history over the course of two or more assessment sessions. A second session could be as simple as a telephone call that allows the clinician to rule out an etiology that has been hypothesized based on previous history, assessment data, or other information. As Green (1992) notes: "Time between sessions is often an important diagnostic and therapeutic ally" (p. 460).

Family Psychiatric History

A specific etiological agent of increasing importance is familial history. Research conducted in the last two decades suggests that the offspring of schizophrenics are 10 times more likely to suffer from the disorder (even if reared apart from their parents), children with early-onset depression are more likely to have a parent with unipolar depression, and there is family resemblance for ADHD (Orvaschel, Ambrosini, & Rabinovich, 1993). Although it can be a disquieting

experience for parents, taking of family history of psychopathology has implications for age of onset, differential diagnosis, and treatment. In addition, such findings have the potential to affect prevention and screening efforts.

Some disorders that show genetic linkages include (Orvaschel, Ambrosini, & Rabinovich, 1993):

Schizophrenia

Unipolar Depression

Bipolar Disorder

Panic Disorder

Tourette's Syndrome

Obsessive-Compulsive Disorder

Separation Anxiety Disorder

Attention-Deficit Hyperactivity Disorder

School screening is an example of the application of family psychiatric history taking. Pre-kindergarten screening programs often ask questions about child behavior, and the inclusion of family history information may trigger prevention or intervention efforts. If, for example, a father reports a history of separation anxiety as a young child, then follow-up could be planned to monitor this father's offspring upon entry into kindergarten. While some minor separation anxiety symptoms are common at this age, if a child with family resemblance for such problems displays some difficulties then earlier and more aggressive intervention may be warranted (see also the case study of Bradford).

It should be pointed out, however, that although biomedical etiologies are better studied, other etiologies deserve equal attention. Other common etiologies include social, behavioral, and educational causes (AAMR, 1992).

Case Study

Bradford is a 10-year-old male who is referred for school difficulties. He has always had school problems, but they have worsened in the fifth grade. His teachers complain that he is unmotivated, moody, irritable, and oppositional.

(Cont.)

Case Study   *(Continued)*

father has had difficulty getting him to complete homework. These sessions usually turn into power struggles and Bradford ends up crying. He also seems unusually emotional in comparison to his younger brother. He angers quickly and cries easily. His mother describes him as brooding.

Bradford's developmental history is unremarkable, with the exception of the continuing problems with work completion. Recently, however, he has had problems interacting with his peers. He cannot identify a best friend, and he is less frequently invited over to other children's homes.

Assessment results did not reveal any problems of note. His intelligence and academic achievement scores ranged from average to above average. His mathematics scores suggest that he is paying a heavier price for work incompletion in this area than in others.

His self-report personality measures and parent and teacher rating scales did not produce any significant T-scores. His scores on internalizing scales such as anxiety and depression were slightly elevated (in the 60s).

Bradford's developmental history and test results leave the clinician puzzled. The results suggest that he has internalizing problems, but he does not display symptomatology that approaches the severity necessary to meet diagnostic criteria for depression, dysthymia, or anxiety disorders. The clinician began to question the parents' reason for the referral. Why are the parents so concerned about what appears to be a circumscribed problem with homework completion and achievement motivation? The clinician discovered the real reason for the parents' referral at the feedback session.

After the clinician presented the findings, recommended behavioral intervention for homework incompletion, and did not make a diagnosis, Bradford's father (who had not attended the previous assessment session) spoke. He disclosed his concern about Bradford's internalizing symptoms, saying that Bradford was realizing his worst fears; that he had inherited his father's susceptibility to depression. Bradford's father then disclosed that he had not wanted the clinician to know about his previous and ongoing treatment so as to not bias the clinician. Bradford's dad then revealed that he has suffered from depression since childhood and has found it difficult to control. He has been involved in psychotherapy at various times and is currently in therapy. He has also received pharmacological treatment for depression and is currently taking Prozac. He has been hospitalized previously because

of suicidal ideation. He also said that although he is a highly successful businessman, he has extraordinary difficulty functioning without ongoing psychotherapy and medical management. He also revealed that his father suffered from depression and eventually committed suicide.

These are belated but interesting historical findings that affect the clinician's conceptualization of the case and intervention planning. The clinician changed his recommendations to include psychotherapy as a further assessment tool, and as a means for designing preventive interventions.

Previous Assessment/Treatment/ Intervention

A child's history of previous intervention/treatment and assessment of these factors is primarily available through history taking. Similarly, previous assessment results may affect interpretation of current findings.

A clinician, for example, may encounter a child who has received psychotherapy for depression for 2 years, pharmacological treatment for 3 months, and partial hospitalization for 6 months prior to the current evaluation. If the child during the current evaluation is demonstrating symptomatology that is more severe than previously noted, the child's clinician is more likely to advise aggressive treatment, perhaps even hospitalization. The need for aggressive treatment, however, may not appear compelling without knowledge of the previous intervention failures.

Information about previous assessment also allows clinicians to gauge the accuracy of their current findings. A clinician can validate their current findings by comparing them to previous assessment results. A child who is diagnosed with an anxiety disorder 2 weeks earlier may demonstrate significant anxiety as indicated by current MMPI-A and RCMAS results. This congruence between current and recent findings may lend some validity to the psychologists' current results.

A lack of congruence between recent and current test findings, however, can be equally insightful. In this situation an advised first step would be to check the scoring of the current measures. Previous diagnoses may also help guide further assessment. If a child is diagnosed previously with ADHD, then the examiner will want to conduct more thorough achievement testing in order to rule out a learning disability. Knowledge of the ADHD diagnosis and the approximately 30% comorbidity of LD with ADHD (Frick et al., 1991) gives the clinician a specific hypothesis to test with further assessment results.

CONTENT

There is considerable overlapping content among history measures although varying degrees of emphasis exist. Some of the most common areas of inquiry include (adapted from the Department of Psychiatry and Child Psychiatry, The Institute of Psychiatry, and the Maudesley Hospital of London, 1987):

Complaints
Present illness
Family history
    Mother
    Father
    Siblings
    Other relatives
    Family atmosphere
Personal history
    Early development
    Behavior and temperament
    School
    Occupation
    Adolescence
    Sexual
    Medical history
    Previous Psychiatric problems
    Alcohol, tobacco, and drug use
    Antisocial behavior
    Current life situation
    Developmental delays or disabilities

Personality
    Attitudes toward others in social, family, and sexual relationships
    Attitudes toward self
    Moral and religious attitudes and standards
    Mood
    Leisure activities and interests
    Fantasy life
    Reaction pattern to stress

A history that is of interest to a certain specialty practice may have a differing emphasis. The content of a history that may be taken by a neurologist or neuropsychologist is described by Teodori (1993) as including the following topics:

Birth history
Developmental history
School history
IQ test results
Social history
Nutritional history
History of exposure to chemicals or toxins
History of other family illnesses
Other medical illnesses
Medications
Hospitalizations
Surgery
Review of systems that inquires about all other aspects of the child's physical functioning
Previous records

A history form that is more commonly used by psychologists is shown in Figure 14.1.

FORMATS

History taking is typically conducted via two formats—the interview and a written form. While history taking research has focused on the interview,

Behavior Assessment System for Children

Structured
Developmental
History **S D H**

Cecil R. Reynolds and Randy W. Kamphaus

Completion Format: ☐ Questionnaire ☐ Interview

Interviewer's name _____   Date _____

Child's name _____   Birth date _____ Age _____

Address _____

_____   Phone _____

School _____   Grade _____ Sex ☐ M ☐ F

Teacher _____

Directions

Notes

To the best of your ability, please answer all of the questions, even if some do not seem to apply.
If you do not understand any item, please ask the person who gave you this form to help you.

Person Answering Questions

Name _____

Relationship to this child _____

Address _____

_____

Home phone_____Work phone _____

Referral Information

Why are you seeking help for this child? _____

_____

_____

Who referred you to our service? _____

_____

What kind of services are you seeking for this child (for example, change of school placement, therapy, psychological testing, custody evaluation, etc.)?

_____

_____

_____

_____

_____

FIGURE 14.1A

Excerpts from the BASC Structured Developmental History (SDH)

Parents

Mother's name _____ Stepmother?　No　Yes

Address _____

Home phone _____ Work phone _____

Occupation _____ Employer _____

How long with present employer? _____ Highest grade completed _____

Father's name _____ Stepfather?　No　Yes

Address _____

Home phone _____ Work phone _____

Occupation _____ Employer _____

How long with present employer? _____ Highest grade completed _____

Does this child have other parent(s)/stepparent(s)?　No　Yes
If yes, please provide the following information.

Name _____

Relationship to this child _____ Home phone _____

Address _____

Name _____

Relationship to this child _____ Home phone _____

Address _____

Primary Caregivers

With what adult(s) does this child live? _____

How long in current living situation? _____

Please provide the following information about primary caregivers, if not given previously.

Name _____ Relationship to child _____

Address _____

Home phone _____ Work phone _____

Occupation _____ Employer _____

How long with present employer? _____ Highest grade completed _____

Name _____ Relationship to child _____

Address _____

Home phone _____ Work phone _____

Occupation _____ Employer _____

How long with present employer? _____ Highest grade completed _____

FIGURE 14.1B

Excerpts from the BASC Structured Developmental History (SDH)

Birth

At this child's birth, what was the mother's age?_____ Father's age?_____

Mother's age at birth of first child? _____

Was this child born in a hospital?   Yes   No   If no, where? _____

    Length of pregnancy:_____weeks   Birth weight:_____lbs_____oz

    Length of labor:_____hours   Apgar score _____

    Child's condition at birth _____

    Mother's condition at birth _____

Check any of the following complications that occurred during birth.

   ☐ Forceps used   ☐ Breech birth   ☐ Labor induced   ☐ Caesarean delivery

   ☐ Other delivery complications: Describe _____

   _____

   ☐ Incubator: How long? _____

   ☐ Jaundiced: Bilirubin lights? .... No   Yes   If yes, how long? _____

   ☐ Breathing problems right after birth: Describe _____

       Supplemental oxygen? .... No   Yes   If yes, how long? _____

Was anesthesia used during delivery? ..... No   Yes   If yes, what kind? _____

Length of stay in hospital: Mother:_____days   Child:_____days

Development

At what age did this child first do the following? *Please indicate year/month of age.*

_____	Turn over	_____	Walk down stairs
_____	Sit alone	_____	Show interest in or attraction to sound
_____	Crawl	_____	Understand first words
_____	Stand alone	_____	Speak first words
_____	Walk alone	_____	Speak in sentences
_____	Walk up stairs		

Was this child breast-fed?   .... No   Yes   When weaned? _____

Was this child bottle-fed?   .... No   Yes   When weaned? _____

When was this child toilet trained?   Days:_____   Nights:_____

Did bed-wetting occur after toilet training? ... No   Yes   If yes, until what age? _____

Did bed-soiling occur after toilet training? ... No   Yes   If yes, until what age? _____

Were there any medical reasons for bed-wetting or -soiling?   No   Yes   If yes, please describe.

_____

Has this child experienced any of the following problems? If yes, please describe.

    Walking difficulty ...... No   Yes _____

    Unclear speech .... No   Yes _____

    Feeding problem ...... No   Yes _____

    Underweight problem ... No   Yes _____

FIGURE 14.1C

Excerpts from the BASC Structured Developmental History (SDH)

Overweight problem . . . . No Yes _____

Colic . . . . No Yes _____

Sleep problem . . . . No Yes _____

Eating disorder . . . . No Yes _____

Difficulty learning to ride a bike . . . . No Yes _____

Difficulty learning to skip . . . . No Yes _____

Difficulty learning to throw or catch . . . . . No Yes _____

During this child's first 4 years, were any special problems noted in the following areas?
If yes, please describe.

Eating . . . . No Yes _____

Motor skills . . . . No Yes _____

Sleeping too much . . . . . No Yes _____

Temper tantrums . . . . . . No Yes _____

Sleeping too little . . . . . . No Yes _____

Failure to thrive . . . . No Yes _____

Separating from parents No Yes _____

Excessive crying . . . . . . No Yes _____

Which hand does this child use for writing or drawing? _____

Eating? _____   Other (throwing, etc.)? _____

Has this child been forced to change writing hand?   No   Yes

Medical History

Childhood Illnesses/Injuries

Please check the illnesses this child has had and indicate age (year/month).

☐ Measles _____   ☐ Rheumatic fever _____

☐ German measles _____   ☐ Diphtheria _____

☐ Mumps _____   ☐ Meningitis _____

☐ Chicken pox _____   ☐ Encephalitis _____

☐ Tuberculosis _____   ☐ Anemia _____

☐ Whooping cough _____   ☐ Fever above 104° _____

☐ Scarlet fever _____

☐ Head injury: Describe _____

☐ Coma or loss of consciousness: Describe _____

☐ Sustained high fever: Describe _____

Please describe other serious illnesses or operations:

Illness/Operation	Age
_____	_____
_____	_____
_____	_____

Has this child ever been on long-term medication (more than 6 months)?   No   Yes

If yes, when? _____   What kind?

FIGURE 14.1D

Excerpts from the BASC Structured Developmental History (SDH)

Adaptive Skills

Please indicate whether this child has the following skills.

Dresses self . . . . No Yes   Bathes self . . . . No Yes

Buys gifts or presents for others . . . . No Yes   Helps with household chores . . . . No Yes

Knows how to get help or find home if lost . . No Yes   Has good table manners . . . . No Yes

Says "please" and "thank you" . . . . No Yes   Tells time accurately . . . . No Yes

Does this child receive an allowance? . . . . . No Yes

     If yes, how does he/she spend it? _____

_____

Educational History

Preschool

Does or did this child attend preschool ? . . . No Yes At what age? _____

     Amount of time per day _____   Days per week _____

     Any problems in preschool? . . . . No Yes If yes, describe _____

_____

Does or did this child attend kindergarten?   No Yes

     Any problems in kindergarten? . . . . . . No Yes If yes, describe _____

_____

Elementary/High School

Please indicate whether this child has had any of the following school experiences.

Has been retained a grade in school . . . . . . No Yes If yes, when and why? _____

_____

Has skipped a grade in school . . . . No Yes If yes, when and why? _____

_____

Has difficulty with reading . . . . No Yes If yes, describe _____

_____

Has difficulty with math . . . . No Yes If yes, describe _____

_____

Gets poor grades . . . . No Yes Describe most recent report card results.

_____

Has been tested for special education . . . . . No Yes If yes, when? _____

_____

Currently is placed in special education class No Yes

     If yes, what type of class? _____   Hours per day _____

Dislikes going to school . . . . No Yes

Is absent from school frequently . . . . No Yes If yes, why? _____

_____

If in high school, when will this child graduate? _____

FIGURE 14.1E

Excerpts from the BASC Structured Developmental History (SDH)

there are often occasions where a written form may be used, particularly with the parents of children. Parents are already accustomed to completing such forms while waiting in physicians' offices. Increasingly, parents are also accustomed to completing rating scales in psychologists' offices.

Most history taking forms, however, require considerable English language fluency on the part of parents. Technical topics, such as the type of special education program that their child attends or a previous medical condition, are difficult for even the most sophisticated parents. Regardless, parents may be able to complete part of the history and thereby save the examiner interviewing time. Parents could easily complete the first part of history forms such as the first page of the form shown in Figure 14.1.

In many circumstances, parents may be encouraged to complete written history forms if they are available in their native language. The use of languages other than English may be of particular value to clinicians who serve such a clientele with considerable frequency.

Many clinicians, however, prefer the interview format because it allows them to use a branching procedure to pursue topics that are of particular relevance to issues of onset, course, etiology, and previous treatment history among other factors. A sample scenario is a case where an 8-year-old child is referred due to a decrement in academic achievement. The examiner may discover that the child's performance in school was exemplary until the current academic year, when the child missed 35 days of school due to an automobile accident. The examiner in this case will likely branch to ask questions about the child's length of absence from school and extent of documented head injury. New and detailed information about these problems may profoundly influence intervention planning. Special education may be placed in abeyance in favor of remedial coursework and monitoring to see if the child recovers his premorbid level of functioning with little intervention, as would often be predicted. Hence, the interview or partial interview format allows the clinician the flexibility necessary for thorough exploration of variables that may impact intervention.

The face-to-face approach of the interview format may offer additional advantages beyond the pos

sibility for branching. See, for example, Green's (1992) advice on observing nonverbal cues during history taking given in Box 14.2.

BOX 14.2

Observing Nonverbal Cues during History Taking

Green (1992) provides some advice to pediatricians regarding behaviors to observe during the interviewing process. This compendium is equally useful to the psychologist who, while interviewing, is developing hypotheses about family dynamics and other factors that impact child development. The following is an adapted list of behaviors for which psychologists should observe during history taking with a caregiver informant or set of informants.

Perspiration, blushing or paling; controlled, uneven, or blocked speech; plaintive voice; taling in a whisper; gait; posture; tics, affirmative nodding; negative shaking of the head

Frequent swallowing, tenseness, fidgeting, preoccupied air, avoidance of eye contact, social distance

A sudden glance at the interviewer or someone else in the family precipitated by a statement or question

Clenching, rubbing, wringing hands; scratching or nail biting

Dress and personal grooming

Redenning of eyes or crying

Frowns, smiles

Affect inappropriate to ideation; e.g., a parent smiles when talking about a child's severe behavior problems

Interactions among parents, child, and examiner

Developmentally inappropriate behavior, e.g., older child on parent's lap . . .

The way in which the infant or young child is held or helped during the interview . . .

The parent's ability to have child respond to a parent's request

---

Adopted from Green (1992), p. 455.

Conclusions

This chapter puts forth the argument that history taking is a central, but often overlooked component, of child assessment. Various reasons for making history taking more central to the child assessment process are offered with the focus on the unique contributions that history taking makes to the process. Specifically, history taking is ideal for assessing factors such as age of onset, etiology, course, and previous assessment/intervention outcomes.

Psychologists are advised to select appropriate history forms and practice the branching procedures necessary for integrating psychological science with child history. In fact, history taking provides an ideal venue for the integration of psychopathology, child development, and cognitive science literatures, among others, with child characteristics.

Chapter Summary

1. Most rating scales, self-report inventories, and even diagnostic interviews do not directly assess the age of onset of problems as well as history taking methods.

2. The use of history taking to clarify age of onset is crucial for the diagnosis and conceptualization of several developmental disorders including:

    a. Mental Retardation

    b. Attention-Deficit Hyperactivity Disorder

    c. Learning Disability

    d. Pervasive Developmental Disorder

    e. Autism

3. Etiology refers to the likely presumed cause of a child's difficulties.

4. Knowledge of etiology is of potential importance for at least four reasons:

    a. The etiology may be associated with other problems (e.g., Down syndrome) that may impair other aspects of functioning—physical, social, or other domains.

    b. The etiology may be amenable to treatment/intervention.

    c. Knowledge of etiology may lead to the design of prevention programs.

    d. Etiologies may be useful for forming homogeneous groups for research or administrative purposes.

5. A specific etiological agent of increasing importance is genetic history.

6. Although biomedical etiologies are the better studied, other etiologies deserve equal attention. Such etiologies include social, behavioral, and educational causes.

7. A child's history of previous intervention/treatment, as well as assessment, is primarily available through history taking.

8. The course of a child's difficulties refers to the assessment of the developmental trajectory of symptomatology.

9. While history taking research has focused on the interview, there are often occasions where a written form may be used, particularly with the parents of children.

10. There is considerable overlapping content among history measures, although varying degrees of emphasis exist.

CHAPTER 15

Adaptive Behavior Scales

CHAPTER QUESTIONS

- What is meant by the term *adaptive behavior?*
- What are the typical domains of adaptive behavior scales?
- How is adaptive behavior different from other constructs such as personality or intelligence?
- What are some of the most popular adaptive behavior scales?

HISTORY OF THE CONSTRUCT

The adaptive behavior construct traces its roots to early work in mental retardation, which in turn, is linked to the roots of intellectual assessment (Kamphaus, 1993). Although intelligence tests contributed mightily to the recognition of the mental retardation syndrome, Edgar Doll (1940) noted that intelligence measures lacked sufficient breadth for assessing all of the relevant domains of behavior that needed to be considered in treatment of mentally retarded individuals.

Doll drew on his experience as a psychologist at the Vineland State Training School in New Jersey, where he was charged with the assessment and rehabilitation of individuals with mental retardation. He noted that such individuals not only lacked intellectual abilities necessary for academic attainment but also often appeared to lack day-to-day living skills needed for independent functioning. In Doll's terminology, they lacked social maturity.

In order to intervene and improve a child's social maturity, Doll created a scale to assess specific behaviors that were deemed necessary for successful living. The Vineland Social Maturity Scale (Doll, 1953) was the first of its genre. It included several sets of items that assessed various aspects of social maturity including locomotion, social skills, and grooming. The Vineland yielded a score that was roughly parallel to a composite score offered by many intelligence tests of the day. His total score was christened a "social quotient." The Vineland became the premier

283

measure of adaptive behavior up to the present day. Doll's pioneering work became the basis for all subsequent measures.

The AAMR Criteria

In 1993 the American Association on Mental Retardation published its most recent version of the *Diagnostic and Statistical Manual of Mental Retardation.* Earlier editions of this manual concluded that the identification of deficits in adaptive behavior is central to the diagnosis of mental retardation. The current manual lists 10 domains of adaptive behavior that should be assessed for the purposes of mental retardation diagnosis and intervention planning, including communication, self-care, home living, social skills, community use, self-direction, health and safety, functional academics, leisure, and work.

More recently aspects of social competence have been identified as important buffers against the development of psychopathology. Social competencies may allow a child to resist being overwhelmed by negative life stressors (Tanaka & Westerman, 1988). In this context, adaptive behavior scales may serve an important function in the assessment of all children referred for evaluation, not just those who are suspected of having mental retardation.

Defining Adaptive Behavior

The "social competence" and "social maturity" names for the construct have been replaced by the modern term *adaptive behavior.* Adaptive behavior has been defined as the performance of the daily activities that are required for social and personal sufficiency (Sparrow, Balla, & Cicchetti, 1984). Hence, adaptive behavior is the antithesis of most of the behavioral constructs discussed in this book in that it deals with behavioral competencies and their absence as opposed to assessing behavioral excesses (i.e., problems).

Most definitions of adaptive behavior have some core similarities including the premise that it is an age-related construct (DeStefano & Thompson, 1990). Specifically, adaptive behavior increases with age in the absence of interfering circumstances much as academic achievements accrue over the course of ontogeny. Adaptive behaviors are identified by the standards of others and the social context in which the child functions (DeStefano & Thompson, 1990). Finally, adaptive behavior assessment focuses on typical behavior as opposed to ability. This assessment emphasis is also consistent with the assessment of other developmental accomplishments such as academic achievements.

Uses of Adaptive Behavior Scales

Traditionally adaptive behavior scales have been considered central to the diagnosis of mental retardation (DeStefano & Thompson, 1990). Although this is a circumscribed role, it is an important one given the epidemiology of mental retardation.

In addition, as the counterpoint of behavior problem scales, adaptive behavior scales hold unique potential for intervention design based on assessment results. Adaptive behavior scales measure key skills that contribute to a child's successful functioning in a variety of environments. Adaptive behavior scales serve a valuable function for the child clinician in that they pinpoint specific skills that a child has not acquired, which then may serve as the focus of treatment efforts.

Adaptive behavior scales are particularly useful in educational settings where their results can be integrated with the objectives of individual educational plans (IEPs). Adaptive behavior scales can be used to identify social skills and other target behaviors for classroom intervention planning.

Some adaptive behavior scales also provide helpful task analyses of adaptive skills which can be of assistance for the sequencing of intervention strategies. The Balthazar Scales of Adaptive Behavior II: Scales of Social Adaptation (Balthazar, 1973) are an example of scales that give helpful skill building sequences that provide considerable structure to intervention planning.

CHARACTERISTICS OF ADAPTIVE BEHAVIOR SCALES

Domains Assessed

Adaptive behavior scales are analogous to measures of behavior problems in that the domains assessed vary somewhat from test to test (See Table 15.1). Domains assessing various aspects of independent functioning/daily living, social skills, and communication skills are common to many tests. The domains of behavior that are assessed by a particular test are influenced by its age range. Children's tests, for example, may place less emphasis on occupational skills, independent living, and interpersonal relationships than measures that are more concerned with assess-

ing adult adaptation. Measures of adult functioning require domains aimed at assessing occupational skills, whereas the child's analog is school functioning. The domains of an adaptive behavior scale thus become an important consideration in test selection. A client's age, the institution's treatment program, and other factors may influence test selection.

In a recent study, Widaman, Stacy, and Borthwick-Duffy (1993) applied multitrait/multimethod matrix procedures to the identification of major domains of adaptive behavior. The subjects for this study were 157 persons with moderate, severe, and profound retardation. The authors found clear evidence for the existence of four major domains; cognitive competence, social competence, social maladaptation, and personal maladaptation. These results suggest that, when assessing individuals with mental retardation,

TABLE 15.1   Characteristics of Two Major Adaptive Behavior Scales

Test Name	Publisher	Age Range	Scales/Domains	Administration Time
Vineland Adaptive Behavior Scales	AGS	Survey and Expanded forms, birth–18-11 and adults with disabilities; Classroom Edition; 3–12-11	Communication-Receptive, Expressive, Written, Daily Living Skills, Personal, Domestic, Community, Socialization, Interpersonal Relationships, Play and Leisure Time, Coping Skills, Motor-Gross, Fine, Maladaptive Behavior	Classroom Edition, 20 minutes; Survey form, 30–60 minutes; Expanded Form, 60–90 minutes
Scales of Independent Behavior	The Riverside Publishing Company	Infancy through adulthood	Motor Skills, Gross Motor, Fine Motor, Social Interaction and Communication Skills, Language Comprehension, Language Expression, Personal Independence Skills, Eating and Meal Preparation, Toileting, Dressing, Personal Self-Care, Domestic Skills, Community Independence Skills, Time and Punctuality, Money and Value, Work Skills, Home/Community Orientation	Broad Independence Scale, 45–60 minutes; Short Form Scale, 10–15 minutes; Early Development Scale, 10–15 minutes

measures of at least these four domains would be desirable. Fortunately the majority of adaptive behavior scales measure at least these domains.

Norm versus Criterion Referencing

Prior to the publication of the revised Vineland in 1984, there were no nationally normed adaptive behavior scales. Several scales possessed local or regional norms and many were created locally and interpreted informally. Unfortunately many of these scales were used for making norm referenced decisions such as determining whether or not a child had adaptive behavior deficits that were significant enough to warrant the diagnosis of mental retardation.

Among the adaptive behavior assessment questions most frequently posed by psychologists are the following:

1. Does the child have adaptive behavior deficits that are significant enough to warrant the diagnosis of mental retardation?

2. What are the adaptive behavior deficits that characterize a child's behavior and thus require intervention?

3. What are the adaptive behavior strengths displayed by the child?

Questions 2 and 3 are less likely to require norm referencing, although it may still be of some benefit. In order to answer these questions, the clinician could make intraindividual comparisons and/or gauge deficits based on how the deficits impair adaptation to particular environments (e.g., bothersomeness).

Choice of Informant

The Vineland Social Maturity Scale represents one of the first scales in psychology to place a premium on parents as informants—long before behavior rating scales became popular in child assessment. This approach stood in stark contrast to the popularity at the time of using direct measures of child behavior such as intelligence tests.

Modern adaptive behavior scales such as the Vineland and Scales of Independent Behavior (Bruininks et al., 1986) still emphasize the use of parents as informants. In reality, the word *parents* is often a pseudonym for mothers. For most scales where parents serve as informants, maternal reports are used nearly exclusively for item development, scaling, and norming. Although fathers are used less frequently there are no systematic data currently available that clarify the differences between mothers and fathers as informants regarding adaptive behavior. It may well be that the use of fathers versus mothers creates discontinuity of measurement as has been found for behavior problem ratings. Unfortunately there are fewer data to guide clinicians who use adaptive behavior scales.

Secondarily, teachers often serve as raters of adaptive behavior. However, teachers have different views of a child's adaptive behavior due to the varied demands of school and home settings. Domains that are commonly included on parent scales of adaptive behavior such as toileting, bathing, dressing, budgeting, and health care are impractical for teachers. Similarly, parents have difficulty reporting on functional academics in reading, writing, calculation, and some vocational skills. The differing demands of school and home environments virtually ensure that a clinician will have an incomplete understanding of a child's adaptive behavior if either teacher or parent adaptive behavior ratings are not used.

Other caregivers also serve as important informants regarding a child's adaptive behavior. Caregivers may include psychiatric aides in hospitals, nurses, mental health assistants, nannies, grandparents, teacher aides, work supervisors, or others who have sustained nearly daily contact with a child or adolescent. These individuals may in some circumstances fulfill parent or teacher roles and therefore be competent primary or secondary informants for such scales. Even when parents or teachers complete an adaptive behavior scale, other caregiver information may be of value. An adolescent's work supervisor is one example of an informant who may contribute unique and important information to the pool of assessment data gathered.

Finally, the child as informant should not be overlooked. In other words, the child may be tested directly in order to assess adaptive behavior, although this is a less popular option with many clinicians. Perhaps one reason for its lack of popularity is a dearth of available instruments. The Children's Adaptive Behavior Scale (CABS; Richmond & Kicklighter, 1979) is one of the few direct measures of adaptive behavior available. The CABS uses an individual testing format to assess Language Development, Independent Functioning, Family Role Performance, Economic/Vocational Activity, and Socialization. Obviously these domains are common to many types of adaptive behavior measures.

As is the case with behavior rating scales there is disagreement between the informants used for adaptive behavior scales. Parents and teachers have been found to generally agree on overall adaptive behavior estimates but disagree considerably at the scale or domain levels (Shaw, Hammer, & Leland, 1991). Self- and caregiver reports have been found to sometimes agree on adaptive behavior ratings but to disagree considerably on ratings of maladaptive behavior (Voelker et al., 1990). Factors such as child age and length of involvement in a treatment program may also affect agreement between informants (Shaw, Hammer, & Leland, 1991).

Relationship to Intelligence

The choice of informant is apparently a moderator variable affecting the correlation of adaptive behavior and intelligence (Kamphaus, 1993). Correlations between intelligence and adaptive behavior measures are modest, .40 to .60 (DeStefano & Thompson, 1990) indicating some overlap but independence. This modest relationship, however, is an oversimplification in that the type of informant and domain of adaptive behavior affect the relationship significantly. Specifically, when teachers are used as informants, the correlation between intelligence and adaptive behavior increases, and domains that assess communication and functional academic skills tend to correlate higher with intelligence test results (Kamphaus, 1987). Hence, if one sees a stronger relationship between intelligence and adaptive behavior as desirable, then an emphasis on the assessment of functional academics rated by teachers will provide adap-

tive behavior results of desired value. If, however, one views the adaptive behavior construct as separate or complementary to intelligence assessment, then parent ratings of less academically related skills (e.g., socialization) should be sought.

Harrison (1990), who has made numerous contributions to the adaptive behavior assessment literature, favors the use of parents as informants. She observes:

> The third-party method of administration is particularly appropriate for the assessment of adaptive behavior. Because adaptive behavior is generally conceptualized as the daily activities in which a person engages to take care of himself or herself and get along with other people, the information supplied by a third party will be more valid than the direct administration of tasks. The third-party method also allows for the assessment of individuals who cannot participate in the administration of many tests, such as the severely handicapped and young children. (pp. 472–473)

The modest to small relationship of adaptive behavior to intelligence is punctuated in a recent study by Szatmari et al. (1993). This study followed 129 children of extremely low birthweight (501–1,000 grams) to the ages of 7 or 8 years and compared their performance to that of a control group. They found significant decrements in intelligence for the low birthweight group, but no significant deficits for adaptive behavior. Such results indicate that different mechanisms affect the development of intelligence and adaptive behavior skills. (See Box 15.1.)

Administration Format

Adaptive behavior scales are commonly administered using a checklist or semistructured interview technique, except, of course, in the case of direct assessment of the child. The checklist format is equivalent to the approach used for parent or teacher ratings of behavior problems discussed in previous chapters. The semistructured interview method espoused by Doll (1953) and popularized by Sparrow, Balla, and Cicchetti, et al. (1984) differs substantially from rating scale methods.

The semi-structured interview technique, however, requires a high level of clinical skill. The clinician has to make the interview conversation-like, topical, and empathic, while at the same time collecting the necessary information to allow for accurate rating (scoring) of individual items. By contrast, the rating scale method is more time-efficient and practical in that the clinician does not even need to be present for the administration of the scale.

The semistructured interview technique has many virtues, including:

- Allowing the examiner to clarify questions for the informant by providing examples, etc.

- Contributing to the establishment of rapport between clinician and parent because of the conversation-like nature of the interaction

- Mitigating against response sets such as fake good or fake bad

- Permitting the assessment of adaptive behavior despite poor English-language reading skills

The semistructured interview technique can be easily mastered with practice. Some techniques for mastering the technique follow.

1. Begin by asking general questions and then proceed to the specific information needed to score items. If one started with the Communication domain of the Vineland, for example, a good starting question for a toddler might be something like, "Tell me about some of the things that Tom is saying these days".

2. Ask for examples of day-to-day behavior since adaptive behavior scales are designed to assess typical behavior rather than ability (DeStefano & Thompson, 1990). A follow-up expressive language question might be, "Tell me the words that you can remember Tom saying today".

3. Become very familiar with the scoring criteria for specific items in order to ensure that adequate clarification is sought.

4. Conduct the interview topically. For example, ask all of the items regarding telephone skills (answering appropriately, states telephone number, uses

pay phone, etc.) before proceeding to the next topic.

5. Pursue questioning until you have a clear picture of the child's day to day behavior. Once you have achieved this portrait, you can confidently rate the child's behavior on individual items.

OMNIBUS ADAPTIVE
BEHAVIOR SCALES

Vineland Adaptive
Behavior Scales (The Vineland)

The Vineland (Sparrow, Balla, & Cicchetti, 1984) traces its roots to the originator of the adaptive behavior construct, Edgar Doll. Doll created the first widely used scale of adaptive behavior, the Vineland Social Maturity Scale. The current Vineland represents a substantial revision, adaptation, and extension of Doll's original scale.

The Vineland is more aptly described as a family of scales that each possess unique characteristics that make them well suited for particular purposes. The Vineland components include:

- Classroom Edition: Completed by teachers; designed for ages 3 1/2 through 13; 244 items

- Interview Edition, Survey Form: Administered to parents (or other caregivers) via semistructured interview, designed for ages birth through 18 years; 297 items

- Interview Edition, Expanded Form: Administered to parents (or other caregivers) via semistructured interview, designed for ages birth through 18 years; 577 items.

The Vineland has many uses in addition to its popularity as a method for the assessment and diagnosis of mental retardation. The Vineland also provides up-to-date standards for social and adaptive behavior of children from birth to 18 years of age (DeStefano & Thompson, 1990). In this sense the

Vineland and other adaptive behavior scales provide an assessment of behavioral competencies (as opposed to behavioral excesses) the lack of which may significantly detract from everyday functioning.

Content

The Vineland Expanded and Survey forms include the same domains; Communication, Daily Living Skills, Socialization, Motor Skills, and Maladaptive Behavior. The Motor Skills domain is designed for ages birth through 5 years and for older individuals with motor handicaps. The Maladaptive Behavior domain is essentially a behavior problems checklist that assesses very severe difficulties such as public sexual misbehavior, self-injurious behavior, bed-wetting, and truancy. The Survey Form includes the following domains and subdomains.

Communication
  Receptive
  Expressive
  Written
Daily Living Skills
  Personal
  Domestic
  Community
Socialization
  Interpersonal Relationships
  Play and Leisure Time
  Coping Skills
Motor
  Gross
  Fine
Maladaptive Behavior

Administration and Scoring

The Vineland Survey and Expanded forms use Doll's well-known semistructured interview technique—a method that is often not followed loyally by Vineland

users. The technique has many advantages; unfortunately, its disadvantages are more salient. Said simply, mastering the semistructured interview technique is not easy.

A central problem with the method is the necessity of organizing the interview topically, while the items are placed on the response form by difficulty order. For example, several items of the Daily Living Skills domain of the Survey Form have to do with telephone skills—answering, dialing, using a pay phone, and so on. The semistructured interview technique involves obtaining adequate information to score these items even though they are scattered throughout the record form. This central contradiction of simultaneously interviewing topically as well as by difficulty undoubtedly leads to routine usage of the Vineland as a rating scale despite the fact that this is a violation of standardized procedure. Given the many advantages of the semistructured interview technique cited earlier it behooves clinicians to acquire this unique skill.

Vineland interpretation features standard scores based on a mean of 100 and standard deviation of 15.

Norming

The Survey Form norming sample of the Vineland was collected based on 1980 U.S. Census Bureau statistics. The sample was made up of 3,000 subjects from birth through 18 years. In addition, the Vineland Survey Form provides several local norms based on separate samples. These supplementary norm groups include:

- Ambulatory and nonambulatory adults with mental retardation in residential facilities
- Ambulatory adults with mental retardation in residential facilities
- Nonambulatory adults with mental retardation in residential facilities
- Adults with mental retardation in nonresidential facilities
- Children with emotional disturbance in residential facilities

- Children with visual handicaps in residential facilities
- Children with hearing-impairments in residential facilities

Reliability

At first blush the notion of a reliable semistructured interview technique seems oxymoronic. Despite the use of the semistructured interview method, the reliability of the Survey Form is quite good. The internal consistency coefficients of the subdomains are consistently in the 80s. The coefficients of the domains range from a median of .83 for Motor Skills to .90 for Daily Living Skills.

Reliability estimates for the Adaptive Behavior Composite (ABC) are very high. The average internal consistency coefficient for the ABC is .94 and the test-retest coefficient is .88 (Sparrow, Balla, & Cicchetti, 1984). These stability coefficients have been transformed to standard errors of prediction and confidence intervals for clinical assessment purposes by Atkinson (1990).

Validity

Many aspects of validity are addressed in the Vineland Survey Form manual. Age differentiation validity (Anastasi, 1988) of the Vineland is well established. The mean raw scores of the Survey Form domains increase lawfully from age to age lending credence to the argument that the Vineland measures adaptive behavior, which is considered a developmental phenomenon.

Factor analysis of the Vineland subdomains lends support to the organization of the domains (Sparrow, Balla, & Cicchetti, 1984). Some of the subdomains contribute less to the domains because of the limited applicability of their age range. The Receptive subdomain of the Communication domain is most appropriate for young children, and the Written subdomain of the Communication domain is only important for children of school age and older.

The content validity of the Vineland is supported by the method of initial item development. Items were selected for the item pool based on a thorough review of previous scales and the child development literature.

A differential validity study conducted by Douthitt (1992) found the Vineland capable of discriminating between regular curriculum and gifted children. Gifted children scored higher on the Communication, Socialization, and Daily Living Skills domains, but not on the Motor Skills domain. The Vineland Socialization domain has also been shown to differentiate between samples of children with autism, Down syndrome, and normal development. Rodrigue, Morgan, and Geffken (1991) found that children with autism scored significantly lower than the other samples on the Socialization domain of the Vineland Survey Form. These findings of predictable differences between samples of exceptional children offer substantial support for the clinical utility of the Vineland.

Strengths and Weaknesses

The Vineland benefits from a long history of successful use, numerous research investigations, and the creation of a multimethod/multidimensional system in 1984. The Vineland's noteworthy strengths include:

1. Multiple components that are useful for a variety of diagnostic and intervention planning purposes

2. A supportive research base that suggests that the Vineland possesses lawful correlations with measures of similar (convergent validity) and dissimilar constructs (discriminant validity)

3. An exhaustive item pool, particularly in the Expanded Form, which allows for the ready identification of treatment goals and objectives

4. A large national normative sample and several local norm samples, which make it particularly well suited for diagnostic decision making

Among the Vineland's limitations are:

1. The considerable training that is required to properly use the semi-structured interview technique

2. Age-equivalent scores for the subdomains that have a highly restricted range suggesting that they should rarely, if ever, be used

3. A lack of transfer of training across forms that have varied administration, scoring, and interpretation procedures

4. A rather limited computer scoring program

Vineland Sample Case

Name: Joan

Age: 12 years

Grade: 6

Evaluation Procedures

Differential Abilities Scale (DAS)

Stanford-Binet Intelligence Scale: Fourth Edition (SB-IV)

Kaufman Test of Educational Achievement (KTEA)

Woodcock-Johnson Tests of Achievement (WJTA)

Achenbach Behavior Checklist

Parent Form

Teacher Form

Behavior Assessment System for Children (BASC)

Parent Rating Scales (PRS)

Teacher Rating Scales (TRS)

Self-Report of Personality (SRP)

Structured Developmental History (SDH)

Parenting Stress Index (PSI)

Piers-Harris Children's Self Concept Scale (PHCSCS)

Structured Interview for the Diagnostic Assessment of Children

(SIDAC)

Vineland Adaptive Behavior Scales (VABS)

Classroom Edition

Interview Edition

Reason for Referral

Joan was referred for evaluation by her father to determine if she is receiving the special education services that she needs in school. Joan is a sixth-grade special education student who is currently in a fifth-grade inclusion classroom where she is receiving extra help from the special education teacher and an aide throughout the day. Reading has always been the most difficult subject for her; she is presently on a first-grade reading level. According to Joan's mother, her school has recommended retaining Joan in the sixth grade next year, and Mr. Jordan would like a second opinion.

Background Information

Joan has lived with her birth parents and paternal grandparents for the last 10 years. Mrs. Jordan is a legal secretary and Mr. Jordan works at a lumberyard. Joan has no other siblings. At birth Joan weighed 7 lb., 11 oz. and was described as a healthy baby. Joan's development during infancy was normal, and she did not have any serious diseases or other difficulties.

Joan is involved with her church youth group and the local 4H Club. She recently won an award at a 4H Club contest. She enjoys caring for her pet rabbit, goat, and two dogs. Joan also enjoys making crafts with her grandmother.

Previous Evaluations

Joan was in a speech program until 3rd grade for fluency and articulation difficulties. She continues to have problems with expressive speech, but her teachers report that this is not a significant problem. Joan is able to speak relatively clearly in class. Joan was recently prescribed glasses, but she fails to wear them in class, and she did not wear them during this evaluation.

Joan was initially evaluated when she was in the first grade. She was diagnosed as mildly intellectually delayed and placed in a self-contained classroom. Joan's Mental Processing Composite on the Kaufman Assessment Battery for Children at that time was in the moderately below average range (MPC = 70). She was reevaluated 3 years later, and her Full Scale score on the Wechsler Intelligence Scale for Children—Revised was also in the moderately below average range (FSIQ = 74). Her Adaptive Behavior Composite on the Vineland Adaptive Behavior Scale was also in the moderately below average range (ABC = 72).

Joan has been in the fifth-grade inclusion classroom for about half a year. She was reportedly placed in the fifth grade based on her ability. Joan was evaluated in January prior to this evaluation with the PIAT-R, and her standard scores were in the significantly below average range with the exception of general achievement (standard scores ranging from 65 to 72).

Teacher Information

Joan's inclusion teacher and the special education teacher were interviewed. Both teachers are impressed and pleased with Joan's progress since being placed in the inclusion classroom. She was described as a nice, sweet kid who works hard. Reading continues to be Joan's weakest area, and math is a relative strength. Joan is easily frustrated with reading assignments. She is described as a sight reader. Joan's socialization skills in the classroom and the community have improved. She gets along well with her peers and adults in her environment.

According to her mother, the school team recommends placing Joan in a sixth-grade inclusion class next year in order to give her another year to develop, so that she may be promoted to the middle school in 2 years. Although her socialization skills have improved, they believe that she needs the additional year to mature before she transfers to the middle school. Joan's father reports that Joan would prefer to go to the middle school next year.

Test Behavior

Rapport was easily established. Joan enjoyed working on puzzles before each testing session. Joan was not talkative during the evaluation and she did not initiate conversation. At times she was difficult to understand because she mumbled. However, she willingly answered the examiner's questions and smiled frequently. She appeared to be nervous in the beginning, but she became more relaxed, as suggested by more frequent smiling and relaxed body posture, as testing progressed. Joan was cooperative and polite. She remembered to complete the homework that the examiner asked her to bring to the second session. Although Joan worked hard during testing, she became frustrated easily, especially during reading exercises. When frustrated, Joan would respond more impulsively, shift often in her seat, rub her face, avoid eye contact, and adopt a flat affect.

Observations during testing suggest that Joan's self-report personality test results are somewhat suspect. Her limited reading abilities and verbal expression skills, and impulsivity on such tasks limits the value of these findings.

Test Results and Interpretation

COGNITIVE ASSESSMENT   Joan is currently functioning in the significantly below average range of intelligence. Cognitive functioning was assessed using the DAS and the SBIV. There is a 90% probability that Joan's DAS General Conceptual Ability score falls between 54 and 64, indicating that her performance meets or exceeds less than 1% of her peers. Both her Verbal and Nonverbal scores fall within this range, but her Spatial score is somewhat higher, falling in the significantly below average to moderately below average range.

Joan also obtained a Test Composite on the SBIV in the significantly below average range. Her SBIV Test Composite score corresponds to a percentile rank of 1, indicating that she performed better than approximately 1% of other 12-year-olds taking the test and worse than 99%. All of the area scores were significantly below average except her Quantitative Reasoning area composite, which was in the moderately below average range (see Psychometric Summary). These indications of intellectual limitations are consistent with Joan's previous evaluations.

These results are also highly consistent with Joan's performance on the academic achievement measures. Individual academic and composite standard scores on the KTEA—Comprehensive Form range from 48 to 64, which corresponds to percentile ranks of less than 1. Her individual academic and composite standard scores on the WJTA range from 7 to 75, which corresponds to percentile ranks ranging from less than 1 to 5. All of the academic skill areas assessed were significantly below average. These results are supported by Joan's prior evaluations, curriculum-based measures taken at her school, and teacher reports.

SOCIAL/EMOTIONAL/BEHAVIORAL ASSESSMENT Joan's mother and both of her teachers completed the Achenbach Child Behavior Checklist (CBCL-P and CBCL-T). Neither her mother nor her teachers rated Joan as having any significant problems. The BASC-PRS and the BASC-TRS were also completed. Mrs. Jordan rated Joan's anxiety as significant, and one of her teachers also rated her high on the Anxiety scale, although not significantly so. This finding is supported by the reports of Joan's behavior during reading exercises. Also, the recent death of her grandfather may contribute to Joan's level of stress.

Joan's mother also completed the Parenting Stress Index. Her Total Stress Score was in the above average range, but it was not clinically significant. However, some of her subset scores were in the significant range. She seems to experience stress from Joan's inability to adequately respond to changes in her physical or social environment, which is consistent with her ratings on the Vineland (discussed later). Joan's emotional difficulties and deficits in communication may contribute to her mother's high stress because she may have trouble understanding her emotional needs. Communication between Joan and her mother is limited, which in turn may affect how each person feels about the relationship. Mrs. Jordan's scores also indicate that she may need some intervention in order to address her emotional needs, as well as Joan's.

Mr. Jordan completed the SIDAC during the interview with the examiner. He endorsed the required number criteria for a DSM-IV diagnosis of Dysthymia, which supports Joan's score on the Depression scale of the self-report and his rating of her anxiety. However, she did not meet the depression criteria for the DSM-IV. This result indicates that Joan is having some emotional difficulties. Mr. Jordan also endorsed the criteria for a DSM-IV diagnosis of

Separation Anxiety Disorder. The Jordans show some signs of familial enmeshment, so this result is not unexpected. In addition, Joan frequently slept in her parents' bed until a few months ago. The recent death of Joan's grandfather may increase Joan's display of symptoms such as somatic complaints when away from home, worrying about her parents, and distortions of her own physical complaints. These results are consistent with Joan's need to improve her social and coping skills and with her expression of unhappiness.

On the BASC-SRP, Joan scored significantly high on the Somatization and Depression scales, and her scores on the Locus of Control, Social Stress, and Sense of Inadequacy scales were also high. Through interviews the examiner learned that Joan had some somatic complaints lately, especially after the death of her grandfather. For example, on one occasion she had a stomachache and was afraid that she would die. Joan may not have the coping skills necessary to deal with her feelings, such as her grief about her grandfather's death, her frustration with reading, and her realization that she is limited by her abilities. She may feel self-doubt due to her frustration with her limited abilities. However, Joan's scores on this measure should be interpreted with caution because her responses are suspect. Joan also completed the Piers-Harris Children's Self Concept Scale. Her score on the Anxiety subscale was low, indicating that Joan may feel unhappy, nervous, worried, or other related emotions. Joan responded positively to items such as I give up easily, I am nervous, I am slow at finishing my work, I am often afraid, and I am different from other people. These responses support her ratings on the BASC. These scores are also supported by her father's and one teacher's rating on the Anxiety scale of the BASC. Mr. Jordan's ratings on the SIDAC are consistent with these results as well.

Adaptive Behavior

The Vineland was completed by interviewing Joan's father, who indicated that Joan's adaptive behavior is significantly below average for her age. There is a 90% probability that her overall estimate of adaptive behavior meets or exceeds less than 1% to 2% of her peers. Her Socialization and Daily Living Skills domain scores were in the below average range, suggesting that Joan is able to interact with others and care for herself to some degree. Her rating for the Communication Domain suggests that Joan has difficulty communicating with others. Her score seems inconsistent with her mother's and teachers' report of her ability to successfully interact with her peers.

Joan's teacher's report on the Vineland Classroom Edition revealed more adaptive behavior strengths. This measure produced an overall adaptive behavior score in the below average range, suggesting that Joan's adaptive behavior is stronger in the classroom. Her score on the Communication Domain is below average, supporting the ratings of Joan's father on the Vineland Interview Edition Survey Form.

The results of the Vineland Survey Form suggest that the following behaviors should be considered as objectives for intervention.

Communication: Reading simple stories, printing three- and four-word sentences, reading vocabulary of at least 10 words, and writing vocabulary of at least 10 words

Daily Living Skills: Dressing appropriately for the weather, avoiding individuals with contagious diseases, telling time by 5-minute segments, caring for her hair and fingernails, and using household cleaning products

Socialization: Ending conversations appropriately, controlling anger when denied own way, and attending after school or evening activities with same age/grade peers

Summary

Joan is a 12-year-old girl who was referred for evaluation to determine what services she needs in school. Her evaluation indicates that she possesses significantly below average–range intellectual skills. Joan's adaptive behavior is also in the significantly below average range. Both of these results are necessary for a diagnosis of mental retardation, so it is appropriate to confirm her school's previous diagnosis. Her achievement scores and visual motor scores lend further support to these findings. The results of this

evaluation are also consistent with Joan's previous evaluations.

Emotionally Joan displays considerable unhappiness and anxiety. Her self-• report and her father's ratings indicate that this is the case. The recent death of her grandfather and Joan's realization that she has limited abilities may be some of the source for these feelings. Joan also lacks adequate coping skills for dealing with these negative feelings. However, Joan is in a supportive environment in her present classroom and she has shown some progress since being placed in the inclusion classroom.

Diagnostic Impressions

309.21 Separation Anxiety Disorder
317.00 Mild Mental Retardation

Recommendations

GENERAL RECOMMENDATIONS

1. Joan should not be expected to make 1 year of academic progress for each year of attendance in school. Therefore, slow academic attainment by itself may not warrant another retention in grade.

2. Mrs. Jordan is advised to read some literature on other children functioning at Joan's intellectual level to understand how she learns, what reasonable expectations are for her, and what her needs are and how to meet them.

3. The focus of academics for Joan should be to help her develop minimal competency in independent living skills, including vocational skills.

4. Joan should receive vocational counseling to guide her educational program.

5. Joan may need to be reevaluated for the speech program at school.

6. If a computer is available, Joan could use software designed to increase her reading, math, and spelling skills. She could work on the computer alone or with a teacher. Computer usage would

increase her independence, give her the attention that she needs, and provide individualized instruction.

7. Joan should be allowed as much as possible to be around her regular classroom peers, so that she can learn socialization, coping, and behavioral skills by observing and interacting with them.

8. Joan should be asked if she wants to be retained or promoted. Her attitudes could significantly affect her adaptation next year.

9. Joan should visit the middle school with a highly mainstreamed student in the next few weeks in order to gauge her reaction.

10. If Joan decides that she wants to go to the middle school, then a mentor (or older student) would help her adjust to the new environment.

11. Joan would benefit from individual counseling through the counselor at the school or the local mental health center to address her emotional needs.

12. Mrs. Jordan would benefit from support services from a local mental health service provider to address her emotional needs. Parent training to develop techniques for supporting a child with Joan's needs would also help her in her role as a the primary caregiver.

13. If Mrs. Jordan feels that Joan could benefit from a positive role model, then Big Brother/Big Sister would be a good organization to contact.

14. Because Mrs. Jordan expressed concern about Joan's weight, a healthy diet and daily exercise could help her. Local organizations such as their church could be a good resource.

The following are instructional interventions that may be of value. They have not previously been attempted.

READING

1. Joan's reading skills may be improved by being tutored by someone who has been trained to help someone with Joan's difficulties.

2. Opportunities for success in reading may reduce Joan's anxiety and frustration during reading exercises.

3. A structured reading program with small steps and multisensory techniques may increase Joan's interest and competence in reading.

4. Skills and concepts should be repeated and reviewed often for Joan to master them.

5. Joan needs to be taught at a very concrete and practical level, using many manipulative and teaching aids, to increase her interest and improve her performance.

   a. Playing games could make reading fun for Joan while increasing her vocabulary. The use of flashcards could be continued with some variations. Joan could have a Word Bank. The words could be written on one side of the card. On the other side, Joan would draw a picture or cut one out of something and write a sentence. These cards could be kept in a box for Joan, so that he could practice and drill with them at school and at home.

   b. Joan seemed to enjoy doing puzzles during the evaluation, and this may be another fun way for her to increase her word recognition. She could begin with two part puzzles. One piece could have an initial sound on it; the other could have a word family. Joan could put the pieces together and pronounce the words. More pieces could be added for contractions, compound words, root endings, etc. The pieces could be pictures from magazines or comic strips that Joan enjoys.

   c. Words could be written on cards to create a deck. Joan could play Go Fish with friends in school or at home with her family.

6. Joan should increase her functional vocabulary, including words such as *all, can, said,* etc.

7. Joan should increase her survival vocabulary, including words such as *walk, help, wanted, stop, caution,* etc.

8. The group reading in the classroom should b continued for Joan to aid her in other sub such as science and social studies, thus ´

her to participate in classroom lessons despite her reading difficulty. An alternative would be to have a student read lessons or reading assignments for various subjects into an audiotape for Joan to follow the lesson.

9. A study buddy might be assigned to Joan. Another student who would ensure that Joan understands instructions and has the materials that she needs to complete the assignments may lessen her frustration. This student may also want to read written directions for Joan when needed.

Psychometric Summary

DIFFERENTIAL ABILITY SCALES   The DAS is an individually administered intelligence test consisting of six core subtests and several diagnostic subtests. Only the core subtests are used in the calculation of the General Cognitive Ability (GCA) score, an estimate of overall intelligence. The DAS core subtests are also used to calculate composite scores for verbal abilities, nonverbal reasoning, and spatial abilities.

The following composite standard scores have a mean of 100 and a standard deviation of 15. Scores between 90 and 110 are considered average. Scores between 110 and 120 are considered above average, scores between 120 and 130 are considered well above average, and scores above 130 are considered extremely high. (See Table 15.2.)

T-scores in Table 15.3 have a mean of 50 and a standard deviation of 10. Scores between 40 and 60 are in the average range. Scores between 60 and 70 are above average, and scores above 70 are very high.

TABLE 15.2   Joan's DAS Composite Standard Scores

Composite	I/Q Index	90% Confidence Interval	Percentile
GCA	58	54–64	less than 1
Verbal	52	56–73	1
Nonverbal	58	52–68	less than 1
Spatial	70	64–78	2

TABLE 15.3   Joan's DAS T-Scores

Subtests	T-Scores
VERBAL REASONING	
Word definitions	24
Similarities	30
NONVERBAL REASONING	
Matrices	28
Sequential & Quantitative Reasoning	20
SPATIAL REASONING	
Recall of Designs	39
Pattern Construction	23

STANFORD-BINET INTELLIGENCE SCALE—FOURTH EDITION   The SBIV is a battery of subtests grouped into Verbal Comprehension, Nonverbal Reasoning/Visualization, Quantitative Reasoning, and Memory Factors, which form the four area scores. The four area scores are combined to convert into a Composite score used to reflect the best estimate of general intelligence. Raw scores are converted into three types of standard scores: Standard Age scores (SAS) for the subtests (m = 50, SD = 8), Area scores (m = 100, SD = 16), and a Composite score (m = 100, SD = 16). Scores between 84 and 116 are considerded average. See Table 15.4.

KAUFMAN TEST OF EDUCATIONAL ACHIEVEMENT   The KTEA is an individually administered measure of the school achievement of children and adolescents. The individual subtests offer standard scores in the following global areas: Reading Composite, Math Composite, and Battery Composite. The KTEA yields standard scores with a mean of 100 and a standard deviation of 15. Standard scores between 85 and 115 are considered average. See Table 15.5.

WOODCOCK-JOHNSON TESTS OF ACHIEVEMENT   The WJTA is an individually administered

TABLE 15.4   Joan's SB-IV Scores

	Standard Age Scores	Area and Composite Scores	90% Confidence Bands
VERBAL REASONING			
Vocabulary	31		
Comprehension	35		
SAS		63	
ABSTRACT/VISUAL REASONING			
Pattern Analysis	38		
SAS		76	
QUANTITATIVE REASONING			
Quantitative	28		
SAS		56	
SHORT-TERM MEMORY			
Bead Memory	39		
Memory for Sentences	34		
SAS		68	
Test Composite		61	55–67

TABLE 15.5   Joan's KTEA Scores

	Standard Scores	90% Confidence Bands
Math Applications	64	56–71
Reading Decoding	59	53–65
Spelling	55	49–61
Reading Comprehension	61	54–68
Math Computation	48	39–57
Reading Composite	59	54–44
Math Composite	54	48–60
Battery Composite	55	51–59

test of school achievement relevant for determining educational progress and the presence of intra-achievement discrepancies. The WJTA yields standard scores with a mean of 100 and a standard deviation of 15. Standard scores between 85 and 115 are considered average. See Table 15.6.

ACHENBACH CHILD BEHAVIOR CHECKLIST—PARENT FORM   The CBCL-P is a parent rating scale designed to be used to assess social competence and behavior problems. Two major syndromes, internalizing and externalizing, are isolated on the Behavior Problems scale. The CBCL-P yields T-scores with a mean of 50 and a standard deviation of 10. Scores between 67 and 70 are considered to be borderline significant. A score above 70 is considered to be clinically significant. See Table 15.7.

ACHENBACH CHILD BEHAVIOR CHECKLIST—TEACHER FORM   The CBCL-T is designed to obtain ratings of social competence and

TABLE 15.6   Joan's WJTA Scores

	Standard Scores	90% Confidence Bands
Letter-Word Identification	43	38–48
Passage Comprehension	40	34–46
Calculation	46	41–51
Applied Problems	75	69–81
Dictation	24	18–30
Writing Samples	26	20–32
Science	56	49–63
Social Studies	70	64–76
Humanities	52	46–58
Broad Reading	32	27–37
Broad Mathematics	49	45–53
Broad Written Language	7	2–12
Broad Knowledge	53	49–57
Skills	36	32–40
Word Attack	29	24–34
Basic Reading Skills	31	27–?

TABLE 15.7   Joan's CBCL-P Scores

	T-Scores
Internalizing	50
Withdrawn	50
Somatic Complaints	53
Anxious/Depressed	53
Externalizing	45
Social Problems	66
Thought Problems	57
Attention Problems	55
Delinquent Behavior	50
Aggressive Behavior	55
Total T	53

behavior problems as well as the adaptive behavior and school performance of a student. There are eight scales that are divided into three scales used to reflect area syndromes of behavior: Internalizing, Mixed, and Externalizing. The CBCL-T yields T-scores with a mean of 50 and a standard deviation of 10. Scores between 67 and 70 are considered to be borderline significant. A score above 70 is considered to be clinically significant. See Table 15.8.

TABLE 15.8   Joan's CBCL-T Scores

	T-Scores	
	TEACHER 1	TEACHER 2
Internalizing	45	57
Withdrawn	50	51
Somatic Complaints	57	57
Anxious/Depressed	50	60
Social Problems	52	52
Thought Problems	50	50
Attention Problems	50	58
Externalizing	51	51
Delinquent Behavior	56	50
Aggressive Behavior	50	52
Total T	48	55

PARENTING STRESS INDEX   The PSI was designed to be an instrument whose primary value would be to identify parent–child systems that are under stress and at risk for the development of dysfunctional parenting behaviors or behavior problems in the child involved. The PSI yields raw scores and percentiles with scores above the 90th percentile considered significantly high. See Table 15.9.

BEHAVIOR ASSESSMENT SYSTEM FOR CHILDREN—PARENT RATING SCALES   The BASC-PRS is a parent rating scale designed to be used to assess social competence and behavior problems. Two major syndromes, Internalizing and Externalizing, make up the Behavioral Symptoms Index. In addition, an Adaptive Skills Composite is composed of Social Skills and Leadership. The BASC-PRS yields T-scores with a mean of 50 and a standard deviation of 10. Scores above 70 are considered significantly high on the Behavioral Symptoms Index. Scores below 30 are considered significantly low on the Adaptive Skills Composite. See Table 15.10.

TABLE 15.9   Joan's PSI Scores

	Raw Scores	Percentile Rank
Total Stress Score	237	70
Child Domain Score	118	85
Adaptability	32	95
Acceptability	13	60
Demandingness	20	70
Mood	10	60
Distractibility/Hyperactivity	28	80
Reinforces Parent	15	95
Parent Domain Score	119	45
Depression	18	35
Attachment	17	90
Restriction of Role	15	25
Sense of Competence	29	55
Social Isolation	18	90
Relationship with Spouse	11	15
Parent Health	11	50

TABLE 15.10   Joan's BASC-PRS Scores

	T-Scores
Behavioral Symptoms Index	65
Externalizing Problems Composite	50
Hyperactivity	52
Aggression	52
Conduct Problems	47
Internalizing Problems Composite	63
Anxiety	82
Depression	63
Somatization	38
Atypicality	54
Withdrawal	57
Attention Problems	65
Adaptive Skills Composite	46
Social Skills	49
Leadership	43

TABLE 15.11   Joan's BASC-TRS Scores

	T-Scores	
	TEACHER 1	TEACHER 2
Behavioral Symptoms Index	48	60
Externalizing Problems Composite	48	47
Hyperactivity	49	48
Aggression	47	45
Conduct Problems	48	48
Internalizing Problems Composite	49	54
Anxiety	55	67
Depression	42	49
Somatization	49	44
School Problems Composite	58	64
Attention Problems	51	64
Learning Problems	65	63
Atypicality	47	47
Withdrawal	44	47
Adaptive Skills Composite	51	60
Social Skills	43	53
Leadership	58	71
Study Skills	53	53

BEHAVIOR ASSESSMENT SYSTEM FOR CHILDREN—TEACHER RATING SCALE   The BASC-TRS is designed to obtain ratings of social competence and behavior problems as well as the adaptive behavior and school performance of a student. Two major syndromes, internalizing and externalizing, make up the Behavioral Symptoms Index. In addition, an Adaptive Skills Composite is composed of Social Skills, Leadership, and Study Skills. The BASC-TRS yields T-scores with a mean of 50 and a standard deviation of 10. Scores above 70 are considered significantly high on the Behavioral Symptoms Index. See Table 15.11.

PIERS-HARRIS CHILDREN'S SELF CONCEPT SCALE   The PHCSCS is a brief self-report measure designed to aid in the assessment of self-concept in children. All cluster scales are scored in the direction of positive self-concept, so that a high score on a particular cluster scale indicates a high level of assessed self-concept within that specific dimension. The PHCSCS provides T-scores with a mean of 50 and a standard deviation of 10. A T-score below 35 is considered to be significantly low. See Table 15.12.

BEHAVIOR ASSESSMENT SYSTEM FOR CHILDREN—SELF REPORT OF PERSONALITY   The BASC-SRP is a self-report measure designed to evaluate the personality and self-perceptions of children. Two major syndromes make up the Emotional Symptoms Index, Clinical Maladjustment and Personal Maladjustment.

TABLE 15.12   Joan's PHCSCS Scores

	T-Scores
Behavior	39
Intellectual and School Status	52
Physical Appearance and Attributes	56
Anxiety	34
Popularity	31
Happiness and Satisfaction	47
Total Score	46

In addition, a School Maladjustment Composite consists of Attitude to School and Teacher and Sensation Seeking. The BASC-SRP yields T-scores with a mean of 50 and a standard deviation of 10. Scores above 70 are considered significantly high on the Emotional Symptoms Index. Scores below 30 on the Personal Adjustment Composite are considered significantly low. See Table 15.13.

VINELAND ADAPTIVE BEHAVIOR SCALES—INTERVIEW EDITION   The VABS is a measure of adaptive behavior, or the ability to perform daily activities required for personal and social sufficiency. In this version of the scale, adaptive behavior is measured in three domains: Communication, Daily Living Skills, and Socialization. The combination of these domains forms the Adaptive Behavior Composite. The VABS provides standard scores (m = 100; SD = 15) and age equivalents. The domain scores are used to determine an overall adaptive behavior composite and age equivalent. Scores between 85 and 115 are considered average. See Table 15.14.

TABLE 15.14   Joan's VABS Scores (Interview Edition)

Domain	Standard Scores	Age Equiv-alent	90% Con-fidence Bands
Communication	45	5-8	34–56
Receptive		7-10	
Expressive		7-5	
Written		5-3	
Daily Living Skills	71	8-7	63–79
Personal		6-4	
Domestic		8-10	
Community		9-10	
Socialization Skills	82	8-11	71–93
Interpersonal Relationships		8-8	
Play and Leisure Time		7-11	
Coping Skills		9-8	
Adaptive Behavior Composite	61		54–68

TABLE 15.13   Joan's BASC-SRP Scores

	T-Scores
Emotional Symptoms Index	63
School Maladjustment Composite	57
Attitude to School	60
Attitude to Teachers	51
Sensation Seeking	56
Clinical Maladjustment Composite	67
Atypicality	64
Locus of Control	68
Somatization	70
Social Stress	68
Anxiety	49
Depression	74
Sense of Inadequacy	69
Personal Adjustment Composite	51
Relations with Parents	52
Interpersonal Relations	48
Self-Esteem	50
Self-Reliance	52

VINELAND ADAPTIVE BEHAVIOR SCALES—CLASSROOM EDITION   The VABS Classroom Edition is a teacher questionnaire that assesses the student's adaptive behavior, or the ability to perform daily activities required for personal and social sufficiency in the classroom. In this version of the scale, adaptive behavior is measured in three domains: Communication, Daily Living Skills, and Socialization. The combination of these three domains forms the Adaptive Behavior Composite. The VABS provides standard scores (m = 100; SD = 15) and age equivalents. The domain scores are used to determine an overall adaptive behavior composite and age equivalent. Scores between 85 and 115 are considered average. See Table 15.15.

STRUCTURED INTERVIEW FOR THE DIAGNOSTIC ASSESSMENT OF CHILDREN   The SIDAC consists of a list of questions to which parents and teachers answer yes or no to indicate the presence of symptoms relating to DSM-III and DSM-III-R diagnoses. Questions relating to Dysthymic Disorder and Sepa-

TABLE 15.15   Joan's VABS Scores (Classroom Edition)

Domain	Standard Scores	Age Equivalent	90% Confindence Bands
Communication	73	7-8	66–80
Receptive		8-4	
Expressive		14-9	
Written		7-2	
Daily Living Skills	91	10-4	83–98
Personal		12-3	
Domestic		10-6	
Community		9-2	
Socialization Skills	101	12-3	94–108
Interpersonal Relationships		7-2	
Play and Leisure Time		12-3	
Coping Skills		13-9	
Adaptive Behavior Composite	86		79–93

ration Anxiety Disorder were administered. The criteria for determining a significant problem for Dysthymia according to DSM-III-R is at least one symptom of eight or symptoms 3, 4, 5, 6, 8, 9 for Major Depression positively endorsed. The criteria for Separation Anxiety Disorder according to DSM-III-R is at least three symptoms positively endorsed.

DYSTHYMIA

DSM-III-R endorsed: none

DSM-III items endorsed: (Joan met the criteria for DSM-III)

1. Feeling very pessimistic or sorry?

4. Feeling angry, irritable, or resentful?

5. Drop in grades or school performance?

SEPARATION ANXIETY DISORDER

DSM-III-R items endorsed:

1. Worrying a lot of the time about something very bad happening to you?

2. Worrying a lot of the time that something bad would happen so he couldn't be with you—like being kidnapped, lost, killed, or hurt in an accident?

4. Really didn't want to go to sleep without you around or had to sleep away from home?

CURRICULUM BASED READING PROBE (CBRP) The CBRP is an educational measure used to assess a student's reading fluency. Two one minute probes, a week apart, were done. The student read a passage from one of her reading books from school, and the number of words pronounced correctly for 1 minute were counted. See Table 15.16.

Scales of Independent Behavior (SIB)

The SIB (Bruininks, et al., 1984) in many ways resembles the Vineland; it is a broad-based assessment of adaptive behavior that includes 226 items spanning an age range of infancy through adulthood. The SIB is a newer entrant onto the adaptive behavior scene that lacks a specific predecessor. (See Box 15.2.)

Content

The SIB includes 14 subscales that are subsumed under four clusters that in turn are summarized by a Broad Independence scale composite score. The four clusters include Motor Skills, Social Interaction and Communication Skills, Personal Independence Skills, and Community Independence Skills. The clusters and their subscales are:

TABLE 15.16   Joan's CBRP Scores

Probe	Number of Words Correct
Week 1	2
Week 2	3

Motor Skills

    Gross Motor

    Fine Motor

Social Interaction and Communication Skills

    Social Interaction

    Language Comprehension

    Language Expression

Personal Independence Skills

    Eating and Meal Preparation

    Toileting

    Dressing

    Personal Self-Care

    Domestic Skills

Community Independence Skills

    Time and Punctuality

    Money and Value

    Work Skills

    Home/Community Orientation

An Early Development scale is provided for assessing the adaptive skills of infancy through age 3. This scale may also be of benefit for the assessment of more significantly impaired individuals beyond the age of 3 years.

Flexible use of the SIB is further enhanced by the availability of an Inventory for Client and Agency Planning (ICAP; Bruininks et al., 1986). The ICAP is a brief form of the SIB that aids the process of intervention planning through needs identification and progress monitoring.

Another valuable feature of the SIB is the provision of a short form that can be administered in 10 to 15 minutes. The short form consists of 32 items from the longer scale that give a quick indication of the overall presence or absence of adaptive behavior deficits. A low score on this scale would trigger the administration of the complete form or another adaptive behavior scale.

A Problem Behaviors scale is also included. This scale measures eight areas of problem behavior:

Hurtful to Self

Hurtful to Others

Destructive to Property

Disruptive Behavior

Unusual or Repetitive Habits

Socially Offensive Behavior

Withdrawal or Inattentive Behavior

Uncooperative Behavior

An additional advantage of this scale is that problem behaviors are not only rated according to frequency but also by severity. The severity ratings provide the clinician with more guidance to follow in a problem-solving assessment paradigm.

Administration and Scoring

The SIB is administered via structured interview in approximately 45 to 60 minutes. The questions are merely posed to a parent, teacher, or other caregiver as they are written; the response options are given on the parent's side of the easel. Parents are given four response options for each item:

1. Never or rarely; even if asked

2. Does, but not well, or about 1/4 of the time; may need to be asked

3. Does fairly well, or about 3/4 of the time; may need to be asked

4. Does very well, or always or almost always; without being asked

In this way the SIB is more like a test or rating scale that an examinee completes. While this technique is easily used, it can become repetitive and uninteresting for the parent near the end of the hour-long session.

The items are worded as precise behavioral objectives that require little comprehension on the part of the informant. The format of the SIB items thus encourages valid responding.

The SIB offers a large and useful variety of derived scores including age equivalents, percentile ranks, and standard scores. The more novel scores include instructional ranges, a relative performance index, and an expected range of independence.

Norming

A sample of almost 1,800 subjects from over 40 locations was used for norming the SIB. The age range of the sample extended from infancy through 40 years. An additional sample of over 1,000 individuals with and without disabilities was selected for research investigations.

Reliability

Split-half coefficients for the clusters are reported in the test manual to be in the .80s to low .90s. The Broad Independence scale reliability estimates were commonly in the mid to high .90s. Test-retest reliabilities for the clusters and the Broad Independence scale were similarly high.

Validity

DeStefano and Thompson (1990) laud the SIB for its evidence of content validity by observing: "The SIB shows good content validity, in that its structure and content cover a broad range of skills and traits included in current models of adaptive and maladaptive behavior" (p. 461).

Roberts et al. (1993) conducted a correlational study of the SIB and Vineland Survey Form that demonstrates considerable criterion related validity for both instruments. This study involved 128 4- to 7-year olds with developmental disabilities. Both tests were found to correlate moderately with intelligence, and both were found to produce one large factor. Similarly, McGrew, Bruininks, and Thurlow (1992) found the SIB to correlate significantly with community adjustment for 239 adults with mild to severe levels of mental retardation. While the SIB is not as well researched as the Vineland, the few studies available show lawful evidence of criterion-related validity.

Strengths and Weaknesses

The SIB possesses many admirable traits that make it a very practical tool. Its strengths include:

1. Flexibility of administration with the availability of a short and long form

2. An objective item scoring scheme that eases scoring.

3. Its link to the other Woodcock-Johnson tests, which fosters transfer of training to the SIB

4. Broad item coverage, i.e., content validity

The weaknesses of the SIB include:

1. A mechanistic easel administration format that may interfere with parental cooperation and/or interest

2. Relatively complex scoring algorithms (which are eased considerably by the use of its accompanying Compuscore software program)

3. A lack of factor-analytic and criterion-related validity studies

MEASURING SOCIAL SKILLS

A universally accepted definition of adaptive behavior remains elusive resulting in scales that may have a variety of domains (Merrell & Popinga, 1994). One aspect of adaptive behavior, social competence or social skills, is of such importance that scales which measure this construct exclusively are available.

A recent study (Merrell & Popinga, 1994) helped clarify the relationship between social competence, as measured by the Social Skills Rating System (SSRS, Gresham & Elliott, 1990), and Adaptive Behavior as measured by the SIB. The results of this study suggests that social skills are a subset of adaptive behavior. Merrell & Popinga (1990) found that:

The average correlation between the SIB Social and Communication cluster score and the five SSRS scores was .51, and the average correlations of the subtests within the three subscales (Social Interaction, Language Comprehension, Language Expression) ranged from .44 to .58. These data indicate a moderately strong relationship between the social and interpersonal communication component of adaptive behavior and social skills, as measured by the instruments used in this study. (pp. 44–45)

Social Skills Rating System

The SSRS (Gresham & Elliott, 1990) is a comprehensive measure of social skills that incorporates multiple domains and raters. Teacher, parent, and student forms are provided for measuring a variety of social skills across settings. Although the SSRS also measures externalizing, internalizing, and hyperactivity problem behaviors, social skills are the focus of the system. The teacher form of the SSRS also includes a rating of academic competence.

Content

The SSRS differs from other crude assessments of social skills by including multiple domains of social skills. The domains corresponding to each form are shown in Table 15.17.

Administration and Scoring

Each of the SSRS forms is straightforward to use. The parent and teacher forms do possess a somewhat unique rating scale in comparison to many of the measures reviewed thus far. In addition to requiring the rater to assess the frequency of a behavior, the rater is also asked to indicate the importance of the behavior for a child's development. The availability of importance ratings allows the clinician to better prioritize behaviors for intervention.

A full range of scores are offered by the SSRS, including standard scores, percentile ranks, and a behavior level. Behavior levels are somewhat like stanines in that they divide up portions of the distribution of scores into three levels where $> +1sd$ = more, $< -1sd$ = fewer, and the middle of the distribution = average.

Norming

The SSRS norming samples consisted of 4,170 children, 1,027 parents, and 259 teachers who completed forms in 1988 (Gresham & Elliott, 1990). The sample used for the Student Form is well described in the manual. On the other hand, the Parent and Teacher Form samples are described in only a few paragraphs. The characteristics of the children rated on the Teacher Form, such as their SES and ethnicity, are not given. The SES of the parent sample is heavily skewed toward high levels of SES. The lack of detailed information given for the Teacher and Parent forms norming, as well as the negative information about the Parent Form that is given, does not lend credence to the utility of these norms.

Reliability

The reliability estimates for the Teacher and Parent forms are generally adequate. Mean coefficient alpha

TABLE 15.17   Domains Assessed by SSRS Forms

	Cooperation	Assertion	Responsibility	Empathy	Self-Control
Teacher Form					
Preschool	X	X			X
Elementary	X	X			X
Secondary	X	X			X
Parent Form					
Preschool	X	X	X		X
Elementary	X	X	X		X
Secondary	X	X	X		X
Student Form					
Elementary	X	X		X	X
Secondary	X	X		X	X

reliability estimates for the Teacher Form subscales were in the high .80s and .90s. Parent Form coefficients are slightly lower with more coefficients in the .70s. Student Form reliabilities are generally low. Coefficients for the Cooperation, Assertion, and Self-Control scales never exceed .70, which makes these subscales of dubious value for individual interpretation. The test-retest coefficients for the Student Form are even more disappointing, with none of the values exceeding .70, including the Total Scale value, which is only .68 (Gresham & Elliott, 1990).

Validity

Conducting criterion-related validity studies with the SSRS may be difficult because of debate about the appropriate criterion. In the case of intelligence testing the WISC-III would likely be widely accepted as the criterion. In the area of social skills, however, there is not a clear criterion; in fact, the SSRS may over time emerge as the criterion for establishing the validity of other measures. Some sense of criterion-related validity, however, may be gained from the studies reported in the manual (Gresham & Elliott, 1990).

A study of the SSRS Teacher Form correlations with the Social Behavior Assessment (SBA) lends some criterion-related validation to the Teacher Form. The majority of correlations were significant for a sample of 79 cases, suggesting that the two measures share considerable overlap. The Cooperation subscale of the Teacher Form was most highly correlated with scores from the SBA. This scale correlated −.70 with the Interpersonal domain of the SBA and −.73 with the Task-Related domain of the SBA.

A study of the relationship of the Teacher Form to the Achenbach Child Behavior Checklist— Teacher Report Form (CBCL-TRF) provided mixed support for the Problem Behavior scales. The Externalizing scale correlated .69 with its counterpart on the CBCL, but the Teacher Form correlated only .33 with its CBCL counterpart (Gresham & Elliott, 1990).

Similar results were obtained for the SSRS Parent Form. In a study of 45 parent ratings of children, the Externalizing scale correlated .70 with the Externalizing score of the CBCL-PRF. Again, however, the Internalizing scale correlated only .50 with the Internalizing scale of the CBCL-PRF (Gresham & Elliott, 1990). These studies of the Problem Behaviors scales of the SSRS suggest that the Internalizing scale measures something different from the corresponding scale of the widely used Achenbach.

The factor analyses provided in the SSRS manual provide limited insights into the underlying traits assessed by the SSRS primarily because of the methods used. Principal components were extracted, but factor analysis was not conducted. Furthermore, the components were apparently derived solely based on empirical methods; a formal attempt to match components to a priori models via structural equation modeling was not made. The authors also only report the loadings of each item on one component, thus not allowing for inspection of co-loadings. It could be said that a thorough factor-analytic investigation of the SSRS is yet to be completed.

Strengths and Weaknesses

The SSRS provides a unique assessment tool for child clinicians in that it is a thorough method for assessing behaviors that are often labeled as social skills. Furthermore, although the norming of the SSRS is not ideal, it is far superior to other measures that do not possess adequate norms and yet are used to make norm referenced decisions. Other strengths of the SSRS include:

1. A multidomain assessment of social skills
2. The use of multiple informants
3. An integrated method of interpretation and intervention planning

Some of the weaknesses of the SSRS include:

1. Inadequately described norm samples for the Teacher and Parent forms
2. Poor reliabilities for some of the subscales, especially those on the Student Form

3. Less than adequate criterion-related validity for the Internalizing scale of the Problem Behaviors domain

CONCLUSIONS

Adaptive behavior scales may be riding a wave of popularity. Although Doll introduced this intuitive concept in the 1930s, adaptive behavior was not formally included as central to the mental retardation diagnostic process until the 1950s.

Components of adaptive behavior scales are now being included on behavior problem checklists such as the Achenbach and BASC. Furthermore, the centrality of adaptive behavior to the mental retardation diagnostic process has been reaffirmed by the AAMR diagnostic criteria (AAMR, 1993).

Another interesting trend is for adaptive behavior scales to be single-domain measures. The SSRS is an excellent example of the trend toward developing assessment measures of what may be called subconstructs of adaptive behavior.

This chapter highlighted several of the most popular adaptive behavior scales but the reader should be aware that there is a substantial universe of such scales available. The Balthazar Scales of Adaptive Behavior I: Scales of Functional Independence (Balthazar, 1971), the Balthazar Scales of Adaptive Behavior II: Scales of Social Adaptation (Balthazar, 1973), the Children's Adaptive Behavior Scale (Richmond & Kicklighter, 1979), and the Adaptive Behavior Inventory for Children (Mercer & Lewis, 1978) are some of the available measures that should be considered as candidates for specific uses. (See Box 15.2.)

havior and cognitive measures. While the low to moderate relationship between intelligence and adaptive behavior scales is well documented (Kamphaus, 1993), the relationship between adaptive behavior and academic achievement is of considerable importance given that academic achievement is often *the* criterion variable of interest to child clinicians.

In the diSibio (1993) investigation the relationship of adaptive behavior to achievement is put to a strict empirical test. The relationship of adaptive behavior to achievement was assessed after the variance attributable to intelligence was removed. If adaptive behavior scales share some variance with achievement above and beyond general intelligence then adaptive behavior becomes a more important construct to consider when one is interested in maximizing a child's school adjustment. If adaptive behavior does not correlate significantly with achievement then the construct is of dubious value for child clinicians.

The participants for this study were 82 nonreferred Kindergarten children. Attrition resulted in a sample of 51 children after 2-year follow-up. Children were administered the Wechsler Preschool and Primary Scale of Intelligence—Revised (WPPSI-R) and the Vineland Adaptive behavior Scale—Classroom Edition (VABS) during the second half of their kindergarten year. At the end of the second grade the children were tested with the Comprehensive Test of Basic Skills (CTBS) as the criterion measure.

While intelligence scores were more highly correlated with achievement, the VABS added 11% of the variance to the prediction of achievement beyond that predicted by the WPPSI-R. Said another way, the VABS composite score correlated .39 with total achievement of the CTBS.

The results of this study are significant in that they support the importance of assessing adaptive behavior and intervening in order to enhance a child's behavioral competencies, which in turn provides another approach to enhancing academic achievement. While this study provides evidence to support the importance of the adaptive behavior construct, many questions remain unanswered. This study does not identify specific aspects of adaptive behavior as most important for positively influencing academic achievement. Although much needs to be learned about this relationship before day-to-day intervention planning is practically affected, the importance of adaptive behavior assessment is affirmed.

Box 15.1

Research Update

A recent study by diSibio (1993) updates and extends the many findings on the relationship between adaptive be-

SOURCE: M. diSibio (1993), "Conjoint Effects of Intelligence and Adaptive Behavior on Achievement in a Nonreferred Sample," *Journal of Psychoeducational Assessment, 11,* 304–313.

CHAPTER SUMMARY

1. Edgar Doll created the construct of adaptive behavior by drawing on his experience as a psychologist at the Vineland State Training School, where he was charged with the assessment and rehabilitation of individuals with mental retardation. He noted that such individuals not only lacked intellectual abilities that were necessary for academic attainment, but they also often appeared to lack day-to-day living skills needed for independent functioning.

2. In 1993 the American Association on Mental Retardation published a revised version of the *Diagnostic and Statistical Manual of Mental Retardation* (AAMR, 1993). Earlier editions of this manual concluded that the identification of deficits in adaptive behavior is central to the diagnosis of mental retardation. The current manual lists 10 domains of adaptive behavior that should be assessed for the purposes of mental retardation diagnosis intervention planning including communication, self-care, home living, social skills, community use, self-direction, health and safety, functional academics, leisure, and work.

3. Adaptive behavior has been defined as the performance of the daily activities that are required for social and personal sufficiency.

4. Adaptive behavior scales serve a valuable function for child clinicians in that they pinpoint specific deficits that a child has not acquired, which in turn may serve as the focus of treatment efforts.

5. Widaman, Stacy, and Borthwick-Duffy (1993) found clear evidence for the existence of four major adaptive behavior domains; cognitive competence, social competence, social maladaptation, and personal maladaptation.

6. Prior to the publication of the revised Vineland in 1984, there were no nationally normed adaptive behavior scales. Many adaptive behavior scales that are currently available do not have adequate norms for making norm referenced decisions.

7. Parents, teachers, and other caregivers are most often used as informants for adaptive behavior scales. Children may also be used as self-informants for some adaptive behavior scales.

8. Correlations between intelligence and adaptive behavior measures are modest, .40 to .60, indicating some overlap but independence.

9. Adaptive behavior scales are commonly administered using a checklist or semistructured interview technique.

10. The semistructured interview technique requires a high level of clinical skill. The clinician has to make the interview conversation-like, topical, and empathic, while at the same time collecting the necessary information to allow for accurate rating (scoring) of individual items.

11. The Vineland Adaptive Behavior Scale meets up-to-date standards for assessing social and adaptive behavior of children from birth to 18 years of age.

12. The Scales of Independent Behavior (SIB) in many ways resembles the Vineland. It is a broad-based assessment of adaptive behavior that includes 226 items spanning an age range of infancy through adulthood.

13. The AAMR Adaptive Behavior Scale—School, Second Edition (ABS-SE:2) is an update of a major adaptive behavior scale that was originally published in 1981. Two editions of the ABS are available: the ABS-SE:2 and the AAMR Adaptive Behavior Scale—Residential and Community (ABS-RC:2). The ABS-SE:2 is designed for teacher report for children ages 3–16.

14. One aspect of adaptive behavior, social competence or social skills, is of such importance that scales that measure this construct exclusively are available.

15. The Social Skills Rating System (SSRS) is a comprehensive measure of social skills that incorporates multiple domains and raters. Teacher, parent, and student forms are provided for measuring a variety of social skills across settings.

16. Adaptive behavior scales may be riding a wave of popularity. Components of adaptive behavior scales are now being included on behavior problem checklists such as the Achenbach and BASC.

BOX 15.2

An Alternative to the Vineland and SIB

AAMR Adaptive Behavior Scale—School, Second Edition (ABS-S:2)

The ABS (Lambert, Nihira, & Leland, 1993) is an update of a major adaptive behavior scale that was originally published in 1981 (Nihira et al., 1981). Two editions are available, the ABS-S:2 and the AAMR Adaptive Behavior Scale—Residential and Community (ABS-RC:2). The ABS-S:2 will be the focus here. The ABS scales are designed for teacher report for children ages 3–16.

The ABS includes two sections. Part 1 includes nine domains that measure personal independence behaviors such as daily living skills, eating and dressing. The nine domains are Independent Functioning, Physical Development, Economic Activity, Language Development, Numbers and Time, Prevocational/Vocational Activity, Self-Direction, Responsibility, and Socialization. Part 2 has seven domains that assesses behavior problems such as interfering with the work of others and damaging property. The seven problem behavior domains are labeled Social Behavior, Conformity, Trustworthiness, Stereotyped and Hyperactive Behavior, Self-Abusive Behavior, Social Engagement, and Disturbing Interpersonal Behavior.

Five composite scores are produced: Personal Self-Sufficiency, Community Self-Sufficiency, Personal-Social Responsibility, Personal Adjustment, and Social Adjustment. The derivation of these composites is based on factor analysis.

This scale is structured as a checklist of 95 behaviors. It is usually completed by teachers, but it may also be completed by school psychologists or others, and parent information may be incorporated. Raw scores are converted to standard scores with a mean of 10 and standard deviation of 3 for the domains. Quotients, with a mean of 100 and standard deviation of 15, and percentile ranks are offered for the composite scores.

The ABS-SE:2 offers several components, including scoring and intervention planning devices. The components include an examiner's manual, examination booklets, and profile and scoring forms. IBM-compatible and Macintosh software is also available.

The ABS-SE:2 has two norm samples: a group of 1,000 children without disabilities and a group of 1,000 children with developmental disabilities.

The ABS-S:2 and its predecessors have a long history of successful use. The revised edition has substantially bolstered the reliability of the scales.

On the other hand, the ABS-S:2 item pool does not take as broad a sampling of adaptive behavior as do the longer SIB and Vineland. In addition, the ABS-S:2 has relatively complicated scoring procedures that may invite clerical errors.

Integrating and Interpreting Assessment Information

CHAPTER QUESTIONS

- What are some reasons why assessment information may differ depending on who is providing it?

- What are the issues involved in using simple (equal weighing) or complex (unequal weighing) methods of combining information from different sources?

- How might age of the child and type of behavior affect the agreement between different sources on a child's or adolescent's adjustment?

- What steps should one go through to integrate information from different sources, from different methods, and across different areas of functioning?

INTRODUCTION

Throughout this book we have emphasized the need for a comprehensive evaluation when testing children and adolescents in most circumstances. Com-

prehensive means that (1) many areas of functioning should be assessed, (2) assessments should be conducted using multiple techniques, and (3) assessments should obtain information from many sources (e.g., child, parent, teachers, peers). If one follows this advice, one is confronted with a dizzying array of information gathered during the assessment. In the previous chapters we discussed each individual component of the assessment in isolation. However, the most important—and most difficult—part of the evaluation is the *integration* of this information into a clear case formulation that answers the referral questions and points the way to the most appropriate intervention.

Although we discuss integrating information across multiple domains of functioning and across multiple assessment techniques, a main focus of this chapter will be on integrating information from different informants. This is a particularly difficult endeavor because one is theoretically obtaining the same information on a child's adjustment from different sources. One would think that there would be a high degree of correlation between information provided by different informants. Unfortunately this is not the case. A large body of research has indicated that there are generally quite small correlations between the same type of information provided by different informants (Achenbach, McConaughy, & Howell, 1987).

One explanation for this low rate of agreement between informants is that different people see a child in different settings. That is, the low correlations between informants may reflect *real differences* in a child's behavior across different settings. The meta-analysis conducted by Achenbach, McConaughy, and Howell (1987) provides some support for this possibility. Across the 119 studies that they reviewed the average correlation in child ratings between informants who see a child in different settings (e.g., parent/teacher) was .28. In contrast, the average correlation between informants who see a child in the same setting (e.g., pairs of parents or pairs of teachers) was .60. This substantial increase in agreement between informants who see a child in the same setting provides evidence that the lack of informant agreement reflects, at least in part, real *situational variability* in children's behavior.

This situational variability has important implications for clinical assessments. It suggests that to make sense of information on a child's emotional and behavioral functioning, a clinical assessor must also assess the contextual demands that might influence a child's behavior and thereby account for the discrepant information one is obtaining. For example, a clinical assessor might be quite puzzled over a teacher's report of significant problems of inattention, disorganization, and hyperactivity at school, when it appears to be in stark contrast to only minimal problems being reported by a child's parent. However, further assessment of the home context may indicate that the parents do not put many demands for sustained attention, organization, or sitting still on the child in the home. As a result, the behaviors are not problematic in this setting.

Another important aspect of the lack of agreement between informants is determining the *level of analysis* at which agreement is being measured. Individual behaviors tend to show less consistency across informants than broader dimensions or *composites* of multiple behaviors. A good example of this phenom-

enon comes from a study by Biederman, Keenan, and Faraone (1990). In a clinic sample of children and adolescents the average correlation between parent and teacher reports of individual symptoms of attention-deficit hyperactivity disorder (ADHD) on a structured interview was quite low (r = .21). However, these authors found that if one looked at the diagnostic level, the level of agreement between parents and teachers was quite high. If a parent reported that a child had ADHD on the structured interview, there was a 90% probability that the child's teacher would report the presence of the disorder.

There are two ways one can conceptualize this level of analysis issue. On a psychometric level, classic measurement theory states that an aggregate measure shows higher reliability than its individual components (Peterson, Kolen, & Hoover, 1989). Alternatively, the same issue can be framed as another aspect of the situational specificity of behavior. That is, the same underlying construct or psychological dimension may be present across situations, but the behavioral manifestation may change depending on the situational demands. If one frames it in this way, the implication for clinical assessment is the same as that discussed previously. To understand the different behavioral manifestations, one must understand the demands of the different contexts under consideration.

One final issue on informant disagreement is the fact that some apparent disagreement may be an artifact of *different measurement techniques* used across informants. An example is a case in which a child is showing indications of depression on a projective technique but this is not reported by parent and teacher on rating scales. A clinical assessor may consider this a disagreement across informants. In fact, this is more a function of the lack of agreement across methods, since studies have shown that the agreement between projective and objective self-report measures is generally low (Ball et al., 1991). However, even within the same method, what is assessed may differ across informants. For example, some rating scales include very different items for parents and teachers (Conners, 1989). As a result, it becomes unclear whether disagreements are due to actual differences in perceptions between parents and teachers or whether they are due to different questions being asked of the two informants.

Considering these issues, clinical assessors should first try to determine if seemingly discrepant information can be attributed solely to varying situational demands or to the level of analysis or to differences in the assessment strategy. If the discrepant information can be explained by these factors, one has gone a long way in explaining the reasons for a child's problems and one usually has obtained important information for designing treatment. For example, if a child is only displaying highly anxious behavior in the school setting, one should then look for what aspects of the school environment are leading to the anxiety (e.g., social-evaluative situations). In doing this, one has pointed the way to one route of intervention, that is, to systematically desensitize the child to the anxiety-provoking stimuli. Unfortunately, in many situations one cannot be confident that any of these factors are contributing to the discrepant information. In such cases, one is confronted with the difficult decision of what to do with conflicting information in developing a case formulation.

INTEGRATING INFORMATION ACROSS INFORMANTS

Simpler May Be Better

To deal with this issue of conflicting information, clinical assessors have often developed their own algorithm or methods of deciding how to weigh the reports of different informants. In Box 16.1 we summarize the results of a survey of child mental health professionals in which respondents rated the importance of different informants for assessing various types of childhood psychopathology. This provides a good illustration of common practice in weighing different informants. In Box 16.2 we summarize an explicit diagnostic decision tree that was developed by two noted researchers to standardize the diagnostic decision-making process. This decision tree was designed for use with structured diagnostic inter

---

BOX 16.1

A Survey of Mental Health Professionals' Use of Different Informants to Assess Childhood Psychopathology

Loeber, Green, and Lahey (1990) conducted a survey of 105 members of the Society for Research in Child and Adolescent Psychopathology assessing their perceptions of the relative usefulness of pre-pubertal children, their mothers, and their teachers as informants on emotional and behavioral problems in children. Two-thirds of the respondents had Ph.D's and one-third had M.D.'s. Fifty-nine percent described themselves as child researchers and clinicians, 34% described themselves as researchers only, 2% described themselves as clinicians only, and 5% described themselves in an "other" category. Respondents rated the utility of information provided by mothers, teachers, and 7–12-year-old children on a 0 (not useful) to 3 (very useful) scale. There were 44 behaviors rated covering the domains of inattention/hyperactivity, oppositional problems, conduct problems, anxiety, and depression.

These authors found that the perceived relative usefulness of children, mothers, and teachers varied as a function of the domain being assessed. Specifically, teachers were rated as more useful than both parents and children in the assessment of inattention/hyperactivity. In contrast, parents were rated as more useful than teachers and children in assessing severe antisocial behavior and aggression. Both parents and teachers were rated as more useful in assessing children's oppositional behavior than children themselves, although there was no difference in the perceived usefulness of parents and teachers within this domain. In general, parents and children were judged more useful in assessing internalizing problems (anxiety and depression) than teachers. Somewhat surprisingly, parents were judged significantly more useful than children in assessing internalizing problems.

In sum, these authors found that there were systematic preferences for certain informants over others in assessing childhood psychopathology, and these preferences varied as a function of the behavioral domain being assessed. These authors correctly point out that the results were limited to mental health professionals' perceptions of pre-pubertal (ages 7–12) children. The results may have been different, especially in the relative importance placed on child self-report, if the assessment of psychopathology in adolescents had been the focus of the survey.

(Cont.)

BOX 16.1   *(Continued)*

SOURCE: R. Loeber, S. M. Green, & B. B. Lahey (1990), "Mental Health Professionals' Perception of the Utility of Children, Mothers, and Teachers as Informants on Childhood Psychopathology," *Journal of Clinical Child Psychology, 19,* 136–143.

BOX 16.2

An Attempt to Develop Rules for Combining Multiple Sources of Information on Childhood Psychopathology

The struggle to develop standardized methods of integrating information from multiple informants is exemplified in an article by Reich and Earls (1987). These researchers set out to develop "a replicable strategy to make psychiatric diagnoses when reports are obtainable independently from parents and children" (p.601). The authors clearly state that the goal was not to achieve perfect parent–child agreement but to learn how to evaluate these different sources of information. The following is a summary (see appendix of research article for full criteria) of the decision tree used by these authors to make diagnoses according to the DSM-III (American Psychiatric Association, 1980). We present this approach not so much as a recommended decision tree, but as an example of strategies that assessors have developed to resolve the problem of discrepant information.

1. Attention-Deficit Disorder

   a. Minimum of eight symptoms from parent report, at least six symptoms from child report, and an age of onset before 7.

   b. Evidence of impairment in school from teacher's report either of significant inattention, disruptive behavior, academic underachievement, or peer difficulties.

   c. If parent reports six or seven symptoms and child report shows four or five, diagnosis can be made with compelling evidence from teacher.

2. Oppositional Disorder

   a. Minimum of two symptoms from both parent and child and a report of at least 6 month duration.

   b. Teacher indicates a pattern of negativistic and defiant behavior.

3. Conduct Disorder

   a. Two or more symptoms from either parent or child.

   b. Confirmation of antisocial behavior from at least one other source.

4. Major Depression

   a. For children over 13, a diagnosis can be made from child report alone if (1) child reports dysphoric mood or anhedonia for 2 weeks or longer; (2) at least four vegetative symptoms from DSM-III criteria are present for 2 weeks or longer; (3) there is evidence of impairment, such as grades dropping, irritability, social withdrawal, etc.

   b. A diagnosis of depression would normally not be made by parents report alone unless child report was just under threshold.

5. Separation Anxiety and Overanxious Disorder

   a. Diagnosis can be made from either parent or child report alone only if other informant provides some evidence of anxiety and/or depressive symptoms.

SOURCE: W. Reich, & F. Earls (1987), "Rules for Making Psychiatric Diagnoses in Children on the Basis of Multiple Sources of Information: Preliminary Strategies," *Journal of Abnormal Child Psychology, 15,* 601–616.

views. We feel that these two pieces of research illustrate the problems one faces when attempting to systematically integrate discrepant assessment information either in clinical practice or in clinical research.

Piacentini, Cohen, and Cohen (1992) provide an interesting discussion on developing ideal weighing systems for combining information across multiple informants. These authors label systems in which one source of information is weighed more heavily than others (e.g., teachers' report of inattention given more weight than parents' report) as *complex schemes*. In contrast, *simple schemes* are those where information from all sources is weighed equally. These simple schemes can also be called the *either/or rule,* since a finding is considered significant if it is reported by any informant (e.g., parent, child, or teacher).

These authors provide both a theoretical and empirical rationale for why simple schemes are either as good as or better than complex schemes. First, these authors argue that most weighing systems are based on clinical judgment, in the absence of any clear research base to guide decisions. They cite numerous findings that "expert judgments" are "almost always inferior to equal weighing in predicting outcomes based on multiple variables" (p. 54). This rationale, however, would only hold for weighing systems based on clinical judgment. What about empirically derived weighing systems?

The authors cite a study in which a complex method of combining information was developed based on logistic regression analyses. When Bird, Gould, and Stagheeza (1990) compared their empirically derived weighing procedure with a simple either/or scheme, there were no differences in how well either system predicted clinicians' diagnoses. Moreover, weighing systems based on regression analyses from one sample are likely to underperform simple schemes when applied in a different sample, since the weighing system is at least partially dependent on the idiosyncratic characteristics of the sample. In summary, Piacentini, Cohen, and Cohen (1992) provide compelling arguments for the use of simple schemes to combining discrepant reports.

Although in principle this advice seems to be sound and we advocate this approach as being the primary or default option for most clinicians, there are several issues that one needs to consider when using this approach. First, this approach assumes that false positives (i.e., a clinically significant finding from an informant that is not true) are rarer and less harmful than false negatives. While for many clinical situations this emphasis on ensuring that children in need of treatment are not missed is appropriate, we also feel that such a decision should not be made blindly. Clinicians should always be careful in diagnosing and classifying childhood problems and carefully consider both positive and negative consequences of any decision (see Chapter 3 for issues in diagnosis and classification). Therefore, one must carefully consider the risks and benefits of both false positives and false negatives when developing case formulations.

A second issue was raised by Piacentini, Cohen, and Cohen (1992), who noted that simple schemes are better only if informants are asked to provide "only

that information they would ordinarily be expected to know" (p. 59). In essence, this implies that there will be certain informants who have better knowledge of a child's adjustment than others. For example, teachers may not have knowledge about certain behaviors that occur outside of the school setting, such as fire setting or cruelty to animals or needing to sleep with parents. In addition to the type of adjustment being assessed, we feel that there are other factors that may make some informants better than others in a given case. In the next several sections we discuss these factors that may affect the quality of information obtained from specific sources. From the outset we should note that most of these factors largely will affect the planning of the evaluation rather than the interpretation. Specifically, many of the factors will affect the choice of informant and of the method used to obtain information.

Informant Discrepancies and the Type of Problem

The survey by Loeber, Green, and Lahey (1990) cited in Box 16.1 indicated that clinicians tend to weigh adult informants (e.g., parents, teachers) more heavily for observable behaviors and tend to weigh child self-report more heavily for emotional problems. The logical basis to this argument is that emotional distress is largely an internal subjective event that is more difficult to tie to behavioral referents that can be observed by others. However, there is a growing body of research that has largely supported this method of clinical practice.

First, research has found that adults tend to report more conduct problems and overactivity than is reported by child self-report (Kashani et al., 1985; Reich & Earls, 1987) and children tend to report more emotional symptoms than do parents or teachers (Bird, Gould, & Stagheeza, 1992; Edelbrock et al., 1986). This differential prevalence in reporting would support the common clinical practice of emphasizing adult informants in the assessment of externalizing problems and emphasizing children in the assessment of internalizing problems, if one assumes that false positives are rare. This view is consistent with the either/or approach discussed in the previous section.

However, there are other studies that have attempted to go beyond simply documenting differences in prevalence to test the differential validity of various informants on child adjustment. These studies test the *differential validity* of various informants across behavioral domains using some external and clinically important criteria. A good example of this approach is a study by Loeber et al. (1991). In a clinic-referred sample of boys between the ages of 6 and 13, these authors tested the correlations between parent, child, and teacher report of disruptive behaviors and several important impairment criteria (e.g., school suspensions, police contacts, grade retention, special education placement) assessed 1 year later. Supporting common clinical practice, teachers' report of inattentive/hyperactive behaviors were the best predictors of impairment 1 year later. For conduct problem behaviors, parental report tended to show the most consistent prediction of impairment, although teachers' and children's information also had utility in predicting school suspensions. These findings should be interpreted in light of the age of the sample studied. Specifically, this study focused on elementary school–age children. As we will discuss in more detail in the next section, there is some evidence that the age of the child may influence the importance of different sources of information. For example, the importance of child report for assessing antisocial behavior, especially covert antisocial behavior (e.g., lying, stealing), may increase in adolescents, while the importance of parental report may decrease as parents' knowledge of their child's behaviors decrease (e.g., Elliott, Huizinga, & Ageton, 1985).

The validation of different informants requires the measurement of some independent and clinically important criteria against which to judge the usefulness of information provided. This has been very problematic for testing the differential validity of informants' reports of internalizing child behavior because it is difficult to determine what should be the validating criteria. One notable exception was a study by Frick, Silverthorn, and Evans (1994) that used a maternal history of anxiety as a way of validating informants' reports of childhood anxiety. Specifically, these authors studied the correlations between parent, child, and teacher reports of anxiety in children and a history of an anxiety disorder in the mothers of the children. In the sample of children ages 9–13, these authors found that teacher report of anxiety was not related to a family history of anxiety, but both parent and child reports of anxiety were. However, there was additional support for the relative importance of children's self-report of anxiety. Children's self-reports of anxiety disorders were always accompanied by confirmation by their parents. However, parental report was not always confirmed by the child, and parent–child disagreements on the presence of an anxiety disorder were systematically related to the parents' own level of anxiety. These authors concluded that there was evidence for parental projection of their own anxiety onto their reports of anxiety in their children. This provides some preliminary support for the relative emphasis on children's self-report of anxiety, at least in this age group (9 to 13 years) of children.

Informant Discrepancies and Age of Child

Another factor that might affect the quality of information provided by different informants is the age of the child or adolescent being assessed. First, one would expect that as a child grows older, parents would have less knowledge of the child's emotions and behaviors, especially as parent–child relationships change in adolescence (Paikoff & Brooks-Gunn, 1991). Similarly, as a child leaves early elementary school, the likelihood of a single teacher spending a great deal of time with a child decreases. Third, as a child develops cognitively, he or she may become better able to report on such abstract concepts as emotions and thoughts. As a result of these factors, one would expect that the importance of parents and teachers as informants decreases with age, and the importance of children's self-report increases.

Edelbrock et al. (1985) tested these hypothesized age effects on parent and child reports using structured diagnostic interviews. Using 2-week test-retest correlations as the index of reliability, these authors found that the reliability of parent report decreased with age as predicted, although the reliability generally remained at an acceptable level into adolescence. Children's self-report showed a more dramatic age trend. Children's self-report on the structured interviews showed a clear increase in reliability with age. Importantly, the reliability of child self-report on the structured interviews was quite poor before age 9. Evidence for the predicted decrease in reliability of teacher's report is obtainable from another source. Specifically, in the development of the Behavioral Assessment System for Children it was found that the reliability for the Teacher Report Form decreased with age (Reynolds & Kamphaus, 1992).

One question in interpreting these results is whether the changes in reliability across age are confined to structured techniques like structured interviews and behavior rating scales. At least the findings for children's self-report are not confined to structured techniques. The reliability of children's responses to projective techniques has also been found to increase with age (Exner, Thomas, & Mason, 1985). Therefore, the hypothesized age-related changes in the reliability of various informants have generally been supported in research across a number of assessment domains. These findings on the limited reliability of child self-report for very young children may not be surprising for may clinicians who work with young children. However, clinical assessors who work largely with older children, adolescents, or adults tend to use a traditional approach to assessment that relies heavily on self-report and may be uncomfortable with a reduced role of self-report in the assessment of young children.

Informant Discrepancies: Other Factors

In addition to type of behaviors and age of the child, there are other factors that might influence the report of various informants and which therefore should be considered when interpreting discrepant information. In the previous chapter we discussed factors within the family, such as *parental adjustment* and *marital conflict,* that may affect the information pro-

vided by a parent on a child's adjustment. Also, informants might have differing motivations, both conscious and unconscious, that can affect the information they provide. For example, a child may not want to admit to problem behavior or a teacher may be invested in getting a child placed outside of his class. Several rating scales discussed in previous chapters include validity scales that attempt to detect such response sets and aid in the interpretation of information provided. It is also important to note *testing conditions* when interpreting the report of different informants. For example, a child may have been administered a self-report questionnaire after a long testing session and it is obvious in watching him complete the questionnaire that he is not reading the items carefully.

Summary

From this discussion it is clear that, although the simple scheme of equally weighing the report of different informants using an either/or approach is a good starting point, a clinical assessor cannot use this approach blindly. There are numerous factors that must be considered in trying to explain seemingly discrepant information from different sources. The previous discussion outlines some of the more important issues that have been uncovered in research that can help guide clinical decision making. However, the final case formulation that results from the integration of multiple types of assessment information involves a number of complex clinical decisions. To aid in this process, in Box 16.3 we provide a sum-

---

BOX 16.3

Research Note: Common Errors in Clinical Reasoning and a Problem-Solving Model for Developing a Case Formulation

---

Nezu and Nezu (1993) conceptualize clinical assessment as a method of translating a client's complaints of distress

(Cont.)

BOX 16.3   *(Continued)*

into a meaningful set of target problems and treatment goals. This is what we have referred to in this chapter as developing a case formulation. Nezu and Nezu conceptualize this process as delineating instrumental outcomes (target problems) that are believed to directly or indirectly relate to a desired outcome for the client (treatment goals). For clinicians to use assessment information in delineating instrumental outcomes, they must go through a complex problem-solving process. Nezu and Nezu first present several common cognitive strategies that can lead to errors in the problem-solving process. Next, these authors outline an orientation to problem solving that should limit these errors in clinical reasoning.

Errors in Clinical Reasoning

1. The *availability heuristic* occurs when clinicians attempt to estimate the probability of an event based on the ease with which examples of that event come to mind. Nezu and Nezu use the example of a clinician who may overestimate the risk of suicide in a new client if the clinician was recently involved in a case of a client who committed suicide but was judged to be of low risk.

2. The *representative heuristic* occurs when a schema is accessed by a given characteristic to the exclusion of other schemas. For example, the symptom of sadness (representative characteristic) may automatically lead the clinician to consider major depression (diagnostic schema) to the exclusion of other possible diagnostic schemas (e.g., medically related mood disorder, personality disorders).

3. The *anchoring heuristic* occurs when predictions or decisions are overly dependent on initial impressions and later information is discounted, even if the new information is in disagreement with the initial impressions. For example, if a depressed client discusses interpersonal problems in the initial meeting with the clinician, the anchoring heuristic would lead the clinician to select poor social skills as the primary target of intervention to the exclusion of other information (e.g., presence of negative cognitions) obtained in subsequent assessment.

4. *Confirmatory search strategies* involve using procedures that seek only to confirm initial impressions, failing to seek disconfirming evidence. For example, a child referred for problems of inattention and motor restlessness is assessed only for other symptoms of ADHD, without considering other possible reasons for his or her symptoms (e.g., learning disability, depression, anxiety).

Problem Orientation

Nezu and Nezu propose that a systematic problem-solving approach to clinical decision making helps to limit the use of these cognitive heuristics. The key to this approach is the clinician's problem orientation. This refers to the clinician's overall theoretical orientation for viewing problem behavior, which defines the proper content and methods of assessment. These authors recommend an orientation of *planned critical multiplism*, which assumes that clinical outcomes are brought about by a multiplicity of interacting factors. The basis of this problem orientation is that:

> A variety of biological (e.g., genetic, neurochemical, physical), psychological (e.g., affective, cognitive, behavioral) and social (e.g., social and physical environment) variables can serve to act and interact as causal agents or maintaining factors. Such variables can influence the pathogenesis of a symptom, disorder or both in either a proximal (e.g., immediate antecedent stimulus) or distal (e.g., developmental history) manner. (p. 256).

Nezu and Nezu state that even if this model is incorrect in a given case (i.e., there is an unitary cause), by starting with the planned critical multiplism orientation, the clinician is less likely to selectively focus on any single type or class of instrumental outcomes. As a result, this problem orientation limits the potential for cognitive biases.

SOURCE: A. M. Nezu, and C. M. Nezu (1993), " Identifying and Selecting Target Problems for Clinical Interventions: A Problem-Solving Model," *Psychological Assessment, 5,* 254–263.

mary of an article by Nezu and Nezu (1993) that outlines (1) some of the common cognitive strategies that are used by people in making decisions but which could lead to errors in clinical reasoning and (2) a general orientation to clinical reasoning that can minimize the effects of these errors in clinical judgment. Using this general problem orientation as a basis, the following section outlines a step-by-step strategy that can help to guide the clinician in the integration of assessment information.

A MULTISTEP STRATEGY FOR INTEGRATING INFORMATION

The following strategy assumes one has conducted a comprehensive clinical evaluation of the child or adolescent. The prerequisites are (1) having information on a child's adjustment from various sources and using multiple methods; (2) having information on the child's developmental, medical, and psychiatric history; (3) having information on multiple areas of functioning, such as information on academic capabilities and peer relations, in addition to information on multiple areas of behavioral and emotional functioning; and (4) having information on the important contexts (e.g., home, school, work) in which a child functions. Once this information is obtained, the following multistep procedure can be used to develop a case formulation. In Boxes 16.4 and 16.5 we provide two case examples that illustrate this interpretive process.

BOX 16.4

Case Study to Illustrate the Multistep Interpretive Procedure: A 7-Year-Old Boy with Behavior Problems

Alex was a 7 year, 1 month–old boy who was referred to an outpatient psychological clinic for a comprehensive psychological evaluation by his mother. His mother reported that Alex was having great difficulty completing school work and he was extremely oppositional and hard to manage at home. Alex was administered a comprehensive battery of tests that included (1) an unstructured clinical interview; (2) an extensive family background assessment; (3) a psychoeducational assessment; (4) an assessment of his emotional and behavioral assessment through structured interviews conducted with his mother and teacher and rating scales completed by his mother, his teacher, and by Alex himself; (5) a sociometric exercise conducted with his class; and (6) an objective assessment of his classroom performance (e.g., amount of work completed, accuracy of work).

Step 1: Document all clinically significant findings on the child's adjustment.

On structured interviews (Diagnostic Interview Schedule for Children [DISC-2.3; Shaffer et al., 1992]), Alex met criteria for ADHD according to both his mother and his teacher. On the Child Behavior Checklist—91 (CBCL-91; Achenbach, 1991), he had T-scores above 70 on both the Thought Problem scale and the Attention Problem scale according to the father and T-scores of 70 and 67 on the Attention Problem and Thought Problem scales, respectively, according to his mother's report. On the teacher-completed Comprehensive Behavior Rating Scale for Children (CBRSC; Neeper, Lahey, & Frick, 1990), he obtained a T-score of 71 on the Daydreams scale and a T-score of 65 on the Motor Hyperactivity scale.

Also on the DISC-2.3, Alex met criteria for Oppositional Defiant Disorder (ODD) according to his mother's report. Similarly, he obtained T-scores above 70 on the Aggressive Behavior scale of the CBCL-91 by both mother and father report.

A final significant finding was the report of a sufficient number of depressive symptoms to meet criteria for current Major Depression according to maternal report on the DISC-2.3.

Step 2: Look for convergent findings across sources and methods.

It was clear that there were convergent findings for significant problems of inattention-disorganization and impulsivity-hyperactivity associated with ADHD, according to parents and teachers and across structured interviews and rating scales. However, for the oppositional behaviors the teacher report gave no indications of these behaviors in the school environment either on rating scales or on structured interviews. For the parental report of depression, although Alex's teacher did not report symptoms of depression of sufficient severity to warrant a diagnosis solely on her report, she did endorse several symptoms, such as feeling sad and irritable, feeling bad about himself, and often seeming as if he was about to cry. However, on the Children's Depression Inventory (CDI; Kovacs, 1992), Alex did not report significant feelings of depression.

Step 3: Try to explain discrepancies.

In talking to Alex's teacher, it appeared that she had a very structured classroom with a teacher's aide who implemented behavioral programs for students. Alex's parents were divorced, and his mother seemed quite distressed over Alex's behavior. As a result, she seemed to be very unsure

(Cont.)

Box 16.4   *(Continued)*

of how to discipline Alex, leading to a great deal of inconsistency and sometimes harshness in her discipline attempts. These differences in teacher and parent handling of Alex's behavior seemed to explain the fact that he was not showing significant oppositional behaviors at school. While there was some support for the depressive behaviors by Alex's teacher, Alex did not report such behaviors. However, given Alex's young age, there was some concern over his ability to accurately report on internal feelings using the structured CDI.

Step 4: Developing a profile and hierarchy of problem areas.

Alex exhibited a common profile of showing both ADHD and ODD. However, there were several reasons why ADHD was considered primary. First, the ADHD behaviors had been present throughout Alex's life, and they were the only behaviors shown at both home and school. Second, Alex's teacher reported that Alex's grades were primarily affected by his failure to complete work or his hasty completion of work that led to careless errors. This teacher report was consistent with a psychoeducational assessment that revealed an IQ in the average range and academic achievement also in an age-appropriate range. A sociometric exercise indicated that Alex was disliked by a significant number of his classmates (5 out of a class of 17). Therefore, the ADHD was considered to be causing a high level of impairment for Alex, educationally and socially. Third, Alex's biological father reported that he had had significant problems with inattention and hyperactivity as a child.

Alex's depressive features were also considered to be secondary to the ADHD. His mother reported that they started after the past semester in school, when he had received his worst grades ever and he and his mother had been constantly arguing about his school performance and home behavior.

Step 5: Determine critical information to place in the report.

Alex's mother had seen a counselor for 6 months following her divorce from Alex's father, 3 years prior to the evaluation. This piece of information did not seem to be crucial for understanding our case formulation of Alex. Also, because the psychoeducational testing did not reveal any significant strengths or weaknesses in cognitive processing or in various areas of academic achievement, this information was only briefly summarized, indicating that it was not suggestive of the presence of a cognitive deficit or a learning disability.

Box 16.5

Case Study to Illustrate Multistep Interpretive Procedure: A 14-Year-Old Boy with a Language Disorder and Social Phobia

Jarrod was 14 years, 2 months old when his school referred him for a comprehensive psychological evaluation. They were concerned about Jarrod's inability to complete schoolwork and his extreme shyness. His teachers reported that Jarrod rarely initiated conversations with either peers or teachers and responded to other people with only one word answers. Jarrod had been receiving resource help at school in a learning disabilities classroom for the past 2 years.

Jarrod was administered a comprehensive battery of tests that included an unstructured clinical interview, an extensive family background assessment, a psychoeducational assessment, assessment of his emotional and behavioral assessment through structured interviews conducted with his mother and Jarrod and rating scales completed by Jarrod and his mother.

Step 1: Document all clinically significant findings on the child's adjustment.

On structured interviews, Jarrod met criteria for Social Phobia on the DISC-2.3 (Shaffer et al., 1992) by both his own self-report and the report of his mother. In the psychoeducational assessment, Jarrod scored 25 points lower on his Verbal IQ than on his Performance IQ on the Wechsler Intelligence Scale—Third Edition (WISC-III: Wechsler, 1992). This verbal deficit was consistent with previous testing conducted by his school. In addition to the verbal weakness, Jarrod scored poorly on tests of processing speed.

Step 2: Look for convergent findings across sources and methods.

Although not in the clinically significant range, there was support for Jarrod's social anxiety and social withdrawal on parent- and child-completed rating scales. On the

(Cont.)

Box 16.5   *(Continued)*

CBCL-91 (Achenbach, 1991) completed by Jarrod's mother, the Withdrawal scale had a T-score of 68. On the self-report Personality Inventory for Youth, Jarrod obtained a T-score of 65 on the Social Withdrawal scale. This was consistent with reports from his teachers and from behavioral observations during testing that indicated that Jarrod was very quiet and withdrawn. The other main areas of convergence were Jarrod's good adjustment in most behavioral domains and the positive and stable home environment provided by his parents.

Step 3: Try to explain discrepancies.

In this case the only discrepancy was the somewhat milder level of social withdrawal being reported at home than was being reported by teachers at school, although clearly the shyness was still evident in the home. This was likely due to Jarrod's higher level of comfort with family members, which made him more willing to converse with family members.

Step 4: Developing a profile and hierarchy of problem areas.

It seemed as though Jarrod had an expressive language disorder and a deficit in processing speed. As a result, Jarrod was likely to be uncomfortable conversing in social situations, leading to the high rate of social withdrawal. The language disorder and processing speed deficit were judged to be primary in the case because (1) they had been chronic throughout his life and (2) Jarrod did not show a high rate of anxiety in other situations that did not require verbal expression.

Step 5: Determine critical information to place in the report.

A great deal of the information on Jarrod's family background, current family functioning, and functioning in other behavioral and emotional areas (e.g., conduct and depression) were only summarized briefly in the report. They were felt to be important to document Jarrod's many psychological strengths, but a detailed discussion of these areas was not felt to be needed in the written report.

Step 1: Document all clinically significant findings regarding the child's adjustment.

The first step of the procedure follows the either/or rule. The assessor sifts through all of the information on a child or adolescent's adjustment from all sources and methods and determines if there are any significant findings, such as norm-referenced elevations on rating scales, diagnoses based on structured interviews, or clinically significant material from projective tests. As discussed previously, this is a very sensitive procedure that can result in high rates of significant findings. We feel that it is a good starting point in the interpretive process. However, we also feel that stopping at this point would result in an unacceptably high rate of false positives; the subsequent steps help to increase the specificity of the process.

Step 2: Look for convergent findings across sources and methods.

After noting all of the significant findings across methods and sources, the next step is to isolate areas that are consistent across the various pieces of assessment information. In looking at cross-method and cross-informant convergence, it is recommended that one take a closer look at the assessment information and not simply determine whether or not a score has crossed some threshold or elevation. We have discussed at several points in this book the arbitrary nature of many clinical cut-offs, such as elevations on a scale of a behavior rating scale or a diagnosis on a structured interview. How different is a child with a T-score of 69 from a child with a T-score of 70 on a given scale? How different is a child with seven symptoms of ADHD from a child with eight?

Therefore, when looking for convergent pieces of evidence, one should look at the full range of scores, problems, or symptoms. For example, suppose a child reports a high level of anxiety on a self-report questionnaire, passing a clinical cut-off point as required in Step 1. However, on a parent structured interview there are no diagnoses of anxiety disorders reported, but the parent has reported three symptoms of overanxious disorder and two symptoms of separation anxiety disorder. Further, a teacher rated a child with a T-score of 64 on the anxiety scale of a behavior rating scale. If one just viewed scores that exceeded a clinical cut-off, this pattern would look like the child's self-report of anxiety was unsupported by other informants, when, in fact, we would argue that there is fairly consistent support for the presence of anxious behaviors, although the anxiety is not being perceived as being as severe by parents and teachers.

Step 3: Try to explain discrepancies.

The complexity of the assessment process is dramatically reduced when assessment information is consistent across methods and sources—the dream of every clinical assessor. Unfortunately, existing research and clinical experience suggest that in most cases there will be numerous discrepancies between the information provided by different sources after steps 1 and 2. At this stage one should take the information discussed in previous sections of this chapter and try to develop explanations for the discrepancies. Can the discrepancies be explained by different demands in the various settings in which a child is observed? Can the discrepancies be explained by differences in the measurement techniques used or by certain characteristics/motivations of the informants? Can the discrepancies be explained by differing knowledge of the child's behavior across informants? As mentioned previously, if one can answer these questions and account for discrepant information, one has gone a long way in developing a good case formulation and developing goals for treatment.

Step 4: Develop a profile and hierarchy of strengths and weaknesses.

Both research and clinical practice indicate that children rarely have problems that are specific to one area. As a result, the next step in the interpretive process is to develop a profile of a child's or adolescent's strengths and weaknesses across the different domains of psychological functioning that have been assessed. In addition, we feel that this process needs to go beyond simply documenting the different areas of strength and weaknesses, to also *prioritizing* the different areas of concern. This prioritization should be both a conceptual and practical endeavor.

Conceptually, one should consider what problematic area may be primary and which areas may be secondary, with secondary being defined as areas that seem to be largely a result of some other primary factor. For example, for a child who becomes depressed because of her frequent school suspensions and police contacts for antisocial behavior, the depression may best be considered secondary to the antisocial behavior. Practically, one needs to consider what area should be the primary focus of intervention. This may follow closely with the determination of primary and secondary problems, where intervention targeting primary areas (e.g., antisocial behavior) may also alleviate problems considered to be secondary (e.g., depression). However, these two levels of analysis do not necessarily have to be congruent. For example, a child with ADHD may have developed conduct problems secondary to the ADHD because of the effects of a child's behavior on parent–child interactions. However, given the current problems caused by the conduct disturbance and the prognostic significance of these behaviors, intervention targeting the conduct problems may be the primary treatment recommendation, rather than treatment for ADHD.

Most assessors would agree with the need to prioritize problem areas, but most would also agree that this is difficult to accomplish with any degree of reliability and validity. We must admit that prioritizing areas of need and determining primary and secondary areas of dysfunction are often largely based on clinical intuition in the absence of a clear research base to guide this process. However, we feel that there are three primary factors to consider in prioritizing areas within a child's profile.

First, one should look at the *degree of impairment* associated with different areas of dysfunction. As a standard part of any assessment one should have measures of the degree to which various behaviors are affecting a child's functioning in at least three major life areas: in school, with peers, and at home. Then several questions can be asked in an effort to determine if some problem areas are contributing more to impairment than others. Are the problematic areas differentially affecting a child's ability to learn or to perform well academically? Has one or more of the areas significantly affected a child's ability to form or maintain meaningful relationships with same-age peers? Is any problem area causing a higher level of conflict with parents and/or siblings than others? This method of prioritization is one of the most important clinically, since areas that cause the greatest degree of impairment typically are the most important targets of interventions.

Second, one can look at the temporal sequencing of when problem behaviors developed to help to determine what might be primary or secondary. Did symptoms of depression develop after a chronic pattern of antisocial behavior? A good example of the therapeutic implications of temporal sequencing comes from a study in which children with major depression who only showed conduct problems *after the onset of the depression* showed a significant reduction of conduct problems after the depression was successfully treated (Puig-Antich et al., 1978).

Third, viewing family history data can help in making a determination of primary and secondary areas of disturbance. As we discussed in Chapter 13 in the section on assessing a child's family history, information on parental psychiatric history can often aid in making differential diagnoses. This is largely due to the fact that (1) adult psychological disturbance tends to be more easily defined and (2) many forms of childhood disturbance show a familial link. As a result, assessing parental adjustment patterns can provide clues as to what is the primary area of dysfunction in their child or adolescent. Box 13.2 in Chapter 13 provides a case example of how obtaining a family history can aid in making differential diagnoses.

Step 5: Determine critical information to place in the report.

In the next chapter we provide a detailed discussion of report writing. However, it is important to note that the last stage of integrating information is a filtering process. After one has developed a profile of the child that explains the referral problems and suggests treatment goals, it is likely that many pieces of information gathered will have either minimal or no bearing on the final case conceptualization. A good assessor will limit the amount of unessential information that is collected in an evaluation by carefully tailoring the evaluation to the needs of an individual child. However, much information cannot be determined to be irrelevant until after it is collected.

Many clinicians feel that if information was collected, it should be included in the written and/or oral report of the assessment results. Our feeling is that too much irrelevant information detracts from the case formulation, making it unduly confusing. Therefore, we feel that the final step in the interpretive process is determining what information is essential for understanding the case formulation and subsequent recommendations for treatment and what information should be omitted or discussed only minimally in the report. This final step sets the stage for the writing of a clear, concise, and readable summary of the assessment results.

CONCLUSIONS

In this chapter we discuss some of the issues involved in integrating assessment information across informants, across methods, and across psychological domains. One of the more difficult aspects of this endeavor is integrating discrepant information from different informants on the same dimension of functioning. We discussed evidence that simple decision rules that equally weigh information given by various informants may be as good or better than more complex methods of differentially weighing information provided by various informants. However, this simple rule needs to be qualified by whether the informant is knowledgeable about the child's behavior and whether the informant can report the information effectively. These two factors can be influenced by many factors, such as age of the child and the specific behavioral domain being assessed. We conclude the chapter with a multistep procedure for integrating the various pieces information from a comprehensive evaluation into a clear case formulation that answers the referral question and points the way to a recommended course of intervention.

CHAPTER SUMMARY

1. Because most clinical assessments of children and adolescents must be comprehensive, one of the most difficult parts of the assessment process is integrating assessment information into a clear case formulation that points the way to the most appropriate interventions.

2. The most difficult task is integrating information on the same behavior provided by different informants. Research has shown that high rates of discrepancy are the rule, rather than the exception.

   a. These discrepancies may reflect real differences in a child's functioning in different contexts (e.g., home, school, clinic). Therefore, assessing the characteristics of the different contexts can help to explain some discrepancies.

   b. Some discrepancies may be an artifact of the level of analysis. For example, individual symptoms may be very discrepant across informants, whereas the presence of a disorder may show greater concordance.

   c. Discrepancies can also be an artifact of different measurement techniques used to obtain information from different informants.

3. Unfortunately, in many cases it is difficult to attribute discrepant information solely to varying situational demands, to the level of analysis, or to differences in assessment strategy. In these cases there is evidence that a simple either/or system for combining information works best—that is, a finding is considered significant if reported by any informant.

   a. This approach assumes that false positives are rarer and less harmful than false negatives.

   b. This approach also assumes that informants are only asked to provide information that they should be expected to know.

4. The quality of information provided by different informants seems to vary depending on the domain of functioning being assessed and the age of the child being assessed.

   a. Research suggests that teacher report of inattentive-hyperactive behaviors, parent report of conduct problems, and child report of anxiety seem to be relatively most important in preadolescent children.

   b. The usefulness of child self-report increases with age and the usefulness of teacher report decreases with age. Age related changes in parental report are less consistently found, although there are some indications that the usefulness of parental report also decreases somewhat as the child gets older.

5. Other factors such as a parent's emotional adjustment, the degree of marital conflict, idiosyncratic motivations of an informant, and testing conditions can influence informant agreement.

6. A multistep procedure for integrating diverse assessment information is recommended.

   Step 1: Document all clinically significant findings on the child's adjustment.

   Step 2: Look for convergence across sources and methods.

   Step 3: Attempt to explain discrepancies.

   Step 4: Develop a profile and hierarchy of findings.

   Step 5: Determine what critical information to place in the formal report.

CHAPTER 17

Report Writing*

- What is the best way to tell parents of their child's test results?

- What are the common mistakes made in report writing?

- How should assessment results be reported to parents in conferences?

- How does a clinician clarify the referral question?

REPORTING PROBLEMS AND CHALLENGES

Presenting assessment results orally or in writing can be a foreboding task. Fears of litigation, insecurities about interpretive skill, and nightmares of embar-

*This chapter is an adaptation of an earlier chapter written by the first author that appears in R. W. Kamphaus, *Clinical Assessment of Children's Intelligence* (Boston: Allyn & Bacon, 1993).

rassing spelling or grammatical errors have all contributed to making the process onerous. Because of concerns such as these, a chapter on report writing is crucial for an assessment text. As clinicians know full well, their written products will live in infamy.

Effective psychological report writing is taking on increased importance for practicing psychologists. Psychological reports are frequently made available to parents, judges, lawyers, and other nonpsychologists, creating the opportunity for improper interpretation of the results by untrained individuals. More positively, psychological reports remain particularly useful to other clinicians who evaluate a child who has previously been seen by a psychologist. A previous psychological report can provide a valuable baseline against which a clinician can gauge response to treatment, the emergence of a comorbid problem, and other factors. A previous diagnosis of conduct disorder, for example, may encourage the evaluating psychologist to screen for depression because of known comorbidity (DeBaryshe et al., 1993). A clinician can significantly enhance the quality of work conducted by a successor through the productions of an articulate written report. As Glasser and

Zimmerman (1967) correctly recognize, the clarity of the report will determine the use made of the results at a later date.

Despite its importance, the topic of report writing is relatively neglected in the research literature (Ownby & Wallbrown, 1986). While a number of treatises are available on this topic (Teglasi, 1983; Tallent, 1988), little research has been conducted to assess the effects of report writing on important outcomes such as the likelihood that a recommendation will be followed (Ownby & Wallbrown, 1986).

From the research on psychological report writing collected to date, Ownby and Wallbrown (1986) draw several discouraging conclusions. They conclude that psychological reports are:

- Considered useful to some extent by consumers such as psychiatrists and social workers

- Frequently criticized by these professional groups on both content and stylistic grounds

- May (or may not) make substantial contributions to patient management

In addition to the opinions of psychiatrists and social workers, a number of studies have assessed teachers' satisfaction with psychological reports and have found that they are frequently dissatisfied with them (Ownby & Wallbrown, 1986). One can get a sense of why teachers and other professionals are dissatisfied with psychological reports by reading the following excerpt that was taken verbatim from a report. All of the conclusions drawn by the evaluator in this case are based on *one test* requiring the child to simply reproduce nine designs with pencil and paper (the Bender-Gestalt Test). We quote:

> The Bender-Visual Motor Gestalt test suggests delinquency and an acting out potential. He is anxious, confused, insecure and has a low self-esteem. He may have difficulties in interpersonal relationships and tends to isolate himself when problems arise. . . . [He] also seems to have a lot of anxiety and tension over phallic sexuality and may be in somewhat of a homosexual panic.

This clinician was apparently using a cookbook approach to interpretation. A report like this is of no help to anyone, especially not the child being evaluated.

One of the difficulties with report writing is that different audiences require different reports. For example, a psychometric summary (a portion of the report that presents only test scores and is usually given as an appendix at the end of a report) given without context is likely to be of little use to parents but of great potential use to colleagues and perhaps teachers. An important decision that each psychologist must make prior to report writing is to determine the primary audience for the report. For example, a psychometric summary may be of minimal use to parents who have contracted with the psychologist in private practice for an evaluation. In this case it is more sensible to present test results in context in order to communicate effectively with the parents. A psychometric summary is more in order in a clinic situation where it is imperative that a psychologist communicate effectively with knowledgeable colleagues.

PITFALLS OF REPORT WRITING

As Norman Tallent (1976) observes, complaints about psychological reports persist. Norman Tallent produced a landmark textbook (now in its third edition) on report writing in which he summarized the literature on the strengths and weaknesses of reports as identified by psychologists' colleagues in mental health care, most notably social workers and psychiatrists. Some of the highlights of Tallent's (1988) review are outlined in the next section.

Vocabulary Problems

As the reader may surmise from reading the report vignette given previously, the problem of using vague or imprecise language in report writing persists. The colloquial term used to describe such language is "psychobabble". Siskind (1967), for example, studied the level of agreement between psychologists and psychiatrists in defining words such as the following.

Abstract	Bright
Affective	Compulsive
Aggression	Control
Anxiety	Constriction
Bizarre	Defense
Dependent	Hostility
Depressive	Immaturity
Emotional	Impulsive
	Normal

The results of the study showed very little correspondence between the definitions offered by the two groups of professionals.

Harvey (1989) explains how this problem of vague or imprecise language applies to school psychologists, who probably do the greatest amount of assessment work with children and adolescents. She also points out that because of the passing of the Buckley Amendment and the increasingly common practice of giving reports to parents, the educational level of the typical consumer of psychological reports is lower than in the past. While many writers of psychological reports use language consistent with their graduate level training, such language may be at a reading level far beyond the capability of the target audience of the report. Harvey (1989) notes that even respected magazines are written at a high school level. The *Atlantic Monthly* is written at a 12th-grade level and *Time* and *Newsweek* at 11th-grade levels.

Tallent (1988) refers to one aspect of this problem with language as exhibitionism, which seems to be a frequent criticism of reports, particularly on the part of other psychologists. One commentator stated, "They are written in stilted psychological terms to boost the ego of the psychologist." (p. 33)

Other pertinent observations (Tallent, 1988, pp. 36–37) on the use of language by psychologists in reports include the following.

- Often padded with meaningless multisyllabic words to lengthen report.
- Gobbledygook.
- Semantics have a tendency to creep in, and the phenomenon of "verbal diarrhea" occurs too often.
- They are too often written in a horrible psychologese—so that clients manifest overt aggressive

hostility in an impulsive manner—when, in fact—they punch you on the nose.

- They are not frequently enough written in lay language. I believe it requires clear thinking to write without use of technical terms. Scores have little meaning even to the psychologist who understands their rationale, unless he knows how they fit together in terms of cause and effect regarding behavior. To cover up his ignorance he resorts to the reporting of percentages, ratios, etc., and overwhelms his reader with such technical language that little information is conveyed.
- They are not clear enough to be wrong.

Of course, psychology cannot be singled out as the only profession with a preference for its own idiosyncratic terminology, as anyone who reads a physician's report or legal contract will attest. Perhaps psychologists can, however, lead the way toward competent reporting of findings.

Eisegesis

Eisegesis is the problem of faulty interpretation based on personal ideas, bias, and idiosyncracies (Tallent, 1988). The problem is most readily seen when the psychologist is clearly using the same theories or drawing the same conclusions in every report. A psychologist may conclude that all children's problems are due to poor ego functioning, neuropsychological problems, or family system failure. A psychologist who adheres exclusively to behavioral principles, for example, will attribute all child problems to faulty reinforcement histories. The savvy consumer of this psychologist's reports will eventually become wary of the psychologist's conclusions, as the relevance of the favored theory to some cases is questionable. One can imagine the skepticism that may be engendered by a psychologist who concludes that a child whose school performance has just deteriorated subsequent to a traumatic head injury merely needs more positive reinforcement to bring his grades up to pre-trauma levels.

The problem of eisegesis may also occur if a psychologist draws conclusions that are clearly in conflict with the data collected for a child. A psychologist may decide to not make a diagnosis that seems contrary to Achenbach CBCL findings of significant T-scores on the majority of scales. If a clear argument for resolving this incongruity is not made, the consumer of the report may well suspect biases. The psychologist who routinely does not reconcile high T-scores with a lack of a diagnosis may soon be labeled as unwilling to diagnose regardless of assessment results. Teachers, pediatricians, or other referral sources who receive this interpretation consistently from the same psychologist may eventually pay more attention to the data presented in the reports and ignore the psychologist's conclusions, or they may simply refer elsewhere.

Report Length

Psychologists, more so than other groups, complain about the excessive length of reports (Tallent, 1988). However, length may not be the real issue. Perhaps long reports are used to disguise incompetence, fulfill needs for accountability, or impress others. The possibility that length is a cover for other ills is offered in the following quote:

> A certain business executive likes to relate the anecdote about the occasion when he assigned a new employee to prepare a report for him. In due time a voluminous piece of writing was returned. Dismayed, the executive pointed out that the required information could be presented on one, certainly not more than two, pages. But sir, pleaded the young man, I don't know that much about the matter you assigned me to. (Tallent, 1988, p. 72)

It may also be worth considering that the Ten Commandments are expressed in 297 words, the Declaration of Independence in 300 words, and the Gettysburg Address in 266 words.

Number Obsession

The clinician must always keep clearly in mind that the child is the lodestar of the evaluation, and the numbers obtained from personality tests and the like are only worthy of emphasis if they contribute to the understanding of the child being evaluated. One way to think of the scores is as a means to an end, the end being better understanding of the child. The same numbers for two children can mean two quite different things. Just as a high temperature reading can be symptomatic of a host of disorders from influenza to appendicitis, so, too, a pathognomic behavioral sign can reveal a host of possible conditions.

One horrendous error often made when reporting test scores is a psychologist reporting a score and then saying that it's invalid. Then why report it (Tallent, 1988)? If a test score is invalid, how does it serve the child to have this score as part of a permanent record? Reporting apparently invalid scores is akin to a physician making a diagnostic decision based on a fasting blood test where the patient violated the fasting requirements. In all likelihood the flawed results would not be reported; rather, the patient would be required to retake the test. We suggest that *one does not have to report scores for a test just because it was administered.*

Failure to Address Referral Questions

Tallent (1988) points out that psychologists too often fail to demand clear referral questions and, as a result, their reports appear vague and unfocused. This very obvious point is all too frequently overlooked. Psychologists should insist that referral sources present their questions clearly and, if not, the psychologist should meet with the referring person to obtain further detail on the type of information that is expected from the evaluation (Tallent, 1988). Many agencies use referral forms to assist in this process of declaring assessment goals. A form similar to those used by hospitals is shown in Figure 17.1 and one suitable for use by school systems is given in Figure 17.2.

On occasions the referral question(s) can be insidious and, consequently, place the psychologist in the position of disappointing the referral source before the evaluation is initiated. Under these circumstances the psychologist may feel helpless or betrayed because of the negative reaction of the referral source to the presentation of results and recommendations. Psychologists may often need to pursue the true

Patient Name _____

Medical Record Number _____

Attending Physician _____

Type of Consultation:

Signed _____ Title _____ Date _____

Results of Consultation:

Date of Consultation _____

Signature of Consultant _____ Title _____ Date _____

FIGURE 17.1

Referral for consultation used by hospitals

Student's Name _____ Date of Referral _____

Referring School _____ Age _____ Grade _____ Grades Repeated _____ Days Absent _____

Is the student now receiving speech therapy? _____ yes _____ no

	Never	**Sometimes**	**Often**
COMMUNICATION PROBLEMS			
Expressive Language (problems in grammar, limited vocabulary)			
Receptive Language (comprehension, not following directions)			
Speech (poor enunciation, lisps, stutters, omits sounds, infantile speech)			
PHYSICAL PROBLEMS			
Gross Motor Coordination (eye–hand, manual dexterity)			
Visual (cannot see blackboard, squints, rubs eyes, holds book too close)			
Hearing (unable to discriminate sounds, asks to have instructions repeated, turns ear to speaker, often has earaches)			
Health (example: epilepsy, respiratory problems, etc.)			
Medications	(yes)	(no)	(Type)
CLASSROOM BEHAVIOR			
Overly energetic, talks out, out of seat			
Very quiet, uncommunicative			
Acting out (aggressive, hostile, rebellious, destructive, cries easily)			
Inattentive (short attention span, poor on-task behavior)			
Doesn't appear to notice what is happening in the immediate environment			
Poor Peer Relationships (few friends, rejected, ignored, abused by peers)			
ACADEMIC PROBLEMS			
Reading (word attack, comprehension)			
Writing (illegible, reverses letters, doesn't write)			
Spelling (cannot spell phonetically, omits or adds letters)			
Mathematics (computation, concepts, application)			
Social Science, Sciences (doesn't handle concepts, doesn't understand relationships, poor understanding of cause and effect)			

Other Problems _____

What methods/materials have you tried to solve the problems? _____

_____

Signature and position of referring person _____

FIGURE 17.2

Referral for consultation used by schools

referral question. Some examples of stated and true referral questions are shown below.

Stated Referral Question	True Referral Question
A child's teacher wants to know if a child has ADHD.	The teacher is convinced that the child has ADHD and expects the psychologist to confirm it.
A parent wants to know why a child is failing in school.	The parent wants to know if the child is showing symptoms of depression, a problem for which the parent has been treated since adolescence.
A psychiatrist wants to know if a child is depressed.	The psychiatrist has made the diagnosis of depression and has placed the child on medication. The referral was made simply because a second opinion is required for reimbursement purposes.
A psychologist wants to know if the child is neurologically impaired.	The psychologist is seeking a diagnosis of traumatic brain injury in order to bolster her court testimony.

In all of these scenarios it would behoove the psychologist to use counseling skills to ferret out referral source needs and/or desires early on in the referral/evaluation process.

The Consumer's View

A few studies have evaluated psychological reports from the viewpoint of the consumer (Mussman, 1964; Rucker, 1967; Brandt & Giebink, 1968). One rather recent study (Wiener, 1985) evaluated teacher preferences for and comprehension of varying report formats. This study required a group of elementary school teachers to read and rate their comprehension of and preferences for three different reports for the same child.

The three reports used were a short form, the psychoeducational report, and question-and-answer. The short-form report was one page, single spaced. It used some jargon, such as acronyms, to shorten length; conclusions were drawn without reference to a data source; and recommendations were given without elaboration. The psychoeducational report format was three and a half single-spaced pages. It used headings such as Reason for Referral, Learning Style, Mathematics, Conclusions, and Recommendations. Observations were stated in behavioral terms with examples used freely. Recommendations were given and elaborated, and acronyms and other jargon were only used when they were defined in text. The question-and-answer report was similar to the psychoeducational report in many ways, but it did not use headings per se. This report listed referral questions and then answered each question in turn. This report was four and a half pages long.

Amazingly, in this study, the participants preferred length. First, teachers comprehended the two longer reports better. Second, of the two longer reports the teachers preferred the question-and-answer report over the psychoeducational report. The short form was clearly least preferred. These are intriguing results in that they hint that length may be overrated as a problem in report writing, and that teachers may prefer a question-and-answer report format. This finding is interesting because this format is rarely used.

Do parents have different preferences from teachers? In a follow-up study with parents using the same methodology, Wiener and Kohler (1986) found that teachers and parents have similar preferences. In this second study the same three report formats were used. As was the case with teachers, parents comprehended the two longer reports significantly better than the short-form report. An interesting additional finding was that parents with a college education comprehended reports better than parents with only a high school diploma. Parents also tended to prefer the question-and-answer format to the other two formats, although the difference in preference scores between the psychoeducational and question-and-answer reports failed to reach statistical significance.

The results of these two studies suggest that the two most frequent consumers of child and adolescent psychological reports, parents and teachers, consider the clarity of reports to be more important than their absolute length. They also show a preference for reports that have referral questions as their focus. Cognizance of these two findings may benefit psychologists who write reports for children and adolescents.

SUGGESTED PRACTICES

Report Only Pertinent Information

One of the most difficult decisions to make when writing a report involves gauging the relevance of information to include (Teglasi, 1983). Clinicians happen onto a great deal of information during the course of an evaluation, some of which is tangential. Say, for example, a child is referred for an evaluation of ADHD. During the course of an interview with the child's father, he recounts at length his disappointment with his wife. He tells the clinician that she is dating other men, and he believes that she is not spending adequate time with their children. When writing the report on this case, the clinician has to determine whether or not this information is pertinent to the ADHD evaluation.

Clinicians must think critically about the information that they include in reports and consider its relevance to the case. If information is not relevant to the referral problem, and it is very personal, the psychologist should consider carefully the decision to invade a family's privacy by including the information in the report.

Define Abbreviations and Acronyms

Acronyms are part of the idiosyncratic language of psychological assessment. They can greatly facilitate communication among psychologists, but they hinder communication with nonpsychologists. Psychologists, just like other professionals, need to use nontechnical language to communicate with parents, teachers, and other colleagues in the mental health field. A pediatrician would not ask a mother if her child had an emesis; rather, the physician would inquire whether or not the child vomited.

When writing a report, psychologists should try to avoid using acronyms, at least undefined ones. To simply use the acronym SAD for separation anxiety disorder, for example, is questionable practice.

Emphasize Words Rather Than Numbers

Particularly in the test results section of a report, clinicians must resist the wizardry of numbers (Zimmerman & Woo-Sam, 1967). Words communicate more effectively than numbers because they communicate more directly. The typical question of a referral source has nothing to do with the obtained T-scores but, rather, the psychologist's interpretation of these scores.

Reduce Difficult Words

The issue of using simple language is by now obvious. The difficult part for report writers is following through on this advice. Consider the following two paragraphs, which differ greatly. The first excerpt uses vocabulary that is unnecessarily complex for most consumers of reports. The second example is a rewrite of the first paragraph that uses a more practical vocabulary level.

> There is also evidence from the test data to suggest that Pam is obdurate in response to anxiety. She may also tend to be very concrete and not notice some of the subtleties of interpersonal discourse. Given these idiosyncrasies, she may find it difficult to generate ef-

fective social problem-solving strategies and mechanisms for coping with life's stressors.

The next paragraph tries to communicate more clearly by using, among other things, simpler language.

Pam responds to stress by withdrawing from others (e.g., going to her room or leaving a group of friends on a social outing), which seems to be the only method she uses for dealing with stress. She also has trouble understanding and responding to messages given by others in social situations (e.g., body language or verbal hints). Because of these behavior patterns, Pam has trouble making friends.

Related to the use of difficult words is the issue of using the correct person. We have occasionally seen reports where instead of using the child's name, he or she was referred to as "the child" or "the subject." This usage sounds too mechanistic and impersonal for a psychological report. In most cases the use of the child's name is better. For a sentence such as "The child scowled at the clinician," we suggest this alternative: "Sandy scowled at the clinician."

Describe the Instruments Used

In many cases it is safe to assume that the reader of the report has little knowledge of the tests being used. When practical, we suggest that report writers describe the nature of the assessment devices being used. Prior to the ready availability of personal computers this task would have been impractical. Now including such descriptions is relatively easy, since a description of each test can be stored, retrieved, and inserted as necessary.

The naive reader of a report will also be helped by descriptors of the nature of a scale or subscale that is being discussed. This observation is particularly true for scales that are not adequately described by their names. Depression scales are a good example of scales that may be perceived inappropriately. The name Depression could conjure up a variety of images in a report reader's mind including the image of a child that is incapacitated by sadness. It may well be that a Depression score indicates significance but, depending on the items endorsed, may not warrant the formal diagnosis of depression. In this case the clinician should try to describe the nature of the scale content and/or its interpretive meaning in order to discourage misuse of results.

Edit the Report at Least Once

We have found that a number of our students do not take a critical eye toward editing their own work. Editing is necessary to ensure the most accurate communication in the least amount of space. Tallent (1988) provides the following excellent example of how an editor (and the articulate psychologist) thinks:

There is the tale of the young man who went into the fish business. He rented a store, erected a sign, FRESH FISH SOLD HERE, and acquired merchandise. As he was standing back admiring his market and his sign, a friend happened along. Following congratulations, the friend gazed at the sign and read aloud, FRESH FISH SOLD HERE. Of course it's here. You wouldn't sell it elsewhere, would you? Impressed with such astuteness, the young man painted over the obviously superfluous word. The next helpful comment had to do with the word *sold*. You aren't giving it away. Again impressed, he eliminated the useless word. Seemingly that was it, but the critic then focused on the word *fresh*. You wouldn't sell stale fish, would you? Once more our hero bowed to the strength of logic. But finally he was relieved that he had a logic-tight sign for his business; FISH. His ever alert friend, however, audibly sniffing the air for effect, made a final observation: You don't need a sign. (p. 88)

Psychologists do not need to engage in such severe editing, but they should at least make an attempt to think critically about their word usage in order to reduce report, sentence, and paragraph length. Judicious editing can go a long way toward clarifying meaning in a report.

Sometimes new clinicians are not used to critiquing their own writing. One readily available option is to have a colleague read reports. Confidentiality, however, should be kept in mind if an editor is used.

Use Headings and Lists Freely

Headings and lists can enhance the clarity of communication (Harvey, 1989). If, for example, a clinician draws a number of conclusions about a child, these can sometimes lose their impact if they are embedded in paragraphs.

As one would predict, the use of headings and lists to excess has a downside. A report that uses too many lists, for example, appears stilted, and it may not communicate all of the texture and subtleties of the child's performance. Report writers should consider using additional headings if a section of their report stretches for nearly a page (single spaced) without a heading. Clinicians should consider lists if they want to add impact to statements and/or conclusions.

Use Examples of Behavior to Clarify Meaning

Since there is some disagreement regarding the meanings of particular words, report writers should clarify their meaning in order to ensure accuracy. Words that may conjure up a variety of interpretations include *anxiety, cooperation, dependent, hyperactive,* and *low self-esteem.* One way to foster clarity is to use examples (behavioral referents) of the child's behavior. Here, for example, are two ways to say that Emilio was anxious.

> Emilio exhibited considerable anxiety during the testing.

Or, alternatively:

> Emilio appeared anxious during the testing. He frequently asked whether or not he had solved an item correctly, he would occasionally look at the ticking stopwatch during an item and then hurry, and his face became flushed when it was obvious to him that he did not know the answer to a question.

An additional benefit of using examples of behavior generously is that it forces the psychologist to consider the extent of supporting evidence for a conclusion about a child's behavior. If a psychologist writes that a child is anxious but cannot think of behaviors to help explain this, then the conclusion should not be drawn, as it is insupportable.

Direct quotes are also helpful for clarifying meaning. If a clinician concludes that an adolescent is suicidal, a quote from the child may help clarify this statement considerably. The child may have said, "I thought about taking some pills once" or "I feel like I want to run out in front of a car tonight and if that doesn't work, I will steal my father's gun and kill myself". These statements convey varying degrees of suicidal intent that are most clearly differentiated by quotes.

Reduce Report Length

Tallent (1988) gives the following instances as indices of undue length. A report is too long when:

- The psychologist is concerned that it took too long to write it.
- The psychologist has difficulty organizing all of the details for presentation.
- Some of the content is not clear or useful.
- The detail is much greater than can be put to good use.
- Speculations are presented without a good rationale for them.
- The writing is unnecessarily repetitious.
- The organization is not tight.
- The reader is irritated by the length or reads only a few sections such as the summary or recommendations sections.

The issue of length is primarily a concern of other psychologists, and it is intertwined with other issues, such as clarity. Hence, the psychologist in training should not assume that shorter is better. Quality may be a more important issue than quantity. At this early point in training the new report writer should keep the issue of length in mind while writing reports. Concerns about length, however, should never interfere with the need to portray a child's performance accurately.

Check Scores

An all too frequent and grievous error is to report scores that are incorrect. Computerized scoring represents a breakthrough that limits errors. In fact, if the facilities are available, we suggest that each test protocol that is scored by hand be checked against computer scoring. If this is not possible, the test scores should at least be doublechecked prior to finalizing a report.

One way of checking scores is to be alert to inconsistencies. If an adjudicated adolescent who was referred for conduct problems obtains an elevated T-score on depression measures and no elevations on conduct problem scales, then the score should be doublechecked to see if a scoring error is the source of the incongruity. If a score doesn't seem sensible, then the clinician should always check for a scoring error in order to rule out this possibility.

Check Spelling

Another problem with reports that detracts from the credibility of the clinician is the presence of spelling errors. Clinicians are advised to take the time to electronically and visually check their spelling.

Many psychologists now have more sophisticated tools at their disposal, such as an electronic thesaurus and grammar/usage checker. These tools can also be beneficial in that they can help to further polish the final report.

ADAPTING REPORTS TO AUDIENCE AND SETTING

There is probably no optimal report format. Psychologists often find that they have to adapt their reports to meet the needs of an ever changing audience. Audiences have varying characteristics, such as literacy levels, and, more importantly, they have differing referral questions.

In a school setting, where most of the psychological assessment of children is conducted, many referrals are for learning problems. Teachers may also be seeking information to assist them in curriculum decisions. These are very different referral questions than those that may be of interest in other questions.

In a psychiatric hospital setting, issues such as suicide potential and coping strategies may be of greater concern. These questions are very different than those of the school setting, requiring a focus on topics such as diagnosis and implications for pharmacological treatment.

Parents are yet another audience with specific questions. When conducting an evaluation for parents in a private practice setting, the emphasis may be on advising the parents on what they can do to effect change in their child's behavior. The reports used throughout this book were taken from a variety of settings with differing referral questions. The reader is advised to think carefully about the needs of referral sources when reading these reports.

THE SECTIONS OF THE PSYCHOLOGICAL REPORT

Identifying Information

Most report formats provide some identifying information on the top of the first page of the report. This section can include information such as name of the child, age, grade, birth date, and perhaps the name of the school or agency where the child is currently attending or being served. Also, most reports indicate that the report content is confidential.

Assessment Procedures

This section typically lists the assessment methods (both quantitative and qualitative) and tests that were used in the evaluation. Evaluation procedures can and frequently do include interviews, reviews of records, and classroom or other observations.

Referral Questions

This section is crucial because the referral questions dictate the design of the evaluation accompanied by their acronyms. In addition, the lack of clear referral questions may lead to consumer or referral source dissatisfaction with the report. As Tallent (1988) suggests, psychologists may have to speak more than once with the referral source to clarify the nature of the question(s).

Background Information

This section should include all of the pertinent information that may affect interpretation of a child's scores. The key word here is *pertinent*. The clinician should report only information that is relevant to the current evaluation, not information that is superfluous or an undue invasion of privacy (Teglasi, 1983). Material should only be included if it has some potential impact on the interpretation of the child's scores in order to answer the referral question(s).

While parental occupation and marital status are generally private subjects, these may be important pieces of information, given what is currently known about the effects of parental variables on child functioning.

The report writer should also be clear about the sources of information. If the father views his son as lazy, then this statement should be attributed to the father. Statements that could be used for making such attributions include the following:

According to . . .

His father/mother said . . .

His mother'/father's opinion is . . .

His teacher's view of the situation is . . .

_____ reports that . . .

_____ acknowledges that . . .

If care is not taken to make clear the sources of information, questions may arise at the time that feedback is given to involved parties.

Sensitive background information should also be corroborated, or excluded from the report if it is inflammatory and cannot be corroborated. For example, a 5-year-old may say something like "Mother shoots people," and later the psychologist discovers that the child's mother is a police officer.

Previous assessment results should also be included in this section (Teglasi, 1983). Also, previous experi-

ences with psychological or educational interventions should be noted here.

If several evaluations are already available, the report writer can simply refer the reader to another source (Zimmerman & Woo-Sam, 1976). Referring to previous evaluations can substantially reduce written report bulk.

Observations and Interview Results

In this section the behaviors that the child exhibits during the assessment are recorded. When writing this section, the number of observations made, the setting where the observations were made (e.g. school, clinic, etc.), and the person who made the observations should be identified (Teglasi, 1983).

This section is also the place to enter interview results that may assist in corroborating or rejecting hypotheses. Quotes are particularly helpful for communicating the essence of the child's self-report. A clinician may report that the child dislikes school or the clinician could report that the child dislikes school as was indicated by this quote: "My teachers have not taught me anything for the past 4 years. I think that they have cheated me by just passing me on. I haven't done more than 2 days of work in school in the last year. I'm not going back to school—it's a waste of time." The quote in this circumstance more clearly communicates the child's distaste for schooling.

Assessment Results and Interpretation

This section is where the test results for the child are reported. Some report writers prefer to integrate the results from various measures into a single section. Still others opt to divide this section into subsections according to domains assessed. The domains may include: cognitive/intellectual, academic achievement, adaptive behavior, visual/motor, and behavioral/personality. This latter section is of primary interest for this text.

Organization within the behavioral/personality section can be according to theoretical orientation, training, or other preferences of the psychologist. Most importantly, this section should provide coherent interpretations of results that relate logically to one another and to other sections, such as sections devoted to providing diagnostic considerations. Hence, this section should not simply report numerical findings that are devoid of interpretation.

Diagnostic Considerations

The decision about whether or not to include a separate portion dealing with diagnostic issues is likely influenced by setting and referral questions. Nonmedical settings, for example, may discourage the inclusion of a discussion of this nature in the psychologist's report. The omission of such a section may be in keeping with interdisciplinary approaches to making classification/diagnostic/eligibility decisions.

The format for this section can be lists or in paragraphs. A psychologist may simply list diagnoses in a manner consistent with the DSM-IV multiaxial approach. Others prefer to use a paragraph or two to more fully explain the rationale for or against making certain diagnoses.

Summary

The final section of the report is intended to give an overview of the major findings. This review helps ensure that the reader understands the major points made in the report. A rule of thumb for writing summaries is to use one sentence to summarize each section of the report. In addition, a sentence should be devoted to each major finding presented in the test results section and to each recommendation. In some cases one sentence can be used to summarize multiple findings and recommendations.

One of the common pitfalls of preparing summaries is including new information in the summary section. If a clinician introduces a new finding in the summary, then the reader is lost. The reader has no idea as to the source or rationale behind the conclusion. We suggest that students read their draft summaries carefully and check every conclusion made in the summary against the body of the report.

Signatures

Reports typically require signatures attesting to their authenticity. An important component of this seemingly unimportant aspect of the report is the necessity for clinicians to use titles that represent them accurately. Some states, for example, do not have specialty licensure, and as such, the use of a title such as Licensed Pediatric Psychologist is not appropriate. In this case a more generic term such as Licensed Psychologist should be used.

Students should also be careful to represent themselves accurately. A title such as Practicum Student, Intern, Trainee, or something similar should be used. Psychological custom also dictates the inclusion of the highest degree obtained by the clinician.

Recommendations

The recommendations part of a report is often the most difficult for new students to write. It is difficult primarily because it requires students to draw on information from a host of graduate training, practicum, and internship experiences. Regardless of the source of knowledge for writing recommendations, some common principles may be followed. Recommendations should be specific and clear (Teglasi, 1983). A recommendation for individual psychotherapy may be difficult to carry out if the specific problems that need to be addressed and other aspects of the recommendation are not made explicit. Some recommendations may also be difficult to communicate succinctly in writing. Some psychologists prefer to include handouts for treating certain problems that are much more specific than can be included in the typical recommendation section of a report. A handout detailing some specific recommendations for a teacher responding to inattentive behaviors in the classroom may be more valuable to the teacher than an abbreviated recommendation. In almost all cases the clinician should relay recommendations in person to psychiatrists, teachers, parents, and other colleagues (Teglasi, 1983) in order to ensure that they are followed.

Another way of offering suggestions in a way that increases the chances they will be carried out is to offer a sliding scale (Zimmerman & Woo-Sam, 1967). If, for example, special class placement is warranted but not practical, then perhaps tutoring should be recommended in lieu of school intervention services.

Psychometric Summary

Some clinicians include a listing of all of the child's obtained scores with the report. While this summary will be of limited value to the less knowledgeable reader, it may be of great value to another clinician who reviews the report. This summary is best placed on a separate sheet(s) of paper, which makes it convenient for the clinician to be selective about who receives the summary. Some psychologists may prefer to not send the summary to parents and virtually always send it to other psychologists.

The Report Writing Self-Test

A report-writing self-test is provided in Figure 17.3. This checklist allows the psychologist to periodically and quickly review principles of report writing.

COMMUNICATING RESULTS ORALLY

Parent Conferences

It is increasingly difficult to define the term *parent* in modern society. For the purposes of this text, *parent* is used generically to include any consistent caregiver in the child's life. Examples of such caregivers include step-parents, residential caretakers, and grandparents, among others.

Imparting assessment results to parents requires considerable savvy, as the individual differences between families are myriad. Because of this diversity there is not a singular methodology that will be effective with all parents. This section will present some ideas for sharing results with parents or other caregivers. However, it is vital for the psychologist to remain flexible in order to adapt the format of the feedback session to the needs of the parent, other caregiver, or family.

In an old but insightful article, Ricks (1959) summarized the heart of the parent conference dilemma.

> The audience of parents to which our test-based information is to be transmitted includes an enormous range and variety of minds and emotions. Some are ready and able to absorb what we have to say. Reaching others may be as hopeless as reaching TV watchers with an AM radio broadcast. Still others may hear what we say, but clothe the message with their own special needs, ideas, and predilections. (p. 4)

Regardless of the potential pitfalls, parents must be informed of the results of a psychological evaluation of their child (the legal, ethical, and regulatory mandates for this practice are given in Chapter 4).

Some helpful suggestions for communicating test results to parents are given next.

1. Avoid excessive hedging or deceit. The problem with hedging or failing to report bad news is that many parents sense this deceit and respond to the psychologist with appropriate mistrust. Honesty is also easily sensed by parents, which ultimately enhances the credibility of the psychologist.

2. Use percentile ranks heavily when describing norm referenced test results.

3. Instead of lecturing, allow parents opportunities to participate by asking about topics such as their opinion of the results and how they fit with their knowledge of their child. Moreover, listening carefully to parents helps the psychologist determine the psychological needs of the parents that are relevant to the evaluation.

4. Anticipate questions prior to the interview and prepare responses. How would a psychologist answer the question, Will my daughter outgrow her ADHD? Psychologists can gauge the probability that such questions will arise by listening carefully in the intake interview and prepare answers as part of the ongoing assessment process.

5. Schedule adequate time for the interview. Parent conferences often become more involved than one has planned. Adequate time allows the psycholo-

Item	True	False
	(circle one)	
1. Was the report edited?	T	F
2. Are there unnecessary invasions of privacy?	T	F
3. Is the referral question(s) explicitly stated?	T	F
4. Is the referral question answered?	T	F
5. Does the report emphasize numbers over words?	T	F
6. Can a person with a high school education understand the wording used?	T	F
7. Is the report so long that the major findings are lost?	T	F
8. Are the conclusions drawn without undue hedging?	T	F
9. Do the conclusions fit the data?	T	F
10. Are invalid results presented?	T	F
11. Are percentile ranks included for the benefit of parents and client?	T	F
12. Was a spellchecker used?	T	F
13. Are supporting data integrated with conclusions?	T	F
14. Are the recommendations clear and specific?	T	F
15. Are headings and lists included to enhance impact?	T	F
16. Are acronyms defined?	T	F
17. Are acronyms overused?	T	F
18. Is new information included in the summary?	T	F
19. Were scores doublechecked?	T	F
20. Are examples of behavior used to clarify meaning?	T	F
21. Are test instruments described adequately?	T	F
22. Is a conference scheduled to accompany the written report?	T	F
23. Was written parental consent obtained prior to releasing the report to interested agencies or parties?		
24. Is a feedback session scheduled with the child or adolescent?	T	F
25. Are the type and paper of professional quality (e.g., laser-quality print)?	T	F

FIGURE 17.3

Report writing self-test

gist time to use counseling skills to bring a parent feedback conference to adequate closure. Certainly, the psychologist does not want to be in the situation of delivering dire news and then sending a weeping parent home on a treacherous interstate highway. Ideally, 2 hours could be allocated for such a parent session. If a session ends early, then the psychologist is the recipient of a precious gift—extra time.

6. It is often helpful to seek practice communicating with parents from a variety of backgrounds. Some parents can be addressed as colleagues, while others may have only a limited grasp on the issues being discussed. Translators, ministers, teachers, trusted family friends, and others may serve as allies in the feedback process.

7. Avoid questionable and/or overly explicit predictions (Kamphaus, 1993). Phrases to be avoided would be statements like, "She will never go to college," or "She will always have trouble with school." These types of statements can be offensive to parents, not to mention very inaccurate.

8. Use good, basic counseling skills. Every parent likes to talk about the trials and successes of raising a child. Give parents at least some opportunity to do this, as it allows you to show interest in the child by listening to the parent's story.

9. Do not engage in counseling that is beyond your level of expertise (Lyman, 1965). Parents are often very eager to obtain advice from a professional. It is inappropriate (and unethical by most standards) for a psychologist to provide services for which he or she is not trained. If, for example, a parent requests marital counseling and you have no training in this area, you should inform the parent of this fact and offer a referral. In fact, the psychologist is wise to have referral sources readily available for such eventualities.

10. Be aware that some parents are not ready to accept some test results. Parents may impugn your skills because psychologically they cannot accept the fact that their child has a severe handicap. They may leave the session angry, and you may feel inept. The idea that every parent conference will end on a happy note is unrealistic. Examine your skills critically in response to parent feedback, but realize that some parents simply will not accept the results because of their own personal issues. An example of such a situation may involve a parent with the same handicapping condition as the child. If a parent was labeled handicapped and ridiculed by peers, then this parent may become defensive and angry at the suggestion that his or her child may have a handicap. The session with such a parent will likely end on a tense note. In many of these cases, however, the parent will adapt and accept the news after developing the psychological resources to cope with the attendant stresses. The psychologist may find this same parent to interact more positively in the next encounter. Some additional advice for oral reporting to parents is given in Box 17.1.

BOX 17.1

Research Report: Interacting with Parents

Some additional advice for oral reporting is provided in a chapter by Tuma and Elbert (1990), who give some advice for understanding and dealing with parents in the assessment process. According to these authors, parents are most concerned about child problems that increase the child's demands on them, while they may be less responsive to a child's problems at school, preferring to attribute these problems to the teacher or school situation. Parents of a delinquent child may have other issues that require consideration in the assessment process. These parents may be unwilling or reluctant to obtain an evaluation and complain that they have been compelled by some authority to seek help with their child or adolescent.

Guilt is another issue that may arise with parents. Sometimes parents are wracked with guilt about their child's behavior problems, assuming perhaps too much responsibility for their etiology. Another group of parents that may be difficult to deal with in the assessment situation is the parent(s) who is reluctant to become involved for fear that his or her own problems, learning disabilities, or psychopathology may be discovered. Such parents may delay seeking help for their child until late adolescence or early adult-

(Cont.)

BOX 17.1   *(Continued)*

hood (Tuma & Elbert, 1990), when they are seeking help primarily in order to get the child to leave the nest.

Tuma and Elbert (1990) identify four important phases of the parent feedback conference. The four components are: (1) initial conference analysis, where parents are asked for their own observations, impressions, and/or concerns about the child's behavior during an evaluation or any other concerns about the assessment process; (2) problem discussion, where the psychologist presents the various assessment findings and discusses the implications of the assessment results; (3) a consultation-like, process where recommendations and intervention planning are considered and recommendations may include those related to family, the child, the clinical facility, or the child's school; and (4) a summary, where the clinician reiterates the nature of the referral, significant assessment findings, and the recommendations and interventions to be carried out.

Tuma and Elbert (1990) further recommend that if a psychologist also has to present findings at the child's school where a large meeting will be called, it is incumbent upon the clinician to meet with the parents prior to the larger school conference. This procedure allows the parents and the psychologist to discuss aspects of the evaluation that would be inappropriate in a larger meeting because some topics may be invasions of the child's (or parents') privacy and confidentiality.

SOURCE: J. M. Tuma and J. C. Elbert, "Critical Issues and Current Practice in Personality Assessment of Children," in C. R. Reynolds and R. W. Kamphaus (Eds.), *Handbook of Psychological and Educational Assessment of Children: Personality, Behavior, and Context*, pp. 3–29 (New York: Guilford Press, 1990).

Teacher Conferences

Many of the principles used in parent conferences also apply to teachers. Several nuances, however, will be outlined here.

1. Do not monopolize a teacher's break from teaching. Some teachers get few breaks in a day. Most get a brief lunch, when they prefer to unwind with colleagues and prepare for the remainder of the day. A clinician is unlikely to command a teacher's undi-

vided attention during such breaks. If a teacher has an additional free period, it may be a good time for a conference. After school is frequently the best time to get a teacher's undivided attention for a meeting. Teachers are generally very busy people, so the pace of the meeting will be quicker than is the case for parents.

2. Teachers are interested in schooling issues. The diagnosis of conduct disorder is of less concern to teachers than getting specific recommendations for helping the child in the classroom (Teglasi, 1983). If a psychologist is not trained and/or has little experience in teacher consultation, then the assistance of someone like a qualified school psychologist should be enlisted to assist with the teacher conference.

The most important point to remember about teacher conferences is that they should take place (Zimmerman & Woo-Sam, 1967; Teglasi, 1983). Such a conference is desirable because teachers are usually involved somehow in the treatment of children and adolescents. An accurate portrayal of a child's personality can assist teachers in designing interventions to assist a child the school.

Child Feedback

This session may be the most challenging for many clinicians. The practice of giving a child feedback about an evaluation has received more emphasis recently and has even been included as part of the ethical guidelines of the National Association of School Psychologists (NASP, 1985).

The major decision that a clinician needs to make before giving feedback to a child regards the type of information that is appropriate for a child's developmental level. Clearly, the kind of feedback given to parents is inappropriate for a 5- or 6--year-old who may have extraordinary difficulty understanding the concept of a percentile rank. A child this age, however, may be able to understand the consequences of the evaluation. In this situation the child may be able to understand something like: "Remember those tests I gave you? Well, your scores were low on a couple of them. Because of this I suggested to your parents that you be tutored after school. So now, you will be going to visit a teacher after school who will help you with schoolwork."

The older the child, the more similar the feedback session becomes to the one for parents. One dramatic difference, however, is that negative feedback to a child or adolescent can have the opposite of the intended effect. That is, in most cases the goal is to improve variables such as peer-related social skills. A child who is told that he or she has poor social skills may decide to stop trying to interact with peers. In some cases the clinician's honesty could harm the child. A few options are available in cases where a clinician is concerned about such negative consequences. One option is to have someone who knows the child well and has a positive relationship with him or her help the psychologist communicate the results in a nonthreatening way to the child. A good person to fill this role is a teacher or other professional caregiver. A second possibility is to have the child's primary therapist or counselor eventually share the results with the child in a counseling session, when he or she could help the child cope with the results in a supportive setting.

In all cases involving feedback to children or adolescents it is advisable to consult with a fellow professional (e.g., teacher, counselor, speech therapist, etc.) who knows the child extremely well. This colleague can help the psychologist gauge the ability of the child to deal appropriately with the assessment results and associated interventions.

CONCLUSIONS

Report writing and oral reporting are central, not ancillary, considerations in the assessment process. The most insightful and elegant of evaluations is lost if not translated to usable information in written reports and intervention planning meetings. Unfortunately, these central assessment skills are easily overlooked in the training of clinicians who are left to acquire these skills through trial and error. Clinicians are advised to seek out expert supervision in this area if it is not readily offered. In addition, enlisting the

aid of a competent editor can markedly enhance the quality of written work. Writing is not easy. Writing skills, however, can be acquired and improved with diligence and patience. George Orwell described the writing process well when stating why he writes. Orwell said that writing a book is a horrible, exhausting struggle, like a long bout of some painful illness. Writing good assessment reports can be just as laborious and the product proportionally influential.

CHAPTER SUMMARY

1. Psychological reports are essentially public domain as they are frequently made available to parents, judges, lawyers, and other nonpsychologists, creating the opportunity for improper interpretation of the results by untrained individuals.

2. Psychological reports can be useful to other clinicians who evaluate a child who has previously been seen by a psychologist.

3. Ownby and Wallbrown (1986) conclude that psychological reports are:

    a. Considered useful to some extent by consumers such as psychiatrists and social workers

    b. Frequently criticized by these professional groups on both content and stylistic grounds

    c. May (or may not) make substantial contributions to patient management

4. Different audiences require different types of written reports.

5. Some of the common problems with report writing include:

    a. Vocabulary problems

    b. Eisegesis

    c. Report Length

    d. A number emphasis

    e. Failure to address referral questions

6. Some research has shown that teachers prefer a question-and-answer report format.

7. Parents also tend to prefer a question-and-answer

format to other formats, although the difference in preference scores between the psycho-educational and question-and-answer reports in one study failed to reach statistical significance.

8. Suggested report writing practices include:

   a. Report only pertinent information.

   b. Define abbreviations and acronyms.

   c. Emphasize words rather than numbers.

   d. Reduce difficult words.

   e. Describe the tests used.

   f. Edit the report at least once.

   g. Use headings and lists freely.

   h. Use examples of behavior to clarify meaning.

   i. Reduce report length.

   j. Check scores.

   k. Use a spellchecker.

9. Psychological reports often include some or all of the following headings.

   a. Identifying Information

   b. Assessment Procedures

   c. Referral Questions

   d. Background Information

   e. Observations and Interview Results

   f. Assessment Results and Interpretation

   g. Diagnostic Considerations

   h. Summary

   i. Signatures

   j. Recommendations

   k. Psychometric Summary

10. Hints for communicating intelligence test results to parents include:

    a. Avoid excessive hedging or deceit.

    b. Use percentile ranks heavily when describing test results.

    c. Allow parents opportunities to participate.

    d. Anticipate questions prior to the interview and prepare responses.

    e. Schedule adequate time for the interview.

    f. Practice communicating with parents from a variety of backgrounds.

    g. Avoid questionable predictions.

    h. Use good, basic counseling skills.

    i. Do not engage in counseling that is beyond your level of expertise.

    j. Be aware that some parents are not ready to accept some of the conclusions offered.

11. Teacher conferences are important for ensuring cooperation with recommendations.

12. The major decision that a clinician needs to make before giving feedback to a child regards the type of information that is appropriate for the child's developmental level.

Assessment of Disruptive Behavior Disorders

CHAPTER QUESTIONS

- What are some findings from research on attention-deficit hyperactivity disorder (ADHD) that have important implications for designing clinical assessments for children suspected of having ADHD?

- What are some practical guidelines for designing an assessment battery for children suspected of having ADHD and interpreting assessment results?

- What are the implications of research on childhood conduct problems for designing clinical assessments for children with these problems?

- What basic questions should be addressed in clinical assessments of children with conduct problems?

INTRODUCTION

This chapter is the first of a series of chapters focusing on the assessment of several specific types of childhood emotional and behavioral problems. These chapters are designed to help an assessor apply information on the various assessment strategies discussed in previous chapters to the assessment of some of the more common types of psychopathology exhibited by children and adolescents. We start with the assessment of disruptive behavior disorders, sometimes called externalizing behaviors (Achenbach & Edelbrock, 1978) or disorders of undercontrol (Quay, 1986). It is appropriate to start our syndrome-by-syndrome discussion with this class of behaviors because they tend to be the most common reason for referral to child mental health clinics (Frick et al., 1993).

This predominance in clinic referrals is out of proportion to the prevalence of disruptive behavior disorders in the general population, where emotional difficulties are often as prevalent (Anderson et al., 1987). This high referral rate for disruptive behavior disorders is likely due to two factors. First, unlike adult mental health referrals, children and adolescents are rarely self-referred. Instead, they are often referred by significant others (e.g., parents, teachers, physicians) in their environment. Second, disruptive behavior disorders, as the name implies, are syndromes of behavior that cause significant disruptions in a child's environment, often directly affecting those responsible for referring a child for assessment and treatment. Thus, anyone working in a clinical setting with children and adolescents must have a firm understanding of these types of behavioral difficulties.

To reiterate a common theme of this book, our recommendations for assessing children with disruptive behaviors disorders are based on research on the basic characteristics of these disorders. In each of the following sections we first provide a brief discussion of the most clinically relevant research findings and then discuss specific recommendations for assessment procedures based on these findings. Consistent with a large body of research (see Hinshaw, 1987), we divide our discussion into two sections corresponding to the major subdivisions within the disruptive behavior disorders. The first section involves a discussion of a syndrome of behaviors involving inattention-disorganization and impulsivity-motor hyperactivity labeled as Attention-Deficit Hyperactivity Disorder (ADHD) by the DSM-IV (American Psychiatric Association, 1994). The second section focuses on conduct problems and aggression subsumed under the categories of Oppositional Defiant Disorder (ODD) and Conduct Disorder (CD) (American Psychiatric Association, 1994).

ATTENTION-DEFICIT HYPERACTIVITY DISORDER

Classification and Subtypes

History

The syndrome of ADHD has long been recognized in the medical and psychological literature. However, there has been considerable disagreement over what are the core features of the disorder. As a result of this confusion, there have been numerous changes in diagnostic definitions (see Frick & Lahey, 1991). This evolution in our conceptualization of ADHD is reflected in changes in the diagnostic criteria for

ADHD over the most recent revisions of the *Diagnostic and Statistical Manual of Mental Disorders.* The second edition of the DSM included a syndrome of the Hyperkinetic Reaction of Childhood to emphasize the belief that motor hyperactivity is the core feature of the disorder (DSM-II; American Psychiatric Association, 1968). In the third edition of the DSM the disorder was reconceptualized to emphasize deficits in sustained attention, coining the term attention-deficit disorder (DSM-III; American Psychiatric Association, 1980). Also in the DSM-III, it was explicitly recognized for the first time that children could have attention deficits in the absence of motor hyperactivity. The next revision, DSM-III-R, softened this emphasis on attention deficits, placing it on equal footing with motor hyperactivity in its definition of Attention-Deficit Hyperactivity Disorder (American Psychiatric Association, 1987). The DSM-III-R criteria also did away with subtypes based on the presence or absence of motor activity.

Before discussing the most recent revision of the DSM (DSM-IV; American Psychiatric Association, 1994), it is important to highlight two main sources of variation in these various conceptualizations of the disorder. First, a main source of debate has been over what are the *core features* of the disorder. For example, DSM-III proposed three core dimensions of behavior associated with attention-deficit disorders: (1) inattention (e.g., very distractible, difficulty finishing things), (2) impulsivity (e.g., acts without thinking, interrupts others, loses things, makes careless mistakes), and (3) hyperactivity (e.g., fidgety and restless, running around and climbing excessively). In contrast, DSM-III-R eliminated any distinctions among these behaviors and considered all three dimensions to be indicative of a single domain of behavior.

Research has fairly consistently suggested that the truth is somewhere in between. Specifically, factor analyses have generally been able to document two partially independent dimensions of behavior: inattention/disorganization and impulsivity/overactivity (Lahey et al., 1988). The behaviors that are generally considered to be the core features of ADHD are listed in Box 18.1.

The second source of contention evident through the revisions of the DSM is the debate over whether

Box 18.1

Core Features of Attention-Deficit Hyperactivity Disorder

Inattention-Disorganization	Impulsivity-Hyperactivity
Doesn't follow through on instructions	Has difficulty waiting in line
Fails to finish things	Has difficulty awaiting turn
Has difficulty sustaining attention	Interrupts others
Doesn't seem to listen	Intrudes on others' activities
Loses things	Blurts out answers to questions
Fails to give attention to details	Has difficulty playing quietly
Has difficulty organizing tasks	Has trouble remaining seated
Is forgetful	Runs around and climbs excessively
Avoids tasks requiring sustained effort	Fidgets and squirms in seat
Is easily distracted	Talks excessively
Daydreams	Cannot sit still
Seems sluggish or drowsy	Impulsively engages in physically dangerous activities
Seems unmotivated	

NOTE: These symptoms formed the initial item pool for the DSM-IV field trials for the Disruptive Behavior Disorders and were selected based on reviews of the literature and reanalyses of existing data sets (Frick et al., 1994). Not all symptoms were selected for the final DSM-IV criteria (American Psychiatric Association, 1994), and some symptoms were combined and reworded.

there are *valid subtypes* of ADHD. DSM-III proposed the existence of two types of attention-deficit disorder: Attention Deficit Disorder without Hyperactivity (ADD/WO) and Attention Deficit Disorder with Hyperactivity (ADD/H). These subtypes shared the core features of inattention and impulsivity but differed on the presence of motor hyperactivity. Frick and Lahey (1991) summarize a significant body of research attesting to the validity of this distinction. Children with ADD/H tend to exhibit more conduct problems, to be more impulsive, and to be more socially rejected than children with ADD/WO. In contrast, children with ADD/WO tend to be more sluggish and drowsy (often described as unmotivated), to be more anxious and shy, and to be more likely to show an optimal response to low doses of stimulant medication than children with ADD/H. Based on their review of the research, these authors concluded that the decision to eliminate the subtypes in the DSM-III-R was not consistent with this body of research.

DSM-IV

The DSM-IV definition of ADHD was designed to reflect the research findings on both of these issues (American Psychiatric Association, 1994). First, there are two symptom lists, which closely correspond to the two dimensions of behavior described in Box 18.1. Second, the DSM-IV recognizes the existence of subtypes based largely on the presence of hyperactivity. There is an ADHD—Inattentive Type to designate children with problems of inattention and disorganization but without problems of impulsivity and overactivity. In addition, there are the ADHD—Hyperactive Type and ADHD—Combined Type to designate children with significant problems of impulsivity-hyperactivity, either in combination with or in isolation from problems of inattention and disorganization.

The DSM-IV definition of ADHD also attempted to incorporate research on two additional issues related to the diagnosis of ADHD that also have important implications for the assessment process: (1) the question of a minimum age at which symptoms of ADHD must be present and (2) the situational variability of symptoms. The designation of a minimum age at which symptoms must be evident is based on the fact that most people conceptualize ADHD as part of a life-long temperament (Barkley, 1990). Consistent with this way of viewing ADHD, research has documented that many of the behaviors associated with ADHD are first evident very early in a child's life (Loeber et al., 1992). As a result, most classification systems place a minimum age of onset based on the assumption that if symptoms first appeared after this age, it should not be considered ADHD. For example, DSM-IV places the minimum age of onset as no later than 7 years old.

The problem with the age-of-onset criterion for clinical assessments is a practical one. It is often difficult to obtain an accurate estimate of the age at which the child first started to show symptoms. For many children, the symptoms are not noticeable until demands are placed on them to sit still and pay attention, such as when they begin to attend school (Barkley, 1990). Even then, the demands on children to sustain attention and to be organized are minimal in the first several years of school and, as a result, children solely with problems of inattention and disorganization may not be detected until much later in school (Loeber, Green, & Lahey, 1990). As a result, it is often difficult to disentangle behavioral tendencies of the child and when they first became problematic due to changes in the situational demands placed on a child.

The *situational variability* in a child's ADHD symptoms has led some authors to conceptualize ADHD as a problem in behavioral regulation (e.g., Barkley, 1990). That is, the primary deficit in ADHD may be the inability of a child to regulate his or her behavior to differing situational demands. Research indicates that there are individual variations in this factor. Some children with ADHD show problematic behaviors in only a few situations and other children with ADHD show problems in multiple situations. These two groups have been labeled as situationally and pervasively hyperactive children, respectively (Schachar, Rutter, & Smith, 1981).

There are three main implications of the situationality of the primary symptoms of ADHD for clinical assessments. First, assessors should expect situational variability in ADHD behaviors when assessing a child in different contexts. Second, one should assess the environmental demands of a situation to see if this can explain the variations in behavior. Third, a child should show ADHD behavior in multiple situations with equivalent demands, so that one can rule out the possibility that the child's behavior is *solely* a function of some aspect of his or her environment. To capture this last aspect of ADHD, the DSM-IV criteria includes the requirement that impairment from symptoms is present in two or more settings (American Psychiatric Association, 1994). Because of the dependence of ADHD behavior on the demands of the situation, we interpret this criterion to mean that impairment must be present in two or more settings *with equivalent demands on the child.*

Comorbidities

Children with ADHD are an excellent example of the fact that children with problems in one area of adjustment are at risk for problems in other areas as well. Problems that often co-occur with ADHD are quite important clinically. They often cause more disruptions for the child and predict poorer outcome than the primary ADHD symptoms themselves (Frick & Lahey, 1991). As a result, the secondary features are often a major focus of intervention (Abikoff & Klein, 1992).

Conduct Problems/Aggression

The most common co-occurring problems experienced by children with ADHD are conduct problems and aggression, with research suggesting that 60–75% of children referred to clinics with ADHD show significant levels of these problems (Hinshaw, 1987). It is often these conduct problems that lead to a great deal of disruption for children with ADHD, leading to multiple disciplinary confrontations with parents and teachers, school suspensions, and problems in peer relations. In addition, these conduct problems are often predictive of poor outcomes in adolescence and young adulthood, especially for predicting delinquency and substance abuse (Mannuzza et al., 1989).

Other Comorbidities

Another condition that often occurs with ADHD is academic underachievement or a learning disability, both of which are frequently defined as school achievement below a level predicted by a child's age and intellectual level. Approximately 30% of children with ADHD show such learning problems (Frick et al., 1991). In addition, children with ADHD tend to show a high rate of conflict with peers (Johnston, Pelham, & Murphy (1985), with parents (Befera & Barkely, 1985), and with teachers (Whalen, Henker, & Dotemoto, 1980). And not surprisingly, given the amount of difficulty and conflict the ADHD child often experiences in his or her environment, children with ADHD often show low self-esteem that persists throughout childhood and into adolescence (Weiss, Hechtman, & Perlman, 1978).

Alternative Causes of Attention Deficits and Motor Restlessness

Most conceptualizations of ADHD consider it a neurologically based temperament that is present through the majority of a child's life and which significantly interferes with a child's functioning in one or more major life areas (Barkley, 1990; Frick & Lahey, 1991). However, there are several medical and psychological conditions that can lead to problems in sustained attention and to problems in motor restlessness that most people would not consider to be ADHD. In many cases, children with these other conditions do not show the severity or chronicity of symptoms that children with ADHD typically display. Therefore, a careful assessment of the number and severity of ADHD symptoms is an important part of ruling out alternative causes for the symptoms. When asked to assess for possible ADHD, a clinical assessor should

be aware of conditions that could lead to ADHD symptoms and mimic the disorder.

Neurological trauma (e.g., head injuries) and other more subtle neurological dysfunctions (e.g., absence seizures) can affect a child's ability to sustain attention (Corbett & Trimble, 1983; Rutter, Chadwick, & Shaffer, 1983). In fact, children with ADHD were at one time labeled minimal brain-damaged because ADHD symptoms resembled the behaviors of patients with neurological trauma (Strauss & Lehtinen, 1947). Several metabolic and endocrine disorders (e.g., diabetes), if not appropriately controlled, can affect attention (Johnson, 1988). Even certain medications prescribed to children for physical illnesses can affect a child's ability to sustain attention and increase his or her motor restlessness (Hynd & Willis, 1988).

Alternative causes for a child's attentional difficulties need not be medical. Children with mental handicaps (Crnic & Reid, 1989) or children with learning disabilities (Rourke & Strang, 1983) can show attentional problems secondary to other deficits in cognitive processing. Attentional problems are often one manifestation of emotional distress. In fact, most definitions of depression include an inability to concentrate and motor restlessness as part of the diagnostic criteria (American Psychiatric Association, 1994). Similarly, children with anxiety disorders often show a marked degree of motor tension and restlessness that is difficult to distinguish from the fidgetiness and restlessness often displayed by children with ADHD (Strauss, 1990).

The implication of this discussion is that the clinical assessor must decide whether or not the symptoms of ADHD are *solely* due to another physical or emotional condition. This is a difficult task because, as mentioned previously, children with ADHD are at risk for showing most of these problems *secondary to the ADHD*. The clinical assessment then becomes largely a task of deciding what is most likely to be primary and what is most likely to be secondary, a process that was discussed in more detail in Chapter 16.

Implications for Assessment

In Box 18.2 we summarize the main implications of research on ADHD for designing an appropriate assessment battery for children or adolescents suspected of having ADHD. (In addition, in Boxes 18.5 and 18.6 we provide two case examples of a typical ADHD assessment battery, with Box 18.5 describing the assessment of a child with ADHD—Hyperactive Type and Box 18.6 describing the assessment of a child with ADHD—Inattentive Type.)

Assessing Core Behaviors

Guided by the research on classification of ADHD, the first goal of the assessment is to assess the core features of ADHD. Many of the behavior rating scales (Chapters 6, 7, and 8) and structured interviews (Chapter 12) discussed in previous chapters provide scales or sections that assess for these core behaviors. These behaviors can also be assessed through behavioral observations (Chapter 9; see also Barkley, 1991).

In selecting specific scales to assess the core features of ADHD, several key factors should be considered. First, one should pay close attention to item content. Many measures are based on outdated conceptualizations of ADHD or the scales were formed strictly on the basis of statistical covariation, without any guiding theory to help in scale definition. As a result, many scales that purport to measure behaviors associated with ADHD also include behaviors that are not currently viewed as being part of the primary symptom clusters. Unfortunately, these less relevant behaviors are intermixed with core behaviors, and, as a result, many measures have no pure indicator of ADHD symptoms. Some of the more common omnibus rating scales with subscales that assess ADHD behaviors are presented in Box 18.3 to illustrate this point. Evident from this table is the fact that a child may have elevations on many scales that purport to measure ADHD *without actually*

BOX 18.2

The Nature of ADHD and Implications for Assessment

Focus of Research	Implications for Assessment
Classification and Presence of Subtypes	Assess for presence of two core dimensions of behavior—inattention/disorganization and impulsivity/overactivity.
	Assess developmental inconsistency of core behaviors.
	Assess for subtypes based on presence of impulsivity/overactivity.
	Assess duration to determine if behaviors are chronic and stable.
	Assess situational variability of behaviors.
Presence of Multiple Comorbidities	Assess for presence of conduct problems/aggression.
	Assess for presence of learning problems.
	Assess self-esteem.
	Assess social relationships and peer social status.
	Assess level of parent–child and teacher–child conflict.
Potential Alternative Causes	Obtain a developmental and medical history.
	Assess for intellectual and learning deficits.
	Assess for emotional difficulties.

Box 18.3

Commonly Used Behavior Rating Scales with Subscales Related to ADHD: An Illustration of Item Heterogeneity

As mentioned in the text, many of the more commonly used parent and teacher rating scales have very heterogeneous item content with respect to ADHD. Most of the scales that purport to measure constructs related to ADHD contain a large number of behaviors not considered to be part of the core symptoms of ADHD. To illustrate this, we list the item content of subscales purporting to measure ADHD behaviors from commonly used omnibus rating scales and we highlight in boldface type the items that are not tied to the two core dimensions of ADHD: inattention-disorganization and impulsivity-hyperactivity (see Box 18.1).

Behavior Assessment System for Children (Reynolds & Kamphaus, 1992)

Parent Rating Scales (ages 6–11)		Teacher Rating Scales (ages 6–11)	
ATTENTION PROBLEMS (7 ITEMS)	HYPERACTIVITY (10 ITEMS)	ATTENTION PROBLEMS (8 ITEMS)	HYPERACTIVITY (13 ITEMS)
Listens to directions	Cannot wait to take turn	Gives up easily when learning something new	Rushes through assigned work
Forgets things	**Needs too much supervision**	Does not pay attention to lectures	Taps foot or pencil
Gives up easily when learning something new	Interrupts others when they are speaking	Has trouble concentrating	Interrupts others when they are speaking
Completes work on time	Makes loud noises when playing	Forgets things	**Acts silly**
Is easily distracted	Leaves seat during meals	Is easily distracted from classwork	**Bothers other children when they are working**
Completes homework from start to finish without taking a break	Is restless during movies	Listens attentively	Acts without thinking
	Climbs on things	Has a short attention span	Is overly active
	Throws tantrums		Talks too loud
	Fiddles with things while at meals		Calls out in class
			Hurries through assignments
			Cannot wait to take turn
			Seeks attention while doing schoolwork
0% not part of core ADHD symptoms	*20% not part of core ADHD symptoms*	*0% not part of core ADHD symptoms*	*23% not part of core ADHD symptoms*

(Cont.)

BOX 18.3 *(Continued)*

Child Behavior Checklist—1991 Version

Parent and Teacher Report Forms

ATTENTION PROBLEMS (11 ITEMS)

Acts too young for his/her age
Can't concentrate, can't pay attention for long
Can't sit still, restless, or hyperactive
Confused or seems to be in a fog
Daydreams or gets lost in his/her thoughts
Impulsive or acts without thinking
Nervous or high strung
Nervous movements or twitching
Poor schoolwork
Poorly coordinated or clumsy
Stares blankly

45% not part of core ADHD symptoms

Comprehensive Behavior Rating Scale for Children (Neeper, Lahey, & Frick, 1990)

INATTENTION-DISORGANIZATION (11 ITEMS)	MOTOR HYPERACTIVITY (4 ITEMS)	DAYDREAMING (3 ITEMS)
Looks around the room or leaves tasks when he or she shouldn't	Fidgets and squirms	Daydreams a great deal
Has difficulty with tasks that require sustained attention	Makes distracting hoises	Stares into space
Responds to questions before thinking through answers	Acts impulsively	Seems to be in world of his or her own
Seems less mature than other children of same age and sex	Is constantly in motion	
Becomes disorganized when changing from one task to another		
Is easily distracted		
Doesn't seem to listen; acts as if he or she never hears teacher instructions		
Seems scatterbrained or confused; is unable to organize and focus on a specific task		
Does not complete class assignments		
Does not try again if he or she fails at a task		

(Cont.)

BOX 18.3   *(Continued)*

Comprehensive Behavior Rating Scale for Children (Neeper, Lahey, & Frick, 1990)

INATTENTION-DISORGANIZATION (11 ITEMS)	MOTOR HYPERACTIVITY (4 ITEMS)	DAYDREAMING (3 ITEMS)
Shifts from one task to another before finishing first task		
9% not part of core ADHD symptoms	*0% not part of core ADHD symptoms*	*0% not part of core ADHD symptoms*

Conners Parent Rating Scale—93		Conners Parent Rating Scale—48	

Conners Rating Scales (Conners, 1989)

RESTLESS-DISORGANIZED (8 ITEMS)	HYPERACTIVE-IMMATURE (17 ITEMS)	LEARNING PROBLEMS (4 ITEMS)	IMPULSIVE-HYPERACTIVE (4 ITEMS)
Restless or overactive	**Picky and finicky**	**Difficulty learning**	Excitable, impulsive
Excitable, impulsive	Restless	Fails to finish things	**Wants to run things**
Constantly fidgeting	**Gets stiff and rigid**	Distractible/short attention span	Restless or "squirmy"
Always climbing	**Twitches, jerks, etc.**	**Easily frustrated**	Restless, always on the go
A very early riser	**Shakes**		
Demands must be met immediately	Runs to bathroom constantly		
Can't stand too much excitement	**Bites or picks nails**		
Acts as if driven by a motor	**Chews on clothes, blankets, or other things**		
	Picks at things such as hair, clothing, etc.		
	Cries easily		
	Wants help doing things s/he should do alone		
	Clings to parents or other adults		
	Lets him/herself get pushed around by other children		
	Feelings easily hurt		
	Restless or overactive		
	Excitable, impulsive		

(Cont.)

BOX 18.3   *(Continued)*

Conners Parent Rating Scale—93		**Conners Parent Rating Scale—48**	
RESTLESS-DISORGANIZED (8 ITEMS)	HYPERACTIVE-IMMATURE (17 ITEMS)	LEARNING PROBLEMS (4 ITEMS)	IMPULSIVE-HYPERACTIVE (4 ITEMS)
	Fails to finish things s/he starts; short attention span		
38% not part of core ADHD symptoms	*50% not part of core ADHD symptoms*	*50% not part of core ADHD symptoms*	*25% not part of core ADHD symptoms*

Conners Teacher Rating Scale—28

HYPERACTIVITY (7 ITEMS)	INATTENTIVE-PASSIVE (8 ITEMS)
Restless in the squirmy sense	Distractibility or attention span problems
Makes inappropriate noises	Daydreams
Demands must be met immediately	**Appears to be easily led by other children**
Disturbs other children	**Appears to lack leadership**
Restless	Fails to finish things
Excitable, impulsive	**Childish/immature**
Excessive demand for teacher attention	**Easily frustrated in efforts**
	Difficulty learning
29% not part of core ADHD symptoms	*63% not part of core ADHD symptoms*

Personality Inventory for Children—Revised (Lachar, 1984)

HYPERACTIVITY SCALE (38 ITEMS)

Others think my child is mean	When my child gets mad, watch out
My child often cheats other children in deals	My child tends to be pretty stubborn
My child loses most friends because of his/her temper	My child usually comes when called
My child seems to enjoy destroying things	My child will do anything on a dare
My child usually doesn't trust others	My child is shy with adults
Speaking up is no problem for my child	My child has usually been a quiet child
My child is shy with children his/her own age	My child seems to be serious minded
My child doesn't seem to care to be with others	My child is exceptionally neat and clean
My child always insists on wearing clean clothes	My child seems to get along with everyone
Usually my child gets along well with others	My child tends to brag
The school says my child needs help in getting along with other children	My child worries about hurting others
My child learned to count by age 6 years	My child usually runs rather than walks
My child shows a lot of affection for a pet	My child's behavior makes others angry
	My child stays close to me when we go out
	My child is adopted

(Cont.)

Box 18.3   *(Continued)*

HYPERACTIVITY SCALE (38 ITEMS)

My child can't seem to keep attention on anything
School teachers complain that my child can't sit still
My child tends to swallow food without chewing it
How to raise the child has never been a problem at our house

My child has been difficult to manage
There is a lot of tension in our home
My child sweats very little
My child seems to enjoy talking about nightmares

87% not part of core ADHD symptoms

Revised Behavior Problem Checklist (Quay & Peterson, 1983)

ATTENTION-PROBLEM IMMATURITY (16 ITEMS)	MOTOR EXCESS (5 ITEMS)
Short attention span; poor concentration	Restless; unable to sit still
Inattentive to what others say	**Tense, unable to relax**
Irresponsible, undependable	Hyperactive; "always on the go"
Passive, suggestive; easily led by others	**Nervous, jittery, jumpy; easily startled**
Distractible; easily diverted from the task at hand	Squirms, fidgets
Sluggish, slow-moving, lethargic	
Drowsy; not "wide awake"	
Answers without stopping to think	
Unable to work independently; needs constant help and attention	
Impulsive; starts before understanding what to do; doesn't stop and think	
Slow and not accurate in doing things	
Does not finish things; gives up easily; lacks perseverance	
Absentminded; forgets simple things easily	
Acts like he or she were much younger; immature, "childish"	
Has trouble following directions	
Schoolwork is messy, sloppy	

19% not part of core ADHD symptoms	*40% not part of core ADHD symptoms*

---

showing the core features of the disorder. Therefore, when selecting a scale to use in an assessment of possible ADHD, an important consideration is whether it contains scales that are largely composed of ADHD symptoms. Further, when interpreting scale elevations on a given rating scale, one must be sure that the elevations were actually due to the behaviors associated with ADHD.

Second, many measures simply do not have sufficient coverage of the core ADHD behaviors to aid in the differentiation of the two subtypes of ADHD. Often behaviors indicative of inattention-disorganization are intermixed with impulsive and overactive behaviors, providing no method of determining subtypes. For example, from Box 18.3 one notices that the CBCL-91 (Achenbach, 1991) Attention Problems scale includes items associated with inattention-disorganization and impulsivity-motor hyperactivity. As a result, use of this overall clinical scale does not aid in distinguishing subtypes of ADHD. Typically, structured interviews that are tied to diagnostic classification systems and are updated as the classification system is updated have the best symptom coverage. Structured interviews also allow one to determine the duration and stability of ADHD behaviors, which, as discussed previously, is crucial in the assessment of ADHD.

Third, when selecting measures to assess the core features of ADHD, one must obtain information from multiple sources (parents and teachers). This helps one determine the situational variability of behaviors. Also, if the core features of ADHD can be assessed through multiple modalities (e.g., rating scales and behavioral observations), this negates the need to rely on any single imperfect assessment instrument. Therefore, one must choose a set of assessment instruments that provides a multi-informant and multimodal assessment of the core ADHD behaviors.

Fourth, one should have information that allows comparison to age norms. Most definitions of ADHD either implicitly or explicitly state that the symptoms should be inconsistent with a child's developmental level (American Psychiatric Association, 1994). Therefore, an assessment must provide information that allows one to compare a child's behaviors to the behaviors of other children of a similar developmental level. Typically, behavior rating scales are best suited for this task because of their extensive normative base. However, one important caution is in order in using norm-referenced rating scales. Many scales (e.g., the Conners' Rating Scales and the CBCL-91) often only provide norm-referenced scores broken down by *age and gender*. Definitions of ADHD do not make the restriction that the behaviors be inconsistent for a child's gender. In fact, it is well accepted that boys are six to nine times more likely to show ADHD than girls (American Psychiatric Association, 1994). Using gender-specific norms ignores

this widely found and accepted gender ratio and artificially equates the number of girls and boys with significant levels of ADHD behaviors. This will lead to more girls and fewer boys being considered to have significant ADHD behaviors than if cross-gender norms are used.

Fifth, researchers on children with ADHD have often used *laboratory measures* of inattention and impulsivity in the assessment of the core ADHD behaviors. One of the most frequently used laboratory measure for the assessment of ADHD is the Continuous Performance Test (CPT). There are many variations of the CPT, but a prototypical CPT is the one developed by Gordon (1983). In the Gordon CPT a child is told to view a screen on which numbers are presented. The child is instructed to press a button each time a predetermined number is presented. Two responses are measured. Omissions are the number of times the designated number is presented to the child and the child fails to press the button. Number of omissions is considered to be a measure of sustained attention, especially increases in omissions over time. Commissions are the number of times the child incorrectly presses the button when the designated number is not presented, which is considered a measure of impulsivity.

There are many variations of the CPT, with some tasks presenting auditory rather than visual stimuli and other tasks presenting distracters with the target stimuli. By varying different aspects of the laboratory measures, researchers have begun to tease apart the types of attentional deficits that underlie ADHD. However, despite their success as research tools, their use in clinical assessments is less well established. Scores from the laboratory measures generally show low correlations with behavioral observations and parent and teacher reports (e.g., interviews and rating scales) of ADHD symptoms (Barkley, 1991; DuPaul et al., 1992). Since treatment decisions are frequently based on the more ecologically valid measures, the role of laboratory measures in clinical assessments is uncertain at this point. In Box 18.4 we summarize Barkley's (1991) review of laboratory measures of ADHD symptoms, which highlights the issue of their ecological validity.

One final note is in order for assessing the core

Box 18.4

Research Note: Ecological Validity of Laboratory Measures of Attention and Impulsivity

Barkley (1991) provides a critical discussion of laboratory measures (LM) used to assess attention and impulsivity, two aspects of the core symptoms of ADHD. The focus of much of Barkley's discussion is on reaction time tasks (RTT), continuous performance tasks (CPT), and the Matching Familiar Figures Test (MFFT). Although Barkley also discusses analogue observations of motor activity, these were discussed previously in Chapter 9.

Concept of Ecological Validity

The first issue addressed in this article is the concept of ecological validity. Barkley defined ecological validity as the "degree to which LMs represent the actual behaviors of interest (i.e., inattention and impulsivity) as they occur in naturalistic settings" (p. 150). This aspect of validity is crucial for clinical assessments. In contrast, most research projects have the goal of determining the "core deficit" in ADHD, which may not be manifested in the natural setting. Therefore, a LM "need not be ecologically valid to be useful in research on ADHD" (p. 151).

Evidence for Ecological Validity

One type of research on the ecological validity of LMs are studies testing group differences on LMs between ADHD and control children. In general, Barkley's review suggested that all of the LMs have consistently differentiated ADHD from normal control children. However, most studies indicate that these affects are weakened or eliminated when differences in intellectual level are controlled. Also, LMs do not differentiate ADHD children from other clinic-referred children. As a result, scores on the LMs are not useful in making differential diagnoses within clinic referrals.

A second type of research investigates the effect of stimulant medication on a child's performance on the LMs. Barkley's conclusion was that the research evidence was mixed. Several studies found significant effects for stimulant medication on commonly used LMs, whereas many studies found no such reliable effect.

A third type of research investigated the correlations between scores on LMs and parent and teacher ratings of ADHD behavior. Studies have generally found significant but modest (.21–.51) correlations between LM measures of attention and impulsivity and parent and teacher ratings of behaviors considered to be indicative of these constructs.

Conclusions

Barkley concludes that the ecological validity of LMs should be considered limited based on the existing research. As a result, clinical research should avoid using LMs as the "gold standard" against which other measures of attention and impulsivity are judged. For clinical assessments, one should recognize the limited usefulness of LMs in an assessment battery. Most clinical decisions are based on the more ecologically valid measures of parent and teacher report of a child's behavior in the naturalistic setting. Barkley concludes, "Where LM results conflict with those obtained from other sources, such as parent and teacher behavior ratings, history, and observations in natural settings, the LM results should probably be disregarded in favor of these more ecologically valid sources" (p. 173). As a result, the incremental benefit of adding LMs to an assessment battery seems to be minimal.

SOURCE: R. A. Barkley (1991), "The Ecological Validity of Laboratory and Analogue Assessment Methods of ADHD," *Journal of Abnormal Child Psychology, 19,* 149–178.

features of ADHD. Despite widespread cautions against the practice (e.g., Barkley, 1990; Kamphaus, 1993; Kaufman, 1994), clinical assessors continue to use the Freedom from Distractibility (FD) factor from the Wechsler Intelligence Scales for Children (Wechsler, 1974, 1989) as an indicator of the presence of ADHD symptoms. This inappropriate use of FD is largely maintained simply because of the name given the factor, which is a significant source of distress to the person who first applied the FD label to the WISC subtests. Alan Kaufman states, "The label should have been trashed years ago. I cringe whenever I read it" (Kaufman, 1994, p. 212).

As Kaufman (1994) goes on to explain, the use of the FD as a measure of inattention or distractibility is inappropriate because these scales are affected by multiple emotional and behavioral factors, not just distractibility. To illustrate the point, Kaufman reviewed 19 studies in which the FD was lower in samples of children with learning disabilities, children with leukemia, children with emotional difficulties, heterogeneous psychiatric samples of inpatient or outpatient children, children with autism, children with schizophrenia, children with conduct disorder, and children with muscular dystrophy. The author then makes the cogent point that the FD factor is important because of its robust ability to differentiate abnormal (medically, behaviorally, educationally) from normal populations, but it is basically meaningless for identifying a specific type of exceptionality, such as ADHD.

Assessing Comorbid Problems

Many of the problems that often co-occur with ADHD can be assessed in conjunction with the assessment of the core ADHD behaviors. For example, many of the omnibus rating scales and structured interviews discussed in previous chapters include items that assess for conduct problems, anxiety, depression, self-esteem, and social competence. Like the ADHD behaviors themselves, potential co-occurring problems are best assessed through multiple informants and using multiple formats. Given the overlap with learning problems, psycho-educational testing should also be a part of most ADHD assessments. Learning difficulties are not reliably assessed through rating scales, interviews, behavioral observations, or projective testing; standardized intelligence and achievement tests are often required as part of a comprehensive evaluation for ADHD.

Some omnibus behavior rating scales include items that assess the degree of family conflict and other aspects of a child's family context. However, as discussed in Chapter 13, some assessments may require a more in-depth assessment of specific areas of family functioning that are better obtained through methods that specifically focus on the child's family context. Each aspect of family functioning that was highlighted in Chapter 13 (parenting styles and behaviors, marital conflict, and parental adjustment) is important in understanding the family context of a child with ADHD.

Assessing Potential Alternative Causes

One of the most confusing parts of assessing for ADHD is ruling out alternative causes for the symptoms. Probably the most important pieces of information for this purpose have already been discussed. If one has adequately determined that the symptoms of ADHD are of sufficient number, severity, and duration to warrant a diagnosis, most of the alternative explanations for symptoms can be ruled out as a *sole* explanation for the behaviors. Many of the alternative explanations for ADHD symptoms result in behaviors similar to ADHD, but of lower intensity and of shorter duration than is typical for children with ADHD.

Given that some medical and neurological disorders can manifest in problems of inattention-disorganization and impulsivity-hyperactivity, it is important that a thorough developmental and medical history be obtained on a child. Where the history is suggestive of the possible presence of a medical or neurological disorder, the child can be referred to a physician for a more comprehensive medical and/or neurological exam. However, most experts on ADHD feel that a full medical exam need not be a standard part of a diagnostic assessment of ADHD, since the diagnosis is primarily based on behavioral data (Barkley, 1990).

The greatest difficulty in ruling out alternative explanations for ADHD symptoms is the problem of determining what is primary and what is secondary, a general issue in clinical assessments that was previously discussed in Chapter 16. Based on the research on co-morbidities, we know that ADHD children are at risk for many other problems in adjustment, most of which can also mask as ADHD (e.g., learning disabilities, emotional disorders). The distinction between primary and secondary is largely a clinical one, based on a complex weighing of various pieces of assessment information. To summarize our suggestions from Chapter 16, several types of information may be helpful in making this difficult case formulation. Considering the level of impairment associated with different areas of dysfunction (i.e., which problem areas seem to be causing the most problems for the child) and the temporal sequencing of problem behaviors (i.e., which problems seem to predate others) can help in distinguishing primary or secondary areas of dysfunction. In addition, viewing family history data and determining if a child might be at risk for a certain type of problem given its occurrence in relatives may also aid in making differential diagnoses. Specifically for ADHD, determining if a child's parents or other first degree relatives had childhood histories of ADHD symptoms can provide valuable information in making an ADHD diagnosis.

BOX 18.5

Case Study: Evaluation of an 8-Year-Old Girl with Attention-Deficit Hyperactivity Disorder—Combined Type

Claire was 8 years, 9 months old when her mother referred her to an outpatient mental health clinic for a comprehensive psychological evaluation. Claire's mother was concerned about Claire's aggressive behavior, describing Claire as having an "uncontrollable temper" and being very defiant. Maternal report also indicated that Claire has had very inconsistent academic performance throughout her first 3 years of school, primarily because she fails to complete work and makes a lot of careless mistakes. To illustrate the effect of Claire's carelessness on her school performance, her mother described an incident the previous school year in which Claire rushed through an arithmetic test and completed all the questions as addition, even though half of the problems were subtraction and Claire knew how to do subtraction problems.

Assessment of Core Symptoms

The core symptoms of ADHD were assessed through a structured diagnostic interview conducted with Claire's mother and her teacher (DISC-2.3; Shaffer et al., 1991) and behavior rating scales completed by her mother (CBCL—1991; Achenbach, 1991) and her teacher (CBRSC; Neeper, Lahey, & Frick, 1990). On the DISC-2.3, Claire's mother and teacher both reported significant problems of inattention-disorganization, such as difficulty sustaining attention, having difficulty finishing tasks, often losing things, frequently making careless mistakes, and

having very messy work habits. In addition, these problems in attention were accompanied by significant problems of impulsivity and motor hyperactivity. Both mother and teacher indicated that Claire frequently interrupted others; often talked out in class; was very fidgety and restless in class; and could not stay in her seat, either in class or at home to eat dinner.

Consistent with a diagnosis of ADHD—Combined Type, Claire's mother reported on the structured interview that these problems have been evident since very early in Claire's life, especially the motor overactivity. In fact, maternal report indicated that Claire had been asked to leave two preschools because she was too "rambunctious" and could not sit still. Claire's teacher indicated that these symptoms of ADHD were currently interfering with her school performance to a substantial degree. On the Academic Performance Rating Scale (APRS; DuPaul, Rapport, & Perriello, 1991), Claire's teacher indicated that she was turning in less than half of the work required by the class and it often was inaccurate, despite Claire knowing the material.

Finally, parent and teacher report on the omnibus rating scales suggested that the core ADHD behaviors were more severe than would be expected in children her age. Using the age- and gender-specific norms of CBCL-91, Claire had elevations on both the Attention Problems (T-score of 75) and Thought Problems (T-score of 76) scales. Similarly, Claire's teacher on the CBRSC rated her as elevated on the Motor Hyperactivity scale, with a T-score of 79 based on the entire normative sample (across ages and gender). Whereas the CBCL-91 elevations may have been spuriously high due to comparisons restricted to girls, the elevation on the CBRSC based on a comparison to both boys and girls clearly indicated the developmental inconsistency of her behavior.

Assessment of Comorbidities

Like many children with ADHD—Combined Type, Claire also exhibited significant conduct problems. On the DISC-2.3 her parent and teacher described Claire as showing frequent temper tantrums, often arguing with adults, often refusing adults' requests, blaming others for her mistakes, and being grouchy and easily annoyed. These behaviors were rated as severe on both parent and teacher rating scales, with T-scores above 70 being obtained on the Delinquent and Aggressive Behavior scales of the parent-completed CBCL-91 and the Oppositional-Conduct Disorders scale of the teacher-completed CBRSC.

On the CBCL-91 Social Problems scale and the CBRSC Social Competence scale, mother and teacher also indi-

(Cont.)

BOX 18.5 *(Continued)*

cated that Claire's behavioral problems seemed to be affecting her peer relations. She was described by parent and teacher as being bossy and domineering in peer interactions, which had led to difficulties in making friends. However, a sociometric exercise did not indicate that Claire's social status was negatively affected by this behavior. In a class of 13, she was nominated as "Liked most" by 3 children and "Liked least" by only 2 children.

A psychoeducational evaluation did not reveal any significant learning problems. Claire's scores on the Wechsler Intelligence Scales for Children—Third Edition (WISC-III; Wechsler, 1991) were in the average to high average range in both verbal and nonverbal abilities. She did not show any significant weaknesses on the subtests of the WISC-III. Even more importantly, Claire obtained age-standard scores in the high average range on both the Reading and Math clusters of the Woodcock-Johnson Tests of Achievement—Revised (Woodcock & Johnson, 1989). Thus, there were no indications of cognitive deficits, and her achievement scores indicated that she seemed to be learning at or above a level expected for her age.

Ruling Out Alternative Causes

Claire's birth, medical, and developmental history did not suggest the presence of any medical or neurological disorder. As mentioned previously, the psychoeducational evaluation did not reveal any cognitive or learning problems that could account for the behaviors. An unstructured clinical interview did reveal that Claire reported being sexually abused over a period of 1 month during the previous summer by a paternal uncle. This alleged abuse had been reported to the local child protection agency, and Claire had been seen at the community mental health center for 3 months following the incident. However, it did not appear that Claire's difficulties could be solely accounted for by an emotional reaction to sexual abuse, for several reasons. First, the ADHD behaviors were more severe than would be expected from such a reaction, and they clearly predated the alleged abuse incident. Second, she did not show any other signs of anxiety and depression that would suggest a significant degree of emotional distress.

ADHD in the Schools: Special Education Placement

ADHD is a psychological syndrome that requires collaboration between professionals across multiple spe-

cialties (i.e., psychology, education, medicine) for assessment and treatment. Clinical assessors must be able to effectively utilize the expertise of other professionals and tailor their assessments to provide useful information to many professionals. Because ADHD often has its most dramatic and noticeable effect on a child in the school setting, collaboration with educators is particularly crucial. It is essential that assessments for ADHD be designed to provide information helpful to educators in developing appropriate interventions.

We feel strongly that not all children with ADHD require special education placement. There is ample evidence that some children with ADHD can successfully function in a regular education classroom with medication, with specific modifications of the classroom environment, and/or with structured behavioral interventions design to reduce the disrupted behaviors (see Abramowitz & O'Leary, 1991). However, designing a successful intervention program for a child with ADHD requires a clear documentation of a child's strengths and weaknesses (behaviorally, emotionally, cognitively, and academically). Simply knowing that a child has ADHD gives educators only limited information on which to base interventions, given the great diversity within children with ADHD. As a result, clinical assessments should clearly outline an individual child's competencies and deficits, with suggestions on how these abilities will influence a child's functioning in a classroom setting.

Unfortunately, some children with ADHD may require more intensive educational services, such as those offered in special education programs. To serve children in special education programs, school systems must operate under federal and state guidelines, the former of which may vary in implementation from state to state and the latter of which may vary both in content and implementation. It is imperative that clinical assessors understand the guidelines under which a school system is operating, in order to design assessments and make recommendations that enhance a school's ability to appropriately meet the educational needs of a child.

The primary piece of federal legislation that guides provision of special education services to children and adolescents is the Individuals with Disabilities Act (IDEA), which was originally passed in 1975 as

BOX 18.6

Case Study: Evaluation of an 8-Year-Old Boy with Attention-Deficit Hyperactivity Disorder—Inattentive Type

Sean was 8 years, 1 month when his teacher referred him to a child mental health clinic for a comprehensive psychological evaluation. Sean was failing most subjects in the third grade and his teacher attributed this poor performance primarily to problems in concentration. At home, Sean's mother also reported that he had difficulty completing things, was often daydreaming, and seemed to have little motivation for anything.

Assessment of Core Symptoms

The core ADHD behaviors were assessed by structured interviews (DISC-2.3) completed by Sean's parent and teacher and by parent (CBCL-91) and teacher (CBRSC, APRS) behavior rating scales. On structured interviews, both parent and teacher reported that Sean showed significant problems of inattention and disorganization, such as being very distractible, frequently daydreaming, having difficulty finishing tasks, often seeming unmotivated, and seeming very sluggish and drowsy. Although Sean was described by his mother as somewhat fidgety, neither his mother nor his teacher reported significant problems of impulsivity or overactivity.

Consistent with these reports on the structured interviews, Sean was rated as showing attentional problems on parent and teacher rating scales out of a normative range. On the CBCL-91 completed by his mother, Sean had a T-score of 69. On the teacher-completed CBRSC, he had T-scores of 76 and 71 on the Sluggish Tempo and Daydreams scales, respectively. He also had a T-score of 69 on the Inattention-Disorganization scale of the CBRSC. Consistent with a diagnosis of ADHD—Inattentive Type, his teacher's rating of Motor Hyperactivity on the CBRSC was within a normative range (T-score of 57).

Assessment of Comorbidities

On parent and teacher structured interviews, Sean was reported as having some signs of mild anxiety, including frequent stomachaches, self-conscious behaviors, and concerns about his appearance. These symptoms did not seem severe enough to warrant a diagnosis of an anxiety disorder and they did not appear out of age-normative ranges on the CBCL-91, on the CBRSC, or on the self-report

Revised Children's Manifest Anxiety Scale (Reynolds & Richmond, 1985). A psychoeducational assessment did not reveal any evidence of a learning disability. Sean's scores on the WISC-III were all within age-appropriate limits, as were his scores on the Woodcock-Johnson Tests of Achievement—Revised. An assessment of Sean's peer relations did not indicate any problems in this psychological domain, based on parent and teacher rating scales and a sociometric exercise conducted with Sean's classmates. Similarly, there were no indications from any assessment source that Sean exhibited significant conduct problems.

Ruling Out Alternative Causes

A birth, medical, and developmental history obtained from Sean's mother did not reveal any indications of significant medical or neurological problems. He reportedly had some difficulties breathing immediately following birth, but he was quickly stabilized with oxygen. Also, he had some mild allergies to dust and pollen, but these were not severe enough to require medication.

Although Sean exhibited some anxiety symptoms, they did not seem severe enough to be causing his problems in attention. Also, his anxiety seemed to be focused largely around school (e.g., stomachaches on school days, worry about tests). Therefore, it seemed more likely that Sean's anxiety was secondary to the problems caused by his attentional difficulties.

Public Law 94-142 and amended and renamed in 1990. IDEA mandates that children with disabilities be provided specially designed instruction and related services in the least restrictive environment (i.e., most contact with children without disabilities) necessary for a child to learn. Providing services to children with ADHD under IDEA has been a source of contention in many school systems, since ADHD is not listed as one of the disabilities explicitly covered under IDEA. However, many children with ADHD have secondary features that may allow them to be served under IDEA guidelines, such as speech or language impairments, emotional disturbance, or specific learning disabilities. In fact, most of the children with ADHD who require intensive special education services do so not because of the ADHD itself, but because of the additional disruptions caused by these secondary features.

Although rare, it is possible that some children with ADHD may need special education services but do not qualify under IDEA guidelines. In recent years these children have been served under a civil rights law, Section 504. Section 504 is part of the Rehabilitation Act Amendments of 1973 (PL93-112) and was designed to protect individuals with handicaps. Section 504 specifically mandates that,

> No otherwise qualified individual with handicaps in the United States, shall, solely by reason of her or his handicap, be excluded from participation in, denied the benefits of, or be subjected to, discrimination under any program or activity receiving Federal financial assistance. (29 U.S.C. Sec. 794)

It is generally accepted that ADHD qualifies as a handicap under Section 504 (Madsen, 1990) and therefore, schools must make accommodations for the individual needs of children with ADHD under this statute. Unfortunately, unlike IDEA, Section 504 does not allocate federal funding for educational interventions.

This discussion of special education laws may seem irrelevant or at least peripheral for clinical assessors who operate outside of the school system. In fact, many such assessors prefer to remain ignorant of such legal guidelines, so as not to be confined to the limits delineated in such laws. However, if one wants to aid a child with ADHD to receive needed educational services, one should understand the legal guidelines so as to be able to work collaboratively with school personnel in developing an appropriate educational plan.

CONDUCT PROBLEMS

Classification and Diagnosis

Like ADHD, conduct problems in children represent a critical mental health concern because they are highly disruptive to others in a child's environment and because they are chronic and predictive of problems later in life (Frick et al., 1993). Also like ADHD, there is considerable agreement that children with conduct problems are a very heterogeneous group. Therefore, a substantial body of research has been directed at determining the most appropriate method of classifying conduct problems into meaningful subtypes.

The most commonly used method of classifying conduct problems in children is a two-dimensional approach originally described in DSM-III and continued with some modifications in the later revisions of this manual. This system divides conduct problems into two syndromes: Oppositional Defiant Disorder (ODD) and Conduct Disorder (CD). ODD refers to a pattern of negativistic, oppositional, and stubborn behaviors, whereas CD refers to more severe antisocial and aggressive behaviors that involve serious violations of others' rights or deviations from major age-appropriate norms. A summary of the behaviors indicative of these two dimensions is provided in Box 18.7.

A detailed discussion of the validity of the ODD/CD distinction is beyond the scope of this chapter (see Frick et al., 1993; Lahey et al., 1992). However, the relationship between ODD and CD behaviors is important conceptually. First, there appears to be a hierarchical relationship between the two diagnoses. That is, most children with the more severe symptoms of CD also show the symptoms of ODD (Spitzer, Davies, & Barkley, 1990). However, the reverse is not true. There are many children with ODD who do not show the more serious conduct problems associated with CD. Second, there seems to be a developmental relationship between ODD and CD. A 3-year longitudinal study of clinic-referred boys found that 82% of the new cases of CD (n = 22) that emerged during the study period had received a diagnosis of ODD in the preceding year (Lahey et al., 1992). Therefore, ODD behaviors can be viewed as a risk factor for the development of the more severe CD.

In addition to this division of ODD and CD, several attempts have been made to distinguish among subtypes within the CD category. Distinctions have

Box 18.7

Two-Dimensional Classification of Conduct Problems

Oppositional Defiant Disorder	Conduct Disorder
Loses temper	Bullies or intimidates others
Argues with adults	
Actively defies adults	Initiates physical fights
Refuses adults' requests or rules	Has been physically cruel to others
Deliberately annoys others	Steals things of nontrivial value
Blames others for mistakes	Forced someone into sexual activity
Is angry and resentful	
Is spiteful and vindictive	Stays out after dark without parental permission, before age 13
Is touchy and easily annoyed	
	Lies to obtain goods or favors
	Has been physically cruel to animals
	Has deliberately destroyed others' property
	Has set fires with intention of causing serious damage
	Has run away from home overnight more than once
	Is often truant from school, beginning before age 13
	Has broken into someone's house, building, or car

been made between youths with CD who are capable of maintaining social relationships and/or commit antisocial acts primarily with delinquent peers (socialized/group type) and youths with CD who do not form lasting relationships and/or commit antisocial acts primarily alone (undersocialized/solitary type). Further, distinctions are also made between children who display primarily aggressive or prima-

rily nonaggressive CD symptoms and between children who show an early onset of CD symptoms (prior to age 11) or a late onset of symptoms. The literature on the validity of these methods of subtyping is often contradictory (see Lahey et al., 1992). However, undersocialized, aggressive, and early-onset forms of CD seem to indicate a more severe disturbance and one that is more persistent into adulthood. As a result of the research on age of onset, DSM-IV makes a distinction between Childhood-Onset Type (at least one symptom of CD prior to age 10) and Adolescent-Onset Type (no CD symptom prior to age 10) in its criteria for CD (American Psychiatric Association, 1994).

Comorbidities

The most common problem co-occurring with conduct problems is ADHD. We have already cited research illustrating that 60–75% of children with ADHD have a co-occurring conduct problem diagnosis. When this comorbidity is viewed from the other direction, 75–90% of children with conduct problems have a comorbid ADHD diagnosis (Abikoff & Klein, 1992; Hinshaw, 1987). This degree of overlap has led to a debate as to whether or not ADHD and conduct problems should even be considered separate psychological domains (see Rutter, 1983). We feel that the research indicates that these domains are at least partially independent (Frick, 1994; Hinshaw, 1987). However, the substantial overlap with ADHD has important clinical implications. The presence of ADHD usually signals the presence of a more severe (Walker et al., 1987) and more chronic (Abikoff & Klein, 1992) form of conduct problems in children. Also, there is growing evidence for a reduction of conduct problems among children with ADHD who have been treated with stimulant medication (Hinshaw, 1991). Therefore, clinical assessment of children with conduct problems should routinely assess for the presence of ADHD.

Children with conduct problems also frequently have a comorbid emotional disorder. In a large clinic sample (n = 177) using DSM-III-R diagnoses, 62% of a sample of children with CD had a comorbid diagnosis of an anxiety disorder (Walker et al., 1991).

Children with CD and a comorbid anxiety disorder tend to be less impaired, they tend to respond better to treatment, and they tend to have a better long-term prognosis (Quay & Love, 1977; Walker et al., 1991). Children with conduct disorders also show a high rate of depression (Harrington et al., 1991; Kovacs et al., 1988; Puig-Antich, 1982), although there is no convincing evidence that the presence of depression affects the severity or prognosis for CD (Harrington et al., 1991).

Research also indicates that approximately 20–25% of children with CD are underachieving in school relative to a level predicted by their age and intellectual abilities (Frick et al., 1991). The reason for this association is not clear, possibly because the mechanisms involved may differ depending on the age of the sample studied (Hinshaw, 1992). For example, in elementary school–age samples, much of the overlap between CD and academic underachievement seems to be due to the presence of ADHD (Frick et al., 1991). However, learning difficulties seem to predict adolescent-onset conduct problems independent of other factors (Hinshaw, 1992). Despite the lack of a definitive explanation for the correlation between learning and conduct problems, the simple fact that they co-occur so consistently warrants the assessment of learning problems when assessing children and adolescents with conduct problems.

Correlates with Potential Causal Roles

Most researchers agree that conduct problems are the result of a complex interaction of multiple causal factors (Frick, 1994). Determining what are the important causal agents and how they interact to cause conduct problems is still an area in need of more research. Past research has uncovered several factors that are *associated* with conduct disorders and *likely* play a role in their development. These factors can be summarized by four categories: biological factors, family context, social ecology, and peers. The research on the biological correlates of conduct problems in children, while crucial for developing causal theories, is not reviewed here because the current state of knowledge is not sufficiently developed to have clear implications for assessment (see Raine, 1993).

In contrast, the link between family dysfunction and conduct disorders is crucial to assessment and intervention. There seem to be at least three dimensions of family functioning that are consistently related to childhood conduct problems: parental psychiatric adjustment, marital instability/divorce, and parental socialization practices (see Frick, 1994). A meta-analysis of the research on the relationship between family functioning and conduct disorders in youth found that parental socialization practices were especially important (Loeber & Stouthamer-Loeber, 1986). To be specific, parental involvement in their child's activities, parental supervision of their child, and the use of harsh or inconsistent discipline tended to show the strongest relationships with conduct problems in children of all the variables included in the meta-analysis.

Another clinically important class of correlates are factors within the child's larger social ecology that may play a causal role in the development of conduct problems. One of the most consistently documented of these correlates has been low socioeconomic status (Frick et al., 1989). However, several other ecological factors, many of which are related to low socioeconomic status, such as poor housing, poor schools, and disadvantaged neighborhoods, have also been linked to the development of conduct problems in children (see Rutter & Giller, 1983).

Finally, research has documented a relationship between peer rejection in elementary school and the later development of conduct problems (Roff & Wirt, 1984). In addition, peer rejection in elementary school is predictive of an association with a deviant peer group (i.e., one that shows a high rate of antisocial behavior and substance abuse) in early adolescence (Dishion, Patterson, & Skinner, 1989). This relationship is important because association with a deviant peer group leads to an increase in the frequency and severity of conduct problems (Patterson & Dishion, 1985). Therefore, peer rejection may be directly related to the development of conduct problems but also may indirectly influence conduct problems by increasing the chance that the child or adolescent will associate with a deviant peer group.

multiple informants and multiple assessment techniques.

Implications for Assessment

This body of psychological research forms the basis for designing an appropriate assessment for children with conduct problems. In Box 18.8 we summarize the critical areas of research and their relevance to the assessment process. In Box 18.9 we provide a case study of a comprehensive evaluation of a child with severe conduct problems. As evident from Box 18.8, assessment of conduct problems shares several important characteristics with the assessment of ADHD. The complex and pervasive nature of conduct problems requires a comprehensive evaluation that assesses many aspects of the child's functioning and psychosocial environment. Further, conduct problems and other relevant aspects of a child's psychosocial functioning should be assessed using

Assessment of Core Features

The first goal of the assessment is to thoroughly assess the types and severity of conduct problems being exhibited by a child. This involves (1) assessing the behaviors that form the different sub-types of conduct problems, (2) assessing the age of onset of conduct problems, and (3) assessing the severity and impairment associated with conduct problems. The primary methods of assessing these important facets of conduct problems are structured interviews, behavior rating scales, and behavioral observations.

Many structured interviews and behavioral rating scales provide good coverage of the conduct problem behaviors and allow for multi-informant assessments. However, they each offer unique advantages in other respects. Behavior rating scales are more

---

BOX 18.8

The Nature of Conduct Problems and Implications for Assessment

---

Focus of Research	Implications for Assessment
Classification and Presence of Subtypes	Assess presence of ODD and CD.
	Assess undersocialized/socialized and aggressive/nonaggressive type.
	Assess age of onset of conduct problems.
Presence of Multiple Comorbidities	Assess for the presence of ADHD.
	Assess for the presence of anxiety and depression.
	Assess for the presence of learning disabilities.
Correlates with Potential Causal Roles	Assess family functioning, especially parental psychiatric status, marital conflict, and parental socialization practices.
	Assess social ecology such as community support, economic stressors, and living environment.
	Assess peer relations and association with deviant peer groups.

SOURCE: Table is adapted from Frick and O'Brien (1994).

Case Study: 14-Year-Old Adolescent Male with Severe Conduct Problems

Patrick was 15 years, 1 month old when his mother requested a comprehensive psychological evaluation from a university-based outpatient psychological clinic. His mother was concerned about Patrick's poor grades in school and his frequent lying. His mother also expressed concerns about his frequent fights both at school and in his neighborhood. Because of his fighting at school, Patrick had been placed in a full-time class for children with behavioral problems.

Assessment of Core Features

On the DISC-2.3, both Patrick and his mother reported the presence of a number of severe conduct problems. They both reported repeated instances of lying, repeated instances of stealing items from stores, and several school suspensions for physical fights. His mother also reported several instances of truancy, and Patrick admitted to breaking into a neighbor's house to steal things and using a knife in a fight. Patrick further admitted to occasional use of marijuana. The severity of these conduct problems is supported by parental report on the CBCL-91, on which Patrick had T-scores of 79 on both the Delinquent Behavior and Aggressive Behavior scales. On the Personality Inventory for Youth (PIY; Lachar & Gruber, 1994), Patrick obtained a T-score of 69 on the Delinquency scale.

According to both Patrick and his mother, much of Patrick's aggressive and antisocial behavior occurred alone. In fact, Patrick reported problems in peer relations, as evident by T-scores of 68 and 73 on the PIY Social Withdrawal and Social Skills scales. Patrick's mother reported that his aggressive and antisocial behavior is of longstanding duration. He had averaged about two suspensions per year since the first grade, mostly because of fighting.

Assessment of Comorbidities

Both Patrick and his mother reported that Patrick goes through frequent periods of depression, often lasting for as long as a month. At the time of the assessment, Patrick had been experiencing significant periods of sadness for the past 3 weeks. He had also lost interest in activities, he had not been sleeping well at night, and he had lost his appetite resulting in significant weight loss. His mother had also noticed a decrease in energy and a decrease in his ability to concentrate. Patrick reported on the DISC-2.3 that he had twice in the past 2 years thought of killing himself by cutting his wrist and on one occasion had actually started to use a knife but was stopped by a classmate. Both Patrick and his mother reported that the episodes of depression seemed to coincide with disciplinary confrontations, such as being suspended from school.

Patrick and his mother reported some problems of attention and concentration, but these seemed to occur during periods of depression and therefore did not seem to be associated with ADHD. Also, a psychoeducational assessment revealed that Patrick was functioning in the low average range of intellectual abilities and he scored in a range commensurate with this intellectual level on an achievement screener.

Assessment of Correlates with Potential Causal Roles

Patrick lived alone with his mother, who worked full-time outside of the home as a secretary. Patrick's parents had divorced when he was 6 years old and he had had minimal contact with his father, who according to maternal report was in and out of prison and had a substance abuse problem. Patrick's mother reportedly had limited social contacts. Her extended family mostly lived in a different region of the country and she had not developed a good network of friends. Patrick's mother also reported that she had great difficulty disciplining Patrick. Because he was so moody, she rarely tried to make him do things. Also, whenever he did something wrong (e.g., getting suspended from school), she did not punish him because it would simply make him angrier and more difficult to live with. There was no indication that Patrick was involved with a deviant peer group. In fact, his mother was concerned with his lack of any connectedness with any peers.

time-efficient and provide some of the best norm-referenced information for determining the severity of conduct problems. In contrast, diagnostic interviews often provide important information on the degree of impairment associated with the conduct problems and a structured means of assessing the age of onset of the problem behaviors. As discussed in Chapter 9, behavioral observations provide a third way of assessing conduct problem behaviors. Behavioral observations in a child's natural setting can make a unique contribution to the assessment process by providing an assessment of a child's behavior that is not filtered through the perceptions of an informant and by providing an assessment of the immediate environmental context of a child's behavior. Unfortunately, for older children and adolescents, many of the common conduct problems are by nature covert (e.g., lying and stealing), which makes them difficult to capture through some observational technique.

It should be apparent that the assessment process for children with conduct problems is quite similar to the one recommended for assessing ADHD. Given the many similarities between these types of behavioral difficulties, this is not surprising. One important difference, however, is the relative importance of a child's self-report of conduct problems, especially in adolescence (Loeber et al., 1991). This is again largely due to the covert nature of many conduct problems in older children and adolescents, which, in addition to being unobservable through observational techniques, may go undetected by parents and teachers. Although some adolescents may be unwilling to admit such antisocial behaviors, self-report is often the only possibility for detecting these behaviors in adolescents.

Assessment of Comorbidities

Co-occurring problems can be assessed conjointly with the assessment of the conduct problems themselves, through the use of omnibus rating scales, structured interviews, or multi-domain observational systems. However, they can also be assessed through the addition of domain-specific rating scales or projective testing. Given the association between conduct problems and learning disabilities, a psychoeducational evaluation that includes a standardized intelligence test and academic achievement screener should also be a part of most evaluations of children and adolescents with conduct problems.

Assessment of Correlates with Potential Causal Roles

Uncovering which of the many potential causal factors may be operating on a child referred for an evaluation could be crucial for making recommendations for treatment. Of primary importance are correlates within the child's family environment (Frick, 1994). In Chapter 13, we discussed some basic issues and methods in assessing crucial elements in a child's family environment.

Research also indicates that peer rejection is predictive of the development of conduct problems and is associated with an adolescent's association with a deviant peer group. Therefore, assessing a child or adolescent's peer relationships is a critical assessment goal. Several of the omnibus rating scales discussed in previous chapters provide an assessment of a child's peer functioning. Also, several rating scales focus specifically on a child's or adolescent's social functioning (see also Hughes, 1990). Social status can also be assessed directly through a sociometric exercise, if a child is in elementary school (see Chapter 10) (Hughes, 1990; Gresham & Little, 1993). Given that a child's association with a deviant peer group is associated with an increase in the severity of conduct problems, some method of assessing this aspect of a child's social functioning (e.g., Elliott, Huizinga, & Ageton, 1985) should also be included in a comprehensive assessment.

Finally, a child's social ecology is often crucial for understanding the development of conduct problems in many cases. Therefore, it is important to assess such variables as the economic situation of the family, the level of social and community support provided to the child and his or her family, and other aspects of a child's social climate (e.g., neighborhood, quality of school).

CONCLUSIONS

In this chapter we discuss two specific applications of the assessment procedures and techniques reviewed in previous chapters. We discuss the assessment of two related types of childhood psychopathology: attention-deficit hyperactivity disorder and conduct problems/aggression. To continue our basic premise that clinical assessments should be guided by basic psychological research, we provide a brief overview of some of the more important research findings with particular relevance to the assessment process. For both domains, assessments should be structured around our current knowledge of the core features of each domain. In addition, the most frequent co-occurring problems associated with both types of psychopathology should be routinely assessed in children and adolescents, since these comorbidities often have important prognostic and treatment implications. For ADHD a difficult part of the assessment is ruling out other medical or psychological disorders that could solely account for the ADHD symptoms. Also, in assessing ADHD, one must be knowledgeable of educational laws related to legally mandated services for children with ADHD, so one can work with educators in designing a treatment plan for the child or adolescent with ADHD. For conduct problems the myriad of potential causal factors should be assessed to determine which ones may be operating for a given child and which ones should therefore be a focus of intervention.

CHAPTER SUMMARY

1. Disruptive or externalizing behaviors are the most common reason for referral to child mental health clinics.

2. Assessments of disruptive behaviors should be based on the most current research on the basic characteristics of these types of psychopathology.

3. Based on research on ADHD:

    a. Assessments should include a multi-informant and multisource assessment of the core ADHD behaviors: inattention-disorganization and impulsivity-hyperactivity. Assessment of these

core features must be placed within a developmental perspective.

   b. Assessments should screen for the presence of the most common co-occurring problems that may accompany ADHD: conduct problems/aggression, emotional disturbance, low self-esteem, problematic social relationships, learning difficulties, and family conflict.

   c. Assessments should rule out alternative causes for the core symptoms: medical/neurological disorders, mental handicap, learning disorders, and adjustment reactions to environmental stressors.

   d. Because ADHD often has a major impact on a child's or adolescent's school functioning, the assessment should be conducted in collaboration with school personnel and with a knowledge of local educational statutes relevant to services for students with ADHD.

4. Based on research on conduct problems and aggression in children and adolescents:

   a. Assessments should provide a multisource and multimethod assessment of conduct problems including determining the types and severity of conduct problems and determining the age of onset.

   b. Assessments should screen for the most common co-occurring problems that often accompany conduct problems: ADHD, emotional disturbance, and learning disabilities.

   c. Assessments should assess known correlates to conduct problems that could play a role in causing or maintaining the problem behavior and therefore should be a major focus of intervention: family functioning, social ecology, peer relations, and associations with a deviant peer group.

Assessment of Depression and Anxiety

- What are the core symptoms of childhood depression and anxiety?

- What are the DSM-IV criteria for the diagnosis of depression and anxiety?

- Which informant is most useful for the diagnosis of depression and anxiety?

- How common is it for a child to have problems of both depression and anxiety?

INTERNALIZING DISORDERS

Depression and anxiety difficulties can be subsumed under the more global set of adjustment difficulties of childhood commonly referred to as internalizing difficulties/disorders (Achenbach & Edelbrock, 1978). Children with internalizing difficulties have been described as having a personality problem syndrome with difficulties of anxiety, withdrawal, and feelings of inferiority (Peterson, 1961); anxious-fear-

ful (Behar & Stringfield, 1974); inhibited (Miller, 1967), anxious-immature (Conners, 1970); and over-controlled (Edelbrock, 1979). Children with internalizing problems are easily distinguished from children with externalizing problems, but this does not imply that such difficulties are easily diagnosed and treated.

Internalizing disorders are among the most difficult to diagnose because of the nature of the symptomatology. The child's symptoms take more of a toll on the child's subjective mental state than on significant others or on the child's adjustment to school or other settings. Furthermore, children with internalizing problems have been found to be more well adapted than children with externalizing difficulties, achieving higher reading and intelligence test scores, and performing better in school (Cohen et al., 1985). The following quote from William Reynolds (1990) eloquently summarizes the central assessment challenge that is presented by the most common internalizing syndromes of depression and anxiety.

Internalizing disorders, including depressive disorders, anxiety disorders, obsessive compulsive disorder, somatic disorders, and suicidal behaviors, among others, are associated with overcontrolled behaviors. Phenomenologically, internalizing disorders are characterized by covert, inner-directed symptomatology. The covert nature of these disturbances presents challenges to professionals, particularly with regard to assessment and treatment. As noted in this article, internalizing disorders as a function of their insidious nature, do not readily come to the attention of psychologists. Because of this, professionals need to be vigilant to the potential existence of internalizing disorders in children and adolescents. This article emphasizes the need for psychologists and other mental health professionals to attend to these potentially severe problems in children and adolescents. (p. 137)

Within the broad category of internalizing problems, depression and anxiety syndromes can be reliably differentiated, although it has been theorized that a third disorder that is symptomatically and etiologically related to both disorders may be present (Clark & Watson, 1991). Clark and Watson (1991) propose the use of three syndrome labels—depression, anxiety, and a mixed anxiety-depression disorder. While it is beyond the scope of this chapter to consider the evidence for this third disorder and the shared etiology of depression and anxiety, it is important for the reader to be aware that, although this chapter will discuss these syndromes as if they differ in many respects (including etiology and course), this view may not account for all of the data. The present discussion is influenced primarily by the structure of the DSM-IV which lists anxiety and depression disorders as separate entities although comorbidity is recognized.

CHILDHOOD DEPRESSION

Diagnostic Criteria

In order to meet the most accepted diagnostic criteria for Major Depressive Disorder, at least five of nine symptoms must be present for at least a 2-week period and one of the symptoms must be either depressed mood or loss of interest or pleasure (APA, 1994). In shortened form, the nine symptoms include (1) depressed or irritable mood, (2) loss of interest in daily activities, (3) significant weight loss or failure to make expected weight gains, (4) frequent insomnia or hypersomnia, (5) motor agitation or retardation, (6) frequent fatigue, (7) feelings of worthlessness or guilt, (8) impaired concentration, and (9) suicidal ideation or suicide attempt.

For many years the need for diagnostic criteria for childhood depression was not clear as researchers debated whether or not the disorder could exist in childhood. There is increasing evidence that children and adolescents display much of the same symptomatology as adults, including cognitive distortion (Haley et al., 1985). Unfortunately, it is now clear that depression exists in childhood, and its course is more persistent and more impairing than thought previously (Kovacs, 1989). In fact, the existence of childhood depression is no longer a point of contention (Kovacs, 1989).

Despite some of the previous controversy regarding the existence of childhood depression, clinicians are fairly reliable in their diagnosis of the condition. When using structured diagnostic interviews such as those described in Chapter 10, the interrater reliability of the diagnosis ranges from about .75 to .90 (Christ, 1990; Eason et al., 1985). Emerging agreement regarding the existence of the depression syndrome in childhood, the widespread application of the DSM criteria, and evidence of interrater reliability have all contributed to forming a consensus that childhood depression is an important public health problem that warrants significant research attention.

Regardless of the accuracy of diagnosis, as Reynolds (1990) observes, the need to assess for the presence of depression is not always obvious. Consequently, the psychologist must develop some strategies and/or cues that trigger a search for depression. Strategies for assessing for depression can be gleaned from an understanding of the nature of the syndrome including its risk factors and course. Some methods for identifying the need to assess for the presence of depression are discussed next.

Characteristics of Childhood Depression

Although prevalence rates are often debated, it is reasonable to expect that about 2% of children may be suffering from depression at any point in time (Semrud-Clikeman, 1990), although a larger proportion of children may show some symptoms of depression (Kashani & Simonds, 1979). This rate of occurrence is significant when one considers that it is similar to the epidemiology of mental retardation. A prevalence rate this large warrants vigilance to the existence of depression in referral populations. In clinical populations, in fact, the prevalence for depression may be high; in the 25–50% range depending on the population (Semrud-Clikeman, 1990).

The prevalence of childhood depression may also be age-related, with the disorder emerging more as age increases. A higher rate of depression may be expected in adolescence because of the attendant stressors associated with this age range (Cooper, 1994). The prevalence rate for adolescents may be double that for children at about 5% (Kashani, Carlson, Beck, Hoeper, Corcoran, McAllister, Fallahi, Rosenberg, & Reid, 1987). Adolescents are presented with increasing developmental demands and stressors for which they may often be ill-prepared (Petersen et al., 1993).

Several studies have suggested that the expression of depression differs by age. While children and adolescents both report dysphoria as a central symptom of depression, younger children more frequently exhibit sleep disturbances (Christ, 1990). Less than half of children and adolescents report suicidal attempts, increased appetite, hypersomnia, hallucinations, or delusions (Christ, 1990). A recent study found that a community sample of adolescents reported significantly more somatic complaints on the CDI than preadolescents (Cooper, 1994). Further analyses revealed, however, that this finding was primarily due to gender differences; adolescent females acknowledged more somatic complaints than preadolescents (boys and girls) and adolescent boys. Perhaps excessive somatic complaints should trigger assessment for depression.

Depression is also distinctive as a syndrome because of the high rate of family resemblance that has been identified. Between a third and a half of depressed adolescents have a positive family history of depression (Puig-Antich et al., 1989; Puig-Antich & Weston, 1983). Knowledge of such significant re-

semblance is often helpful for conceptualizing cases. Family resemblance data may affect assessment and intervention planning for a child who has several symptoms of depression but does not meet diagnostic criteria. If this child's mother has a history of depression, more assessment and intervention would be warranted than if no family resemblance was present. This information also indicates that the psychologist should routinely and carefully gather family history data regarding a history of depression for the child suspected of having an internalizing disorder.

The duration of a depressive disorder can be substantial. In an interesting study, 105 children who entered a special school for children who lost a parent due to death, divorce, or separation were divided into depressed and nondepressed groups based on the CDI cut score of 13 or greater indicating depression. The elevated groups was found to, for the most part, exceed the cut score again 4 years later (Mattison et al., 1990). Mattison et al. (1990) found the depressed group to show considerable impairment over the 4-year duration of the study. They concluded that:

> They further showed significantly poorer academic performance, received significantly more counseling, and more often separated from the school under negative circumstances. The most pathological scores overall were demonstrated by the children in the original depressed group who separated from the school during the 4 years under negative circumstances. (p. 169)

Mattison et al. (1990) hypothesized that perhaps the high-scoring CDI group suffered from dysthymia, which may explain the chronicity of their difficulties. Perhaps this study also supports the contention of Clark and Watson (1991) that there is a third disorder that is associated with chronic mixed symptoms of anxiety and depression.

The chronicity of depressive symptomatology has even been documented in first-graders. In a study of 677 first-grade children from the Baltimore, Maryland public schools, CDI scores tended to be most stable for children with scores in the upper quartile of the scale. Impressively, all of the children who scored in the upper quartile in the fall of the academic year remained in the upper quartile when re-tested in the spring. Children who scored below the upper quartile showed considerably more fluctuation from the fall to the spring (Edelsohn et al., 1992).

Similarly, a longitudinal study of over 1,000 New York State high school students further reinforces the conclusion that adolescent depressive symptoms persist, and that they significantly impair functioning well into young adulthood (Kandel & Davies, 1988). This large sample was reevaluated in adulthood (m = 24.7 years) with a six-item depressive symptom checklist based on the DSM III, an interview, and the Hopkins Symptom Checklist—90 items (SCL-90). The adult cohort was subsequently divided into two groups, not highly depressed versus highly depressed, based on previously validated cut scores. Some of the more pertinent findings of the Kandel and Davies (1988) study included the following. Depression in adolescence:

- Predicted later psychiatric hospitalization for women.

- Predicted poorer physical health among men. (Both men and women were less likely to describe themselves as healthy.)

- Was associated with a greater likelihood of dropping out of high school.

- Was associated with more divorces for women, and more unemployment for men.

- Produced greater use of cigarettes by men and women, and increased use of prescription tranquilizers among women.

- Was associated with less religious affiliation, and more delinquent and deviant activities as young adults. In fact, men who were depressed as adolescents were more likely to have been involved in an automobile accident within the previous year.

- Was associated with less closeness to spouses for men and women, and less closeness to parents for women.

These findings are rather disturbing in that they point to an unfavorable prognosis for adolescents who experience significant depressive symptoms. Such re-sults also punctuate the need for careful monitoring of depressive symptomatology over the course of treatment, and they emphasize the need for ongoing follow-up assessment.

Comorbidity

When a child is diagnosed with depression, there is a high probability (a third to two-thirds of cases) that the child will simultaneously be diagnosed with an anxiety disorder (Weller et al., 1990). One study found that every child who was diagnosed with depression over a 4-year period was at some point also diagnosed with an anxiety disorder (Christ, 1990). This overlap is striking, but it does not indicate that depression and anxiety are the same syndrome. In addition to being reliably differentiated with diagnostic measures, the two problems differ in family resemblance and course (Stavrakaki & Ellis, 1989).

Also of interest is the comorbidity of depression and disruptive behavior disorders. Christ (1990) reports that 11–46% of depressed children and 14–34% of depressed adolescents also have a comorbid diagnosis of conduct disorder. Relatedly, a study of 120 delinquent boys found that 18% of the sample suffered from comorbid depression, and over one third of all of the parents had a history of depression (Kashani et al., 1982). Semrud-Clikeman (1991) concludes that 20–30% of children with ADHD have co-occurring depression. She notes further that comorbidity is particularly high when family resemblance for depression is present.

Hall and Haws (1989) found considerable comorbidity for depression among a sample of children being served in a learning disability special education program. They studied fourth- (n = 17), fifth- (n = 18), and sixth-grade (n = 15) LD students who were compared to nonhandicapped controls (NLD). CDI scores were significantly higher for children in the LD program than for NLD students (m = 13.34, SD = 7.37 and m = 8.24, SD = 5.43, respectively). In addition, the LD students were rated significantly higher in terms of demonstrating depressive symptomatology by teachers who completed a checklist of depressive symptoms based on DSM criteria. The mean CDI score for the LD group is high when one considers that it lies at the advised cut score for indicating depression.

Issues of comorbidity can also be confused with the notions of primary and secondary conditions. The primacy of the condition can be especially important for these disorders because they often have to be treated simultaneously because of considerable comorbidity. It may also be important to differentially intervene based on knowledge of primacy. A child with both depression and anxiety may require intervention for depression first, for example, if the child is presenting risk factors for suicidal behavior. Relatedly, a child suffering from anxiety and depression may require intervention for anxiety symptoms initially if compulsive hand washing behavior has resulted in impaired functioning in school, at home, and among peers. Determining primacy of condition is fraught with problems (Winokur, 1990), and the implications of doing so are not yet clear at this early stage of research on the comorbidity of these disorders in children. The skillful clinician, however, will often attempt to distinguish the primacy of anxiety and depression for the purpose of problem-solving assessment aimed at targeting behaviors for intervention. Some characteristics that may be useful in problem-solving assessment include symptomatology, course of symptoms and condition, family resemblance and background, test results, and response to prior treatment/interventions (Winokur, 1990).

Some research suggests that one should often screen for depression when a medical illness is present. In one study, depression and anxiety had a 41% higher prevalence rate in individuals with medical illness (Cassen, 1990). Depression that is secondary to medical illness may have different outcomes, thus also requiring differing approaches to intervention (Cassen, 1990).

Measuring Affectivity

A specialized assessment method for assessing depression is the measurement of positive and negative affectivity. The constructs of positive (PA) and negative affectivity (NA) have been identified as important determinants of self-reported mood states in adults (Clark & Watson, 1991). Clark and Watson (1991) provide the following definitions of NA and PA.

> Briefly, NA represents the extent to which a person is feeling upset or unpleasantly engaged rather than peaceful and encompasses various aversive states including *upset, angry, guilty, afraid, sad, scornful, disgusted,* and *worried*; such states as *calm* and *relaxed* best represent the lack of NA. In contrast, PA reflects the extent to which a person feels a zest for life and is most clearly defined by such expressions of energy and pleasurable engagement as *active, delighted, interested, enthusiastic,* and *proud*; the absence of PA is best captured by terms that reflect fatigue and languor (e.g., *tired* or *sluggish*). (p. 321)

NA is present in both depression and anxiety. It is the lack of PA that distinguishes the depressed individual from the person who only suffers from anxiety (Clark & Watson, 1991). Since much of this research program, however, has been conducted on adults using self-report measures, the applicability of the concepts of NA and PA to child assessment is not yet firmly established.

The importance of assessing a child's cognitions and self-reported feelings is, on the other hand, well established in the assessment of child depression and anxiety (Kendall & Ronan, 1990). Given considerable support for the use of PA as a distinguishing variable for depressed individuals, the child clinician could include interview questions assessing PA as part of depression assessment on a clinical trial basis until research with child populations is completed.

Specialized Measures of Depression

Hopelessness Scale

The Hopelessness Scale is a 17 item self-report inventory designed to assess a child's feelings of pessimism and hopelessness about the future (Kazdin et al., 1983). The measure is designed for use with children ages 8 to 13 years. This scale has yielded moderate estimates of reliability (less than .80), and the results correlate moderately with self-report depression measures. Two factors have been identified: (1) feeling that the future would likely be negative, and (2) feeling that nothing could be done to change this eventuality (Semrud-Clikeman, 1990). As an experimental measure the scale may be more useful as a method of data collection about feelings of hopelessness rather than serving as a norm-referenced diagnostic tool.

Children's Depression Rating Scale (CDRS-R)

The CDRS-R is a brief inventory of depressive symptomatology for children ages 6 through 12 that is completed by pooling information from the child, parents, teachers, clinicians, and others (Poznanski, Cook, & Carroll, 1979). The CDRS-R items are rated on a 7-point scale with higher scores indicating depressive problems. Items assess depressed mood, physical symptoms, and vegetative signs. Evidence of interrater reliability and test-retest reliability has been favorable, and CDRS-R scores have been found to correlate with clinicians' ratings of depression (Merrell, 1994). The CDRS-R is a unique tool that may help clinicians integrate information from a variety of informants in a qualitative if not quantitative sense.

Peer Nomination Inventory for Depression (PNID)

The PNID includes 20 items that assess three aspects of depression: depression, happiness, and popularity (Lefkowitz & Tesiny, 1980). It is designed for classroom-based assessment; a child's score on each item is the number of nominations divided by the number of students who rated the child in the classroom. The item scores are then summed to yield a total score. Normative data for the PNID have been collected for grades 3 through 5. Reliability data for the PNID are adequate, but correlations with self-report measures of depression have been low (Merrell, 1994) to moderate (Semrud-Clikeman, 1990). Although not a strong measure of clinical depression per se, the PNID could serve as an additional data source in the evaluation of children by gauging a child's popularity, social interaction, and happiness

as perceived by peers. Information of this nature could assist in targeting for intervention classroom behaviors that improve a child's adaptation in this important setting.

AN ASSESSMENT STRATEGY FOR DEPRESSION

Similar to previous chapters, we recommend a five stage assessment process for the assessment of depression; screening, classification, comorbidities, alternative causes, and treatment considerations (see Figure 19.1).

In light of the substantial epidemiology and comorbidity of depression, its adverse effects on development in a variety of domains, and its less than flagrant symptomatology, we recommend that every child who is seen by a clinician should be screened for depression. Even individuals with mental retardation are at higher risk for depression (AAMR, 1993). These research findings support the need for screening all referrals that are seen not only by psychologists, but also by other professionals (e.g., pediatricians, teachers). The screening process can be time-efficient and may include:

- Administering a brief, self-report inventory to the child with adequate reading ability.

- Asking parents whether or not their child exhibits symptoms given in the DSM-IV criteria.

- Querying teachers, nurses, grandparents, or others about symptoms of depression.

Any one of these screening methods takes only a few minutes. In fact, querying the child and a parent both would take only a few minutes. Screening efforts may allow the clinician to implement intervention in order to avert considerable suffering (see Box 19.1).

Classification of a child as depressed requires meeting the DSM-IV criteria, and by this we mean meeting all criteria based on apparently valid information. Possessing the necessary symptomatology is

Assessment Question	Implications for Assessment
Screening	Administer screening measures.
	Determine need for further assessment.
Classification	Assess for presence of symptoms that meet DSM-IV criteria.
	Determine stability and duration of symptoms.
	Determine onset.
	Determine family resemblance.
Comorbidities	Assess for presence of anxiety disorders, ADHD, or conduct disorder.
	Determine the influence of depression on school performance, absenteeism, etc.
	Assess social relationships and peer social status.
	Assess for presence of substance abuse, particularly in adolescents.
Alternative Causes	Obtain developmental and medical histories.
	Rule out dysthymia and post-traumatic stress disorder.
	Rule out medical problems that are associated with depression.
Treatment Considerations	Assess for presence of maladaptive cognitions (e.g., negative affectivity).
	Assess parental depression and parenting style.
	Evaluate response to previous interventions (e.g., psychotropics).

FIGURE 19.1

The assessment questions related to childhood depression
and implications for assessment

BOX 19.1

A Case of Individual Screening for Depression

Screening for depression is crucial because of the nature of internalizing symptomatology, and it is time-efficient in most settings. This case example illustrates the importance and practicality of screening.

Chris came to the psychologist's office because of concern about his academic progress. He is an 18-year-old college freshman who was referred by one of his college professors in order to rule out a reading disability.

Chris cited a long history of academic problems. He reported considerable speech delays as a youngster. He was enrolled in speech therapy throughout his elementary school years. He was often ridiculed by his peers for misarticulations and stuttering. He said that his speech problems abated somewhat in high school. He has, however, had longstanding problems with reading

and spelling. He says that he always felt that his writing was inferior.

When asked why he was never tested for a reading disability, he remarked that he was well behaved. He feels that he was passed along from grade to grade because he was very quiet and never caused any problems. In fact, he was reluctant to speak because of his speech difficulties.

In his freshman year in college he is having trouble in most of his classes. He is performing adequately in college algebra, but he complains that he has trouble taking notes and comprehending them after he takes them. He failed his freshman English class and Portuguese. He is very distraught about these failures because of his desire to become an elementary school counselor and his concern about disappointing his parents. Chris also reported some other recent stressors in his life. He recently broke off a 3-year relationship with a girlfriend, and he is receiving rehabilitation for a severe back injury that he incurred in a bicycle accident. Chris also has two sisters who were diagnosed

(Cont.)

BOX 19.1 *(Continued)*

with developmental disorders, one with a reading disability and the other with ADHD.

Chris gave the impression of being well adjusted and socially skilled. He was impeccably groomed and a good conversationalist. He even asked the examiner questions about his interests and offered his full cooperation with the assessment process. Chris described many successes in his life, including selection for the "male review" at his high school and being chosen as captain of the baseball team. He apparently has an active and successful social life. He currently serves on the interfraternity council at his college.

Chris was asked to complete the Beck Depression Inventory (BDI) while waiting in the office for his appointment. He was then administered a battery of achievement and intelligence measures.

The results produced clear evidence of a reading disability. He obtained intelligence test results in the average range and far below average reading scores.

Surprisingly, Chris acknowledged enough symptoms on the BDI to fall into the mild/moderate range of depression. He acknowledged guilt about past failures, uncontrollable sadness, insomnia, hopelessness, decreased appetite, increased fatigue, low self-esteem, self-deprecation, concerns about his appearance, worry about his physical well-being, lack of interest in social activities, and occasional thoughts of hurting himself, among other symptoms. The incongruence between the symptoms he marked and his presentation was striking. During the feedback session Chris was apprised of these findings and asked to verify their validity, which he did. He was then referred for follow-up assessment and intervention for his depression.

This case illustrates how time-efficient screening for depression can be of potential importance. In this scenario, depression was not suspected by the referral source, the examining psychologist, or the client.

He may discern that it is wise to deny all of these difficulties if he thinks that he may be a candidate for inpatient or partial hospitalization treatment. Clinicians who treat adolescents have seen cases where the young adult denies suicidal ideation although he may have been transferred from a hospital emergency room because of a suicide attempt. An array of assessment methods is necessary in order to ensure adequate documentation of symptoms:

- Structured and semistructured interviews with children, their parents, teachers, and other caregivers are necessary to assess for the presence of symptomatology and their effects on the child's functioning in different environments.

- Self-report inventories and parent and teacher rating scales can provide further documentation of symptoms, screen for comorbid problems, and assess for the presence of response sets or other threats to validity.

- History taking from the child and/or parents is necessary in order to establish adequate duration and pervasiveness of symptoms.

Anxiety disorders are especially important to consider when ruling out comorbidities. Anxiety symptomatology should be assessed concurrently with all of the data collection necessary for classification. Omnibus rating scales that include a well-validated anxiety scale and interview schedules that also assess for anxiety are helpful in this regard. The full realm of anxiety problems should be routinely ruled out. Somatization problems, phobias, milder fears, obsessive-compulsive disorder, and separation anxiety disorder should be distinguished.

One of the alternative causes that looms large in cases of depression is a medical difficulty that can cause depression. We recommend that a clinician assessing a child who displays the symptoms of depression should have access to the results of a recent physical exam, or an exam should be scheduled if one has not been conducted within a few months of the psychological evaluation.

The psychological evaluation must also rule out other conditions that may appear to be a major

only a first step in meeting criteria. The psychologist has to be sure that malingering, response sets, or other threats to validity have not had an effect on the report of symptoms. An adolescent, for example, may be asked if he has experienced decreased appetite, fatigue, sleeplessness, agitation, and suicidal ideation.

depressive episode. In this regard, thorough history taking is necessary in order to rule out transient states such as bereavement (e.g., depression due to a child's mother being called away to active duty in the armed forces), adjustment disorder with depressed mood, or dysthymia.

Finally, assessment methods must be selected that help direct intervention efforts. Rating scales may be used to broadly sample behavior in home, school, and other settings. A broad sampling of behavior allows the clinician to consider depressive problems and other difficulties that may in some way adversely affect the child's adaptation. If, for example, the child also shows considerable evidence of worry about school difficulties, an adjustment in the child's curriculum may have a positive effect on the child's perceived level of stress, which, in turn, could help abate depressive symptoms.

An assessment of academic achievement may also be necessary in order to determine whether or not a child is suffering from academic underachievement associated with long term depressive symptomatology. Teacher interviews and norm-referenced and curriculum-based measures may be helpful in this regard.

Self- and other informant ratings are also useful for monitoring response to psychological, educational, or medical interventions. The previous research citing long-term adaptation difficulties for children with depressive problems suggests that careful monitoring of the effects of treatment is necessary, and post-treatment follow-up is warranted in order to prevent or effectively deal with indications of relapse.

Sample Case: Corin

The application of several assessment methods are applied next to the case of Corin. The report is given as it would be written in a typical psychological report, with commentary regarding interpretation.

Initially Corin was referred for a psychological evaluation by her mother due to academic problems. According to Mrs. Jacobs, Corin has trouble concentrating in school and she thought that Corin's school problems may be caused by ADHD.

Corin is a 16-year-old female who lives with her mother and younger brother. Corin's parents are divorced and she rarely sees her father.

Mrs. Jacobs reports that there were no difficulties during pregnancy. During birth, Corin was in fetal distress and Mrs. Jacobs had an emergency cesarean delivery. Corin was born full-term and weighed 8 pounds, 7 ounces. Corin's mother described her development as normal; she reached all motor and language developmental milestones at age-appropriate times. Corin is in very good health. She is supposed to wear contact lenses, but her mother reports that Corin rarely wears them.

Corin's parents divorced when Corin was 5 years old. Corin was very close to her maternal aunt who died earlier this year. Corin states that her mother is constantly on her back, and she has to do too much work around the house. There is a family history of alcohol abuse on both her mother's and father's sides of the family. Corin's mother and father both have a history of alcohol abuse.

Corin's mother reports that Corin did well in elementary school, always receiving A's or B's. Starting in the seventh grade, Corin's academic performance deteriorated. Her mother noticed that she had problems reading aloud and problems with mathematics.

Corin received her first failing grade in the ninth grade and was moved from algebra back to pre-algebra, which she had in eighth grade. Her grades continued to deteriorate and currently she is receiving an F in history and English, a C in science, algebra, and Spanish, and an A in photography.

Corin's teachers feel that she is smart but that she does not put forth significant effort. They report that she is a behavior problem in the classroom. She is constantly talking and disrupting the class. Her algebra teacher reports that she is fond of Corin, but that she horses around too much. She talks back to her teachers, which is consistent with the reports from last year's teachers. They also report that she frequently sleeps through class.

According to records kept by the school for the past 2 years, Corin is often excessively tardy and absent from class. In the fall of this year she served 2 days of suspension in study hall for being rude to a new teacher. Subsequent to this incident, a parent conference at school resulted in Mrs. Jacobs agreeing to have Corin evaluated in order to rule out ADHD.

Corin has been seen in counseling at a community clinic for 2 years. Her current counselor reports that she is under a great deal of stress due to her parents' divorce, her aunt's death, and her continuing academic problems. Mrs. Jacobs says Corin also often has stomachaches and dizzy spells, which she attributes to stress. Corin complains of not being able to go to sleep; once asleep, she has nightmares about dying. She reports that she worries about getting cancer. She told the examiner that one time she felt a bump on her leg and she thought she had cancer.

Mrs. Jacobs reports that Corin drinks alcohol regularly and at times she drinks quite heavily, 12 to 15 beers. She told the examiner that she sometimes blacks out on the weekends. She admits to frequent use of marijuana and she smokes at least one pack of cigarettes a day. A few weeks before the evaluation, Corin was detained by police because of skipping school and being intoxicated.

In two interview sessions, Corin described herself as being depressed. She told the examiner that for the past 3 weeks she has felt angry, sad, and hopeless.

Corin's intellectual functioning was evaluated with the Wechsler Adult Intelligence Scale—Revised (WAIS-R). Her overall intelligence score of 115 indicates that she is functioning in the above average range. Her Performance Composite score of 126 meets or exceeds 96% of her age mates. She did well on tests that were timed and involved physical manipulation of materials. Her Verbal Composite score of 96 meets or exceeds 48% of her age mates. She had the most difficulty with the Vocabulary and Arithmetic subtests. This result is consistent with both her mother's and her own report of problems with math. The Verbal Composite score is consistent with her academic performance.

Corin was administered two tests of academic achievement, the Kaufman Test of Educational Achievement (K-TEA), and the Woodcock Johnson Psychoeducational Battery—Revised Tests of Achievement (WJ-R). Corin's performance on the two tests was similar in that all of her scores were in the average range, like her WAIS-R Verbal composite.

Several measures were given to assess Corin's behavior. Rating scales were completed by Mrs. Jacobs, two of Corin's teachers, and Corin. Corin's mother and a teacher completed the Achenbach Child Behavior Checklist (CBCL). This teacher rated Corin high in the areas of attention problems, delinquent behaviors, and somatic complaints. Mrs. Jacobs did not indicate any significant problems on the Achenbach. The Behavior Assessment System for Children (BASC) was also completed by the mother and teacher. Again the teacher rated Corin high for attention problems. She also rated her high for hyperactivity. She indicated that Corin has poor social, leadership, and study skills. Mrs. Jacobs rated Corin high on hyperactivity, aggression, conduct problems, and attention problems. Both her counselor and Mrs. Jacobs indicated that they did not believe that Corin has ADHD.

Corin completed several self-report measures that were used to determine her self-perceptions. She was given the Behavior Assessment System for Children—Self Report of Personality (BASC), Piers-Harris Self-Concept Scale (PHCSCS), and the Millon Adolescent Personality Inventory (MAPI). On the BASC and the PHCSCS, Corin rated herself high for anxiety, depression, somatization, and locus of control. On the BASC, Corin indicated significant problems on the School Maladjustment Composite. Her attitude toward school, attitude toward teachers, and sensation seeking scores were significantly high, which is consistent with Corin's complaints about school and the types of behaviors that she exhibits at school. On the MAPI, Corin's responses were similar to the other self-report measures. Her profile on the MAPI included concerns about academic problems and tension in the home. Corin marked questions that indicate problems with impulse control and compliance. She also cited tensions in the home that were consistent with her statements during the interviews.

On all of the self-report measures it appears that Corin has a good self-concept. She describes herself as being good looking. She feels that she has good peer relationships. She says that all of her friends like her because she is funny. Her peer relationships and social life at school are the areas in Corin's life that are not currently stressful for her.

As a follow-up measure, Corin was given the Structured Psychiatric Interview. It consists of questions to which parents and adolescents respond yes or no in order to indicate the presence of symptoms relating to DSM diagnoses. Questions relating to Major Depression, Dysthymia, and Alcoholism were administered. Corin endorsed all of the items in the area of Major Depression with the exception of suicidal ideation. Corin described herself as being anxious, and she told the examiner that she often has stomachaches and dizzy spells that she associates with stress. Corin meets the DSM criteria for Alcohol Abuse. She stated that she frequently drinks large quantities of alcohol, and occasionally she has blackouts. Corin also admitted to the examiner that she smokes marijuana quite a bit. Throughout the interview Corin appeared to be agitated.

From the information gathered a diagnosis of ADHD does not seem appropriate. Corin's acting-out behaviors are more than likely caused by the stress and depression that she currently feels. Current diagnostic impressions are Major Depression, Single Episode, Moderate, and Alcohol Abuse.

Recommendations for Corin included:

1. Corin was referred to a psychiatrist, to rule out the need for inpatient psychiatric care and interdisciplinary treatment of Major Depression.

2. It is also recommended that Corin receive psychological counseling from a therapist who has experience working with adolescents.

3. Referral to an addictions counselor who works with adolescents who are abusing alcohol. (Mrs. Jacobs was given several appropriate names).

4. Corin would benefit from group counseling for her alcohol abuse. The best group would be one made up of teenagers.

5. The Jacobs family should seek family counseling to improve the home situation. Mrs. Jacobs may also benefit from individual counseling to help alleviate some of the stress in her life.

6. Corin's teachers reportedly enjoy having Corin in their classroom and seem eager to do what they can to help her. The school psychologist can devise behavior modification plans to be imple-

mented by Corin's teachers to increase appropriate behaviors. Corin should take part in the development and implementation of the plans.

7. Communication between the school and home is necessary. Weekly reports of Corin's behaviors should be discussed with Mrs. Jacobs in order to devise problem solutions.

8. After 6 months to a year of therapy, Corin needs to be reevaluated to see if there are still issues of attention problems in the classroom.

9. Corin would benefit from tutoring in algebra.

Psychometric Summary

See Table 19.1 through Table 19.3.

TABLE 19.1   Corin's CBCL—Parent Form Scores

	T-Score (Mother)
Withdrawn	55
Somatic Complaints	59
Anxious/Depressed	56
Social Problems	50
Thought Problems	50
Attention Problems	59
Delinquent Behavior	50
Aggressive Behavior	60
Intrnalizing Composite	*55*
Externalizing Composite	*58*
Total Composite Score	*58*

TABLE 19.2   Corin's BASC-PRS Scores

	T-Score (Mother)
Hyperactivity	63
Aggression	72
Conduct Problems	61
Externalizing Problems Composite	*68*
Anxiety	63
Depression	47
Somatization	52

(Cont.)

TABLE 19.2 *(Continued)*

	T-Score (Mother)
Internalizing Problems Composite	55
Atypicality	39
Withdrawal	47
Attention Problems	68
Behavioral Symptoms Index	62
Social Skills	46
Leadership	64
Adaptive Skills Composite	55

BASC Self-Report

	T-Score
Attitude to School	67
Attitude to Teachers	70
Sensation Seeking	74
School Maladjustment Composite	75
Atypicality	58
Locus of Control	65
Somatization	60
Social Stress	52
Anxiety	56
Clinical Maladjustment	60
Depression	64
Sense of Adequacy	54
Relations with Parents	42
Interpersonal Relations	57
Self-Esteem	54
Self-Reliance	15
Personal Adjustment	39
Emotional Symptoms Index	53

TABLE 19.3 Corin's SADS Scores

Major Depression

8 out of 9 items were endorsed. The exception was the question about suicidal ideation.

Generalized Anxiety Disorder

14 out of 19 items endorsed.

Alcoholism

Corin meets criteria for Alcohol Abuse.

ANXIETY DISORDERS OF CHILDHOOD

The term *anxiety* can be traced to the Latin root *angere*, which means to cause distress or strangle. That is, unpleasant feelings of anxiety, including potentially intense feelings of fear, dread, and worry, evoke emotions associated with strangulation (Stavrakaki, 1989). Disorders and symptoms that are commonly discussed under the general rubric of anxiety include generalized anxiety disorder, separation anxiety disorder, agoraphobia, social phobia, simple phobia, school phobia, other fears, obsessive compulsive disorder, post-traumatic stress disorder, and panic disorder, among others. In the space allotted, this chapter will primarily discuss the diagnosis of childhood anxiety disorders that are most thoroughly addressed by the recently published DSM-IV. Specifically, generalized anxiety disorder and separation anxiety disorder will be the focus here.

The crux of the DSM-IV criteria for Generalized Anxiety Disorder is the following provisions: The symptoms of anxiety and worry about several events or activities (such as school) must occur more days than not for a period of at least 6 months; the child must have difficulty controlling the worry; the anxiety and worry must be associated with one of six symptoms—(1) restlessness or feeling keyed up or on edge, (2) being easily fatigued, (3) difficulty concentrating or mind going blank, (4) irritability, (5) muscle tension, and (6) sleep disturbance; the symptoms must cause significant distress or impairment in important areas of functioning; and the symptoms may not be due to other causes such as medical conditions (APA, 1994).

The diagnosis of separation anxiety disorder requires that a minimum of *three* of the following criteria be met for a period of at least 4 weeks: (1) excessive distress when separated from home or family members, (2) excessive worry about the well-being of attachment figures, (3) worry that some event (such as a kidnapping) will cause the child to be separated from family members, (4) school refusal, (5) fear of being alone, (6) refusal to sleep without an attachment figure present, (7) nightmares about separation, and (8) excessive somatic complaints when separated from an attachment figure. The phenomenology of SAD may become more clear by comparing it to that of Depression. Such a comparison is made in Box 19.2.

Characteristics of Childhood Anxiety Disorders

Comparatively speaking, much less is known about childhood anxiety disorders compared to the knowledge base for depression, and classification schemes are primarily based on research on adult anxiety disorders (Last, 1993b). There are some findings, however, that have importance for assessment practice:

BOX 19.2

Two Dimensional Classification of Depression and Separation Anxiety Disorder

---

DEPRESSION	ANXIETY
Depressed or irritable mood	Excessive distress when separated from home or family members
Loss of interest in daily activities	Excessive worry about the well-being of attachment figures
Significant weight loss or failure to make expected weight gains	Worry that some event (such as a kidnapping) will cause the child to be separated from family members
Frequent insomnia or hypersomnia	
Motor agitation or retardation	School refusal
Frequent fatigue	Fear of being alone
Feelings of worthlessness or guilt	Refusal to sleep without an attachment figure present
Impaired concentration	Nightmares about separation
Suicidal ideation or suicide attempt	Excessive somatic complaints when separated from an attachment figure

---

- One follow-up study of children with anxiety disorders found that the majority of children did not meet criteria for anxiety disorders at follow-up and, relatedly, these children were at no greater risk for experiencing a depressive episode at a later date than were children without disorders (Last, 1993b).

- Kappa coefficients, when taken as indices of interrater reliability for anxiety disorders, can be perilously low. Sample coefficients from studies of diagnostic interview schedules cited by Silverman (1993) include .47 for the Schedule for Affective Disorders and Schizophrenia, .37 for the Child Assessment Schedule, and .27 to .39 for the Diagnostic Interview Schedule for Children.

- The phenomenology of childhood anxiety disorders is very similar to that of adults (Silverman, 1993).

- While anxiety often is apparent in cases of depression, anxiety disorders often occur in the absence of depression (Silverman, 1993).

- In cases of both depression and anxiety there is evidence of poorer prognosis, more severe symptomatology, and poorer response to treatment (Silverman, 1993).

- Anxiety disorders occur about as frequently in childhood (8%) as they do in adolescence (8.7%) (Moreau & Weissman, 1993).

- Most children who are experiencing an anxiety disorder do not seek or receive psychological services (Moreau & Weissman, 1993).

- Separation anxiety disorder typically occurs in children less than 13 years of age (Strauss, 1993).

- Fears of animals, the dark, and heights are more likely to occur at younger ages than social phobias which, in turn, occurs at younger ages than agoraphobia (Strauss, 1993).

- There are two main types of school phobia: those that come on acutely in a child who has functioned reasonably normally before onset, and those that arise in a child who has had similar problems from the preschool years and has never developed the social skills that would permit normal functioning (Berg, 1993).

- Obsessive-compulsive disorder (OCD) usually has its onset in late adolescence and early adulthood, with a mean age of onset of about 23 years (Francis & Borden, 1993). Regarding OCD, Last (1993b) draws the following conclusions: (1) Obsessions rarely occur without accompanying compulsions, (2) the most commonly occurring compulsion is washing/cleaning, and (3) anxiety disorders are often comorbid with OCD.

- Children as young as the first and second grades have been found to be capable of reporting symptoms of both state and trait anxiety (Biedel & Stanley, 1993).

- The central symptoms of Post-Traumatic Stress Disorder, increased arousal, psychic numbing, and reexperiencing the trauma, occur in children as well as adults who are diagnosed with the condition (Last, 1993a).

Specialized Measures of Anxiety

Self-Report Measures

Three relatively popular measures of anxiety symptomatology in children include the Fear Survey Schedule for Children—Revised (FSSC-R; Ollendick, 1978), Revised Children's Manifest Anxiety Scale (RCMAS; Reynolds & Richmond, 1985), and the State-Trait Anxiety Inventory for Children (STAIC; Spielberger, 1973). Some of the assessment domains offered by these measures are as follows:

FSSC-R DOMAINS

Total Fear score

Failure/criticism

Fear of Unknown

Injury/small animals

Fear of danger/death

Medical Fears

RCMAS DOMAINS

Total score
Physiological Anxiety

Worry/Oversensitivity
Concentration Anxiety
Lie

STAIC DOMAINS

Total State Anxiety
State—cognitive
State—somatic
Total Trait Anxiety
Trait—cognitive
Trait—somatic

In a large-scale investigation of three groups of children, with anxiety disorder, with ADHD, and without disorders, the tests were unable to reliably differentiate the groups. Last (1993a) concluded that "the two patient groups did not differ on any of the three anxiety measures, suggesting that the measures may not be tapping the phenomenology of childhood anxiety per se, but rather may be assessing a more general or global index of psychopathology or distress" (p. 1). Such findings support a cautious approach to interpretation of these measures because of a lack of discriminant validity. At best, these measures may indicate that a problem of some unknown nature may exist.

Cognitive-Behavioral Assessment

A more recent emphasis in the assessment of children's anxiety symptomatology is to get away from tests per se. Kendall and Ronan (1990), among others, emphasize the importance of a child's information processing as a mediating variable in the development and expression of anxiety symptoms. Some of the cognitive variables that may mediate anxiety are self-statements, irrational beliefs, current concerns, images, problem-solving capacities, expectancies, and attributions. Methods for assessing these cognitive variables include (Kendall & Ronan, 1990):

- Self-monitoring

- Recordings of spontaneous verbalizations

- Think aloud methods

- Role playing

- Imagery assessment
- Thought sampling and thought listing techniques
- Interviews
- Endorsement measures

These informal methods of assessment are not yet well developed, but they do show promise. Cognitive-behavioral methods currently serve the clinician, even in experimental form, by providing corroborating data for test-based findings, and by providing insights that may be useful for intervention design. Because of encouraging preliminary data, it has been suggested that failure to incorporate these measures in an assessment battery will drastically limit the clinician's ability to examine the role of cognitive mediation in childhood fear and anxiety (Kendall & Ronan, 1990).

AN ASSESSMENT STRATEGY FOR ANXIETY

We again recommend a five-stage assessment process for the assessment of anxiety: screening, classification, comorbidities, alternative causes, and treatment considerations (see Figure 19.2).

Screening for anxiety can be accomplished using both informal and formal means. A few questions about anxiety symptoms may be more appropriate for many settings than the use of self-report or other more formal psychometric devices. The reader should note, however, that this advice is based on practical experience rather than on a research base. The sensitivity of informal screening measures is not well documented. The most important screening principle to remember is to do it, since failure to screen for anxiety may result in underserving children with less obvious problems.

Classification of anxiety difficulties is complicated by debate regarding the appropriateness of existing criteria, including the DSM-IV. It has been suggested by some that school phobia should be considered as a separate syndrome rather than being considered a

symptom of SAD. Furthermore, recent studies reveal that the diagnosis of Generalized Anxiety Disorder rarely occurs in children (Last, 1993a). The DSM-IV only lists SAD as an anxiety disorder that is marked by childhood onset.

We suggest that clinicians obtain specialized instruction regarding the diagnosis of anxiety disorders in children. Continuing education workshops and/or supervised experience or consultation from a colleague would help the new clinician who anticipates work with child anxiety problems or the experienced clinician who has rarely encountered anxiety problems in the past. The differentiation of SAD, various phobias, adjustment disorders, and other syndromes requires careful study of the DSM as well as considerable experience. The vicarious acquisition of experience will likely foster the clinician's feeling of competence in dealing with childhood anxiety disorders.

Anxiety disorders are most likely to be comorbid with other internalizing disorders such as other anxiety disorders or depression. Moreover, the nature of the symptomatology may vary over time. A child may, for example, initially be diagnosed with SAD and not have school difficulties. School refusal, however, may appear at a later time.

Medical problems should be ruled out as alternative causes because of the role that physical illness and medical procedures can play in initiating or exacerbating anxiety symptoms. In fact, one of the first hypotheses to consider when somatic symptoms are present (e.g., headaches, stomachaches, diarrhea) is the possibility that the child is physically ill. Although it seems obvious, it should be stated that a medical evaluation should be conducted when somatic complaints are evident.

Treatment considerations for anxiety disorders should also include prevention. As noted, (Last, 1993b), children with anxiety disorders are at greater risk of having an anxiety disorder occur again in the future. Hence, the young child with SAD should be periodically monitored and prevention steps taken in order to reduce future risk. If, for example, school refusal is easily treated for a child with SAD over the course of a few weeks, the psychologist should remain involved. The parents in this case could be asked to alert the psychologist if new fears, obsessions, or

Assessment Question	Implications for Assessment
Screening	Administer assessment.
	Determine need for further assessment.
Classification and Subtypes	Assess for presence of symptoms that meet DSM-IV criteria.
	Determine stability and duration of symptoms.
	Determine onset.
Comorbidities	Assess for presence of depression, school or other phobias, or obsessive-compulsive disorder.
	Determine the influence of anxiety on school performance, absenteeism, etc.
	Assess social relationships and peer social status.
Alternative Causes	Obtain developmental and medical histories.
	Rule out depression, dysthymia, and post-traumatic stress disorder.
	Rule out medical problems that are associated with anxiety.
Treatment Considerations	Assess for presence of maladaptive cognitions.
	Assess parental depression and parenting style.
	Evaluate response to previous interventions (e.g., pharmacotherapy, counseling by parents or others).

FIGURE 19.3

The assessment questions related to childhood anxiety
and implications for assessment

compulsions emerge so that intervention can be initiated in a timely manner that will prevent development of a new anxiety disorder or relapse.

Sample Case: Thurman

Thurman is a 9-year-old male who was referred for academic difficulties subsequent to being transferred to a new school. He was referred in May of the school year. His grades are lower in the new school than the old, he makes frequent self-deprecating statements; he requires more attention and supervision to complete his homework; and he gives up easily on academic activities, often refusing to complete them. He has trouble separating from his mother, and he often seeks attention in the classroom. On the positive side he is described as endearing to teachers, creative, and artistically talented.

Thurman's background information is significant.

He was born 3 months preterm and weighed approximately 3 pounds. He was treated in neonatal intensive care for 2 months after delivery. He did not walk until 16 months and he did not speak in single words until 24 months. He had considerable difficulty with all motor milestones including skipping and riding a bike.

He was diagnosed at age 5 with a motor delay, ADHD, and ODD. He continues to receive occupational therapy for his motor problems.

His teachers have always indicated that he responds better in a structured classroom. His grades have usually been above grade level with the exception of mathematics. He has not been retained nor has he been served in special education. He often complains of headaches and stomachaches at school.

Thurman's test behavior was also remarkable in that he refused testing initially. He clung to his mother in the waiting room and whined. He cried and requested that his mother join him for the test ing. During testing (with his mother in the room) he cried, tantrumed, threw objects, refused to answer questions, and responded impulsively. Several times he remarked, "I'm an idiot". He was rescheduled for testing a week later.

During the second assessment session, Thurman cooperated fully. He again pleaded with his mother to join him, but she refused. He did not display any of the previous behavior problems, and he did not make self-deprecating statements.

Based on findings from rating scales and historical information, Thurman was diagnosed with Separation Anxiety Disorder based on the rationale that he displayed the minimum of three symptoms for a minimum of 4 weeks. His symptoms included:

1. Excessive distress when separated from family members
2. Worry about the well-being of family members
3. Somatic complaints when separated

An interesting aspect of this case is that the previous diagnoses of ADHD and ODD were not confirmed. The diagnosis of SAD, hence, suggested several treatments that were at variance with previous diagnoses.

CONCLUSIONS

The assessment of child anxiety and depression requires a well-trained clinician. The less flagrant nature of their symptomatology and the range of disorders related to anxiety and depression make identification of these problems a professional challenge.

Further complicating assessment practice is the lack of research on some issues, especially child anxiety problems. Although our understanding of child depression and anxiety has increased exponentially within the last two decades, our understanding of these problems still lags behind the available knowledge base for adults. Clinicians are advised to make a concerted effort to remain abreast of changes in the emerging research base.

CHAPTER SUMMARY

1. Depression and anxiety difficulties can be subsumed under the more global set of adjustment difficulties of childhood commonly referred to as internalizing difficulties/disorders.

2. Internalizing disorders are among the most difficult to diagnose because of the nature of the symptomatology.

3. Clark and Watson (1991) propose that there are three syndromes: depression, anxiety, and a mixed anxiety-depression disorder.

4. In order to meet the diagnostic criteria for Major Depressive Disorder, at least five of nine symptoms must be present for at least a 2-week period, and one of the symptoms must be either depressed mood or loss of interest or pleasure (APA, 1994). The nine symptoms include (1) depressed or irritable mood, (2) loss of interest in daily activities, (3) significant weight loss or failure to make expected weight gains, (4) frequent insomnia or hypersomnia, (5) motor agitation or retardation, (6) frequent fatigue, (7) feelings of worthlessness or guilt, (8) impaired concentration, or (9) suicidal ideation or suicide attempt. (See Box 19.3 on p. 383–384.)

5. Approximately 2% of children may be suffering from depression at any point in time.

6. Depression is marked by differing epidemiology for children and adolescents, differing symptoms by age, considerable family resemblance, lengthy episodes, and substantial chronicity of problems.

7. A specialized assessment method for assessing depression is the measurement of positive and negative affectivity. The constructs of positive affectivity (PA) and negative affectivity (NA) have been identified as important determinants of self-reported mood states in adults.

8. Specialized measures that may be useful for assessing childhood depression include the Hopelessness Scale, Children's Depression Rating Scale, and the Peer Nomination Inventory for Depression.

9. Some methods for screening for depression in-

clude: administering a brief self-report inventory to the child with adequate reading ability; asking parents whether or not their child exhibits symptoms given in the DSM-IV criteria; or querying teachers, nurses, grandparents, or others about symptoms of depression.

10. A five-step method for assessing for depression and anxiety involves assessing for (1) screening, (2) classification, (3) comorbidities, (4) alternative causes, and (5) treatment.

11. The central diagnostic criteria for Separation Anxiety Disorder (SAD) require that a minimum of three of the following criteria be met for a period of at least 4 weeks: (1) excessive distress when separated from home or family members, (2) excessive worry about the well-being of attachment figures, (3) worry that some event (such as a kidnapping) will cause the child to be separated from family members, (4) school refusal, (5) fear of being alone, (6) refusal to sleep without an attachment figure present, (7) nightmares about separation, and (8) excessive somatic complaints when separated from an attachment figure.

12. Some findings regarding anxiety disorders in-clude: children with a history of a psychiatric disorder are at greater risk for later development of an anxiety disorder; some studies have found poor indices of interrater reliability for interview schedules designed to assess anxiety disorders; the phenomenology of childhood anxiety disorders is very similar to that of adults; anxiety disorders often occur in the absence of depression; in both depression and anxiety there is evidence of poorer prognosis, more severe symptomatology, and poorer response to treatment, most children who are experiencing an anxiety disorder do not seek or receive psychological services; SAD typically occurs in children less than 13 years of age; and OCD usually has its onset in late adolescence and early adulthood, with a mean age of onset of about 23 years.

13. Three relatively popular measures of anxiety symptomatology in children include the Fear Survey Schedule for Children—Revised, the Revised Children's Manifest Anxiety Scale, and the State-Trait Anxiety Inventory for Children.

14. Cognitive behavioral assessment have also been espoused as important measures of anxiety that have implications for intervention planning.

BOX 19.3

Commonly Used Omnibus Scales with Subscales Related to Depression: The Match and Mismatch to DSM-IV Criteria

---

As we noted in Chapter 18 for ADHD, many of the more commonly used parent and teacher rating scales have heterogeneous item content with respect to ADHD. This heterogeneity of item content also applies to the assessment of depression, which can make scale-level interpretation unclear. In order to illustrate this interpretive problem for depression, we list here item content of subscales that purport to measure depression, that is not tied to the symptoms of Major Depression as identified in the DSM-IV. Additionally, we identify in this table the number of DSM symptoms that are not assessed by each scale in order to give the clinician an indication of how well each scale overlaps with DSM criteria. We did not assume by doing this that the DSM is the gold standard for defining the content of a depression scale, but it seems to us to be at least one important standard for the clinician to consider during interpretation.

(Cont.)

BOX 19.3   *(Continued)*

Behavior Assessment System for Children (Reynolds & Kamphaus, 1992)

Parent Rating Scales (ages 6–11)	Teacher Rating Scales (ages 6–11)
Changes moods	**Changes moods**
Lacks friends	**Is teased**
	Lacks friends
	Stays disappointed if something is cancelled
6 of 9 DSM items not assessed	*6 of 9 DSM items not assessed*

Child Behavior Checklist and Teacher Report Form (Achenbach, 1991)

CBCL Anxious/Depressed Scale (6–11)	TRF Anxious/Depressed Scale (6–11)
Loneliness	**Loneliness**
Fears impulses	**Fears impulses**
Perfectionistic	**Perfectionistic**
Feels persecuted	**Feels persecuted**
Nervousness	**Nervousness**
Fearful, anxious	**Fearful, anxious**
Feels self-conscious	**Feels self-conscious**
Suspicious	**Suspicious**
Worry	**Worry**
	Conformity
	Sensitive to criticism
	Eager to please
	Fears mistakes
7 of 9 DSM items not assessed	*7 of 9 DSM items not assessed*

Devereux Scales of Mental Disorders (Naglieri, LeBuffe, & Pfeiffer, 1994)

DSMD Depression Scale (5–12)

Difficulty making or keeping friends	**Appears unaware of how others feel toward him/her**
Fails to show pride in accomplishments	
Appears unconcerned about how others feel toward him/her	**Has a blank expression**
Avoids physical contact with others	**Refuses to speak**
	Shows little interest in adult approval or praise

5 of 9 DSM items not assessed

(Cont.)

Box 19.3 *(Continued)*

Minnesota Multiphasic Personality Inventory—Adolescent (Butcher et al., 1992)

MMPI-A Depression Core Clinical Scale

Worry about my health	Work under tension
Nausea and vomiting	Constipitation
Impaired judgment	Reluctance to greet acquaintances
Tease animals	Worry about catching diseases
Vomit blood or cough up blood	Sensitivity to criticism
Fit or convulsion	Impaired reading comprehension
Impaired memory	Sweating when embarrassed
Hay fever or asthma	Flirting
Nervousness	Sweaty even on cool days
Worry about whether doors are locked and windows closed	Laughs at a dirty joke
	Occasionally feeling unusually cheerful

9 of 9 DSM items assessed

Personality Inventory for Children—Revised (Lachar, 1989)

PIC-R Depression Scale

Does not play with a group of children	Perfectionism
Worries	Self-pity
Poor sense of humor	Loneliness
Worries about sin	Sensitive to criticism
Lacks self-confidence	Afraid of dying
Too serious	Seldom talks
Easily embarrassed	Whines
Talks about death	

3 of 9 items not assessed

Personality Inventory for Youth (Lachar & Gruber, 1992)

Psychological Discomfort Depression Subscale

Unsure of self

5 of 9 DSM items not assessed

(Cont.)

BOX 19.3   *(Continued)*

Self-Report of Personality (Reynolds & Kamphaus, 1992)

BASC SRP Depression Scale (8–11)	BASC SRP Depression Scale (12–18)
In trouble at home or **I am always in trouble with someone** **Prefers to not be noticed**	
6 of 9 DSM items not assessed	*6 of 9 DSM items not assessed*

Youth Self-Report (Achenbach, 1991)

	YSR Anxious/Depressed Scale
Loneliness	**Anxiety**
Fears	**Self-conscious**
Perfectionistic	**Suspiciousness**
Feeling of persecution	**Worry**
Nervousness, tense	

6 of 9 DSM items not assessed

*Because of space limitations, only those items that do not seem to be similar to the DSM-IV symptoms are listed here to give the clinician some sense of the heterogeneity of items for each scale.

CHAPTER 20

Assessment of Autism

CHAPTER QUESTIONS

- How are the syndromes of autism and schizophrenia defined by the DSM-IV?
- How is autism differentiated from mental retardation?
- What types of scales are most useful for the assessment of children with these syndromes?
- What are some of the problems with autism rating scales?

DEFINITIONAL ISSUES

DSM-IV Criteria

In the DSM-IV, Autistic Disorder is part of a class of problems known as Pervasive Developmental Disorders (PDD). Other disorders that are included under the rubric of PDD include Childhood Disinte-grative Disorder, Asperger's Disorder, Rett's Disorder, and PDD Not Otherwise Specified (APA, 1994). This chapter will be limited to a discussion of Autistic Disorder, a condition that has long been of interest to psychologists. The DSM-IV describes Autistic Disorder as "the presence of markedly abnormal or impaired development in social interaction and communications and a markedly restricted repertoire of activity and interests" (p. 66).

Autistic Disorder is also known by other terms such as *autism* or *early infantile autism*. Autistic Disorder is also known to be frequently comorbid with mental retardation (APA, 1994). With comorbidity estimates ranging as high as 75%, the differential diagnosis of autism and mental retardation can be challenging.

The most recent edition of the DSM emphasizes three classes of symptoms that are central to the disorder: social interaction problems, communication problems, and repetitive and stereotyped behaviors. The onset of these symptoms must occur by age 3. The DSM criteria require that a total of six symptoms with a minimum of one from each of the three classes of problems be present in order to make a diagnosis. Furthermore, at least two of the symptoms from the social interaction class of problems must be present.

The social interaction symptoms include:

1. Failure to engage in appropriate nonverbal behaviors such as appropriate eye contact, facial expressions, body postures, and social gestures
2. Poorly developed peer relationships
3. Failure to share pleasurable interests, activities, or achievements with others
4. Lack of social reciprocity

Communication symptoms include:

1. Delayed development of spoken language
2. When speech is present, inability to begin or maintain a conversation
3. Stereotyped or repetitive use of language
4. Lack of imaginative play

Problems with repetitive or stereotyped play include:

1. Preoccupation with one or more behavior patterns
2. Preoccupation with nonfunctional routines or rituals
3. Inappropriate motor movements
4. Preoccupation with specific objects

Characteristics of Autism

Autism is often described as an etiologically diverse disorder, but, perhaps most importantly, specific etiological agents have not been identified. Some studies have found factors such as vaginal bleeding, maternal infection, maternal medication use, small weight for gestational age, and hyperbilirubinemia to be associated with a greater incidence of autism (Piven et al., 1993). Similarly, other syndromes such as Fragile X and Tuberous Sclerosis have been found

to be overrepresented in populations of autistic children. Although it is not known whether or not birth order is an etiological agent, autistic children are more commonly first or fifth or later-born children (Piven et al., 1993). A recent study by Piven et al. (1993) highlights the problems involved in identifying specific etiologies for autism by finding that etiological risk factors were not significantly different between autistic children and their siblings when the effects of birth order were controlled. Thus, it appears that much remains to be learned about risk factors that may be etiologically involved in autism. This lack of scientific clarity implies that clinicians should not place undue importance on etiological agents when conceptualizing cases of autism or when providing feedback to others.

Although they are sometimes assumed to be similar, autism can be reliably differentiated from schizophrenia; moreover, autism does not place a child at greater risk for schizophrenia (Volkmar & Cohen, 1991). In fact, the DSM-IV (APA, 1994) notes that schizophrenia rarely occurs in children, and the typical age of onset is between late adolescence and the mid-thirties. The major symptoms of schizophrenia are delusions, hallucinations, disorganized/incoherent speech, disorganized or catatonic behavior, and so-called negative symptoms such as flat affect (APA, 1994). These symptoms bear some relationship to autism, but experienced child clinicians will testify as to the rarity of such problems in children. (See Box 20.1.) The behavior of children with autism also differs qualitatively from that of children with psychotic symptoms in that they have poorer language and social skills (Matese, Matson, & Sevin, 1994).

Differentiation of autism from Pervasive Developmental Disorder—Not Otherwise Specified (PDD-NOS) and mental retardation, however, is more difficult. Although many of the scales discussed later have been found to adequately differentiate mental retardation or other developmental disorders from autism, more cross-validation studies are needed. A study by Mayes et al. (1993) found that children with language disorder could be more easily differentiated from children with autism, but autism and PDD-NOS were more difficult to differentiate.

It has also been argued that autism is a heteroge-

BOX 20.1

The Mental Status Exam

One of the hallmark symptoms of schizophrenia is poor reality contact or reality distortion (DSM-IV). The mental status examination is a tool that is commonly used to assess such problems. Reprinted below is an outline that may be used by the clinician to evaluate reality contact/distortion among other behaviors that have been associated with schizophrenia.

Appearance

1. Does the client look healthy?
2. Does he look his age? If not, does he appear older or younger?
3. Does he have any obvious physical deformities? Describe.
4. Is he appropriately dressed?
5. Is his clothing clean?
6. Does he walk or move in an unusual way?
7. Does he sit in a comfortable posture?
8. Does he have any visible scars?
9. Do his height and weight appear to be appropriate?
10. Does he have any visible tics or unusual movements of the body, face, or eyes?
11. Does he make eye contact? If so, consistently or intermittently?
12. What is the client's facial expression? Does it change over the course of the interview?

Speech

1. Does the client speak?
2. Does he speak unusually rapidly or slowly?
3. Does he have a speech impediment?
4. Does he speak unusually loudly or softly?

Emotions

1. What is the client's predominant mood? Describe the comments and behavior on which you base this observation.
2. What is his predominant affect? Describe the comments and behavior on which you base this observation?

3. Does his affect vary over the course of the interview?
4. Does his affect seem excessive at any time? Describe.
5. Does he exhibit labile affect?
6. Is his affect appropriate to the content of the interview?

Thought Processes and Content

1. Is the client's thought process circumstantial?
2. Is it perseverative?
3. Is his thinking tangential?
4. Does he demonstrate loose associations or flight of ideas?
5. Does he exhibit somatic delusions, or delusions of grandeur, persecution, or control? On what comments do you base this observation?
6. Does he appear to exhibit thought broadcastiang or ideas of reference? On what comments do you base this observation?
7. Does he suffer obsessive thoughts or experience compulsive behavior? If so, describe.
8. Is he phobic? If so, what is the nature of this phobic?
9. Are there indications of homicidal or suicidal ideation? If so, on what comments do you base this observation?
10. Is there a particular subject that seems to preoccupy the client's thoughts? If so, describe.

Sensory Perception

1. Does the client appear to have any hearing problems?
2. Does the client appear to have any sight problems?
3. Does the client suffer from illusions or hallucinations? If so, are the latter auditory, visual, olfactory, tactile, or gustatory? On what comments or behavior do you base this observation?

Mental Capacities

1. Is the client oriented to time, place, and person?
2. Does the client appear to be of average intelligence or above?
3. Does he exhibit a capacity for concentration within the normal range?
4. Does he exhibit appropriate recent, remote, and

(Cont.)

immediate memory? If not, on what do you base this observation?

5. Does his judgment appear impaired in any way? If so, on what comments or behavior do you base this observation?

6. Does he have an appropriate sense of self-worth? If not, on what comments or behavior do you base this observation?

7. Does he appear to understand the consequences of his behavior?

8. Does he exhibit a capacity for insight?

Attitude toward the Interviewer

1. What is the client's attitude toward you?

2. Does it change over the course of the interview?

3. Does he respond to empathy?

4. Does he appear to be capable of empathy?

Adapted and reprinted with permission from Lukas (1993).

neous disorder that benefits from subtyping (Castelloe & Dawson, 1993). In fact, three subgroups of autism have been identified based on different qualities of social interaction. An aloof subgroup of individuals rarely initiates social interaction except to meet basic needs, and these individuals do not respond to unsolicited social overtures. A passive subgroup similarly does not initiate interaction but will respond to structured social overtures by others. The active-but-odd subgroup initiates social interaction with others, but they do so in a peculiar, naive, or one-sided way (Castelloe & Dawson, 1993).

A similar cluster-analytic study revealed four subtypes (Eaves, Ho, & Eaves, 1994). The largest group was characterized as typically autistic; the second largest group possessed similarities to the first, but they were defined by moderate to severe mental retardation. The two smaller groups included a group of high-functioning children who were Asperger-like, and the last group had impaired social and language skills and a family history of learning problems. This

subtyping study is interesting in that it supports the role of intelligence as an important factor contributing to heterogeneity within the autistic population (Eaves, Ho, & Eaves, 1994).

Comorbidity

The most frequent comorbid problem for autism is mental retardation (Ghaziuddin, Tsai, & Ghaziuddin, 1992). In a study of 68 children age 2 to 17 years with autism, Ghaziuddin et al. (1992) found that 57 children met criteria for mental retardation, 3 cases were identified with a mood disorder (2 of these were major depression), 1 with OCD. 1 with trichotillomania, and 1 with a tic disorder. Interestingly, none of the subjects was diagnosed with schizophrenia.

SPECIALIZED MEASURES
OF AUTISM

Autism Behavior
Checklist (ABC)

The ABC is a 57-item, teacher-completed checklist that is purported to be useful primarily for screening purposes. One study found the ABC to reliably discriminate between a group of 56 children with mental retardation and learning disabilities and 67 autistic children (Wadden, Bryson, & Roger, 1991), although another investigation cast doubt on the utility of cut scores used to indicate the presence of autism on the ABC (Sevin et al., 1991). Wadden, Bryson, and Roger (1991) also found that a three-factor model fit the instrument better than a previously proposed five-factor model. This latter finding is congruent with the identification of three symptom clusters by the DSM-IV.

Infant Behavioral Summarized
Evaluation (IBSE)

The IBSE is a rating scale that is appropriate for infants and preschoolers. One study evaluated some psychometric properties of the scale for a sample of 39 children with autism, 33 with mental retardation, and 17 with other handicaps (Adrien et al., 1992). Good interrater reliability was found. A factor analysis of 31 items found two factors, with the first factor accounting for most of the items. Adrien et al. (1992) also concluded that first factor scores were capable of differentiating the autism group from the other two samples.

Autism Diagnostic Interview— Revised (ADI-R)

The ADI-R is a semistructured diagnostic interview designed to be used with a child's primary caregiver (Le Couteur et al., 1989). According to the authors, "It aims to provide a lifetime assessment of the range of behaviors relevant to the differential diagnosis of pervasive developmental disorders in individuals of any chronological age from 5 years to early adulthood, and with any mental age level from two years upward" (p. 365). The ADI focuses on three domains of behavior that are largely consistent with the DSM-IV criteria: reciprocal social interaction; communication, and repetitive, restricted, or stereotyped behavior. An overview of the procedure for using the ADI is provided in the following excerpt from Le Couteur et al. (1989).

> Because the interview is concerned with the differential diagnosis of developmental disorders, the standardized history-taking begins (after a general orienting section) with questioning on when and how the parents first became aware that something might be wrong with the child, and on key developmental milestones. It then proceeds to cover the child's behavior during the 5 first years of life, because certain diagnostic features are usually most evident during this age period. The questioning then shifts to the subject's current behavior, that is during the 12 months prior to the interview. However, for many items, the interviewer also determines whether specified behaviors have ever been present. (p. 366)

Le Couteur et al. (1989) report favorable evidence of interrater reliability for the ADI. Intraclass correlations (a measure of interrater reliability) for area scores ranged from .91 for the language/communication area to .96 for reciprocal social interaction. Differential validity was also assessed in this same investigation with favorable results. The ADI was able to reliably differentiate subjects with autism from subjects with mental handicaps. All of the autism subjects and none of the nonautistic subjects met the full criteria for the diagnosis of autism according to the ADI (Le Couteur et al., 1989; see Box 20.2 on p. 400).

The ability of the ADI to differentiate children with autistism from children with other developmental disabilities was assessed more recently in a study of 43 children (Fombonne, 1992). In this study Fombonne (1992) concluded that the ADI was better able to diagnose autism than the DSM III-R criteria. Another recent study again found the ADI-R to reliably differentiate between samples of children with autistism and children with mental retardation (Lord, Storoschuk, Rutter, & Pickles, 1993). This investigation, however, identified problems when trying to differentiate these samples for children with mental ages of less than 18 months, reflecting the continuing dilemma of diagnostic accuracy with low-functioning children.

Parent Interview for Autism (PIA)

The PIA, a newer alternative to the ADI-R, was developed at Vanderbilt University (Stone & Hogan, 1993). While generally based on the three core dimensions of autism, the PIA has items that were rationally/theoretically grouped into the following scales (Stone & Hogan, 1993):

Social Relating

Affective Responses

Motor Imitation

Peer Interactions

Object Play

Imaginative Play

Language Understanding

Nonverbal Communication

Motoric Behaviors

Sensory Responses

Need for Sameness

Parents are asked to rate the frequency of the behavior for each item on a 5-point scale. The scale is designed to be administered via interview.

The psychometric properties of the PIA are varied. Internal consistency indices for the scales range from a low of .55 for Object Play to a high of .83 for Relating. Test-retest coefficients were more variable, ranging from a low of .48 for Object Play to a high of .90 for Need for Sameness (Stone & Hogan, 1993).

Differential validity was documented for several of the scales. Three of the scales, Motoric Behaviors, Sensory Responses, and Need for Sameness, did not differentiate samples of 58 subjects with autism and 36 with mental retardation (Stone & Hogan, 1993).

While the PIA shows some promise, the validity of the subscales is not documented. Empirical methods should be used in concert with rational methods in order to refine the subscales.

Childhood Autism Rating Scale (CARS)

The CARS is a rating form that is typically completed by an observer of the behavior of a child who has reached a developmental age of approximately 3 years. In some cases an observation period of only about 30 minutes is used (Sevin et al., 1991). Items are rated on a 7-point continuum for the 15 subscales. The CARS is composed of nine portions. It included items such as a puzzle-like task and a set of toy objects designed to assess make-believe play activity.

The CARS produces a moderately high correlation with the ABC of .67 (Eaves & Milner, 1993). Although this correlation is significant, the two instruments did classify children at differing rates. The CARS correctly identified 98% of the children with autism and the ABC 88% of the sample (Eaves & Milner, 1993).

In an investigation by Sevin, et al. (1991), 24 children were assessed with the CARS. The interrater reliability of the CARS for these subjects was found to be highly variable. Coefficients were as low as .10

(Activity Level) and .14 (Intellectual Response), and as high as .85 (Relating to People). The interrater reliability coefficient for the total score was .68.

In spite of such modest reliability coefficients, the CARS results showed fairly good concordance with clinician diagnoses of autism (Sevin et al., 1991). The CARS classified 19 of the 24 subjects with autism correctly. Only two of the subjects were incorrectly classified with autism, although this study provided a weak test of differential validity because of the small sample of subjects without autism.

Autism Diagnostic Observation Schedule (ADOS)

The ADOS (Lord et al., 1989) is designed for the assessment of autism in the classroom setting for children age 6 years and older. It is a unique measure for the assessment of autism in several ways. It emphasizes the assessment of reciprocal social interaction and communication rather than restricted or repetitive behavior, and it is structured in an unusual way. In a sense the ADOS is like a test, in that the environment for the observation is structured in a standardized way and the examiner presents predefined challenges to the child in this structured setting. In this way the examiner serves as both the stimulus for interaction and as the recorder of behavior. The challenges presented by the examiner (Lord et al., 1989) are:

TASK	TARGET BEHAVIOR(S)
Construction task	Asking for help
Unstructured presentation of toys	Symbolic play
	Reciprocal play
	Giving help to interviewer
Drawing game	Taking turns in a structured task
Demonstration task	Descriptive gesture and mime
Poster task	Description of agents and actions
Book task	Telling a sequential story

Conservation

Socioemotional
   questions

Reciprocal communication

Ability to use language to
   discuss socioemotional
   topics

The interrater reliability of the ADOS was found to be adequate but less robust than for the ADI, with some coefficients from a test-retest study being as low as .57 (Lord et al., 1989). The differential validity of the ADOS in one investigation was found to be acceptable (Lord et al., 1989). In this study, none of the subjects without autism were diagnosed as having autism based on the ADOS. However, half of the subjects with autism were classified as possibly abnormal as opposed to having autism (Lord et al., 1989). Such a result suggests that the ADOS may serve well as a complementary measure of autism, as opposed to being a central arbiter of the differential diagnosis.

Ritvo-Freeman Real Life Rating Scale for Autism (RLRS)

This 47-item rating scale is completed by adult caregivers. The RLRS takes a different approach to the assessment of autism by including five domains instead of the three emphasized in the current edition of the DSM. The five scales include Sensory Motor, Social Relationship to People, Affectual Responses, Sensory Responses, and Language. Items were grouped into scales based on rational/theoretical considerations (Aman, 1994). Limited research is available for this instrument although the RLRS has shown some utility for assessing the effectiveness of pharmacological interventions for children with developmental disabilities (Aman, 1994).

AN ASSESSMENT STRATEGY FOR AUTISM

Autism is increasingly recognized as being a disorder with heterogeneous etiologies and highly variable

symptomatology among those affected (Campbell et al., 1991). Such within syndrome variability suggests that children who are either suspected of or diagnosed with the disorder should have access to multidisciplinary assessment procedures (see Figure 20.1). The severity of autistic symptoms, as demonstrated by the overlap with mental retardation, further emphasizes the need for a range of professionals to be involved in assessing the affected child. Such interdisciplinary work, however, can be challenging if there are not adequate structures for encouraging interdisciplinary practice. Consequently, the psychologist may have to make a concerted effort to go beyond the typical practice regimen and communicate more frequently with colleagues who practice related specialties.

Marcus, Lansing, and Schopler (1993) describe one of the better methodologies for fostering multidisciplinary assessment of autism. They describe the State of North Carolina TEACCH evaluation system as follows:

> This process includes a developmental/ psychoeducational assessment of the child, psychological assessment, detailed parent interviewing including assessment of adaptive functioning, and a medical screening. This integrated and multiperspective approach generates comprehensive data on diagnosis, intellectual and adaptive functioning, motor, language, and social functioning, behavior problems, medical factors, family functioning and school or community factors. The data are sufficiently detailed and objective to be organized into dimensions or axes that both overlap with and extend beyond the DSM-III-R system. (p. 350)

The severity and frankness of the symptomatology of autism requires us to emphasize different aspects of our five-stage paradigm: screening, classification, comorbidities, alternative (see Figure 20.1).

The screening process for autism is aimed primarily at the population of children with developmental disorders as opposed to the general population. We advise that clinicians consider the possibility of autism in all samples of young children with developmental disabilities. Because the nature of autism does not allow the child to serve as a source of screening information, parent and teacher ratings are likely

Characteristic	Implications for Assessment
Screening	Administer screening measures; target young children with signs of developmental delay.
	Determine need for further assessment.
Classification	Assess for presence of symptoms that meet DSM-IV criteria.
	Determine stability and duration of symptoms.
	Determine age of onset.
Comorbidities	Assess for presence of mental retardation.
	Determine the influence of autism on school performance, adaptive behavior, development, etc.
	Assess social relationships and peer social status.
Alternative Causes	Obtain developmental and medical histories.
	Rule out Rhett's disorder, Asperger's syndrome, language disorders, mental retardation, and hearing impairment.
Treatment Considerations	Assess adaptive behavior assets and deficits.
	Identify behavior problems that require intervention.
	Assess caregiver stress and caregiver ability to provide adaptive behavior instruction and behavior problem management.
	Evaluate response to previous interventions.

FIGURE 20.1

Assessment questions related to childhood autism and
implications for assessment

to be the most fruitful. The time-efficiency of such ratings argues for their routine use with these populations.

Classification of the child as having autism requires meeting the DSM-IV criteria outlined earlier. The classification process will depend heavily on caretaker information such as histories and child behavior ratings. Furthermore, medical, language, and other assessment data will need to be integrated in order to make differential diagnoses.

The most likely comorbid condition for autism is mental retardation. An in-depth assessment of intelligence and adaptive behavior development is therefore required in every comprehensive study of a child suspected of autism. Sensory impairments must also be ruled out by other clinicians.

The process of ruling out alternative causes is a lengthy one requiring full participation by medical and other professionals in the assessment process. Neurological problems, in particular, should be ruled out as primary etiologies for the child's behavior.

A central aspect of psychological intervention for children with autism is skill development in a variety of domains. A comprehensive measure of adaptive behavior can be useful for defining needed skills and evaluating the effectiveness of intervention.

A SAMPLE CASE OF AUTISM IN A CHILD WITH NEUROLOGICAL IMPAIRMENT

Julie was a 5 year, 1 month–old female who was referred by her parents.

Assessment Instruments

Behavior Assessment System for Children (BASC)

Parent interview

Teacher interview

Review of medical records

Kaufman Assessment Battery for Children (K-ABC)

McCarthy Scales of Children's Abilities (McCarthy)

Developmental Test of Visual-Motor Integration (VMI)

Bracken Basic Concept Scale (Bracken)

Woodcock Johnson Psychoeducational Battery—Revised (WJ-R) Tests of Achievement

Vineland Adaptive Behavior Scales (Vineland)—Interview Edition, Survey Form (Mother)

Vineland Adaptive Behavior Scales (Vineland)—Classroom Edition (teacher)

Parenting Stress Index (PSI)

Referral Information

Julie was referred for a psychological evaluation by her parents. Original referral questions included concern about delayed language development, short attention span, difficulty in her kindergarten class, and a possible learning disability. Subsequently, however, Julie had two seizures and was diagnosed as having tuberous sclerosis and seizure disorder. Upon learning that tuberous sclerosis often affects a child's intelligence, her parents requested a thorough evaluation to determine Julie's current level of functioning.

Background Information

Julie is a 5-year-old girl who lives with both parents. Her mother reports that she had no serious difficulties when she was pregnant with Julie. Julie was born full-term and weighed 7 pounds, 0 ounces. Both Julie and her mother were in good condition at the time of birth. Julie did, however, have an open sore on her back that was surrounded by a purple mark. The doctor remarked that this type of wound was very unusual.

According to her mother, Julie has had two seizures. The first was about 6 weeks prior to this evaluation. Her mother describes these seizures as lasting about a minute and not involving severe convulsions. Julie was seen by a neurologist. According to Julie's medical reports, she was somewhat difficult to understand and hyperactive during the medical examination. Her doctor had difficulty obtaining her cooperation. Her physical condition appeared to be normal, except for a large scar on her right hip and skin lesions on her face and extremities. Based on Julie's physical condition, recent seizures, EEG results, and CAT scan results, she was diagnosed as having seizure disorder and tuberous sclerosis, a genetic disorder associated with tumors in the brain and internal organs and skin lesions on the face and body. Her doctor prescribed Tegretol for seizure control.

According to her mother, Julie has also had frequent ear infections, beginning at 8 months old and continuing until May of this year. At that time, she had tubes placed in her ears. She has had no difficulties since then. She had a hearing examination in June that indicated a slight hearing loss in the right ear. Julie has also had frequent colds. Her mother thinks that Julie's vision is normal.

According to her mother, Julie's development was inconsistent. She seemed to learn gross motor skills at a normal rate but her fine motor and language development appeared to be delayed. She spoke her first words at 9 months, but by 18 months she could still speak only four words. She did not speak in sentences until she was 2 years old. Her speech articulation is clear, but her language is still delayed. She was in speech therapy for language development until recently.

Her mother states that Julie is sweet, has a good sense of humor, and enjoys singing. Julie, however, can also be stubborn and sometimes does not seem to listen to or obey her mother. Her mother says that Julie likes to play by herself rather than with other children. She also reports that Julie can be easily overstimulated, is very energetic and active, has a short attention span, and is impulsive. She adds that Julie requires much parental attention.

Julie has been in a preschool program since she was 2 years old. Her mother reports that Julie's teachers have been concerned because Julie did not communicate in school, had difficulty doing age-appropriate work, required much teacher attention, and seemed to lack self-esteem and confidence. Julie is now enrolled in a kindergarten class. Her current teacher reports that Julie is a sweet child and seems to want to please. Julie memorizes well and knows many songs. She also states, however, that Julie shows many behaviors that make it difficult to teach her. She spends most of the day by herself, talking only to herself or inanimate objects. She seems to repeat over and over phrases that she has heard adults say. She does not interact with the other children. When called on in class, she seems embarrassed, then blurts out any answer. She has a very short attention span. She also sometimes leaves the room without teacher permission. She chews on her clothes and mat. She is teased by the other children because of her behavior. According to her teacher, Julie has not learned many academic skills. She seems to have learned a few basic concepts, such as shapes. She can also make a capital *A,* but it is frequently upside down. She does many things upside down and does not seem to recognize that they are incorrect. She cannot do worksheets; she just draws lines up and down the page or colors the whole page one color. Sometimes she does better with one-on-one assistance, but other times she will not accept help from her teacher.

Julie was briefly observed at school during lunch. She was sitting at the end of the table by herself and did not interact with the other children. Although she had talked with the observer previously, she showed little response to her at this time. When asked if she remembered the observer, she said that she did, but still did not interact with her. She just continued eating.

Behavioral Observations

Julie was tested over a 2-day period. Three examiners participated in her evaluation. She was brought to the first testing session by her mother. She seemed very uncomfortable meeting strangers and clung to her mother. Her mother carried her to the testing room and stayed for a while until Julie was more comfortable. Julie did not become relaxed with the examiners for some time. Adequate rapport for testing purposes was finally established.

During testing, Julie was very active and distractible. The examiners had difficulty keeping her attention on the test materials. She required much direction and attention from the examiners to stay on task. She frequently wanted to play with the other toys. At one point, she sat on the floor, facing the wall. When asked what she was doing, she said she was in time-out. Upon further questioning, she responded that she was put there because she did not pay attention. Later she again sat on the floor, this time repeating "Stephanie, it's time to go to school." The examiner had difficulty distracting her from this behavior. This type of behavior seemed to occur most when Julie was being asked to perform a task that was difficult for her. After this last time, Julie could not be enticed to pay any more attention to the test materials. She got up and left the room without the examiner's permission.

Julie was more cooperative during the second testing session. She seemed much more comfortable with the examiners and accompanied them readily to the testing room. She was, however, still very distractible and active and required much examiner attention to stay on task.

Tests Results and Interpretations

Intellectual Functioning

Julie's intellectual functioning was evaluated with the K-ABC and the McCarthy. Taken together, her performance on both of these tests indicates that her current level of intellectual functioning is far to well below average. This level of functioning is consistent with her teacher's and mother's reports of her ability and with her current school performance. The two tests, however, differ in their estimation of her ability. This difference can be attributed to differences in the tests' requirements of examinee cooperation and participation. The K-ABC requires that the child look at an easel and respond mostly by saying the answer or pointing to it. The McCarthy, on the other hand, requires the child to perform a variety of physical and manipulative tasks.

Julie's performance on the K-ABC suggests that there is a 90% probability that her level of intellectual functioning meets or exceeds that of 1–5% of her agemates. Her performance on the subtests was consistent, showing no relative strengths or weaknesses. Although the examiner attempted to administer the achievement subtests, they were not all completed. Those achievement subtests that were finished suggest below average achievement in expressive vocabulary, factual information, and mathematical concepts.

Julie's performance on the McCarthy, was poorer, meeting or exceeding that of less than 1% of her agemates. She did especially poorly on subtests that required attention and concentration. She did somewhat better on recall of pictures, gross motor skills, and verbal fluency.

Visual Motor Integration

Julie was also given the VMI to assess her ability to coordinate what she sees with what she is doing. This test required Julie to copy designs in a booklet. Her performance on this task was at or above that of 8% of children her age, suggesting that her visual motor integration and fine motor skills are well below average. Her mother and teacher also reported difficulty with fine motor tasks, such as drawing and writing.

Academic Achievement

Julie was administered two tests of academic readiness and achievement. The Bracken measures understanding of simple concepts, such as color, letter and number recognition, shape, direction, size, texture, quantity, and time. Her performance on this test indicates that her understanding of these concepts is far below that of the average child. This result is consistent with her results on the intelligence tests given. The WJ-R, Tests of Achievement were administered to determine what basic reading and math skills Julie had learned. Her performance on the subtests administered was well to far below average. Her score on the Letter-Word Identification

subtest meets or exceeds that of 0.5–2% of her agemates, while her score on the Applied Problems (math) subtest meets or exceeds that of 1–5%. On these subtests and informal assessment, Julie showed the ability to sing the alphabet and count objects with one to one correspondence.

Adaptive Behavior

The Vineland was completed by the examiner interviewing Julie's mother. The Vineland is a measure of Julie's ability to take care of herself, get along with others, and live in the community appropriately for her age. It includes four domains: Communication, Daily Living Skills, Socialization, and Motor Skills. Her mother indicates that Julie's overall ability in these areas is below average for her age. There is a 90% probability that her ratings meet or exceed those of 9–30% of her agemates, which is somewhat higher than her intelligence test scores. Most of her scores were consistent with her overall score, suggesting below average performance. Her score in the Socialization domain, however, was higher than the others, indicating average ability in getting along with others. This score, however, is not consistent with teacher and parent reports or behavioral observations.

Julie's teacher also completed the Vineland, Classroom Edition. Her teacher indicates that Julie's adaptive behavior is variable. Her score on the Daily Living Skills domain is similar to that given by her mother and is in the below average range. However, her other scores are in the far to well below average range, more consistent with her intelligence test scores. Her Socialization domain score is inconsistent with that of her mother's rating, but more consistent with other assessment findings. It indicates far below average socialization skills.

Rating Scales

Julie's mother, father, and teacher each completed the Achenbach CBCL. This rating scale assesses behavioral and emotional problems of children. Although the raters show similar behavioral patterns, only Julie's father indicates that Julie has any serious problems. He rates Julie as significantly above average in social withdrawal and hyperactivity. Julie's mother and teacher also rate her as high in these areas, but not significantly high. These findings are consistent with teacher and parent report and behavioral observations.

Summary and Conclusions

Julie is a 5-year-old girl referred by her parents to determine her current level of functioning. She has been diagnosed as having seizure disorder and tuberous sclerosis. Her mother reports that her language and fine motor development were delayed. Her teacher reports that she has made little progress in adjusting to kindergarten or learning basic readiness skills. Parent and teacher reports indicate that she is very active and inattentive and requires much adult attention and supervision. These behaviors were also observed in the testing situation, in which examiners had much difficulty getting Julie to cooperate and attend to the tasks. She was very active and distractible. Parent and teacher reports, as well as observation during testing, also suggest that Julie displays several unusual behaviors, such as talking to herself or inanimate objects, repeating the same phrases or motions, panting heavily at times, chewing on clothes, preferring to stay by herself, and not interacting with other children.

Most of Julie's test results, including intellectual, achievement, visual motor, and some adaptive behavior areas, are in the well to far below average range. Other adaptive behavior scores, however, were in the below average range. Information from rating scales indicates that Julie is socially withdrawn, hyperactive, distractible, slow to learn or adapt to new situations, and sometimes fussy.

Taking all of the assessment information together, the diagnosis of Pervasive Developmental Disorder Not Otherwise Specified (299.80) seems appropriate. At this time a diagnosis of mental retardation does not seem applicable. Although her intelligence test scores are within the mild mentally retarded range, her adaptive behavior scores lie outside the mental retardation range. Both of these areas of functioning must be significantly below average to warrant a diagnosis of mental retardation.

Recommendations

Julie should be evaluated again at the end of this academic year to assess her progress. At this time the following recommendations are made for Julie:

1. Julie needs to be in a very structured educational environment where she can get the attention and supervision she needs to learn. Her parents should consult school personnel in order to find such an educational setting.

2. Julie will need much individual instruction, gradually moving to small-group instruction.

3. Julie's classroom assignments should be within the range appropriate for her intellectual and academic level.

4. Julie should be allowed to learn and work at her own pace.

5. Instructional tasks should be organized into short, structured units.

6. Julie will need to be taught at a very concrete and practical level, using many manipulatives and teaching aids.

7. Skills and concepts will need to be repeated and reviewed often for Julie to master them.

8. Julie may be helped by being tutored by someone who has been trained in tutoring children like her.

9. Julie's parents and teachers should continue to search for activities that she does well and enjoys and encourage her in these activities.

10. Julie's parents and teachers should continue to use behavior management strategies, such as positive reinforcement and time out, to help her learn appropriate behavior. Her parents may wish to attend behavior management training sessions to become more facile with these techniques.

11. Inappropriate behavior should be ignored as much as possible, while appropriate behavior is rewarded with praise and other appropriate reinforcers.

12. Communication between school and home should be maintained. A home-school contract, in which Julie is rewarded at home for appropriate behavior at school, may be helpful.

13. Julie should be allowed as much as possible to be around normal children her own age, so that she can learn socialization and behavioral skills by observation and interaction with them.

14. Julie's overactivity may be channeled by assigning classroom duties.

Psychometric Summary

For Julie's scores on individual assessment methods, see Tables 20.1 through 20.6.

TABLE 20.2   Julie's McCarthy Scores

Verbal Scale	28
Perceptual-Performance	> 22
Quantitative Scale	24
General Cognitive Index	> 50
Memory Scale	26
Motor Scale	28

TABLE 20.3   Julie's VMI Scores

Standard Score	Percentile
79	8

TABLE 20.1   Julie's K-ABC Scores

	Standard Score	Percentile
Sequential Processing	78	5
Simultaneous Procession	69	2
Mental Processing Composite	69	2
Faces and Places	80	9
Arithmetic	83	13

SEQUENTIAL SCALED SCORES

Hand Movements	7
Number Recall	6
Word Order	5

SIMULTANEOUS SCALED SCORES

Gestalt Closure	5
Triangles	5
Matrices	6
Spatial Memory	5

OUT OF LEVEL TESTING
(usually given to younger children)

Magic Window	4	(Simultaneous scaled score)
Face Recognition	7	(Simultaneous scaled score)
Expressive Vocabulary	78	(standard score)

TABLE 20.4   Julie's Bracken Basic Concepts Test Scores

	Score	Percentile
STANDARD		
Total test	63	1
SCALED		
School Readiness Composite	5	5
Direction/Position	5	5
Social/Emotion	3	5
Size	2	0.4
Texture/Material	5	5
Quantitative	3	1
Time/Sequence	4	2

TABLE 20.5   Julie's Scores on the WJ-R—Tests of Achievement

	Standard Score	Percentile
Letter-Word Identification	65	1
Applied Problems	69	2

TABLE 20.6   Julie's Scores on the Vineland

	Interview Edition (mother)		Classroom Edition (teacher)	
	Standard Score	Percentile	Standard Score	Percentile
Adaptive Behavior Composite	86	18	72	3
Communication domain	82	12	78	7
Daily Living Skills domain	87	19	86	18
Socialization domain	108	70	67	1
Motor domain	82	12	70	2

BOX 20.2

Research Note: ADI-R Items That Differentiated Samples with Autism from Samples without Autism

---

Le Couteur et al. (1989) systematically investigated the ability of the ADI-R to differentiate a sample of 16 children with autism from 16 children with significant mental handicaps. Thus, this is a strict test of the differential validity of the ADI-R, since previous studies have shown that the major diagnostic conundrum associated with autism is the confounding of mental retardation. The following table lists the items within the three commonly cited domains of autism that significantly differentiated the two samples.

Reciprocal Social Interaction Items	Communication/Language Items	Repetitive, Restricted, and Stereotyped Behavior Items
Anticipatory gesture	Abnormality in pointing	Unusual preoccupations
Social intentionality	Abnormality in gesture	Unusual attachments to objects
Social reciprocity	Lack of conversation	Compulsions/rituals
Vocal expression	Abnormality in amount of social communication	Hand-finger mannerisms
Range of facial expression	Stereotyped utterances	Unusual sensory interests
Appropriate facial expression	Pronominal reversal	Resistance to change
Friendship	Idiosyncratic language	
Affection	Neologisms	
Offers comfort	Verbal rituals	
Seeks comfort	Abnormality in intonation/volume/ rhythm/rate	
Separation anxiety	Abnormality in social play	
Greeting	Abnormality in imitation	
Shares activities		
Pleasure/excitement		

SOURCE: Le Couteur et al., "Autism Diagnostic Interview: A Standardized Investigator-based Instrument," *Journal of Autism and Developmental Disorders, 19,* 363–387.

CONCLUSIONS

Autism is among the most difficult of the developmental disorders to reliably classify, yet classification is central to research efforts aimed at prevention and intervention. Considerable progress has been made in the past decade in defining the three core dimensions of impairment that separate this condition from other developmental disabilities.

The practicing clinician, however, is left with a dearth of instruments that reliably differentiate autism from mental retardation, particularly in very young children and those with more severe developmental delays. While new methods of assessment have made strides in terms of differential validity, considerably more progress is needed. The most promising method for assessing and classifying autism at this time is a thorough and standardized interview of the child's primary caregiver.

CHAPTER SUMMARY

1. Autistic Disorder is part of a class of problems known as Pervasive Developmental Disorders (PDD).

2. The most recent edition of the DSM emphasizes three classes of symptoms that are central to the disorder: social interaction problems, communication problems, and repetitive and stereotyped behaviors.

3. Much remains to be learned about risk factors that may be etiologically involved in autism.

4. Autism can be reliably differentiated from schizophrenia; moreover, autism does not place a child at greater risk for schizophrenia.

5. Differentiation of Autism from Pervasive Developmental Disorder - Not Otherwise Specified (PDD-NOS) and mental retardation is difficult.

6. Some have asserted that autism is a heterogeneous disorder that benefits from subtyping.

7. The most frequent comorbid problem for autism is mental retardation.

8. The Autism Diagnostic Interview—Revised (ADI-R) is a semistructured diagnostic interview that is designed to be used with a child's primary caregiver.

9. The Autism Diagnostic Observation Schedule (ADOS) is designed for the assessment of autism in the classroom setting for children age 6 years and older.

10. The within-syndrome variability associated with autism suggests that children who are either suspected of or diagnosed with the disorder should have access to multidisciplinary assessment procedures.

REFERENCES

Abidin, R. R. (1986). *Parenting Stress Index manual* (2d ed.). Charlottesville, VA: Pediatric Psychology Press.

Abikoff, H., & Klein, R. G. (1992). Attention-deficit hyperactivity and conduct disorder: Comorbidity and implications for treatment. *Journal of Consulting and Clinical Psychology, 60,* 881–892.

Abramowitz, A. J., & O'Leary, S. G. (1991). Behavioral interventions for the classroom: Implication for students with ADHD. *School Psychology Review, 20,* 220–234.

Achenbach, T. M. (1982). Assessment and taxonomy of children's behavior disorders. In B. B. Lahey & A. E. Kazdin (Eds.), *Advances in clinical child psychology* (vol. 5, pp. 1–38). New York: Plenum.

Achenbach, T. M. (1986). Child behavior checklist— direct observation form (rev. ed.). Burlington: University of Vermont.

Achenbach, T. M. (1991a). *Integrative guide for the 1991 CBCL/4-18, YSR, and TRF profiles.* Burlington: University of Vermont Department of Psychiatry.

Achenbach, T. M. (1991b). *Manual for the Child Behavior Checklist/4-18 and 1991 profile.* Burlington: University of Vermont, Department of Psychiatry.

Achenbach, T. M. (1991c). *Manual for the Teacher's Report Form and 1991 profile.* Burlington: University of Vermont, Department of Psychiatry.

Achenbach, T. M., Conners, C. K., Quay, H. C., Verhulst, F. C., & Howell, C. T. (1989). Replication of empirically derived syndromes as a basis for taxonomy of child/adolescent psychopathology. *Journal of Abnormal Child Psychology, 17,* 299–323.

Achenbach, T. M., & Edelbrock, C. S. (1978). The classification of child psychopathology: A review and analysis of empirical efforts. *Psychological Bulletin, 85,* 1275–1301.

Achenbach, T. M., & Edelbrock, C. (1983). *Manual for the Child Behavior Checklist and Revised Child Behavior Profile.* Burlington: University of Vermont.

Achenbach, T. M., & Edelbrock, C. (1986). *Manual for the Teacher's Report Form and teacher version of the Child Behavior Profile.* Burlington: University of Vermont, Department of Psychiatry.

Achenbach, T. M., & Edelbrock, C. (1991). *Manual for the Youth Self-Report and Profile.* Burlington: University of Vermont Department of Psychiatry.

Achenbach, T. M., Howell, C. T., Quay, H. C., & Conners, C. K. (1991). National survey of problems and competencies among four-to sixteen-year-olds: Parents' reports for normative and clinical samples. *Monographs of the Society for Research in Child Development, 56*(3), 1–131.

Achenbach, T. M., & McConaughy, S. H. (1987). *Empirically based assessment of child and adolescent psychopathology: Practical applications.* Newbury Park, CA: Sage.

Achenbach T. M., McConaughy, S. H., & Howell, C. T. (1987). Child/adolescent behavioral and emotional problems: Implications of cross-informant correlations for situational specificity. *Psychological Bulletin, 101,* 213–232.

Adams, C. D., & Drabman, R. S. (1994). BASC: A critical review. *Child Assessment News, 4*(1), 1–5.

Adrien, J. L., Barthelemy, C., Perrot, A., & Roux, S. (1992). Validity and reliability of the Infant Behavioral Summarized Evaluation (IBSE): A rating scale for the assessment of young children with autism and developmental disorders. *Journal of Autism and Developmental Disorders, 22,* 375–394.

Agras, W. S., Chapin, H. N., & Oliveau, D. C. (1972). The natural history of phobias: Course and prognosis. *Archives of General Psychiatry, 26,* 315–317.

Albert-Corush, J., Firestone, P., & Goodman, J. T. (1986). Attention and impulsivity characteristics of the biological and adoptive parents of hyperactive and normal children. *American Journal of Orthopsychiatry, 56,* 423–423.

Allen, J. C., & Hollifield, J. (1990). Using the Rorschach with children and adolescents: The Exner Comprehensive System. In C. R. Reynolds & R. W. Kamphaus (Eds.), *Handbook of psychological and educational assessment of children: Personality, behavior, and context* (pp. 168–185). New York: Guilford Press.

Aman, M. D., Werry, J. S., Fitzpatrick, J., Lowe, M., & Waters, J. (1983). Factor structure and norms for the Revised Behavior Problem Checklist on New Zealand children. *Australian and New Zealand Journal of Psychiatry, 17,* 354–360.

Aman, M. G. (1994). Instruments for assessing treatment effects in developmentally delayed populations. *Assessment in Rehabilitation and Exceptionality, 1,* 1–19.

Amanat, E., & Butler, C. (1984). Oppressive behaviors in the families of depressed children. *Family Therapy, 11,* 65–77.

Amato, P. R., & Keith, B. (1991). Parental divorce and the well-being of children: A meta-analysis. *Psychological Bulletin, 110,* 26–46.

Ambrosini, P. J., Metz, C., Prabucki, K., & Lee, J. (1989). Video tape reliability of the third revised edition of the K-SADS. *Journal of the American Academy of Child and Adolescent Psychiatry, 28,* 723–728.

American Psychiatric Association (1968). *The diagnostic and statistical manual of mental disorders* (2d ed.). Washington, DC: Author.

American Psychiatric Association (1980). *The diagnostic and statistical manual of mental disorders* (3d ed.). Washington, DC: Author.

American Psychiatric Association (1987). *The diagnostic and statistical manual of mental disorders* (3d ed., rev.). Washington, DC: Author.

American Psychiatric Association (1994). *The diagnostic and statistical manual of mental disorders* (4th ed.). Washington, DC: Author.

American Psychological Association (1994). Guidelines for child custody evaluations in divorce proceedings. *American Psychologist, 49,* 677–680.

American Psychological Association (1985). *Standards for educational and psychological testing.* Washington, DC: Author.

American Psychological Association (1992). Ethical principles of psychologists and code of conduct. *American Psychologist, 47,* 1612–1628.

Ames, L. B., Metraux, R., Rodell, J. L., & Walker, R. (1974). *Child Rorschach responses* (rev. ed.). New York: Bruner/Mazel.

Anastasi, A. (1988). *Psychological testing* (6th ed.). New York: Macmillan.

Anastasi, A. (1992). Introductory remarks. In K. F. Geisinger (Ed.), *Psychological testing of Hispanics* (pp. 1–7). Washington, DC: American Psychological Association.

Anderson, J. C., Williams, S., McGee, R., & Silva, P. A. (1987). DSM-III disorders in preadolescent children. *Archives of General Psychiatry, 44,* 69–76.

Archer, R. P. (1992). MMPI-A: *Assessing adolescent psychopathology.* Hillsdale, NJ: Erlbaum.

Archer, R. P., Belevich, J. K. S., & Elkins, D. E. (1994). Item-level and scale-level factor structures of the MMPI-A. *Journal of Personality Assessment, 62*(2), 332–345.

Asher, S. R., & Hymel, S. (1981). Children's social competence in peer relations: Sociometric and behavioral assessment. In J. D. Wine & M. D. Smye (Eds.), *Social competence* (pp. 125–157). New York: Guilford Press.

Asher, S. R., Singleton, L. C., Tinsley, B. R., & Hymel, S. (1979). A reliable sociometric measure for preschool children. *Developmental Psychology, 15,* 443–444.

Atkins, M. S., Pelham, W. E., & Licht, M. (1985). A comparison of objective classroom measures and teacher ratings of attention deficit disorder. *Journal of Abnormal Child Psychology, 13,* 155–167.

Atkinson, L. (1990). Standard errors of prediction for the Vineland Adaptive Behavior Scales. *Journal of School Psychology, 28,* 355–259.

Ball, J. D., Archer, R. P., Gordon, R. A., & French, J. (1991). Rorschach depression indices with children and adolescents: Concurrent validity findings. *Journal of Personality Assessment, 57,* 465–476.

Balthazar, E. F. (1973). *Scales of social adaptation.* Palo Alto, CA: Consulting Psychologists Press.

Balthazar, E. E. (1971). *Scales of functional independence.* Palo Alto, CA: Consulting Psychologists Press.

Barker, P. (1990). *Clinical interviews with children and adolescents.* New York: Norton.

Barkley, R. A. (1981). *Hyperactive children: A handbook for diagnosis and treatment.* New York: Guilford Press.

Barkley, R. A. (1988). Attention deficit disorder with hyperactivity. In E. J. Mash & L. G. Terdal (Eds.), *Behavioral assessment of childhood disorders* (2d ed., (pp. 69–104). New York: Guilford Press.

Barkley, R. A. (1990). *Attention deficit hyperactivity disorder: A handbook to diagnosis and treatment* (2d ed.). New York: Guilford Press.

Barkley, R. A. (1991). The ecological validity of laboratory and analogue assessment methods of ADHD. *Journal of Abnormal Child Psychology, 19,* 149–178.

Barkley, R. A., & Edelbrock, C. (1987). Assessing situational variation in children's problem behaviors: The home and school situations questionnaires. In R. J. Prinz (Ed.), *Advances in behavioral assessment of children and families* (vol. 3, pp. 157–176). New York: JAI.

Baron-Cohen, S., Allen, J., & Gillberg, C. (1992). Can autism be detected at 18 months? The needle, the haystack, and the CHAT. *British Journal of Psychiatry, 161,* 839–843.

Barrios, B. A. (1988). Fears and anxiety. In E. J. Mash & L. G. Terdal (Eds.), *Behavioral assessment of childhood disorders*, (2d ed., pp. 196-264). New York: Guilford Press.

Barrios, B. A. (1993). Direct observation. In T. H. Ollendick & M. Hersen (Eds.), *Handbook of child and adolescent assessment* (pp. 140–164). Needham Heights, MA: Allyn & Bacon.

Barrios, B A., & Hartmann, D. P. (1988). Fears and anxiety. In E. J. Mash & L. G. Terdal (Eds.), *Behavioral assessment of childhood disorders* (pp. 167–221). New York: Guilford Press.

Bauer, D. H. (1976). An exploratory study of developmental changes in children's fear. *Journal of Child Psychology and Psychiatry, 17,* 69–74.

Baumrind, D. (1971). Harmonious parents and their preschool children. *Developmental Psychology, 4,* 99–102.

Beck, S. T., Steer, R. A., & Garbin, M. G. (1988). Psychometric properties of the Beck Depression Inventory: Twenty-five years of evaluation. *Clinical Psychology Review, 8,* 77–100.

Befera, M. S., & Barkley, R. A. (1985). Hyperactive and normal girls and boys: Mother–child interactions, parent psychiatric status, and child psychopathology. *Journal of Child Psychology and Psychiatry, 26,* 439–452.

Behar, L. B., & Stringfield, S. A. (1974). A behavior rating scale for the preschool child. *Child Development, 10,* 601–610.

Bellak, L., & Bellak, S. (1949a). *A manual for the Children's Apperception Test.* Larchmont, NY: CPS.

Bellak, L., & Bellak, S. S. (1949b). *The Children's Apperception Test.* New York: CPS.

Berg, I. (1993). Aspects of school phobia. In C. G. Last (Ed.), *Anxiety across the lifespan: A developmental perspective* (pp. 78–93). New York: Springer.

Biedel, D. C., & Stanley, M. A. (1993). Developmental issues in the measurement of anxiety. In C. G. Last (Ed.), *Anxiety across the lifespan: A developmental perspective* (pp. 167-203). New York: Springer.

Biederman, J., Keenan, K., & Faraone, S. V. (1990). Parent-based diagnosis of attention deficit disorder predicts a diagnosis based on teacher report. *Journal of the American Academy of Child and Adolescent Psychiatry, 29,* 698–701.

Bird, H. R., Gould, M. S., & Stagheeza, B. (1992). Aggregating data from multiple informants in child psychiatry epidemiological research. *Journal of the American Academy of Child and Adolescent Psychiatry, 31,* 78–85.

Bird, H. R., Gould, M. S., & Staghezza, B. M. (1993). Patterns of diagnostic comorbidity in a community sample of children aged 9 through 16 years. *Journal of the American Academy of Child and Adolescent Psychiatry, 32,* 361–368.

Bird, H. R., Yager, T. J., Staghezza, B., Gould, M. S., Canino, G., & Rubio-Stipec, M. A. (1990). Impairment in the epidemiological measurement of childhood psychopathology in the community. *Journal of the American Academy of Child and Adolescent Psychiatry, 29*(5), 796–803.

Black, K. (1994). A critical review of the MMPI-A. *Child Assessment News, 4*(2), 1, 9–12.

Blashfield, R. K. (1984). *The classification of psychopathology: Neo-Kraepelinian and quantitative approaches.* New York: Plenum.

Block, J. H. (1965). *The child rearing practices report.* Berkeley: Institute of Human Development, University of California–Berkeley.

Block, J. H., Block, J., & Morrison, A. (1981). Parental

agreement-disagreement on child-rearing orientations and gender-related personality correlates in children. *Child Development, 52,* 965–974.

Blum, G. S. (1950). *The Blacky Pictures: Manual of instructions.* New York: The Psychological Corporation.

Borgen, F. H., & Barnett, D. C. (1987). Applying cluster analysis in counseling psychology research. *Journal of Counseling Psychology, 34,* 456–468.

Bornstein, M. R., Bellack, A. S., & Hersen, M. (1977). Social-skills training for unassertive children: A multibaseline analysis. *Journal of Applied Behavioral Analysis, 10,* 183–195.

Bower, E. M. (1982). Severe emotional disturbance: Public policy and research. *Psychology in the Schools, 19,* 55–60.

Bowlby, J. (1969). *Attachment and loss: I., Attachment.* New York: Basic Books.

Brandt, H. M., & Giebink, J. W. (1968). Concreteness and congruence in psychologists' reports to teachers. *Psychology in the Schools, 5,* 87–89.

Brody, G., Stoneman, Z., & Burke, M. (1987). Family system and individual child correlates of sibling behavior. *American Journal of Orthopsychiatry, 57,* 561–569.

Brody, G., Stoneman, Z., & Burke, M. (1988). Child temperament and parental perceptions of individual child adjustment: An intrafamilial analysis. *American Journal of Orthopsychiatry, 58,* 532–542.

Bruininks, R. J., Hill, B. K., Weatherman, R. F., & Woodcock, R. N. (1986). *Inventory for client and agency planning.* Allen, TX: DLM Teaching Resources.

Bruininks, R. J., Woodcock, R. W., Weatherman, R. F., & Hill, B. K. (1986). *Scales of independent behavior.* Allen, TX: DLM Teaching Resources.

Burns, G. L., & Patterson, D. R. (1990). Conduct problem behaviors in a stratified random sample of children and adolescents: New standardization data on the Eyberg Child Behavior Inventory. *Psychological Assessment: A Journal of Consulting and Clinical Psychology, 2*(4), 391–397.

Burns, R. C., & Kaufman, S. H. (1970). *Kinetic family drawings (K-F-D): An introduction to understanding children through kinetic drawings.* New York: Bruner/Mazel.

Butcher, J. N., Williams, C. L., Graham, J. R., Archer, R. P., Tellegen, A., Ben-Porath, Y. S., & Kaemmer, B. (1992). *MMPI-A, Minnesota Multiphasic Personality Inventory—Adolescent: Manual for administration, scoring, and interpretation.* Minneapolis: University of Minnesota Press.

Campbell, S. B. (1986). Developmental issues in childhood anxiety. In R. Gittelman (Ed.), *Anxiety disorders of childhood* (pp. 24–57). New York: Guilford Press.

Campbell, M., Kafantaris, V., Malone, R. P., & Kowalik, S. C. (1991). Diagnostic and assessment issues related to pharmacotherapy for children and adolescents with autism. Special Issue: Current perspectives in the diagnosis, assessment, and treatment of child and adolescent disorders. *Behavior Modification, 15*(3), 326–354.

Cardell, C. P., & Parmar, R. S. (1988). Teacher perception of temperament characteristics of children classified as learning disabled. *Journal of Learning Disabilities, 21,* 497–502.

Carlson, C. L., & Lahey, B. B. (1983). Factor structure of teacher rating scales for children. *School Psychology Review, 12,* 285–291.

Carlson, C. L., Lahey, B. B., & Neeper, R. (1984). Peer assessment of the social behavior of accepted, rejected, and neglected children. *Journal of Abnormal Child Psychology, 12,* 189–198.

Cassen, E. H. (1990). Depression and anxiety secondary to medical illness. In G. Winokur (Ed.), *The psychiatric clinics of North America: Anxiety and depression as secondary phenomena* (pp. 597–612). Phildelphia, PA: W. B. Saunders.

Castelloe, P. & Dawson, G. (1993). Subclassification of children with autism and pervasive developmental disorder: A questionnaire based on wing's subgrouping scheme. *Journal of Autism and Developmental Disorders, 23*(2), 229–241.

Chambers, W. J., Puig-Antich, J., Hirsch, M., Paez, P., Ambrosini, P. J., Tabrizi, M. A., & Davies, M. (1985). The assessment of affective disorders in children and adolescents by semi-structured interview: Test-retest reliability of the Schedule for Affective Disorders and Schizophrenia for School-aged Children, Present Episode. *Archives of General Psychiatry, 42,* 696–702.

Chandler, L. A. (1990). The projective hypothesis and the development of projective techniques for children. In C. R. Reynolds & R. W. Kamphaus (Eds.), *Handbook of psychological and educational assessment of children: Personality, behavior, & context* (pp. 55–69). New York: Guilford Press.

Christ, M. G. (1990). A four-year longitudinal study of

depression in boys: Phenomenology and comorbidity of conduct disorder. Ph.D. diss., University of Georgia, Athens.

Christensen, A., Margolin, G., & Sullaway M. (1992). Interparental agreement on child behavior problems. *Psychological Assessment, 4,* 419–425.

Clark, L. A., & Watson, D. (1991). Tripartite model of anxiety and depression: Psychometric evidence and taxonomic implications. *Journal of Abnormal Psychology, 100*(3), 316–336.

Cohen, N. J., Gotlieb, H., Kershner, J., & Wehrspann, W. (1985). Concurrent validity of the internalizing and externalizing profile patterns of the Achenbach Child Behavior Checklist. *Journal of Consulting and Clinical Psychology, 53,* 724–728.

Coie, J. D., Dodge, K. A., & Coppotelli, H. (1982). Dimensions and types of social status: A cross-age perspective. *Developmental Psychology, 18,* 557–570.

Coie, J. D., & Kupersmidt, J. B. (1983). A behavioral analysis of emerging social status in boys' groups. *Child Development, 54,* 1400–1416.

Connell, J. P. (1985). A new multidimensional measure of children's perception of control. *Child Development, 56,* 1018–1041.

Conners, C. K. (1969). A teacher rating scale for use in drug studies with children. *American Journal of Psychiatry, 126,* 884–888.

Conners, C. K. (1970). Symptom patterns in hyperkinetic, neurotic, and normal children. *Child Development, 41,* 667–682.

Conners, C. K. (1989). *Conners rating scales.* Toronto, Canada: Multi-Health Systems.

Conners, C. K. (1990). *Conners rating scales manual.* New York: Multi-Health Systems.

Conoley, J. C., & Conoley, C. W. (1991). Collaboration for child adjustment: Issues for school and clinic-based child psychologists. *Journal of Consulting and Clinical Psychology, 59,* 821–829.

Constatino, G. (1986). *TEMAS (Tell me a story).* Los Angeles: Western Psychological Services.

Cooper, D. K. (1990). Developmental trends in Children's Depression Inventory responses across age and gender. Master's thesis, University of Georgia, Athens.

Corbett, J. A., & Trimble, M. R. (1983). Epilepsy and anticonvulsant medication. In M. Rutter (Ed.), *Devel-*

opmental neuropsychiatry (pp. 112–132). New York: Guilford Press.

Costa, P. T., & McCrae, R. R. (1985). *The NEO personality inventory manual.* New York: Psychological Assessment Resources.

Costello, A. J. (1983). The *NIMH diagnostic interview schedule for children.* Pittsburgh, PA: University of Pittsburgh.

Costello, A. J., Edelbrock, C., Dulcan, M. K., Kalas, R., & Klaric, S. (1987). *Diagnostic interview schedule for children (DISC).* Pittsburgh, PA: Western Psychiatric Institute and Clinic, School of Medicine, University of Pittsburgh.

Costello, E. J. (1989). Child psychiatric disorders and their correlates: A primary care pediatric sample. *Journal of the American Academy of Child and Adolescent Psychiatry, 28,* 851–888.

Costello, E. J., Edelbrock, C. S., & Costello, A. J. (1985). Validity of the NIMH Diagnostic Interview Schedule for Children: A comparison between psychiatric and pediatric referrals. *Journal of Abnormal Child Psychology, 13,* 579–595.

Crnic, K. A., & Reid, M. (1989). Mental retardation. In E. J. Mash & R. A. Barkley (Eds.), *Treatment of childhood disorders* (pp. 247–346). New York: Guilford Press.

Cuellar, I., Harris, I. C., & Jasso, R. (1980). An acculturation scale for Mexican American normal and clinical populations. Hispanic *Journal of Behavioral Science, 2,* 199–217.

Cummings, J. A. (1986). Projective drawings. In H. M. Knoff (Ed.), *The assessment of child and adolescent personality* (pp. 199–244). New York: Guilford Press.

Curry, J. F., & Craighead, W. E. (1993). Depression. In T. H. Ollendick & M. Hersen (Eds.), *Handbook of child and adolescent assessment* (pp. 251–268). Needham Heights, MA: Allyn and Bacon.

Cytryn, L., & McKnew, D. H. (1974). Factors influencing the changing clinical expression of the depressive process in children. *American Journal of Psychiatry, 131,* 879–881.

Dahlstrom, W. G. (1993). Small samples, large consequences. *American Psychologist, 48,* 393–399.

Dalby, J. T. (1985). Taxonomic separation of attention deficit disorders. *Contemporary Educational Psychology, 10,* 228–234.

Dana, R. H. (1993). *Multicultural assessment perspectives for professional psychology.* Needham Heights, MA: Allyn and Bacon.

Daniel, M. H. (1993, August). Diagnostic specificity of parents' and teachers' behavior ratings. Paper presented at the annual meeting of the American Psychological Association, Washington, DC.

Darling, N., & Steinberg, L. (1993). Parenting style as context: An integrative model. *Psychological Bulletin, 113,* 487–496.

The Departments of Psychiatry and Child Psychiatry, The Institute of Psychiatry, & The Maudsley Hospital London (1987). *Psychiatric examination. Notes on eliciting and recording clinical information in psychiatric patients.* Oxford: Oxford University Press.

DeBaryshe, B. D., Patterson, G. R., & Capaldi, D. M. (1993). A performance model for academic achievement in early adolescent boys. *Developmental Psychology, 29*(5), 795–804.

DeStefano, L., & Thompson, D. S. (1990). Adaptive behavior: The construct and its measurement. In C. R. Reynolds & R. W. Kamphaus (Eds.), *Handbook of psychological and educational assessment of children: Personality, behavior, and context.* New York: Guilford Press.

Dishion, T. J., Patterson, G. R., & Skinner, M. S. (1989). A process model for the role of peers in adolescent social adjustment. Paper presented at the biennial meeting of the Society for Research in Child Development. Kansas City, MO.

diSibio, M. (1993). Conjoint effects of intelligence and adaptive behavior on achievement in a nonreferred sample. *Journal of Psychoeducational Assessment, 11,* 304–313.

Dodge, K. A. (1983). Behavioral antecedents of peer social status. *Child Development, 54,* 1386–1399.

Dodge, K. A., Coie, J., Brakke, N. (1982). Behavior patterns of socially rejected and neglected adolescents: The roles of social approach and aggression. *Journal of Abnormal Child Psychology, 10,* 389–410.

Dodge, K. A., McClaskey, C. L., & Feldman, E. (1985). Situational approach to the assessment of social competence in children. *Journal of Consulting and Clinical Psychology, 53,* 344–353.

Doleys, D. M. (1977). Behavioral treatments for nocturnal enuresis in children: A review of the recent literature. *Psychological Bulletin, 84,* 30–54.

Doll, E. A. (1940). A social basis of mental diagnosis. *Journal of Applied Psychology, 24,* 160–169.

Doll, E. A. (1953). *Measurement of social competence: A manual for the Vineland Social Maturity Scale.* Circle Pines, MN: American Guidance Services.

Douthitt, V. L. (1992). A comparison of adaptive behavior in gifted and nongifted children. *Roeper Review, 14,* 149–151.

Downey, G., & Coyne, J. C. (1990). Children of depressed parents: An integrative review. *Psychological Bulletin, 108,* 50–76.

Dresden, J. (1994). Gender, temperament, and mathematics achievement. Ph.D. diss., University of Georgia, Athens.

Drotar, D., Stein, R. E. K., & Perrin, E. C. (1995). Methodological issues in using the child behavior checklist and its related instruments in clinical child psychology research. *Journal of Clinical Child Psychology, 24*(2), 184–192.

DuBois, P. H. (1970). *A history of psychological testing.* Needham Heights, MA: Allyn and Bacon.

DuPaul, G. J., Anastopolous, A. D., Shelton, T. L., Guevremont, D. C., & Metevia, L. (1992). Multimethod assessment of Attention-deficit Hyperactivity Disorder: The diagnostic utility of clinic-based tests. *Journal of Clinical Child Psychology, 21,* 394–402.

DuPaul, G. J., Rapport, M. D., & Perriello, L. M. (1991). Teacher ratings of academic skills: The development of the Academic Performance Rating Scale. *School Psychology Review, 20,* 284–300.

Eason, L. J., Finch, A. J., Brasted, W., & Saylor, C. F. (1985). The assessment of depression and anxiety in hospitalized pediatric patients. *Child Psychiatry and Human Development, 16*(1), 57–64.

Eaves, R. C., & Milner, B. (1993). The criterion-related validity of the Childhood Autism Rating Scale and the Autism Behavior Checklist. *Journal of Abnormal Child Psychology, 21*(5), 481–491.

Eaves, L. C., Ho, H. H., & Eaves, D. M. (1994). Subtypes of autism by cluster analysis. *Journal of Autism and Developmental Disorders, 24*(1), 3–22.

Edelbrock, C. (1979). Empirical classification of children's behavior disorders: Progress based on parent and teacher ratings. *School Psychology Digest, 8,* 355–369.

Edelbrock, C., & Costello, A. J. (1988). Convergence between statistically derived behavior problem syndromes and child psychiatric diagnoses. *Journal of Abnormal Child Psychology, 16,* 219–231.

Edelbrock, C., Costello, A. J., Dulcan, M. K., Conover, N. C., & Kalas, R. (1986). Parent–child agreement on child psychiatric symptoms assessed via structured interview. *Journal of Child Psychology and Psychiatry, 27,* 181–190.

Edelbrock, C., Costello, A. J., Dulcan, M. K., Kalas, R., & Conover, N. C. (1985). Age differences in the reliability of the psychiatric interview of the child. *Child Development, 56,* 265–275.

Edelsohn, G., Ialongo, N., Werthamer-Larrson, L., Crockett, L., & Kellam, S. (1992). Self-reported depressive symptoms in first-grade children: Developmentally transient phenomena? *Journal of the American Academy of Child and Adolescent Psychiatry, 31,* 282–290.

Education for All Handicapped Children's Act of 1975, P.L. 94-142, 20 U.S.C. Section 1401 (1975).

Eisenstadt, T. H., Eyberg, S., McNeil, C. B., Newcomb, K., & Funderbunk, B. (1993). Parent–child interaction therapy with behavior problem children: Relative effectiveness of two stages and overall treatment outcome. *Journal of Clinical Child Psychology, 22,* 42–51.

Elliot, D. S., Huizinga, D., & Ageton, S. S. (1985). *Explaining delinquency and drug use.* Newbury, Park, CA: Sage.

Emery, R. E. (1982). Interparental conflict and the children of discord and divorce. *Psychological Bulletin, 92,* 310–330.

Endicott, J., & Spitzer, R. L. (1978). A diagnostic interview: The Schedule for Affective Disorders and Schizophrenia. *Archives of General Psychiatry, 35,* 57–63.

Erikson, E. H. (1968). *Identity, youth, and crisis.* New York: Norton.

Exner, J. E. (1974). *The Rorschach: A comprehensive system, I.* New York: Wiley.

Exner, J. E. (1978). *The Rorschach: A comprehensive system, II: Recent research and advanced interpretation.* New York: Wiley.

Exner, J. E. (1983, June 13). The depression index. *1983 Alumni Newsletter* (p. 7). Bayville, NY: Rorschach Workshops.

Exner, J. E. (1990, April 16). The depression index. *1990 Alumni Newsletter* (pp. 12–13). Asheville, NC: Rorschach Workshops.

Exner, J. E., & Martin, L. S. (1983). The Rorschach: A history and description of the comprehensive system. *School Psychology Review, 12,* 407–413.

Exner, J. E., Thomas, E. A., & Mason, B. (1985). Children's Rorschachs: Description and prediction. *Journal of Personality Assessment, 49,* 13–20.

Exner, J. E., Jr., & Weiner, I. B. (1982). *The Rorschach: A comprehensive system. III: Assessment of children and adolescents.* New York: Wiley.

Eyberg, S. M., & Robinson, E. E. (1982). Conduct problem behavior: Standardization of a behavioral rating scale with adolescents. *Journal of Clinical Child Psychology, 12,* 347–354.

Eyberg, S. M., & Robinson, E. A. (1983). Dyadic Parent-Child Interaction Coding System: A manual. *Psychological Documents, 13,* 24 (Ms. No. 2582).

Eyberg, S. M., & Ross, A. W. (1978). Assessment of child behavior problems: The validation of a new inventory. *Journal of Clinical Child Psychology,* Summer, 113–116.

Eysenck, H. J. (1965). [Review of the Wittenborn Psychiatric Rating Scales.] In O. K. Buros (Ed.), *Mental Measurements Yearbook* (5th ed.). Highland Park, NJ: Gryphon Press.

Faraone, S. V., Biederman, J., Keenan, K., & Tsuang, M. T. (1991). Separation of DSM-III Attention Deficit Disorder and Conduct Disorder: Evidence from a family genetic study of American child psychiatric patients. *Psychological Medicine, 21,* 109–121.

Farrington, D. P. (1993). Motivations for conduct disorder and delinquency. *Development and Psychopathology, 5,* 225–242.

Feighner, J. P., Robins, E., Guze, S. B., Woodruff, R. A., Winokur, G., & Munoz, R. (1972). Diagnostic criteria for use in psychiatric research. *Archives of General Psychiatry, 26,* 57–63.

Feinberg, T. L., Crouse-Novak, M. A., Paulauskas, S. L., & Finkelstein, R. (1984). Depressive disorders in childhood: I. A longitudinal prospective study of characteristics and recovery. *Archives of General Psychiatry, 41,* 229–237.

Figueroa, R. A. (1990). Assessment of linguistic minority group children. In C. R. Reynolds & R. W. Kamphaus (Eds.), *Handbook of psychological and educational assessment of chidren: Intelligence and achievement.* New York: Guilford Press.

Finch, A. J., & Belter, R. W. (1993). Projective techniques. In T. H. Ollendick & M. Hersen (Eds.), *Handbook of child and adolescent assessment* (pp. 224–238). Needham Heights, MA: Allyn and Bacon.

Finch, A. J., Lipovsky, J. A., & Casat, C. D. (1989). Anxiety and depression in children and adolescents: Negative affectivity or separate constructs? In P. C. Kendall & D. Watson (Eds.), *Anxiety and depression: Distinctive and overlapping features* (pp. 171–202). New York: Academic Press.

Finch, A. J., Saylor, C. F., & Edwards, G. L. (1985). Children's depression inventory: Sex and grade norms for normal children. *Journal of Consulting and Clinical Psychology, 53,* 424–425.

Fisher, P., Wicks, J., Shaffer, D., Piacentini, J., & Lapkin, J. (1992). *NIMH Diagnostic Interview Schedule for Children: Users manual.* New York: New York State Psychiatric Institute.

Fombonne, E. (1992). Diagnostic assessment in a sample of autistic and developmentally impaired adolescents. Special Issue: Classification and diagnosis. *Journal of Autism & Developmental Disorders, 22*(4), 563–581.

Forness, S. R., & Knitzer, J. (1992). A new proposed definition and terminology to replace "serious emotional disturbance" in the Individuals with Disabilities Act. *School Psychology Review, 21,* 12–20.

Fowler, P. (1982). Factor structure of the Family Environment Scale: Effects of social desirability. *Journal of Clinical Psychology, 38,* 285–292.

Francis, G., & Borden, J. (1993). Expression and treatment of obsessive-compulsive disorder in childhood, adolescence, and adulthood. In C. G. Last (Ed.), *Anxiety across the lifespan: A developmental perspective* (pp. 148–166). New York: Springer.

Franco, J. N. (1983). An acculturation scale for Mexican-American children. *Journal of General Psychology, 108,* 175–181.

Freeman, B. J., & Schroth, P. C. (1984). The development of the Behavioral Observation Scale (BOS) for autism. *Behavioral Assessment, 6,* 177–187.

Freeman, B. J., Ritvo, E. R., Yokota, A., & Ritvo, A. (1986). A scale for rating symptoms of patients with the syndrome of autism in real life settings. *Journal of the American Academy of Child Psychiatry, 25*(1), 130–136.

French, J. L., & Hale, R. L. (1990). A history of the development of psychological and educational testing. In C. R. Reynolds & R. W. Kamphaus (Eds.), *Handbook of psychological and educational assessment of children: Intelligence and achievement* (pp. 3–28). New York: Guilford Press.

Frick, P. J. (1990). *The Alabama parenting questionnaire.* Tuscaloosa: University of Alabama.

Frick, P. J. (1993). Childhood conduct problems in family context. *School Psychology Review, 22,* 376–385.

Frick, P. J. (1994). Family dysfunction and the disruptive behavior disorders: A review of recent empirical findings. In T. H. Ollendick & R. J. Prinz (Eds.), *Advances in clinical child psychology* (vol. 16. pp. 203–226). New York: Plenum.

Frick, P. J., & Jackson, Y. K. (1993). Family functioning and childhood antisocial behavior: Yet another reinterpretation. *Journal of Clinical Child Psychology, 22,* 410–419.

Frick, P. J., Kamphaus, R. W., Lahey, B. B., Loeber, R., Christ, M. A. G., Hart, E. L., & Tannenbaum, L. E. (1991). Academic underachievement and the disruptive behavior disorders. *Journal of Consulting and Clinical Psychology, 59,* 289–294.

Frick, P. J., & Lahey, B. B. (1991). The nature and characteristics of attention-deficit hyperactivity disorder. *School Psychology Review, 20,* 163–173.

Frick, P. J., Lahey, B. B., Applegate, B., Kerdyck, L., Ollendick, T., Hynd, G. W., Garfinkel, B., Greenhill, L., Biederman, J., Barkley, R. A., McBurnett, K., Newcorn, J., & Waldman, I. (1994). DSM-IV field trials for the disruptive behavior disorders. *Journal of the American Academy of Child and Adolescent Psychiatry, 33,* 529–539.

Frick, P. J., Lahey, B. B., Christ, M. G., Loeber, R., & Green, S. (1991). History of childhood behavior problems in biological relatives of boys with Attention-deficit Hyperactivity Disorder and Conduct Disorder. *Journal of Clinical Child Psychology, 20,* 445–451.

Frick, P. J., Lahey, B. B., Hartdagen, S., & Hynd, G. W. (1989). Conduct problems in boys: Relations to maternal personality, marital satisfaction, and socioeconomic status. *Journal of Clinical Child Psychology, 18,* 114–120.

Frick, P. J., Lahey, B. B., Loeber, R., Stouthamer-Loeber, M., Christ, M. G., & Hanson, K. (1992). Familial risk factors to oppositional Defiant Disorder and Conduct Disorder: Parental psychopathology and maternal parenting. *Journal of Consulting and Clinical Psychology, 60,* 49–55.

Frick, P. J., Lahey, B. B., Loeber, R., Tannenbaum, L. E., Van Horn, Y., Christ, M. A. G., Hart, E. A., & Hansen, K. (1993). Oppositional Defiant Disorder and Conduct Disorder: A meta-analytic review of factor analyses and cross-validation in a clinic sample. *Clinical Psychology Review, 13,* 319–340.

Frick, P. J., Lahey, B. B., Strauss, C. C., & Christ, M. A. G. (1993). Behavior disorders of children. In H. E. Adams & P. B. Sutker (Eds.), *Comprehensive handbook of psychopathology* (2d ed., pp. 765–789). New York: Plenum.

Frick, P. J., & O'Brien, B. S. (1994). Conduct disorders. In R. T. Ammerman & M. Hersen (Eds.), *Handbook of child behavior therapy in the psychiatric setting* (pp. 199–216). New York: Wiley.

Frick, P. J., Silverthorn, P., & Evans, C. S. (1994). Assessment of childhood anxiety using structured interviews: Patterns of agreement among informants and association with maternal anxiety. *Psychological Assessment, 6,* 372–379.

Frick, P. J., Strauss, C. C., Lahey, B. B., & Christ, M. A. G. (1993). Behavior disorders of children. In P. B. Sutker & H. E. Adams (Eds.), *Comprehensive handbook of psychopathology* (2d ed., pp. 765–789). New York: Plenum.

Friedlander, S., Weiss, D. S., & Traylor, J. (1986). Assessing the influence of maternal depression on the validity of the Child Behavior Checklist. *Journal of Abnormal Child Psychology, 14,* 123–133.

Fuchs, D. (1987). Examiner familiarity effects on test performance: Implications for training and practice. *Topics in Early Childhood Special Education, 102,* 90–104.

Fuchs, D., & Fuchs, L. S. (1986). Test procedure bias: A meta-analysis of examiner familiarity effects. *Review of Educational Research, 56,* 243–262.

Funderbunk, B. W., & Eyberg, S. M. (1989). Psychometric characteristics of the Sutter-Eyberg Student Behavior Inventory: A school behavior rating scale for use with preschool children. *Behavioral Assessment, 11,* 297-313.

Gallucci, N. T. (1989). Personality assessment with children of superior intelligence: Divergence versus psychopathology. *Journal of Personality Assessment, 53,* 749–760.

Galton, F. (1884). Measurement of character. *Fortnightly Review, 42,* 179–185. Reprinted in L. D.

Goodstein & R. I. Lanyon (Eds.), *Readings in Personality Assessment.* New York: Wiley

Gantner, A. B., Graham, J. R., & Archer, R. A. (1992). Usefulness of the MAC scale in differentiating adolescents in normal, psychiatric, and substance abuse settings. *Psychological Assessment, 4*(2), 133–137.

Garber, J. (1984). Classification of childhood psychopathology: A developmental perspective. *Child Development, 55,* 30–48.

Garcia, M., & Lega, L. I. (1979). Development of a Cuban ethnic identity questionnaire. Hispanic *Journal of Behavioral Sciences, 1,* 247–261.

Geisinger, K. F. (1992). Fairness and selected psychometric issues in the psychological testing of Hispanics. In K. F. Geisinger (Ed.), *Psychological testing of Hispanics* (pp. 17–42). Washington, DC: American Psychological Association.

Gelfand, D. M., & Hartmann, D. P. (1984). *Child behavior analysis and therapy* (2d ed.). New York: Pergamon Press.

Geller, B., Fox, L. W., & Fletcher, M. (1993). Effect of tricyclic antidepressants on switching to mania and on the onset of bipolarity in depressed 6- to 12-year olds. *Journal of the American Academy of Child and Adolescent Psychiatry, 32,* 43–50.

Ghaziuddin, M., Tsai, L., & Ghaziuddin, N. (1992). Comorbidity of autistic disorder in children and adolescents. *European Child & Adolescent Psychiatry, 1*(4), 209–213.

Ghiselli, E. E., Campbell, J. P., & Zedeck, S. (1981). *Measurement theory for the behavioral sciences.* San Francisco: W. H. Freeman.

Gittelman-Klein, R. (1986). Questioning the clinical usefulness of projective psychological tests for children. *Developmental and Behavioral Pediatrics, 7,* 378–382.

Gittelman, R., Mannuzza, S., Shenker, R., & Bonegura, N. (1985). Hyperactive boys almost grown up: I. Psychiatric status. *Archives of General Psychiatry, 42,* 937–947.

Glasser, A. J., & Zimmerman, I. L. (1967). *Clinical interpretation of the Wechsler Intelligence Scale for Children.* New York: Grune & Stratton.

Glueck, S., & Glueck, E. (1968). *Delinquents and nondelinquents in perspective.* Cambridge, MA: Harvard University Press.

Glutting, J. J., & Kaplan, D. (1990). Stanford-Binet Intelligence Scale: Fourth Edition: Making the case for reasonable interpretations. In C. R. Reynolds & R. W. Kamphaus (Eds.), *Handbook of psychological and educational assessment of children: Personality, behavior, and context.* New York: Guilford Press.

Goldberg, L. R. (1992). The development of markers for the big-five factor structure. *Psychological Assessment, 4,* 26–42.

Gordon, M. (1983). *The Gordon diagnostic system.* DeWitt, NY: Gordon Systems.

Gorsuch, R. L. (1988). *Factor analysis* (3d ed.). Hillsdale, NJ: Erlbaum.

Goyette, C. H., Conners, C. K., & Ulrich, R. F. (1978). Normative data on revised Conners parent and teacher rating scales. *Journal of Abnormal Child Psychology, 6,* 221–236.

Green, K., Vosk, B., Forehand, R., & Beck, S. (1981). An examination of differences among sociometrically identified accepted, rejected, and neglected children. *Child Study Journal, 11,* 117–124.

Green, M. (1992). *Pediatric diagnosis: Interpretation of symptoms and signs in infants, children, and adolescents (5th ed.).* Philadelphia: Saunders.

Gresham, F. M., & Little, S. G. (1993). Peer-referenced assessment strategies. In T. H. Ollendick & M. Hersen (Eds.), *Handbook of child and adolescent assessment* (pp. 165–179). Needham Heights, MA: Allyn and Bacon.

Gresham, R. M., & Elliott, S. N. (1990). *Social skills rating system.* Circle Pines, MN: American Guidance Service.

Gutterman, E. M., O'Brien, J. D., & Young, J. G. (1987). Structured diagnostic interviews for children and adolescents: Current status and future directions. *Journal of the American Academy of Child and Adolescent Psychiatry, 26,* 621–630.

Haak, R. A. (1990). Using the sentence completion to assess emotional disturbance. In C. R. Reynolds & R. W. Kamphaus (Eds.), *Handbook of psychological and educational assessment of children: Personality, behavior, and context* (pp. 147–167). New York: Guilford Press.

Haley, G. M. T., Fine, S., Marriage, K., Moretti, M. M., & Freeman R. J. (1985). Cognitive bias and depression in psychiatrically disturbed children and adolescents. *Journal of Consulting and Clinical Psychology, 53,* 535–537.

Hall, C. W., &. Haws, H. D. (1989). Depressive symptomatology in learning-disabled and nonlearning-disabled students. *Psychology in the Schools, 26,* 359–364.

Hammen, C., Gordon, G., Burge, D., Adrian, C., Jaenicke, C., & Hiroto, G. (1987). Maternal affective disorders, illness, and stress: Risk for children's psychopathology. *American Journal of Psychiatry, 144,* 736–741.

Hammer, E. F. (1958). *The clinical application of projective drawings.* Springfield, IL: Thomas.

Harrington, R. G., & Follett, G. M. (1984). The readability of child personality assessment instruments. *Journal of Psychoeducational Assessment, 2,* 37–48.

Harrington, R., Fudge, H., Rutter, M., Pickles, A., & Hill, J. (1991). Adult outcomes of childhood and adolescent depression: II. Links with antisocial disorders. *Journal of the American Academy of Child and Adolescent Psychiatry, 30,* 434–439.

Harris, F. C., & Lahey, B. B. (1982a). Recording system bias in direct observational methodology: A review and critical analysis of factors causing inaccurate coding behavior. *Clinical Psychology Review, 2,* 539–556.

Harris, F. C., & Lahey, B. B. (1982b). Subject reactivity in direct observational assessment: A review and critical analysis. *Clinical Psychology Review, 2,* 523–538.

Harrison, P. L. (1990). Assessment with the Vineland Adaptive Behavior Scales. In C. R. Reynolds & R. W. Kamphaus (Eds.), *Handbook of psychological and educational assessment of children: Personality, behavior, and context.* New York: Guilford Press.

Hart, D. H. (1972). *The Hart sentence completion test for children.* Salt Lake City: Educational Support Systems.

Hart, D. H. (1986). The sentence completion techniques. In H. M. Knoff (Ed.), *The assessment of child and adolescent personality* (pp. 245–272). New York: Guilford Press.

Hart, D. H., Kehle, T. J., & Davies, M. V. (1983). Effectiveness of sentence completion techniques: A review of the Hart Sentence Completion Test for Children. *School Psychology Review, 12,* 428–434.

Hartmann, D. P., Roper, B. L., & Bradford, D. C. (1979). Some relationships between behavioral and traditional assessment. *Journal of Behavioral Assessment, 1,* 3–21.

Harvey, V. S. (1989, March). Eschew obfuscation: Support of clear writing. *Communique,* p. 12.

Hasegawa, C. (1989). The unmentioned minority. In C. J. Maker & L. W. Schiever (Eds.), *Defensive programs for cultural and ethnic minorities* (vol. 2). Austin, TX: Pro-Ed.

Hathaway, S. R., & McKinley, J. C. (1940). A multiphasic personality schedule (Minnesota): I. Construction of the schedule. *Journal of Psychology, 10,* 249–254.

Hathaway, S. R., & McKinley, J. C. (1942). *Minnesota Multiphasic Personality Inventory.* Minneapolis: University of Minnesota Press.

Hathaway, S. R., & McKinley, J. C. (1989). *MMPI-2: Minnesota Multiphasic Personality Inventory—Second Edition.* Minneapolis: University of Minnesota Press.

Hayvren, M., & Hymel, S. (1984). Ethical issues in sociometric testing: Impact of sociometric measures on interaction behavior. *Developmental Psychology, 20,* 849–884.

Heber, R. (1959). A manual on terminology and classification in mental retardation (2d ed.). (Monograph supplement). *American Journal of Mental Deficiency.*

Heber, R., & Helzer, J. E. (1988). Schizophrenia: Epidemiology. In R. Michels, J. O. Cavenar, A. M. Cooper, S. B. Guze, L. L. Judd, G. L. Klerman, & A. J. Solnit (Eds.), *Psychiatry.* New York: Lippincott.

Helzer, J. E. (1988). Schizophrenia: Epidemiology. In R. Michels, J. O. Cavenar, A. M. Cooper, S. B. Guze, L. L. Judd, G. L. Klerman, & A. J. Solnit (Eds.), *Psychiatry.* New York: Lippincott.

Hetherington, E. M., & Martin, B. (1986). Family factors and psychopathology in children. In H. C. Quay & J. S. Werry (Eds.), *Psychopathological disorders of childhood* (3d ed., pp. 332–390). New York: Wiley.

Hill, A. B., Kemp-Wheeler, S. M., & Jones, S. A. (1986). What does the Beck Depression Inventory measure in students? *Personality and Individual Differences, 7,* 39–47.

Hinshaw, S. P. (1987). On the distinction between attentional deficits/hyperactivity and conduct problems/aggression in child psychopathology. *Psychological Bulletin, 101,* 443–463.

Hinshaw, S. P. (1991). Stimulant medications and their treatment of aggression in children with attention deficits. *Journal of Clinical Child Psychology, 20,* 301–312.

Hinshaw, S. P. (1992). Externalizing behavior problems and academic underachievement in childhood and adolescence: Causal relationships and underlying mechanisms. *Psychological Bulletin, 111,* 127–155.

Hodges, K., Cool, J., & McKnew, D. (1989). Test-retest reliability of a clinical research interview for children: The Child Assessment Schedule (CAS). *Psychological Assessment, 1,* 317–322.

Hodges, K., Kline, J., Stern, L., Cytryn, L, & McKnew, D. (1982). The development of a child assessment schedule for research and clinical use. *Journal of Abnormal Child Psychology, 10,* 173–189.

Hodges, K., & Saunders, W. (1989). Internal consistency of a diagnostic interview for children: The Child Assessment Schedule. *Journal of Abnormal Child Psychology, 17,* 691–701.

Hodges, K., & Zeman, J. (1993). Interviewing. In T. H. Ollendick & M. Hersen (Eds.), *Handbook of child and adolescent assessment* (pp. 65–81). Needham Heights, MA: Allyn and Bacon.

Holtzman, W. H., & Swartz, J. D. (1990). Use of the Holtzman Inkblot Technique (HIT) with children. In C. R. Reynolds & R. W. Kamphaus (Eds.), *Handbook of psychological and educational assessment of children: Personality, behavior, and context* (pp. 187–203). New York: Guilford Press.

Hoza, B. (1994). Review of the Behavior Assessment System for Children. *Child Assessment News, 4*(1), 5, 8–10.

Huesmann, L. R., Eron, L. D., Lefkowitz, M. M., & Walder, L. O. (1984). Stability of aggression over time and generations. *Developmental Psychology, 20,* 1120–1134.

Hughes, J. (1990). Assessment of social skills: Sociometric and behavioral approaches. In C. R. Reynolds & R. W. Kamphaus (Eds.), *Handbook of psychological and educational assessment of children: Personality, behavior, and context* (pp. 423–444). New York: Guilford Press.

Hutt, M. L. (1980). *The Michigan picture test—revised.* New York: Grune & Stratton.

Hynd, G. W., & Willis, W. G. (1988). *Pediatric neuropsychology.* Needham Heights, MA: Allyn and Bacon.

Inclan, J. E., & Herron, D. G. (1985). Puerto Rican adolescents. In G. T. Gibbs & L. N. Huang (Eds.), *Children of color.* San Francisco: Jossey-Bass.

Jersild, A. T., & Holmes, R. (1935). *Children's fears* (Child Development Monograph No. 20). New York: Columbia University Press.

Jesness, C. F. (1988). *Jesness inventory of adolescent*

personality. North Tonawanda, NY: Multi-Health Systems.

Johnson, S. B. (1988). Diabetes mellitus in childhood. In D. Routh (Ed.), *Handbook of pediatric psychology* (pp. 9–31). New York: Guilford Press.

Johnston, C., Pelham, W. E., & Murphy, H. A. (1985). Peer relationships in ADHD and normal children: A developmental analysis of peer and teacher ratings. *Journal of Abnormal Child Psychology, 13,* 89–100.

Jones, K. M., & Witt, J. C. (1994). Rating the ratings of raters: A critique of the Behavior Assessment System for Children. *Child Assessment News, 4*(1),10–11.

Jonsen, A. R., Siegler, M., & Winslade, W. J. (1992). *Clinical ethics* (3d ed.). New York: McGraw-Hill.

Jung, C. J. (1910). The association method. *American Journal of Psychology, 21,* 219–235. Reprinted in L. D. Goodstein & R. I. Lanyon (Eds.), *Readings in Personality Assessment.* New York: Wiley.

Kachigan, S. K. (1982). *Multivariate statistical analysis: A conceptual introduction.* New York: Radus Press.

Kagan, J., & Snidman, N. (1991). Temperamental factors in human development. *American Psychologist, 46,* 856–862.

Kamphaus, R. W. (1993). *Clinical assessment of children's intelligence.* Needham Heights, MA: Allyn and Bacon.

Kamphaus, R. W., Morgan, A. W., Cox, M. R., & Powell, R. M. (1995). Personality and intelligence in the psychodiagnostic process. In D H. Saklofske & M. Zeidner (Eds.), *International handbook of personality and intelligence.* New York: Plenum Press.

Kandel, D. B., & Davies, M. (1988). Adult sequelae of adolescent depressive symptoms. *Archives of General Psychiatry, 43,* 255–262.

Kashani, J., Carlson, G. A., Beck, N. C., Hoeper, E. W., Corcoran, C. M., McAllister, J. A., Fallahi, C., Rosenberg, T. K., & Reid, J. C. (1987). Depression, depressive symptoms, and depressed mood among a community sample of adolescents. *American Journal of Psychiatry, 144,* 931–934.

Kashani, J. H., Henrichs, T. F., Reid, J. C., & Huff, C. (1982). Depression in diagnostic subtypes of delinquent boys. *Adolescence, 17*(68), 943–949.

Kashani, J. H., Orvaschel, H., Burk, J. P., & Reid, J. C. (1985). Informant variance: The issue of parent-child disagreement. *Journal of the American Academy of Child and Adolescent Psychiatry, 24,* 437–441.

Kashani, J., & Simonds, T. F. (1979). The incidence of major depression in children. *American Journal of Psychiatry, 136,* 1203–1205.

Kaufman, A.S. (1994). *Intelligent testing with the WISC-III.* New York: Wiley

Kazdin, A. E. (1981). Behavioral observation. In M. Hersen & A. S. Bellack (Eds.), *Behavioral assessment: A practical handbook* (pp. 59–100). New York: Pergamon Press.

Kazdin, A. E. (1988). Childhood depression. In E. J. Mash & L. G. Terdal (Eds.), *Behavioral assessment of childhood disorders* (2d ed., pp. 157–195). New York: Guilford Press.

Kazdin, A. E. (1989). Childhood depression. In E. J. Mash & R. A. Barkley (Eds.), *Treatment of childhood disorders* (pp. 135-166). New York: Guilford Press.

Kazdin, A. E., French N. H., Unis A. S., Esveldt-Dawson, K., & Sherick, R. B. (1983). Hopelessness, depression, and suicidal intent among psychiatrically disturbed inpatient children. *Journal of Consulting and Clinical Psychology, 51,* 504–510.

Keller, H. R. (1986). Behavioral observation approaches to personality assessment. In H. M. Knoff (Ed.), *The assessment of child and adolescent personality* (pp. 353–390). New York: Guilford Press.

Kendall, P. C., & Braswell, L. (1985). *Cognitive-behavioral therapy for impulsive children.* New York: Guilford Press.

Kendall, P. C., & Clarkin, J. F. (1992). Introduction to special section: Comorbidity and treatment implications. *Journal of Consulting and Clinical Psychology, 60,* 833–834.

Kendall, P. C., & Ronan, K. R. (1990). Assessment of children's anxieties, fears, and phobias: Cognitive-behavioral models and methods. In C. R. Reynolds & Kamphaus, R. W. (Ed.), *Handbook of psychological and educational assessment of children: Personality, behavior, and context* (pp. 223–244). New York: Guilford Press.

Keogh, B. K. (1994). A matrix of decision points in the measurement of learning disabilities. In G. R. Lyon (Ed.), *Frames of reference for the assessment of learning disabilities: New views on measurement issues* (pp. 15–26). Baltimore, MD: Paul H. Brookes.

Kleinmuntz, B. (1967). *Personality measurement: An introduction.* Homewood, IL: Dorsey Press.

Kline, R. B. (1995). New objective rating scales for

child assessment, II. Self-report scales for children and adolescents: Self-report of Personality of the Behavior Assessment System for Children, the Youth Self-Report, and the Personality Inventory for Youth. *Journal of Psychoeducational Assessment, 13,* 169–193.

Knoff, H. M. (1983). Justifying projective/personality assessment in school psychology: A response to Batsch and Peterson. *School Psychology Review, 12,* 446–451.

Kochanska, G., Kuczynski, L., & Radke-Yarrow, M. (1989). Correspondence between mothers' self-reported and observed child-rearing practices. *Child Development, 60,* 56–63.

Koocher, G. P. (1993). Ethical issues in the psychological assessment of children. In T. H. Ollendick & M. Hersen (Eds.), *Handbook of child and adolescent assessment.* Needham Heights, MA: Allyn and Bacon.

Koppitz, E. M. (1968). *Psychological evaluation of children's human figure drawings.* New York: Grune & Stratton.

Koppitz, E. M. (1983). Projective drawings with children and adolescents. *School Psychology Review, 12,* 421–427.

Kovacs, M. (1985). The Interview Schedule for Children (ISC). *Psychopharmacology Bulletin, 21,* 991–994.

Kovacs, M. (1989). Affective disorders in children and adolescents. *American Psychologist, 44*(2), 209–215.

Kovacs, M. (1991). *The children's depression inventory (CDI).* North Tonawanda, NY: Multi-Health Systems.

Kovacs, M. (1992). *The Children's Depression Inventory manual.* New York: Multi-Health Systems.

Kovacs, M., Feinberg, T. L., Crouse-Novak, M. A., Paulauskas, S. L., & Finkelstein, R. (1984). Depressive disorders in childhood: I. A longitudinal prospective study of characteristics and recovery. *Archives of General Psychiatry, 41,* 229–237.

Kovacs, M., Paulauskas, S., Gatsonis, C., & Richards, C. (1988). Depressives disorders in childhood: III. A longitudinal study of comorbidity with and risk for conduct disorders. *Journal of Affective Disorders, 15,* 205–217.

Kuehne, C., Kehle, T. J., & McMahon, W. (1987). Differences between children with Attention Deficit Disorder, children with Specific Learning Disabilities, and normal children. *Journal of School Psychology, 25,* 161–166.

Kuper, K. K., Frick, P. J., & Wootton, J. M. (1994). The *assessment of parenting practices in school-aged children.* Manuscript submitted for publication.

Lachar, D. (1982). *Personality inventory for children— revised (PIC-R).* Los Angeles: Western Psychological Services.

Lachar, D. (1990a). *Multidimensional description of child personality: A manual for the Personality Inventory for Children.* Los Angeles: Western Psychological Services.

Lachar, D. (1990b). Objective assessment of child and adolescent personality: The Personality Inventory for Children. In C. R. Reynolds & R. W. Kamphaus (Eds.), *Handbook of psychological and educational assessment of children: Personality, behavior, and context* (pp. 298–323). New York: Guilford Press.

Lachar, D. (1993). Symptom checklists and personality inventories. In T. R. Kratochwill & R. J. Morris (Eds.), *Handbook of psychotherapy for children and adolescents* (pp. 38–57). Needham Heights, MA: Allyn and Bacon.

Lachar, D., & Gruber, C. P. (1992). *Personality Inventory for Youth (PIY).* Los Angeles: Western Psychological Services.

Lachar, D., & Gruber, C. P. (1993). Development of the Personality Inventory for Youth: A self-report companion to the Personality Inventory for Children. *Journal of personality assessment, 61*(1), 81–98.

Lachar, D., & Gruber, C. P. (1994). *The Personality Inventory for Youth.* Los Angeles: Western Psychological Services.

LaCombe, J. A., Kline, R. B., Lachar, D., Butkus, M., & Hillman, S. B. (1991). Case history correlates of a Personality Inventory for Children (PIC) profile typology. *Psychological Assessment, 3,* 678–687.

Lahey, B. B., Applegate, B., McBurnett, K., Biederman, J., Greenhill, L. Hynd, G. W., Barkley, R. A., Newcorn, J., Jensen, P., Richters, J., Garfinkel, B., Kerdyck, L., Frick, P. J., Ollendick, T., Perez, D., Hart, E. L., Waldman, I., & Shaffer, D. (1994). DSM-IV field trials for Attention-Deficit Hyperactivity Disorder in children and adolescents. *American Journal of Psychiatry, 151,* 1673–1685.

Lahey, B. B., Loeber, R., Quay, H. C., Frick, P. J., & Grimm, J. (1992). Oppositional defiant disorder and conduct disorders: Issues to be resolved for DSM-IV. *Journal of the American Academy of Child and Adolescent Psychiatry, 31,* 539–546.

Lahey, B. B., Loeber, R., Stouthamer-Loeber, M., Christ, M. A. G., Green, S. M., Russo, M. F., Frick, P. J., & Dulcan, M. (1990). Comparison of DSM-III and DSM-III-R diagnoses for prepubertal children: Changes in prevalence and validity. *Journal of the American Academy of Child and Adolescent Psychiatry, 29,* 620–626.

Lahey, B. B., Pelham, W. E., Schaughency, E. A., Atkins, M. S., Murphy, A., Hynd, G. W., Russo, M., Hartdagen, S., & Lorys-Vernon, A. (1988). Dimensions and types of attention deficit disorder. *Journal of the American Academy of Child and Adolescent Psychiatry, 27,* 330–335.

Lahey, B. B., & Piacentini, J. C. (1985). An evaluation of the Quay-Peterson Revised Behavior Problem Checklist. *Journal of School Psychology, 23,* 285–289.

Lambert, N. M. (1988). Adolescent outcomes for hyperactive children: Perspectives on general and specific patterns of childhood risk for adolescent educational, social and mental health problems. *American Psychologist, 43,* 786–799.

Lambert, N., Nihira, K., & Leland, H. (1993). *AAMR adaptive behavior scale—school* (2d. ed.)(ABS-S:2). Austin, TX: Pro-Ed.

Last, C. G. (1987). Developmental considerations. In C. G. Last & M. Hersen (Eds.), *Issues in diagnostic research* (pp. 201–216). New York: Plenum.

Last, C. G. (1993a). Introduction. In C. G. Last (Ed.), *Anxiety across the lifespan: A developmental perspective* (pp. 1–6). New York: Springer.

Last, C. G. (1993b). Conclusions and future directions. In C. G. Last (Ed.), *Anxiety across the lifespan: A developmental perspective* (pp. 204–213). New York: Springer.

Last, C. G., Hersen, M., Kazdin, A. E., Francis, G., & Grubb, H. J. (1987). Psychiatric illness in the mothers of anxious children. *American Journal of Psychiatry, 144,* 1580–1583.

Le Couteur, A., Rutter, M., Lord, C., Rios, P., Robertson, S., Holdgrafer, M., & McLennan, J. (1989). Autism Diagnostic Interview: A standardized investigator-based instrument. *Journal of Autism and Developmental Disorders, 19,* 363–387.

Lefkowitz, M. M., & Tesiny, E. P. (1980). Assessment of childhood depression. *Journal of Consulting and Clinical Psychology, 48,* 43–50.

Locke, H. J., & Wallace, K. M. (1959). Short marital-adjustment and prediction tests: Their reliability and validity. *Marriage and Family Living, 21,* 251–255.

Loeber, R. (1991). Antisocial behavior: More enduring than changeable? *Journal of the American Academy of Child and Adolescent Psychiatry, 30,* 393–397

Loeber, R., Green, S. M., & Lahey, B. B. (1990). Mental health professionals' perception of the utility of children, mothers, and teachers as informants on childhood psychopathology. *Journal of Clinical Child Psychology, 19,* 136–143.

Loeber, R., Green, S. M., Lahey, B. B., Christ, M. A. G., & Frick, P. J. (1992). Developmental sequences in the age of onset of disruptive child behaviors. *Journal of Child and Family Studies, 1,* 21–41.

Loeber, R., Green, S. M., Lahey, B. B., & Stouthamer-Loeber, M. (1991). Differences and similarities between children, mothers, and teachers as informants on disruptive child behavior. *Journal of Abnormal Child Psychology, 19,* 75–95.

Loeber, R., & Stouthamer-Loeber, M. (1986). Family factors as correlates and predictors of juvenile conduct problems and delinquency. In M. Tonry & N. Morris (Eds.), *Crime and justice* (vol. 7, pp. 29–149). Chicago: University of Chicago Press.

Longman, Inc. (1984). *Longman dictionary of psychology and psychiatry.* New York: Author.

Lord, C., Rutter, M., Goode, S., Heemsbergen, J., Jordan, H., Mawhood, L., & Schopler, E. (1989). Autism Diagnostic Observation Schedule: A standardized observation of communicative and social behavior. *Journal of Autism and Developmental Disorders, 19,* 185–212.

Lord, C., Storoschuk, S., Rutter, M., & Pickles, A. (1993). Using the ADI-R to diagnose autism in preschool children. *Infant Mental Health Journal, 14*(3), 234–252.

Lorr, M. (1965). [Review of the Wittenborn Psychiatric Rating Scales]. In O. K. Buros (Ed.), *Mental measurements yearbook* (5th ed.). Highland Park, NJ: Gryphon Press.

Love, A. S., & McIntosh, D. E. (March, 1994). Differential diagnosis of attention deficit hyperactivity disordered and emotionally/behaviorally disordered children using the Temperament Assessment Battery for children. Paper presented at the National Association of School Psychology annual meeting, Seattle, WA.

Lubin, B., Larsen, R., & Matarazzo, J. (1984). Patterns of psychological test usage in the United States: 1935–1982. *American Psychologist, 39,* 451–454.

Lukas, S. (1993). *Where to start and what to ask: An*

assessment handbook. New York: W. W. Norton.

Lytton, H. (1990). Child and parent effects in boys' conduct disorder: A reinterpretation. *Developmental Psychology, 26,* 683–697.

Maccoby, E. E., & Martin, J. A. (1983). Socialization in the context of the family: Parent–child interaction. In P. H. Mussen & E. M. Hetherington (Eds.), *Handbook of child psychology: IV, Socialization, personality, and social development* (pp. 1–101). New York: Wiley.

Machover, K. (1949). *Personality projection in the drawing of the human figure.* Springfield, IL: Charles C. Thomas.

Madsen, C. J. (1990, September). Attention deficit disorders and application of the EHA and Section 504. Paper presented to the Seventh Annual Pacific Northwest Institute on Special Education and Law.

Mannuzza, S., Gittelman-Klein, R., Konig, P. H., & Giampino, T. L. (1989). Hyperactive boys almost grown up, IV. Criminality and its relationship to psychiatric status. *Archives of General Psychiatry, 46,* 1073–1079.

Marcus, L. M., Lansing, M. D., & Schopler, E. (1993). Assessment of the autistic and pervasive developmentally disordered child. In D. J. Willis & J. L. Culbertson (Eds.), *Testing young children.* (pp. 319–344). Austin, TX: Pro-Ed.

Marin, G. (1992). Issues in the measurement of acculturation among Hispanics. In K. F. Geisinger (Ed.), *Psychological testing of Hispanics* (pp. 235–252). Washington, DC: American Psychological Association.

Marin, G., Sabogal, F., VanOss Marin, B., Otero-Sabogal, R. & Perez-Stable, E. J. (1987). Development of a short acculturation scale for Hispanics. *Hispanic Journal of Behavioral Science, 9,* 183–205.

Martin, R. P. (1983). The ethical issues in the use and interpretation of the Draw-a-Person Test and other similar projective procedures. *The School Psychologist, 38,* 6, 8.

Martin, R. P. (1988a). *Assessment of personality and behavior problems: Infancy through adolescence.* New York: Guilford Press.

Martin, R. P. (1988b). *The Temperament Assessment Battery for Children: Manual.* Brandon, VT: Clinical Psychology Pub.

Martin, R. P. (1989). Activity level, distractibility, and persistence: critical characteristics in early schooling. In G. A. Kohnstamm, J. E. Bates, & M. K. Rothbart (Eds.), *Temperament in childhood* (pp. 451–462). London: Wiley.

Martin, R. P., & Holbrook, J. (1985). Relationship of temperament characteristics to the academic achievement of first grade children. *Journal of Psychoeducational Assessment, 3,* 131–140.

Martin, R. P., Nagle, R., & Paget, K. (1984). Relationships between temperament and classroom behavior, teacher attitudes and academic achievement. *Journal of Psychoeducational Assessment, 1,* 377–386.

Martin, R. P., Wisenbaker, J., Matthews-Morgan, J., Holbrook, J., Hooper, S., & Spalding, J. (1986). Stability of teacher temperament ratings over 6 and 12 months. *Journal of Abnormal Child Psychology, 14,* 167–179.

Martinez, R., Norman, R. D., & Delaney, H. D. (1984). A children's Hispanic Background Scale. *Hispanic Journal of Behavioral Sciences, 6,* 103–112.

Mash, E. J., & Terdal, L. G. (1988). Behavioral assessment of child and family disturbance. In E. J. Mash & L. G. Terdal (Eds.), *Behavioral assessment of childhood disorders* (2d ed., pp. 3–68). New York: Guilford Press.

Matese, M., Matson, J. L., & Sevin, J. (1994). Comparison of psychotic and autistic children using behavioral observation. *Journal of Autism and Developmental Disorders, 24*(1), 83–94.

Mattison, R. E., Handford, H. A., Kales, H. C., Goodman, A. L., & McLaughlin, R. E. (1990). Four-year predictive value of the Children's Depression Inventory. *Psychological Assessment, 2,* 169–174.

Mayes, L., Volkmar, F. R., Hooks, M., & Cicchetti, D. V. (1993). Differentiating pervasive developmental disorder not otherwise specified from autism and language disorders. *Journal of Autism & Developmental Disorders, 23,* 79–90.

McArthur, D. S., & Roberts, G. E. (1982). *Roberts Apperception Test for children.* Los Angeles: Western Psychological Services.

McCarney, S. B. (1989a). *Attention deficit disorders evaluation scale—home version.* Columbia, MO: Hawthorne Educational Services.

McCarney, S. B. (1989b). *The attention deficit disorders evaluation scale—home version technical manual.* Columbia, MO: Hawthorne Educational Services.

McCarney, S. B. (1989c). *Attention deficit disorders evaluation scale—school version.* Columbia, MO: Hawthorne Educational Services.

McConaughy, S. H., & Achenbach, T. M. (1989). Empirically based assessment of serious emotional disturbance. *Journal of School Psychology, 27,* 91–117.

McConaughy, S. H., Achenbach, T. M., & Gent, C. L. (1988). Multiaxial empirically based assessment: Parent, teacher, observational, cognitive, and personality correlates of child behavior profile types for 6- to 11-year old boys. *Journal of Abnormal Child Psychology, 16,* 485–509.

McConaughy, S. H., Stanger, C., & Achenbach, T. M. (1992). Three year course of behavioral/emotional problems in a national sample of 4- to 16-year-olds: I. Agreement among informants. *Journal of the American Academy of Child and Adolescent Psychiatry, 31,* 932–940.

McConell, S. R., & Odom, S. L. (1986). Sociometrics: Peer-referenced measures and the assessment of social competence. In P. S. Strain, M. J. Guralnick, & H. M. Walker (Eds.), *Children's social behavior: Development, assessment, and modification* (pp. 215–286). New York: Academic Press.

McGrew, K. S., Bruininks, R. H., & Thurlow, M. L. (1992). Relationship between measures of adaptive functioning and community adjustment for adults with mental retardation. *Exceptional Children, 58,* 517–529.

McNally, S., Eisenberg, N., & Harris, J. D. (1991). Consistency and change in maternal child-rearing practices and values: A longitudinal study. *Child Development, 62,* 190–198.

McNeil, C. B., Eyberg, S., Eisenstadt, T. H., Newcomb, K., & Funderbunk, B. (1991). Parent-child Interaction Therapy with behavior problem children: Generalization of treatment effects to the school setting. *Journal of Clinical Child Psychology, 20,* 140–151.

Meehl, P. E. (1973). *Psychodiagnosis: Selected papers.* Minneapolis: University of Minnesota Press.

Mendoza, R. H. (1989). An empirical scale to measure type and degree of acculturation in Mexican-American adolescents and adults. *Journal of Cross-Cultural Psychology, 20,* 372–385.

Mercer, J. R., & Lewis, J. E. (1978). *Adaptive behavior inventory for children.* New York: Psychological Corporation.

Merrell, K. W. (1994). *Assessment of behavioral, social, and emotional problems: Direct and objective methods for use with children and adolescents.* New York: Longman.

Merrell, K. W., & Popinga, M. R. (1994). The alliance of adaptive behavior and social competence: An examination of relationships between the Scales of Independent Behavior and the Social Skills Rating System. *Research in Developmental Disabilities.* 15(1), pp. 39–47.

Milich, R. (1984). Cross-sectional and longitudinal observations of activity level and sustained attention in a normative sample. *Journal of Abnormal Child Psychology, 12,* 261–276.

Milich, R., Loney, J., & Landau, S. (1982). The independent dimensions of hyperactivity and aggression: A validation with playroom observations. *Journal of Abnormal Psychology, 91,* 183–198.

Miller, L. C. (1967). Louisville Behavior Checklist for males 6–12 years of age. *Psychological Reports, 21,* 885–896.

Milner, J. S. (1986). *The Child Abuse Potential Inventory: Manual—Second Edition.* De Kalb, IL: Psytec.

Milner, J. S., & Wimberley, R. C. (1980). Prediction and explanation of child abuse. *Journal of Clinical Psychology, 36,* 87–884.

Mischel, W. (1968). *Personality and assessment.* New York: Wiley.

Moore, S. G., & Updegraff, R. (1964). Sociometric status of preschool children as related to age, sex, nurturance-giving, and dependency. *Child Development, 35,* 519–524.

Moos, R. H., & Moos, B. S. (1986). *Family Environment Scale Manual—Second Edition.* Palo Alto, CA: Consulting Psychologists Press.

Moreau, D. L., & Weissman, M. M. (1993). Anxiety symptoms in nonpsychiatrically referred children and adolescents. In C. G. Last (Ed.), *Anxiety across the lifespan: A developmental perspective* (pp. 37–62). New York: Springer.

Morris, R. J., & Kratochwill, T. R. (1983). *Treating children's fears and phobias: A behavioral approach.* New York: Pergamon Press.

Murray, H. A. (1943). *Thematic apperception test.* Cambridge, MA: Harvard University Press.

Mussman, M. C. (1964). Teacher's evaluations of psychological reports. *Journal of School Psychology, 3,* 35–37.

Naglieri, J. A., LeBuffe, P. A., & Pfeiffer, S. I. (1993). *Devereux behavior rating scales—school form.* New York: The Psychological Corporation.

Naglieri, J. A., LeBuffe, P. A., & Pfeiffer, S. I. (1994). *Devereux scales of mental disorders.* New York: The Psychological Corporation.

National Association of School Psychologists (1985). *Principles for professional ethics.* Silver Springs, MD: Author.

Neeper, R., & Lahey, B. B. (1986). The Children's Behavior Rating Scale: A factor analytic developmental study. *School Psychology Review, 15,* 277–288.

Neeper, R., Lahey, B. B., & Frick, P. J. (1990). *Comprehensive behavior rating scale for children.* New York: The Psychological Corporation.

Newman, J., & Matsopoulos, A. (1994, March). Temperament precursors of early reading ability. Paper presented at the annual meeting of the National Association of School Psychologists, Seattle, WA.

Nezu, A. M., & Nezu, C. M. (1993). Identifying and selecting target problems for clinical interventions: A problem-solving model. *Psychological Assessment, 5,* 254–263.

Nicholls, J. G., Licht, B. G., & Pearl, R. A. (1982). Some dangers of using personality questionnaires to study personality. *Psychological Bulletin, 92,* 572–580.

Nihira, K., Foster, R., Shellhaas, M., Leland, H., Lambert, N., & Windmiller, M. (1981). *AAMD adaptive behavior scale, school edition.* Monterey, CA: Publisher's Test Service.

Nihira, K., Leland, H., & Lambert, N. (1993). *AAMR adaptive behavior scales—residential and community* (2d. ed.) (AAMR-RC: 2). Austin, TX: Pro-Ed.

Nitko, A. (1983). *Educational tests and measurement: An introduction.* New York: Harcourt Brace Jovanovich.

Offord, D. R., Boyle, M. H., Fleming, J. E., Blum, H. M., & Grant, N. I. R. (1989). Ontario child health study: Summary of selected results. *Canadian Journal of Psychiatry, 34,* 483–491.

Ollendick, T. H., & Hersen, M. (1993). *Handbook of child and adolescent assessment.* Needham Heights, MA: Allyn and Bacon.

Olmedo, E. L., Martinez, J. L., Jr., & Martinez, S. R. (1978). Measure of acculturation for Chicano adolescents. *Psychological Reports, 42,* 159–170.

Orvaschel, H., Ambrosini, P., & Rabinovich, H. (1993). Diagnostic issues in child assessment. In T. H. Ollendick & M. Hersen (Eds.), *Handbook of child and adolescent assessment.* Needham Heights, MA: Allyn and Bacon.

Orvaschel, H., Welsh-Allis, G., & Ye, W. (1988). Psychopathology in children of parents with recurrent depression. *Journal of Abnormal Child Psychology, 16,* 17–28.

Ownby, R. L. & Wallbrown, F. (1986). Improving report writing in school psychology. In T. R. Kratochwill (Ed.), *Advances in school psychology* (vol. 5). Hillsdale, NJ: Erlbaum.

Paikoff, R. L., & Brooks-Gunn, J. (1991). Do parent-child relationships change during puberty? *Psychological Bulletin, 110,* 47–66.

Parker J. G., & Asher, S. R. (1987). Peer relations and later personal adjustment: Are low-accepted children at risk? *Psychological Bulletin, 102,* 357–389.

Patterson, G. R. (1982). *Coercive family process.* Eugene, OR: Castalia.

Patterson, G. R., & Dishion, T. J. (1985). Contributions of families and peers to delinquency. *Criminology, 23,* 63–79.

Payne, A. F. (1928). *Sentence completions.* New York: New York Guidance Clinic.

Pearson, D. A., & Lachar, D. (1994). Using behavioral questionnaires to identify adaptive deficits in elementary school children. *Journal of School Psychology, 32* (1), 33–52.

Pearson, K. (1901). On lines and planes of closest fit to systems of points in space. *Philosophical Magazine* (Series 6), *2, 559*–572.

Pelham, W. E., Gnagy, E. M., Greenslade, K. E., & Milich, R. (1992). Teacher ratings of DSM-III-R symptoms for the disruptive behavior disorders. *Journal of the American Academy of Child and Adolescent Psychiatry, 31,* 210–218.

Perry, M. A. (1990). The interview in developmental assessment. In J. H. Johnson & J. Goldman (Eds.), *Developmental assessment in clinical child psychology: A handbook* (pp. 58–77). New York: Pergamon Press.

Petersen, A. C., Compas, B. E., Brooks-Gunn, J., Stemmler, M., Ey, S., & Grant, K. E. (1993). Depression in adolescence. *American Psychologist, 48,* 155–168.

Peterson, D. R. (1961). Behavior problems of middle childhood. *Journal of Consulting Psychology, 25,* 205–209.

Petersen, N. S., Kolen, M. J., & Hoover, H. D. (1989). Scaling, norming, and equating. In R. L. Linn (Ed.), *Educational measurement* (3d ed.). New York: Macmillan.

Phares, E. J. (1984). *Clinical psychology: Concepts, methods, and profession* (rev.). Homewood, IL: Dorsey Press.

Piacentini, J. (1993). Checklists and rating scales. In T. H. Ollendick & M. Hersen (Eds.), *Handbook of child and adolescent assessment* (pp. 82-97). Needham Heights, MA: Allyn and Bacon.

Piacentini, J. C., Cohen, P., & Cohen, J. (1992). Combining discrepant diagnostic information from multiple sources: Are complex algorithms better than simple ones? *Journal of Abnormal Child Psychology, 20,* 51–63.

Piacentini, J., Shaffer, D., Fisher, P., Schwab-Stone, M., Davies, M., & Gioia, P. (1993). The Diagnostic Interview Schedule for Children-Revised Version (DISC-R): III. Concurrent criterion validity. *Journal of the American Academy of Child and Adolescent Psychiatry, 32,* 658–656.

Piven, J., Simon, J., Chase, G. A., Wzorek, M., Landa, R., Gayle, J., & Folstein, S. (1993). The etiology of autism: Pre-, peri-, and neonatal factors. *Journal of the American Academy of Child and Adolescent Psychiatry, 32,* 1256–1263.

Porter, B., & O'Leary, K. D. (1980). Marital discord and childhood behavior problems. *Journal of Abnormal Child Psychology, 8,* 287–295.

Poznanski, E. O., Cook, S. C., & Carroll, J. B. (1979). A depression rating scale for children. *Pediatrics, 64,* 442–450.

Puig-Antich, J. (1982). Major depression and conduct disorder in prepuberty. *Journal of the American Academy of Child and Adolescent Psychiatry, 21,* 118–128.

Puig-Antich, J., Blau, S., Marx, N., Greenhill, L. L., & Chambers, W. (1978). Prepubertal major depressive disorders. *Journal of the American Academy of Child and Adolescent Psychiatry, 17,* 695–707.

Puig-Antich, J., & Chambers, W. (1978). *The schedule for affective disorders and schizophrenia for school-aged children (Kiddie-SADS).* New York: New York State Psychiatric Institute.

Puig-Antich, J., Goetz, D., Davies, M., Kaplan, T., Davies, S., Ostrow, L., Asnis, L., Twomey, J., Ivengar, S., & Ryan, N. D. (1989). A controlled family history study of prepubertal Major Depressive Disorder. *Archives of General Psychiatry, 46,* 408–418.

Puig-Antich, J., & Weston, B. (1983). The diagnosis and treatment of Major Depressive Disorder in childhood. *Annual Reviews in Medicine, 34,* 231–245.

Quay, H. C. (1986). Classification. In H. C. Quay & J. S. Werry (Eds.), *Psychopathological disorders of child-hood* (3d ed., pp. 1-34). New York: Wiley.

Quay, H. C., & Love, C. T. (1977). The effect of a juvenile diversion program on rearrests. *Criminal Justice and Behavior, 4,* 377–396.

Quay, H. C., & Peterson, D. R. (1983). *Interim manual for the Revised Behavior Problem Checklist.* Coral Gables, FL: Author.

Rabin, A. I. (1986). Concerning projective techniques. In A. I. Rabin (Ed.), *Projective techniques for adolescents and children* (pp. 3–13). New York: Springer.

Raine, A. (1993). *The psychopathology of crime: Criminal behavior as a clinical disorder.* New York: Academic Press.

Ramirez, M., III (1984). Assessing and understanding biculturalism-multiculturalism in Mexican-American adults. In J. L. Martinez, Jr., & R. H. Mendoza (Eds.), *Chicano Psychology* (pp. 77–94). Orlando, FL: Academic Press.

Reed, M. L., & Edelbrock, C. (1983). Reliability and validity of the direct observational form of the Child Behavior Checklist. *Journal of Abnormal Child Psychology, 11,* 521–530.

Reich, W., & Earls, F. (1987). Rules for making psychiatric diagnoses in children on the basis of multiple sources of information: Preliminary strategies. *Journal of Abnormal Child Psychology, 15,* 601–616.

Reich, W., Herjanic, B., Welner, Z., & Gandhy, P. R. (1982). Development of a structured psychiatric interview for children: Agreement in diagnosis comparing child and parent interviews. *Journal of Abnormal Child Psychology, 10,* 325–336.

Reynolds, C. R., & Kamphaus, R. W. (1992). *Behavior assessment system for children (BASC).* Circle Pines, MN: American Guidance Services.

Reynolds, C. R., & Richmond, B. O. (1985). *Revised children's manifest anxiety scale (RCMAS).* Los Angeles: Western Psychological Services.

Reynolds, W. M. (1986a). A model for screening and identification of depressed children and adolescents in school settings. *Professional School Psychology, 1,* 117–129.

Reynolds, W. M. (1986b). *Reynolds adolescent depression scale.* Odessa, FL: Psychological Assessment Resources.

Reynolds, W. M. (1989). *Reynolds child depression scale.* Odessa, FL: Psychological Assessment Resources.

Reynolds, W. M. (1990). Introduction to the nature and study of internalizing disorders in children and adolescents. *School Psychology Review, 19*(2), 137–141.

Richmond, B. O., & Kicklighter, R. H. (1979). *Children's adaptive behavior scale.* Atlanta, GA: Humanics Limited.

Richters, J. E. (1992). Depressed mothers as informants about their children: A critical review of the evidence of distortion. *Psychological Bulletin, 112,* 485–499.

Ricks, Jr., J. H. (1959). On telling parents about test results. *Test Service Bulletin, 54,* 1–4.

Roberts, C., McCoy, M., Reidy, D., & Crucitti, F. (1993). A comparison of methods of assessing adaptive behaviour in pre-school children with developmental disabilities. *Australia and New Zealand Journal of Developmental Disabilities, 18,* 261–272.

Roberts, G. C., Block, J. H., & Block, J. (1984). Continuity and change in parents' child-rearing practices. *Child Development, 55,* 586–597.

Roberts, M. A., Milich, R., & Loney, J. (1984). *Structured observations of academic and play settings (SOAPS).* Iowa City, IA: University of Iowa.

Roberts, M. A., Ray, R. S., & Roberts, R. J. (1984). A playroom observational procedure for assessing hyperactive boys. *Journal of Pediatric Psychology, 9,* 177–191.

Robertson, D., & Hyde, J. (1982). The factorial validity of the Family Environment Scale. *Educational and Psychological Measurement, 42,* 1233–1241.

Robins, L. N. (1966). *Deviant children grown up.* Baltimore: Williams & Wilkins. Robins, L. N., & Helzer, J. E. (1985). *The National Institute of Mental Health diagnostic interview schedule—version IIIA.* St. Louis, MO: Washington University.

Robins, L. N., Helzer, J. E., Croughan, J., & Ratcliff, K. S. (1981). The National Institute of Mental Health Diagnostic Interview Schedule: Its history, characteristics, and validity. *Archives of General Psychiatry, 38,* 381–389.

Robinson, E. A., & Eyberg, S. M. (1981). The Dyadic Parent–Child Interaction Coding System: Standardization and validation. *Journal of Consulting and Clinical Psychology, 49,* 245–250.

Rodrigue, J. R., Morgan, S. B., & Geffken, G. R. (1991). A comparative evaluation of adaptive behavior in children and adolescents with autism, Down syndrome, and normal development. *Journal of Autism and Developmental Disorders, 21,* 187–196.

Roff, J. D., & Wirt, R. D. (1984). Childhood aggression and social adjustments as antecedents of delinquency. *Journal of Abnormal Child Psychology, 12,* 111–126.

Rohde, A. R. (1957). *The sentence completion method: Its diagnostic and clinical application to mental disorders.* New York: Ronald Press.

Rorschach, H. (1921). *Psychodiiagnostik.* Bern: Bircher.

Rorschach, H. (1951). *Psychodiiagnostics: A diagnostic test based on perception* (P. Lemkau & B. Kronenberg, Trans.). New York: Grune & Stratton.

Ross, A. O. (1981). *Child behavior therapy: Principles, procedures, and empirical basis.* New York: Wiley.

Rotter, J. B., & Rafferty, J. E. (1950). *Manual for the Rotter Incomplete Sentences Blank, College Form.* New York: The Psychological Corporation.

Rourke, B. P., & Strang, J. D. (1983). Subtypes of reading and arithmetical disabilities: A neuropsychological analysis. In M. Rutter (Ed.), *Developmental neuropsychiatry* (pp. 473–488). New York: Guilford Press.

Routh, D. K. & Ernst, A. R. (1983). Somatization disorder in relatives of children and adolescents with functional abdominal pain. *Journal of Pediatric Psychology, 9*(4), 427–437.

Rucker, C. N. (1967). Technical language in the school psychologists' report. *Psychology in the Schools, 4,* 146–150.

Rutter, M. (1983). Behavioral studies: Questions and findings on the concept of a distinctive syndrome. In M. Rutter (Ed.), *Developmental neuropsychiatry* (pp. 259–280). New York: Guilford Press.

Rutter, M., Chadwick, O., & Shaffer, D. (1983). Head injury. In M. Rutter (Ed.), *Developmental neuropsychiatry* (pp. 83–111). New York: Guilford Press.

Rutter, M., & Garmezy, N. (1983). Developmental psychopathology. In E. M. Hetherington (Ed.), *Manual of child psychology, IV: Social and personality development* (pp. 775–912). New York: Wiley.

Rutter, M., & Giller, H. (1983). *Juvenile delinquency: Trends and perspectives.* London: Penguin.

Sandberg, D. E., Meyer-Bahlburg, H. F. L., & Yager, T. J. (1991). The child behavior checklist nonclinical standardization samples: Should they be utilized as norms? *Journal of the American Academy of Child and Adolescent Psychiatry, 30,* 124–134.

Sandberg, S. T., Wieselberg, M., & Shaffer, D. (1980). Hyperkinetic and conduct problem children in a primary school population: Some epidemiological considerations. *Journal of Child Psychology, Psychiatry and Applied Disciplines, 21,* 293–311.

Sandoval, J. & Echandia, A. (1994). Behavior assessment system for children. *Journal of School Psychology, 32(4),* 419–425.

Sandoval, J. & Mille, M. (1979, September). Accuracy judgments of WISC-R item difficulty for minority groups. Paper presented at the annual meeting of the American Psychological Association, New York.

Sargent, J., Liebman, R., & Silber, M. (1985). Family therapy for anorexia nervosa. In D. M. Garner & P. E. Garfinkel (Eds.), *Handbook of psychotherapy for anorexia nervosa and bulimia* (pp. 257–279). New York: Guilford Press.

Sattler, J. M. (1988). *Assessment of children (3d ed.).* San Diego, CA: Author.

Schachar, R., Rutter, M., & Smith, A. (1981). The characteristics of situationally and pervasively hyperactive children: Implications for syndrome definition. *Journal of Child Psychology and Psychiatry, 22,* 375–392.

Schaughency, E. A., & Lahey, B. B. (1985). Mothers' and fathers' perceptions of child deviance: Roles of child behavior, parental depression, and marital satisfaction. *Journal of Consulting and Clinical Psychology, 53,* 718–723.

Schaughency, E. A., & Rothlind, J. (1991). Assessment and classification of attention-deficit hyperactivity disorder. *School Psychology Review, 20,* 187–202.

Schwab-Stone, M., Fisher, P., Piacentini, J., Shaffer, D. Davies, M., & Briggs, M. (1993). The Diagnostic Interview Schedule for Children—Revised Version (DISC-R): II. Test-retest reliability. *Journal of the American Academy of Child and Adolescent Psychiatry, 32,* 651–657.

Semrud-Clikeman, M. (1990). Assessment of childhood depression. In C. R. Reynolds & Kamphaus, R. W. (Ed.), *Handbook of psychological and educational assessment of children: Personality, behavior, and context* (pp. 279–297). New York: Guilford Press.

Semrud-Clikeman, M. (1991). ADHD and major depression in children and adolescents. *Child Assessment News, 1,* 6–7.

Sevin, J. A., Matson, J. L., Coe, D. A., & Fee, V. E. (1991). A comparison and evaluation of three commonly used autism scales. *Journal of Autism and Developmental Disorders, 21,* 417–432.

Shaffer, D., Fisher, P, Piacentini, J., Schwab-Stone, M.,

& Wicks, J. (1991). *NIMH diagnostic interview schedule for children—version 2.3.* New York: New York State Psychiatric Institute.

Shaffer, D., Schwab-Stone, M., Fisher, P., Cohen, P., Piacentini, J., Davies, M., Conners, C. K., & Regier, D. (1993). The Diagnostic Interview Schedule for Children-Revised Version (DISC-R): I. Preparation, field testing, interrater reliability, and acceptability. *Journal of the American Academy of Child and Adolescent Psychiatry, 32,* 643–650.

Shapiro, E. S. (1987). *Behavioral assessment in school psychology.* Hillsdale, NJ: Lawrence Erlbaum.

Shapiro, E. S., & Skinner, C. H. (1990). Principles of behavioral assessment. In C. R. Reynolds & R. W. Kamphaus (Eds.), *Handbook of psychological and educational assessment of children: Personality, behavior, and context* (pp. 343–363). New York: Guilford Press.

Shaw, J. G., Hammer, D., & Leland, H. (1991). Adaptive behavior of preschool children with developmental delays: Parent versus teacher ratings. *Mental Retardation, 29,* 49–53.

Shepard, L. A. (1989). Identification of mild handicaps. In R. L. Linn (Ed.), *Educational measurement* (3d ed.). New York: Macmillan.

Shoham-Salomon, V. (1991). Introduction to the special section on client-therapy research. *Journal of Consulting and Clinical Psychology, 59,* 203–204.

Shopler, E., Reichler, R. J., & Renner, R. R. (1988). *Child autism rating scale.* Los Angeles: Western Psychological Services.

Silverman, W. K. (1993). DSM and classification of anxiety disorders in children and adults. In C. G. Last (Ed.), *Anxiety across the lifespan: A developmental perspective* (pp. 7–36). New York: Springer.

Silverman, W. K., & Nelles, W. B. (1989). The stability of mothers' ratings of child fearfulness. *Journal of Anxiety Disorders, 3,* 1–5.

Silverthorn, P. (1994). Assessment of attention-deficit hyperactivity disorder using the attention deficit disorders evaluation scale (ADDES): A review. *Child Assessment News, 4,* 1, 5, 12.

Singleton, L. C., & Asher, S. R. (1979). Peer preferences and social interaction among third-grade children in an integrated school district. *Journal of Educational Psychology, 69,* 330–336.

Siskind, G. (1967). Fifteen years later: A replication of a semantic study of concepts of clinical psychologists and psychiatrists. *Journal of Psychology, 65,* 3–7.

Snyder, M., Tanke, E. D., & Berscheid, E. (1977). Social perception and interpersonal behavior: On the self-fulfilling nature of social stereotypes. *Journal of Personality and Social Psychology, 35,* 656–666.

Solomon, I. L., & Starr, B. D. (1968). *School apperception method: SAM.* New York: Springer.

Spanier, G. B. (1976). Measuring dyadic adjustment: New scales for assessing the quality of marriage and similar dyads. *Journal of Marriage and the Family, 38,* 15–28.

Sparrow, S. S., Balla, D. A., & Cicchetti, D. V. (1984). *Vineland adaptive behavior scales.* Circle Pines, MN: American Guidance Services.

Spielberger, C. D., Gorsuch, R. L., & Lushene, R. E. (1970). *STAI manual for the State-Trait Anxiety Inventory.* Palo Alto, CA: Consulting Psychologist Press.

Spitzer, R., & Cantwell, D. (1980). The DSM-III classification of psychiatric disorders of infancy, childhood, and adolescence. *Journal of the American Academy of Child and Adolescent Psychiatry, 19,* 356–370.

Spitzer, R. L., Davies, M., & Barkley, R. A. (1990). The DSM-III-R field trials of disruptive behavior disorders. *Journal of the American Academy of Child and Adolescent Psychiatry, 29,* 690–697.

Spivack, G., & Spotts, J. (1966). *Devereux child behavior rating scale.* Devon, PA: The Devereux Foundation.

Spivack, G., Spotts, J., & Haimes, P. E. (1967). *Devereux adolescent behavior rating scale.* Devon, PA: The Devereux Foundation.

Stavrakaki, C., & Ellis, J. (1989). The relationship of anxiety to depression in children and adolescents. In C. Stavrakaki (Ed.), *The psychiatric clinics of North America: Affective disorders and anxiety in the child and adolescent* (pp. 777–789). Philadelphia, PA: W. B. Saunders.

Stein, M. A., Szumowski, E., Blondis, T. A., & Roizen, N. J. (1995). Adaptive skills dysfunction in ADD and ADHD children. *Journal of Child Psychology and Psychiatry, 36*(4), pp. 663–670.

Steinberg, L., Lamborn, S., Dornbusch, S., & Darling, N. (1992). Impact of parenting practices on adolescent achievement: Authoritative parenting, school involvement, and encouragement to succeed. *Child Development, 63,* 1266–1281.

Stone, W. L. & Hogan, K. L. (1993). A structured parent interview for identifying young children with autism. *Journal of Autism and Developmental Disorders, 23*(4), 639–652.

Strauss, A. A., & Lehtinen, L. E. (1947). *Psychopathology and education of the brain-injured child.* New York: Grune & Stratton.

Strauss, C. C. (1990). Overanxious disorder in childhood. In M. Hersen & C. G. Last (Eds.), *Handbook of child and adult psychopathology* (pp. 237–246). New York: Pergamon Press.

Strauss, C. C. (1993). Developmental differences in expression of anxiety disorders in children and adolescents. In C. G. Last (Ed.), *Anxiety across the lifespan: A developmental perspective* (pp. 63–77). New York: Springer.

Strauss, C. C., Lahey, B. B., Frick, P. J., Frame, C. L., & Hynd, G. W. (1988). Peer social status of children with anxiety disorders. *Journal of Consulting and Clinical Psychology, 56,* 137–141.

Strupp, H. H. (1973). On the basic ingredients of psychotherapy. *Journal of Consulting and Clinical Psychology, 41,* 1–8.

Sundberg, N. D. (1961). The practice of psychological testing in clinical settings in the United States. *American Psychologist, 16,* 79–83. Reprinted in L. D. Goodstein & R. I. Lanyon (Eds.), *Readings in Personality Assessment.* New York: Wiley.

Sutter, J., & Eyberg, S. M. (1984). *Sutter-Eyberg student behavior inventory.* Gainseville, FL: University of Florida.

Swensen, C. H. (1968). Empirical evaluations of human figure drawings: 1957–1966. *Psychological Bulletin, 70,* 20–44. Reprinted in L. D. Goodstein & R. I. Lanyon (Eds.), *Readings in Personality Assessment.* New York: Wiley.

Szapocznik, J. & Kurtines, W. (1980). Acculturation, biculturalism and adjustment among Cuban Americans. In A. M. Padilla (Ed.), *Acculturation: Theory, models and some new findings* (pp. 139–159). (American Association for the Advancement of Science Selected Symposium 39.) Boulder, CO: Westview.

Szapocznik, J., Scopetta, M. A., & Aranalde, M. A. (1978). Theory and measurement of acculturation. *Interamerican Journal of Psychology, 12,* 113–130.

Szatmari, P., Saigal, S., Rosenbaum, P., & Campbell, D. (1993). Psychopathology and adaptive functioning among extremely low birth weight children at eight years of age. *Development and Psychopathology, 5,* 345–357.

Tallent, N. (1988). *Psychological report writing* (3d ed.). Englewood Cliffs, NJ: Prentice-Hall.

Tanaka, J. S., & Westerman, M. A. (1988). Common dimensions in the assessment of competence in school-aged girls. *Journal of Educational Psychology, 80,* 579–584.

Teglasi, H. (1983). Report of a psychological assessment in a school setting. *Psychology in the Schools, 20,* 466–479.

Tellegen, A., & Ben-Porath, Y. S. (1992). The new uniform T-scores for the MMPI-2: Rationale, derivation, and appraisal. *Psychological Assessment, 4,* 145–155.

Teodori, J. B. (1993). Neurological assessment. In T. H. Ollendick & M. Hersen (Eds.), *Handbook of Child and Adolescent Assessment.* Needham Heights, MA: Allyn and Bacon.

Thomas, A., & Chess, S. (1977). *Temperament and development.* New York: Bruner/Mazel.

Thompson, C. T. (1949). *Manual for Thematic Apperception Test—Thompson modification.* Cambridge, MA: Harvard University Press.

Thurber, S., & Hollingsworth, D. K. (1992). Validity of the Achenbach and Edelbrock Youth Self-Report with hospitalized adolescents. *Journal of Clinical Child Psychology, 21*(3), 249–254.

Trites, R. L., Bouin, A. G. A., & Laprade, K. (1982). Factor analysis of the Conners teacher rating scale based on a large normative sample. *Journal of Consulting and Clinical Psychology, 50,* 615–623.

Tuma, J. M., & Elbert, J. C. (1990). Critical issues and current practice in personality assessment of children. In C. R. Reynolds & R. W. Kamphaus (Eds.), *Handbook of psychological and educational assessment of children: Personality, behavior, and context* (pp. 3–29). New York: Guilford Press.

Tuma, J., & Pratt, J. (1982). Clinical child psychology practice and training: A survey. *Journal of Clinical Child Psychology, 11,* 27–34.

Tupes, E. C., & Christal, R. E. (1961). Recurrent personality factors based on trait ratings. *Technical Report ASD-TR-61-97.* Lackland Air Force Base, TX: U.S. Air Force.

Vance, F. L. (1965). I was an imaginary playmate. *American Psychologist, 20,* 990.

Van Hasselt, V. B., Hersen, M., Bellack, A. S., Rosenblum, N. D., & Lamparski, D. (1979). Tripartite assessment of the effects of systematic desensitization in a multi-phobic child: An experimental analysis. *Jour-nal of Behavior Therapy and Experimental Psychiatry, 10,* 51–55.

Vaughn, B. E., & Langlois, J. H. (1983). Physical attractiveness as a correlate of peer status and social competence in preschool children. *Developmental Psychology, 19,* 561–567.

Voelker, S. L., Shore, D. L., Brown-More, C., & Hill, L. C. (1990). Validity of self-report of adaptive behavior skills by adults with mental retardation. *Mental Retardation, 28,* 305–309.

Volkmar, F. R., & Cohen, D. J. (1991). Comorbid association of autism and schizophrenia. *American Journal of Psychiatry, 148*(12), 1705–1707.

Wadden, N. P., Bryson, S. E., & Rodger, R. S. (1991). A closer look at the Autism Behavior Checklist: Discriminant validity and factor structure. *Journal of Autism & Developmental Disorders, 21,* 529–541.

Walker, C. E., Milling, L. S., & Bonner, B. L. (1988). Incontinence disorders: Enuresis and encopresis. In D. K. Routh (Ed.), *Handbook of pediatric psychology* (pp. 363-398). New York: Guilford Press.

Walker, H. M., & McConnell, S. R. (1988). *The Walker-McConnell scale of social competence and school adjustment.* Austin, TX: Pro-Ed.

Walker, J. L., Lahey, B. B., Hynd, G. W., & Frame, C. L. (1987). Comparison of specific patterns of antisocial behavior in children with conduct disorder with or without coexisting hyperactivity. *Journal of Consulting and Clinical Psychology, 55,* 666–678.

Walker, J. L., Lahey, B. B., Russo, M. F., Frick, P. J., Christ, M. A. G., McBurnett, K., Loeber, R., Stouthamer-Loeber, M., & Green, S. M. (1991). Anxiety, inhibition, and conduct disorder in children: I. Relations to social impairment. *Journal of the American Academy of Child and Adolescent Psychiatry, 30,* 187–191.

Ward, J. H. (1963). Hierarchical grouping to optimize an objective function. *Journal of the American Statistical Association, 58,* 236–244.

Wechsler, D. (1974). *Wechsler intelligence scale for children—revised.* New York: The Psychological Corporation.

Wechsler, R. D. (1991). *Wechsler Intelligence Scale for Children—Third Edition.* New York: Psychological Corporation.

Weiner, I. B. (1986). Assessing children and adolescents with the Rorschach. In H. M. Knoff (Ed.), *The assessment of child and adolescent personality* (pp. 141–172). New York: Guilford Press.

Weiss, B., & Weisz, J. R. (1988). Factor structure of self-reported depression: Clinic-referred children versus adolescents. *Journal of Abnormal Psychology, 97,* 492–495.

Weiss, G., Hechtman, L., & Perlman, T. (1978). Hyperactives as young adults: School, employer, and self-rating scales obtained during ten-year follow-up evaluation. *American Journal of Orthopsychiatry, 48,* 438–445.

Weissman, M. M., Warner, V., & Fendrich, M. (1990). Applying impairment criteria to children's psychiatric diagnosis. *Journal of the American Academy of Child Adolescent Psychiatry, 29*(5), 789–795.

Weissman, M. M., Warner, V., Wickrmaratne, P., & Prusoff, B. A. (1988). Early-onset major depression in parents and their children. *Journal of Affective Disorders, 15,* 269–277.

Weller, E. B., Weller, R. A., Fristad, M. A., & Bowes, J. M. (1990). Dexamethasone suppression test and depressive symptoms in bereaved children: A preliminary report. *Journal of Neuropsychiatry and Clinical Neurosciences, 2,*(4), 418–421.

West, M. O., & Prinz, R. J. (1987). Parental alcoholism and childhood psychopathology. *Psychological Bulletin, 102,* 204–218.

Whalen, C. K., Henker, B., & Dotemoto, S. (1980). Methylphenidate and hyperactivity: Effects on teacher behaviors. *Science, 208,* 1280–1282.

Widaman, K. F., Stacy, A. W., & Borthwick-Duffy, S. A. (1993). Construct validity of dimensions of adaptive behavior: A multitrait-multimethod evaluation. *American Journal on Mental Retardation, 98,* 219–234.

Widiger, T. A., Frances, A. J., Davis, W., & First, M. (Eds.). (1994). *DSM-IV sourcebook* (vol. 1). Washington, DC: American Psychiatric Association.

Widiger, T. A., Frances, A. J., Pincus, H. A., Davis, W. W., & First, M. B. (1991). Toward an empirical classification for the DSM-IV. *Journal of Abnormal Psychology, 100,* 280–288.

Wiener, J. (1985). Teachers' comprehension of psychological reports. *Psychology in the Schools, 22,* 60–64.

Wiener, J. & Kohler, S. (1986). Parents' comprehension of psychological reports. *Psychology in the Schools, 23,* 265–270.

Williams, C. L., Butcher, J. N., Ben-Porath, Y. S., & Graham, J. R. (1992). *MMPI-A Content Scales: Assessing psychopathology in adolescents.* Minneapolis: University of Minnesota Press.

Winokur, G. (1990). The concept of secondary depression and its relationship to comorbidity. In G. Winokur & Wesner, R. B. (Ed.), T*he psychiatric clinics of North America: Anxiety and depression as secondary phenomena* (pp. 567–583). Philadelphia, PA: W. B. Saunders.

Wirt, R.D., Lachar, D., Klinedinst, J. K., & Seat, P. S. (1984). *Multidimensional description of child personality: A manual for the Personality Inventory for Children* (1984 revision by Lachar). Los Angeles: Western Psychological Services.

Wirt, R. D., Lachar, D., Klinedinst, J. K., & Seat, P. S. (1990). *Personality inventory for children—1990 edition.* Los Angeles: Western Psychological Services.

Witt, J. C., Heffer, R. W., & Pfeiffer, J. (1990). Structured rating scales: A review of self-report and informant rating processes, procedures, and issues. In C. R. Reynolds & R. W. Kamphaus (Eds.), *Handbook of psychological and educational assessment of children: Personality, behavior and context.* New York: Guilford Press.

Wolf, T. H. (1966). Intuition and experiment: Alfred Binet's first efforts in child psychology. *Journal of History of Behavioral Sciences, 2,* 233–239

Wolfe, D. A. (1988). Child abuse and neglect. In E. J. Mash & L. G. Terdal (Eds.), *Behavioral assessment of childhood disorders* (2d ed., pp. 401-444). New York: Guilford Press.

Wolfe, D. A., Edwards, B., Manion, I., & Koverola, C. (1988). Early intervention of parents at risk for child abuse and neglect: A preliminary investigation. *Journal of Consulting and Clinical Psychology, 56,* 40–47.

Woodcock, R. W., & Johnson, M. B. (1989). *Woodcock-Johnson tests of achievement—revised.* New York: Riverside.

Woodworth, R. S. (1918). *Personal data sheet.* Chicago: Stoelting.

Zimmerman, I. L., & Woo-Sam, J. M. (1985). Clinical applications. In B. B. Wolman (Ed.), *Handbook of intelligence: Theories, measurements, and applications* (pp.873–898). New York: Wiley.

Zuckerman, M. (1990). Some dubious premises in research and theory on racial differences: Scientific, social, and ethical issues. *American Psychologist, 45,* 1297–1303.

AUTHOR INDEX